A
01-05-02
#1

ELIZABETH BAYLEY SETON
COLLECTED WRITINGS

Volume I

ELIZABETH BAYLEY SETON
COLLECTED WRITINGS

VOLUME I

Correspondence and Journals 1793–1808

Edited by:

Regina Bechtle, S.C.
Judith Metz, S.C.

Published in the United States by New City Press
202 Cardinal Rd., Hyde Park, NY 12538
© 2000, Elizabeth Seton Federation, Inc.

Library of Congress Cataloging-in-Publication Data:

Seton, Elizabeth Ann, Saint, 1774-1821.
    [Works. 2000]
    Collected writings / Elizabeth Bayley Seton ; edited by Regina Bechtle,
Judith Metz.
        p. cm.
    Contents: v. 1. Correspondence and journals, 1793-1808.
    ISBN 1-56548-148-8 (v. 1)
    1. Spiritual life--Catholic Church.   I. Bechtle, Regina M. II. Metz,
Judith. III. Title.
BX4700.S4A2 2000
271'.9102--dc21   00-042362

Printed in Canada

TABLE OF CONTENTS

Part I

Part II

Part III

Part IV

Appendix

ILLUSTRATIONS

Facing Page 242:
Elizabeth Ann Bayley and William Magee Seton
Dr. Richard Bayley
The Rt. Rev. John Henry Hobart, D.D.

Facing page 243:
The second Trinity Church (1788-1839)
No. 8 State Street, the Setons' home (1801-1803)

Facing page 306:
Amabilia and Antonio Filicchi
Elizabeth Seton

Facing page 307:
View of the port of Leghorn, Italy
Elizabeth Seton's journal entry for the day of her husband's death

Facing page 378:
St. Paul's Episcopal Chapel, New York
St. Peter's Catholic Church, New York, circa 1831

Facing page 379:
Crucifixion scene by Vallejo, St. Peter's Church, New York
Archbishop John Carroll
Bishop John Cheverus

ACKNOWLEDGEMENTS

The dawn of the new millennium marks the twenty-fifth anniversary of the canonization of Elizabeth Bayley Seton as the first American-born saint of the Roman Catholic Church. With the publication of this first volume of her collected writings, we celebrate Mother Seton and the fire of charity that continues to warm our church and our world through her followers. Gratefully, we commemorate all who contributed to this project, even though only a few can be mentioned here.

Since 1993 when our work began, we have been blessed by the support of the Sisters of Charity Federation, especially Mary Louise Brink, S.C., Katherine Hoelscher, S.C., Sandra Barrett, S.C.I.C., and Joyce Serratore, S.C., leadership liaisons to the Seton Writings Project. As a widow and a foundress, Elizabeth Seton relied on the kindness of benefactors to support her family and community. In like manner this project has received generous financial support from the Sisters of Charity Federation, the Vincentian Studies Institute, the Alumnae Association of St. Joseph's College, Emmitsburg, MD, and several private donors. For the incalculable benefit of in-kind contributions, we thank De Paul University, Chicago, IL; the College of Mount St. Vincent, Riverdale, NY; and the Sisters of Charity of Cincinnati, OH.

All who find inspiration in the life and spirituality of Elizabeth Bayley Seton owe a profound debt of gratitude to our manuscript editor, Ellin Kelly, affiliate of the Daughters of Charity, and to authors Annabelle Melville and Joseph Dirvin, C.M., among others, for their meticulous and pioneering work in Seton scholarship.

The cheerful grace of the members of the Advisory Committee, currently Kathleen Flanagan, S.C., Vivien Linkhauer, S.C., and Betty Ann McNeil, D.C., sustained the project through endless iterations as much as did their scholarly wisdom. Their commitment to this labor of love for Elizabeth Seton has modeled charity in action.

Betty Ann McNeil, D.C., provincial archivist of the Daughters of Charity, Emmitsburg, MD, freely and graciously shared organizational and procedural suggestions. Her sleuth-like ability to find obscure information saved the editors untold hours of work. The practiced editorial eye and proofreading expertise of Victoria Marie Forde, S.C., greatly enhanced the readability and reliability of the finished product. Vivien Linkhauer, S.C., and Betty Rensing, Cincinnati S.C. associate, contributed hours of painstaking work to compile the index.

To our research requests, no matter how tedious or obscure, archivists, present and former, and their staff were unfailingly helpful and prompt. We are particularly indebted to those whose archives hold the majority of Seton manuscripts: Betty Ann McNeil, D.C., Aloysia Dugan, D.C., Rita King, S.C., and Anne Courtney, S.C., Judith Metz, S.C., and Benedicta Mahoney, S.C., Elizabeth McLoughlin, S.C., Mary Catherine Seli, S.C., Genevieve Keusenkothen, D.C., Bonnie Weatherly, and Andrew Cooperman. Irene Fugazy, S.C., Mary Elizabeth Earley, S.C., and Jessica Silver of Trinity Episcopal Church, Manhattan, helped to locate illustrations and references.

For advice, assistance, and support, we thank publisher Patrick Markey and staff, New City Press, Hyde Park, NY; Edward Udovic, C.M., and Nathaniel Michaud, Vincentian Studies Institute; Marie Poole, D.C., Vincentian Translation Project; John Freund, C.M., St. John's University, NY; Professors Christopher Kauffman, Catholic University of America; and Professor Scott Appleby, University of Notre Dame. Thanks also to Susan McMahon, Halifax S.C. Associate, for business and marketing assistance; Joe Moretti, for his computer wizardry; and Neal Daniel, cover artist.

Directors and novices at the Sisters of Charity Collaborative Novitiate, Fort Lee, NJ; the Sisters of Charity at Mount St. Joseph, OH; and the Daughters of Charity at St. Joseph's Provincial House, Emmitsburg, MD, extended warm hospitality during committee meetings and work sessions. A vast array of senior Sisters of Charity in New York and Cincinnati kept lists, mailed order forms, and prayed without ceasing for the success of the Seton Writings Project.

Finally, with immense gratitude to our God whose name is Love, we dedicate these volumes to all the Sisters and Associates of the Sisters of Charity Federation in the Vincentian-Setonian Tradition and to their benefactors and colleagues in ministry.

"The charity of Christ impels us." (2 Cor. 5:14)

November 1, 1999, Feast of All Saints
Regina Bechtle, S.C., and Judith Metz, S.C., Editors

INTRODUCTION

"Elizabeth Seton did more for the Church in America than all of us bishops together."
Archbishop Francis P. Kenrick

On September 14, 1975, Elizabeth Ann Bayley Seton (1774-1821) became the first native of the United States of America to be canonized a saint of the Roman Catholic Church. This event focused attention for a brief time on a woman whose life was intertwined with many notable figures of the young republic and the growing Catholic church in America.

Elizabeth Seton's education, family life, and social practice were typical of women of her class in late eighteenth century America. In her early life in New York, she mingled with figures of post-Revolutionary society, religion, government, and business. As a devout Episcopalian wife and mother, she was a founding member of the first benevolent society in the United States initiated and directed by women. Her conversion to Catholicism in 1805 brought her to the attention of such priests as John Carroll, John Cheverus, and Louis Dubourg, who came to view her as an instrument, even a partner, as they sought to shape the emerging identity of the American Church. The school which she began in Emmitsburg, Maryland, in 1809 educated the daughters of prominent families, Catholic and non-Catholic alike, from Baltimore, New York, Philadelphia, and elsewhere. Her personal magnetism and spiritual depth sustained lifelong networks of friendship that spanned oceans and decades. Among American women of her time, particularly Catholic women, she is one of the earliest for whom substantial documentation is available.

But, despite Elizabeth Seton's prominence in the history of American Catholicism, there has been little critical scholarship about her. One major reason has been the difficulty of accessing relevant documents since her writings are located in a number of archives throughout North America. Another reason is that American Catholic historiography until recently paid little attention to the contributions of women and lay people in general. Finally, Elizabeth did not compose the theological tracts or compendia of spiritual teachings that historians would have been likely to notice. Rather, she wrote letters and journals, women's traditional medium of communication, singularly revealing, but often overlooked.

THE HISTORY OF THE PROJECT

The Sisters of Charity Federation in the Vincentian-Setonian Tradition, previously the Elizabeth Seton Federation, is an association of women's religious congregations in the United States and Canada which trace their roots to Mother Seton's 1809 foundation of the Sisters of Charity in Emmitsburg, Maryland, or which follow the rule of St. Vincent de Paul and St. Louise de Marillac. In 1992 the Federation sponsored the first Seton Legacy, a major research conference on the life and spirituality of Elizabeth Seton, in which the co-editors and manuscript editor of the present work were involved. A second Seton Legacy was held in 1996-1997.

Presenters at the 1992 conference pointed out the difficulty of locating the various Seton papers housed in a number of archives. It was evident that further research would be greatly aided by the publication of the complete Seton corpus. As a result, in 1993 the Federation authorized a committee of Sisters of Charity to begin this work. Its first members were Regina Bechtle (New York), Mary Louise Brink (Halifax), Theresa Corcoran (Halifax), and Judith Metz (Cincinnati), all of whom combined scholarly expertise with a deep desire to spread knowledge of Elizabeth Seton.

Phase I of the project sought to locate and identify all original Seton writings. Written inquiries verified that original letters, journals, notes, translations, and other material existed in twelve archives, with the largest collection at St. Joseph's Provincial House, Emmitsburg, Maryland. Additional materials were later discovered in four more archives. As a useful tool for researchers and a step toward publication of the writings, an annotated list of the holdings in all archives was prepared. This list was published in several installments in *Vincentian Heritage*, a journal of the Vincentian Studies Institute, beginning with volume 18, number 1 (1997).

In March 1996, Ellin Kelly, professor emerita at De Paul University, Chicago, joined the committee as manuscript editor. Dr. Kelly took over the formidable task of transcribing newly found material and verifying the accuracy of existing transcriptions. Sisters Regina Bechtle and Judith Metz were named co-editors of the project in the spring of 1996. They assembled the Advisory Committee with representatives from each of the six congregations which traced their roots to the community founded by Elizabeth Seton in Emmitsburg, Maryland, in 1809. Sisters and scholars who have served on the committee include Kathleen Flanagan, S.C., (Convent Station, NJ); Anne Harvey, S.C., and Elizabeth Bellefontaine, S.C., (Halifax, NS); Vivien Linkhauer, S.C., (Greensburg, PA); and Betty Ann McNeil, D.C., (Southeast Province).

PREVIOUS STUDIES

Rev. Charles I. White wrote *Life of Mrs. Eliza A. Seton* (New York, 1853), the first full-scale biography of Elizabeth Seton, thirty-two years after her death. White's work was translated and adapted by Madame Hélène Bailly de Barberey and published in French as *Elizabeth Seton et Les Commencements de L'Eglise Catholique aux Etats-Unis* (Paris, 1868). After six French editions Joseph B. Code, C.M., translated de Barberey's work back into English as *Elizabeth Seton by Madame de Barberey Translated and Adapted from the Sixth French Editon,* adding newly discovered material. Inevitably, the two processes of translation resulted in some deviations from White's biography and the original sources on which it was based.

Sisters of Charity played an early and significant role in advancing Seton scholarship. New letters were published in the *Life of Mother Elizabeth Boyle of New York* by Maria Dodge, S.C., (New York, 1893). In her 1917 *History of Mother Seton's Daughters* Mary Agnes

McCann, S.C. (New York, 1917), brought to light new documents from archives in Baltimore and Cincinnati. Rose Maria Laverty, S.C., traced the saint's Bayley and Le Conte ancestry in *Loom of Many Threads* (New York, 1958).

In her 1950 dissertation at The Catholic University of America on the life of Elizabeth Seton, historian Annabelle Melville made extensive use of the Seton manuscripts. Subsequently published as *Elizabeth Bayley Seton, 1774-1821* (New York, 1951) this book has come to be regarded as the definitive scholarly biography of the saint. Melville with Ellin Kelly edited *Elizabeth Seton: Selected Writings* (New York, 1987) and thereby introduced a wider audience to the depth of Mother Seton's spiritual life. Until the publication of the current work, this study represented the most comprehensive publication of Seton writings available. Dr. Kelly, manuscript editor for the present volumes, has made numerous major contributions to Seton scholarship over the years, notably as compiler and editor of *Elizabeth Seton's Two Bibles: Her Notes and Markings* (Huntington, IN, 1977) and *Numerous Choirs: A Chronicle of Elizabeth Bayley Seton and Her Spiritual Daughters* (2 vols., Evansville, IN, 1981, 1996).

Papers from the two Seton Legacy symposia on the significance of Elizabeth's life and spirituality have been published in *Vincentian Heritage*, [14 (1993) and 18 (1997)].

Besides Melville's dissertation five others have dealt with aspects of Elizabeth Seton's life. Kathleen Flanagan, S.C., studied the influence of Rev. John Henry Hobart (Union Theological Seminary, 1978). Rose Marie Padovano, S.C., explored Elizabeth's ministerial leadership qualities and educational innovations (Drew University, 1984). Gail Giacalone used Elizabeth's experience as a case study in loss and bereavement (New York University, 1987). Jenny Franchot analyzed the ante-bellum encounter of American Protestants with Catholicism through the writings of Elizabeth Seton and other converts (Stanford University, 1986). William Jarvis focused on Elizabeth and the early Sisters of Charity to critique the influence of religion on nineteenth century women (Columbia University, 1984).

Works in a more popular and reflective vein which have also drawn on many of the Seton manuscripts include *Letters of Mother*

Seton to Mrs. Julianna Scott by Joseph B. Code, C.M. (New York, 1960); *Mrs. Seton: Foundress of the American Sisters of Charity* (New York, 1962, 1975) and *The Soul of Elizabeth Seton: A Spiritual Portrait* (San Francisco, 1990), both by Joseph Dirvin, C.M.; *Praying with Elizabeth Seton* by Margaret Alderman and Josephine Burns, D.C. (Winona, MN, 1992); *Elizabeth Ann Seton: a Woman of Prayer* (New York, 1993), *The Intimate Friendships of Elizabeth Ann Bayley Seton* (New York, 1989), and *Elizabeth Ann Seton: A Self-Portrait* (Libertyville, IL, 1986), all by Marie Celeste Cuzzolina, S.C.; and *A Retreat with Elizabeth Seton: Meeting Your Grace* by Judith Metz, S.C. (Cincinnati, 1999).

These works, of necessity, have been able to select only a small sample of Elizabeth's letters, personal journals, meditations and instructions to her sisters. Some of these hundreds of manuscripts have never been published in full or in part. With the publication of this comprehensive and chronologically arranged edition of Elizabeth Seton's writings, the full depth of her spirituality and the breadth of her achievements and relationships over her short lifetime are finally accessible to the interested reader and serious researcher alike. An authentic portrait can begin to emerge of Elizabeth Bayley Seton as a woman firmly rooted in her times, yet able to transcend them.

THE STRUCTURE OF THE WORK

Volume One consists of Elizabeth Seton's letters, journals, and notes from 1793 through June 1808. Part I covers her life as an Episcopalian daughter, wife, and mother in New York from 1793, just before her marriage, until October 1803, when she sailed for Italy with her ailing husband and her eldest daughter, Anna Maria. Part II (October 1803 to June 1804) includes the journal and other material written on the Italian journey during which her husband died. Part III (June 1804 to July 1805) contains the journal of her spiritual conflict and conversion on her return to New York. The last section, Part IV, includes letters, notes and the journal she kept after her conversion as a widow and mother in New York (July 1805 to June 1808).

Volume Two will comprise Elizabeth's life in Baltimore (June 1808 to June 1809) and her years as foundress of the Sisters of Charity of St. Joseph's in Emmitsburg, Maryland (June 1809 to December 1820). Volume Three will include material from Elizabeth's notebooks, instructions, and meditations as well as excerpts from works she translated for the Sisters. The latter is significant for an understanding of the spirituality that Mother Seton bequeathed to her young community.

A NOTE ON SOURCES

Since the death of Elizabeth Seton in 1821, her papers have found their way by circuitous routes into numerous archives, including but not limited to those of the original congregations that stemmed from her Emmitsburg foundation. The Seton-Jevons Collection is one example. These family letters formerly in possession of the Jevons family, Elizabeth's great-grandchildren, were given to the Mother Seton Guild, which promoted the Seton cause for canonization. Subsequently, they were distributed among various Sisters of Charity archives by Salvator Burgio, C.M., who also gave photostats of the letters back to the donors. A fire at the motherhouse in 1951 destroyed manuscripts the Sisters of Charity of Halifax possessed. In 1967 the last direct descendant of Elizabeth Seton, Ferdinand Jevons, willed the bulk of his photostats to the Sisters of Charity of New York. Thus these volumes include both original manuscripts and copies under the designation "S-J."

Many Seton manuscripts have simply disappeared. Only fragmentary citations survive in early works by Rev. Simon Bruté, Rev. Charles I. White, and Msgr. Robert Seton, Elizabeth's nephew. Internal evidence in letters written by some of her correspondents, including Bishop John Cheverus and Rev. John Henry Hobart, indicates that additional Seton letters once existed. In these cases the editors made every attempt to locate the original manuscripts. Where this proved impossible, a typescript or transcription from an archival photostat or printed source was used, and this is so indicated in the accompanying notes.

A FINAL NOTE

This project of the Sisters of Charity Federation is focused on making the Seton writings accessible in as close a form as possible to the original manuscripts while at the same time providing adequate information to situate the writings in context. These volumes provide scholars with much material for further research. Yet to be probed in depth, for example, are themes such as the trajectory of Elizabeth's spiritual development; the influence of political, intellectual, and religious movements of her day; her philosophy and practice of education; her exercise of leadership; and the manner in which she adopted or transcended the conventional role of women. Those who guided this project to completion share the hope that these volumes will mark the beginning of a new and fruitful phase of exploration into the life of Elizabeth Bayley Seton, wife, mother, widow, convert, educator, foundress, and saint.

BIOGRAPHICAL NOTE

Elizabeth Ann Bayley Seton began the Sisters of Charity, the first religious community of women founded in the United States. She was born into a prominent Episcopalian family in New York City, August 28, 1774. Her father, Dr. Richard Bayley, was a physician, professor of medicine, and one of the first health officers of New York City. Her mother, Catherine Charlton Bayley, daughter of an Episcopal minister, died when Elizabeth was only three years old.

Elizabeth married William Magee Seton, scion of a wealthy New York mercantile family with international connections, January 25, 1794, at Trinity Episcopal Church. Five children were born between 1795 and 1802, Anna Maria, William, Richard, Catherine, and Rebecca. As a young society matron, Elizabeth enjoyed a full life of loving service to her family, care for the indigent poor, and religious development in her Episcopal faith, nurtured by the preaching and guidance of Rev. John Henry Hobart, an assistant at Trinity.

As the eighteenth century drew to a close, a double tragedy visited Elizabeth. Political and economic turmoil took a severe toll on William Seton's business and on his health. He became increasingly debilitated by the family affliction, tuberculosis. Hoping to arrest the disease, Elizabeth, William, and Anna Maria embarked on a voyage to Italy. On their arrival in Leghorn, they were placed in quarantine; soon after, December 27, 1803, William died. Waiting to return to their family, Elizabeth and Anna Maria spent several months with the Filicchi brothers of Leghorn, business associates of her husband.

For the first time Elizabeth experienced Roman Catholic piety in her social equals. She was deeply impressed, especially by the doctrine of the real presence of Christ in the Eucharist. She returned to New York in June 1804, full of religious turmoil. After almost a year of searching, she made her profession of faith as a Roman Catholic in March 1805, a choice which triggered three years of financial struggle and social discrimination. At the invitation of several priests, she moved with her family to Baltimore in June 1808 to open a school for girls.

Catholic women from around the country came to join her work. Gradually, the dream of a religious congregation became a reality. The women soon moved to Emmitsburg, Maryland, where they formally began their religious life as Sisters of Charity of St. Joseph's July 31, 1809. Elizabeth Seton was named first superior and served in that capacity for the next twelve years.

As the community took shape, Elizabeth directed its vision. A Rule was adapted from that of the French Daughters of Charity, a novitiate was conducted, and the first group, including Elizabeth, made religious vows in July 1813. In 1814 the community accepted its first mission outside Emmitsburg, an orphanage in Philadelphia. By 1817 sisters had been sent to staff a similar work in New York.

During her years in Emmitsburg, Elizabeth suffered the loss of two of her daughters to tuberculosis, Anna Maria in 1812 and Rebecca in 1816. By that time she herself was weak from the effects of the disease. She spent the last years of her life directing St. Joseph's Academy and her growing community. She died January 4, 1821, not yet forty-seven years old.

Elizabeth Seton was canonized September 14, 1975, by Pope Paul VI as the first native-born saint of the United States.

GENEALOGY

The Bayley Line

William Bayley (1708?-1758?) of Hertfordshire, England, later of Fairfield, Connecticut, m. (1742/3) Susannah Le Conte (Le Compte) (b.1727?), daughter of William LeConte (LeCompte) and Marianne Mercier of New Rochelle, New York
Children:
Richard Bayley, Sr. (1744-1801)
   [1] Married (January 9, 1767) Catherine Charlton (d.1777), daughter of Mary Bayeux and Rev. Richard Charlton
      Children:
      Mary Magdalen Bayley (1768-1856) m. (1790) Dr. Wright Post (1766-1828)
        Children:
        Catherine Charlton Post (b.1798) m. James Van Cortlandt Morris
        Richard Bayley Post m. Harriet Wadsworth Terry
        Eugene Post (1810-1884) m.
           [1] (1835) Pricella Ridgely Howard (1814-1837)
           [2] (1838) Margaret Elizabeth Howard (1816-1901)
        Lionel (Leo) Post (d.1819?)
        Edward Post (d.1816)
        Mary Post m. Robert Hawthorne
        Emily Post m.
           [1] Frederick Gore King
           [2] William Meredith Hawthorne
      Elizabeth Ann Bayley (1774-1821) m. (1794) William Magee Seton (1768-1803)
        Children: See below.
      Catherine Bayley (1777-1778)

   [2] Married (June 16, 1778) Charlotte Amelia Barclay (1759?-1805), daughter of Helena Roosevelt and Andrew Barclay of New York
      Children:
      Charlotte Amelia (Emma) Bayley (1779?-1805) m. (1799) William Craig
      Richard Bayley, Jr., (1781-1815) m. (1812) Catherine White
      Guy Carlton Bayley (1786-1859) m. (1813) Grace Roosevelt
      Mary Fitch Bayley m. Sir Robert Bunch
      William Augustus Bayley (d.1805)
      Andrew Barclay Bayley (d.1811)
      Helen Bayley (1790-1848) m. (1814) Samuel Craig

William Le Conte Bayley (1745-1811) m. Sarah Pell, daughter of Phoebe and Joseph Pell
   Children:
   William Le Conte Bayley, Jr. (b.1772)
   Susannah Bayley (b.1774) m. Jeremiah Schureman II
   Joseph Bayley (b.1777) m. Susan (?)
   Richard Bayley (b.1779)
   Ann (Nancy) Bayley (b.1782) m. Captain James Hague
   John Bayley (b.1784)

The Charlton Line

Rev. Richard Charlton (1706?-1777) of Ireland, later of Staten Island, New York, m.
Mary Bayeux, daughter of Thomas Bayeux and Madeleine Boudinot, French
Huguenot settlers of New Rochelle, New York
Children:
Catherine Charlton (d.1777) m. (1769) Dr. Richard Bayley (1744-1801)
    Children:
    Mary Magdalen Bayley (1770-1856) m. (1790) Dr. Wright Post (1766-1828)
    Elizabeth Ann Bayley (1774-1821) m. (1794) William Magee Seton (1768-1803)
    Catherine Bayley (1777-1778)
Mary Magdalen Charlton m. Thomas Dongan (1717-1765)
    Child: John Charlton Dongan
Dr. John Charlton m. Mary de Peyster
    Child: Mary Magdalen Charlton

The Seton Line

William Seton, Sr., (1746-1798) of London, later of New York City, son of John and
Elizabeth Seton, clan of Parbroath, Scotland, and of London
[1] Married (March 2, 1767) Rebecca Curson (Curzon) (d.1775?), daughter of
    Richard Curson, Sr., and Elizabeth-Rebekah Beker of Baltimore, Maryland
    Children:
    William Magee Seton (1768-1803) m. (January 25, 1794) Elizabeth Ann
    Bayley (1774-1821)
    James Seton (b.1770) m. (1792) Mary Gillon Hoffman (d.1807)
    John Curson Seton (d. before 1816) m.
        [1] (1799) Mary Wise (d.1809)
        [2] Mrs. Gorham
    Henry Seton (b.1774)
    Anna Maria Seton (b.1775?) m. (1790) John Middleton Vining (1758-1802)

[2] Married (November 29, 1776) Anna Maria Curson (Curzon) (d.1792),
    daughter of Richard Curson, Sr., and Elizabeth-Rebekah Beker of Baltimore,
    Maryland
    Children:
    Elizabeth Seton (1779-1807) m. (1797) James Maitland (d.1808)
    Rebecca Seton (1780-1804)
    Mary Seton (b. 1784?) m. Josiah Ogden Hoffman
    Charlotte Seton (1786-1853) m. Gouverneur Ogden (1778-1851)
    Henrietta (Harriet) Seton (1787-1809)
    Samuel Waddington Seton (1789-1869)
    Edward Augustus Seton (b.1790) m. Bazilide Belome
    Cecilia Seton (1791-1810)

Elizabeth Ann Bayley and William Magee Seton

Elizabeth Ann Bayley (1774-1821) m. (January 25, 1794) William Magee Seton (1768-1803)

Children:

Anna Maria (Annina) Seton (1795-1812)

William Seton II (1796-1868) m. (1832) Emily Prime (1804-1854)

Children:

William Seton III (1835-1905) m. (1884) Sarah Redwood Parrish (1844-1895)

   Child: William Seton V (1886-1886)

Henry Seton (1838-1904) m. (1870) Ann Foster

Children:

John Gray Foster Seton (1871-1897)

William Seton IV (b.1873)

George Seton (d. infancy)

Robert Seton (1839-1927), ordained priest (1865); archbishop (1905) of Heliopolis

Elizabeth Seton (1840-1906)

Emily Seton (1845-1868)

Helen Seton (d.1906) entered Sisters of Mercy of New York (1879), known as Mother Mary Catherine, R.S.M.

Isabella Seton m. (1870) Thomas Jevons

Children:

Marguerite Jevons (d.1954)

Reginald Seton Jevons (d.1907)

Thomas Seton Jevons (d.1963)

Ferdinand Talbot Roscoe Jevons (1876-1967)

Infant Seton (d. infancy)

Richard Bayley Seton (1798-1823)

Catherine Charlton (Josephine) Seton (1800-1891) entered Sisters of Mercy of New York (1846), known as Mother Mary Catherine, R.S.M.

Rebecca Seton (1802-1816)

EDITORIAL PROCEDURES
FOR VOLUME ONE

1. All letters, journals, etc., are original autograph documents unless indicated. To produce clear and accurate transcriptions of the original documents written by Elizabeth Seton, the transcribed texts follow the originals as exactly as possible, given the condition of the documents. A clearer idea of the writer is obtained by retaining the unique and significant features of her writings.

2. Conventions of spelling, grammar, and punctuation were not standardized in Elizabeth's time. For example, she often used *ie* where *ei* is usual, and she did not consistently indent paragraphs. In general these volumes follow her punctuation, capitalization, spellings, and misspellings in English and other languages as closely as possible except where such retention would result in confusion.

3. Dates are uniformly placed at the beginning of letters. Dates appearing within the text have been retained as in the original in the case of letters written over a period of several days or longer. Brackets around a date indicate that it does not appear in the manuscript but has been determined from internal or other evidence. Undated letters are grouped based on the internal contents of documents.

4. Salutations are placed on a separate line even though this was not always Elizabeth's practice.

5. Square brackets [] enclose missing dates, letters, words, or punctuation added by the editors for clarity.

6. Complete words are substituted for abbreviations not in current use. Elizabeth used either *and* or the ampersand; *and* is used throughout this edition.

7. Accent marks in French names and expressions do not always appear in the original manuscripts, but they are added in this text.

8. Elizabeth's style of frequently using equal sign (=), short dash (-), and long dash (—), as terminal punctuation is followed as closely as possible.

9. Elizabeth's favorite devices for emphasis were underlining and exclamation marks. Underlined words and phrases appear in this edition in italics. Multiple underlinings and other unusual notations in the text are indicated in footnotes.

10. Material crossed out in the original appears in angle brackets (< >).

FOOTNOTES

1.   The archival citation precedes the footnotes of each document.

2.   Where possible, footnotes identify persons, places, and events named in the text in their relationship to Elizabeth Seton.

3.   To minimize the number of notes, frequently mentioned persons, abbreviations, and nicknames are listed at the beginning of each part. Elizabeth often bestowed nicknames or pet names on her family and friends, names not always easy to identify precisely. As was the custom of the day, the Setons had household servants to whom they usually referred by first names only.

4.   The first citation gives full biographical or geographical data. Within a document a person's name or a place is footnoted only the first time that it appears.

5.   Besides quoting the Bible directly, Elizabeth used many scriptural allusions. "Cf." indicates a probable biblical citation. All biblical footnote citations refer to contemporary Catholic translations.

6.   Names of immigrants to the United States have been anglicized; the French or Italian usage has been retained for those who lived in Europe.

LIST OF ABBREVIATIONS

The following archival designations are used:

AAB Archives of the Archdiocese of Baltimore, Baltimore, MD

ACS Archives of the Sisters of Charity of St. Elizabeth, Convent Station, NJ

ACU Archives of the Catholic University of America, Washington, DC

AGU Archives of Georgetown University, Washington, DC

AMPH Archives of Marillac Provincial House, Daughters of Charity, St. Louis, MO

AMSJ Archives of the Sisters of Charity of Cincinnati, Mount St. Joseph, OH

AMSV Archives of the Sisters of Charity of St. Vincent de Paul, Mount St. Vincent, Riverdale, NY

ASCH Archives of the Sisters of Charity of St. Vincent de Paul, Halifax, NS, Canada

ASCSH Archives of the Sisters of Charity of Seton Hill, Greensburg, PA

ASJPH Archives of St. Joseph's Provincial House, Daughters of Charity, Emmitsburg, MD

AUQ Les Archives des Ursulines de Quebec, Quebec, Canada

AUND Archives of the University of Notre Dame, South Bend, IN

ACM Archives of the Carmelite Monastery, Baltimore, MD

MHS Maryland Historical Society, Baltimore, MD

OCL Old Cathedral Library, Vincennes, IN

SAB Sulpician Archives, Baltimore, MD

S-J Seton-Jevons Collection (Photostatic collection in AMSV)

Other abbreviations used in the text and footnotes include the following:

C.M.   Congregation of the Mission (Vincentians)

D.C.   Daughters of Charity of St. Vincent de Paul

O.S.A.   Order of St. Augustine (Augustinians)

S.C.   Sisters of Charity

S.S.   Society of the Priests of St. Sulpice (Sulpicians)

S.J.   Society of Jesus (Jesuits)

PART I

New York Episcopalian Daughter, Wife, Mother (1793-1803) Letters and Notes

1793[1]

In Part I Elizabeth makes frequent references to the following family members: her husband, William Magee Seton (Will, Bill, My William, Seton, W.M., Friend William, W.M.S., Willy); her father, Dr. Richard Bayley (Father, papa, Grandfather B, grandpa); her sister, Mary Bayley Post (my sister, Aunt Post, Sister Post); her brother-in-law, Dr. Wright Post (Post, Brother Post); her children Anna Maria Seton (Anna), William (little William, Will, son William, Bill), Richard (Ricksy, Dick, Dox, Doxie, Doxy, Pinté, Dicksy), and Catherine (Kate, Kit, Cate, Fin); and her sisters-in-law Rebecca Seton

---

[1]The following note (ASJPH 1-3-3-9:66a) appears with the notes and letters from 1793: " + the old nameless writings of Miss Bayley—soon to become Mrs. Seton and years after—the 1st Mother of the Daughters of Charity truly models of light innocent writings worth preserving + Bruté." Bruté used Daughters of Charity and Sisters of Charity interchangeably.

Rev. Simon Gabriel Bruté de Remur, S.S., (1779-1839), returned from France to America with Bishop-elect Benedict Flaget, S.S. and served at both St. Mary's College and Seminary, Baltimore, Maryland, and Mount St. Mary's, Emmitsburg, Maryland, where he developed deep spiritual bonds with Elizabeth Seton. He became the spiritual director and chaplain for the Sisters of Charity of St. Joseph's (1818-1834) and later the first bishop of Vincennes, Indiana (1834-1839).

The Sulpicians were founded in Paris in 1642 by Jean-Jacques Olier (1608-1657). Their mission is the formation and education of candidates for the priesthood. With Pierre de Bérulle (1575-1629) and St. John Eudes (1601-1680), Olier is considered one of the founders of the French school of spirituality. Olier was a friend and colleague of St. Vincent de Paul (1581-1660) in the spiritual renewal of the Catholic Church in France after the Council of Trent.

While in Europe for his episcopal consecration, John Carroll invited the Sulpicians to open a seminary in the United States. In 1791 the first Sulpicians, led by Rev. Charles Nagot, S.S., came to Baltimore and began St. Mary's Seminary.

(Beck, my own), Harriet Seton (Hatch, Ha), and Cecilia Seton (Celia, Cely, Cele). No information is available on some persons mentioned in the letters in which case they have not been footnoted.

1.1 To William Magee Seton[2]

[n.d.]

My dearest Will—

I have resolved to do my *duty* and go and see Mrs. Dwight this afternoon and If the weather remains clear it is my intention to pass an hour with Mrs. Wilks[3] in the Evening where you may have the honor of seeing me if you please—

Your EB

1.2 To William Magee Seton

[n.d.]

Your Eliza is well—and would be perfectly happy if she could enjoy the Society of her Friend

---

1.1 ASJPH 1-3-3-9:66b

[2]William Magee Seton (1768-1803) was the son of William and Rebecca Curson Seton. He was educated in England for six years and served briefly in the Bank of New York. In 1788 he toured the important counting houses in Europe and developed a friendship with Filippo Filicchi of the Filicchi firm in Leghorn (Livorno), Italy. Upon his return he joined Seton, Maitland and Company. His marriage to Elizabeth Ann Bayley January 25, 1794, was witnessed by the Episcopal bishop, Rev. Samuel Provoost. The couple had five children, two boys and three girls. Despite a sea voyage for his health, William Magee died of tuberculosis December 27, 1803, at Pisa, Italy, and is buried in the cemetery of St. John's Anglican Church in at Leghorn, Italy.

[3]Mary Seton Wilkes (d. 1801) was the wife of John Wilkes and a first cousin of William Magee Seton. John and his brother Charles were nephews of John Wilkes, a famous liberal member of Parliament and mayor of London. They came to New York in 1780 with letters of introduction to William Seton, Sr., from the Berrys, Seton relatives in England. Charles Wilkes succeeded William Seton, Sr., as cashier of the Bank of New York. He worked at the bank forty years, eventually becoming its president as well as being involved in a number of civic endeavors. John Wilkes was also a business associate and friend of the Setons.

1.2 ASJPH 1-3-3-9:66c

I have wished very much to see you, and knew that Indisposition only could have prevented my wish—Tomorrow I will wait in anxious expectation—

Believe me Your *own*

1.3 To William Magee Seton

[n.d.]

My dearest *Will*—

Mrs. Sadler[1] is not going to the Concert and wishes very much to see *us* there this Evening—do not be too late—

Yours *EB*

1.4 To William Magee Seton

[n.d.]

Your Eliza's Eye is very *Ugly* but not very painful, but It will prevent the possibility of my going out Therefore you must devote a great deal of your time to me—come as early as possible—We shall dine at one to day as Post[1] is going out of town—

Yours EB

1.3 ASJPH 1-3-3-9:66d

[1]Eliza Craig Sadler was a cherished friend of Elizabeth Seton and wife of Henry Sadler. Elizabeth frequently referred to her as Sad.

1.4 ASJPH 1-3-3-9:67a

[1]Dr. Wright Post (1766-1828) studied medicine under Dr. Richard Bayley and in Europe in 1792-93. He was a prominent New York surgeon and professor at Columbia College. Beginning in 1802, he served on the medical board of the Institution for the Inoculation of Kine Pox with the objective of instructing physicians in the method of inoculation, preparing the vaccine, and providing free vaccine for the poor. He married Mary Magdalen Bayley June 10, 1790, thus becoming the brother-in-law of Elizabeth Bayley Seton. He died June 14, 1828.

1.5 To William Magee Seton

[n.d.]

An unavoidable Something obliges Mrs. [Eliza] Sadler to drink tea with Mrs. Constable—If you are *anxious* to see your Eliza you will find her at Mrs. Atkinsons at the Piano

Your own—

1.6 To William Magee Seton

[n.d.]

My Father[1] dined with us and has gone I dont know where—I do not think you will meet him until the Evening.—Your apology is already made for one who is most earnestly interested in his good opinion of you—*Your E* will be in Wall Street[2] by five oclock and you shall then know more on the subject—

1.5 ASJPH 1-3-3-9:67b
1.6 ASJPH 1-3-3-9:68

[1]Dr. Richard Bayley (1744-1801) was the son of William and Susannah LeConte Bayley. He studied medicine under Dr. John Charlton and three times traveled to England to study, twice under the famous Dr. William Hunter. He married Catherine Charlton January 9, 1767. The couple had three children, Mary Magdalen, Elizabeth Ann, and Catherine who died as a young child. After the death of his first wife, he married Charlotte Amelia Barclay June 16, 1778. They had seven children, three girls and four boys. A well known surgeon, he had a special interest in public health and was one of the first health officers of the Port of New York as well as a noted authority on yellow fever. He died at the quarantine station on Staten Island August 17, 1801. See Appendix A-1.6a for a description of Richard Bayley in Elizabeth's handwriting.

Catherine Charlton (?-1777) was the daughter of Rev. Richard and Mary Bayeux Charlton. Rev. Charlton was the rector of St. Andrew's Episcopal Church, Staten Island, from 1747 until his death October 7, 1777. Catherine died at Newtown (later Elmhurst), New York, May 8, 1777. At this time Newtown was in the hands of the British. Her brother Dr. John Charlton had a home there.

Dr. John Charlton was the son of Rev. Richard and Mary Bayeux Charlton. He studied medicine in England and upon his return became a prominent New York physican. Becoming head of the Medical Society in 1792, he oversaw its reorganization in 1794 as well as taking an active part in pressing for public health regulations. In addition he was active in Trinity Church. He married Mary de Peyster, the daughter of Abraham and Margaret van Courtlandt de Peyster.

[2]According to the 1790 census, Dr. Bayley resided at 51 Wall Street.

1794

1.7 To William Magee Seton

23rd July 1794—

Oh my dearest treasure how my heart does bless you for those two dear affectionate letters, and think of my not recieving either 'till six this afternoon, the person who left the first one said he had entirely forgot he had it.

He little knew the happiness it would give or he could not have been so Inhuman as to have neglected sending it, while my eyes were rivited on it and I was revolving in my mind all the circumstances of your absence and the fatigue and vexations you might experience from the frenchman etc. in came Jackson[1] with the other letter and then I was too happy and most grateful for your attention to the wishes of your little girl, ah my dearest Husband how useless was your charge that I should "think of you," that I never cease to do for one moment and my watery Eyes bear witness of the effect those thoughts have for every time you are mentioned they prove that I am a poor little weak Woman—

I dined with our Father[2] and was so fortunate as to meet Mr. Fisher,[3] He is really the most charming company that can be and I think I never was in my life more pleased with a stranger—We talked of you, you may be sure and he said that I must learn one thing which few women could acquire the first year of their marriage which was to let their Husbands "Act for the best"—We drank a bumper to-

---

1.7 AMSV 110:MII S-J#454-457

[1]Probably one of the household servants

[2]Elizabeth often used this term to refer to her father-in-law, William Seton, Sr., (1746-1798), who married Rebecca Curson March 2, 1767. The couple had four sons and one daughter. Seton was a principal in the import-export firm of Seton and Curson. After Rebecca Curson Seton's death William Seton, Sr., married his sister-in-law, Anna Maria Curson in 1776. They had eight children, six girls and two boys. Anna Maria Curson Seton died August 22, 1792. Even though William Seton, Sr., was a Loyalist during the Revolutionary War, he retained most of his holdings after the war. In 1784 he became the cashier of the newly organized Bank of New York, a position he held for ten years. In 1794 he became a principal in another mercantile firm, Seton, Maitland and Company. He died June 9, 1798, as a result of a fall on the ice several months earlier.

[3]Probably a friend or business associate of William Magee Seton

gether to your health and speedy return[4] and He addressed me with all the familiarity and affection of Old friendship "Well Eliza if thee should ever visit Philadelphia come and stay with us" etc. You dont know how much he delighted me for it was certainly Complimenting my Husband in being so kind to his wife whom he can esteem only from her being such—for he cannot judge me worthy of his friendship on any other ground

I drank tea with Mrs Fitch[5] at Mrs. Whites (my neighbor) and from there went to papas, not finding him home I went [to] your Aunt Farquhars[6] because I knew you would wish it and from there returned to papa's ate our Supper and here we are at 1/2 past ten, Eliza[7] Asleep and your little Darly[8] cheerful *as may be* gratifying her self for I am sure you will be tired of my small-talk

Oh my love think of our poor little friend [Eliza] Sadler[.] She has been ran away with and thrown against a tree by the Crazy horse and almost Bruised to Death, *Post* happened very fortunately to be at Mrs. M. Hoffmans (at Mr. Willetts) where she was going and gave her every possible assistance but he thinks (altho' no bones are broke) that she cannot be moved for some time. I hope to go and see her tomorrow as I pass the day with Mr. Fitch and then I will tell you more—It really makes my heart ache to think of her melancholy Situation—

If I could have but one peep at you to know you were comfortable—but the Idea of the Inconveniences you may be suffering while these arms Heart and bed are all forlorn without you—I will not go to bed as I did last night for altho it was twelve I did not close my Eyes 'till three there fore I will take my Bible and read till I am sleepy—Heaven Bless and Protect you—

Thursday morning—

---

[4]William Magee Seton was on a business trip to Philadelphia.

[5]Mary Fitch, an intimate family friend, became one of the godparents of Elizabeth's first child.

[6]Elizabeth Curson Farquhar was a maternal aunt of William Magee Seton. Elizabeth often referred to her as Auntie F.

[7]Elizabeth Seton Maitland (1779-1807) was the oldest child of William and Anna Maria Curson Seton and a sister-in-law of Elizabeth Seton. In 1797 she married James Maitland (d. 1808), a business associate of William Magee Seton. She was known as Eliza and left five young children at the time of her death in March 1807.

[8]Elizabeth herself

I tremble for you my Darly on account of the weather the day will be almost insupportably hot, but I must trust that Mercy which alone can preserve you from every danger, it is past nine and I think you arrived or near it, and if you write by today's post tomorrow I shall have a letter, in the hope of which I will be as cheerful as possible—My father just past in a Charriage and nodded his head I suppose he is just arrived, 'tis strange I've seen nothing of the letter you mentioned—

the little picture surprised you I scarcely know what I meant by putting it there, I wish it could express what the Original does, you must fancy it smiles and is continually beconing you to return—Your picture is so melancholy that I dont love to look at it in your absence, it indulges too many fancys which my dismal imagination is ready enough to represent—two days are quite gone thank fortune and the third begun. I must look forward to tomorrow and tomorrow—O [unclear] desires his love to his dear papa. Hope travels on nor quits us till we die—love your dear little girl[9] and give her as much of your leisure time as you can without fatiguing yourself—good-by

Your Own E.A.Seton[10]

1796

1.8 To Eliza Sadler

New York 8th February 1796—

At last I have recieved your letter by Morison and as it is nearly five months old[1] I hope I shall recieve a fellow to it soon—and really Mrs. Sad *il facto* you go to Balls on Sunday night, you depraved creature, and what Balls or amusement can compensate for that quiet calm tranquility which Sunday and particularly Sunday Evening affords with Husband shaking his Slipper by a good coal fire and a volume of

---

[9]Elizabeth herself
[10]The signature is enclosed in a box and a circle.
1.8 ASJPH 1-3-3-7:1
[1]Eliza Craig Sadler, who frequently traveled to Europe, was in Paris at the time.

Blair[2] opened on the table. but avast I am an American savage I suppose and should not mention these dull Insipidities to a Lady in the largest Matropolis in the world and who can go to see Blond perugues[3] on Sunday Eve and I suppose jump among the gayest and after all my Sad the effects of their manner may be as useful as ours and as I think the first point of Religion is cheerfulness and Harmony they who have these in view are certainly right

According to my calculations with *Post* counting our fingers to the names of the months you are on the Eve of your departure from France, and so much the better for tho' you may be settled as if seven years had passed since you are there yet I would rather hear that you was almost any where else, Peace and a potatoe for me I care not for rooms as big as a Church, great Buildings, busy servants or Perugues and as for your Boul[e]vards I dare say they are very inferior to the pure air, fine prospect and gliding cement of our Battery[4]—I grant that the society of it might be improved but never mind, that we will form that to each other—But certainly my Sad I almost envy you the view of so fine a country and your description of the people awakens what formerly was a reigning passion in my breast, a curiosity to see the world and Europeans in particular, but all that is long ago laid aside—a half a dozen form my World—

At this moment William is playing "rosy dimpled Boy," "pauvre Madelon return," "enraptured hours" and "Caermignol" all as fast as the violin can sound them in rotation[5] so you may suppose my thoughts have a great deal of consistance—as they are addressed to

---

[2] A book of sermons by Hugh Blair, minister of the High Church and professor of rhetoric and belles-lettres at the University of Edinburgh. In their original publication the ninety-one sermons formed five volumes.

[3] Wigs worn by men of the period

[4] A section of New York at the tip of lower Manhattan at water's edge. Beginning in 1789, the city of New York began a program to refurbish this area which was the site of the original colonial fortification. By 1793 a spacious walk ran along the water's edge shaded by elm trees. It became a popular promenade for "genteel folk" as well as a fashionable residential area.

[5] William Magee Seton, Elizabeth's husband, brought the first known Stradivarius violin to America. William Magee enjoyed playing the violin while Elizabeth was accomplished on the piano. Throughout the years of their married life, music brought a great deal of enjoyment to their family.

you it is no matter how they are formed, they must all tell that I love you—

Respecting a certain pair of eyes,[6] they are much nearer to black than any other color which with a small nose and mouth, dimpled cheek and chin, rosy face and never ceasing animation, and expression forms an object rather too interesting for my pen Her grand Father B will tell you that he sees more sense expression Intelligance and enquiry in that little face than any other in the world, that he can converse more with her than any woman in New York in short she is her mothers own Daughter, and you may be sure her Fathers pride and Treasure—So some little Beings are Born to be treasured while others are treated with less attention by those who give them Being than they recieve from their hirelings—but it is all right, and often those who want the fostering indulgent bosom of a Parent to lean on, get cheerful thro' the world whilst the child of Hope will have its prospects darkened by unthought of disappointments—and so we go, there is a Providence which never slumbers or sleeps—But as my husband begins to gap, the clock strikes ten, and my fingers are cold I must say good by tho' suddenly for my friend William only gave me 'till tomorrow, or the vessel will go without this my assurance that neither time or absence can change my unvaried affection for you—

My William says he waits impatiently for the letter you promise for which you shall have a very long N.B. The Box which contains my Music is not yet opened, I shall learn it I am sure with very little difficulty as Simplicity is your taste—

My very best regards to my friend H[7]—Yours ever E A Seton—

---

[6]Anna Maria Seton (1795-1812) was born May 3. She was the oldest child of Elizabeth Bayley and William Magee Seton and accompanied her parents to Italy in 1803. She came to Emmitsburg in June 1809 with her mother and expressed a desire to die as a Sister of Charity of Saint Joseph's. She made her vows shortly before she died March 12, 1812. She is buried in the original cemetery at Emmitsburg.

[7]Henry Sadler, husband of Eliza Craig Sadler, was a wealthy English merchant who had settled in New York. Located at 215 Water Street, the firm of Sadler and Bailie was a dealer in "cloths, wines, indigo, and tobacco."

1.9 To Eliza Sadler

11 August 1796

Do you not think that after all the anxiety I have lately known on your Account, I kissed the letter and placed it in my Bosom, which told me that you were *quietly* living among all the tumults which surround you.[1] The first of June was also a later date than I expected, and from some other circumstances also this dear letter conveys a greater Joy to my Heart than any I have recieved since we parted. You love me, and yet call me *dearest*—The longer I live and more I reflect and know how to value the realities of Friendship, the more precious that distinction becomes, and I look forward to the dear Hope that my Sweet Child[2] will also enjoy it—You need not fear to lose me—no my *Sad* every hour I pass shows me the Instability of every expectation which is not founded on reason. I have learnt to commune with my own Heart, and I try to govern it by reflection, and yet that Heart grows every day more tender and softened, which I in great measure I attribute to the state of my Williams Health,[3] that Health on which my every Hope of Happiness depends and which continues me either the most perfect *Human* felicity or sinks me in the lowest depths of sorrow—That Health certainly does not mend and I often think very much decreases, and altho' it is my fixed principle both as a Christian and a reasonable Being never to dwell on thoughts of future events which do not depend on myself, yet I never view the setting sun or take a solitary walk but melancholy tries to seize me, and if I did not fly to my little Treasure[4] and make her call Papa and kiss me a thousand times I should forget myself—This disposition is also increased by the expectation of another precious Sharer of my self[5] whether it be

---

1.9 ASJPH 1-3-3-7:2

[1] Elizabeth may have been referring to the fact that military and political tensions between Britain and France in the 1790s led the French to declare that all United States ships en route to Britain were subject to search.

[2] Anna Maria Seton, Elizabeth's oldest child

[3] Tuberculosis ran in the Seton family. William Magee Seton was beginning to show signs of it.

[4] Anna Maria Seton

[5] Elizabeth's second child was due in November.

happy or the reverse; therefore my Sad I am become a looker-up which is certainly the only remedy for my description of sorrow. Yes dear *Sad* I shall have an Ang[el] in each hand to recieve you—and how will you express your emotion—who will you fix your eye on—how often will you say dear dear Eliza—

Next November will be the month of my confinement and in that time how many thoughts of my Sad will be mixed with others dear and interesting. Mama Fiter has no longer the same cares and attentions for me, without being particularly the reverse. My William dines and sups with her constantly and every office of good will and kindness is fulfiled quietly and uniformly. It is all right and perhaps the failure on *her part* is greatly owing to my not having the same leisure I once had for Intercourse of a different discription—But on *my Part* my Sad (You are not to be decieved) *I* am Irrecoverably lost to Her and where Esteem does not exist how can I express friendship—the moon might as well meet the Sun—but be assured I never will forget that she is in Years—a Stranger—and has fought many a hard battle for me added to which her kindness and attention have been those of a Mother, feeling these things as I do, do not fear—

Julia[6] is a little vain Shadow and never Interests me but when she is in sickness or sorrow—then I fly to her, hold her in my Bosom till the Storm is past, and only care enough for her to hold the chain together until it comes round again W.C.[7] is the best and most valuable Male Friend I have in the world except my two bests,[8] I do not know his equal and never before saw a man who I would so readily choose for a Brother[.] every body who knows him thinks well of him and he rather seems to enjoy the respect given to a man of forty, settled in Life than

---

[6]Julianna (Julia) Sitgreaves Scott (1765-1842) was the first daughter of William and Susanna Deshon Sitgreaves. She was born in Philadelphia and after her marriage to Lewis Allaire Scott January 15, 1785, she lived in New York. The couple had two children, John Morin Scott and Maria Litchfield Scott. Julia moved from New York to Philadelphia in 1798 shortly after her husband's death and lived with her sister, Mrs. Charlotte Sitgreaves Cox. She was a lifelong confidante and benefactor whose friendship Elizabeth Seton cherished. They carried on an extensive correspondence until Elizabeth's death in 1821.

[7]William Craig was the brother of Eliza Craig Sadler. He later married Elizabeth's half-sister, Charlotte Amelia Bayley.

[8]William Magee Seton, Elizabeth's husband, and Dr. Richard Bayley, her father

the passing Approbation generally bestowed on men so young and in-experienced—

Do you know that it is two months since I have written to you and yet those months are spent in scenes familiar to you and which forever remind me of you. I cannot *Spell* you the place that is past my art, but it is certainly one of the pleasantest and best calculated for real retirement of any I ever met with. You remember your situation on Long Island[9] with Mrs.White[.][10] I am about two miles nearer the Narrows,[11] enjoying every comfort of the country without a single Interruption of visitors, servants or any other difficulty—My Will[12] comes three times a week, and when the moon shines every evening—

You are surprised to hear we are not at Mr. [John] Wilkes or rather I believe you forsaw it would be so—however my William has managed it so as not to give offence and my Daughter having the Lax[13] with cutting her teeth made the necessity for Sea-air evident—I never before enjoyed the pleasures of the country so perfectly. Sister Post[14] is within a hundred yards on one side and if I but had you my *Sad*, the other I should have every charm of society—My Father is Health officer of New York and runs down in his Boat very often to see us, and when he meets me and little love he says there never was such a pair, that he sees no such cheerful welcome expression in any other eyes in the world—You may believe it for there never was truer affection in any Heart than in Mine towards him—

You do not tell me if you preserve your Health—I well remember those violent head-achs you used to suffer and my friend H[enry Sadler] is he merry and cheerful as ever? You must tell me many many

---

[9]The Sadlers had a summer home on Long Island, an island roughly parallel to the shore of New York and Connecticut.

[10]A neighbor of Elizabeth

[11]A strait connecting upper and lower New York Bay and separating Staten Island from Brooklyn

[12]William Magee Seton worked in the city while Elizabeth and her daughter were at a summer home on Long Island.

[13]A nineteenth century term for diarrhea

[14]Mary Magdalen Bayley Post (1768-1856), Elizabeth's sister, was the oldest daughter of Dr. Richard and Catherine Charlton Bayley. She married Dr. Wright Post in 1790 and had nine children, seven of whom lived, Edward, Lionel (Leo), Catherine Charlton, Richard Bayley, Eugene, Mary, and Emily .

things my *Sad*, if we are still to be so long separate—and may you long enjoy the singing of sweet Birds, but not in Europe, come here and hear my Bird sing, it has the sweetest voice—and you may take it Home and enjoy it both Summer and Winter—

I am very glad that I have written you to day as I find a vessel sails on Sunday and so much I have at heart your Remembrance of me as your *Dearest* that I would not have missed the chance of your hearing from me on any account W[illiam] C[raig] was to tell me where to write you, but he is a man of business and I forgive him, tho' in future I will write if only five lines by every opportunity as I am sure you will have many anxieties for me—

Dearest *Sad* may every blessing of a contented mind be yours think of me as one who often thinks of you and who hopes notwithstanding all the changes and chances, to meet you soon with the welcome of true affection—

most Sincerely Your *E.A.S.*

1797

1.10 To Dr. Richard Bayley

New York 13th February 1797

My Father

This is to intreat and implore you to smile on me when we meet, and not to punish me with the well merited reproof my Conscience has prepared for me. as an Apology is useless when the person who is to offer it is convinced of the fault committed, and as it often occasions embarrassment and additional error, I hope you will admit in its place the plain Truth, that I am well My Husband better my Son and

Daughter[1] *Admirable* etc. etc.—that the most pleasant day I have yet experienced or anticipate in this month of February is the one which will return you to me, a circumstance very generally wished, but most particularly by your very affectionate Daughter E.A.Seton
   The Soap Boilers and Tallow chandlers talk of petitioning the Legislature for a removal of the Health Officer[2]

1.11 To Eliza Sadler

Long Island 18th June 1797

My Precious *Sad*—

   as I scarcely know any thing necessary to the completion of my present comforts and satisfaction but the assurance of your Health and safety, I mean in the course of general events, for if instead of hearing from you, you were with me, I should be too well contented. The mild, peaceful flow of the river before our dwelling,[1] always inspires me with ideas of you, and increases the malancholy of regret which thoughts of absent friends inspire, but I have no friends to cause that regret, and no bosom to sigh for but yours, for I have none which calls forth the same kind of affection with yourself, none that I would unite with my William to increase the delight of my Evening hours.

---

[1] Anna Maria Seton and William Seton (1796-1868). He was born November 25 and was the oldest son of Elizabeth Bayley and William Magee Seton. He attended both Georgetown College in Washington, D.C., and St. Mary's College in Baltimore and was among the first students at Mount St. Mary's College, Emmitsburg. From 1815 to 1817, he learned mercantile procedures under the tutelage of the Filicchi family in Leghorn, Italy. He served in the United States Navy (1818-1834) and married (1832) Emily Prime (1804-1854), the daughter of a New York banker. They had nine children of whom seven lived. He led the life of a country gentleman, dividing his time between travel and residence at his wife's beautiful estate, Cragdon, in Westchester County, New York. He and some members of his family are buried in the old cemetery at Mount St. Mary's near the entrance to the present National Grotto of Our Lady of Lourdes.

[2] Dr. Richard Bayley, health officer of the newly created Board of Health Commissioners, was responsible for public health issues. In 1797 the powers of the Health Office commissioners were strengthened by conferring on them the right to make ordinances for cleaning the city. Standing water and sewage in the streets where the soap and candle makers worked were the objects of part of their attempts to clean up the streets.

1.11 ASJPH 1-3-3-7:3

[1] They were at a summer home on Long Island facing the East River.

You may probably recollect a House of Mr. Livingstons[2] on the East river opposite the Battery and facing Governers Island[3]—Sister Post divides the House with us, and the pleasure of recieving our Husbands together in the Evening, the company and protection we are to each other, when they are detained from us, counterbalances every inconvenience which a union of families always occasions,—we have as yet recieved nothing but pleasure and comfort from our Establishment and the offering of fresh Bread, Butter, and coffee to the dear well beloved Father of us, after a fatiguing sail in his Health Office employment is a satisfaction of which you can well form an Estimate.

last Evening when my William, Sister, Post, and some Gentlemen were walking, *I* was detained at Home to put my Boy[4] asleep, sitting on the sill of the door with my Baby sleeping at my Breast, the Heavenly tranquil view of every thing round me—you will readily believe when I tell you that I felt my face wet with tears whilst thinking how far distant you were from what we could so well enjoy together—I am always anticipating pleasure, and in my imagination I have painted scenes for next summer which far exceed even *these*, which I so well know how to value—

29th June

I have been too melancholy and depressed this week past to attempt writing for I should only unnecessarily distress you by communicating feelings to you which time and reason only can alleviate. Catherine Cooper with whom so many of my past days have been spent in friendship and affection is dying in the most melancholy manner, unconscious of the change she is making of this world for the next. Can there be a subject of more sorrowful reflections. Miss Colden[5] is passing the same scene with her, which she has already done with Mrs. O. Hoffman[6] and I really believe her to be a far greater sufferer than my poor friend in all the horrors of the cramp and a rapid

---

[2]There were several prominent Livingston families in New York at the time.

[3]The southern tip of Manhattan and a small island in New York harbor

[4]William Seton, Elizabeth's oldest son

[5]The Coldens, a prominent New York family, were neighbors of the Setons. Miss Colden later became Mrs. E. W. Laight.

[6]Possibly Mrs. Ogden Hoffman, the wife of a prominent attorney

consumption. Sweet amiable girl, may her latter days be more peaceful and fortunate than the present. I have much to lament in the loss of Mrs. Cooper for it is not easy to meet with such unreserved affectionate attachment as she has always expressed to me more by manner than by words—but my Sad I have already made the estimate of Human life too-well to grieve for her fate unconnected with the distressing effect it must have on those she leaves behind her.

—W[illiam] C[raig] has passed one Afternoon with me since I have been here, and I very much fear, that without great care he will suffer in his Health, as he is scarcely ever without pain in the Head and uneasiness of the Breast. When I caution him, he gives that throw of the chin which expresses, "and what matter is it"—he is too good and too valuable not to excite the greatest interest in his friends when his health is in question. He confirms the Hope you have given me that four or five months will end our seperation, and I am sure I have no expectation more cherished and indulged than that of meeting you again—My Father says Heavens how I wish I could see her, and my William in his mild manner answers Yes I wish we had them well over their dangers and difficulties, your friend smiles on them and secretly prays, Heaven grant it—

I am rocking the cradle with one hand, with a book on my knee to substitute my cabinet which is left in New York. Anna Maria is close by my side putting her Dolly to sleep and I will cut a lock of her beautiful hair for you which curls in a thousand ringlets over her head. She is one of the loveliest beings my Eyes ever beheld. *Yours* may have seen many more so, but a Mother sees thro' a vail which renders the object as she wishes it—My father says you will take her from me, but I deny it for she does not possess those gentle expressions of sensibility which you so much admire—*I* only have the least influence with her, because her disposition is exactly my own.

Give my affectionate Rememberance to my friend H[enry Sadler] and may the best blessings of Heaven be Yours—

Your *E.A.S.*

1.12 To Eliza Sadler

Long Island 1st August 1797—

The great length of time since we heard from our dear *Sad* has now become a serious concern to me, and if our friend H[enry Sadler] had not written to one of his correspondants in N[ew] Y[ork] I should certainly think that some new evil had seperated us still further from the desired point, for if ever we meet again it will be gaining a point to me on which hangs many of my favourite expectations—A Mr. Lawrence also has told my William that Mrs. S[adler] was well two months ago, enjoying the *agréments de Paris*,[1] more in earnest than any one there, that she was in one continued scene of amusement—This was repeated at the Breakfast table, on which my Sister addressed me with a look of sagacity "there you see what your gentle, sentimental friend has come to." I observed that it was one of the fixed sentiments of my friend, to submit to all matters of necessity with a good grace and that as you probably would never see Paris again you were right in enjoying all the good it affords. It has several times been insinuated to me that in your absence you will lose that interest you once took in a little retired uninformed personage, who possesses neither fashion nor fancy. but the idea has never given me a moments pain, for when I recieved the first carresses of my Sad she knew as much of the world as she does now, and I dread no alleniation from a Heart that values candour and nature more than refinement and grace, where *they* are not to be found—the only subject of reflection with me is, that you will find me in a situation which I fill with all the carelessness of an old possessor, whilst to you, unaccustomed to see me in it, every blemish will be instantly discovered, and of them (Heaven knows my consciousness and desire of doing better) there are too many—

My little Daughter[2] is the object of all others which I most fear to present to you, tho' I dare say she is the one you most wish to see, she possesses from her Mother a most ungovernable temper and with all

1.12 ASJPH 1-3-3-7:4
[1]The pleasures of Paris
[2]Anna Maria Seton, Elizabeth's oldest child

my endeavours is past all management. My William leaves her to me, My Father tells me, conquer her by gentleness. Post and my Sister recommends *Wipping*, which is to me an unnatural resource, and the last I shall have recourse to—Send me a word of advice on this subject, or rather make hast to set me right, and assist me in a case which demands more resolution, than any situation I have hitherto experienced—

10th August—

And where are all my dreams and fancys fled, you again delay your long wished for return,—and next spring promises what so many seasons have disappointed, that I scarcely dare look forward even to that—The happy Evenings I have pictured to my Imagination music, reading, all must be given to the winds, for I will not indulge expectations which it is in the power of chance again to deprive me of—You speak of me as independant of you; do you not know that there is not an hour of my Life in which I do not want either the advice or soothings of Friendship, and I sacredly declare that you *Eliza S.* are the only person to whom I could commit the guidance of my conduct in preferance to the impulse of my own Judgement, therefore never again say that you are not necessary to me, for it is utterly impossible that any one else should fill that place in my estimation which *affection* and *experience* has assigned to you. I know that this declaration is unnecessary but my heart has so often made it, that I can not refuse myself the indulgance of expressing it—

15th August

My beloved little William was very unwell when I wrote the above, and he has since been so ill, with inflamation in his bowells that my Father thought he could not recover.—Could I speak to you in the language of my feelings, should I attempt to express what passed in my Heart in any moment of that time whilst his recovery was uncertain, you would lament that Heaven had allowed me the privilege of being a Mother, for what is there in the uncertainty of human happiness to repay the agonizing convulsion of those twenty four hours in which I witnessed his sufferings.

yet it is all past, and he is quietly sleeping in his cradle—[unclear] forgetfulness of sufferings and appears as well as if he had not been ill.

My bosom is yet trembling and dares not trust itself with the joyful emotions which present themselves, and takes the pleasures of the present hours with the same silent submission with which it has endured the past.—

I will write again very shortly, and tho' time and chance and sorrow comes to all, and I must take my share, they all united will only draw me nearer to that friend to whom I look for comfort and Sympathy in all events, and with whom I hope to share much Peace and pleasure in time to come. in the meanwhile may *they* attend you every where—

E.A.S.

1.13 Draft to Mrs. John Seton[1]

[n.d. 1797]

Surely my dear Grandmother will not be surprised at my writing to her, to express a small share of that sincere affection I have always felt for her since I have been the wife of her W. M. and the Daughter of a son[2] who so affectionately loves her, and thro' whom I have had the happiness to recieve her good wishes for our <happiness> wellfare. <My William> If we could but be so happy as to present our Son and daughter to you, then indeed we should show our claims to your love for there never was two sweeter children. little William is all a mothers heart can wish in health, Life, and Beauty and from his promise of goodness sweetness of temper I have reason to hope he will indeed be a *third* William. Our little Anna Maria is Our<companion and> hearts delight and already our companion and dearest amusement<she promises>

1.13 ASJPH 1-3-3-7:70
[1]Elizabeth Seton Seton (1719-1797) was the paternal grandmother of William Magee Seton. She and her husband, John Seton (1712 - ?), had two sons, John and William, and five daughters, Isabella Seton Cayley, Jane Seton Synnot, Elizabeth Seton Berry, Margaret Seton Seton, and Barbara Seton Seton. Elizabeth usually first wrote her formal letters in draft form before copying them. Many times this draft is the only extant copy of the correspondence.
[2]William Seton, Sr., Elizabeth's father-in-law

1798

Elizabeth's extensive correspondence with Julia Scott began in 1798. In these letters she frequently referred to members of Julia's family: her siblings, Charlotte Sitgreaves Cox (sister, Sister Charlotte), Samuel Sitgreaves (Brother Samuel, Brother S.), and John Sitgreaves (Brother, Brother John); and her children, Maria and John (Jack) Scott.

After the death of William Seton, Sr., in June 1798, Elizabeth and William Magee Seton inherited responsibility for William's younger half-sisters and -brothers, Mary, Charlotte, Harriet, Samuel, Edward, and Cecilia. Elizabeth made frequent references in her letters to "the girls" and "the boys" who were away at school. She also frequently referred to her sister-in-law, Elizabeth Seton Maitland (Lidy, Eliza, Sister Maitland, Lize, Lizé). Household workers of whom she spoke are Mammy Huler, Malta, Phoebe, Luke, Sukey, and Pete.

1.14 To Eliza Sadler

—27 March 1798—

My own dear Sad—

Friend William has just left me, and with him has carried Hopes which has for many days been cherished with more than usual delight, for the certainty of seeing you in the spring has for some time past so forceably pressed on my mind, that you have been concerned in every plan of comfort, and a sharer of every certainty of pain (which I know must come) in the approaching season. But now he tells me that he will not be surprised if the next letter from London declares your intention of remaining in Europe—He is perfectly sick at the idea, nor do I ponder, for a state of Uncertainty is terrible indeed—

The last time I wrote you (almost two weeks ago[1]) I meant to have had a letter ready for whatever opportunity presented, but Fate orders all things, and since that time has ordered the *Husband* of my poor little Julia Scott,[2] to the regions of Peace—I have not left her night or day

---

1.14 ASJPH 1-3-3-7:5

[1]This letter is not extant.

[2]Lewis Allaire Scott (1759-1798) was the oldest son of Helena Rutgers and John Morin Scott. He served as secretary of state of New York from 1789 to 1793. He married Julianna Sitgreaves January 15, 1785.

during the excess of her Sorrows and such scenes of terror I have gone thro' as you nor no one can concieve—'tis past—little Julia goes to Philadelphia next week, where she is to fix her residence, as her Family connections are all there. and I am once more *Home* ten thousand times more delighted with it than before, from witnessing the Horrors of a Seperation and derangement in that of my friend.

My precious children[3] stick to me like little Burrs, they are so fearful of losing me again, the moment I shake one off one side another clings in the opposite, nor can I write one word without some sweet interruption—the *Charlotte* sails to-morrow, and I was determined to tell you myself that we are well, and that *dear Aunt Sad* is lisped by both my Angels on every occasion which conveys an idea of future pleasure, and that the thought of seeing her is one of the dearest Hopes of

E.A.S.

1.15 To Julia Scott[1]

New York 16th April 1798

Colonel [Aquila] Giles[2] has just called to say that his Deputy leaves New York for Philadelphia at three oclock. My children are both in my charge poor Mammy[3] being sick a bed, but nothing shall ever interrupt the course of my affection for you or prevent my expressing it whenever it is in my power. I am very anxious to hear of your arrival and I hope you will satisfy me, if it is only by putting the pen in Maria's[4] hand, who will be an excellent Substitute when you are either busy or lazy, with the advantage also of giving her the habit of writing, and do

---

[3]Anna Maria and William Seton

1.15 ASJPH 1-3-3-6:1

[1]Julia Scott's husband died in March 1798. Elizabeth spent many hours with Julia in her time of sorrow, helping her to pack her belongings and close her house in preparation for her and her children's move to Philadelphia. Until the time of her death, Elizabeth maintained a correspondence with Julia.

[2]Colonel and Mrs. Aquila Giles were New York friends of Julia Scott. Aquila Giles was a lawyer and wealthy landowner in the Flatbush section of Brooklyn.

[3]A servant in the Seton household

[4]Maria Litchfield Scott (1789?-1814) was the daughter of Lewis Allaire and Julia Sitgreaves Scott. In 1812 she married Peter Pederson, consul general and chargé d'affaires of His Majesty, the King of Denmark, to the United States. She died in Copenhagen, Denmark, November 7, 1814.

not fear to lessen my pleasure in hearing from you by so doing for you know that one of the first rules of my happiness is to be satisfied with good in whatever degree I can attain it, besides which it is very material that absence should not efface me from Maria's remembrance as I have not yet lost the Hope that my Anna may one day be as dear to her as you are to me—difference of Age after a certain period is very immaterial and rather adds to affection by creating that kind of confidence we have in those who are at an age to Judge of our particular feelings, and yet have more experience to give weight to advice—I forget that Futurity has no part in your calculations, but where it is the source of pleasurable Ideas I am very fond of dwelling on the good it offers—

You meeting with your Family must have been a scene of so much pain to you as well as pleasure, that I please myself with the Hope that it is over—And may Heaven grant you Peace in return for all the sorrow and confusion you have passed thro' Here—

Poor Miss Chippy[5] will write I suppose by this opportunity—She is a proof with respect to myself, how liable we are to err in our Judgments respecting others except we thoroughly know the motives of their actions for unfeeling and unkind as I must appear to her in affecting not to understand her oddities of behaviour I really and truely pity her Situation—She was at church yesterday; tho' I had not the pleasure of meeting her Eye—My Father is murmering still at the manner of your departure, and never comes in without saying something about you—

Give my very best love to dear Sister Charlotte,[6] and tell Brother John[7] that I never shall forget him.

Kiss your children for me and think of me as I am,

Yours most affectionately *E.A.Seton*

---

[5]Probably Miss Shipton, a mutual friend of Elizabeth and Julia

[6]Charlotte Sitgreaves, sometimes called "Lott," was the daughter of William and Susanna Deshon Sitgreaves and the sister of Julia Sitgreaves Scott. After her sister Mehitabel's death Charlotte married her widower brother-in-law, James Cox, January 4, 1787, at St. Paul's Church in Philadelphia. James Cox was the president of the Pennsylvania Insurance Company.

[7]John Sitgreaves (1763-1798) was born in Philadelphia, the son of William and Susanna Deshon Sitgreaves and brother of Julia Sitgreaves Scott. He never married and died of yellow fever.

1.16 To Julia Scott

New York 23rd April 1798

Dearest Julia

I recieved your precious letter last Friday, and it added a particular share of pleasure to a day which I always appropriate to Content and Peace, the 20th of April is the Birth day of Him who gives me *every thing*[1]—Your letter proved to me that I sometimes look on the dark side of the question as well as my neighbours, for nothing but the assurance from yourself could have persuaded me that you would have arrived in Philadelphia in any other state than that of serious Illness; I bless the Merciful Providence Who has granted us this Indulgence and implore the care of your good angel for the future, who if it should ever be inclined to remissness or inattention in your concerns will recieve many a check from *mine*—Perhaps you do not believe in the Doctrine of Angels But I think I can trace the truth of it both from Reason and Scripture; and a certain proof I had of it on Friday night—I went thro' all the storm, with my sister to the Theatre *for a frolick*, we came out in a violent thunder gust and got in our Hack with carriages before behind and a side—the coachmen quarrelling, first one wheel would crack, than another, and we passed a full half hour in the embarrassment, you know how much I like such situations, but my Guardian Angel landed me safe in Wall Street[2] without one single Hysteric—indeed I think [I] ought to take a review of my adventures last week for your Amusement as I know every thing I can say about your friends in New York will please you.

—Poor Nany Brown recieved my first visit and I declare to you that she perfectly made me love her by her affectionate kind expressions about you—her situation is deplorable but I believe is getting

---

1.16 ASJPH 1-3-3-6:2

[1]William Magee Seton, Elizabeth's husband, was born April 20, 1768, on board the ship *Edward* while his parents were returning to America from a visit with relatives in England.

[2]27 Wall Street was the Seton residence from 1795 to 1798. The Wall Street of the 1790s was lined with splendid private residences and the walls of the rebuilt Trinity Church rose after 1790 to grace the upper end of the street. The beauty of the remodeled City Hall made Wall Street the focal point of all civic and official life.

better every day—Mrs. Giles and Miss S_[3] recieved my next attention, (*all in due order*) and shewed me the very extremes of Civility
and good humour I mentioned with all the necessary expression, your
message of regards, which was recieved by Mrs. G_ with a Bow of infinite Grace, but very few words. *Miss S.* indulged her tears indeed she
has had quite a fit of sickness which she attributes chiefly to the struggle of seperating from the only friend she has in America—this she
communicates to every body. Mrs. Arden was there—She says we
must be good neighbour[s] on Long Island next summer—Alas!—
    Mrs. Governeur and Mrs.Startin[4] I have also been to see, and now
the *heavy labour* is over, I feel Home more sweet as its pleasures are
not interrupted one moment with the thought of what I *have* to
do—Colonel G[iles] is so good as to call whenever he has news direct
or indirect, from Philadelphia and I now feel a regard for him from *a*
combination of Interests which is as real as his own goodness of
Heart, and I hope my dear Julia it is on as sure a foundation—My dear
Seton was delighted with Brother John's kind attention in writing to
him, and would have told him so before now, but my Father Ss[5] indisposition has so much increased and with the additional distress of
Jack[6] being intirely confined to his room for this week past, that my
poor Hub has been in a worse situation than any Slave—
    My Father was very anxious to see your letter, but you had forbid
my shewing it, and therefore I told him that Maria had bruised her
cheek, John[7] had the mumps, and my dear little Julia was very much

---

[3]Wife of Colonel Giles and probably Miss Shipton

[4]Sarah Startin, the widow of Charles Startin and godmother of Elizabeth Bayley in the Episcopal
Church, was a rich and childless widow. She provided financial assistance to Elizabeth when she
returned from Italy, but after Elizabeth's conversion to Catholicism, Mrs. Startin excluded
Elizabeth from her will.

[5]William Seton, Sr., Elizabeth's father-in-law, had had a bad fall on the ice the previous winter.

[6]John (Jack) Curson Seton (b. 1772) was the son of William and Rebecca Curson Seton. He
married Mary Wise in 1799 and lived in Alexandria, Virginia, until she died in 1809. He later
married a widow, Mrs. Gorham, of Boston. After his death she became a Catholic in 1816.

[7]John Morin Scott (1789-1858) was the son of Lewis Allaire and Julianna Sitgreaves Scott. He
moved to Philadelphia with his mother after the death of his father in 1798. He was educated there
and at Princeton after which he practiced law and served several terms in the Pennsylvania House of
Representatives. He married Mary Emelen (1795-1881) May 15, 1817. She was the daughter of
George and Sarah Fishbourne Emelen, a prominent Quaker family. John and Mary Emelen Scott
had seven children.

distressed (You know he always declares against long story's) —He said he foresaw it all He knew that in the course of things you must meet with many difficulties, and prayed heaven to avert them in future earnestly wishing that it was in his power to alleviate or lessen them—When I wrote I was to tell you that neither time or distance could lessen the Interest he takes in every thing that relates to your happiness—And my Interest dear Julia do you think it will diminish—no my little Soul—without any professions vows or resolutions, I tell you from my Heart, that you are inexpressably dear to It—that I would give the greatest share of any good I enjoy to add to your comfort—but what I most desire and wish for you now is *Peace* that first and most perfect of all earthly attainments. In the arms and affection of our dear Charlotte I Hope you will regain it, tell her she must guard *my* priviledge until we all meet, and not leave room for any new Friend (for I know there will be enough to solicit it) to charm themselves into that place which I desire always to retain in your Heart.

Remember me Affectionately to your dear Children; and to every one of your Family, particularly to *my Brothers.*[8] I will soon write again as I know you wish it—time is very precious to me, I write this at seven in the morning for I had not written one side to you yesterday, before My Father, Brother, Hub, and the *Colonel* [Giles] called me away in rotation—Heaven Bless and Protect you—

E.A.Seton
24th April

---

[8]John and Samuel Sitgreaves. Samuel Sitgreaves (1764-1827) was the son of William and Susanna Deshon Sitgreaves and a brother of Julia Sitgreaves Scott. He was a lawyer in Easton, Pennsylvania. From 1794 to 1798 he served as a member of the House of Representatives and from 1798 to 1802 as a commissioner representing the United States government to the British government. He married Mary Kemper.

1.17 To Julia Scott

[n..d.]¹

I think that by this time my dearest Julia You are in some degree
settled, and your mind as far as present circumstances can affect it,
reconciled in part to the inevitable decree—
I was always sensible that I loved you truely, and that I could not be
absent from you, without the power and priviledge of enjoying your
Society, without the knowing if you were well or sick, and not feel a
pain peculiar to my Affection for you, but my love I had never fancied
that moment when I should pass that door I had been so constantly accustomed to stop at, when I should wish to take little Anna a walk and
not know which way to direct my steps—and altho' I have passed
sometimes a week without seeing you, now that I have not the *choice*
it is a constant source of melancholy reflection to me—Anna is now
begging me for a pen to write and when I refuse her, she says "do let
me write to poor Aunt Scott["] I cannot resist the demand and she has
the pen at all risques—the *Good Col*[Giles], who I believe is always
on some errand of attention and kindness, has called to tell me that
Brother John had written to him without mentioning one word of you
or your childrens Health, therefore as I am always willing to believe
the *best* I Judge that you and they are at least as well as usual, and that
there are no serious consequences from Maria's fall, or Jack's Indisposition—Your mind I know must be in that state of gloomy sorrow
that neither the fine wheather nor Spring nor exercise can be more
than partial relief, but I hope that these blessings will do a great deal in
re-establishing you and preventing the effects of the Struggles and
Agitations you have endured. I think I have heard you say that in former days you had a Physician in Philadelphia who you could confide
in and I hope you will not triffle or delay asking his advice when you
find it necessary, if it is for even a trivial occasion, for you have been

---

1.17 ASJPH 1-3-3-6:25
¹This letter was written in 1798. It refers to Julia's brother John who died later in 1798.

accustomed to that care and attention my love, and you must yet use the good that is in your power—

Poor Miss Chippe[2] is going to leave her dear Friend and adviser. She has actually, and past the power of wavering, taken her passage with the Berry's and will sail in one week at furthest—only think—poor Soul, she flatters herself that she is flying from trouble, but (as I have candidly told her) she carries the sting in her own bosom, and until she conquers *self* she may as well live with Mrs. G[iles] as any one else who I really begin to have rather a better opinion of, for only in the Quarter of an hour I was in her house, she recieved reproofs and marks of ill humor from Miss Chippy with that kind of *Graceful forbearance*, that I could not sufficiently admire—

I have met Mrs. Platt at the Widows Society,[3] and she shewed me so many of her sweet Fascinations, that I shall be ten times more careful than ever I was, not to form opinions of people *at a distance*, for no one can ever persuade me that she is not truely a sweet woman, and let those who have no faults of their own, indulge themselves in speaking of hers—

how is dear Charlotte and her hopeful family, lovely little souls, I should not murmur any more at *two* than I shall at one. *All* are welcome as long as I am capable of fulfilling *all* the duties—

---

[2]Probably Miss Shipton

[3]Elizabeth Seton's compassion for the poor and her commitment to social justice shows itself as early as 1797 when she and other public-spirited women met at the home of Mrs. Isabella Marshall Graham to form a society to aid destitute widows with children in New York City. They established the Society for the Relief of Poor Widows with Small Children, and Elizabeth served as treasurer for a time. Many of her friends, including Catherine Dupleix, Rebecca Seton, Sarah Startin, and Eliza Sadler, took an active part. This association was the first charitable organization in the United States managed by women. The current child welfare agency, The Graham-Windham Agency, traces its roots to this society.

In a 1798 letter Isabella Graham described the work of the society: ". . . I mentioned in my last that we had planned a society for the relief of poor widows with small children, the success has been beyond our most sanguine expectations. We have now a hundred and ninety subscribers, at three dollars a year, and nearly a thousand dollars in donations. We have spent three hundred dollars this winter, and nearly all upon worthy objects. The poor increase fast: emigrants from all quarters flock to us, and when they come they must not be allowed to die for want. There are eight hundred in the almshouse, and our society have helped along many, with their own industry, that must otherwise have been there. The French, poor things, are also starving among us: it would need a stout heart to lay up in these times. . . ." (*The Unpublished Letters and Correspondence of Mrs. Isabella Graham . . . selected and arranged by her daughter Mrs. Bethune* (New York, 1838.)

Whenever you see Brother S_, Harriet[4] give her such a kiss, and press her to your Bosom as you know I would do—I have an Interest in her which seems to have become a part of myself—and your dear Children and Charlotte—I am already longing for the time when I shall see them, and fetch you to William's Musqueto-Hall—this time next year Julia—according to custom we are always looking forward—it is the pleasure of my Life, tho' I already enjoy more than I can expect should continue at least without [the u]sual Interruptions of the good of this world—but my Af[fection] for you I hope will meet no Interruption

truely yours E.A.Seton—

good Miss Brown is much better with Broken ribs—

1.18 To Julia Scott

New York 9th May 1798—

At Eleven Oclock *my dear Colonel* [Giles] is to call for a letter,—Yours my dearest Julia I recieved when I came Home from Church last Sunday, and I found it a delightful addition to the excellent Ideas I had recieved from Mr. Moore[1]—Yes my dear little Soul you must learn the severe lesson of Submission, and that once gained, all that follows becomes Easy,—to resign our dearest Hopes, and console ourselves with *reason* in the hours when anguish rends the Heart—to rouse from the torpor of grief, and enter into scenes in which the Heart has no concern, or at best can recieve no comfort, is the lot of Virtue, and Superior minds—Have I not before remarked to you that this World would have too many Sweets if we did not view disappointments forever in the back ground and often pursuing us in

---

[4]Samuel Sitgreaves' daughter
1.18 ASJPH 1-3-3-6:3
[1]Rev. Benjamin Moore (1748-1816) was at the time assistant rector at Trinity Episcopal Church. He later became rector of Trinity and bishop of the Protestant Episcopal church of New York. He also served for many years as president of Columbia College.

our most favorite haunts of happiness—do you remember the day we rode as far as Hornbrooks on the East River, when we had ascended the Hill and were viewing the delightful scenery in every direction I told you that this world would be always good enough for me, that I could willingly consent to be here forever—but now Julia—since that short space of time, so thoroughly is my mind changed, that nothing in this World were all its best pleasures combined they would not tempt me to be otherwise than what I am—a Passenger—

You will recieve with this a letter from Miss Shipton. She has been on Board the Vessel, and obliged to return because they cannot find the Sailors—Heaven defend me from her threatnings which are that She would make me love her in the course of one twelvemonth at furthest, surely if so, it would be against both my reason and conscience, but there is no answering for what a Woman might do—She tell[s] me she will send this, that, etc—I tell her I cannot recieve her gifts, that Obligations must be preceded by Affection, and that I never had decieved her with the idea that I entertained more for her than was necessary to make me her Well-wisher. She says she likes candour, and that I shall not forget Her—Poor soul, may she have *Peace*, if so Heavenly a guest can reside in her bosom—Where passion reigns—

I have been on Long Island, and with *due* ceremony, with proper Witnesses, (and dearest Julia I cannot tell you with what sensations of Pleasure and delight)—I have marked *your room* and Heaven grant that I may recieve you there—with *tranquility*, and *Health* your Son and Daughter. I heard more satisfactory Intelligence from *my friend* than from my Father, respecting your purchase, I believe he would rather have purchased a Situation on our Batterey for you, for all your friends here are of opinion that the Heat of Philadelphia will incommode you very much—there is the expected rap—I left writing to the last hour for Miss S_ for a week past has not allowed me any other—May Heaven Bless you and yours—my best love to dear Charlotte—

E.A.Seton.

I will write very soon again and mind my pen—

1.19 To Julia Scott

New York—16th May 1798—

Dear precious Julia—

Your letter was handed me last evening by our ever watchful Friend, who never loses the opportunity of giving pleasure, and at the same time was informed of Miss G__s intention to visit Philadelphia tomorrow—And she will see you, and perhaps for a moment hold you in her arms—could I ever wish to be *her*?—Yes for that moment I would give ten thousand other precious ones, for I wish extremely and of all things to have if it was only for one hour, the satisfaction of being near you, but I must be content with the comfort yet left—that of writing to you, at this time when pain and a thousand nameless anxieties remind me continually of that hour in which the soul wavers between its future and its present Home—*mine* is transported at even the probability, for the bonds that hold it have scarcely strength to restrain it, and sure I am if it does escape, it will not be to any state of *Medium*, it is too active in its exertions ever to be disappointed, and if reason and the best Affections of this World did not withhold, and draw back with more than common force its flying propensities I should have renounced every other desire and aim long ago.—and is your dear little Heart yet throbbing?—unable to procure tranquility. Well Julia dear if it must be so, let these hours of Affliction lay a foundation of future enjoyment, and let the same hand which gave the blow heal and embalm it—Sorrow exhausts itself, and afflictions will find alleviations from time, if there are no other sources, but you my love have many, and have also good sense and strength of mind to profit by them—All I wish for you is that nature may take its course, and Affliction be allowed its advantages, as it certainly has the power of giving the mind a Peaceful course, and procuring future tranquility—the sweet Miss Bowdler[1] says, "that Fortitude

---

1.19 ASJPH 1-3-3-6:4

[1] The first edition of *Poems and Essays* appeared in 1786 as the work of the late Miss Bowdler. By 1798 nine editions had been published. Later editions identified the author as Jane Bowdler, and her work was printed for the benefit of the General Hospital, Bath, England.

does not consist in being insensible to the afflictions which come upon us in this World, but he who when his heart is pierced with sorrow can still love his God with unabated fervour, and submit with intire resignation to his Will,—who can struggle with his Affliction and resolutely persist in a constant endeavour to perform all the duties of his Station—that man acts with real fortitude, and when the time shall come that all his trials are drawing towards a conclusion, when from the brink of the Grave he looks back on all the various scenes of his past life those seasons of Affliction which once appeared so severe will be then what he can recollect with the greatest Satisfaction, and the remembrance of them will afford him solid consolation when all the little pleasures of this world are vanished and forgotten."

—I have returned Miss Bowdler to Mrs. P_ but not without transcribing in Anna's Book[2] all those Observations I thought most valuable, and which we will read together on Long Island in happier days, indeed I have written almost half the Volume. Miss G_ will tell you every thing about New York, and about our fears for Poor Chippy[3]—a person has returned from a Vessel which sailed a day before hers who was taken by a Privateer which he left in chase of another Vessel which is supposed to be the one she is in—how queer it would be if after all the *figitations* she should be *returned* to us—oh—oh—oh—

My sweet Treasure[s][4] are quite well, a little drop of Aunt Scotts Lavender on the little *HKf* [handkerchief], or a short story about John and Maria will delight my Anna for an hour, and keep her as quiet as a mouse—*Will* listens too very attentively and every now and than calls out *Anté-ca*. My W.M.S. is very anxious about your sufferings from the *heat*, tho' *I* with all my love of *air* have been Obliged to keep the House shut this week past—I am more anxious about your threats from those French *Scounds*,[5] tho' I think if Brother John is awake you need not fear—

---

[2]Elizabeth kept a copybook of quotes, passages, and poems for her daughter Anna Maria.
[3]Probably Miss Shipton
[4]Anna Maria and William Seton, Elizabeth's children
[5]Beginning in November 1798, the United States and France were engaged in an undeclared naval war which continued for two years.

I took both my children to see *Mama*,[6] and delivered your message, She said that *Mrs S.* had written, but that I must tell you She was going to try and recover her health at New Rochelle[7]—I stayed an hour with her, and endeavoured to impress on her mind that you leaving us so suddenly was a matter of Necessity, but the poor old Lady's passions are irritated, and she does not try to calm them. She is much to be pitied, but her sorrows will soon have rest for She looks I may say shockingly. She spoke a great deal of your children and of yourself very Affectionately—

It is nine oclock, and I have yet a letter to write to Richard[8] before I sleep—*My W.* is at the Theatre, and my *dear Dad* I have not seen to day—*My truest love to Charlotte* dear Julia

your own Friend E.A.Seton.

1.20 To Julia Scott

[Postmarked May 29, 1798]

My dear Julia

I write tho' only a few lines, because I know it will satisfy you more than any thing Mr.Ogden[1] could tell you respecting us—and should have written before but have been obliged to recieve my share of the prevailing Fever and Sore Throat which confined me for a week; you will almost dread to recieve my hand writing any more for it seems it is no longer to express any thing but sickness and disappointment. My children are so reduced by the Dissentary that I have been persuaded to consent to quit My Husband and take them for a fortnight to Long

---

[6]Julia Scott's mother-in-law, Mrs. John Scott

[7]A city in New York, northeast of New York City on Long Island Sound.

[8]Richard Bayley (1781-1815) was the son of Dr. Richard and Charlotte Barclay Bayley and half-brother of Elizabeth Seton. He married Catherine White in 1812.

1.20 ASJPH 1-3-3-6:5

[1]Abraham Ogden, a business associate, who was possibly traveling to Philadelphia. He was the brother of Gouverneur Ogden who later married Charlotte Seton.

Island where Mrs. [Eliza] Sadler will accommodate us with a room, until our little summer residence is in order to recieve us. —Do not think by this account that we are ill, They are running about and I am almost as strong as before—I long to hear from you, Julia, and pray that you may be now enjoying healthy breezes somewhere. I have never had a line from you since you mentioned your Malancholy forbodings of Evil—Heaven avert it, and preserve my precious Friend, and do write, and tell me particularly every thing that concerns you—in great haste but always

Yours *E.A.S.*
Wednesday 10 Oclock

1.21 To Julia Scott

New York 3rd June 1798

I have had the Satisfaction and comfort in the midst of all my Sorrows and perplexities to hear that you and your precious children were well, and that you were very much occupied which is a good antidote against the sadness and depression of your Spirits. I think I have never in my life suffered so much from the Anticipation of Evil (as it is a source of uneasiness which I never indulge) as during the last fortnight for in that space of time we have every hour expected to lose our dear Papa Seton[1] and dreadful has been the hours we has passed for my poor William has been lost I may say in mute anguish. his disposition is of that kind which does not admit of the soothings of sympathy, but wraps its grief in the stillness of despair which but little suits the anxious solicitude of my cares for him, but I Hope now that we shall have at least a temporary relief as Papa appears considerably better tho' I think by no means out of danger—

So you see dear Julia the debt we pay for this beautiful creation and the many enjoyments of this life, is to be borne in some degree by us all. Human life and sorrow are inseperable—

1.21 ASJPH 1-3-3-6:6
[1]William Seton, Sr., Elizabeth's father-in-law

My children *are well* and that in itself is so great a good that I can never be sufficiently grateful. We are decidedly not going to Long Island this summer, at least not until my confinement[2] is over as my Husband could give me so little of his time on account of his Fathers ill Health, that I could expect very little comfort there—

Colonel Giles leave[s] us tomorrow, and expects to be with you the day After, and he will present you with the long promised little pictures which I hope you will like;—not the lively animated Betsy B_[3] but the softened Matron with traces of care and anxiety on her Brow, and this is much more expressed in the large Picture than in the small ones—Present one pair to my Brother Samuel and one to the Batchelor [John] and tell them I wish they may recieve half the pleasure I do when I contemplate theirs; they shall always retain their place over my darling cabinet.—

Eliza Maitland was this Morning brought to bed of a Son. a Warning for me to be ready, I have laid a mat on my drawing room and put up a misqueto net, and there I may comfort myself, and happy I am it is no worse—[unclear] to be sure ours is the hottest House in the street having no draft thro' it—I do not know if I mentioned to you that Maitland[4] has brought your china. Knowing you did not want it at present I believe I neglected mentioning it in my last—William did not tell me if he meant to send it or if it waited your orders—if you should not recieve it by the time you write to me, say what you wish respecting it—

Heaven Bless you dearest Julia, with my Kindest remembrance to my Friends.

I am Your *E.A.S.*

My William's likeness will strongly remind you of a Manager at the Assembly, he committed the same fault as Brother John, not having his hair cut—

---

[2]Elizabeth was expecting her third child in July.

[3]A name Elizabeth often used to refer to herself

[4]James Maitland was a business partner with William Magee Seton in the firm of Seton, Maitland and Company. He married Eliza Seton in 1797.

1.22 To Julia Scott

New York 5th July 1798

It is realy true my dear Julia, that tho' I have not written to you, my pen has been scarcely one hour out of my hand these few weeks past except to sleep, or rather to weep for I have had much more of the latter than the former—My poor William has kept me constantly employed in copying his letters and assisting him to arrange his Papers for he has no friend or confident now on Earth but his little wife; his attachment to his Father was so particularly affectionate and uniform that his loss is one of the most severe afflictions to him that could possibly have happened[1]—most men have the resource in an event of this

---

1.22 ASJPH 1-3-3-6:7

[1]William Magee Seton's father died June 9, 1798, and was buried in Trinity churchyard. Following is the death notice and a brief eulogy which appears to be a brief note to young William Seton. There is a question whether these documents are in Elizabeth Seton's handwriting.

Death Notice ASJPH—Died New York on the 9th of June 1798—

William Seton Esquire in the 52nd year of his age, a Native of Great Britain and a resident of America for upwards of thirty years. From his earliest youth his time was occupied by pursuits of commerce in which he soon acquired and invariably preserved the fairest reputation—with the most persevering assiduity he combined the most generous conduct. Never addicted to Vice of any kind nor to Pride nor to ostentation, his heart was replete with every virtue, a real friend, and a friend to mankind—his whole life was marked uniformly by Sincerity of Heart, dignity of Manners, and Active Liberality of Mind. but alas he is no more! the destitute Orphan is deprived of its kindest patron, the helpless widow, and the unfortunate of their best friend—his afflicted children of an indulgent and beloved Parent, and the community of a citizen who in early life gained and never lost their confidence and approbation, their affection and esteem, and one they will never cease to Lament.

Eulogy of William Seton, Sr. **ASJPH 1-3-3-18:1**

[June 9, 1798]

My dear William

This is not one of those efforts of Friendship which endeavors to shade the defects of a Departed Friend by bringing his Virtues in a conspicious point of view—but the genuine truth imperfectly and feebly expressed in comparison with the merits it attempts to describe—it is necessary to have seen him in the several situations of Husband Father Friend Protector—to form any just idea of the perfections of his character which bright example impress indelibly on your mind—You bear his name—and I pray to Heaven with all the fervor of a Mother's Hopes that you will preserve it as unblemished and yield it to the author of your Being as spotless as he did.

kind either of particular friends, or habits to disipate sorrow but my Husband has neither, for he has been so long accustomed to leave my Society only for his Fathers, and his Fathers for mine that all now center in the survivor and you may Judge if I do not try to sustain myself and reconcile every decree of Fate—to be sure for me who so dearly loves quiet and a small Family to become at once the Mother of six children and the Head of so large a Number,[2] is a very great change, and Death or Bread and Water would be a happy prospect in comparison when I consider *Self*—but you well know how long ago I have accustomed that to yield to Affection for my Will and when I consider his vexations and cares I bless my God who allows me to share and lessen them—

9th July—Monday—

My Friend I did propose writing you a long letter, but find myself so woefully fatigued, and so unwell that I must defer it till another opportunity—I have this Morning dispatched our two dear little Boys[3] to Connecticut where they will be in the family of a Respectable clergyman and get a much more regular Education than this city could afford them—If my confinement was over we would soon get arranged, but I cannot expect to move to Stone Street until the last of August[4]—and then—

—but Julia could I have expected *a Life* of such happiness as I have known these four years past?—I trust all to the Mercy of Him who never forsakes those who confide in Him—

You cannot think how much I was hurt at my thoughtless behaviour to Sister Charlotte—I can only say that the trouble and confusion

---

[2]Elizabeth and her husband inherited the responsibility for William's younger half-brothers and sisters upon the death of his father. They were Mary, Charlotte, Henrietta (Harriet), Samuel Waddington, Edward Augustus, and Cecilia.

[3]Samuel Waddington Seton (1789-1869) and Edward Augustus Seton (1790-?) were sons of William and Anna Maria Curson Seton and brothers-in-law to Elizabeth Seton. Edward (Ned), a talented artist, went south and married Bazilide Balome in Opelousas, Louisiana. Samuel served as an agent and superintendent of the public schools in New York.

[4]Elizabeth and her family were planning to move to the Seton family home on Stone Street in New York after the elder Mr. Seton's death. She and William Magee had lived there during the first year of their marriage and were now planning to return in order to assume responsibility for William's younger half-sisters and brothers. After their return to Stone Street, the house at 27 Wall Street was occupied for several years by the Wright Posts.

of my mind at that time was such, that if she knew only one part of it she would forgive me—another reason, I recollect that my Seton brought only the three pair which were struck off expressly because the Colonel [Giles] was expected to set off immediately—if there had been more copies I might have had more reflection.

Kiss your precious children for me, and tell Maria that Anna is happy as the day is long with her dear Dolly she calls it dear Mariva and takes it in her crib every night—

I see my Father very seldom and when I do my Family is now so large that I never see him alone, but I am sure I may venture to say that he always will be Interested in your Health and comfort.

—Heaven Protect you my Julia—E.A. Seton.

1.23 To Lady Isabella Cayley[1]

New York 6 July 1798

My dear Aunt Caley.

We received your letter No.2 written to our dear Father[2] the 3rd of April last and happy should I be were it in my power to offer you the kind affectionate [unclear] contained in it. but alas we have every thing to lament and deplore without one source of comfort but that submission to the disposer of all events which we know is our duty to pay even when the heart is rent with anguish—and how shall I rend yours and what can I say to prepare your mind for the sad and distressing intelligence that our beloved one, best of parents, is no more—You have heard of the melancholy accident he met with on the 25th of January by a fall at his door, since which he has never been free

---

1.23 AMSV Seton-Jevons #566-567 (photostat) No original exists. The copy that does exist is not in Elizabeth Seton's handwriting.

[1] Isabella Seton was the daughter of John and Elizabeth Seton of Scotland and the sister of William Seton, Sr. She lived in England and married Thomas Cayley, a Yorkshire baronet, in 1763. The couple had two children, George and Ann who married George Worsley.

[2] William Seton, Sr., Elizabeth's father-in-law, had died June 9.

from pain, and almost constantly confined to his room, except now and then riding to his country retreat for exercise, of which unfortunately he had never been in the habit of taking enough—His complaint increased rapidly with the warm season and he so entirely lost his spirits as to think himself in danger some weeks before the event took place—He died on the 9th of June after several hours of severe pain but possessing his senses to the last, and with him we have lost every hope of fortune, prosperity and comfort, and shall feel his loss irreperable

Perhaps there never was an instance of any person being so universaly beloved and lamented. Nearly five hundred people attended him to the grave, chiefly dressed in black with every mark of unaffected sorrow—those in the higher station of life regretting a friend and social companion—the Poor mourning a father and benifactor always their resource in misfortune and their assistant in every difficulty—and by us his children who were accustomed constantly to receive his dearest affection and to look up to him as the soul of our existance, his loss will be for ever severely felt and deplored.

My dear William who was ever his favourite and most beloved child, his partner in trade and the one in whom he placed every confidence and trust feels himself at once the Provider and head of a numerous family. Rebecca[3] is the eldest daughter unmarried and there are six younger than herself, but our beloved father brought up his family in such harmony and affection and they have such good and amiable dispositions that if *William* can but make them a comfortable maintenance we shall yet have some hopes of domestic enjoyment when the family gets in some degree settled, but in these hours of sorrow I have not only my poor husbands spirits to support but also to sustain myself expecting every day the birth of another little dependent in addition to our son and daughter—How my William has come thro' each severe trial and anguish of heart as our heavy loss has caused him, particularly being the one on whom the weight of the blow has fallen is only

---

[3]Rebecca Seton (1780-1804) was the daughter of William and Anna Maria Curson Seton and sister-in-law of Elizabeth Seton. A dear friend and confidante of Elizabeth, she died immediately after Elizabeth's return from Leghorn, Italy. Elizabeth often referred to Rebecca as her "soul's sister."

to be accounted for by referring every thing to Him who gives us power to support those evils which every Human being must endure their proportion of. As yet his health has not suffered much but his mind is in a state scarcely to be endured for besides our family sorrow the situation of our affairs with the French and the constant preparation for war makes every one uncertain how long they may be permitted to enjoy their homes or what their future prospects may be—

Our dear Father unfortunately did not leave a will which places my husband in a difficult and uncomfortable situation with respect to his property, which tho' not very great may with Williams industry and unremitting care prove sufficient to maintain and educate a numerous family, if he can but arrange and collect it. But in these melancholy times every thing is scattered and uncertain—and all we can do is to keep united and contribute as much as we can to each others happiness of which Heaven knows we expect but little share, until time which softens all things shall reconcile or rather accustom us to a change which is now the loss of all we valued most. My Williams unremitting labour in the arrangement of the business of the House,[4] which is very extensive and the disturbing confusion and perplexity of his mind at this moment prevents his having the power to write to you himself tho' he very much wishes it, but the constant expression of his affection and g[rateful] remembrance of your goodness to him when he was with you has so familiarized me with the Idea of your family that I hope it will be a sufficent excuse for the manner in which I have ventured to write, and he anxiously wishes that you will from time to time have the goodness to let him hear from you as every thing which interest you will be interesting to us and to him particularly who knows and remembers every branch of your family so well—When circumstances of hurry or necessity prevent his answering your letters I can promise that they shall not remain unanswered as I am always happy to be his scribe and should be particularly so in this case—our father recieved a letter a week or two before his death from

---

[4]Seton, Maitland and Company, an import-export mercantile firm, was managed by William Magee Seton and James Maitland after the death of the elder Mr. Seton. At this time the company was beginning to experience financial difficulties.

Lady Synnot[5] announcing the death of Hon. George Seton[6] which was a very great shock to him, as likewise that of our Grand mother[7] for tho' he could not expect to see her, her letters and the certainty of her fond affection were his greatest pleasures—And in short he had no other gratifications than the happiness and welfare of all his numerous friends and relations, and altho we who were in the constant enjoyment of his affections have reason most to feel his loss there are many who sincerely share with us our sorrows who only knew him for his virtues—and to you my dear Aunt who so well knew and estimated them I can not help again lamenting that the sad tidings should come from my pen—My William desires his affectionate regards to your self and Lady Synnet and Sir Walter and the rest of the family in which I beg leave sincerely to join and remain yours most truly—

Eliza Ann Seton.[8]

1.24 Draft to Julia Scott

New York 20th August 1798

If wishes and thoughts could form letters without any assistance from the Pen you would have recieved at least some thousands since I last wrote to you my Julia—My Pains and Aches are all over and I have one of the loveliest Boys,[1] to repay me that my fond Imagination

---

[5]Jane Seton, a sister of William Seton, Sr., had married Sir Walter Synnot of County Armagh, Ireland.

[6]The husband of Barbara Seton, a sister of William Seton, Sr.

[7] Elizabeth Seton, William Magee Seton's paternal grandmother

[8]A note beside the first line of page #567 states, "word obliterated in original by the seal probably 'grateful.'" The following note appears at the bottom: "Addressed to the Dowager Lady Cayley at Sir Walter Synnots Dublin or Balanoye Newry. Copied by E.S. [or G.S.] Cayley Jan 20, 18[68?]: great grandson of the said Lady Cayley. the original letter being in the possession of Sir Digby Cayley." According to Robert Seton, the copy was made for him by E.S. [or G.S.] Cayley.

1.24 ASJPH 1-3-3-6:8

[1]Richard Bayley Seton (1798-1823) was born July 20, 1798. He was the second son of William Magee and Elizabeth Bayley Seton and attended both Georgetown College in Washington, D.C., and St. Mary's College in Baltimore and was among the first students of Mount St. Mary's College, Emmitsburg. He later served in the United States Navy (1822-23) and became the United States Assistant Agent in Monrovia. He was serving in this capacity at the time of his death which was a result of an illness contracted while nursing the first American consul in Liberia, Jehudi Ashmun, who recovered. Richard was buried at sea.

could have formed, not a little additionally dear to me for bearing the name of Richard Bayley which softened by Seton at the end are sounds which very much delight me and are the promise of much future Hope and Comfort—

My Illness was so severe that both Mother and child were some hours in a very doubtful Situation, and to save the Mother the child was nearly lost, but the *Grand Father*[2] (think what were my sensations who had just enough life to see it) on his Knees blew the Breath of Life into its Lungs and by his skill and care restored it, and need I say doubly endeared it—dear Julia what a subject for my full Heart.

1.25 To Julia Scott

20th August 1798

If wishes and thoughts could form letters without the assistance of the Pen you would have recieved at least some thousands from me within these last six weeks, but from a variety of troubles, such as my nurse leaving me before the time expected, Mammy Hulers[1] sickness during which time I had the care of my *three,*[2] and little Will and Anna both ill of the dissentary which has obliged me to send them out to Mrs. [Eliza Seton] Maitland at my Father Setons country place[3] with at least a half dozen other reasons the worst of the[m] the loss of my fine eyes for some weeks from excessive pain occasioned by the severity of my pains in the Birth of my Son, all combined to prevent my writing to you, but believe me my friend not from often *very often*, anxiously thinking of you—

I have so much to say that I can scarcely Know how to begin the half I have to tell you—I was so terribly ill in my hours of sorrow that

---

[2]Dr. Richard Bayley, Elizabeth's father, attended her in this childbirth.

1.25 ASJPH 1-3-3-6:9

[1]The children's nurse employed by the Setons

[2]Anna Maria, William, and the new-born, Richard Seton

[3]Cragdon at Bloomingdale, located at approximately 78th Street on the west side of present day Manhattan, was the Seton's summer home. The Bloomingdale Road, opened in 1703, ran between what are now 23rd and 147th Streets and followed roughly the route of the present Broadway. Elizabeth went to Cragdon the last week of August because of the illness of her two older children who had been sent there during her confinement. The infant Richard did not do well there, so she returned to the city about August 29.

my Poor Father could scarcely perform his office, tho' every exertion was necessary to save me. The dear little son was for some hours thought past Hope and the Mother within one more pain of that rest she has so often longed for—but which Heaven I hope for good purposes has again denied—my Father may truely be said to have given the breath of Life to my child for when it neither Breathed or moved he went on his Knees and placing his Mouth to its lips breathed or I may say forceably blew it into its Lungs—and now the little Soul is the most lovely healthy Being you ever saw, and not a little additionally dear to his Mother for bearing the name of Richard Bayley which with Seton at the end are sounds truely delightful to me—

30th August

I was hastily summoned by my William to go with him to see our poor little Anna who has been extremely ill, and have been ever since with her until yesterday, when the ill effect of the sudden change of weather on my Baby obliged us to return Home where the first and most wellcome object that met my eyes was your letter which might well reproach me for not writing—

Your dear children I Hope are better but I shall write a note to my Father (for fear I should not see him) to tell your wish, and will send my letter by tomorrows Post.You do not say one word of your own Health therefore I will indulge the Hope that it is as I wish it to be. I have not heard any thing latterly of the Fever in Philadelphia,[4] whether it will not be as bad with us Heaven only knows, but I am sure it bids fair to be as bad as it can be—My Father says it is the most deadly kind and more like the Plague than Fever and that the *mischief* in[cre]ases fast—Ah Julia this Life is not worth one ha[lf th]e anxious moments that I suffer in one single day. Husband[,] Father and my good Brother [Post] are continually in the midst of it—Our moving is deferred for some weeks, as Stone Street[5] is the very center of the Fever therefore I can say but little of my Family—the girls[6] are all with

---

[4]Yellow fever was currently rampant in Philadelphia.

[5]The location of the home to which the Seton family was moving

[6]William Magee's four younger half-sisters, Mary, Charlotte, Cecilia, and Harriet, for whom he and Elizabeth had assumed responsibility

me and as yet have given me much more satisfaction that I can express to you, for it is impossible to meet with more amiable dispositions—I wrote Our Dear Charlotte six lines some time ago in answer to a most Affectionate letter she wrote me to thank me for the Engravings I sent her by Seton—Heaven Preserve and Bless her—

My Julia do not tell me that Family or occupations, or chances or changes shall hinder me from giving you the only proof that absence and Fate have left me of expressing to you my Affection—I will write again very soon—

Yours truely and affectionately

31st August—My Father particularly directs me to tell you that there is no cure for the Hooping Cough[7]—Nature must have its course—but if they have pain i[n th]e Breast & oppressed Breathing you must have recourse to [unclear] and Blistering[8] as in any other complaint of the Breast. [He wou]ld have written this direction himself but he has scarcely time to Breath and never pretends to sit down except at meals—[I t]ell you as he bid me word for word—*E.A.S.*

1.26 To Julia Scott

8th September 1798

My Darling Julia,

It is now indeed that I feel the bitterness of Our Separation, While all your Sorrows are renewed and your Heart is again torn with affliction, I fear too much for you to bear. And is our poor Brother[1] gone—Almighty Disposer of all events we must bow in Silence to thy decrees,—but I tremble for the Consequences of this unlooked for blow to you my friend whose future comfort and satisfaction in Life seemed so nearly

---

[7] A highly infectious respiratory disease

[8] Blisters on the skin were formed by applying a sharp, irritating ointment, plaster or other application.

1.26 ASJPH 1-3-3-6:10

[1] Julia's brother John Sitgreaves died of yellow fever September 3, 1798.

connected and dependant on those affectionate attentions of which you will so much feel the Want, and that never failing cheerful mind which extended its happy influence to all within its Sphere, Oh Julia I could indulge myself in reflections which are too unavailing—but it seems the last tribute within our Power to the departed worth of one whom we have Affectionately loved—our Brother will long recieve that tribute and I have fully paid it accompanyed by many tears—

You are I am sure very anxious for your friends in New York in this season of horrors—and I believe we are the only ones who remain—Poor Seton is chained, and where he is, there am I also—our little Darlings are out of Town with Mrs. Maitland[2] and so are all the family occasionally, but our neighborhood is intirely deserted—We are all perfectly well how long we shall be so Heaven only Knows for several have died in this street, one Person three doors off—I have not seen my Father for a whole week until last Evening and he then told me that he spent every hour in the Hospitals and Lazaretto[3]—While one so dear to me is so much exposed I infinitely prefer remaining in the City Independent of my William being here

—Julia I cannot say more until I hear from you which I pray and intreat you may be soon, and very soon—

My affectionate remembrance to Brother Samuel and your darlings—

Yours most truely—E.A.Seton—

1.27 To Julia Scott

Bloomingdale 28th September 1798[1]

My Beloved Julia,

I have experienced nothing but sorrow and anxiety since I recieved your letter of the 15th it arrived at a moment well calculated to give force to the melancholy it expressed, and which has affected me beyond

---

[2]Elizabeth's older children, Anna Maria and William, were with Eliza Seton Maitland, Elizabeth's sister-in-law, at Cragdon outside the city.

[3]A place where the sick were confined during contagious epidemics

1.27 ASJPH 1-3-3-6:11

[1]Elizabeth was often not consistent in her spelling as in this letter in which she uses both Bloomingdale and Blooming Dale to refer to the location of the Seton home, Cragdon.

measure that you are suffering both in mind and Body and so far from the reach of that affection which at this time would so much contribute to soothe the pangs of sorrow—that affection so intirely your own—Oh Julia how bitter are these days of seperation to me—When you are well, in Health and cheerfulness I can resign you and persue my path without regret and think it is for the best, but when you are in sorrow I feel an exclusive right and could fly over mountains to support that aching head—If I thought your situation in mind and Body was as you describe it, habitually, I should think it almost insupportable, but I hope from self experience that your sensibility to your present misfortunes will exhaust and destroy itself, for believe me my darling Julia you were not born to be unhappy, or Heaven would never have given you *such a Brother* [Samuel] as is still left to you, and tho' I well know that it is impossible to reconcile you to the distressing afflictions that have attended you, I also know how capable he is of lessening their weight—look up my love and be thankful for the Good that yet remains.—how much I wish again to hear from you, and to hear that those distressing sensations you describe to me are past.

—I should have written Immediately on recieving your letter but my William my Husband and *My All* was at that time ill with the prevailing Fever[2]—he has happily had but a slight attack but sufficient to terrify me for the consequences, particularly as our Being at Blooming Dale prevented my Father attending him—He is now most happily intirely restored and is going to stay some time from the city which is in a state truely deplorable—My Sister and Brother Post have also both been attacked but are on the recovery and gone to Long Island—My Father resides intirely at Bellvue Hospital.[3] Dear Julia consider the lot of Humanity is to *suffer* and bow with me in Patient submission to our All-Wise Director.—I am in extreme pain while I write occasioned by a Bile[4] on my arm therefore must say Adieu

4th October May Heaven restore you to Peace prays your *E.A.S.*

---

[2]There was a yellow fever epidemic at the time.

[3]Bellevue Hospital was a municipal hospital opened in 1736 as the almshouse infirmary on the site now occupied by City Hall. Later, in 1794, the city bought a building at 26th Street and First Avenue to house victims of epidemics. Dr. Bayley was associated with Bellevue.

[4]Probably a boil

1.28 To Julia Scott

[postmarked New York, October 13]

My best Beloved Julia

I wrote you last week, and should have again written you as I feel how anxious you must be for our present situation, but really it appears to me that I am not to be myself again. I have been almost blind of my best eye, and had a gathering under my Arm occasioned by cold which settled my Milk there, besides which my head is absolutely turned with anxiety about my Husband who is obliged to go every day in the city, and my Father who still resides at *Bellvue* and has almost exhausted himself with the excessive fatigues he daily endures. I would have returned Home long ago if I could have gained permission from my Father as our House having been open all the summer renders it much safer for us than Others who left no one at Home. You may Imagine that eighteen in Family,[1] in a House containing only five small rooms is rather more than *enough*, and I cannot help longing again for the *rest* which I have never known but in Wall Street[2]—

But my love what are my troubles compared with your Perpetual Sorrow—could I but share it with you, I could willingly quit Home and all its charms with only the priviledge of my little *nurseling*[3] with me, if I could be allowed the comfort of being with you in the season of Affliction,—dearest Julia—a thousand times nearer to my Heart than when in the days of Ease and cheerfulness, what would I give to hold you to that Heart which shares with yours every pain. how much I long to hear of Our dear Charlotte—May Heaven shield her from danger and spare her the anguish of witnessing the sufferings of those she loves—

1.28 ASJPH 1-3-3-6:12

[1] This number included Elizabeth's immediate family as well as her husband's younger half-brothers and sisters.

[2] Wall Street was Elizabeth and William Magee Seton's residence prior to the death of William Seton, Sr. They were now residing on Stone Street.

[3] Richard Seton, Elizabeth's third child

My Julia, you must not Indulge the extreme dejection which I am persuaded you have resigned yourself to. You have two precious Objects[4] sufficient to tye you to that existance you now seem careless of possessing. You must nurse yourself and look forward, at all events this life is worth possessing if it were only because while we have it we are candidates for a better—think of your *Daughter* my love, think what is the difference to her if you preserve your Health or lose it—you never knew the want of a Mothers tender care, or you would tremble at the thought that *your child* should ever want it.

Sunday Evening 14th October

You say my love that you wish the latest Intelligence of the Health of your friend, could I save you one moments anxiety it would be the source of hours of pleasure to me therefore you may suppose how willingly I obey your request. This day has been clouded and Melancholy as the present season, and nothing but the smiles and Health of my precious Children could have saved me from its Influence, but I am so intirely occupied with them having only Mammy Huler to assist me, that I have no time to indulge reflection. If I retire one moment I hear a half dozen voices calling Sister, or Mamma,—My Father has been ill the last week and altho' now better, I cannot help feeling great anxiety.—My Sister[5] was last Friday in momentary expectation, and I have not heard from her since—Immagine Yourself in my situation, in its extent, for a few moments, and you will find that there are yet many sources of regret and disappointment that you have not Experienced and I hope never may;—but the Merciful conductor of All—mixes the sweet with the bitter, and whenever the Evil has most force; he throws the veil of Peace over the Soul that confides in Him—May He Protect you my beloved Prays

your E.A.Seton

---

[4]Julia's children, Maria and John Scott
[5]Mary Bayley Post was pregnant and close to her time of delivery.

1.29 To Julia Scott

Sunday 21st October 1798

I have two letters to write, one to My Sister and one to Richard,[1] but I cannot take hold of my Pen, but my thoughts fly to you, and to you they shall go, tho' without any new occurrences to give rise to them—We are, and are likely to be in a state of confusion, and where there is not Peace, the mind loses all those delightful communications and Reflections which mine so much delights in, and which I fear it has lost for many years to come, for if I get thro' *my task* with the Sacrifice of the most incessant care and attention, and in the end feel the Satisfaction of having performed it well, it is as much as I can expect, and more than I dare to Hope—but this is a subject it is vain to Indulge, for who shall dare to look into futurity—how different were my prospects in the last year, from the present, and if I now plan the futurity it may never be realized, and if it is, the causes for apprehension may be lessened—perhaps removed—therefore to intend the best, and be thankful for the present, is the only plan I can resolve on—

Sunday Evening

My dear Julia I can only add good Night to the above which I was interrupted in writing this morning, and assure you that you are inestimably dear to the Heart of

Your *E.A.S.*

The Fever is better—

1.29 ASJPH 1-3-3-6:13
[1]Richard Bayley, Elizabeth's half-brother

1.30 To Julia Scott

Sunday Night *28th* October *[17]98*

My darling Julia

Saturday Night always brings to my recollection that it is in my power to do something you wish, and if it is not then in my power to accomplish it, I am restless and dissatisfied until I can procure an hour of leisure that indeed is but seldom, for I am constant Nurse to my Infant[1] and when he is out of my arms the two padlers[2] are always after me praying to go in the Garden the Woods or the Bread and Butter closet, so you may imagine I am well occupied and happy for me it is so, for reflection in these times can only augment the evils we have to endure.

My William lectured me for half an hour last Sunday for sending you so short a letter as I wrote you on that day—he said it was not worth its postage, but I would give something at this moment to have one from you if it contained only half the number of lines, for I am extremely anxious to hear of our dear Charlotte—What a sorrowful reflection for me, who loves her so well that she is in the very center of danger—may Heaven avert it from her and her family; for any one being ill would afflict her more than any Personal suffering—Julia dear when shall we meet in a State of *Certainty*, surely the next blessing in our future existance to that of being near the source of Perfection, will be the enjoyment of each others Society without dread of interruption from evil—*no seperation*, but free communication of affection unshackled by the why's and wherefores of this World—Who that is toiling thro' the scenes of vexation that this life continually presents, but must sigh for futurity, and yet it is thought wonderful and even incredible that a person free from Poverty and the greatest ills of Life, should wish to change this for another—I resign the present and the future to Him who is the Author and conductor of both—but most

---

1.30 ASJPH 1-3-3-6:14

[1]Richard Seton

[2]Anna Maria and William Seton, Elizabeth's two young children

certainly I have no enjoyment so great as to induce me to remain Here one moment longer, if it depended on me to make the change—even as the Mother of my children I would not stay if I were sure they would not be deprived of the Protection of their Father

—Why do I tell you all this? how it is that I never can preserve any consistancy in a letter to you, but always involuntarily express my *thoughts* as they arise?—I write some letters where the words drop so heavily that I can scarcely form them at all, but when I begin "Dear Julia" they flow faster than the pen can write them.

Well to tell you what I ought to tell, and what you will wish to know, the Evil that afflicts us[3] is lessining, tho' the very uncommon weather renders the degree of it very changeable and uncertain, one day every Hope is revived, and the next the number of Deaths is again doubled—Heaven only knows when it will end—My poor girls are all getting the Fever Ague[4] and my children take colds which keep me in continual alarm which added to my William's fatigues, and the very great inconvenience of being here, has determined us to go to Town to-morrow, We go to Wall Street at first and arrange our Winter habitation as fast as possible—My Sister Post is happily delivered of a Daughter[5]—on Long Island at the Narrows where her husband[6] remains with her—you may easily imagine their Joy on the occasion—My Father still resides at Bellvue Hospital if I were taken ill tomorrow I should wish to go *there*. Richard has arrived at Leghorn[7] in perfect Health and de[lighted] with his situation—Emma[8] is engaged to marry Craig, and they only wait the arrival of Mr. and Mrs. Sadler who are hourly expected—it rejoices my Heart that she is chosen by so good a man, for tho' he is very far from those brilliant

---

[3] The yellow fever epidemic

[4] An attack of fever accompanied by chills or shivering

[5] Mary Bayley Post's daughter Catherine was born at this time.

[6] Dr. Wright Post

[7] Richard Bayley, Elizabeth's half-brother, went to Leghorn, Italy, to work in the firm of Filippo and Antonio Filicchi, business associates of the Setons.

[8] Charlotte Amelia (Emma) Bayley (1779-1805) was a daughter of Dr. Richard and Charlotte Barclay Bayley and the half-sister of Elizabeth Seton. She married William Craig, the brother of Eliza Craig Sadler, June 19, 1799, and died giving birth to a child in 1805.

qualities which the World so much admires, he has those of a true and upright Heart with a very well informed mind.—May she be happy.

—and for you my Julia my wishes have not a name, the only Word that approaches their meaning is *Peace* It is what *I* covet, and oh that we may one day share it together. I have not recieved a letter from you since the sixth October—pray write soon—

Yours ever affectionately *E.A.S.*

1.31 To Rebecca Seton

31st October [1798]

How glad you will be to see the heads of old Speeds Horses[1]—come my Rebecca and enjoy the comfortable coal fire and every thing in my power to make you happy.—I send every thing I can muster to make you warm coming home, and be sure to wrap Harriet[2] well up in the Shawl and coat, and bring the Blankets I sent yesterday with you for fear we have not enough without them.—We would have sent Speed immediately but he was not at Home—

Willy says be sure to bring *all the Girls*

Yours most Sincerely

1.31 AMPH Seton-Jevons #1-2

[1] A coach was sent to Bloomingdale to bring the Seton girls back to the city.

[2] Henrietta (Harriet) Seton (1789-1809) was the daughter of William and Anna Maria Curson Seton and the half-sister of William Magee Seton. She accompanied her sister Cecilia to Baltimore in 1809 for a visit with their sister-in-law Elizabeth Seton. Once engaged to Elizabeth's half-brother Andrew Barclay Bayley (d.1811), Harriet broke the engagement after her conversion to Roman Catholicism. She made her profession of faith July 22 and her First Communion September 24, 1809.

1.32 To Julia Scott

New York 3rd November 1798—

Once more returned to my happy Home, and doubly enjoying its sweets from the long privation I have endured,[1] my thoughts turn to you dear Julia with whom I have so often shared the cheerfulness of the blazing fire, and the *feeling tones* of my sweet *Piano*. I could not help falling on my knees the moment I entered the dear scene of past happiness and shed tears as Abundantly as if I was the next moment going to quit it. Oh Julia, Julia *never again.*—those hours are past which tho' I enjoyed them, I never knew their value. Who can help looking back on Innocent and past pleasures without sorrow, I can more forceably say *anguish*, I could cry like a child at the thought of them, but resolved to *brave the future*, I turn over the Page with rapidity, and looking towards Heaven *there* fix my aim—*there is no change.*

My Father is in perfect Health, and in a state of exultation at his escape from Bellvue,[2] and the recollection of all the Good which his resolution and undaunted spirit has effected there—you may imagine how much I was rejoiced to see him after the many dangers he has past.—Dear Julia, how much have I to be thankful for—Post is also well, and my *William* enjoying better Health than for many months before. but our long residence in the country, and without proper winter cloathing has given Our Girls the fever ague and little *Anna* a serious illness, which she is but slowly recovering from. Richard has also had a fever and rash—I am well Occupied, and expect notwithstanding these difficulties to be peaceably sleeping in Stone Street by this night a week.—We have painted Papered and White-washed, so I hope there is no danger, tho' the Man who took care of the House was ill there with Fever, and not one House in the neighbourhood escaped

---

1.32 ASJPH 1-3-3-6:15
[1] The Setons had been living out of the city because of the yellow fever epidemic.
[2] Dr. Richard Bayley had been working at Bellevue Hospital during the epidemic.

—You say that "No news is good news"—thank Heaven, for you do not mention either Yours or your childrens Health. I am therefore to Hope that those disagreeable symptoms you wrote of in a former letter are past. I am rejoyced that our dear Charlotte has had so fortunate an escape, I know no one except yourself I have been more anxious for. that you may both enjoy Health and Peace is the sincere prayer of her who never can forget you—

E.A.Seton.

1.33 To Julia Scott

New York 25th November 1798—

My dearest Julianna

Three Saturdays are past without writing one line to you; not that you have been thought of less than usual for I have been in trouble, and it is then I think most of you. at Bloomingdale my right arm was visited, and this fortnight past I have been unable to move my left, from a similiar gathering which my Father was obliged to operate upon, and was so painful as to cause a constant slow Fever. Since my recovery Pantrys, closets, store rooms, cellar etc have Occupied me well, and I suppose I shall have the same reason from you for not writing, for I hope by this time you are settling your Home, or rather your House Julia, for I cannot think that you will make Philadelphia your Home, Brother [Samuel] being with you is I am sure a very great consolation, but he cannot devote so much of his time to you as to compensate for the many disadvantages you will experience, for my William says your House is a long walk for you to your Family, and except you enter in the trouble of keeping a Equipage[1] you might better be in New York. I rejoice that Harriet[2] is with you, I wish extremely to see her

---

1.33 ASJPH 1-3-3-6:16
[1]An elegantly equipped carriage
[2]Julia's niece

and to know if she is that kind of disposition which wants nothing but a short residence with *Madam Particular* to perfect it—if she is, she is not *my sort,*—I am more interested for her than you can imagine, and have always felt a presentiment that I shall one day know more of her.

Your children you never mention; for want of time I suppose, poor Julia you have always a great deal to do, or *make* a great deal. Suppose you had a Nurseling and half a dozen besides—Suppose the providing and arranging my family—and suppose yourself a teacher of Reading, writing, sewing etc for I devote the whole Morning—that is from ten till two to my three Girls[3]—Going to school thro' snow and wet will give me more trouble than keeping them at Home[.] I have tried it one week, and as yet it has been only a pleasure at all events I shall go thro' it this winter—The two oldest girls are at Brunswick at Boarding School,[4] which is a very great relief to me—Girls of twelve and fourteen are much more difficult to manage than at any other time of Life, and I am sure it will be greatly for their own advantage they are all sweet amiable children, and I love them as my own—Rebecca is without any exception the most truely amiable estimable young woman I ever knew. her Virtues are such as would ornament any Station, and does honor to the Memory of my poor Father[5] who was her only Director in every thing. her Society is a source of pleasure to me, such as is altogether new and unexpected, for until I was under the same roof with her I always thought her an uninformed Girl, with many good qualities, but very much neglected.—but I prove the contrary every day—

And Myself—am jogging on Old style, trying to accomplish every duty, and *Hoping* for the reward—without *that* in View heaven knows this life would be a scene of confusion and vexation *to me*, who neither values it nor desires it. I always thought and ever shall, that *Husbands*

---

[3]Elizabeth's sisters-in-law Harriet and Cecilia Seton and her daughter Anna Maria Seton.

[4]Elizabeth's sisters-in-law Mary and Charlotte Seton were attending a boarding school operated by Miss Hay in (New) Brunswick, New Jersey.

Mary Seton and Charlotte Seton (1786-1853) were the daughters of William and Anna Maria Curson Seton. Mary married Josiah Ogden Hoffman. Charlotte married Gouverneur Ogden (1778-1851). He was from a prominent New York family and graduated from Columbia (1796). He entered the legal profession and was a partner of Alexander Hamilton.

[5]William Seton, Sr.

can be consoled, Children sometimes prosper as well without, as with Parents, and at all events Life has such varieties of disappointments that they may as well proceed from one cause as another, —but when Existance is the Gift of Heaven in order that certain duties may be fulfilled, and the path that leads to a state of Immortality and perfection—in this point of view I am Grateful for the gifts, and wait with *cheerful Hope*. Good night dear Julia, Kiss dear Sister Charlotte for me and believe me

Yours most truely. *E.A.S.*

1.34 To Julia Scott

Sunday Evening 19th December 1798

Dear Precious Julia—

Whilst I was dozing over a volume of Sermons (such is the frailty of Human nature) I recollected that I had not written to you these ten days—and in one moment my eyes were open, thoughts awake and every tender affection of my Heart in exercise. dear precious little friend—I never will even in appearance neglect her.—Your last letter gave me much uneasiness as it regards my Brother Henry,[1] who I am extremely Anxious should have some provision and altho' I knew him to be sometimes irregular in his conduct, I had no Idea that it had ever excited so much attention as materially to injure him—My poor William is indeed to be pitied and has a dreadful struggle with them all—how he will get thro' it I know not, and it is well for me I have a perfect reliance on Superior Providence, or my Spirits would be unequal to the task of supporting His—Our Friend G[iles] and his Brother from Baltimore passed an hour with us this Morning, I always feel in his company an interest I never do in any other persons since

1.34 ASJPH 1-3-3-6:17

[1] Henry Seton (b. 1774) was the son of William and Rebecca Curson Seton. He became a lieutenant in the United States Navy and accompanied the Setons until they left the New York harbor en route to Italy in 1803.

your departure He speaks so much of our Poor Brother John,[2] and all your affairs that he seems more nearly connected with the Idea of you than any other Person I know—

With what mingled and various sensations I touched the rapper of your door this Morning, inquiring for Mrs. Laight the Bride[3]—She is there as Mistress of the House at present, and will be I suppose if Mr. Hoffman remain[s] unmarried. I had not the melancholy pleasure of entering it and did not know whither or no to regret her not being at Home, but think I should have liked to have viewed the scene of so many past hours, and some very happy ones—

If I do not conclude my letter to night, you will not recieve it in several days, for Monday is a busy day with me, as it formerly was with you and Tuesday a part of *the family* dines with us and of course make more to do than usual. When you speak of me to Brother Samuel, as I am sure you sometimes will, remember to *remember* him, that I always was and *believe* ever will be of the number of those who dearly love him—

Kiss your precious children for me and take the prayers and fondest Affection of

your E.A.S.

1.35 To Anna Maria Seton[1]

December 31, 1798

The last the first and every day of the year my thoughts and time are yours my Anna,—but I enjoy a peculiar pleasure in devoting an hour generally appropriated to Amusements, to you my precious Child, in whom my greatest delight and amusements are centered. May the

---

[2]Julia's brother John Sitgreaves had died in September 1798.

[3]Formerly Miss Colden

1.35 UNDA II-1-a

[1]Anna Maria Seton was three and a half years old when this was written. It appears on a piece that had a rather moral subject, which has been crossed out, presumably by Elizabeth, and the page has been cut; clearly the moral piece was longer.

Giver of all good, grant his Protection to you, and assist me in my Endeavours to promote your future good and Advantage. The Blessing and attentions of the tenderest Parents and most affectionate friends are constantly yours, and by your conduct you will confer the gratification of our fondest wishes, or inflict the most Bitter disappointment. In you I view the Friend, the Companion, and Consolation of my future years—delightful Reflection

1799

1.36 To Julia Scott

3rd January 1799

My Julia

The last year has been to *us* the reverse of Our dearest Hopes, the Grave of every enjoyment—yes to *us* my Julia, I feel a melancholy satisfaction in the expression, and the first pleasant thought I enjoyed in the opening of this year was that the terrible ninety-eight was past—but the effects of those events which are past with it, must remain as long my existance—may the similitude fail here my love, and Heaven grant you that Peace you covet—and Bless your children who I am sure are real Blessings to you—

The Colonel [Giles] has been terrifying me with apprehensions for your Health and is sure that you are ill because you have not written, but I am so well accustomed to your Lazy pen that I have better Hopes tho' I cannot altogether divest myself of fears for you as young Giles mentioned your having been Indisposed—do write one line to clear the cloud—for dearest Julia absence does not shake Affection, and *Friendship Make[,]* it strengthens. I write only to wish you a happy

New Year and to beg that you will soon let me hear that you are well; for Rebecca Seton[1] is very ill, and I am just going to lay a Blister on her Breast, but will write again next week. I am

Yours most truely and surely *E.A.S.*

1.37 To Julia Scott

New York 20th January 1799

Mrs. Julia

I should be happy to know if the key of your memory is lost, or if you have a Felon[1] on your Finger—something certainly must have happened to make you so very indifferent to my wishes on the subject of hearing from you. the Colonel [Giles] and even his amiable Lady are favoured but as you have not *business* to transact with me I can excuse you on the score of your numerous correspondants provided you had substituted Maria or John, for I have really been unhappy about you, having once heard you were ill, I did not know how far that illness might have extended until the Colonel called to inform me that you were neither dying nor Dead. thank Heaven for that and whenever you have leisure please to remember me.—

I have had a siege of Sorrow these three weeks, but it is now happily past, and my poor Sister is better and my children who were all down with a cold the most violent they ever had, are quite recovered. Mrs. [Eliza] Sadler is also arrived after being four months at Sea, and my Poor Sister Emma[2] is released from her terrible doubts and anxieties, and I suppose her Wedding will now take place as soon as she pleases—for myself, I can but reflect on the perverseness of Human Affairs for Mrs. S's arrival once so much my earnest wish is now

---

[1]Elizabeth's sister-in-law had tuberculosis which was flaring up.

1.37 ASJPH 1-3-3-6:19

[1]An infection at the end of a finger near the nail

[2]Charlotte Amelia Bayley, Elizabeth's half-sister, was engaged to marry William Craig, Eliza Craig Sadler's brother.

converted into, I could almost say a misfortune, except as far as respects her Personal Safety; for my Father perseveres in his resolution that I shall never admit a reconciliation with Mrs. B[ayley][3] and in that case my Intercourse with Mrs. Sad[ler]—will be so much mixed with vexation, and our difference will be a source of so much mortification to her, that I can never visit her without expecting to meet those I do not wish to meet, and would now rather wish to avoid what was once so great a pleasure—my *Home* too is changed Julia—I am now never alone, have no leisure hours, and care less than ever for the World or its enjoyments.

Your friend told me that you were in the cruelest state of depression of Spirits, but Julia I know you well and if you are not changed I do not care for your expressions at the moment of writing to an Absent Friend, for I have known you to write to your Father[4] or Brother in the morning on the most melancholy Subjects, and in the Afternoon dress, go visiting, and be the most cheerful of the company—this you may remember and I hope it is so now, tho' your mind has been but too much exercised I believe, and I fear Sorrow has gained but too great an ascendance over it. Cheer up my love, remember the Storm is in part blown over, and the remaining cloud may pass by harmless—O Julia if my wishes or exertions could gain you Peace you should enjoy it in its most perfect state, but Heaven alone can bestow it for it is Heaven.

How is my Sister Charlotte and her prosperous train, how much I would give to see you both and those that belong to you—If my Son[5] gets well over his Innoculation in time nothing is more probable than

---

[3]The stepmother of Elizabeth Bayley Seton, Charlotte Amelia Barclay Bayley (d.1805), became the second wife of Dr. Richard Bayley June 16, 1778. By 1799 Dr. Bayley was estranged from his second wife and had instructed Elizabeth not to associate with her. With the impending marriage of Elizabeth's half-sister to her friend Eliza Sadler's brother, she found herself in a tense situation.

[4]William Sitgreaves (?-1800), Julia's father, arrived in Philadelphia in 1729 and became a prominent merchant. He married Susanna Deshon.

[5]Richard Seton, Elizabeth's infant son, had a mild case of smallpox due to his inoculation and was quarantined in the nursery. Dr. Edward Jenner had publicly introduced the use of coxpox vaccine to create immunity to smallpox in 1798. This use of the inocualtion would have been among the earliest in the United States.

that I shall surprise you with a visit—Heaven bless and preserve my Julia—

E.A.S.

1.38 To Dr. Richard Bayley

New York 2nd February [17]99

Should you be in your Retirement, unoccupied by cares and Solicitudes that generally accompany you, a letter from your Daughter will be very acceptable—if otherwise, it will be read in haste and the Idea "Bett is a Goose" will pass your mind,—I send it to take its chance, hoping as the children say, it may find you well, as I am the same. It is currently reported that you are gone to New London[1] to inquire the origin of "the Fever," and that you are to proceed to Boston to see your Children,[2] but I hope you will very soon return and convince the Ladies who chatter on the subject that the origin is not the object of your pursuit, but the remedy.

I have passed one of the most Elegant Evenings of my Life. it is now Eleven oclock, and since seven I have never quited my seat, and scarcely changed my posture. Part of my Family are asleep, and part abroad—I have been reading of the "High and lofty One who inhabits Eternity," and selecting such passages as I wish to transmit to my Daughter.[3] How the World lessens and recedes—how calm and peaceable are hours spent in such Solitude, they are marked down for useful purposes and their Memory remains—

I close my Evening Employment with "Orasons for Thee." Peace be with my Father.

E.A.S.

1.38 ASJPH 1-3-3-9:79

[1] A city in southeast Connecticut on Long Island Sound, forty-five miles east of New Haven
[2] Probably some of the children of Dr. Bayley's second marriage
[3] Anna Maria Seton

1.39 To Julia Scott

New York 20th February 1799

My dearest Julia

Your last letter filled me with Sorrow and renewed every recollection of former days. that fate which has seperated you from those who love you so well can never reconcile me to your absence except I could call you to my imagination happy, and in the enjoyment of more than you left behind you in N[ew] York, but Julia sick and in sorrow are images which are too painful to dwell on, and my imagination always on the fairest side, loves to pourtray you in the midst of those whose society you used so much to covet, your tranquility restored and all those little family arrangements made which are so necessary to your repose—it is a melancholy reflection. And no one can make it oftener than I do, that our Peace and pleasure should so much depend on hirelings and circumstances so trivial, but it always will be so while artificial wants and habits affect us as much as they now do

Oh Julia how happy must have been the former days of Simplicity and ease, when cooks and Waiters had their proper rank in existance and had not the power of overturning whole Families and tormenting us poor little Ladies until Life is almost a burthen—but better days will come—there is another and a better world, and as my Poor Father says "hail, to the period when we will be at rest." I recieved a very long letter from Him Yesterday, He has been dancing attendance on the Legislature[1] these three weeks and is likely so to do, but he is well and in a situation perfectly agreeable to Him, at the Lieutenant Governors where he finds those attentions and formalities he is so fond of recieving. I also have a long letter from Miss Shipton who I suspect is on the road to Matrimony or Disappointment, for I think it very evident by her expressions respecting Mr. Morgan that if he regains his

---

1.39 ASJPH 1-3-3-6:20

[1]From 1798 to 1801 Dr. Bayley made regular trips to Albany each winter to report to the New York State Legislature in his capacity as health officer of the New York City Board of Health Commissioners. He usually stayed in Watervliet and received his mail in care of Lieutenant-Governor Steven van Rensselaer.

Health and returns from Lisbon he will marry her but Mr. Ogden who saw him embark says that he was the picture of Death and scarcely able to stand without support. She has sent dear little Anna the Scripture lessons such as Maria has—Anna is extremely altered since you were here and has grow[n] a most lovely girl indeed she is every thing *you* would most wish in a child, Will is a Bouncer and would rule the house if permitted, but my little Richard rules all Hearts for you never did see a lovelier Baby, very like Anna but a much milder expression—

Col[onel] Giles has promised me that he will send this letter—Oh Julia how it grieves me to hear that you have so much vexation on account of Mr.Grien and that miserable Sam Smith, I wish you may not find these mortifications too much for You, and I hope you will exert your mind and look forward to better days. Mrs. G[iles] says she has pressed you to pass the summer with her at Long Island, but whether it will add to your happiness or not you are the only Judge, happy should I be were it in my power to make you a similar proposition—but alas I am out of my proper Sphere, cloged and shackled, without the power of one free act of the Will, in a narrow path from which I never expect to step until I arrive on that blest shore "where weary travellers rest.["] dear Julia rest assured that small as your portion of happiness may appear to you,—you have not more than almost any person has to contend with who has suffered a reverse of family affairs, to feel all our Old habits infringed or altered, to extend our ideas to the affairs of other people and make exertions we are unaccustomed to, is not so easily to be reconciled—but acting well our part in present difficulties is the only way to insure the Peace of futurity.—Kiss your precious children for me and remember me most affectionately to Sister C[harlotte] and Brother Samuel and believe me ever

Yours—*E.A.Seton*

1.40 To Dr. Richard Bayley

New York 24th February 1799

Your most Welcome letter arrived safe, but not before it was too late to answer it by the next Post. it was also without a date which deprived me of the pleasure of knowing when it was written, but the good intelligence it contained of your Health and expected return was as much pleasure as could possibly be afforded by any circumstance, and exhilirated my Spirits to so great a degree that Madam Olive who had passed the day with me, declared that her *chere fille* was *charmante* and gave me *mille baisérs.*[1] She has confided her eldest Son to my care, a confidence so flattering from one who is so particularly attentive to the Morals and Manners of her Children that I purpose on our return from their neighborhood next Summer to leave my Son William with her, as it will be the means of his gaining the French Language with facility and giving him a Knowledge of it which with practice will be permanent, an advantage I think incalculable—besides weaning him from Old Mammy [Huler]

—Your Friends are all well, Mrs. F. is better Mr. Forbes from Jamaica dined with us Yesterday and says the long-looked for Gentlemen will certainly be here this year if the *Crops* are good. good-good. If you should have any leisure moments think of my Brother, dear Sir—You are a Philosopher—I rejoice in your acquisition of *Firmness, Stability,* O my Father treasure up the Blessed Spirit, and place me in the Path to attain it. Mr. Olive says *I* am a Specimin of Philosophy, one who reasons and reflects on the Consequences of actions, and superior to exterior appearances, *"pas une femme savant c'est ci que je deteste le plus"*[2]—He little thinks how the frail Bark is tost by contending commotions, and how dearly earned is that spirit of accomodation he thinks so great an ornament. I wrote Julia [Scott] this

---

1.40 ASJPH 1-3-3-9:80

[1] That is, "her dear daughter was charming and gave me a thousand kisses"

[2] That is, "what I detest most is a woman who is not wise."

day. She is well. and so are all my *Darlings*, and your Own dear
Daughter *E.A.Seton*

Who made the Heart, 'tis he alone
Decidedly can try us,
He knows each chord its various tone,
Each Spring its various bias:
Then at the balance let's be mute,
We never can adjust it;
What's done we partly may compute,
But know not what's resisted.

1.41 To Julia Scott

15th March [1799]

Your letter my Julia afflicts me beyond measure—And have I
added pain to your Accumulated causes of vexation who would do
any thing in this World to lessen or sooth your sorrows—I have also
had my Share, notwithstanding my resolution to bear up against all
evil with Patience and fortitude, but Alas, Nature will have its vent
and maintain its ascendancy in every Bosom unarmed with apathy—a
blessing I fear I never shall attain—but it is all in vain to think or
grieve, my cup must be filled, and when all is over, when the Silver
cord is loosed, and the Spirit returned to Him who gave it, then He who
has witnessed its struggles will give it Rest.—in the mean time exertions and sacrifices must be made. in the midst of your sorrows you
have the sweetest Consolations your Daughter particularly will soon
supply a thousand sources of happiness—

I think if mine could possibly ever approach her in the amiable
qualities of her mind and temper I should think Her unequalled—but
my Julia, she is of a different mould and tho' a pliant good disposition
she possesses too much of that lively genius which tho' flattering in its

first appearances very often is the ruin of its possessor—Perhaps you may in a future day be permitted to assist me in my duty towards Her, and I feel the most perfect assurance of your rediness to do so—My Father in addition to his former uneasiness has new sources of distress which make me tremble. two of my Brothers[1] have already shewn the most unquestionable marks of unsteady dispositions—*We* cannot Wonder—but this is a sacred subject, and appears to have affected him above all other Evils. Richard begs me particularly in his last letter to remember him to you—My Father has obtained permission from the Legislature to perform all the plans he has contemplated on Staten Island—He is building a *Hospital* and *dwelling House* but I fear not to recieve his family[2] — Emma's[3] Marriage will be, but when, is uncertain I have not time to write more before the Post goes and if I detain my letter you will not recieve it in two days, and I fear you have already expected it.

tell my Sister Charlotte that one of my most favorite Hopes is that of seeing her again—remember me also affectionately to my Brother and Harriet. tell me something of your Father and Mother,[4] Julia, in your next letter. how they bear their sorrow, and if ever I am mentioned before them, remember me respectfully to them. If you are not [well] enough do not write. let Maria write for you if it is only five lines—Kiss my *J[ohn] Scott* for me and be assured of my truest affection. *E.A.Seton.*

15th March

My Father this moment enters the room—"have you any message to my Julia" "tell her I wish I had her at Quarantine"—

---

[1] Elizabeth's half-brothers Richard and Andrew Barclay Bayley. Andrew Barclay Bayley (d. 1811) was the son of Dr. Richard and Charlotte Barclay Bayley. At one time he was engaged to Harriet Seton. He pursued a mercantile career in Jamaica and the West Indies and died there.

[2] Dr. Bayley's hope was to establish a health station on Staten Island to improve public health and to serve as a quarantine.

[3] Charlotte Amelia Bayley Craig, Elizabeth's half-sister

[4] William and Susanna Deshon Sitgreaves

1.42 To Julia Scott

New York 27th March 1799

My dearest Julia

I wrote to John[1] Yesterday—and altho' I have nothing in particular to tell you, yet feeling a presentiment that I may not be able soon to write again cannot help repeating what I have so often said, that I am *your own*. my little darling Richard was a few days ago Innoculated, and it is impossible to surpress the anxieties of such a period, happy I shall be when it is over—tho' the Season is very favoured and, and my darling in perfect Health. the time is now approaching when your promise of visiting New York *must* be fulfilled—the idea fills me with a thousand pleasant reflections, yet I am convinced there are many reasons why I should not anticipate *too* much happiness from seeing you, as your unavoidable situation and Engagements with *Broadway* will be a sad reverse to the former happy expectation of having you all ` to myself.—

2nd April—

My poor Rebecca has again been ill, and my *whole* attention is requisite to support her when she is sick, as her mind is in so feeble a state that without it she would be in perfect misery. You would suppose that at such a time all her friends would be round her, but their attentions are messages and *visits*, and those are not sufficient to comfort the sick and desponding Soul, or to relieve the aching head which requires the Bosom of Affection for its pillow and the soothing still voice of friendship to sustain it—

that you my Julia should feel the want of these while the one whom affection habit and the most sacred ties has bound to you, while she is far away is an idea insupportable, and which tho' I feel the certainty that it is so, I try to drive away, for when will it be otherways, and where is the remedy?—Charlotte cannot be a great deal with you for

1.42 1-3-3-6:22
[1]Possibly John Curson Seton, Elizabeth's brother-in-law

she has many duties to fulfill—if she could—you will need no other Comforter—

Richard is not yet sick, [unclear] but there always is a difficulty in my children [unclear] the small Pox—my darling Julia farewell—may Peace be with you—

E.A.Seton.

1.43 To Julia Scott

New York 20th April 1799

My Precious friend—

I have the happiness of knowing that your long silence is not in consequence of Indisposition but of the remaining pain in your finger—and also that your former expectations of visiting us are lessened, in other words that you cannot make Sufficient exertion for so serious an undertaking—

23rd April

so much I had said dear Julia when I was called away, and have since seen Col[onel] Giles who says you have not written to Mrs. Pintard[1] as you had promised and consequently we have reason to fear that you are not so well as when you last wrote. pray do let us hear from you as soon as possible.—How impossible it is to form any idea of realizing future plans, I never will trust myself again, even with the most probably appearances, for was I not in this month to have brought you from Philadelphia to have settled you in *my Home* at least for a season—and how many Etceteras might I add, which it is wrong to dwell on because it only embitters the disappointment.—but in this

---

1.43 ASJPH 1-3-3-6:23

[1]The Pintards were a prominent New York family of the time. John Pintard was a wealthy merchant, scholar, and philanthropist who was the guiding light in the founding of several important civic and cultural organizations in New York City during this period.

month I have had every variety of disagreeable circumstances, as sick
ch[amber], dressing blisters, etc—

all our Boys at Home and two strangers they brought with them to
pass their Vacation; added to all, being without a servant, have been
obliged to set my own table and do all the work of a servant man except cleaning knives, as Richard being in the small Pox the two
women were obliged to confine themselves intirely to the Nursery,
and little Sandy was so far in decline we were obliged to send him a
sea voyage—but Richard is now well, Rebecca is better and all goes
well. I tell you these things that you may form some idea of my manner of getting thro' my new situation, and to give you the comfort of
knowing that your friend is in the very same state of affairs with yourself. You can have no derangement no difficulty that I do not endure
every day, but I fear Julia that you do not bear yours as lightly as I do
mine, you do not feel the same Spirits, indeed not enjoying Health
how should you. You will scold me for that word *comfort*—and when
you do, reflect on the soothing power of Sympathy. and also that I
rather welcome these Evils than wish to avoid them, for they bring the
scene nearer to a close.—

26th April

On my Breakfast table I found a letter from You dated 13th April
which the person you intrusted it with thought proper to keep until
yesterday—it has the Post Mark of the 25th on it—and I have been all
the while persuaded that you were ill—

You speak of my Visiting you as a thing that could be easily
done—could you see the exact situation in which I am at this moment
writing you would acknowledge the Impossibility. sitting between
two sick beds, on one Rebecca is laid with an ulcerated sore throat
covered with 2 blisters, and Harriet in the other with the same complaint, and I think it highly probable that it will go thro' the family as
they caught it from Mrs. Farquhar.[2] if we fortunately should escape,
this sweet girl is evidently in a decline and requires the most attentive
care to soothe the remnant of her existance, and I adore that Power that

---

[2]Elizabeth Curson Farquhar, William Magee Seton's aunt

gives me the sacred charge of doing so. added to this the two Eldest girls[3] are to be Home from Boarding School on M[onday] with a little friend they are to bring to pass the Vacation which will last a month, and then it will be more than time for my children to be in the Country—so we go—to take it as quietly as possible is the only remedy.

I am sure the approaching Season as it will render your intercourse with those you love more frequent, and agree so much better with the state of your mind and Body, will restore you in some degree to the tranquility you have lost,—Heaven in Mercy grant it and give you rest my Julia

I am always truely and surely your own E.A.S.—

this is worse than Patch work but if you can understand it I am satisfyed—

1.44 To Julia Scott

New York 14th May 1799

Dear Precious Julia

If it was possible to love you more than I did, how much nearer would it now draw you to my Heart to find you in sorrow and Inquietude, struggling with the vexations and cares of a mind Oppressed—could I relieve it, was it my lot to speak Peace to your Afflicted Heart. —but I am fulfilling my destiny, and I fear will never be permitted to share yours, if I could even Hope to do so, I would rejoice in the change that permitted it, if it were even in other things for the Worse—Your Spirits Julia are too low, your mind so greatly oppressed will sink under its weight, and your promising amiable children will be deprived of that protection and Guideance so necessary to their future happiness; If your situation at Easton[1] is in no way

---

[3]William Magee Seton's younger half-sisters, Mary and Charlotte
1.44 ASJPH 1-3-3-6:24
[1]The home of Julia's brother, Samuel Sitgreaves

particularly disagreeable, I am sure you ought to go there, for Brother ever must be the most proper and effectual comforter of your Heart, he knows all those secret springs so thouroughly and has been so much accustomed to your disposition. I think it very probable that he has himself prevented the visits of his Wife and Sister knowing the deranged state of your family and that it would be too much additional trouble. but all these things You alone can Judge of, and I only pray that you may not remain in Philadelphia during the Summer[.] let what will be the consequence of leaving it. I am pursuaded you will never have any pleasure in a visit Here except it is to a friend, your living at lodgings is intirely out of the question—Oh Julia why cannot I be that friend.

—Every Soul of our thirteen children except little Will has in turn had the Intermitting Fever, they are all recovering but my faithful Mammy [Huler], my attentive friend, the constant companion of all my changes and chances, is sinking fast in the Grave; and she will be a loss not easily repaired—the Second Mother of my Children.—"THY WILL BE DONE"[2]

16th May 1799—

Little Richard has been lying in my arms ill with a violent Fever since the day before yesterday, and this is the first moment I have quitted him—I am very anxious that you should recieve this letter by to days Post and therefore write when I should be sleeping. I dread the shock that you may probably too soon sustain—but Julia endeavour to strengthen your mind, and use that resolution which on a former melancholy occasion you exerted so well, your Father with his precautions and the favourable Season may soon recover, but in course of Nature and his complaints there is every Reason why you should expect the worst.—Heaven preserve and sustain my Julia thro' all her trials, for without that support, all other is of little avail—

I will write very soon again, very often when I read my letters over I almost resolve not to send them I find so many inaccuracies and mistakes of expression. but Julia there are no mistakes of meaning when

---

[2]Matt. 26:42

they express how much I love you and how much I am your own E.A.Seton.

Your letter is dated the 9th and I recieved it the 14th—

1.45 To Julia Scott

Sunday Evening 2nd June 1799

I begin my Long Island Expedition on Tuesday[1] and as Col[onel] Giles is to visit you and will see your dear *little self* I cannot resist writing a line tho' without one word to say except what I have so often repeated. My Sister[2] is to leave me to-morrow for Dover on a visit to Mrs. V[ining].[3] I do not think you will see her as she is too weak and ill to call on you if you are in Town, which I hope and pray you may not be, for it is time my love that you should be in a situation of safety which I am sure Philadelphia cannot be during the Summer—I hear from the Col[onel] that his dear Lady is not in a travelling situation, and that she has relinquished her plan of visiting you—so goes that hope—for with him I cannot expect you to come. My Julia I am tired of Hopes and fears and will take all as it comes tho' I cannot help being very much disappointed in thus losing every hope of seeing you

Monday. I have recieved your dear letter of 31st of May how it wrings my Heart Julia to see it has been wet with tears—this is too much tho' I fear you shed many in silence and sorrow—My Brother [Samuel] has *too many* engagements to satisfy your Heart, and re-membrance recalls the image of one who would have been all a Brother could be.[4] with respect to your Father,[5] you must be resolute,

---

1.45 ASJPH 1-3-3-6:26

[1]Elizabeth was planning to leave the city for the summer.

[2]Rebecca Seton, Elizabeth's sister-in-law

[3]Anna Maria Seton (b. 1775), daughter of William and Rebecca Curson Seton and elder sister of Rebecca, had married (1790) John Middleton Vining (1758-1802). He was a member of the United States House of Representatives from Delaware from 1789 to 1793 and a United States senator from 1793 to 1798. Their home, "The Oakes," was near Dover, Delaware.

[4]John Sitgreaves, Julia's deceased brother

[5]William Sitgreaves

and not indulge melancholy reflections, for you must be persuaded that from his General state of health having been so long impai[r]ed his seperation from you will not be sudden, and he may yet retain what strength he has for many years—think Julia how many we have out-lived whose lives we calculated upon as certainly of longer duration than our own, and how unable we are to Judge of Future Events—and if your fear is realized Remember the sure the never failing Protector we have, but he will not divide your Confidence[.] rely solely on Him, and from experience I can declare that it will produce the most Peaceful sensations and most perfect enjoyment of which the Heart is capable.

Julia I can speak freely to you what I wish to say, you will not call me Preacher or Moralizer, your own Bosom has experienced *that Peace*, and you have not seen so much sorrow in this World without being convinced that our best employment while in it is to improve those sentiments which produce that temper of mind which inspires confidence in Him who has the guidance of our concerns; and without which confidence of a Friend and Father, there can be no enjoyment of that intercourse with him which is to form our greatest felicity in future and I am sure *Here* is the most perfect Peace to those who are blessed with it—What sorrow what vexations and tumults has it carried me th[r]o' and with a peculiar propriety and resolution, that any natural Passion of my Heart was combatting—for this last year—Oh Julia when I look back upon it I tremble.—and now I am free for a while—and we, you and I, might yet pass our Summer together if I knew *where* it was to be passed—

My Husband purchased a long lease of a little place two miles from the city, and after altering it as we wished, the Sheriffs have offered it for Sale because there was not a proper title to it; William is *now* so Angry that he declares he will give up the purchase, but I think by the 10th of the month when it is to be decided he will alter his Mind, as the House and street we are now in, is an insupportable Summer residence—Oh Julia if I could now say there is a room for you and your Darlings—come with the Col[onel Giles]—instead of which I cannot tell if I am not to remain in the city all summer for if we lose our first prospect, there is little chance of another as places on the Island are so much in demand and such exorbitant prices that it is next to impossible to procure one.—

I hope my children may get such a stock of Health at the Sea Shore as will enable them to buffet it a little, they now want it very much or I would not take them; for Mrs. [Eliza] Sadler has but a garret room for us, and I cannot see my poor William while I am there so you may suppose it will not be for long—Heaven Bless you my darling, and make all for the best I am your own

E.A.S.

1.46 To Rebecca Seton

Long Island 8th June 1799

My dearest Rebecca,

I hope your Journey to Philadelphia is finished, and that you have born it as well as the first days Journey, which Ogden[1] says was past even Jacks[2] Sanguine hopes—tho' *I* do not know how to believe all that was said, as I know your never complaining makes them think you much Stronger than you really are. —Heaven grant the best, and guard you thro' it, to Health and Peace. William brought us here on Tuesday and left us the next Morning with a heavy Heart for little *Will* was very sick, but he is now the merriest of the party and runs on the Beech like a Bird. Ricksy is absolutely Rosy and when he goes out he lifts up his little hands to the trees and says do, do with such delight and astonishment and when the wind blows in his face, shuts his little eyes and laughs as he used to when you blew at him. We have every thing very comfortable and the children and Mammy [Huler] enjoy themselves as much as possible.

1.46 AMSJ A111 005 (Seton-Jevons #3-6)

[1]Possibly Abraham Ogden, a business associate of William Magee Seton's

[2]John Curson Seton, Elizabeth's brother-in-law, escorted his sisters Rebecca, who was ill, and the young Cecilia south. He remained in Virginia and later married there.

—and you will enjoy yourself my Dear Rebecca for tho' I am sure you felt a struggle in quitting Stone Street,[3] I am fully persuaded that the change of air, the carresses and attentions you will continually recieve, the affectionate endearments of Jack, (and many etcetra's I could mention) will soon reconcile you to it, and make you feel the change much for the better, and when you return you will bring with you Health, and that tranquility of mind You so much covet, and deserve so well. Sometimes read *Sisters little Book*, and remember tho' there are many ways of expressing affection You have *hers* in full, signed and sealed.—

I am more anxious about your hearing from the children than any thing else, as I know you cannot be happy without it; if you have any particular wish about it, name it, but I know no way better than to tell the Boys to write once a week or fortnight and let it be immediately forwarded to you—You have doubtless arranged all with the Girls—You will easily hear from them. I will write to them to day, I long to hear how they are.—owing to the badness of the weather William did not come yesterday and I do not know when you will recieve this—

How is dear little Cecilia.[4] Write me every thing particularly but do not write when it hurts your chest for I know you will have [unclear] to write to, and I should recieve no pleasure from your letters if I thought you were in pain while writing them.—I have just recieved a large package from our dear little Boys, and have written them a long letter which I will send with the cage and Inkstand they write for. Mr. Som[e]body has sent a bag of nuts and I will make up a little Box and send them some. they shall not feel the distance you are from them more than I can help—Heaven preserve my dear Rebecca and restore her to her affectionate E.A.Seton.

this is the 11th June, and we are all well—

---

[3]61 Stone Street was the Seton family residence.

[4]Cecilia Seton (1791-1810) was the daughter of William and Anna Maria Curson. She was a half-sister of William Magee Seton and a convert to Roman Catholicism (June 20, 1806) despite strong family opposition. She joined Elizabeth in Baltimore in June 1809 and shared the life of the Sisters of Charity of Saint Joseph's at Emmitsburg until her death April 17, 1810, in Baltimore where she had been taken for medical treatment. Known as Sister Cecilia or Cecilia Theresa, she was elected to the first council of the Sisters of Charity in 1809. She is buried in the original community cemetery at Emmitsburg.

1.47 To Julia Scott

Long Island[1] June 11th 1799

The very name of this place must recall many recollections to the mind of my Friend for many it renews to mine who have not passed so many pleasant hours here as you have. I was walking in the wood near Bennets and found the name of Julia Scott written, and fastened on a tree. it really seemed as if I had seen your Ghost—dear precious little name! my companion (*no matter who*) felt nearly the same effect that I did, and put it in his pocket book saying he would carry it to *Flat Bush*.[2] How I long to know if you will come, I am sure if you tasted the sweet breezes and delights of the country as I now do, you would think yourself fully paid for any trouble it might cost you to possess them. tho' I feel almost sure and yet I cannot tell why that if you fall on no other plan but that of going to flat-bush, it will not be—We are yet doubtful about our future destination for the Summer. Oh Julia if it could be that I might have you and your children in all the ease and freedom of a country Life, they surely could be precious days—Polly would come with you, you could share as much of your time with other friends as would hinder you from tireing of Solitude with me, and in so near a tie as we are, triffling inconvenience would be lightly passed over on your part and on mine[.] it could not be felt if I should have the little Box to myself

—I return Home on Monday next as Emma's[3] marriage takes place on Wednesday the 19th and I hope notwithstanding all difficulties I shall be present and forget the past as *far* as possible.[4]

May they be only half as happy as they expect for their calculations are beyond all bounds—

---

[1]Elizabeth was at the Sadlers' summer home on Long Island.

[2]A section of Brooklyn where Julia Scott had friends

[3]Charlotte Amelia Bayley, Elizabeth's half-sister, who was about to be married to William Craig, Eliza Craig Sadler's brother

[4]Elizabeth is referring to family tensions as a result of Dr. Bayley's estrangement from his second wife, Charlotte Barclay Bayley, the mother of the bride.

I have all the enjoyments of Books, Music, walking, etc that my most romantic fancy every formed, for Mrs. [Eliza] Sadler always possesses them as naturally as I do the air I breathe as she has nothing else to employ her, but to me who has so long been tyed to sick rooms and a large family it appears like a change to some better region.

My children are perfectly wild with the change, and if I could see my William oftener I should be in no haste to give up my room to Craig and Emma⁵ which by the by I am obliged to do as this is to be their *retreat* on Thursday—Little Dick calls me—

Heaven preserve my Julia and give her Health and Peace—

I am yours most Affectionately *E.A.S.*

1.48 To Eliza Sadler

Blooming Dale Sunday Morning 23rd June 1799

I do not know Why, but I have never thought of you for a moment since our Seperation without the most melancholy Sensations—are you well my Friend?—I do not ask if you enjoy yourself—it would be like asking you if *our* fortnight was not happy—It was one of those small portions of time never to be forgotten and which never can come again. I have a dear little retirement to share with you, but not one prospect to expand the Soul—nothing but Shade and quiet. and is not that a great deal—and it will be Ours—

My William continues his determination of going to Baltimore,¹ I cannot be left alone, and if dear *J. Jacques* I find it—Rousseau!!!² *and you* are my company I shall have a reproach to make myself I never felt before, that of being satisfied in his absence—and if your Visitors are not gone—it will surely be sufficient excuse—

---

⁵The newlyweds were going to use the room at the Sadlers' summer home after the wedding.
1.48 ASJPH 1-3-3-7:13

¹William Magee Seton, Elizabeth's husband, was going to Baltimore to visit his maternal grandfather, Richard Curson (1726-?), to discuss business affairs.

²Jean Jacques Rousseau (1712-1778) was a French romantic philosopher and author of *Emile*, a popular novel of the period.

Mrs. [Julia] Scott talks of going with Mr. Seton and returning with her children when he returns. but she has not decidedly said so—if she should I shall have the pleasure of making a Season agreeable to her which otherwise would be passed in the heat of Philadelphia and perhaps in the danger of the Yellow Fever for she has no country house—You know the priviledge of giving a friend what no one else could give—how sweet it is—but as She once wished herself Mrs. Sadler, there can be no harm in saying, I wish she was.

—tell me when you have seen my Father[,] if Helen[3] is restored—and a thousand other things I wish to know which you can easily Imagine—every time I recieve Mr. Seton I shall ask for your Note the first question. Peace to my Precious Sad—

E.A.S.

Dick is quite well. Anna and Will also.

1.49 To Rebecca Seton

Craiggdon 27th June [1799]

My friend A[braham] O[gden][1] often asks after you He slept here last Saturday and staid till Sunday Evening[.] took a nap on the Big Rock[2]

My Dearest Rebecca—I have had the most busy bustling Week you can Imagine or my first employment on my arrival in Town would have been writing to you. We came two days sooner than we expected to be present at Emma's Wedding[3] which went off charmingly, and they are at last happy—then was the question whether Busshy Hill or Craigdon would be our summer habitation as Mr. Corp having

---

[3]Helen Bayley (1790-1848) was a daughter of Dr. Richard and Charlotte Barclay Bayley. She married Samuel Craig June 1, 1814.

1.49 AMSJ A111 006 (Seton-Jevons #276-279)

[1]A business associate of William Magee Seton

[2]This introductory note is written at the top of the letter.

[3]Charlotte Amelia Bayley, Elizabeth's half-sister, married William Craig June 19, 1799.

purchased Mr. Pollocks place [unclear] William again to take the latter, and as there was yet the difficulty about the title to Bushy-hill and little Ricksy had a violent dysentary, it was determined we should come to Craigdon[4] and here we are—all Nature Smiling—the children and my Husband well—Rice and milk and stewed cherries from morning till night—and every body pleased with the novelty.

—last Sunday Aunt F[5] dined with Mary Wilks and after Dinner came to see me. She asked a great deal about you and seemed to expect you had written oftener to me than to any one else—I told her I had but the one letter, and we both agreed that you ought when you are well enough to write once a week a few lines if you cannot more to some of the Family but not to make it a task to write to all, for writing is of all things the employment least suited to your feelings, and might injure your health if you do too much—

1st July 1799—

I defered finishing my letter anxious to inform you that you would recieve your cloaths but when I went to Town yesterday to put up WM's things for his Journey to Baltimore, I found that yours had not yet been sent, and Caty to whom I gave your Key of the door thinking that she would make it a point to get them ready I found had not been to the house. We stoped at Eliza's[6] and I asked her if she had not time If I should do it, She said no that Maitland[7] was to let her know when there would be an opportunity. indeed my child you should not wait for them if I knew where to get at the things, but your not having worn them since we have been together I do not know more than the Man in the Moon, and if I was to look till I found them I might not perhaps send half what you want and make it worse than your waiting for them. the black and white muslin I laid on your bed to go in the Box 9 yards was the half, and it must be washed very carefully and dryed immediately or it drys thick and a red cast—

---

[4]William Magee Seton was negotiating for a lease to Bushy Hill as a summer home, but due to legal complications, the property was not available. Cragdon was the Seton family home in Bloomingdale.

[5]Elizabeth Curson Farquhar, William Magee Seton's aunt

[6]Eliza Seton Maitland, Elizabeth's sister-in-law

[7]James Maitland, Elizabeth's brother-in-law

I have recieved charming affectionate letters from the Girls, and from the *Boys*, without number—I have sent them both a Box with sweetmeats and nuts[,] Mary a keg of crackers, the Boys chains for their Squirrils and Harriet shoes—William wrote the Boys since I wrote them—and will call to see the Girls tomorrow—he sets out at eight in the morning and will dine at Brunswick[8]—He says he has not time to see Maria and means to make his jaunt as quick as possible as the Fever is very much talked of in Philadelphia—I must say it is a Sorrowful jaunt to me and I have felt melancholy Since the first moment it was talked of—I have ten thousand things to say to you but there has been such combustion[,] cleaning house[,] packing and un-packing and such a monstrous packet I dare dispatched to Aunt Caley[9] in answer to one we recieved since you left us that I have not had many moments to myself but you shall soon hear from me again—

3rd July—

W.M's departure has been defered till to-morrow—he left me this morning and sleeps in Town to night he wrote me a little note this evening in which he says, "Write Beck that I shall be in Baltimore the 7th and that she must write to me certainly and that the longest stay I make will be 'till the 12th"—Heaven grant it.

I have this evening a letter from both Charlotte and Mary—they are very anxious about You but perfectly well—Charlott says "Miss Hay is very good to us we have cherries currants and Rasberrys very of-ten—but Harriet wishes very much to be Home"—I have also your letter of the [unclear] for which my Sister I more than thank you and will soon reply to it Kiss dear little Cely a thousand times for me and tell her Anna keeps a part of every thing she gets "to put by for Aunt Celia"—Eliza's [Maitland] last son is a lovely fellow very like what Seton was at his age—and she looks wonderfully well—the little dar-lings are perfectly well—Ricksy wistles to little Tufty fifty times a day, who has taken his station in the hall and eats his sallad and sugar all the while he sings—Java and the Eagles are also well—

---

[8]Site of Miss Hay's school in New Brunswick, New Jersey.
[9]Isabella Seton Cayley, William Magee Seton's aunt

Heaven bless my Beck and give her a good nights rest—

E.A.S.

1.50 To Eliza Sadler

[n.d. 1799]

"My day has been, and may be again" so says Mrs. F[1] at whose Desk I am writing. and I pray that my day may be again and that *my Sad* may be released from all Engagements and Visitors and come to her friend any day after Thursday the sooner the better. on Thursday my William takes his departure and I am in Town to day to prepare his little Packet, stopping at the Lady's to see our Ship Northern Liberties[2] Salute, she pressed us in *"her way"* to meet Post at *three* and take a family Dinner—Here I am Dinner past, on the moment of setting out for my little Home and every thought full of you sharing it with me—Oh come, come, come friend H[enry Sadler] says he will come every night, that Long Island is too fatiguing

E.A.S.

1.51 To Eliza Sadler

[n.d. 1799]

My dear Sads pains are I hope all past. a great big tear swelled when we left New York which really was inexplicable, as every sweet was full in view, and therefore I call it Sad. She is suffering and I am

---

1.50 ASJPH 1-3-3-7:6
  [1]Elizabeth Curson Farquhar, William Magee Seton's aunt
  [2]One of the vessels of the Seton, Maitland and Company's fleet
1.51 ASJPH 1-3-3-7:7

happy—The Darlings are too precious, too lovely, and their mother too happy—that you may soon *share* is one of the first wishes of

your *E.A.S.*

1.52 To Eliza Sadler

4th July 1799

Your precious little letter was received with truest Joy—but disappointment followed at finding the time of our meeting yet undecided—is it that Helen[1] detains you—but you say I will be satisfied with your reasons tho' I must acknowledge if that is it, I shall be only mortified—W. M. is gone the Roses are done blowing the cherry's and strawberry's are past, but—Heaven—all Nature smiles on me, I have never known such intire content as since I have been at this little Home[2]—If I had you Eliza and J.J.[3] it would be like a pleasant dream, or an April Sun-shine for my Husband is gone but to get Health and a release from business therefore I am satisfied with his absence—

As to little Julia[4] I cannot answer one of your enquiries respecting her intentions the last time I saw her she was yet undecided but talked of my Husband bringing her two children to her as the Fever is said to be very much dreaded having certainly made its appearance in Philadelphia—But surely her movements need not influence you. She is with the Persons for whom her visit was originally intended and if she does stay, will probably pass the greater part of the Summer there, for my Solitude will illy suit her disposition—at all events let not your Visit be deferred come while W.M. is away, and come when he is here—for he says he will never forgive you if you do not give as much time when he returns as you will while he is away—His longest stay

---

1.52 ASJPH 1-3-3-7:14

[1]Possibly Helen Bayley, Elizabeth's half-sister
[2]Their summer place at Cragdon in the Bloomingdale section of Manhattan.
[3]Jean Jacques Rousseau, whose works she was reading
[4]Julia Scott was visiting in New York at this time.

will be 'till the 14th.—Oh come come come come I could say 'till I see you—

your own *E.A.S.*

1.53 To Julia Scott

5th July [1799]

My dear Julia

I have looked for you both yesterday and today supposing you would take me in your ride and let me [know] how my W.M. and you had planed your change to him. He was a good deal alarmed at the accounts of the Fever, and I believe will be back again sooner than he proposed—Before I thought of the probability of your not going with him to arrange your House I appointed the time of his absence for Mrs. [Eliza] Sadler to return my Long Island visit and therefore my love until she returns I cannot give you your room which I have occupied since my Husband left me and will continue to until its future mistress takes possession—Am I not a pretty one to be up a 1/2 past 12—Good night—"Peace be with you"—pray let me see you soon

Your *EAS*

1.54 To Rebecca Seton

Craigdon 10th July 1799—

My Dear Rebecca's letter gave me great pleasure particularly as it expressed much Affection for old Sister—not that I wanted the assurance, but to tell you the truth since I heard from Aunt F [1] that your

---

1.53 ASJPH 1-3-3-6:48
1.54 ASCSH Seton-Jevons #7-10
[1] Elizabeth Curson Farquhar, William Magee Seton's aunt

staying the winter with Jack[2] was decided, I have felt as if all former days should be forgot for I so well know his decided opinion of me that I am sure if you once get under his roof you will never again call mine your Home, and you cannot know my Sister the melancholy thoughts that presses on me whenever I consider myself without you in Stone Street,[3] it seems to me as if I could as soon enjoy Home without a limb or a part of myself. this no one else can understand, but I am sure you do—and I hope you will consider it in your plans of next winter, tho' it would be very selfish in me to wish you to <consider my> think of my desires yet think of the children, for no one but yourself knows how necessary you are to their happiness and to you only would I mention the circumstance. as for Mary,[4] She will be miserable without you—You have I am sure weighed it all, and am as sure will act for the best.—

My William writes me that I must direct my letters to Dover[5] as he thinks it very probable he will visit you tho' his plan was not yet made—Richard[6] he says is much better than he expected, and the poor old gentleman perfectly[7] overjoyed to see him—I hope he will be able to go to you *for ma[n]y reasons.*

The girls all three wrote me very handsome letters and I answered them the same day—Harriet is wonderfully improved in her writing. they say they have all they want. I had a letter from both the dear little Boys last week and if William had not said decidedly he should not see you I would have sent you some specimins of their writing which would have pleased you exceedingly. tell my dear little Celia I have some beautiful Books for her to read when She returns and kiss her for me—the most Affectionate Brother could not shew me more attention than A[braham] O[gden] has since William is absent—every day I recieve a kind little note from him to know how we are, and if he can

---

[2]John Curson Seton, Elizabeth's brother-in-law, who had married Mary Wise in 1799 and lived in Alexandria, Virginia.

[3]Location of the Seton residence in downtown New York

[4]Mary Seton, Elizabeth's sister-in-law and Rebecca's sister

[5]Home of Anna Maria Seton Vining and United States Senator John Middleton Vining, where Rebecca was staying in Delaware

[6]Richard Curson, William Magee Seton's cousin

[7]Richard Curson, William Magee Seton's grandfather

do any thing. Mrs. [Eliza] Sadler is to stay with me till my William returns—She is delighted with my children and to be sure she could not be otherwise particularly Your Boy[8] who is ten times more lovely than when you left him—I am persuaded he never sees the Birds without thinking of you, for he lifts his little hands and makes that expression of wonder you learnt him, and looks all round as if he wanted Sombody—it was a curious thing He put out his arms to Mrs. [Julia] Scott the moment he saw her and after she took him he hung down his head and cryed to come to me, and looked at her as he does at all other Strangers. I am sure her being intirely in black as he was Accustomed to see you decieved the little darling, and he would not go to her again [page torn] Will, and Mammy [Huler] are very well—we often talk of you—and wish to see you, My Dearest Rebecca take care of yourself, and may Heaven bless you—Remember me to Maria

[Yours] most Affectionately E.A.S.

1.55 To Julia Scott

Sunday Evening 16th July [1799]

My dearest Julia

It is very long since I have heard from you, are you well, and enjoying this fine weather

—My W.M.[1] wrote me yesterday that he was to write to Charlotte the day he set out for Philadelphia as he proposes staying there only one day and that he would be here the 18th or 20th if he did not go to Dover[2] which he was undecided about—

Mrs. [Eliza] Sadler will leave me the day after his return, and I hope to see you immediately with your dear children—my darling Dick has

---

[8]Richard Seton, Elizabeth's third child

1.55 ASJPH 1-3-3-6:49

[1]William was en route to Philadelphia from Baltimore.

[2]Delaware home of William's sister and brother-in-law, the Vinings

had the dissentary which alarmed me very much but is getting better[.] Ann and Will are well and the little place looks charmingly but I fear Long Island will spoil your enjoyment of it—Peace is here dear Julia—that is *Something* and I hope the Affection and attentions of a friend will in some degree make up the rest. I am

your most truely and sincerely *E.A.Seton*

1.56 To William Magee Seton

Craig Don 16th July 1799—Sunday evening

Your letter my Dearest William which I recieved last Evening made me as lively and happy as a Bird—that you pass your time so well, so free from cares is a pleasure quite new, and makes me feel selfish in wishing your return—I also pass my time at least pleasantly, for our little Solitude is so beautiful and Mrs. S[adler] so much pleased with it that between walking reading and our Darlings the time is very well divided, and when Mr. S[adler] comes the laugh and storys never ceases for he has the talent of being pleased or seeming so wherever he is—the Menage[1] goes on very well—and quietly enough but our tranquillity is sorrowfully interrupted by the daily visit we make poor Mr. Olive who has ruptured a blood vessel and reduced so far that I should not be surprised at any hour to hear that all is over—so many things combine to Interest me for him that you may easily imagine how melancholy it is.

I am persuaded you are now at Dover,[2] and hope your visit may give you as much pleasure as the last one you made there—[Abraham] Ogden wrote me that you was to return the 22d you say 18th or 20th come when it may it will be a happy day to your little Wife—Mrs. S[adler] says she will stay to shake hands with you and then Adieu. I

1.56 ASJPH 18:2

[1]Household

[2]Delaware home of William Magee Seton's sister and brother-in-law, the Vinings. William was en route from Baltimore back to New York.

have neither seen nor heard a word of Julia Scott since yesterday week, I will write her what you told me, I suppose she is on Long Island

—little Angel Richard has had the summer complaint all last week, but is very lively and lovely as ever, call Papa and he looks every where for you—Anna and Will are perfectly well, he has had his small cloaths on and cockade on his Hat all day—Sadler perfectly doats on him. Post dined with us and says the city is remarkably Healthy, but Mr. [John] Wilks nurse told Mammy [Huler] that our poor Eliza Maitland is in a great deal of trouble with a gathered Breast and little Seton[3] is suffering with the Disentary. Post did not say a word of it and Stone[4] who was here to day knew nothing of it, so I hope it is not true—

Good night to you, my Dear love may Heaven Bless you, and return you safe to your own

E.A.Seton

1.57 To Eliza Sadler

[July or August 1799]

I am a bond woman, and you are free.—You must come to me, for little Darling[1] is not to be fed, and I am to be faithful to him 'till October. this is in consequence of a derangement of his little stomach last week, which has with great care and anxiety been remedyed, and still requires great care to prevent in future. but I have had some sweet *lonely* walks while the little friend was sleeping and discovered many beauties that quite escaped *us*. last Sunday morning before breakfast I retraced the honey-suckle walk and to my great astonishment found

---

[3]Eliza Maitland's infant son.

[4]A business associate of William Magee Seton

1.57 ASJPH 1-3-3-7:12

[1]Richard Seton, Elizabeth's infant son who had been ill. It appears that Elizabeth had to continue nursing him for several months, hence her reference to being a "bond woman."

that those bushes with buds on them which grow near the honey suckle and in great quantities in other places, bear the sweetest flower you can imagine with the greatest profusion. its fragrance is beyond any wild flower I ever saw. I brought home a load of it on my back—Mr. Olive says its name is Cletera[2] but whether major or minor he does not know—Oh how it would delight me to send you a branch of it, for like other sweets its season is passing but I will transplant a great deal of it next month—

I told Anna I had written to Aunt [Eliza Craig] Sadler that she was a good girl her instantanious exclamation was "then she will tell my Uncle [Henry] Sadler and he will love me dearly and not scold me any more." how much I wish they could see him again for there never passes a day but they call out something about him and whenever a chair turns up the lane they wonder if it is uncle.

—precious little souls they are in most perfect health, and realy seem as if they are relieved from some spirit of contradiction so different are they from when you were here. it was not to be too sweet—

little Lady[3] is to stay but four weeks longer—she says she must be with Mrs. G_[iles] on an interesting occasion—and then—

take great care of the valuable consignment I send you, and take care he does not expose himself too much to the sea-air

Your own own—

My Heart leapt with you at the Sunday Event—thank Heaven for it—

---

[2]Sweet pepper bush
[3]Probably Julia Scott who was visiting in New York

1.58 To Eliza Sadler

[July 1799]

My dearest Sad—

From your Note which I received this afternoon I think you did not get the few lines I wrote you on Friday. My W. M's Indisposition which has prevented my having my usual thoughts about me is the reason why you have not recieved your Watch etc.—

I can easily suppose how great your enjoyment must have been on once more hearing the Dash of the waves and feeling the renovating Breeze—my enjoyments have been very cursory, Mrs. S[cott] staid but three days, and I proposed enjoying *absolute retirement* when Mr. Stone[1] took it in his hand [to] *Keep me company* 'till she returns—Well—Patience—Resignation Heavenly Virtues exercised in little things that keep the Soul in a sense of its dependant State, for I assure you I do not possess them on this occasion without a struggle—

Anna is a perfect Angel. I am about persuaded her fancys are somehow governed by the Moon, for she is as different from what she was, as the present darkness is from the beautiful light of that period when she perplexed me most—

Little Darling stands quite alone, but he does not walk, and Mr. Will[2] is also very much improved—You shall soon hear from me again—bless you my Eliza—

Your own *E.A.S.*
Wednesday Morning

1.58 ASJPH 1-3-3-7:8
[1]A business associate of William Magee Seton
[2]Richard, Elizabeth's infant son, and William, her older son

1.59 To Rebecca Seton

Craig Don. Tuesday Morn[in]g 23rd July [1799]

My Dearest Rebecca

Our Dear William arrived last night—He left Phila[delphi]a Sunday 3 Oclock, and was much better on the road than he expected tho' he does not look so well as when he left me—I think he shall not be off again in a hurry, and I do not know how to express My Joy that he is here—You will hear from me again very soon but for the present must only tell you the good news which you will not recieve this Post if I do not send it by Mr. [Henry] Sadler to go to day, and they are waiting Breakfast—the dear Girls all came running to the Tavern to meet Wm.[1] they are perfectly well—he left them at 10 Oclock Yesterday Morn[in]g I had a letter from Edward[2] yesterday and they too were very well—Will[ia]m is delighted with Marias[3] children particularly little Charles—He will write himself tomorrow—and proposes taking a day of rest to day which he wants very much, the moment Ricksy opened his eyes and saw Papaty he began kissing him and would not quit him a moment—we are all well—

Yours affect[ionatel]y—E. A. Seton

1.59 AMSV Seton-Jevons #280-282 (photostat) No original exists

[1]William Magee had stopped in Brunswick, New Jersey, on his way home from Philadelphia to visit his half-sisters Mary, Charlotte, and Harriet who were attending Miss Hay's school there.

[2]Edward Augustus Seton, William Magee Seton's half-brother

[3]Anna Maria Seton Vining, Elizabeth's sister-in-law

1.60 To Eliza Sadler

[July or August 1799]

My own Sad—

I believe my last Note to you expressed very much the hurry of my mind for I had very serious alarm for my William and several other reasons interrupted my tranquility, but that is past, and all is again going its usual course. the Little Lady returned here last Saturday and her good little daughter,[1] who answers all the good I had anticipated for my Anna who comes down every Morning after Breakfast with the clean hands and Frock, and gets on her ribbon bracers then sets down with her needle. and as the *needle* is the task of the day I have been mending old shirts these three Mornings which has its use I assure you, for it requires the force of example to induce me to do it. Julia called me out to look at the New Moon the night before last, and I cannot account for the abruptness with which I answered "I do not want to see it"—it has marked two periods of past pleasure, but I do not wish to recall the unavailing regrets that will come when I look at it. when are we to meet again. I wish to come to town some day within a fortnight and if you have any errand name a day supposing it a fair one and then I can pass at least some hours with you. one branch of *your* honeysuckle yet lives and I nourish it with a nurses care. the little plant is in a volume of J J.+[2] and I will bring the H kerchief with me to town. —All goes well I hope—do you ever see Helen[3] or my Father. think Eliza how long since I have seen him—my Heart is full when I think of him.—

there is no reading no rambling the mornings are busy and the afternoons we part to read or sleep, or write, or *Something*, and altogether I am very well satisfied that things are as they are, especially if *we* are all the Summer to be so far seperated.—

1.60 ASJPH 1-3-3-7:11

[1] Julia Scott and her daughter, Maria

[2] Jean Jacques Rousseau

[3] Helen Bayley, Elizabeth's half-sister

Dear little Dick might well be cross while you were here, he all the while was suffering with the sprue[4] which is a terrible complaint and is NOT yet over the effects of it. Mammy [Huler] is well and Bill as strong as ever

Heaven Bless you remember me to friend H[enry]

E.A.S.
Wednesday Morning 7 oclock—[5]

1.61 To Rebecca Seton

3d August 1799

I have often told you my Rebecca that I had determined never again to allow myself the enjoyment of any affection beyond the bounds of *moderation*—but really your affectionate letters, the rememberance of past hours, and the thousand thoughts of you that strike me every day at this place, makes it not an easy matter to restrain my expressions when I write you. I never sweep the Hall, or dress the flower Pots, or walk round the Pear-tree walk, but you are as much my companion as if you were actually near me, and last Eve[nin]g finding myself Accidentally by the Garden fence at the head of the lane where we once stood at sun-set last Fall anticipating What we would do this Summer if Willy hired Craggdon, I was so struck with the recollection and the uncertainty of when I should see you again, that I had a hearty crying spell, which is not a very common thing for me, nor do I suppose would have happened but that I have ever since the first moment you left me had a strong presentiment that our seperation was for a long while—my spirits too were very much depressed by a letter I recieved from Aunt Caley[1] with a Box containing the Legacy's of her Mother, one is her Watch left to Mrs. Andrew Seton,[2] and to her

---

[4]A chronic disease characterized by diarrhea

[5]A note at the bottom of the letter, probably written by Rev. Simon Gabriel Bruté, reads "+ Jean Jacques alas!"

1.61 PAHRC MC 44:1,1 (Seton-Jevons #11-14)

[1]Isabella Seton Cayley, William Magee Seton's aunt who lived in England

[2]Margaret Seton, William Magee Seton's aunt who lived in Albany, New York, and her daughter, Elizabeth Seton

Daughter Elizabeth at her death—the other the Picture of our Father[3] which is left to his Eldest Daughter unmarried, consequently is yours my love. I suppose you remember the Picture it was done by Ramage[4] and sent to your GrandMother[5] in the year ninety.—I am to deliver it in your own hands is the direction.—

James,[6] and [James] Maitland were here yesterday Afternoon—Eliza[7] has been very unwell—but is now better. She passed the day with me Sunday week with her darling little Babe and Dick was very Jealous of him as I had him most of the time—it is a fine lovely child.—James says his *Darling Spaz*[8] has had the Dissentary, and seemed very low Spirited. I advised him to give her Rice water, which has cured Richard every time he has had it. poor Mary has really more trouble than she can bear. I have not had a letter from the Girls since Williams return, I suppose it is owing to their want of Quills and Paper. [Abraham] Ogden promised me he would send them a good stock to Aunty and she was to forward them. the Dear little Boys has sent a letter for Cecilia and have both written to me and to Willy also. You dont know how much uneasiness I have had about William since his return he has been so often unwell, tho' nothing very serious, yet enough [to keep] me in constant alarm. Your little Angel[9] too has [had the] Sprue and suffered very much I send you a little curle of his beautiful light hair cap. it will not be more precious to you than Celia's wreath is to Anna, all the Gold and Silver in the world could not be half the Value to her—Kiss the dear little Puss for me a thousand times I wish I could send her something to remind her of her Birth day—but

---

[3]William Seton, Sr.

[4]John Ramage, an Irish artist, lived in New York from 1777 to 1794. He was considered the best miniature painter of his time although he was also skilled at making life-size portraits in crayon and pastel. Many prominent people, including President George Washington, had Ramage record them for posterity.

[5]Mrs. Elizabeth Seton, William Magee Seton's grandmother

[6]James Seton (1770-?) was the son of William and Rebecca Curson Seton. He married Mary Gillon Hoffman March 20, 1792. He was an insurance broker with offices at 67 Wall Street and a business associate of William Magee Seton.

[7]Eliza Seton Maitland, Elizabeth's sister-in-law

[8]Possibly his spouse, Mary Gillon Hoffman Seton (?-1807), the daughter of Nicholas and Sarah Ogden Hoffman of New York, or one of their children

[9]Richard Seton

I will not forget her here—I suppose William told you Mrs. [Julia] Scott is to spend some time with me—She is in very low spirits poor little Soul, and as I am not very high so we jog on but heavily, She came last Saturday, with her Daughter about Harriets[10] age, who is a very fine girl and delights Anna exceedingly for since little Aunty has been away she has been very much at a loss—

Farewell my dearest Girl remember me to Maria—and Believe me yours Most Affectionately

E.A.Seton

1.62 To Julia Scott

[August 1799]

My dearest Julia—

your dear little Note surprised me as I had written you the second Evening after you left us. but it now appears that it was left at the compting House and that you are all this while uncertain respecting the pains etc—which are all past and gone and every things goes on in the old way. Mr. Seton has become so perfectly at home that I keep my room as much as I please—but Mrs. W[ilkes] keeps a room ready for him therefore you need not be afraid of dislodging Him. My Husband expects you in time for the Races, do not disappoint him for he anticipates a great deal of pleasure—I send Maria's Book and a thousand kisses from the Darlings for her—my companions talk so fast they confuse my brain Heaven bless you

E.A.S.
Sunday Evening

---

[10]Maria Scott, Julia's daughter, was about ten years old.
1.62 ASJPH 1-3-3-6:50

1.63 To Eliza Sadler

9th September 1799

My own dear Eliza

You should have heard from your Darlings and your friend three days ago, but our W.M.S. has given us those last three days, and our opportunities to the city are not very frequent for the consternation here is generally felt, and particularly here since poor Mr. Morgue who is at Mr. Olives has been ill—it is truly sorrowful to hear all that I am obliged to hear, whilst you and my friend H[enry] I hope are quietly secured where Peace only abides—Peace—Peace—oh the very sound is harmony—but we have some enjoyments when we get poor Willy out, for himself and the little friend[1] never tire with Romps and Jokes which is so unlooked for a pleasure and gives me so much liberty that take the all in all I am well *content*

Your sweet Dick for the first time, stept this day four steps alone to get to my arms, and you cannot concieve a sweeter expression than When he finds the danger over. He is perfectly well and as merry and busy as his sister and Bill who never passes an hour without naming his Uncle[2] and asks every day if he will come again

Now the cold and comfortless blasts begin I send many a sigh to Staten Island and when I play all the little *favorites*, which is indispensable every Evening it is impossible to chase the thoughts of that life of danger and severity, which my poor Father endures.[3] —but how vain are thoughts and wishes—could they avail I should be for stealing many an hour from Dick—Heaven bless my own Sad—surely we have sufficient trial of our dispositions to make the most of necessity for the distance does not lessen between us—May Peace be yours prays *E.A.S.*

1.63 ASJPH 1-3-3-7:15

[1]William, Elizabeth's oldest son

[2]The children referred to Henry Sadler as uncle

[3]Dr. Richard Bayley, Elizabeth's father, was at the health station on Staten Island, caring for poor immigrants. When Elizabeth played the piano at Cragdon, their summer residence, she thought of him.

9th September 1799—

My own dear The little letter was forgot yesterday—the sun shines
bright this Morning and all are well but the death of Poor Morgue has
brought the prospect [nearer], that the whole family are in [danger]
W.M.S. is *very well* and on the continuation of that little sentence depends the All of comforts—he goes to town every day—but Heaven is
my trust.

Wednesday Morning

1.64 To Eliza Sadler

[n.d. 1799]

My dear Sad was well yesterday at Col. Giles's thank Heaven for
that and the comfort also that we are all enjoying good Health, good
spirits, and every good you could wish us except the Society of a *few*
which privation to be sure is not easily compensated. but there is no
choice—

my heart was with you last Sunday[.] five minutes with the dear
Sad and my Father would have been the happiness of ages to me.—I
share all your pain and anxiety for my friend Henry [Sadler] for I am
sure you never see him depart for the city without suffering—how
much we have both to fear is terrible to think of. My W.M.S. has
passed the three last days with us and I have played the Piano more
than in a year before and my little Lady[1] who you would never take for
a romp throws handkerchiefs, sticks needles in him and chases him
round the room fifty times a day, a kind of mirth he delights in, so that
all goes well—every half hour I can catch goes to Emilius[2]—three
volumes I have read with delight and were I to express half my
thoughts about it particularly respecting his Religious Ideas I should
lose that circumspection I have so long limited myself to and be

---

1.64 ASJPH 1-3-3-7:18

[1] Anna Maria, Elizabeth's oldest child

[2] The novel, *Emile*, by Jean Jacques Rousseau, whom she spoke of as "J.J."

E.A.*B[ayley]* instead of *E.A.S.*—dear JJ. I am yours—and my Sad you have your share of *E.A.S.*

Your Anna Maria is all we can wish her and never forgets her Uncle and Aunt Sadler—[3]

1.65 To Dr. Richard Bayley

Blooming Dale 10th September 1799

My Very Dear Mr. Monitor

That you are in the enjoyment of Health, in the midst of Dangers toils and Death, is a subject of high exultation to me—and if the prayers of a good quiet little Female are supposed to be of any avail it will be long continued to you, with the Hope that the visual rays of our fellow citizens will in time be brightened by your labours, and their attention awakened by the voice of truth and *conscience*[1]

—I had the pleasure to hear a Mr. Delmas a French Phisician refer a number of strangers, both French and English, to a publication called the *Monitor* as the best thing written on the subject of yellow Fever and as the only one that pointed out its true cause and Origin, he said he did not know who was the author but he must be the best friend of Humanity, and should be considered by the Americans as their best adviser[2]—I imagine my Eyes were large and blacker at that moment than usual.

It is impossible my dear Sir even to fancy finer Grandchildren than you have—but *little Richard* Bayley is the center of all Harmony.

---

[3]Rev. Simon Gabriel Bruté added this note at the top: "*Oh Read at the End* O providential 1799 - 1805 - 1821"

1.65 ASJPH 1-3-3-9:81

[1]Dr. Bayley's efforts as public health officer were not supported by all the citizenry.

[2]Dr. Bayley was the author of the article, written in 1796, to which Elizabeth referred. It was entitled *An Account of the Epidemic Fever Which Prevailed in the City of New York During Part of the Summer and Fall of 1795.* He also wrote *Letters From the Health Officer to the Common Council of the City of New York* in 1799.

Is my Helen[3] well, and will she be pleased to remember Her Sister with affection—Your old friend Mrs. Juliana [Scott] is reading by my side—I ask her comment to you, she says tell him that "if the great Gods be Just they shall assist the deeds of Justest Men"—Maria is without exeption the most amiable Being I know—

—If you would sometimes direct Helens pen to Blooming Dale it would be a most grateful substitute for your own which I cannot expect to claim in this season of occupation,—and it would always be punctually replyed to—

Your Child. *E.A.Seton*

1.66 To Eliza Sadler

Wednesday—2nd October 1799

And is it possible my Sad, that you have been so long without hearing from me—My Father presented me the little travelling Note the day before yesterday. Imagine how much his visit surprised and delighted me. he said you were well and on Long Island,[1] O that I could see you too—but my Fate seems to be fixed this Summer,[2] and I fear that nothing less than snows and Nor-westers will again bring us together. Mrs. Scott[3] is gone to Long Island for a week, and Mr. Stone[4] fearful that the time Mr. [William Magee] Seton and myself were to pass together should be tedious, has kindly taken her room until she returns, if Mr. and Mrs. Maitland[5] does not turn him out which they have some thoughts of doing—

---

[3]Helen Bayley, Elizabeth's half-sister
1.66 ASJPH 1-3-3-7:16

[1]The Sadlers had a summer home on Long Island.

[2]Elizabeth and her children had to stay at Cragdon, away from the city, until the cool weather removed the danger of yellow fever.

[3]Julia Scott had gone to visit her friends Col. and Mrs. Aquila Giles.

[4]A business associate of William Magee Seton

[5]James and Eliza Seton Maitland, Elizabeth's brother- and sister-in-law

Well—internal Peace is mine, let them go round and round—the sweet Children are sweet indeed and enjoy this fine weather so much as even *we* could—if you can only imagine Dick running over the grass and garden, tumbles down and turns to see the countenance that is watching him to know if he shall cry, then off again as merry as a Bird—precious Beings—If their Father is preserved thro' this Terrible Fever, we shall do well—He goes every day to Town but only in Broad Way—Heaven will show the Event, but my mind is in a most cruel state of apprehension.—Friend H[enry] of course remains with you therefore your fears are at rest. remember Us 5 to him

—A Mr Zerleder from Hambro',[6] has told me a great deal about Pitcairn and his Pamela[7]—I suppose he brings you letters—he particularly knew Mr. Thierry, and your "very good Friends" was his expression—

—tell me something about who is with you—how the time goes—and how your dear little Self is above all—

Your *E.A.S.*

Mrs. Scott said she certainly should go to see you—

1.67 To Eliza Sadler

[October 1799]

My own Eliza is I hope enjoying this precious Morning Sun which is really delightful—surely you have reason to rejoice that friend H[enry] is so secure in this terrible se[a]son of danger—Our little breathing flute is no more and every note of your favorite air is recollected with melancholy pleasure—Poor Gamble—but his death has not been felt in comparison with Mr. Monique's[1] which was in all its

---

[6]Probably a business associate of Seton, Maitland and Company from Hamburg

[7]The Pitcairn family was related to the English branch of the Seton family.

1.67 ASJPH 1-3-3-7:19

[1]Every day, news of deaths from yellow fever in the city increased Elizabeth's fears for her husband's welfare.

circumstances inconcievably distressing and the daily visit I make Mrs. O[live] has impressed me with more sorrowfull thoughts than I ever voluntarily indulged before. My W.M.S. goes to Town this Morning and the exercise of all my chearfullness and courage is necessary to hide the apprehensions I always feel when the cabriole leaves the door—but the Banks must be attended and Bills paid.

—Yesterday you thought of me, you saw my Father I wrote a little letter to him last week and dreaded that it would not please him for it is difficult to meet the train of his thoughts;—mine are in a tone sufficiently elevated, for trouble always creates great exertions of my mind and give it a force to which at other times it is incapable.

—Your JJ.[2] has awakened many ideas which has long since been at rest, indeed he is the writer I shall always refer to in a season of sorrow for he makes me forget myself whilst reading, but leaves the most consoling impression on every thought—I hope we shall often enjoy his society together—Oh how far preferable to—

—the children of the Abbay *as a Novel*[3] is superior to many, indeed I could not name more than half a doz[en] I would rather read—but without your commendation I believe I should not have been so well satisfied—Your Richard stands by my side with the smile of a little Angel he pads cautiously from room to room delighted with the new power—Anna is a precious Being and attaches me more every hour. Bill is quite a Man, and very much improved—Uncle Sadler is sure to be named whenever there is a romp and whenever I tell Anna she is a good girl she asks, "wont you write it to Aunt Sadler"—All goes quietly and that is saying a great deal Peace be yours.

E.A.S. Monday Morning

William is hurrying me

---

[2]Jean Jacques Rousseau

[3]*The Children of the Abbey* was a Gothic novel by Mrs. Regina Marie Dalton Roach. Popular in England, it was first published in America in 1798.

1.68 To Rebecca Seton

Cragdon October 2, 1799

My dear Rebecca—

I recieved your letter of the 22nd September an hour ago, and altho' I make it a rule never to answer letters whilst under the influence of the first impression I recieve from them, I cannot refrain from immediately replying to it and it is not a very easy task to preserve my usual sincerity with you, for recalling the past is useless and vain, and to pass it over in Silence is doing injustice to the truth of my affection for you; but I believe even that is best[,] for my mind is in a state of anxiety and distress which does not admit of any calculation respecting the enjoyment of this Life—in one short week sisters, friends, and the whole world may be nothing to me there never passes a day but some family is deprived of its support, children of their Parent and the Wife of her Husband even in the number of my acquaintances;—My William[1] goes every day to town and is more exposed than many who have lost their lives—that he should escape depends on that Mercy which has never yet failed and which I have reason to bless every hour of my Life—If he does not the greatest probability is that you and I will never meet again, for never can I survive the scene.

I hope you have written to Eliza, She has seen a great deal of Sorrow this Summer, and Maitland[2] told William the day before yesterday that they were all unwell—yesterday morning I wrote Eliza a Note such as I would have written *you* in similar circumstances, that is the most affectionate I could pen, intreating her to shut up House and to bring her Family to us until they were recovered—William gave it to her, but she has not said wether she will come or not—I hope she will for my Heart achs to think of the fatigues and distress she goes thro'—Mr. Stone[3] at present occupies the room Mrs. [Julia] Scott has

---

1.68 ACS Seton-Jevons #15-17

[1] Elizabeth was referring to the effects of the yellow fever epidemic and her fears for the safety of her husband, William Magee Seton.

[2] Eliza Seton Maitland, Elizabeth's sister-in-law, and her husband, James Maitland

[3] A business associate of William Magee Seton

left—she has gone to Long Island to Mrs. Giles—the Darlings are in perfect health and very much improved, Richard pads all over the grass and walks, down and up again, and is so delighted with his New power that he is as good as a little angel—the Girls were very well last week—Mary has written me charming letters this summer, and the Boys have sent three or four Packets—I shall write them this week—

I saw all James Family and Aunt Farquhars last Sunday they were all well and Mary's children look delightful[.][4] Mr. Stone and William are reading the Papers and request to be remembered to you. William says I must tell you "he is glad you are so well pleased with your situation,"[5] and Sister prays that Peace and content may be yours. *E.A.S.*

Kiss my Cely for me, tell her there never passes a day but Anna talks of her, and is all ways picking nuts and apples for her Aunty.

Miss Hunter is forever asking about her Books. do if there is any opportunity send them even at the risk of losing them for then we might get her another set—She has mentioned it to Stone, Mary Wilks, and to myself five or six times.

1.69 To Julia Scott

New York 20th November 1799

I have not been able to steal even an hour from sleep to write to you my dear Julia, for I have not been in bed for more than two hours any night this week past, and this is the first hour even in the day I have claimed from my Darling Dick who has not been well since you left me, and has for many days had a complaint in his bowells which threatens the most serious consequence, but as my Father has now come to Town I have many Hopes in his care and power to save, tho' I may be very soon obliged to resign the dear little angel who has

---

[4]James and Mary Hoffman Seton and their family; William Magee's aunt, Elizabeth Curson Farquhar

[5]This letter is addressed to Rebecca in Alexandria, Virginia, where she was staying with her brother John and his new wife, Mary.

1.69 ASJPH 1-3-3-6:28

become so more than ever attached to me that it is only while he sleeps that I venture to leave his room—So we go dear Julia—and the Merchants are in such trouble thro' the Hambro' and London faileurs that I have to use every exertion to keep my poor W.M.[1] alive, his present plan is the *back woods* where we shall not calculate the dollars per load, but I hope tomorrow's sun will be brighter, and then we shall be going to Washington City[2] which will be all in your way, I am sure only such a great event will realize your expectations for you have intirely forgotten the 17th September of which there is now no doubt,[3]—if my poor Dick's illness does not change the prospect—the Girls have returned with nothing but their chemieses to their backs, so that I have cut up a piece of Dimmity, Flannel, and two of Calico to great Advantage besides the endless variety of other necessary purchases, among which I paid 13 dollars for their three Hats, which illy comports with the "times" so that if you compare Your *crosses* with mine I think you will sit down quietly in your dear little Home, and bless yourself. things indeed are changed when you can stand cold and wet better than Maria—"Providence allways [fits the] burthen," I hope she is now well and happy with the dear cousins—my love to her and John

—Will and Anna are well, and indeed it is a miracle how we have escaped for the back part of our house has been so offensive added to the circumstance of poor Samuels death that we have been obliged to shut up as much as we could and live in the front.—Col[onel] G[iles] is to forward your Trunk to-morrow; If wishes would do you should have peace—I did not tell you I recieved your dear little letter, for which I thank you a thousand times.

Remember me to Brother [Samuel] and Charlotte—and write as soon as you can to

your *E.A.S.* in great haste

---

[1] William Magee Seton's business was suffering because of shipping conditions between America and Europe.

[2] Washington, D.C.

[3] Elizabeth was now certain she was pregnant with her fourth child.

1.70 Draft to Lady Isabella Cayley[1]

[Fall 1799]

My [last] letter to you was written from our habitation in Wall Street[2] which we were drove from by the Yellow fever and came with all the children to the place we are now at for the summer, which my father had leased and furnished[3] where my poor William had a small touch of the Fever tho not so much as to give us very serious alarm, and I believe the leisure he enjoyed in consequence of an intire cessation from business was more advantageous to him than the Fever was injurious—tho' I should be very sorry to make such another trial. He was the only one of the Family who suffered in the least which as it is so numerous was almost a miracle,—We did not dare venture to Town as inhabitants until the first of November. When we removed immediately to Stone Street the Family House—My Husband with the advice of his friends and the general consent of the family sold the greater part of the furniture as most of it had been in use ever since my fathers first marriage[4] and our keeping it might have created disputes besides which we have *abundance* of our own all new when we were first married those things that were not sold, were valued by competent Judges, and the plate was divided—

Mary and Charlott the two girls next Rebecca[5] are placed at an English Boarding school established in Brunswick[,] state of New Jersey about 30 miles from New York and the two younger Girls[6] passed the winter at Home where Rebecca and myself taught them reading writing and spelling[7] until her ill Health made it impossible to give them the necessary attention—When Mary and Charlott returned

---

1.70 AMSJ A 111 004 (Seton-Jevons #452-453)

[1]Isabella Seton Cayley, William Magee Seton's paternal aunt, residing in England

[2]27 Wall Street, where William Magee and Elizabeth Bayley Seton lived prior to the death of the elder William Seton

[3]Cragdon, the Seton summer home

[4]William Seton, Sr., married Rebecca Curson March 2, 1767.

[5]William Magee Seton's younger half-sisters for whom he and Elizabeth had assumed responsibility after his father's death.

[6]Harriet and Cecilia Seton, Elizabeth's sisters-in-law

[7]This was Elizabeth's first experience at teaching girls.

from their Spring Vacation took Harriet with them to school and Cecilia the youngest accompanies Rebecca—she is a very delicate child, and one of the most amiable little creatures in the World—Samuel and Edward[8] who my Father[9] used to call his little Pillars, and always had one on each side of him at table are the most Promising lovely Boys that ever were they have even a marked Elegance and Grace in their appearance and manners that distinguishes them from any Boys of their Age I ever saw—and a Sweetness of Disposition Unequalled[10]

1.72 To Julia Scott

New York 20th December 1799

My little Son is quite Well the Girls gone, and I can once more sit down in Peace and call my thoughts to their old course—My Julia is then their first object, and I feel that her affectionate letter has been too long unanswered, but if you could have seen my poor little sufferer, and know half the distress I have had to endure, you would not even in thought reproach me—the girls too were to be arranged for the succeeding six months, their cloathing to be measured and managed by me with Dick in my arms for he would not go to Mammy [Huler] night or day for three weeks more than to a Stranger—but "the storm is past and I at rest"—and so much for I.

how does your poor little self do, I dread the effect of your terrors from this terrible fire tho' I can form no idea of the situation of your House, which being in the same street with the buildings destroyed must have made your Situation terrible while the danger lasted—is Brother with you—I am sure you should not be so unprotected as you discribed in your last letter—if you are to be, I should wish Charlottes Suspicions realized that you would form an engagement[,] tho

---

[8]Samuel Waddington Seton and Edward Augustus Seton

[9]William Seton, Sr.

[10]A longer version of this letter appears in Robert Seton's *An Old Family* (New York: Brentano's, 1899), pp. 286-288. It is reprinted in Appendix 1- A1.71. His version of Elizabeth's letters are usually modifications of the original and are therefore not always reliable.

1.72 ASJPH 1-3-3-6:29

independant of that[,] were I you[,] nothing on Earth should tempt me for new schemes of Life are not the thing except there could be more certain of the future, and the very best of these men (one is writing opposite to me) are so unruly and perplexing that nothing should induce a reasonable Woman to wear the Chains of two of them, and that is the plain English of Matrimony Julia—

Old Stone[1] says the extreme cold nights obliges him to wear all the cloaks and great coats he can find and if you could muster a few old flannel petticoats and send them by Post—it would be an estimable favor—he continues to be the Shadow of my Good man[2] but I have had something else to think of besides them therefore they have it their own way—I shall never dare look the Col[onel Giles] in the face again—when he came in Richard and Bill were both figgiting for their soup, and he asking me more questions about you than the little things allowed to answer, I very innocently drew your letter from my Pocket—but oh what a circulation thro' every vein when after he was gone reading it again myself I recollected the September calculations[3]—he must think me the most compleatly impudent Mortal alive—but alas, like many more of my follies it is past recall, and I dare say you are laughing at me with all your heart—You mention your wish to be kind to my poor Beck,[4] but she will not give you the opportunity till the Spring—she suffers so much pain in her breast that she dares not venture travelling at this season—that you can scarcely imagine a more lonely [person] independant of my trio, than I am—Seton is more Engaged than ever, my sister indulges old habits, and Mrs. [Eliza] Sadler and Emma Craig so distant, that they can only get to me in fine weather—so that I have all my pretty Library and musick to myself—Father often comes but as soon as he has five minutes rest falls asleep—Anna often says Mamma play you are Aunt Scott and Bill and I Jack and Maria how do they do how is the Piano, look up Maria or you will never play by note—My paper is very

---

[1] A business associate of William Magee Seton

[2] William Magee Seton

[3] A reference to her pregnancy

[4] Rebecca Seton, Elizabeth's sister-in-law, had tuberculosis.

cross—Heaven Bless you—best love to Charlotte when she behaves well, and the flame that never dies to Brother Sam!—

Your own *E.A.S.*

1.73 To Rebecca Seton

New York 23rd December 1799

Well my dear Rebecca,

you say you have made up your mind to every thing that can happen—and that happiness can never again decieve you—but how will you make up your mind to hear of my poor W.M.S. misfortunes—that Maitland[1] has stoped payment in London and that we are obliged to do the same here—it is a cruel event to William for altho' he has every consolation a man can have under such circumstances, that it is not from his own imprudence and that no part of the blame is attached to him, you may imagine the distress and perplexity it occasions to all—James[2] has been almost crazy but on examination finds less cause of apprehension than he imagined, and it is the general decission of all William's friends and the Directors of the Banks who have been consulted that he must absolutely suspend payments—but you will hear all about it from Jack[3] who has doubtless recieved letters from some of the family[,] bad news travels fast—make the best of it—is an old lesson—

You may think it fortunate that you are so happily situated, and that your wish for action was prevented for if we were a melancholy family last Winter we are something worse this, and Heaven only knows where our troubles are to end—I should have written to you my Sister,

---

1.73 ASJPH 1-3-3-8:1

[1]Mr. Maitland, head of the London branch of Seton, Maitland and Company, stopped payment as a result of the loss of a ship off the coast of Amsterdam.

[2]James Maitland, Elizabeth's brother-in-law and William Magee's business partner in the American branch of the firm

[3]John Curson Seton, Elizabeth's brother-in-law

but for six weeks little Dick never left me night or day, and would not go to Mammy [Huler] more than to a stranger—and when I was released every thing as you may suppose was in such confusion that I had hard work to bring it round again—

I hope the Girls have written to you since their return—Mammy took care of them, and says Miss Hay is beyond every thing kind and attentive to them, and that they seemed very happy[4]—So they seemed at Home there was but one complaint that they were obliged to go out more than they wished, and I did not controul them in any point except their wearing Hand Kerchiefs—Mary with a pain in her Breast and Charlott with a cold to which you know she is liable usually wore their thick Jackonet Handkerchiefs in the Morning and were out in the Evening without any, because it was the fashion—but the moment I represented the imprudence to Mary she was convinced and I gave them Muslin of a finer quality and they were perfectly satisfied—I mention this particularly to you as you may also have another Account of it from those who thought it "foolish to muffle girls like old women"

—well I think we are all muffled now, and shall not be puzzeled to follow the fashion, but my dear Beck[,] Hope must go on with us, for it will not do for hearts and fortunes to sink together—Kiss my little Darling for me, and remember me to your amiable Companion[5] who I hope will now exert herself more than ever to make you forget Sorrow— Heaven Bless you—*E.A.S.*

The dear little Boys are well; I have sent their Coats and a *Box* since I came from the country and yesterday sent Aunty a package of Raisins and almonds to put in the Christmas Box with a letter—

---

[4]Mary and Charlotte Seton, Elizabeth's sisters-in-law, were attending a boarding school run by Miss Hay.

[5]Cecilia Seton and possibly Anna Maria Seton Vining, Elizabeth's sisters-in-law

1800

1.74 To Julia Scott

3rd January 1800

My dearest Julia,

I write only to wish you a happy New Years—and to tell you if the news of our Misfortunes[1] has reached you that you must do as I do, *Hope the best*—My Seton is in a distress of mind scarcely to be imagined partly from the shock he has recieved which was altogether unexpected, and partly from the necessity of immediate Statement of Accounts etc. which is necessary for his personal honor and the satisfaction of his Friends—the Directors of the Banks and all the principal Merchants even those who were concerned with him recommended and strongly advised his suspension of Payments as soon as he had recieved Mr. Maitlands[2] letters—You may suppose how much it has cost him both in Mortification and the uncertainty of the Event—What is to become of his Fathers Family[3] heaven only knows for his Estate has the first claims as he was the principal Partner—for himself he could immediately be in a better situation than before, for so great is the confidence in his integrity that he has had three offers of Money to any amount he would name but he has determined to leave every thing at a stand till the Partnership is expired next June twelvemonth and for the Girls I must do as usual use Economy and in cases of unnecessary demands appeal to their reason—

1.74 ASJPH 1-3-3-6:30

[1]The Seton family business reversals

[2]Head of the London branch of Seton, Maitland and Company. The London branch of the firm failed due to the loss of a ship carrying coined money. The insolvency of the London office contributed to the downfall of the New York branch of the firm. Many New York merchants suffered serious losses at this time because of the conflict between the English and the French which affected trade on the high seas.

[3]After the death of William Seton, Sr., William Magee and Elizabeth assumed responsibility for William's younger half-brothers and sisters.

—dear dear Julia how long I have been tired of this busy scene, but it is not likely to mend, and I must kiss Dick and be thankful for what remains from the ruins of Wall Street[4]—Anna and Will are very much improved and yet talk of Aunty Scott, John, and Maria—how are your children and how do you support your new character of managing for yourself. Bless you little Soul I fear you will not find it very easy—Col[onel] G[iles] is to send my letter, it is now nine Oclock, and I fear I shall be too late—My love to Charlotte and Brother [Samuel] Heaven grant you all a happy *century* if it is but a happy *one*

Yours most truely—*E.A.S.*

1.75 To Rebecca Seton

3rd January 1800

Have you recieved my letter of the last of December? I forget the day.[1] Have you seen A[braham] O[gden] Heaven bless him—his attentions to my William can never be equaled or forgot.[2]

Dear Rebecca The tears flowed fast over your letter—the thoughts of your present state of mind compared to that it described hurt me a thousand times more than if you had not obtained that tranquility and resolution you have so long struggled for—but things are going better than we had at first Imagined and you must keep up good Hopes—you know Willy's disposition sometimes he says he will work it out, at others Nothing but State Prison and Poverty,[3] nor can we know with any certainty how it will go until *Maitland*[4] has arranged finally with his creditors. but as I said before we must Hope the best, for Myself I fear nothing but tremble at the hold these crosses take on Williams Spirits—for one intire week we wrote till one and two in the morning

---

[4]27 Wall Street, where Elizabeth and William Magee had lived before William's father died
1.75 ACS Seton-Jevons #464-467

[1]The letter to which Elizabeth refers is either undated or not extant.

[2]This opening sentence is written above the salutation at the left of the date on the letter.

[3]The possible outcome of her husband's business reversals

[4]Head of the London branch of Seton, Maitland and Company

and he never closed his eyes till daylight and then for not more than an hour—but when things are at the worst they must grow better, and since he has arranged the Statement of his Accounts etc. his mind is more composed, tho' he is really very unwell—

to change this distressing subject my Father sent me twenty pound New Year Cakes and Honey casings with a Box of raisins and Keg Biscuits to be divided between Helen[5] and our Girls which with the addition some Almonds has made a nice Box for them or rather Trunk for with their stays and a few other little things it completely filled their trunk they left at home—they took the large one in your room as the other would not hold half their cloaths now they wear white, and were to have had a Chest of Drawers to hold their small things but as it was not yet purchased, and it is not absolutely necessary I have sent the other Trunk, without saying why, for it would only distress them without understanding it—I had a letter from Charlotte two days ago—they are well dear little Souls, they say they passed Harriets[6] Birthday merrily—

Think how many *thoughts* came on New Years day, Willy, George Bush,[7] and Ann and Will was all our party—William and I each trying to make each other think we did not reflect on past days, for to have touched on the subject, would have knocked up the little pleasures we yet possessed—tho' between *you and I*, it was not the most unpleasant New Years day I ever passed, for where there is Affection and *Hope* there is a great [page torn]

—Christmas day I passed with my Father and Sister and Willy at Home with the children, *can you believe it.* but I had promised ago, and nothing could persuade him to go, or to let me stay, he insisted in the most positive manner—and I went "like a wretch" for so I felt—we dine at James' next Monday—poor Eliza[8] is in a great deal of trouble at Nurse's staying so long, but she is well and so is dear old *Kate*, I have not heard from the Boys since I wrote you—I again repeat

---

[5]Helen Bayley, Elizabeth's half-sister, and her husband's younger half-sisters attended the same school in Brunswick, New Jersey.

[6]Harriet Seton had her eleventh birthday.

[7]A friend of William Magee Seton.

[8]Probably James Maitland, Elizabeth's brother-in-law, and his wife, Eliza Seton Maitland

make yourself as easy as possible—and think it for the best that you do not witness this bustle and distress for it would do no good—Kiss my Cecilia a thousand times for me—and the dear little girls who I am sure you must love almost as much as you do her—Dick is fat he can hardly March to Bill's singing—he sings Hail Columbia[9] as well as I can, and Anna says her Book constantly for fear God-mother should ask her to read and she not know how—

Yours most affectionately E.A.S.[10]

1.76 To Julia Scott

New York 16th January 1800

"only one line will be a Gratification" so said the friend [Colonel] Giles as he closed the door after him, another proof of his Mild and amiable temper for he has been running every day to the Post office for a promised letter from you—I have but two hours before my letter must go, and *I* to Craig's[1] to dine therefore I at first refused writing but there is no resisting when assured it is to please you—

"the Storm is past" and my poor Seton accomodating himself to what cannot be altered—Ogden goes in the Packet to settle as far as possible all difficulties with Maitland, and if it can be done to dissolve the Partnership[2]—until we know the Event, every thing remains quiet except the Pen which as you may suppose has little rest, and keeps us up till one and two Oclock instead of the old regular hour of ten which I dare say you have not forgot—My Sweet Children have perfect

---

[9]The melody of "Hail Columbia" is taken from "The President's March" and was supposedly composed by Philip Phile (d. 1793). It was first performed by a band stationed at Trenton Bridge when George Washington passed over to his inauguration in New York in 1789.

[10]This letter is addressed to Alexandria, Virginia, where Rebecca was visiting her brother John Seton.

1.76 ASJPH 1-3-3-6:31

[1]Elizabeth's half-sister and brother-in-law, Charlotte Amelia Bayley and William Craig

[2]Abraham Ogden, a business associate of William Magee Seton, was sailing to London to resolve difficulties with Seton, Maitland and Company.

Health, and my Fathers redoubled attentions and affection keep my mind more anxious to please him than to attend to itself—

Mrs. [Mary] Wilks has been at the point of Death apparantly for a fortnight I sat up with her two nights and was so intirely overpowered at seeing Mr. [John] Wilk's Sufferings and hers that I have been fainting and weak as any poor Soul you ever saw—but the crisis is past and she is recovering—Jack is married,[3] Rebecca is well and the dear little Girls enjoying themselves unconscious of their misfortunes—

I long for Brother Sam's arrival, I hope he will go in the Packet for Ogdens sake, and for his own sake *considering Miss Hunter and her Brother* goes also—Heaven Bless him— and you my own dear Julia

E.A.S.

The Dimity measures 52 yards which I have divided.[4]

1.77 To Rebecca Seton

New York 5th February 1800

If I would have written to my dear Rebecca as often as I have thought of it, you would have recieved a volume, but every thought that arises when I sit down with my Pen is the very contrary of what I ought to indulge myself, or express to you—for what avails melancholy forboadings, and an indulgence of feelings which can never alter the Event of things—it is all easy to me for I never have thought of my own comforts when there was any other persons depending, but to see my Williams struggles and hear his constant reflections on what is to become of *us* and that us such a number,[1] that at times courage flies—at first Williams hopes were kept up with an idea that Mr. Maitlands[2] next letter would explain the situation of his affairs, and

---

[3]John Curson Seton, Elizabeth's brother-in-law

[4]This last sentence is written on the back of the address page.

1.77 ASJPH 1-3-3-8:2

[1]William Magee and Elizabeth were responsible for their own three children as well as William's six younger half-brothers and sisters.

[2]The head of the London branch of Seton, Maitland and Company

we would then know what there was to expect but on the contrary he only writes that the creditors have attached[3] *all* the Property, and that his mind is in such a state that he can say no more, without considering while he is indulging his sensibilities William does not know if he has a right to Bread for his family—Sweet world! how good you are for them that like you—I should not disturb my poor Rebecca's mind with the truth of our situation but you seemed to reproach me for dissembling with you and so I have, for the most evil I dread is the return of pain in your breast which is always brought on by distress of your mind—the time of your return so much wished for, is now a thing I can not think of without pain for you will meet nothing but sorrow—[several words crossed out] William will give up every thing even his furniture in order to be free of these everlasting struggles, so that what is to follow is still worse than the past, and where we shall be Heaven only knows—the first of June I am to bring another little being to share the common lot,[4] and my Father in consequence is trying to secure us rooms on Long Island but it is still uncertain if he can get them, or what number—but we will see how it will go—we must look up—and trust to the best director—while I have room you may at least be sure of a corner of it—

James has bought a handsome three story house in Greenwich Street,[5] so thank heaven we are not all sinking—

I am writing on my Knee rocking Dicks cradle with one hand I have not my Evenings now, for what with despatching Stone to Leghorn and Ogden for England,[6] the Evening writing is never done 'till 12 and one Oclock—

A. O[gden] has been more than ten Brothers to my William Night and day Sunday or week day he is always busy for him and is to go in the Packet to Maitland to try and arrange matters, and some measure

---

[3] Seized by legal writ

[4] Elizabeth was expecting her fourth child.

[5] William Magee Seton's brother James Seton had purchased a house at 85 Greenwich Street in lower Manhattan.

[6] Mr. Stone and Abraham Ogden were sent by Seton, Maitland and Company to try to sort out its business difficulties.

substitute Williams presence. Never, in no change, or length of Life can his attentions be forgotten—

I have letters from Harriet and Cecilia and Eliza Farqhar saying all are well—and having none from Mary this long while I fear something has reached her respecting late affairs—I told you my reason for not mentioning them to her, and leave it to you to do what is best—perhaps it will be better you should say something to her before her return home—Kiss my precious Cecilia for me and your little Darlings,[7] and remember me Affectionately to our new Sister and to Jack[8]—Heaven Bless and save my Rebecca *E.A.S.*

You will wonder at the erasure, it is one of the many instances, I must supress even the truth, for fear of mischief in case my letter fell in other hands it might injure my Willy's affairs—

1.78 To Dr. Richard Bayley

New York 12th February 1800

My Father.

Your letter of the 8th Instance confered an incalculable favour on your Daughter who would with pleasure employ an hour of every day in writing to insure a repetition of similar favours. I have of late been so much engaged in copying Mercantile correspondance and assisting my friend in making Statements to his Partner in London,[1] that your letter was absolutely necessary to restore my thoughts in their usual channel—I rejoice that yours are so much in the train that Nature and the bent of your mind has marked them for, and altho' from personal considerations your return is a most desirable event to myself, for

---

[7]Cecilia Seton, Elizabeth's sister-in-law who was with Rebecca. The darlings she is referring to were probably the children of Anna Maria Seton Vining and her husband, John Middleton Vinning, who lived in Dover, Delaware.

[8]Mary Wise and John Curson Seton married in 1799.

1.78 ASJPH 1-3-3-9:82

[1]Elizabeth was assisting William Magee Seton, her husband, with business correspondence during the bankruptcy crisis of Seton, Maitland and Company.

yourself I regret that your visit cannot be prolonged—Mr. Sitgreaves[2] thinks that men of active Genius should never be more than one month in the same place—who does that apply to[,] who is it that could not be made happy by an Angel even if the uniting bond was but a Cambric thread[3]—no bonds, no restraints, the Air, the Ocean, the whole Earth, and not even that *I* believe would satisfy the restless Spirit of the object now present to my Mind.

—Poor Sitgreaves on the contrary wants his shelves of Books, his Segar [Cigar], the eye of Affection enquiring his wish, and hastning to fulfil it before it is expressed—and so contrary is the device of fortune that he must engage with the World, sacrifice even his most natural propensities etc etc etc—he has engaged me to fill a long Paragraph to you expressive of his disappointment at your Absence during his visit here, but as he Sails this Morning and regrets are very unavailing I would rather tell you that my little friend and her rib dines with us tomorrow *very quietly* that I anticipate a peculiar pleasure in conveying your <recollection> remembrance and respect[.] her Chest has been very troublesome during the last week so I believe until the Struggle of parting is past, it cannot be restored. Peace to it—I have seen Mary but once since your departure, but she is well tho' little Kate[4] has been indisposed[.] indeed you have escaped a scene of long faces, for every one has been suffering from the last change of weather—

You did not consider in your reflections or calculations that you were indulging one of the most incorrigable failings of your Daughter, who has no right to the privilege as a Woman however pardonable the active unrestrained mind of man may be in his errors.—but Natures Characters can never be erased, and the next best choice is to keep cool and be satisfied with Events—the Darlings are very well and I have the pleasure to subscribe myself

E.A.S. Yours

---

[2]Either Julia's father, William Sitgreaves, or her brother Samuel Sitgreaves
[3]A fine white linen or cotton thread
[4]Elizabeth's sister, Mary Bayley Post, and her daughter Catherine

1.79 To Dr. Richard Bayley

Thursday 20th February 1800

I have just learned that Mrs. Govenour intends setting out for Albany to morrow,[1] and as there is some reason to suppose your return will not be so soon as was first intended, your Betty could not disappoint your wish of a line by every opportunity, tho' there is nothing to communicate which has not already been told, except that the vessel of my friend is *cleared out*, and the Voyage will be commenced on Sunday—that the dear little *Trio* are well, and Seton as usual—he has kept me so much employed that the last Post day escaped me—but I wrote by Monday's which I hope is recieved—

My little friend passed an hour with me yesterday, pale, dejected but boasting the resolution of a *Philoso*, tho' I fear it will not bear Proof—it will have sufficient support for independence of all others, *Mary P[ost]*seems resolved to enter heart and soul in the Interests of the concerned, and speaks with active Indignation of all secondary considerations—"She must and shall be comforted"—true language of female determination, but who can search the Secret Soul, and [turn] the rooted Sorrow from

—Peter has called attention of all the World to his Rush Light—inclosed is his Introduction of it—he certainly may boast the advantages of a persevering spirit, and his Simile of his friend ought to be recorded—

—once more I repeat—"Your spirit" Surrounds your child who checks each word you would prevent, and pursues every action that you would approve, particularly by those where the interest is greatest—a tincture of Vanity in this, but self-confidence is the result of *attention*, to which I cannot be remiss in *your Absence.*

1.79 ASJPH 1-3-3-9:83

[1]Dr. Bayley was in Albany on one of his regular trips to report to the state legislature. During the Revolution the Gouverneurs were business partners of the Cursons, William Magee Seton's maternal relatives.

—Post has just left us—his family are well—Your Daughter Presents herself to you—

Most Affectionately E.A.Seton

1.80 To Dr. Richard Bayley

New York 4th March 1800—

My Father.

A little faithful heart has been conversing with you this hour past, and I have engaged to copy from it a part of its contents—that it regrets your absence, is extremely anxious for your present safety, and will rejoice when you return. the Post goes to-morrow therefore there is no time to wait 'till the brain is in the humour of invention, *and therefore*, you must recieve the present communication from that source which is always ready when you are the person in question; and it has also a particular pleasure in conveying to you the intelligence that its friend who was yesterday a Sufferer, is well to day—*absolutely well*, cheerful, and light as if a weight had been removed; She visited me yesterday Morning and was so much Indisposed that I privailed with her to defer her engagements, and return to her Home, to which I had the good fortune to send Post immediately with the remedy you had prescribed and which had the most desirable effect, and I had the pleasure to find her to-day with Mary Post, quite well and her own expression a "New creature"—to-morrow we are engaged to ride, and pass the day in the *Nursery*—I hope to hear of your arrival as far as Croten[1] by the boatmen, and heaven grant that it has been in safety, and some degree of comfort.

prays your own very dear E.A.Seton

1.80 ASJPH 1-3-3-9:84

[1]Croton is a town on the Hudson River about thirty-five miles north of lower Manhattan. Dr. Bayley was en route from Albany where he made annual trips to report to the state legislature from 1798 to 1801.

1.81 To Dr. Richard Bayley

New York 12th March 1800

The Heart of your Betty jumped for Joy at sight of the letter that was to tell her of your safe arrival, that you were well, and in the midst of friends; and can it be that there is any charm in the visit to Albany[1] to compensate for your absence from New York—dear Sir indeed you mistook, it was but a momentary impression, which I am sure is before this time changed into recollections of those *Douceurs*[2] without which every other gratification loses its charm with its Novelty.

—that ever *you* should observe the distance of the belt from the *chin*—it is true that very conspicuous points must attract attention, so far it is easy to imagine—more so than that your mind should be in that pliant happy mood to admit of amusement from transient objects—I wish it may longer remain in the desirable state your letter left you in; like Holiday to the child that has long been kept in school, and harassed by the severity of its Teacher This is not our dear Helens[3] case, for a letter I have just recieved from her expresses all that Health and life can give, pleased with her little friends and exulting in the idea of vacation which begins the last of April. Miss Hay[4] has written to me for your permission to allow Helen to recieve the attendance of a Dancing Master who excells in his profession, the terms very moderate etc—

I have seen the good Patty, but not her dear Mistress to day, and I know from Post that she is well, and in better spirits than usual—it is next to impossible for us to meet for the streets are absolutely dangerous from the two falls of snow uniting and melting—and for my poor little self, when I can walk over the floor without limping, and making wry faces I shall think myself very fortunate—as soon as possible we will ride again, and I hope, renew all pleasant Ideas tho unfortunately

---

1.81 ASJPH 1-3-3-9:85

[1]Dr. Bayley was in Albany in his capacity as health officer.

[2]Pleasures

[3]Helen Bayley, Elizabeth's half-sister, who was away at boarding school

[4]Director of the boarding school in Brunswick, New Jersey, which Helen attended along with the younger Seton girls

we are both but too much inclined when we are together to indulge *Sympathy*

—I have been copying so many English letters French letters etc that one eye is open the other shut therefore dear Mr. Papa I wish you a night of rest and myself the same

Your most dear daughter *E.A.S.*

My Mr. S-s remembrance to you—1/2 past Eleven Tuesday night

1.82 To Julia Scott

New York 18th March 1800—

My dear Julia may well ask what I am doing, and really I never was in my life so busy or should not have passed six weeks without a word to you. My Seton has a great deal of Private writing just now, which he or I must do, and as I am doomed this Winter to suffer a great deal of pain both of mind and body, and no employment helps me so soon to forget both as writing, I have taken to myself as a comfort what would have been a great deal of trouble to him, besides my knowing all the *why's* and *wherefores* makes me a better companion for him and I am now his only one—Stone, Ogden,[1] and every Body is gone, and I am most truely his *all.*—the plot thickens dear friend not one line of explanation from Maitland,[2] but *Setons* Bills[3] and all those endorsed by him refused and returned gives an appearance not very flattering and makes the future prospect so serious that even *I* cannot bear to dwell on it—I have also had to make every thing new for my children this winter and to ruffle a dozen shirts which for me is quite a serious undertaking and now am not half ready for the month of June[4]—

1.82 ASJPH 1-3-3-6:32

[1]Mr. Stone had been sent to Leghorn and Abraham Ogden to London by the firm of Seton, Maitland and Company to get firsthand information about its failing business fortunes.

[2]Head of the London branch of Seton, Maitland and Company

[3]A bill of exchange is a written order by the writer or drawer to the drawee to pay a certain sum on a given date to the drawer or to a third person named in the bill known as the payee.

[4]Elizabeth was expecting her fourth child in June.

We enjoyed but little of dear Brother Samuels Society, but what I had was sweet and I would not have missed it for the world, he seemed as much himself—that mild amiable expression of satisfaction as if he was to leave us but a week—but who can read the inmost thought and know how far he felt the seperation—he mentioned parting with your mother as if it really cost him a great deal and surely he must have felt it severely—Heaven protect him—Seton says he has had very favorable winds and weather—your earnest expressions about visiting you make me smile—dear little soul who can bear no derangements or exertions yourself even in common cases require your friend with all her *weights and measures* to leave Home *Physician* and a thousand etcetera's to take a Journey thro' roads almost impassible and to return when they certainly must be worse—you might as well say come friend we will make a jaunt to the Moon—besides which Seton cannot leave his Creditors just now there is already one suit against him and Heaven only knows how soon there will be more—

Ah Julia Dear, you little know nor would I wish you to know what the present state of your friends mind is, nor the paleness of her face with pain in the back all day, and in the side at night neither of which I have been one hour without for the last two months but as I believe this to be intirely the consequences of the *Shadow*[5] (which I am sure you have not forgot) the moment the little angel is at the Breast all will be forgot and as soon as my poor Hub is able to work for us again, tho we are a pretty large number, I trust in heaven that the storm will go over, but really at present it is hard times—he at this moment says "my best love to Julia I wish she would send me two or three kisses"—

I do not wonder at your suffering with colds from the account Brother gave of your raking[6]—pray tell Charlotte not to mislead you in a manner of life for which you are so little suited except it was to introduce your dear Maria, for that alone would excuse you—you do not say half enough of your children—[Colonel] Giles says he is going to bring you to us as soon as the roads will allow, and as we have some prospect of being on Long Island and old Stone left his *Buggie* behind

---

[5] Her pregnancy
[6] Acting in a dissolute or dissipated manner

I think we may then talk over every thing with comfort—Miss Hunter went in the Packet *before* and had nearly been one of poor Brothers companions.

Emma[7] had *lost*, and has found *again*, my father is very well. my *loves* are ten times more precious and lovely than ever, and never pass a day without saying something about Aunt Scott or Jack and Maria and dear crazy Don—all that is past dear, and I must yet "rejoice in Hope"—Heaven Bless you both soul and Body prays

your own friend E.A.S.

1.83 To Rebecca Seton

New York 20th March 1800

I find my dear Rebecca is determined I shall not hear from her until she does from me—you make no allowance for the poor *Old Lady*[1] full of pains and troubles for which I shall give you a good scolding when we meet—indeed I have so much writing for William to do that it is as much as I can do to make time for the necessary work that must be done, as you know in my present case I always make every thing for the following six months at least,[2] besides which there is as much time spent in kissing and admiring Ricksy now as there used to be in nursing him—to be sure there never was so lovely a fellow, and I think the moment in which I put him in your arms will repay many a bitter one past since our Seperation—Eliza's[3] last letter from you gives us some hopes that it is soon to end, but indeed my dear Beck there seems to me a fatality in it, and I should not now be surprised at any thing that happened to prolong it—

---

[7]Charlotte Amelia Bayley Craig, Elizabeth's half-sister. This possibly refers to a miscarriage.
1.83 ASCSH Seton-Jevons #23-25
[1]Elizabeth
[2]Elizabeth was expecting a child in June.
[3]Eliza Seton Maitland, Elizabeth's sister-in-law

how I wish I could write you a long letter without saying one word
of *affairs* for in their present state they are too melancholy to think
about, and that not from any impression I have recieved from my William for never did a mortal bear misfortune and all the aggrivated distress of it with so much firmness and Patience as he does—I say
aggrivated for vessel after vessel arrives and Correspondants in London and Hamburg notify him that his Bills are refused and his property
detained there, and not one line of explanation from Maitland[4] either
good or bad—and here we are with funds detained on one side the water, and *transfered* the other, for he is obliged to make over every thing
in trust to his friends, nothing coming in, and one suit already against
him give but too much reason to expect more—but it is all in vain to
think about it—*Patience* is the only choice—and you are lucky my
dear Girl to find yourself with the happy party, tho' I am sure it cannot
suit you whilst such a cloud is suspended over us. I have been obliged
to write to Mary [Seton] on the subject, and recieved such an answer
as would do your heart good as it did mine, Miss Hay writes me that
she is so attentive to her studies as to give her very great satisfaction—

You cannot think how I long to see Cecilia dear little soul[.] Anna's
thoughts and play is as full of her as ever—I hope she has had no more
colds, they weaken her constitution so much—Eliza [Seton Maitland]
is so much fatter and healthier than when you left her that you will
scarcely believe it is her, and her children are lovely little creatures
particularly Bun, I dined with her and Aunt F at Mary's[5] last
Sunday—we have had no letters from the Boys later than February but
expect them next month about the 25th[.] Mr. Tamage is to bring
them, and if there is no better way I will send Mammy [Huler] for the
Girls—

I have ten thousand things to say to you my sweet Beck, but as we
are soon to meet, (I *trust* in Heaven) it is best to wait 'till we get snug at
our work on the sofa, that is supposing you come in May, for after that
I must be at my Summer destination wherever it is, or determine to

---

[4]Head of the London branch of Seton, Maitland and Company

[5]Elizabeth Curson Farquhar, William Magee Seton's aunt. It is not clear if Mary refers to Mary
Bayley Post, Elizabeth's sister, or to another Seton or Farquhar relative.

bear my confinement in Stone Street,[6] which I would not do if I could help it. at all events I will not leave home till all the chicks are ready to return to school—

Heaven bless you prays your *E.A.S.*

1.84 To Rebecca Seton

6 Oclock—thought it was 7—[1800]

My own dearest Sister.

I cannot tell you how well how happily we made our Voyage yesterday[.] we found dear Father at the Wharf with such a welcome as dispelled all the gloom of my heart and made me only wish that you were present.[1] Where is Rebecca the first question—the House so neat, you never would have believed the floors and rooms had been inhabited—the Birds the little garden—every thing so cheerful—

Holy Nature was the first thing required—the bedsteads were up and all righted by six Oclock—and then just as we were going to tea a great Punch bowl of garden strawberrys from Mrs. Vanduzen[2] crowned the feast—the sweet setting sun too—how the heart did melt before him the giver of all—

—I look at *Our* dwelling and see distinctly the street door shut dinning-room windows open, the windows above shut exept one a little way opened and am sure could see you if you were at it—Rebecca—dear Rebecca—*our dwelling* where we will not part—

Remember to write me above all things and name *the day* the moment you see your way clear—I have written to my own Willy.[3] Your

---

[6]Elizabeth, William Magee, and the family lived at 61 Stone Street after the death of the elder Mr. Seton.

1.84 ASJPH 1-3-3-8:20

[1]Elizabeth and the children went by boat to Staten Island where they were to spend the summer with her father, Dr. Richard Bayley. Rebecca remained at their Stone Street residence in the city.

[2]The VanDuzer (or VanDusen) family had a store and farm about a half mile south of the quarantine station on Staten Island. They also operated a tavern and were involved in the ferry service.

[3]William Magee, Elizabeth's husband, remained in the city during the summer.

darlings are as well as possible and Dick too sweet now he *"must not cry"*—Peace—Peace—Peace bless my own Rebecca

---

put away the Paper waiters and leave out the common ones—let my Bedstead which was forgot be carryed in from the yard and show Pat the Matts if they should be asked for.

1.85 To Rebecca Seton

2nd June 1800

My Rebecca—

Imagine the Sweet day I have passed with "Kiss me, Mamma," and all the dear little notes of love continually sounding—I hope your tear is chased by the smile also, and that all will go well—let me hear from you by Willy when he returns. a thousand loves from the darlings

E.A.S.

A great many kisses from own Sis Mary[.][1] Health*

1.87 William Seton to Julia Scott[1]

New York Tuesday 1st July 1800

D[ear] Madam

I have the pleasure to inform you that on Saturday last at the dawn of day your little friend presented us with another Daughter,[2] if possible

---

1.85 ASJPH 1-3-3-8:43

[1]Either Mary Bayley Post, Elizabeth's sister, or Mary Seton, Rebecca's sister

*For document 1.86, see Appendix.

1.87 ASJPH 1-3-3-6:33

[1]This letter was written by William Magee Seton, Elizabeth's husband.

[2]Catherine Charlton Seton (1800-1891) born June 28, the fourth child and second daughter of Elizabeth Bayley and William Magee Seton. After Elizabeth's death Catherine traveled with her brother William and his family before entering the Sisters of Mercy in New York (1846) where she ministered to prisoners and became the assistant of her order (1864-1871). She died in 1891 as a Sister of Mercy and is buried in Calvary Cemetery (section 4-2-D) in Woodside, New York. Josephine was probably her Confirmation name.

more lovely than the first, but as you are acquainted with my sentiments with respect to what is mine, I will forbear all description at present, and let you judge for yourself.—I left her and her Mother yesterday at the *Health Establishment,*[3] where they cannot but thrive and indeed Eliza never was better, so much so as to do without a Nurse.—This is the first opportunity I have had of informing you of this great Event and I am sure no one will participate more in the general joy.—With my *love* to Maria and John and *the same* to yourself believe me

Your friend and humble Servant Wm M Seton

1.88 To Eliza Sadler

[July 1800]

The air is clear, Father singing[,] the Birds singing, Nature refreshed, and above all my Seton restored—yet in looking at the op[p]osite shore bright with the setting sun, I cannot help sending forth a long sigh to the one who would so much value and enjoy the blessing which seems unpossessed by any one. every window is closed all looks solitary, and what are you doing dear Eliza—thought cannot trace you but if peace is your companion the whole beautiful universe can bestow nothing more precious—I wish you could see our Darlings—they are so merry and well—My amiable Sister[1] promises to see you if possible—Remember me to friend Henry and the Craiges's[2]—

Yours affectionately *E.A.S.*

---

[3]Elizabeth gave birth while she was with her father on Staten Island.

1.88 ASJPH 1-3-3-7:20

[1]Possibly Mary Bayley Post, Elizabeth's sister, or Rebecca Seton, her sister-in-law

[2]Henry Sadler and Eliza's brother and his wife, William and Charlotte Bayley Craig

1.89 To Catherine Dupleix[1]

Staten Island 12th July 1800

What would you give my own Du to see us all so well, your little Darlings enjoying themselves most perfectly, my Father at his usual occupations, Seton and Rebecca nursing and kissing little Catherine all day long, and the little *Mother* too happy, for *we* know that human nature cannot bear it.

—I believe our situation and enjoyments have been invariable since you left us. the anticipation of our dear *Du's* return and surmises about the wind and weather you experience mixes with all our conversations and often causes too a silent sigh, every evening we sing "the Sailor Boy" and "may some protecting angel near still hover round our Dué's head" forms the chorus, for our Rebecca is as sincerely attached to you and as anxious for your return as if she had known you as I know you my darling friend, the proof of every Virtue that can give endearment to friendship and affection.

—Father is sure that you have fair winds that you are never sea sick and that you want nothing but one of our Rusk loaves and water from our well. the Note he recieved from friend Duplex[2] was delightful to us tho' written so short a time after you sailed. the truth is that to-morrow is but one week it seems already a month, and the thought of the distance that separates us would be insupportable were it not for hope, nay the certainty that our *Du* will return to us.

—And how are you? —many thoughts occur when asking that question, but it will not do to think of the dark side, while Imagination paints you suffering, you may be quietly enjoying yourself in those occupations you delight in and often I have told you that while your other friends would be pitying your pains and loneliness on your passage I should be reconciled by the thoughts that you were exercising

---

1.89 AJSPH 1-3-3-7:62

[1]Catherine Dupleix was a friend of Elizabeth and the wife of George Dupleix, a naval captain. She had left New York to visit Ireland where she had family ties. She converted to Catholicism sometime after 1808. Elizabeth often referred to her as Du, Dué, or Kate.

[2]Captain George Dupleix

your mind with such reflections as would fortify it in hours of necessity. this was your last promise and I never can doubt the word my friend gave at so sacred a moment—Heaven will protect you and grant you to our prayers in Peace and safety.

—and dear Sister Anna with what tenderness and delight she will hold you to her Bosom, your Mother, dear Brother and all those dear ties which my *Du* has long wanted the consolation of enjoying and which she can enjoy so tenderly. these are the [only] thoughts I wish to connect with the recollection of my Du 'till we meet again.

—Your little Kate continues the same peaceful sweet angel you left her and goes by the name of "Queen of quiet." by your return she will hold out her arms to you and try to share Dick's kisses—He talks every [day] of his Du "gone big ship," and Ann and Will talk of you too and their Mother will take good care none of them shall forget you.

—Emma Craig and Mrs. Sad[ler] and their Husbands[3] dined with us yesterday, all is quiet and cheerful Mrs. Sad says but little you know that is her usual habit—but I think she has an unusual dejection, which may be in my imagination but at all events we cannot alter it. Sister Post is in her country Home and I have not seen her since you had but know that she is well. Mrs. McVickers[4] too is well I heard from her by our little Boys. Patty came down the morning you left us, and staid all day. I hope often to see the good soul while you are away She seems to me like a piece of my Du and I felt a debt of Gratitude to her for loving you so much—

I shall not omit any opportunity of writing to you. Whether you recieve my letters or not, for I love to give you every chance of what to me would be so great a pleasure as hearing from you. let me repeat to you not to fail if it is only by one line to tell us of your safety the moment it is in your power—remember me kindly to your Husband, and to your friends present me as you know I wish them to consider me, the true and sincere friend of their Dear Kate—

---

[3]Charlotte Bayley Craig and her husband, William; Eliza Craig Sadler and her husband, Henry

[4]A mutual friend of Catherine Dupleix and Elizabeth. In the early 1790s a John McVickar operated a store on Water Street which dealt in "printed waistcoats, toilanets and corded dimities" imported from England.

I have a long charge of love to dear Mrs. Duplex, whenever I write—the girls really love you quite enough—they have letters from Brunswick,[5] and your Sister is very well, and well contented. My Father and Husbands Affectionate remembrance to you—Oh that you were at this moment where the "cows are galloping"—

Kate's elbows recieves regularly every day the kiss of remembrance, and a sigh to Dué. May *Peace* be yours my own Darling—prays

your own friend *EASeton*
14th July

1.90 To Rebecca Seton

Sunday evening 9 Oclock [1800]

At 4 Oclock this morning little Kate began to crow and twist her little head about, and after getting a *plenty*, and kisses enough went to sleep again quietly. but Mamma's eyes and heart were awakened, the sky was sober grey, and I took my testament to the Piazza where I had two hours sweet Peace before any of my treasures moved. since that time there has been a *sombody* here all the while and there is still a gentleman talking with my Willy, who is fond of the variety of strangers conversation—but I have been looking at the new moon with thoughts bent to the same direction. will you then be here to enjoy her on the Balcony, or at the Piano—it is so my own Beck that *you* must decide how long you stay, but come *you must*, even if but for a little while.[1] to give the "old lady" one week out of six, especially as you must want recruiting, cannot be doing wrong to anyone.

The darlings are Health itself, and I am very much cheered by My Willy's appearance and good spirits this week, tho' he has been talking to me this morning of *the limits*[2] in next October. I tell him it is an

---

[5]Location of the boarding school attended by Elizabeth's young sisters-in-law

1.90 ASJPH 1-3-3-8:49

[1]Rebecca was in the city while Elizabeth was on Staten Island for the summer.

[2]William Magee feared being put in debtors' prison.

old blister, but he says it is too true—It does not bear thinking of—to commit ourselves to Him who judges righteously and look to him for strength and refuge is the only relief from thoughts which would over-power the mind that did not resist them.—Kiss your dear darlings for me and best love to Eliza and Mary[3]—I have given Willy an orange with a kiss on it from each of the loves little Kate's the largest for she thought it was her dear Tité[4] and almost nestled a hole in it—"more or less"—

write to me as soon as you can for I long to hear the pain in the Breast[5] is gone, I am sure you suffer more than you say—I do not go out[,] therefore the little white hat covered with black is suffi-cient—every blessing be yours—is the warm prayer from the Heart of

your own Sis

Monday morning—very well—wishing for you—

1.91 To Julia Scott

Staten Island 26th July 1800

My Julia says true indeed I am in long arrears with you, and the lit-tle tears would jump out as I closed your last letter which contained so many affectionate expressions to the friend who acknowledges she has too long permitted the appearance of neglect, tho' I am persuaded your friendship has suggested many reasons, and some very sorrowfull ones why I have been so long silent where I should so natu-rally have expressed the cares and anxieties that have occupied my mind for many months past,[1] but Julia dear the bent of Nature cannot easily be changed particularly when confirmed by the long habits of six and twenty years and in that time I cannot remember ever having

---

[3]Eliza Seton Maitland and Mary Seton, Elizabeth's sisters-in-law

[4]Possibly an affectionate name for aunt or auntie, or for Elizabeth's breast

[5]Rebecca had tuberculosis which ran in the Seton family.

1.91 ASJPH 1-3-3-6:34

[1]Elizabeth was referring to the family's financial difficulties.

expressed Suffering when I have the choice of Silence, and I have indeed been a sufferer, partly from the strong impressions of the mind which I could not efface and also from causes sufficiently real, which however we seem<now> reconciled to as they cannot be altered, and now that I have my little Cherub[2] in my arms and every day feel returning Health and chearfulness it seems that I have past a long night of pain and weariness exchanged for the comfort of a bright day in which I enjoy my Fathers Society my Husband and childrens affection, and future hopes of Peace.

I have one more lesson on the uselessness of perplexing the mind with anxieties about fortunes favour—from the time we gave up our country place I was always wondering how we were to get thro' the Summer in Stone Street,[3] and my father was at great pains to procure lodgings on Long Island where the accommodation was so bad that necessity only could reconcile them, and my Fathers house on Staten Island was to recieve us during my confinement, but the habit of "being a Christian" and in some degree "domesticated" to use his own words was not to be dispensed with after 4 weeks enjoyment, and the decission is that we remain all Summer, and certainly was there a choice of all creation I could not wish a pleasanter situation or more delightfull rooms with the addition of an upper Balcony that commands a view fifty miles beyond the Hook.[4] Seton passes four days of the week with me and my Father very seldom quits the House but to visit vessells.

the Boys are indiscribably fine fellows, Richard is a miracle of sweet expression and grace with a size of person and limbs very unusual for his age, William is still more like his grandfather Seton and as sturdy and saucy as ever—Anna continues "little Anna" very healthy but delicately small for 5 years old and the same manner of drawing back and looking downwards or rather side ways, that you see in country children—her disposition is very much improved, and

---

[2]Catherine Seton, Elizabeth's infant daughter

[3]The Setons had been forced to give up the summer home at Cragdon due to their financial difficulties. Their residence in New York City was on Stone Street.

[4]Sandy Hook, a spit of land on the northern New Jersey shore at the outer reach of New York harbor. The lighthouse there, built in 1764, is the oldest in the United States.

her capacity I think uncommon, tho' I am sorry to say her Mother has not been able to attend to it as it deserves, but am just making a serious beginning—and as to our sweet Babe I think you would wish to be its nurse as well as its God-mother for a more Peaceable serene little Being you cannot imagine. Seton may well admire her for she sleeps continually and makes none of those crooked faces children of a month old generally do—You will begin to say as Father does that we are "all wonders" when I tell you that eight days after her Birth I continued my arrangements down stairs as usual and have never had an hours Indisposition since. The season is so favourable and my Seton and Father so uncomfortable without those attentions which servants only can never give that I was anxious to do, what I surely would have condemned in any other circumstances—how pleasant it would be to visit you at the foot of the Hill, and Charlotte at the top, and more pleasant still to have a situation just in the center, where one might run up or run down as the compass pointed. [Colonel] Giles told us you were to be here in a month from the time he left you but the month is past and no Julia, nor do you intimate that you are coming—I should like to have a pinch of Mr. V_s ears. how well we might have managed for you might have personally recieved your little Daughter, but <I think> as it is, I will defer christening her till we go to town, tho' against my Inclination for I think the Covenant should be entered into as soon as possible, and is much too sacred to be trusted to accident—

Father says "at the end of your letter tell her your Father presents his recollections of Friendship; and affection to her children particularly to his darling Maria."—Maria I am sure must be very much improved in the polish of Education I mean for the material requisites I think she possessed more of than any young person I ever knew—Now indeed I pity with regard to John for he is at that age that requires so much attention and of a kind you cannot be altogether equal to, that I am sure he must give you constant anxiety—does Mr. C[ox] superintend it, or how do you manage.[5] I rejoice that you are within reach of your Father and Mother, for Brother told me he

---

[5]Julia Scott had been a widow since 1798. Elizabeth was inquiring if her brother-in-law, Mr. James Cox, was overseeing her son John's upbringing.

thought them both declining very fast, and they must want every attention that you and Charlotte can give them, besides that to you the time passed from them can never be recalled—Courage dear Julia "we are bound to see it out."—

Miss Moon remarks on Education, and a very pretty letter was handed me from Miss Shipton, in which she says she had sent you a Box and a packet a few weeks ago—pray is there any thing one could send her[.] have you who are not more of obligations than [unclear] found out any thing that could with propriety [unclear] to her's. for you know a gift should be easily procurred by the person who is to [unclear] to [page torn] me have literally been so—

My Seton is well—his creditors in Europe (or rat[her] Mait[land][6]) have allowed him two years to settle the con[unclear]; but in that time nothing is coming in, he seems fortunately to have made up his mind, and says but little about his affairs—what he feels is another thing

do tell me something about each of the girls, Where is Harriet and what kind of woman is she likely to make, is Kitty[7] as sweet a girl as when I saw her, and is Maria growing out of the only fault I knew her to possess —meaning gowns ribbons etc—tho' by the by it would be unnaturally if she has except her mind has made a progress incredible and jumped two or three dozen years, for I believe where *taste* is a natural quality of the disposition, nothing can eridicate it but sorrow and Indifference to the world. Dear Julia farewell—

Yours most affectionately. E.A.S.

1.92 To Rebecca Seton

Tuesday Morning [1800]

There are many persons very dear to my Heart, but the moment I saw this blessed Sun this Morning (with Kit in my arms) dear Rebecca

---

[6]The London partner of Seton, Maitland and Company

[7]Kitty was probably a niece of Julia. Harriet Sitgreaves, also Julia's niece, was the daughter of Samuel Sitgreaves. She married William McCall April 18, 1807, in Easton, Pennsylvania.

1.92 ASJPH 1-3-3-8:30

came at once in my thoughts, and if there had been a wish to name it would have been to have you with me. the Morning was so mild I walked the Piazza a half hour with little Darling before even Father was up—precious companion when I am alone with her I always think here is at least one Peaceful spotless Soul, who never offends—how earnest is my prayer that it may continue so as far as Human nature will allow—We will help it—dear God-ma[1] who must always in affection have the first place—

Willy left my Note; to be sure he thought it of no consequence and little thinks how precious our little scraps are—I got your dear *Packet* this afternoon and gave them their second reading on a beautiful Rock we found out behind the cornfield, Kate slept on my lap and the Darlings played Tea in godma's little shells which were distributed in order and Bill cannot tell it often enough that he is saucy Bill and looks so funny and Beautiful you would kiss him to pieces.—Ricksy says "tell her come back," and Anna is learning her *Whatsevers* very fast to say them to godma—Kate is asleep indeed all are asleep and I must write Miss Hay[2] this Evening—Willy is to come to—morrow—if Rebecca too—but that must not be talked of—

I send old Mammy [Huler] to see about House cleaning as quick as possible—

Your Sis—*E.A.S.*
Wednesday Afternoon

1.93 To Rebecca Seton

Staten Island 11th August 1800

Your dear heart has beat with joy at the arrival of *our Liberties*,[1] and you may be sure we have had a scene of pleasure such as does not

---

[1]Elizabeth often referred to Rebecca as "God ma" (Godmother) in relation to the children.

[2]The director of the boarding school which Elizabeth's young sisters-in-law attended

1.93 ASJPH 1-3-3-8:33

[1]The *Northern Liberties* was one of the long-awaited Seton, Maitland and Company ships.

often come, and one that you would have enjoyed as much as I did, except the pouring 50 bowls of tea a day three days running—has hurt the sinews of my arm a little

—Mary went to see Aunty[2] yesterday and she has promised to pass a day with me this week. My Father says he will fetch her to-morrow. Where the treasure is there will the heart be also.[3] the *you* came from the heart, tho I really shall be delighted to see Aunty and shew her *my little Rebecca.*[4] Your not coming a Sunday was a great disappointment, but as Eliza has once been able to decide on such a jaunt I hope it will be *next* Sunday—I long to see her and the dear chicks, but fear it will be a very fatiguing jaunt for her.[5]

Dear *Rebecca* how I long to put little Kate in your arms; but so far from expressing any unavailing regrets you know I have told you ever since your return home that you ought to be as much with our little lonely Sister[6] as possible this Summer. was I in her situation I should think it very unkind if you were not. You well know how much I value your Society and affection but we are not always to have what we like best in this world, thank Heaven! for if we had how soon we should forget the *other*,—the place of endless Peace, where they who were united by Virtue and affection here, will surely enjoy that union so often interrupted while on their journey Home. —the precious Darlings are well. *we all* (Cate in a paper Bonnet) made in Eliza's way, were on the shore an hour yesterday Evening while the General and Mary were on the water.

She calls to come and dress darling *Your own Sis*

Thursday Morning—9 Oclock

---

[2]Possibly Mary Magdalen Charlton (Mrs. Walter) Dongan, the sister of Elizabeth's and Mary's deceased mother, Catherine Charlton Bayley. It is less likely to refer to Elizabeth Seton Farquhar, Elizabeth's aunt by marriage.

[3]Cf. Matt. 6:21.

[4]Catherine, Elizabeth's infant daughter, who reminded her of Rebecca Seton

[5]Elizabeth was hoping for a visit from Eliza Seton Maitland, her sister-in-law, and the Maitland children. Eliza had not been well.

[6]Eliza Seton Maitland

—I send letters for the dear little girls and a little Box with diced sweet-meats.—there are no pineapples for dear Eliza—best love to her

1.94 To Eliza Sadler

[n.d.]

How do you do? it seems as if an Ocean divides us—but you will be happy when I tell you *Peace* is restored—the darlings are well, and *I* am happy in most things.

—Seton expects to bring you with him if the means of returning can be ascertained

My Father is very well—and *so* busy—they are waiting on the warfs—for my Comm[unication]

Your own friend *E.A.S.*
Sunday Morning—

1.95 To Rebecca Seton

Staten Island 14th August 1800

My own Rebecca

I have recieved your dear little note of Tuesday Eve[nin]g at which time you had not heard from poor Maria—happy Maria I hope and believe, for surely so much suffering as she has known must have brought her mind to its Home—Her task is done and she has Peace; while we my dear Sister have still to strive, and take our portion as it is allotted—The little Darlings are all sleeping—it is an agonizing thought to *Nature* how soon *they* may be deprived of a Parent,[1] but to

1.94 ASJPH 1-3-3-7:23
1.95 AMSV Seton-Jevons #27-30 (photocopy) no original exists
[1]William Magee Seton's health was deteriorating due to tuberculosis.

the *Soul* that trusts in its Saviour it is easy to resign for he is most particularly a Father and Protector to the Orphan and his Protection is of more value than what the Whole world united can give—

—your poor Breast I know is suffering what with sorrow and anxiety it has enough to try it, and I shall be very anxious to hear from you. Surely before this your *fatigues* must be relieved or Eliza[2] and yourself must be both knocked up—Mary[3] wishes very much to be with you and it is right she should be, you must my dear Rebecca exert *yourself* and not indulge her sensibility, for it is necessary to her future comfort in Life that her mind should be strengthned, and try to teach her to look at the events of life as they are, guided by a just and merciful Protector who orders every occurrence in its time and place, and often by his trials, and disappointments, strives to turn the Soul to him who is the resource and comforter of the Afflicted—You have more influence with her than *all*, and may from the sensible turn of her mind and affectionate disposition *turn* her thoughts almost any way you wish.

—You say you think differently from Mary on the degree of happiness we can bear—dear Rebecca long may your opinion be the same—I expressed *my Opinion* from sad and cruel experience which tho' it degrades Human Nature that it is so, yet you will find it certified by almost every Author who writes on the subject and from your own observation will find that it is the happiest Beings who are most apt to become careless of Religion and forgetful of their God. Good night my darling Sister

your *E.A.S.*

---

[2] Eliza Seton Maitland, Elizabeth's sister-in-law
[3] Mary Seton, Elizabeth's sister-in-law

1.96 To Eliza Sadler

27th September 1800

Your little Note of Sunday my dear Eliza was a comfort—how have you passed the Storm? it made me think of *Home* for I have little cold hands to rub, and want some necessaries for the Darlings which only Home can afford—however, sweet it is—under all circumstances—and more than the present it promises future good, for my Father cannot do more than he does to prove his regret for the Past[1]—I tell you this because I know I can never repeat too often to you that I am happy in that particular which is *almost* the most interesting of my existance. —Seton has been the last ten days here, and the Darlings are well—Father is more than busy, and has many vexations, but he says he "can never rest in this World and it may as well be one thing as another" [the mela]ncholy truth, and all that can be done is to soothe—cruel would the person be who ever wished to deprive me of that power—but we must hope there is no such Being—Peace be with you

E.A.S.
The pears were truely enjoyed—I return the Basket—

1.97 To John Wilkes

9th October 1800

My Dear friend Mr. Wilks—

The Health Officer[1] sends you his respects with a particular request that if your Servant by name Julius Ceasar is yet disengaged you will

---

1.96 ASJPH 1-3-3-7:21

[1]Dr. Richard Bayley was minimally involved with his daughters Mary and Elizabeth after the death of his first wife and through the early years of his second marriage.

1.97 ASJPH 1-3-3-7:74

[1]Dr. Richard Bayley, Elizabeth's father

do him the favour to secure him for his Service as he is informed you have no essential fault to find with him—this without fail and on any terms—

My dear Mary[2] I hear is well, which rejoices me—many loves to her from our Health Establishment but particularly from him and

your friend *E.A.S.*

Staten Island Thank Mary for the ham—

1.98 To Rebecca Seton

10 Oclock Thursday [1800]

My Darling Girl

this is a cloudy morning to your Sis, Dear Willy is quite sick, but *will* be out and I am very uneasy about him as a pain in the side is no trifle but must *look up*—Rebecca your darlings are well Kit too good and sweet. Bless you the round tables love to you—

1.99 To Julia Scott

New York 19th November 1800

My Dearest Julia

little knows the real true affection of the heart of her friend, or she could never have allowed the idea that my afflictions or troubles or any event of my life should have the power to lessen my intire attachment to her—but habits as you well know are forcable things—and I have allowed myself to lose the enjoyment I once had in writing, and

---

[2]Mary Wilkes, whom Elizabeth had nursed through illness in January 1800
1.98 ASJPH 1-3-3-8:45
1.99 ASJPH 1-3-3-6:35

in truth so much attention was required by my Father during the Summer and so earnest was I in fulfilling every attention to him (more so than ever from some particular circumstances which happened in the Spring and which will better be told when we meet than now) that with the darling little Cate and other Etcetceras, I left things undone which should have been attended to as sacred—however twice I wrote by Covacheche[1] one letter I have now in my secretary and if I had any other opportunity but the Post would inclose it, the other got lost between him and my Seton with whom he had some difference which ended in a law suit and my poor letter paid the Piper and Covacheche has gone most probably never to return—

This day dear friend the 19th November little angel Cate was carried to church and christened Catharine, after my Mother—Her Sponsers (you will laugh when I tell you she had five) were Sister Post; Mrs. Duplex who sent her an elegant christening suit from Ireland with a particular request that she might stand for her, that is by Proxy; myself for *you* (surely you will allow a good representative) and my Father and Mr. Curson God Fathers;[2] the sweet creature mistook Mr. Beach[3] for my Father as he had spectacles on and when he threw the cold water in her face, looked up at him and laughed so drolly that I could hardly keep from laughing and crying both. Oh how you will love her Peace and Sweetness always before you when you see her—The whole family doat on her and you might suppose her the *first* child rather than the fourth—so kindly does Nature provide, for time was when Richard ruled the day, and a darling he still is, and from His winning affectionate temper is likely to be so—Will is as bold and Independent as John Scott was in *Broadway*,[4] and with delight I tell you as Obedient and amiable in his disposition; but I am sorry to say Anna will disappoint you for she is not sufficiently restrained to be

---

[1] A family friend who was godfather to Elizabeth's two sons, William and Richard

[2] Catherine Seton's godparents were Mary Bayley Post, Elizabeth's sister; Catherine Dupleix; Julia Scott; Dr. Richard Bayley; and Richard Curson, Jr., maternal uncle of William Magee Seton.

[3] Rev. Abraham Beach (1740-1828) was assistant minister at Trinity Church.

[4] Elizabeth was comparing her son William with John Scott, Julia's son, when John was a young child and the Scotts lived on Broadway in New York City.

called an *improved* child, tho' she has points of disposition inestimable—

Julia Julia when you come how will it be with us, for the *House*[5] is to be declared Bankrupt within that time or Seton must go to Prison—that is a nerve that shrinks from the touch—and "Faith and Hope" is my only refuge—this twelvemonth past I have been harassed with the anticipation—but how much reason I have had in that time to Bless my Maker for his [unclear] my Childrens who have none of them been ill an [hour] and my own Strength of mind which increases with the storm

—I have expected you here these three months past as [Colonel] Giles said you must come to meet the Chancellor,[6] which is another reason for my not having wrote as it is difficult to write to so near a friend without expressing the uppermost thought and yet you will easily feel for me that it is not a subject to write about—your cold is I hope gone and you regaining health and strength—your friend cannot now hold the head and sooth the mind—dear Maria I hope does it for me—*Bless her*

Rebecca and Cecelia are my companions this Winter—Harriet is at Brunswick[,] Mary and Charlott stay with James Seton—the Boys at school—when you write to *Brother* say every thing for me that affection can say to a dear and valued friend—sorry I am for his Harriet[.] love to dear Charlott how are her *affairs thriving* I hope—be assured Julia that I love you in my heart, from my Heart, and with my Whole Heart—

E.A.S.

---

[5]The firm of Seton, Maitland and Company
[6]Robert R. Livingston (1747-1813) was chancellor of the state of New York from 1777 to 1801.

1.100 To Julia Scott.

Judge Lawrence is to go to Philadelphia tomorrow, and notwithstanding my progress in the lesson of Indifference which way the wind blows, thought will be pressing on and picturing my Julia in her sick bed, are you well[,] are you happy as the nature of your situation admits?— [Colonel] Giles really frightens us, he asks Seton continually "has Mrs. S_ hear[d] from her friend" and twice he has called here so woe begon complaining that you do not write to any of your friends. that is not fair for if ever there was a faithful friend he is one.—how I should like to take a peep at you and your little circle, if Peace is in the midst you must be happy, but every situation has its trouble and well I feel for yours as it respects your children, for as your mind is relieved on account of Maria your cares for John must increase and cause you many anxious hours.

it sometimes lessens personal sorrow to compare our condition with the case of others—therefore when you sit musing and thoughtful about your crosses and accidents turn you[r] mind to your friend and view the changes of the last few years in my lot, and when you have traced it to the present period, figure to yourself Mr. Garret Kittlet[2] as the winder up of the Bankrupts, sitting in our Library taking inventory of our furniture goods etc. this is the anticipation for the following week—but Seton is writing quietly by my side, in as perfect Health as he has ever enjoyed, my Chicks quiet in Bed, and Father smiling over a list of Books he has just made of those he chuses to retain as one of our creditors—

1.100 ASJPH 1-3-3-6:36

[1]The Setons had to move from the house on Stone Street because of William's failing business affairs.

[2]William Magee Seton reluctantly chose to declare bankruptcy rather than go to prison. Mr. Garret Kittlet was the receiver of bankruptcy. All of the Seton possessions, even to the children's clothing, was listed, and the lists placed in the hands of the bankruptcy commissioners. William handed over the key to the business, thus marking the end of Seton, Maitland and Company.

for myself I think the greatest happiness of this Life is to be released from the cares and formalities of what is called the World—my World is *my Family*, and all the change to me will be that I can devote myself unmolested to my Treasure—Seton can never be more a slave than he has been, and for the present season while the cloud hangs heaviest I trust where my trust has never yet failed. this is a little Picture my Julia not to interest your mind too much, but only to afford you a Comparison—let me know the amount of your Market Bills, I engage I shall supply my large family for less than you can your small one[.] the excellence of the provision is another thing, all depends with me on the temper with which I enjoy it.

Peace Peace Father Echos Peace to you—Seton asks if you ever dream of Shadows—never never was there such a sweet Being as our little *Shadow,*[3] on the whole dear Julia I have much more reason to hope, even in the things of this life than to be cast down, in those of the one to come, I have as bright a hope and a faith as strong as ever animated a mortal—Heavens blessing be on you—

Your own friend *E.A.S.*

Mrs. [Eliza] Sadler has been at the point of Death with a paralytic complaint but is now recovering tho' very slowly. I see her as often as "the times" will allow—Emma's long anticipated happiness is fast approaching she has even the promise in appearance of a *Pair.*[4]

1.101 To Julia Scott

New York 26th December 1800

The Philadelphia Paper announced to us this morning that my Julia is in sorrow,[1] which added to the severe indisposition you have before

---

[3]Catherine Seton, Elizabeth's infant daughter
[4]Charlotte Bayley Craig, Elizabeth's half-sister, was soon to deliver, and twins were a possibility.
1.101 ASJPH 1-3-3-6:37
[1]Julia's father, William Sitgreaves, had died.

suffered, will I fear prove too much for the poor little frame—weakened and debilitated as you described it to me—dear dear Julia what would I give to be with you at this time to hold your head and wipe your tears, I might say to mingle mine for indeed independant of the sympathy of Affection, I have cause to sigh and weep from Monday to Saturday and yet viewing this World but as the passage to my Home it all goes by; I have this last week watched and attended the street door to keep out the Sheriffs Officers with as cheerful a Countenance as ever you saw me with, and have given up my list to the Commissioners of Bankruptcy of all we possess, even to our and the childrens cloathing—if you did not know me, you would say my friend is boasting—no dearest that is not the meaning, only try and use *your* powers of exertion also, and do not let unavailing reflections overpower the Strength and fortitude I know you possess—but Nature will have her struggle, and I pray to Heaven to restore you *Peace* write to me as soon as you can, tell me what arrangement your Mother makes, whether she will live with you, and how she supports the trial she has undergone.

Keep up your spirits my friend if possible, do not be uneasy about my Seton, I have him safe and all to myself—they have taken away the key of his Compting House and the Commissioners protect him for the present. your little Angel Daughter[2] is his greatest amusement and is really the Comfort of us all—the darlings are all well remember me to yours, and be assured of the affection of

Your E.A.Seton.

if you are not well enough to write do let my Maria write if only two lines to say if your apprehensions are over with respect to your Lungs being affected, which gives me great uneasiness.

---

[2]Catherine Seton, Elizabeth's infant daughter and Julia's godchild

1.102 To Rebecca Seton

[n.d.]

I spared you the sorrow of knowing Ethelinda was worse yesterday
as to-day she is much better. Mr. Hobart[1] this morning—language
cannot express the comfort the Peace the Hope—but Willy did not understand, that happy hour is yet to come—Kit is in his arms. the rest
round a plate of nuts. love love plenty for you—Kiss Lidy for me tell
her I long for the *Norwester[.]*

Peace to you

1801

1.103 To Julia Scott

New York 16th January 1801

My Julia's letter tho' expressive only of sorrow was still a Comfort
to me, and would have been immediately answered but a sore throat
has interrupted my usual occupations and put all in the wrong.—how
often I have wished to lay my aching head by yours, but these
softning, soothing Ideas increase the inquietudes they are meant to solace, and I always try to shake them off—one reason dear Julia why

1.102 ASJPH 1-3-3-8:44

[1]Rev. John Henry Hobart (1775-1830) was a curate at Trinity Episcopal Church on Broadway in
New York. He was Elizabeth Seton's spiritual director until 1805. In 1803 Elizabeth Seton became
the godmother of his daughter Rebecca, who, after her marriage to Levi Silliman Ives, later became
a Roman Catholic. Henry Hobart was a trusted friend who had agreed to keep some furniture of the
Setons when they left for Italy. He was bitterly opposed to Elizabeth's conversion to Roman
Catholicism. He was named assistant bishop in 1811 and diocesan bishop and rector in 1816.
Elizabeth often referred to him as H, HH, JHH, Hobe and Hobes.

1.103 ASJPH 1-3-3-6:38

instead of your recieving three letters a week full of tenderness and Affection you have had not many more in the year—

[Colonel] Giles still says he thinks the first Tuesday in April will bring you to us, do-tell me when you write again it is it still your plan, for I should delight to have at least the anticipation my friend of seeing you and above all of putting little Kate in your arms, whose shape make and expressions are so exactly suited to them that if you were here I would agree to be only her wet nurse. the dear pet was innoculated yesterday which creates some anxiety for us *all*, as she is the Darling of *All*, but our family has been so favoured in every instance of innoculation that with the many precautions I take, and the blessing of Heaven I trust it will go well—if not—she will be much the gainer—go *right* it certainly will either way—

I shall ask you the first question when we meet, where are your children, and charge you dear Julia not to leave them behind you, for where ever we are or however situated I can answer that we can always give you a room if it is only Rebeccas who can have a bed in the Nursery—at all events whether you stay with Mrs. Giles or me there will always be a bed for whichever of your children you can spare which I wish you to understand more particularly as I think if I remember right you did not wish them to be with Mrs. Giles when you were here before—

I think the arrangement of your mother's[1] being with you will be much more comfortable for you than having her at a distance and still anxious to perform those duties and attentions which her situation must require, but every Event to you will bring its cares until you either leave Philadelphia which now you cannot do while she lives, or until your Family again has a Head, an experiment I should not dare to wish for, as the consequences however well arranged and planned might be so different from our calculations

Dear Dear Julia, not to moralize or repine, but in the common language of every day and hour what is Life except we consider it a passage and are therefore ind[ifferent] to the accommodations or casualties, that happen in the dear, the strong and anxious hope of

---

[1]Susanna Deshon Sitgreaves, newly widowed

soon reaching our happy heavenly Home, where Peace and all we prize most awaits our arrival—You say you are a Mother—I am a Mother too and am far from being so selfish as to wish to leave my Charge while my cares are required but as the time of being called is so little know[n], and the prospect is so sweet a solace and so strong an assistance to the discharge of all our Duties—to keep it before me is the prayer of my Heart, and let it be the prayer of yours—tell me if your cough and anxieties have left you . . and how every thing goes—blessings on your Maria and John and Peace be with you dear friend—

Your *E.A.S.*

Seton is well, his affairs go on as well as the case allows—Father says he wishes he was your Physician

1.104 Draft to Dr. Richard Bayley

1 or 2 [n.d.]

My dear dear Father—

You will know my not writing does not proceed from neglect or forgetfulness of you—no no—rather from too great a disposition to converse with you and indulge a regret which too frequently intrudes—and you might scold me for so childish a reason, but indeed I am obliged to banish the thoughts of you sometimes as we do that of heaven when an excessive desire delays us in our progress towards it—my health has been worse and worse this winter, but is a little mended since the fine weather—the thought that I may so soon depart has brought with it many imaginations about my five darlings[1]—but peace is the result of all my calculations since I can

---

1.104 ASJPH 1-3-3-9:86

[1]William Magee Seton, Elizabeth's husband, and her four children, Anna Maria, William, Richard, and Catherine

but leave them with the good shepherd who laid down his life for them,[2] and human calculations are so uncertain that it is in vain to dwell on them.[3]

1.105 To Rebecca Seton

[February 1801]

My own Rebecca—

at Mary's bedside[1] I repeat the Melancholy sigh—she has passed a wretched night—it was with great difficulty they could keep her in her Bed—but heaven directs—the Angel Cecilia is at the round table having the lessons—and is to give a premium to the best behaved child—Kate is very much oppressed but the *all in order* continues and the lesser evils sink in the sorrow that surrounds men—Joy, Joy, Joy to my Eliza I would give a great deal to press the little angel in my arms—Soon I hope—Hope—there is but *one hope* that never decieves—

your *E.A.S.*

1.106 To Rebecca Seton

[February 27, 1801]

again by Mary's Bedside, but there is no agony now[1]—the scene is closed forever and if the Peace that overspreads her countenance is a token for the soul—happy happy Mary. the groans and Anguish of her

---

[2]Cf. John 10:11.

[3]Rev. Simon Gabriel Bruté noted on the address page: "To her father 1801 (early in the year)."

1.105 ASJPH 1-3-3-8:6

[1]Elizabeth had been nursing Mary Wilkes, a cousin of William Magee Seton, who was seriously ill.

1.106 ASJPH 1-3-3-8:7

[1]Mary Wilkes, whom Elizabeth had been nursing, had died.

poor [John] Wilks is easily concieved he has shed tears over me which I hope will relieve him. Her heart was true to him in its last agony—and perfectly sensible—

Oh Rebecca if I dared to wish[,] how gladly would I drink the cup[2]—but my God knows best. I did not undress last night[.] poor Kate was all night in a burning fever—her teeth I believe The other darlings are well—Kiss Eliza and her little ones for me. Your own Sis loves you too much.

1.107 To Dr. Richard Bayley

New York 1st March 1801

Have you any recollection of the mild quiet evening hour at Staten Island when standing in the door you have observed to your Betty "all Nature is hushed"—*so* is my heart after throbing and aching till nature is exhausted, it sinks to rest almost as profound as that which prevails in the Bosom of our once animated interesting friend,[1] whose last sigh I recieved on Friday Morning, and this Evening the Earth has recieved her remains. "on thy peaceful Bosom laid, pain shall cease nor care invade"—

Mr. [John] Wilks has given me a message to you, expressive of his sense of obligation to you for having so long defered your departure from New York, with many etceteras too affecting to dwell on as they are unavailing, but in the agony of his heart necessary to convey to you the idea that he believed nothing could ha[ve] saved his Mary tho' doubtless her sufferings would have been lessened by your presence—he talked of writing to you, which I ventured to say was unnecessary—

We anticipate your return, some time in the next week—it is useless to say how much I wish it. When the next eight weeks are over a

---

[2]Cf. Matt. 26:39.

1.107 ASJPH 1-3-3-9:87

[1]Mary Wilkes, a relative who recently had died

new scene will open—the blossoms and zephyrs of Spring the gentle but animating colors of Nature heightened by the converse and smiles of "her I love"—that is one side of the scene, the other I dare not look at.[2] —Our little circle has lost its key—Rebecca is away on her usual errand of sharing griefs, She has gone to attend her sister in her confinement[3]—Sweet Cate is suffering, but I hope it will soon be over as it is occasioned by cutting teeth.

—a strong Southerly wind has prevailed these two days, and a great number of arrivals particularly this afternoon amongst which the Packet which left England the twenty sixth January. As the French were within sixty miles of Vienna the Emperor has been obliged to sue for Peace which was on the point of being concluded. alas the poor Arch Duke [Char]les—this is all the news that has yet transpired. the letters cannot be given out before tomorrow—perhaps—but at all events I will write to you by the next Post. Quarantine has begun[.] a Brig from Malaga[4] is at Staten Island. the Health officers Mate[5] is very Active. Mr. Setons respects attend you and the Affection of your Daughter

E.A.Seton

1.108 To Julia Scott

New York 10th March 1801

How I should like to find a quiet corner where I might enjoy an hour of Silence and recollection of the many many things I might say that would interest my friend and perhaps gratify her heart—but so it

---

[2] The continuation of the Seton's financial difficulties

[3] Eliza Seton Maitland, whom Rebecca had gone to assist during the birth of her child

[4] A province in southern Spain

[5] Possibly Joseph Bayley, Dr. Bayley's dedicated assistant who later received a medical degree from Columbia University. Dr. Richard Bayley's brother William had a son named Joseph. It is possible that he was the "young Bayley" working with Dr. Richard Bayley at Staten Island.

1.108 ASJPH 1-3-3-6:39

is that some prattler or interruption is sure to occur when ever I begin to write, and I have frequently put by a letter, which has not been resumed for a fortnight, and then sent off in haste, not so much from the actual want of time as the want of habit in writing, or doing any thing that is not *absolutely necessary* for I have so many indispensable employments that except you could witness the habits of my present life you would scarcely believe any discription of them—the general tenor is to rise early, which must sometimes depend on the degree of sleep I get with my Nurseling[1] who is however generally uncommonly good; but ten oclock all is arranged and the *round table* covered with the different Books used by my Darlings; Cecilia begins Grammer, reading, writing, Spelling of large and small words, marking, sewing, and figures[.][2] You doubtless smile at the idea of my being her Directress, but certainly she makes very great progress and learns thoroughly whatever she applies herself to—her disposition cannot be excelled for mildness and assiduity *rare qualities united*, and Miss Shipton with an attention she herself cannot concieve the value of, has furnished me with books of every kind that are useful in the Education of Children. Anna Maria follows Cecilia as nearly as her inferior age allows and discovers a capacity and amiability of mind that give me a peaceful satisfaction, for a Mother always "rejoices with trembling." William and Richard say their lessons: little Pieces, names of the United States, Divisions of the Globe, *some* of the Commandments etc—all this employs the Morning compleatly, and the Afternoon and Evening is as regularly filled up by my Father and Seton. the Piano and Cribbage party pass them over very chearfully when there are no particular interruptions.

—Seton is now poking the fire scoalding me for writing nonsense to Julia, puzzeling himself about his dream last night, wondering what he should do if he was a single man, and says he believes his best plan is a voyage to the East India—

---

[1] Catherine Seton, Elizabeth's infant daughter

[2] Cecilia Seton, Elizabeth's sister-in-law, was then about ten years old and was teaching Elizabeth's children.

The last ten days of February I att[end]ed Mrs. [Mary] Wilkes every hour except 3 times a day half an hour to nurse *little Kate* who from a cold fallen on her Breast since the small Pox[,] never rested at night—but the old *Knot of Oak* as Seton calls me has not suffered any inconvenience but trouble of mind, of which there was a full share, for my poor friend died a hard and dreadful death. the circumstances and scene of which can never be effaced from my imagination—it has but one effect, that of making me yet more anxious and careful in making ready to meet *that hour*. that hour which without the comfort and support of the Father who gives the call is—My Soul shudders at the thought—*think of it Julia*

Rebecca has done my part at Home while I was away—she is too amiable—too good—to be described—you would not believe if I tryed to tell you what she is—

and here is the end of my paper without a word but Egotism if [Colonel] Giles does not call for my letter to-morrow I will take the other side—if he does you must answer me by following my example and telling me every thing about yourself Your dear little self's own friend *E.A.S.*

We move in May to the Battery[3] next door to Carey Ludlows house which is now a lodging house so that if you persist in your *determination*, we may at *least* be next door no small consolation to those who meet so seldom—Giles *laughs* at the idea of your plans *and well he may*

---

[3]The Setons were planning to move to 8 State Street on the Battery. Their new neighbor, John Corré, had recently obtained permission to make a gate in the Battery Fence just opposite nearby Columbia Garden, and here he offered concerts as well as ice cream to the public on their evening walks along the Battery. The building the Setons occupied and an adjoining one are now preserved as Our Lady of the Rosary Church and Shrine of St. Elizabeth Seton.

1.109 To Rebecca Seton

Wednesday 4 Oclock 11th March

I received my Rebecca's little dear note at 2 Oclock to day after a fatiguing morning, and felt the full meaning of its contents. I pray that you *do* nurse *yourself* for the most amiable dispositions of the Human heart may destroy their possessor if carryed too far. I *cannot* send you cloaths but in very small parcels for so many thoughts go with them that—

yesterday Morning I left *Fin*[1] from 10 till 3 she slept the last 3 hours sound. and to day from *11* till *2* without a wimper. *Angel* how my heart loves her—

She still knows the sound of Godma and I take care she shall not forget it. tell Eliza I am impatient to hold her little darling in my arms and to tell her how much I share her anxieties.

The girls are so happy and well—the Boys so saucy—and Willy so idle that on the whole my hours go more to my mind than you would suppose—tell me about Eliza's *nursing* particularly—Dad is not worse Post says.

"Peace be unto you"[2]

Fin's cold on the Breast still keeps her upstairs she has not been down since you left her, but once and that increased it. therefore—guess the rest

---

1.109 ASJPH 1-3-3-8:46

[1] A nickname for Catherine Seton, Elizabeth's infant daughter
[2] John 20:19

1.110 To Dr. Richard Bayley

Thursday Night 10 Oclock 13th March [1801]

My friend[1] has this moment left me after passing the day pleasantly together preceeded by a ride in the Morning which has doubtless benefited both finding on our way pure air and possessing the disposition to enjoy all the Good to be met with.—her Health is certainly mended, and the mind either is or appears more composed. mutual confidence and free expression of thought might have produced the effect—Peace, rest, and every blessing go with her—

The letter that was to have been long, must be short, for Mr. and Mrs. Olive and family occupied yesterday, and Doux this day—therefore I have done no duty for Seton and there are three letters yet to be ready for to-morrows Post. one letter from my Father in Eleven days is rather hard, but I have hopes of the next Post producing what to me is of inconcieveable value. Seton is puzzling me with a long story for my Father of great numbers of Vessels from the West Indias the captain of the Kingston Brig sent to your Hospital—The Olives asked with great interest if the report of the Quakers having combined against the Health Officer was true, and a variety of reports which was explained to them as far as my Information extended[2]—Olive speaking of the present appearance of things in general observed with the finger on the side of the Nose "*Rien n'est en Equilébre ni dans les Physeques ou dans les Morales, les têtes des Hommes les tournent?*"[3]—I hope your heart is quiet, and that your stay from us will be short as possible—I ventured to read your letter to little Darby which delighted her she begged me to recollect her best wishes to you—

Your own Bet—

1.110 ASJPH 1-3-3-9:88

[1] Catherine Dupleix

[2] Dr. Richard Bayley was the health officer. His progressive public health care techniques sometimes met with opposition.

[3] "Nothing is stable, neither in the physical realm nor in morals, the heads of men are turning around?"

1.111 To Dr. Richard Bayley

2 Oclock Tuesday 24th March [1801]

The Baltimore and Philadelphia Gazettes will remind my Father of the fire place in Stone Street—the Post is arrived twice since my anticipations, but they are vain.—The "free air" of your Establishment is I am sure benificial[1]—Peace to you dear Dear Sir. The little Circle[2] salute you—and your Betty's affection attends you.

E.A.Seton

1.112 To Dr. Richard Bayley

10 Oclock 2nd April 1801

Little Kate is Launched,[1] and will soon bring the wished for visitor.—little Kate—Seton says with many calculations that "the winds are so favorable and vessels from Europe make such short runs." we shall certainly see her in earnest—happy prediction two weeks more, and something must be decided—In the hope of soon seeing my Father and with remembrances and good wishes

Your Betty—

1.111 ASJPH 1-3-3-9:70
  [1]The quarantine station on Staten Island
  [2]Elizabeth's family
1.112 ASJPH 1-3-3-9:89
  [1]This possibly refers to a ship they were expecting or to the return of one of Elizabeth's friends.

1.113 To Rebecca Seton

Friday [n.d.]

My much loved Sisters two notes are received and give comfort to the heart that seemed to have left a portion of itself with you—why are you to be in town again to-day; I hope not for *we* feel the heat and you would find it too much going out and in the same day—take care of yourself my darling girl for if you go I shall be *too impatient* when my watch has 35 minutes past ten

this morning I took my Prayer-book to try and bear a part—happy happy hours when we joined in the sweet employment. thankful for even the remembrance of them the greatest pleasure I can anticipate in this world is that they will again be enjoyed in the same society

—the rules here are so strict that I cannot send to Vanduzers[1] without special permission and none but the boatman—therefore if you do not hear from me as often as you expect—set it down to the right account—Every thing goes on so peaceably and with so much regularity, and particularly with respect to the *little* ones that if I could find a *Home* this side the blue-Vault, I should only wish for you and my Willy and set down without a sigh. but *"thanks be"* there is no home here—

Kit is ta ta ta-ing and the boys stuffing an orange—Anna runs to me with a butter cup for Godmother, she calls it *Kit*, and you will find a kiss from us all on it with ten thousand blessings—

mind you tell the day, the moment you see if fairly—

Your own most truely—*EA.S.*

Friday Afternoon 3 Oclock—send *Waits* for the Piano is too bad.

1.113 ASJPH 1-3-3-8:51

[1]The Vanduzer (or Vanduzen) family had a farm, sold provisions, and ran a ferry on which they probably carried mail. Elizabeth was on Staten Island with the children at the time.

1.114 To Rebecca Seton

4 o'clock [n.d., 1801]

My Rebecca

Your two notes are in my Bosom—they relieve many anxieties tho' really my poor Lidy's trouble makes me melancholy, give her all the comfort you can, and tell her to cheer up for all our sakes. My Father was here part of the day yesterday and the rest of it was *Peace* and *Willy*. Shakespeare amused him all the Evening—Your Kit is yet bigger and saucier than when you left her, and *too too* sweet. she claps hands for "God-ma come home" all the day

Our Lady Cook does not say any thing further—we all wait your coming which I am sure will be as soon as possible—Cecilia is merry and well—Doxy "is No Yoker"—Maitland[1] waits[.] heaven bless you—"Peace be unto you" Kiss the darlings for me and press my little one close to your heart.

4 Oclock dont put such large wafers they tear your notes.

1.115 To Rebecca Seton

Sunday Afternoon 7th June 1801

How are you employed my own Rebecca, and how have *I* been employed—Sad to me is the difference—but there is no distance for Souls and mine has surely been with yours most faithfully—St. Pauls Steeple, Rebecca and H.H.[1] were thought of, but thought did not dwell

---

1.114 ASJPH 1-3-3-8:9

[1]James Maitland, Elizabeth's brother-in-law

1.115 ASCSH Seton-Jevons #35-36

[1]From Staten Island where she was staying, Elizabeth could see lower Manhattan. The steeple of St. Paul's Episcopal Chapel on Broadway between Fulton and Vesey Streets where she and Rebecca often worshiped was visible. This led her to think of Rev. Henry Hobart. St. Paul's, a daughter church of Trinity, completed in 1766, is the oldest functioning church building in New York City.

with *them*. the sweet day of sacred rest is not for me, Emma and Miss Shipton² who arrived last night in the 2 Brothers, did not give me a moment until 12—dear dear Rebecca how I long to see you—Father took you a little note yesterday and a letter for Willy, and Emma will take for you both to-day—the Darlings are well they often talk of you and Kate always gives a long call when I speak your name—the little robin's note who is a prisoner close by me fills my Eyes and Heart—dear Sister I am a prisoner too—with all this wide and beautiful creation before me the restless Soul longs to enjoy its liberty and rest beyond its bound[.] when the Father calls his child how readily he will be obeyed—

I just recollect I must say a word to Mrs. [Eliza] Sad[ler]—where are the congenial thoughts—they only fly to my own own dear Rebecca—

1.116 To Rebecca Seton

Thursday Morning [1801]

My own Rebecca

I long to hear how you passed your day yesterday. Mine went pleasantly enough—came down in the nick of time to give Breakfast before Father went to N[ew] York—a long account and the most interesting one I yet have heard of the yellow fever of Ninety-eight, when Mr.Truman¹ was one of the Seven meritorious commissioners. heard the Darlings lessons—Anne made a shift sleeve intirely and very neatly.

---

²Charlotte Bayley Craig, Elizabeth's half-sister, and Miss Shipton, a friend of hers and Julia Scott
1.116 ASJPH 1-3-3-8:26
¹Member of the Board of Health Commissioners, created in 1798. Dr. Bayley was health officer.

—at twelve recieved the *Book* and yours. J[ohn]W[ilke]s and my own Williams notes, which was quite a treat. Dr. Miller and Post dined here—elegant black fish chicken pye etc. in good order and not one knit of the brow.—a sweet afternoon with a Sun[.] Sat in Peace and elegant light, red clouds over my head at the back door—a quiet Evening the Alderman kept in conversation and I made almost the body of a shift for Kit wrote my *own William* and slept sound from Eleven 'till 1/2 past five. we have now Breakfast in haste and the provision is in the Schooner and her sails up to go to Sandy Hook for the day—So contradictory is our lot dear Rebecca how much would we have given for *three* such days as the past—but "mercy's in every plan" and I hope you have your share too of comfort. and at all events it will comfort you to know that the scene has changed with *me.*

Kit is at my feet with her lap full of play things and the Boys[2] and Anna all devoted to please her while Maté[3] writes to godmother—a thousand loves to dear Lidy and the Darlings—and always give my love to Mammy Dina.[4]

J[ohn]W[ilkes] writes that he "sipps sweets morning and Evening"—poor Soul—how I wish he would find them at the *true fountain.* I have recommended our testament and Doddridge[.][5] write me if you have got one as I told you if not Willy shall get you one—

Your own Sis *EAS*

---

[2]William and Richard Seton, Elizabeth's young sons

[3]A reference to herself as mother

[4]Eliza Seton Maitland and her children. Mammy Dina was probably a servant in the Maitland household.

[5]Philip Doddridge, author of *The Principles of Christian Religion and of Hymns Founded on Various Texts in the Holy Scriptures.*

1.117 To Rebecca Seton

[1801]

My own Rebecca would rejoice to see our chearful countenances at the Norwester—how I wish I could see yours—Kit is calling Mamma as loud as she can hollou and Ann Will and Dick on the Battery only inside the gate—Dick is quite well and Kit would be weaned but a tooth is just coming out—Eliza Sad[ler] is better and Dué¹ is to meet me to morrow morning—Dear Sunday make haste—O that Lidy was coming too—a thousand loves to her—poor Mrs. Myers—how I pity her—do you [plan] to stay on Tuesday—Covecheche has written from Brunswick that he is to be here in a fortnight and will bring the dear little girls²—Kit crys God Bless

EAS

1.118 To Julia Scott

Thursday Afternoon 11th June 1801

My darling Julia—

the Bird Cages were dressed, the flower pots replenished. the children all tip toe, and their mother smoothing all the care worn wrinkles from her forehead, anticipating a day of most perfect pleasure, when the dear Father returned with neither Julia nor her children¹—well—this is one more of the many, is all my reply,

---

1.117 ASHPH 1-3-3-8:4

¹Catherine Dupleix

²Joseph Covechichi, business associate of William Magee Seton, was going to bring William's younger half-sisters home from school in Brunswick, New Jersey.

1.118 ASJPH 1-3-3-6:40

¹Julia and her children, Maria and John Scott, were visiting New York but did not make it to Staten Island where Elizabeth was staying with Dr. Bayley for the summer.

seperated a hundred miles or *nine* I must imagine the distance the same for I have but one Nurse for my four children, and little Kate being still at the Breast I can neither leave her nor take the others—I cannot tell you half that my Seton says of your attentions and kindness to him and his fellow travellers—dear dear Julia is repeated again and again in every letter—

dear Julia I repeat with a sigh but have no other relief for except you could come to me which I find cannot be, I have not the smallest chance of seeing you, and your coming here would make you tremble independant of crossing the Bay, for there is one Vessel of Irish Emigrants just opposite the door who has a hundred sick passengers to land which they are doing as fast as possible and we are not suffered to go further than the Gate,[2] which to you who are so little accustomed to such scenes would be "'horror inexpressible"—but to me who possesses a frame of fibers strong and nerves well strung it is but a passing scene of Natures Sufferings which when closed will lead to happier scenes—

My Father says "two finer children my Eyes never beheld Maria is a perfect creature all mildness and Harmony"—I wish to see them Julia as much almost as I do you.

—remember me to Brother [Samuel], and believe me always and in all places

most Affectionately Yours *E.A.S.*

Remember me to Miss Chippy[3] when you see her—[4]

---

[2]For fear of contracting ship's fever
[3]Miss Shipton, a mutual friend
[4]The outside is addressed to Mrs. Scott in New York.

1.119 To Eliza Sadler

Thursday [June 1801]

My Eliza's Heart would rejoice to know how sweet how good and smoothly every thing goes with our little circle—The welcome was such as drove every care and sigh to the winds—"Holy Nature" and fine garden strawberrys with little questions and answers passed away the Evening and this day is really too happy

Dick now he knows "he must not cry" is an angel. Anna and the boys are above [on] their knees picking clover—and Kit *la ta* all over the House. Grandpa toodle doos and seems much better than when we saw him last. *God bless you Sad* in haste

your E.A.S.
10 Oclock Thursday Morning—

1.120 To Rebecca Seton

3 Oclock Thursday [1801]

My Rebecca must be sure that it was not from neglect that the little note did not go last night—*Kate* and I have suffered but it is going over—Doxy has been limping on one leg but is also better—So we go but how small are those evils *comparatively*

The girls and *two Wills* are as saucy as you please. I long for Saturday—Blessings to my dear Lidy—and Darling—and kiss the Boys for me—

Peace be unto you

1.119 ASJPH 1-3-3-7:10
1.120 ASJPH 1-3-3-8:10

1.121 To Rebecca Seton

Saturday Eve[nin]g 14th June 1801

You are to be in town *to-morrow*, that is certain you say—Heaven grant my dear Sister the Peace she seek[s]—but you are sure of it—it is in your own breast, and thankfully I acknowledge as my greatest blessing that I share it with you, altho' we are 9 miles distant—that it sh[oul]d be for me to say yes or no, to our meeting is hard indeed for poor Bayley[1] having a hundred Patients to provide and visit every day, while it lasts, can hardly be spared to fetch you, and when Father goes it is in such a tangent—but he says you must come and scolds every day that *you* are not here, and that I am such a humdrum—true the "heart is with the treasure . . ." <the treasure is with the heart>

how shall I get at you my Darling—your fixing a [time] is no good, except I c[oul]d be such of a messenger, not to give you a walk in town for nothing—I will write you to-morrow—Monday—or the moment I can find out—No letters from my Willy since those you have—the scenes of misery here are past all description—there are ten large tents and other buildings fitting up as fast as 1/2 doz[en] carpenters, Boatmen, and all hands, spured up continually by my poor Father can do them—We are to be re-inclosed by an outside fence, but the promise of a back gate to the Hills makes all the little ones dance—You will hardly know Kit She is so beautiful[,] too good—Dox never crys—*Anna* [unclear] quite rational and *Will* as submissive as he *can* be—the lessons and work go on regularly—and *I* read *our testament* at least two hours of the day— *too too* happy.

No scolding from the old Lady, few *loud* words from any one and always *peacable* Breakfasts. —so different from formerly. Give H[enry] H[obart] a *look* and a *sigh* for me, such as you will for yourself. but Mercy is every where—and my temple is a large one. remember to tell me the text—

1.121 AMSV Seton-Jevons #468-4721 (photocopy) No original exists
[1]Joseph Bayley, Dr. Bayley's assistant, or Dr. Bayley's servant

the first thing these poor people[2] did when they got their tents was to assemble on the grass and all kneeling adored Our maker for the Mercy and every morn[in]g sun finds them repeating their praises—Praise Him Oh my Soul—

E.A.S.
[On the address side:]

with a letter. A Kiss from all on the rose leaf—a bud from Ann[,] Kit and her Mother she says.

1.122 To Rebecca Seton

1/2 past ten Wednesday Morning 17th June 1801

dear dear Rebecca

my disappointment is beyond expression—You said yesterday you would stay in town last night to wait for the Schooner in case it should come—at five this morning Father was off and at six the windows and door in State Street[1] was open which made your being there certain—I saw the schooner leave New York and more persons in her than Father—more certain still, but as she approaches no Rebecca—no darling Godmother—so goes the outward pleasures, thanks be for those that cannot be disappointed and if you are in town I hope by this hour you are at Peace under the dear roof of His dwelling.[2] I am too much mortified at your losing perhaps the only chance *this* day, especially as your going in and out so often from Eliza will be unpleasant—I cannot bear to send

---

[2]The immigrants arriving at the health station

1.122 ASCSH Seton-Jevons #283-284

[1]No. 8 State Street, near the Battery, was the house the Setons rented when they were forced to move from Stone Street because of financial problems. Rebecca was staying at State Street for the summer.

[2]Church

this till I can learn some certain time for you to be in town which I hope will be at dinner after which the Health commissioner will take this—

Wednesday Afternoon

Think my Father says he did not even call for you—the reason will make you laugh tho' it is vexation to me —You shall know when the happy hour of "face to face" comes.—the Commissioner is to stay all night. I have had the pleasure of seeing three ferry boats go by to N[ew] Y[ork] as fast as the wind could carry them, but cannot get a line on board for no one dares go out side the Gate.³ If I had the Speaking trumpet I should be apt to make the Old Luke's ears ring. the blessing of Patience be with you

1.123 To Rebecca Seton

Thursday morning—6 Oclock [1801]

My own Rebecca

how much I wish you were here to enjoy this beautiful sunset at the corner of the Piazza. Father is visiting vessels, Willy and Charles¹ are gone to see poor Richard² safe to his lodging—Cate is asleep and the three chicks running below. You would have enjoyed the last half hour past as much as I have—imagine a young robbin in a cage, its mother on the top which she never left but to fetch it food, and the male chipping on a tree near it Nelly was its owner and I *coaxed* her to make them happy and open the cage-door, and the moment it was done out went the little one with both the old ones after it. pray bring a handsome ribbon for Nell *to remember it.*

---

³The residents in Dr. Bayley's house could not go beyond the gate to keep them from contact with those in quarantine because of ship's fever.

1.123 ASJPH 1-3-3-8:27

¹William Magee Seton, Elizabeth's husband, and probably Charles Seton, a cousin of his
²Richard Bayley, Elizabeth's half-brother

My Father scolds most terribly at your and Mary's[3] absence, indeed I dont know what account Charles will give of it, he has let the Eagles out, and he says on purpose to prepare it for you when he can catch you again—as I know I never can make him *understand* I generally am silent, or try to laugh it off—He calls Cate *Aunt Rebecca* and all the family have found out that she is *your image*—I pray that she may be both in the interior as well as exterior. indeed she is the sweetest little soul you can imagine and laughs continually while I am nursing her as if she knew who she ought to love best—Whenever I ask Ricksy "where is Godmother" "gone teck a wake will come bymby."—

I rejoice that all goes so well and hope my dear Mary may long continue to acknowledge "dear Miss Hay."[4] my best love to her—and also to Eliza. I am very glad Aunty[5] is in the country for Charles gave a sad account of her. Will says Sister James[6] and all are well—

Heaven bless *you*—the hour of nine has been changed to *ten* lately for Father has been very busy and we seldom have tea before eight—Peace be with *my dear Rebecca*

most affectionately *E.A.S.*—

Monday Evening

a most lovely morning Ann Will Dick and myself have had three turns to the gate and back—William's dear *Liberties*[7] he thinks is coming therefore he will stay to day. *joy joy*. for it relieves him from a heavy weight—He found Richard much better than he expected and delighted to see [him]

---

[3]Mary Seton, Elizabeth's sister-in-law

[4]Director of the school in Brunswick, New Jersey, attended by Mary Seton

[5]Possibly Charles Seton's mother, Margaret Seton

[6]Mary Hoffman Seton, wife of James Seton

[7]One of the ships of the Seton, Maitland and Company fleet

1.124 To Rebecca Seton

Monday afternoon 3 Oclock [1801]

Not even a little farewell look,—my Rebecca's thoughts and mine were the same, for it is a pang that *travellers* ought not to subject themselves to. I was delighted you had such a short passage, and long to know all that happened *after*. Write me soon as possible especially about *yourself*. Kit is as lovely and merry and saucy as a pet can be—the *500* ship is just come too—poor Father—I fear to lose the Boat therefore only say *Peace unto you*

1.125 To Rebecca Seton

[1801]

Kit hindered my seeing you off—Breakfast immediately a Ship in the offing.—Conjectures and Hopes, but not one crooked word—chit chat all the while—Bayley[1] returned with accounts of your arrival at 1/2 past 6 I am set to writing letters to McCormick, Craig, and John Wilks in behalf of our Irish Emigrant Shoe Maker[2]—the Darlings and old Woman making Boats on the back stoop all ordered to keep out of "that Nursery"—Now then the sigh of thankfulness is sent up that there is the beginning of Peace in *some* degree—

ten oclock—Father gone a gunning—Kit asleep, and the day of the month and St. Johns first Epistle makes me sadly recur to who read them with me yesterday[3]—but the hour will come when seperations will not embitter the sweet scene of Peace.

1.124 ASJPH 1-3-3-8:22
1.125 ASJPH 1-3-3-8:34

[1]Joseph Bayley, Dr. Bayley's assistant, or Dr. Bayley's servant

[2]Possibly Elizabeth was seeking help from friends for her work among the poor in which she was active at the time. Craig could refer to either William or Samuel Craig.

[3]Rebecca Seton herself

Dined with the two young Doctors[4] and my children—Slept with Kit by my side till 1/2 past 4 Father wakened me looking out from the Balcony for the ship which appeared, but no angel a signal is up and we are *now* on the lookout again—Just such a sun set as *we* looked at the day before—if it only forboades as Peaceful a day as the past—not one cloud. if you had been with me it would have been too much—played *merrily* in the Evening did not feel sleepy till past Eleven, and after two hours to *myself* slept a blessed sleep until Morning—Breakfasted at 6 all in time and nothing missing—quiet good humour—*dressed* the Birds, washed the Darlings—and now at a quarter past ten Kit is asleep—Mammy [Huler] and the Boys at the wash house and I am going to my *day of the month*—my Master[5] is in his row Boat—the thermometer in the Hall only 77—the other 78—Just about that of a *happy mind* I send you a piece of gold[6]

1.126 To Eliza Sadler

Monday Morning 18th June 1801

My Sad

Your welcome note and the bundle was recieved with particular delight and made a cheerful hour yet more cheerful.—Father is very much interested by *"alone"*
—and how you could think I would not like the Scotch song I dont know for it has been hummed all day long these six weeks and I am very glad to have the music. If you should ever meet with "Kate of Aberdeen" send it for my Father loved it formerly and it might now

---

[4]Probably one was Joseph Bayley
[5]Possibly William Magee Seton,
[6]Written on the outside: *"true love to Lidy"*
1.126 ASJPH 1-3-3-7:24

amuse—how glad I am the uncles[1] could serve you at all,—sweet could you realize your idea of the tent which struck me forcably when I read the poor Lady of the Haystacks who says that trouble and sorrow dwells in Houses and happiness only with fresh air and liberty—a reasonable truth from the poor Lunatic wiser than the Wisdom of the Wise, according to your and my beliefs of happiness—

Emma[2] is not well they say—which really grieves me—for I have been uneasy about her since the first moment. two more emigrant ships loaded arrived yesterday and today which put the period of seeing those I love in N[ew] York still more distant.

I need not tell you how much Anna is delighted with her frock or how well she looks in it exactly fitted to her shape—

tomorrow I expect the Olives and my heart begins to trouble even now at the very idea of the last adieu but it certainly is best so—[3]

Seton says he owes his pleasantest hours to you for the last week, and I hope he will be able to call for them often in the one to come—no Duplexses[4] I hope they have plenty of Provision—The darlings are all well and I am

yours most affectionately E.A.S.

—tell friend Henry [Sadler] there is an Irish girl here who sings "Pats Wedding" from morning till night—I never hear a word of it without thinking I see him. the children all told her it was Uncle Sadlers song.

---

[1]Possibly Seton relatives whom Eliza Sadler had met on her trip abroad
[2]Charlotte Bayley Craig, Elizabeth's half-sister and Eliza Sadler's sister-in-law
[3]The Olives were family friends who were sailing on July 1.
[4]Catherine and Captain George Dupleix

1.127 To Julia Scott

[date on the outside June 20th 1801]

My friend

I was sufficiently unhappy at not being allowed to see you before I recieved your letter, but after recieving it such were the melancholy impressions it conveyed that it seemed to me you were Ill, in Sorrow, and wanting the Bosom that once supported and shared your sufferings—Julia in Health amusing herself and recieving the caresses of her friends is always dear Julia—but Julia in trouble or suffering of any kind touches every nerve of my heart and it always feels that she at that time possesses its strongest affection and is its first its dearest friend.

Miss Chippy[1] writes me that you had very great difficulty in arranging your business and the additional distress of Johns Indisposition, besides not being perfectly well yourself. I long to know how you got Home, and hope your fatigues are over before now. how did you find Miss Chippy She says she has acquired great qualities since she left us which she means now to practice and is sure she possesses a firmness of temper which will guard her from all her former errors—Heaven grant—but I doubt the *firmness* she hopes she can command proceeds solely from a principle which is not so easily acquired, and possessed by few, it must be felt in the hourly occurrences of life and become a habit of temper in order to please Him who alone can give us ability to support it, and our friend did not in the few hours we passed together show any dispositions of that kind—

did she tell you how lovely my Children are, your Child[2] particularly, who is ten times lovelier if possible than she was then for a very few days on Staten Island will restore the most languid looks, and *if*

1.127 ASJPH 1-3-3-6:41

[1]Miss Shipton

[2]Either Anna Maria Seton, Elizabeth's oldest child, who was born while Julia was still living in New York or Catherine who was Julia's godchild

the heart is at rest afford enjoyments which no other place I can have any idea of could equal—well I may be partial to it as it is Fathers Home—You say you wanted his advice—I am sure if you had known it was actually a day of sorrow to him on which he saw you look so ill, you would have asked and recieved it in the way that old friends ought to have done. he never can lose his interest in your Wellfare tho' as is very Common with him he takes little pains to show it. was you not surprised to see him look so well. he cannot forget Marias Grace and Mildness—"the two finest children in the world"

how much I would have given to have presented my family to Brother [Samuel], it was a Chapter of misunderstanding or I might have been gratified with two or three hours such as can never again return and would have been valued by me as a favour of good fortune. but that is past too Julia, and when I shall have the opportunity of seeing either of you again is not to be thought of—to change a sorrowful thought I charge you to send me a kiss by my Husband—*one* mind no more or you will be putting notions in the mans head. he will be with you next Thursday I suppose, and with [me], who will make your *one many* by all the rules of multiplication, next Saturday I hope—I must write him by this post to charge him not to come away without the letters you promise which is a favour almost too great to be reasonable for me to ask.—

tell me about Charlott and ask her why she does not try to improve *her* plan of Multiplication and if two succeeded so well to try three. Your little Box got safe to me and the contents is particularly acceptable as I have long wished for such a neat smart little Affair tho' I do not promise you I will not take off the Bows—if Willy will let me

My rememberances to your Mother[3] and best love to Charlott and your dear Children. how do you all manage this summer, not in the City I hope. Seton speaks of your taking them to church in your Coachee and living in a stile of real elegance, therefore I am sure no consideration should make you neglect the thing that would conduce

---

[3]Susanna Deshon Sitgreaves

to your health which can only be mended by exercise and fresh air—how I wish you could share the sea breeze I now enjoy dear dear Julia farewell—

yours Most affectionately EASeton.

1.128 To Eliza Sadler

Monday 22nd June 1801

My Eliza

Your dear little *Cadeau*[1] arrived safe yesterday. it is my Treasure, and as compleat as my Imagination could have formed. Father says it certainly is a mistake, not intended for *me* but *Him*

little Kit has been very sick but is again merry and well, doats on her Grandfather, dances even at the sound of his voice and when he takes her in his arms looks as—her *Mother* would wish to look. The Clover before our door is reaped and the children are all playing on the Haystacks—Rebecca is mending Fathers cravats and Father himself is reading the papers. this is our interior—within the White pailing but *without* is a scene no human language can describe—[2]

Are you well—the back, the feet—and above all the *trembler* is I hope at rest. do you know the Olives are going the first of July—see them if possible—how much I wish I could.

Blessings on my dear Eliza. *Echo*, blessings on her.

your *EAS*.

I forgot to tell you that I expect my Seton this week—he always sends his remembrances to you and declares he has very *serious* thoughts of

---

1.128 ASJPH 1-3-3-7:25
[1]Gift
[2]The sick immigrants in the quarantine station

accepting his Grandfathers Mercantile situation[3] which he is too old to support himself.—Could such a thing be possible?

1.129 To Eliza Sadler

Sunday Afternoon 26th June 1801

Dear Eliza

I hope you will find some proper punishment if my letter carrier is so negligent in fulfiling this trust as he was the last.—the delight occasioned by the arrival of the long looked for and I began to fear lost friend Dué[1] is not to be described—she has told you how sweet Dick looked and indeed he behaves so well with only the check of Grandpapas voice that you would doat on him more than ever—you wish me to say that he is well, which I cannot with truth for every one who has had any communication with these unhappy Imegrants has been more or less sick and I am more than thankful that He has not been actually ill [they] are now all most gone and those th[at] remain have new buildings to recieve them and there is no danger when they can be kept clean.

dear Eliza if you could enjoy this sweet afternoon—the windows are still shut up at Bergers—Bless them, I hope they have air enough in their Hall—here we are really cold. take care of my Seton for me he is not well, and looks more Indisposed than I have ever before seen him—this is bitter—Good now indeed outweighs the Evil but if I did not trust to infinite Mercy should tremble for the future.—[the] darlings are well—Peace to you Sad.

Your *E.A.S.*

---

[3] William Magee Seton had gone to Baltimore in early June for reasons of business and health. His maternal grandfather, Richard Curson, a businessman in Baltimore, was encouraging William to move his family there.

1.129 ASJPH 1-3-3-7:26

[1] Catherine Dupleix who had returned from abroad

1.130 To Rebecca Seton

Tuesday afternoon [1801]

a very bad headach prevented my writing to my own Rebecca yesterday, and to-day Will was off very unexpectedly—I know you will be disappointed at not recieving a line by him, especially as you will probably be alone this Evening. Eliza surely has not missed so fine a day for her jaunt and I long to know the effects of it on poor little Darling also the effects (and mind I shall pinch you if your next note does not tell me) of your visit to *Miss R.* I know that poor Dué[1] was not with you yesterday which was sorrow enough to me—I know *too* well the cause of her *Indisposition* but think from what her husband[2] told me I may see her soon and then shall know if you was with her etc.—and when I am to see you my darling girl Heaven only knows—Willy is now sowerd and worried and says I must not come home till October[3] he is not as tired as I am of the strange way of living[,] meeting but once a week and then wearied and out of spirits—Father says I shall go as soon as I please the 15th September but *Willys* please must be *my* please.—

our darlings are all well Kits locks are growing *red*, and she so saucy that managing her is out of the question—She held up her little hands with such delight at the beautiful sky last Evening that I could have ate her up—Dicksy still says at every turn I will tell my godmother—Bill and Ann have grown very good, I am ten thousand times more at rest than before, and come what will, *"He is above"* therefore it must work for good—His blessing be with you my own Sister

your EAS

1.130 ASJPH 1-3-3-8:11

[1]Catherine Dupleix

[2]Captain George Dupleix

[3]William wanted Elizabeth to remain in the country air of Staten Island either because of his time-consuming and burdensome business affairs or because of the danger of disease in the hot city.

1.131 To Rebecca Seton

[1801]

My own Sister

I send all that I *know of.* say if there is any thing else—We are well as can be—Mrs. Chenot is here—Willy chatting sweet sleep stealing away the darlings Kit has called Zise[1] till she is hoarse

Peace my darling girl Oh how bright our Moon is but how I long that she should lose that brightness—forever—

1.132 To Rebecca Seton

Wednesday 10 Oclock 15th July 1801

My own own Beck—

you have your share of trouble—and yesterday our Fever which began at daylight and was heightened by an unlucky Pig from Vanduzers[1] almost knocked me up—all day except the meals was past up stairs and the last hour of it was worse than the first for I had been stupid enough to leave the Birds out. went up with a heavy heart, but soon found comfort and sat on the hearth ready to answer Kate until past eleven and than put Doddridge[2] under my pillow hoping to continue the blessed influence—dear Rebecca how great is *our treasure*, the greatest of all blessings. if dear Lidy owned it how light would it make her Burthen in comparison; but if any one can teach her *in this world* I am sure it is you, and remember it is your duty not to leave it untried.

1.131 ASJPH 1-3-3-8:12
[1] A nickname for one of Eliza Seton Maitland's children
1.132 ASJPH 1-3-3-8:47
[1] A neighbor and storekeeper on Staten Island
[2] A religious book of meditations

—poor Mr. W.[3] now he is again in sorrow I could do any thing in the world to lessen it—

—Our young doctor[4] is sick which is truly melancholy—there is two vessels below full of Passengers and new buildings going on night and day—I saw poor *Du*[5] in my sleep in her green gown and hair all falling laying on a litter pale and motionless.—happy would it be for her—but Him above knows best— Your Darling is—I cannot tell you how sweet. the sound of Godma always makes her look round with a call—She stands alone constantly and the first time I saw her in the joy of my heart I called to Anna *My Sister look*, we were alone and poor Pagé looked at me so pitiful "Am I your sister"—poor Harvey. I am in truth

your own Sister *EAS*

not one paper cut till yesterday—they almost beguiled me of my sun set which was bright thro' clouds.

1.133 To Eliza Sadler

[July 20, 1801]

My dear Eliza

I am unwilling to give you any thing to do that I myself dislike so much, but when My Father with some displeasure said this Morning that a *Cook* must be had and he did not know how to set about it, I could only reply that I would write to Mrs. Sad[ler]—if you can procure a decent woman (for a really decent one will hardly come to our Quarantine) her wages may be any thing she pleases so says the old

---

[3]Possibly John Wilkes
[4]Possibly Joseph Bayley, Dr. Bayley's assistant
[5]Catherine Dupleix
1.133 ASJPH 1-3-3-7:17

gentleman who sometimes has been obliged to give ten dollars—and if she likes me for a Mistress she may be sure of going Home with me in the Fall.

—This is Dear Dicks Birth day. the 20th July three years ago recalls many thoughts to me and probably still more to you[1]

take care of my Seton he seems to look to you for all his pleasant hours while our weekly separation continues—he will tel you how well the Darlings are—Father complains for several days, but never seriously—Heaven prevent that. Peace to you Sad dear Sad

EAS[2]

1.134 To Rebecca Seton

[July 20, 1801]

I would give something to know whether or no you got my note by J[ohn] W[ilkes] *last night*—if you were as happy as I wished you it certainly was not recieved till this morning for I was you may be sure anxious that you should not be interrupted and therefore was obliged to give the line he asked for that he might know nothing of your intention to stay in town.—I prompted you on account of the day. What passed *inwardly* it is impossible to describe[.] at 7 several sails were discovered and Breakfast went over cheerfully, "in hopes";—at 9 Darby came running up with a Confirmation of all, and pointed out a private signal between him and the man at the flag staff that the *ship* was below—The Schooner was dispatched with Darby—Father went to bed, Seton to Vanduzurs—the Boys and Anna to walk and Kit to the cradle. As I was going up to watch her and enjoy *my* hour a Man and

---

[1]Elizabeth almost died giving birth to Richard.

[2]A note in Rev. Simon Gabriel Bruté's handwriting opposite the second page of this note reads: "+Never let go this Mother 1797!!!—perverted to Rousseau and *Emile* by her unhappy friend Mrs. Sadler—"

1.134 ACS Seton-Jevons #139-142

Basket containing a *Pig* close covered up appeared before me—the Cambuck and cook turned as cloudy as myself at the sight as "*there was no wood*"—however I had *my Comfort*, and about 12 J[ohn] W[ilkes] Eliza and the Boys appeared[.] Poor Father very much indisposed came from his chamber, and Darby returned with news that "it was all a mistake."—Oh at that hour my hearts Sister how different was your happy lot—

Monday <Afternoon> night—

Afternoon was Eased for a walk on the Fort[1]—with my Willy and the Spy glass—could it be imagined that *All* the scene changes when he is here—*Countenances* every thing wears the Smile, and really *this* has been as happy a day to me as a mortal ought to have—indeed if the Merits and the blessings of every day were compared they are all too good, but this day has really flown—

how sweet it would be to have a peep of my own Beck to know if hers has been light or heavy. this day three years ago you may well remember—Darling Doxey compleats his third year. —I send you one of *Kits curls* after making her kiss it. Now I say Becka is gone—poor God ma, she will turn the back of her hand to her eyes—and then put it to mine to make me cry too—sweet pet when she slaps Dick he tells her he will tell Godmother and she stretches out her neck and calls as loud as when we used to play peep-bo.—this wont do I could write to you all night but something else *is* "*needful*"

—Heavens blessing be with you—my love to dear Eliza and the Darlings—write very soon—

Your Sis *EAS*

I have had *my* five minutes on the Piazza the moon covered with clouds dear dear Rebecca—When *we* were there—

---

[1]Possibly Fort Wadsworth at Fort Hill near the quarantine station or the ruins of a nearby Revolutionary War fort

1.135 To Rebecca Seton

Thursday morning 24th July 1801

My own Rebecca's heart will rejoice when I tell her that the Setting
Sun of last evening and the Glory of this morning were both enjoyed
with Dué[1]—She left me a few minutes ago, and the last words were
that she would write you immediately. I wish you may recieve the first
intelligence from herself—You may safely my love share the Affection you bear me with her as one united by the same link to Him who is
our common Friend and Guardian, and do it freely my Darling without reserve or fear such as we feel in affection found only for this
world.

Your note of Sunday rejoiced my Heart—to find it had been just as
I wished—except the last, tho' I cannot account for you being alone.
Where was Miss B. but *one* protection is sure. the misfortune of the
Afternoon will I hope be a *lesson for life* to my Darling Sister that you
never should violate a strict rule not to leave Home on any persuasion
on *Sacrament* Sunday[2] and to say openly to whoever may request it
that it is *your rule.* it can never be a breach of civility, or seem unkind
even to a sister or the dearest friend, if you say it with the firmness of
one who has been at *his table* who refreshes and strengthens the Soul
in well doing. I have often asked myself the question. Why should any
one be more earnest in prevailing with me for a trifle or a thing of no
consequence in itself than *I*, in maintaining the thing I know to be
right, and that touches the interests of my Souls Peace—You will say I
use many words w[h]ere *one* would do. from the fulness of the heart it
is spoken for indeed my heart is full when one moment of your Peace
is concerned.

1.135 ASJPH Seton-Jevons #31-34

[1]Catherine Dupleix

[2]It was the practice of the Episcopal church at this time to set aside designated Sundays
throughout the year on which Holy Communion was given.

—Is it Possible that you and Dué will go, not Sunday, if you say *yes*, She shall tell Mrs. McVickers[3] to call for you the *Sunday after*. happy happy Rebecca—how I long for and yet fear your next note that tells me about poor Lidy and the Darlings.[4] it seems to me if ever I see her again I will try, after first imploring the blessing if I cannot gently rouse her from her Slumber—

—I got 2 notes Saturday by Willy—and 2 yesterday. J[ohn] W[ilkes] says since you *came from Staten Island* you are "very cross." —think poor Dué is not allowed to wear her *cross* at least the badge of it, for inwardly it is weighty enough—*Sacred*—Dear Dué she has the token in her inmost Soul.—

Heavens blessing be with you I will not leave *this* blank if I can steal time—

Thursday Afternoon

Willy will be jealous of you, there is so much difference in the size of the two notes—again the Peace that passes understanding[5] be yours—

I called Dué God ma and dear Becka, but all the return was scolding, and would not even look at her—never mind the smiles will be the sweeter by and by—Your Note of Tuesday is just presented by Mr. Cambrick—and my heart answers every sigh you have breathed over it—J[ohn]W[ilkes] is a scrub to frighten you so—tho the thing was true—the Darling is quite wild with her teeth to day and yet at intervals saucy and full of play. a gardner and his wife (she a cook) is ushered in to day and Mrs. Davis to her *old walk* the *last* good by I imagine—*Endure and perform for a season* my love, perhaps *for the present* Eliza is happier in her care about the "many things,"[6] than if her *real Sorrows* has possession of her mind.

---

[3]Friend and colleague at the Widows Society
[4]Eliza Seton Maitland and her children, Elizabeth's nieces and nephews
[5]Cf. Phil. 4:7.
[6]Cf. Luke 10:41.

1.136 To Rebecca Seton

Staten Island 29th July 1801—

"Consider the Blessings that are at his right hand for them that love Him "[1] —I was awoke from my sleep this morning with those sweet words still sounding in my Ears. a Bright Sun and every blessing summoning me—often does the perishing Body enjoy this happiness while the soul is still imprisoned in the shades of darkness—this day it flies to Him the merciful giver of these unspeakable blessings without a fear or one drawback but the dread of that frailty returning which has so often sunk it in the depths of sorrow—Merciful Father graciously save it from the worst of all misery that of offending its adored <blessed> Benefactor and Friend—Praise the Lord O my Soul—Praise him that the blessed impulse of Grace may rebound to thy own happiness and glory, for to Him thy praise can add nothing, to thyself it is now the means of Grace and comfort and here after will be thy pleasure and joy thro' Eternity.

Wednesday morning

My own Rebecca I can give you no better Idea of my happiness *this* day than the *within* which was written in Kits Book[2] and on second thoughts torn out.—how I long to hear about little Eliza[.][3] I cannot sit down with out blessing the Mercy that gives me all my Darlings well.

—Dué and my *own* left me yesterday[.][4] Father has gone to shoot snipes—The good Alderman keeps us "a going" and tho' Mrs. *Van*[5] has sent a Pig I do *not* feel apprehensive. Sweet Peace is strongest this day the sun set last Evening without a cloud, I was *busy* at the moment with poor Ann in the garret closet, and afterwards took her on the top

---

1.136 ASJPH 1-3-3-8:42

[1]Ps. 2

[2]Catherine Seton's book is in the archives of St. Joseph's Provincial House, Emmitsburg, Maryland, ASJPH 1-3-3-258.

[3]One of Eliza Seton Maitland's children

[4]Catherine Dupleix and William Magee Seton

[5]Mrs. Vanduzer, a Staten Island neighbor and storekeeper

step of the ladder that leads to the top of the House, to make her feel that the promise she made "to be good" was before God who knows all we say and do. did you never experience the awe (tho I know you have) of a solemn thought greatly highthened by viewing the Heavens in open space without an intervening object—poor little Puss she is very sensible but will have many hard struggles—

—write me very soon the Boat will come soon and I long for what it will bring—

Your own Sis *EAS*

Is Mrs. Foley come the name was last week among passengers

1.137 To Rebecca Seton

Eleven Oclock Thursday night

Rebecca

I cannot sleep—the Dying, and the Dead, possess my mind. Babys perishing at the empty Breast of the expiring Mother—and this is not fancy—but the scene that surrounds me[1]—Father says *such* was never known before that there is actually twelve children that must die for mere want of sustenance, unable to take *more* than the Breast, and from the wretchedness of their Parents deprived of it as they have lain ill for many days in the ship without food, air, or *changing. Merciful Father.* Oh how readily would I give them each a turn of *Kits* treasure [2] if in my choice, but Rebecca they have a provider in Heaven who will smooth the pangs of the suffering innocent

Father goes up early in the morning to procure all possible comforts for the sufferers, and I would not have painted such a scene to

---

1.137 ASJPH 1-3-3-8:52

[1]Elizabeth was horrified at the condition of the sick immigrants at the quarantine station.
[2]Elizabeth was still nursing her infant daughter Catherine

you but to turn your mind from that which I fear too surely surrounds you—write me particularly—my side window is open and wherever I look there are lights—tents are pitched over the yard of the Convalescent House and a large one made joined to the Dead House—we are kept within the white railings—no punishment to me—

What will you think of Willy's "serious thoughts." they do not trouble me where *he* is—is my *present Home*, and our God is everywhere—

Friday morning [unclear]

Father is up and out long ago—sweet comfortable rest with Kit hugged close to a plentiful supply has been my blessing—

1.138 To Rebecca Seton

Friday Morning 10 Oclock [August 1801]

Is it possible says my Rebecca that Sister[1] is so unkind—not one line—dear dear girl my thoughts are often enough with you.—contrary to former times I am not a moment away from my poor Father[2] without being missed and sent for—he tells me in the Morning "come sit by me I have not rested a minute since you left me"—

Kate is very good and allows me to be the greater part of the night in his room, and has never wimpered these three days tho' very seldom nursed. Ana and Will went with my Sister yesterday to stay till it goes better. Post sat up with him and is gone to town this Morning to return with Tillary[3] who will still [stay] 'till there is *a change.*—what that change may be Oh my Rebecca—if I did not in this hour know who to look to, how could it be borne—My head is always

---

1.138 ASJPH 1-3-3-8:21

[1]Elizabeth herself

[2]Dr. Richard Bayley had become ill on August 11.

[3]The doctor who attended Dr. Bayley in his illness

beating—and never free from pain night or day, since you and my Willy left me I do not expect him 'till tomorrow

Do[4] not let Willy lose a minute my own Beck, for such a sweet Sun and sweet prospect will soon be shut out from us—that is one side the question

—the other is very sweet too—but I long to enjoy the scene of the little ones running to meet you, they are half wild with the expectation that Paté and God-ma[5] will soon be here—make haste to your own Sis

Wednesday Morning Kiss dear Mary[6] for me.

1.139 To Rebecca Seton

[August 16, 1801]

try to get Patty to take the inclosed

My own Rebeccas heart asks for me—but all in vain. the chance is so small that hope is folly except as we refer it to Him who can renew both soul and Body in an instant.

He[1] cannot retain any nourishment or get rest for any length of time—knows his dear Betty so as to express *by his looks* his pleasure at seeing her and sometimes puts out his hand—Sister is still here—we were both with him last night except *2 hours*

Kit coughed and would not leave me She is very good and Dick a perfect angel the whole week past. Ann and William very happy at Sisters—All this I know you wish to hear—Your poor Sis's only ref-

---

[4]The remainder of this note appears to be a separate note but it is classified with 1-3-3-8:21 in the St. Joseph Provincial House Archives.

[5]William Magee Seton and Rebecca Seton

[6]Possibly Mary Seton, Elizabeth's sister-in-law

1.139 ASJPH 1-3-3-8:16

[1]Dr. Richard Bayley who was then dying

uge is the *Father that cannot be removed*—Oh how sweet is such refuge in this hour—

Your Sis

9 Oclock Sunday morning *this day* to all human appearance will decide—

1.140 Draft to Rev. Richard Channing Moore

[after her father's death on August 17, 1801]

I cannot leave the Island without offering to Mr. Moor[e][1] the acknowledgements of a grateful heart for the blessing and comfort he has procured for us in the bitter hours of heavy affliction—You have dear Sir placed the remains of my dear Father in a *sacred* resting place,[2] and the only remaining wish I have is that <the> a small space may be reserved on each <by his> side of him for his two eldest children this request is not the impulse of unrestrained sorrow, but <the request> of a heart that knows where its Home is to be and feels the greatest consolation in the Hope that it may be permitted to repose by its dear Parent.[3]

1.140 ASJPH 1-3-3-7:73

[1] Rev. Richard Channing Moore (1762-1841), who conducted the funeral service for Dr. Richard Bayley, studied medicine under Dr. Bayley and theology under Dr. Samuel Provoost. He was the rector of St. Andrew's Church on Staten Island (1789-1809) and St. Stephen's Church in New York City (1809-1814). Consecrated bishop of Virginia in 1814, he founded Virginia Theological Seminary and was a leader in reconstructing the Episcopal church in the United States after the American Revolution.

[2] Dr. Richard Bayley is buried at St. Andrew's Episcopal Church, Richmondtown, Staten Island.

[3] A note in another hand, probably Rev. Simon Gabriel Bruté's, reads: "Thank God Mrs. Seton does not repose by the side of her 'dear Parent.' She many years after his death told her daughter Catherine that she had never heard him [speak] pronounce the word God but once and that was on his deathbed just before expiring he threw up his arms O my God!" Cf. 1.141 for Elizabeth's version.

1.141 To Julia Scott

New York 5th September 1801—

on the 10th August—in the Afternoon My Father was seated at his Diningroom window composed, cheerful and particularly delighted with the scene of shipping and manoeuvering of the Pilots etc., which was heightened by a beautiful sunset and the view of a bright rainbow which was extended immediately Over the Bay—

He called me to observe the different shades of the sun on the clover field before the door and repeatedly exclaimed "in my life I never saw any thing so beautiful"—little Kit was playing in my arms and he pleased himself with feeding her with a spoon from his glass of drink and making her say papa—after tea I played all his favourite musick and he sung two German Hymns and the Soldiers Adieu with such earnestness and energy of manner that even the servants observed how much more cheerful he was than any Evening before, this summer—at ten (an hour later than usual) he went to his room and the next morning when Breakfast was ready (tho' it was then but just sunrise) his servant said he had been out since daylight and just returned home very sick = he took his cup of tea in silence which I was accustomed to and went to the wharf and to visit the surrounding buildings. shortly after he was sitting on a log on the wharf his head leaning on his hands exposed to the hottest sun I have felt this summer and looked so distressed as to throw me immediately in a flood of tears (which is very unusual for me) the umbrella was sent and when he came in he said his legs gave way under him went to bed and was immediately delirious—

—young Bayley[1] who has been one of his family for fourteen years and to whom he was excessively attached was with him and capable of executing every direction, but neither opium or any remedy whatever could give him a moments relief—nor could he even lay still in his bed

---

1.141 ASJPH 1-3-3-6:42

[1] A servant in Dr. Bayley's household.

without constantly holding my arm—"all the horrors are coming my child, I feel them all" with other expressions and the charge he gave me of his keys convinced me he knew the worst from the beginning—Blisters upon blister[2] produced no change for the better, every thing he took his stomach rejected with continual dreadful reachings—he looked earnestly in my face the third day— "*the hand of Heaven is in it all, will not do*"—and often wished it was later in the day—complained it was hard work—and repeatedly called "my Christ Jesus have mercy on me." once in the night he said, "Cover me warm, I have covered many—poor little children, I would cover you more, but it cant always be as we would wish"—he struggled in extreme pain until about 1/2 past two Monday Afternoon the 17th when he became apparently perfectly easy, put his hand in mine turned on his side and sobbed out the last of life without the smallest struggle, groan, or appearance of pain—

I saw his composed quiet countenance several times in the interval of his interment—the Parish of Richmond refused his being carried thro' the Island—his Grave was dug in a corner near the house where my children were accustomed to play—but as if the Mercy of my Heavenly Father directed it we thought of taking Him in his barge to Richmond which could go within half a mile of the church yard, where he was at last laid by young Bayley and his faithful Boatmen—the sexton nor none of the people daring to approach—Mr. Moore[3] of the Island performed the service and two waggons full of relatives and friends paid the last respect—*I* his dear—his darling—child—who[se] Soul doated on Him—without a *perceptible* struggle and [unclear] with the calmness of a subdued spirit, *after once the soul was departed*—saw all, did all, that was to be done—and now review with wonder, and with grateful praise, that *I live*, much less that I have lived thro' it—

---

[2]Blisters on the skin were formed by applying a sharp, irritating ointment, plaster, or other aplication.

[3]Rev. Richard Channing Moore

I and my darlings removed to our only remaining earthly Protector,[4] the following week, and since that time I have suffered so much with the nerves of my teeth and temples that I have been really stupifyed.—the night before my Fathers Death Kit lay all night in a Fever at my breast and Richard on His mattress at my feet vomitting violently—but they have all been perfectly well since

My Seton is very well—has received your letter rejoices you have got the mat the price is *30* dollars, original price *50*, it was only down a few weeks. it can be cut and bound any size you please—the reason you did not get it before Mr. Robinson who had the refusal had it to try, and it did not fit his room—Seton has told Miss Shipton to tell you *we* are coming to visit you in October—Mammy is at Brunswick[5] and all the mistakes you meet must be set down to your child[6] who is pulling me by the gown all the while I write—I am going to be well when I get a little rest from my summer fatigues—"thy will be done" is my constant support—*if it could be*, and not his will—oh Julia—

Bless you Your EAS

1.142 To Rebecca Seton

[n.d.]

My Rebecca

Your Cate continues very sick. She has a sore throat and sore mouth which with the cough and distress of her Breast fairly knocks the Darling up. —Except *my back* all else is well—love to dear Eliza and the precious little one[1] and pray take care of yourself—I have not

---

[4]William Magee Seton, Elizabeth's husband

[5]Mammy Huler, a household servant, was with Elizabeth's younger sisters-in-law at their school in Brunswick, New Jersey.

[6]Anna Maria or Catherine Seton

1.142 ASJPH 1-3-3-8:40

[1]Eliza Seton Maitland and her baby

seen poor [John] Wilks today for Kate will not be away from me a moment—My Cecilia, Anna, and the Boys have been round the battery[2] both yesterday and today and are all very happy—

Bless Bless *you* do not be uneasy about your pet the worst that can happen she will be *an Angel*—

Your Sis

dear *tieze*[3] is well he is very serious in these time and says he wishes to know how to make *that* hour easy

1.143 Draft to Mary Bayley Post

[September 1801]

My own dear Mary

tell me how you are if all your dear ones are well—why do I not hear from you—are you at the wilderness[1]—does the peaceful Spirit of our Celia hover over it, or do the carriages and plumb cake spirits disturb its solitude. is dear Post well—alas and oh I must go to the Visions of fancy to find you all, while the little angel[2] was at the breast I could bring you to my mind at any time knowing so well the looks and position of the dear little Mother—but now whether standing on the rocks watching the passing waves which picture the passage to eternity, wandering in the woods, or pouring tea for the ladies, all is uncertain—and the sinking Sun behind the mountain—calls thought away

---

[2]On their return to New York after Dr. Bayley's death, the Seton family moved into No. 8 State Street, a house on the Battery.

[3]Possibly a nickname for her husband, William Magee Seton

1.143 ASJPH 1-3-3-7:87

[1]Possibly James Seton's country home, called "The Wilderness." It was on a neck of land on the banks of the Hudson River near present day 43rd Street and 11th Avenue in New York City. Water swept past on one side and rocks and woods on the other gave a wild appearance to the place.

[2]Mary Bayley Post's infant daughter Catherine or Elizabeth's own infant daughter Catherine

to that scene w[h]ere all uncertainties shall be made clear—Where we shall find a home large enough for us all, and our different and various perspectives will be as the Doctor say[s] "brought to a focus" where we shall behold! O Mary dear how the soul bounds at the thought—behold the father recieving, and welcoming his children Home—O do be good and do not let the present good (tho' I well know yours is mixed with many a pang) banish or obscure the future prospect You see Mrs. Cruger frequently I hope—from Cecils account of her sweet manners and independent character she must exactly [be] the neighbour you would like

1.144 To Rebecca Seton

1st Sunday in October [1801?]

My own Rebecca was to have seen *Sister Due Kit* and the three Darlings[1] this Morning when your Note by J[ohn] W[ilkes] knocked up our Jaunt and Due as they were all in the carriage was obliged to give them a ride to Mrs. [Eliza] Sadlers who had just returned. I am very uneasy about Maitland, indeed shall always be for any one attacked in that way as it was the beginning of my poor Fathers sufferings[2]—

G[unclear] Ogden[3] was to see us Friday Evening we talked of William little thinking.—did you notice how she was affected by the Sermon on Providence—She has promised to see me very often—who can be Sorry that so good a Soul as her dear Brothers is spared the *struggles*—perhaps the yet worse misery of falling from its high

---

1.144 UNDA MSVY, M 41 (typescript) No original exists

[1]Elizabeth herself, Catherine Dupleix, and Elizabeth's four children, Catherine, Anna Maria, William, and Richard

[2]James Maitland, Elizabeth's brother-in-law, and a partner in Seton, Maitland and Company. Possibly James Maitland was showing symptoms of yellow fever similar to those Dr. Bayley had exhibited before he died.

[3]Possibly Charlotte Seton who had married Gouverneur Ogden in 1800

calling—Heaven's mercy is sure—"thy will be done" should be our unceasing tribute.

I must see Miss R, and really long for it—any day all days are the same you know if you are to bring her. twice with Due *my own William* and our two eldest yesterday—but only to hear strangers—but it was good, and we were well satisfied, *tho'* the Superlative rests with H[enry] H[obart][.] Kit is so good I could almost wish the old w[blank] visit lengthened—Dear Bayley[4] has enquired after you—Bless you *past four* I shall be too late

Your own Sis—

dream we are in the 3rd seat from the Pulpit
9 Oclock Best love to dear Eliza—

1.145 To Rebecca Seton

4 Oclock 14th October 1801

My dearest Rebecca says "do write," but I have nothing to say more than the ever welcome *All is well.* the terror of our fellow citizens[1] seems to be so awakened that I do not believe you ought to come to town as prudence says, *but I* say come dear and "let us keep the feast"—with Sincerity and truth,[2] we do not know that another opportunity will be allowed us—but I would not come on Friday except you could stay till Monday and that I suppose dear Lidy would not wish—thank Heaven she is well again and the little darling—

Kit is so sweet saucy and well that we all love her too much—Mrs. S[adler] I have not heard of to-day but suppose she is as

---

[4]Dr. Bayley's servant

1.145 ASJPH 1-3-3-8:50

[1]Another of the periodic yellow fever epidemics was threatening New York City. Those who could, left the city.

[2]Cf. 1 Cor. 5:8.

yesterday—almost stupifyed poor little Soul—*His* blessing be with you both and the affection of your own *Sis*

E.A.S.

my Will is remarkably well

1.146 To Rebecca Seton

[1801]

My darling Rebecca

who would mind or alter the effusions of a heart as good and amiable as yours, they are such as your dear Mother would have approved, and must be recieved with generosity and redoubled affection by the one to whom they are addressed—they are already in His possession. I am very uneasy about your indisposition, it lasts too long and I charge you to attend to yourself. I send you some of Kates Magnesia, it is calcined, take all I send you, and drink tamarind water or some acid with it. *Her* ear is getting well and the darling Eyes are paying for it. *Mrs. M* has not answered my note so that I hope she is *trying*. William will not hear to my leaving home—

His Will be done Who knows best—but it is the hardest of all trials to see an innocent suffer. William took it in his mind that the Boys would be here yesterday, dear little rogues they have a bad time if on the water to day I will send them with James[1] for you, as soon as they come.—

Bill called out as he opened his Eyes this Morning "dear Henry Hubbard[2] I wish you would preach for me." just those words; they woke me from my sleep and occasioned a long heavy sigh, not

---

1.146 ASJPH 1-3-3-8:25
[1]James Seton, Elizabeth's brother-in-law
[2]Rev. Henry Hobart

unaccountable nor yet accountable. the anxious passage, and hope that he might teach the wisher to be a preacher—Oh what a thought—Heavens will be done—that prayer settles every thing with *me* and I trust with *you*. love to Lidy[.] Peace to you my Sister

Your *EAS*

I will put your letter under lock in your drawer (or say if I shall) Maitland[3] will think us crazy if it goes back

1.147 To Julia Scott

New York 27th October 1801

It makes me sorry when I think how long my own Julia has been expecting an answer to the kind tender proofs of friendship she had offered me—indeed it seems as if I spend my time in wishing to do what is to be done without making any proper exertion, tho' the last three weeks has been tryed to the utmost by my poor little friend, [Eliza] Sad[ler], who has gone thro' more fatigue with a weak frame than the strong could have endured without that all powerful principle which the Creator seems particularly to bestow in the hour of tryal. an innate strength or rather force of the mind which when suffered to relax nearly breaks the powers of life as it has proved in this instance for Mrs. Sadler is more like a lifeless body than any thing liveing, and in fact so stupified, that it seems almost the same situation she was in twelve months ago from a paralytic affection which threatened her life and deprived her for three months of the use of her right side—I mention this to you as you could not, without knowing this circumstance have any idea of the horrors of such a situation which it is feared will occasion the return of her dreadful complaint—you may

---

[3]James Maitland, Elizabeth's brother-in-law
1.147 ASJPH 1-3-3-6:43

be sure I have borne *my part* in the melancholy scene—she staid with poor Sadler[1] to the last and I was (as seems my lot to be) her only Earthly Support. Mrs. [Catherine] Duplex a particular friend of our circle stays with her for the present but it is difficult to imagine a Being more forlorn—

Yellow fever—the very sound drives the blood from my heart, well—dearest what is next to be done, will I be allowed to sit still and enjoy my Sweet Home?—"Thy Will be done"—oh Julia what a comfort and support those four little words are to my Soul—I have repeated them till they are softened to the sweetest harmony. they recall the death bed scene of my own Father, and I counted his Dying pulses so long to that time that whilst repeating them I can imagine I still hold his hand—Surely in my last hour my heart will lean on them—

Our projected visit to you like all other schemes that go against the stream must be defered—how I could leave home at any time is not easy to concieve, but now I have my Sister Matelands Infant[2] in addition to my own, and its wet nurse for a *winter* charge, and our dear little Cecilia and Harriet to be Home from school tomorrow, the former to be *my* Pupil again this winter, (which by the by is a wonderful assistance to my Anna Maria) it is as much impossible as any thing can be. —how Seton is to get out of his scrape with you I cannot tell—he is so much plagued by *family* Crosses (not Domestick ones observe) and disappointments in every way that you must not be hard with him—he sends you a Kiss and says you shall have two when he sees you again if you forgive him—He is in love with you, your House and all that belongs to you—

—your little *Kit* is not weaned yet—to tell the truth I am affraid of the *Shadows*[3] as soon as I give up nursing. She is the most compleat little piece of Delicacy your eyes ever beheld. and Richard and Will a Pair unequalled—even by Charlotts—how does she do—*Wonders* must not be expected twice in her life I suppose—Seton speaks of *herself* as still a

---

[1]Eliza Craig Sadler's husband, Henry, had died in the yellow fever epidemic.

[2]There was sickness in the Maitland household.

[3]Possibly a reference to postpartum depression or a fear of getting pregnant again

wonder and if the comparison had not been with my Julia she would have been the Philadelphia favourite—I wish to see Maria almost as much as yourself—and Kitty and Harriet as much as if I had know[n] them in latter years, but I am sure Maria in my mind would excell both—John must be quite a substitute to you and from the knowledge I have of his disposition I am sure, a great blessing. my love to both and respects to your dear Mother[4]—

I have not seen the Giles's since the 1st September their House is shut up as you may Suppose while the fever fear lasts. there is very little said about it the last two days, tho the weather continues very unfavourable—I wish you joy of Miss Chippy.[5] pray get her a Husband if you can, I would rather she was making caps or feet for childrens stockings.—than covering screens which she has taken in hand for me. [unclear] times for joking—I am as I hope ever to be

> your own friend Eliza the wife of W M Seton
> [On the address side]

I omitted mentioning I received the *30 dollars* safe—WMS respects your punctuality—John Wilkes says Come yourself

1.148 To Rebecca Seton

[1801]

Dear Rebecca

My Spirits are heavy—Willy says so much about my going to-morrow[1] and that we shall not without a carriage—that it is madness the streets almost impassable etc.—*you know him.* that I think it

---

[4]Susanna Deshon Sitgreaves
[5]Miss Shipton
1.148 ASJPH 1-3-3-8:15
[1]Elizabeth is referring to church.

will be best for *me* to go quietly with him, and if the Whether is not really a storm come to you *after*—You must not lose if *I* must You had better go to Mrs. Bogert's pew as she has since pressed me to come there—Kit is quite wild with her teeth but they are almost thro'. Malta and I have drawn her in a little Box all day when she has not been in my arms—the girls are very happy and the Boys saucy—Maté[2] is quite cheary being Saturday. dear dear Blessed Day that follows, while there is life there is *Peace* on that day which ever way enjoyed—and when this life is no more—sweet sweet will be that day without a Night—come come. Mammy [Huler] is quite ill again—Mrs. [Eliza] S[adler] worse in her helplessness than at first—but we do not want any one else—Mrs. *M* is not to be depended on—

—for my part I would rather have a great deal to do that *not*, while it is my duty.—it will be the sooner done.

—Willy bids me inclose ten dollars to Eliza for the Baker and Milkman. I wanted him to do it but he would not —I send you night cloths, and would have sent something to *Zise*[3] but did not know of anything but a knuckle—Bless Bless you. I have not one paper cut—indeed dear you dont know how I am *pushed* have wrote till twelve these 2 nights. *till 11 for Willy*[4] and always something to mend, for there is no one to do any thing, and always faithfully hear the lessons—it will not *always* be so we will soon have rest—have got 40 dollars for H[enry] H[obart]'s.

Your EAS

---

[2]Elizabeth herself
[3]One of the Maitland children
[4]Elizabeth was taking care of her husband's business correspondence.

1802

1.149 To Julia Scott

New York 7th January 1802

My dear Julia,

Seton has been constantly dreaming of you, and as a kiss has often been realized to his imagination which he thinks an unpropitious sign, he fears you are *still* angry with him, and begs you "for pity's sake," to let the offences of the old year pass with it—and his little wife begs you for remembrance sake to write that you are neither sick nor sorry which we have been assured by Mrs. Ryess but can scarcely hope as *Col[onel] G[iles]*, and his Rib have been as long without a lines from you as I have—Surely you will say friend your letters neither by their manner, or frequency call for immediate answers—but my darling *Months* have passed in silence and they are pretty long periods—which added to an interruption of the accidental information we generally recieve of you make us apprehensive that either Body or mind is oppressed—

We are going on quietly—our children the wonders of Perfection they were before, described to you by their Father, Miss White calls your favourite Dick the cherub of New York, indeed it is difficult to imagine a countenance of more expression and beauty he is almost as tall as William and very robust—I keep all at Home, William makes his letters very well and Anna begins to join her's, they spell very well and would read, but I promised my *Father* the first of last Summer that I would keep them back for twelve months. Dear little Kit has her first little red shoes on, and pads about the delight of all hearts—I have a wet nurse and Infant for the winter—of our Sister Maitlands and Cecilia is one of my scholars therefore with the management of my

Widows also, "I rise up early and late take rest,"[1] you may be sure—never before after 12, and oftener one. Such is the allotment and as every body has their *Pride* of some sort, I cannot deny that this is mine—Rebecca continues my *friend and sister*, in all things Mammy Huler is going Home so fast that we can scarcely by an indulgence or care quiet her pains and sufferings.

—It must delight you to hear how well my Brothers[2] are going on—I wrote you how they were employed, and rejoice to say that they have great credit for their industry and good conduct—we look for poor Richard[3] every day—Emma is in the way she has *longed* for,[4] and little Sister[5] very well—Mrs. Sadler[6] is better—I tell you all my concerns—mind that I recieve an exact account of *yours*—

I have written Miss Shipton—rather laconically, but [tri]ed to set her the example of not dealing [unclear] long stories—her account of Mrs. Sitgreaves is *respectful* to a degree—and of Brother [Samuel] as I know he deserves—do tell me about Charlott—I yet love to think of the last Monday I had hold of her hand in the front bedroom upstairs and thought her, next to Father Hub and child, the most precious of created beings—You remember I was miffed with *you* at the time for being *too young.* indeed I think while I live I shall always love her from the bottom of my heart.

dont you think of seeing us in the Spring—dear little Julia I think if I could hold you once more to my heart it would ease it of a heavy weight—it very seldom can unburthen itself since Poor Father is gone except when humbled before Him who made it—

Your EAS

---

[1]Cf. Ps. 127:2

[2]Elizabeth's half-brothers were Andrew, Guy Carleton, Richard, and William Augustus Bayley.

[3]Richard Bayley was associated with the Filicchi firm in Leghorn from 1799 to 1803.

[4]Charlotte Bayley Craig, Elizabeth's half-sister, was expecting a child.

[5]Possibly Rebecca Seton

[6]Eliza Craig Sadler had recently lost her husband.

1.150 To Rebecca Seton

[n.d.]

Dearest Rebecca—

I have cut out my two *suits* to day and partly made one—heard all the lessons too and had a two hours visit from my Poor Widow Veley[1]—no work—no wood—child sick etc—and should I complain with a bright fire within—bright, bright *Moon* over my Shoulder and the Darlings all well hallooing and dancing—I have played for them this half hour, Mr. Jones dressing Willy to sup at Aunté's with six and *30* people[2]—He laments that I will be *Alone* I talk to him of my Companion a *Peaceful Soul*, but he only laughs—think of me at *12* I hope dear Zise[3] and all rest well—Kiss her and her little Maté[4] for me—Mammy [Huler] still in bed and Kit almost as fond of Mrs. Myers as of me[5]—Bless you my own Sister—the within letters were delivered this Evening[.] Anna wrote every word herself—*Malta* by her side[.] take great care of them they will be a treasure in my Cabinet—*last night* I wrote two sheets as full as I could crowd them to Aunt Caley[6] *to please my Will*—went to bed at *12* <last night>. as *you and I understand each other* I may show you the within description to her—with what rapid pleasure the pen ran it over—the Praise of those we love how sweet—how *sweet sweet* will be *His Praise*—when it is our reward for well doing—'till than *His peace be ours*

1.150 ASJPH 1-3-3-8:37

[1]Probably one of the women whom Elizabeth helped through her work in the Society for the Relief of Poor Widows with Small Children

[2]A household servant was assisting William Magee Seton to dress for a dinner at the house of his aunt Elizabeth Curson Farquhar.

[3]One of Eliza Seton Maitland's children

[4]Eliza Seton Maitland

[5]Mammy Huler was sick, and Catherine Seton, the baby, had taken to the new woman who was helping to care for the Seton children.

[6]Isabella Seton Cayley, a paternal aunt of William Magee Seton, who lived in England

1.151 To Rebecca Seton

29th January 1802

I know my Rebecca will wish for a little word tho' there is nothing pleasant to say—Willy is out, and to dine out—but is far from well. Mammy [Huler] not out of bed since breakfast and Kit a jaw tooth to make her cross—Eliza is as good as an angel—and her cold quite better tho' not gone—Malt[,] Ann and the Boys saucy but I suppose it is still comfort compared to your scene—best love to dear Zise[1] Kit is on my lap—

"Thy comforts have refreshed my Soul"[2]—still refresh and may they never leave us or we them—

your Sis

1.152 To Rebecca Seton

[n.d.]

My darling Rebecca

I think the print will be too small for your eyes—if so you shall have the one in church—Bill has a sore throat and Ann pain in her breast—Mammy [Huler] not so well—Aunty[1] has been so kind as to send word she has *prevailed* upon Mrs. Rogers[2] to pass Saturday Evening with us—by way of *preparation* I suppose—indeed I am more sorry for *her* than for myself great as the mortification is

Kits eyes are very hollow and she has a bad cold but I *must* dine at Posts at *3* to return by *5*. that is the promise—

such a sweet Evening as the last 5 hours quiet and the books. Willy and Leffingwell[3] in Counting house—said the sick Prayers for poor

---

1.151 ASJPH 1-3-3-8:55

[1] One of Eliza Seton Maitland's children

[2] Cf. Ps. 22 and Jer. 31:25.

1.152 ASJPH 1-3-3-8:29

[1] Elizabeth Curson Farquhar, William Magee Seton's maternal aunt

[2] Probably a neighbor on State Street

[3] A business associate of William Magee Seton

Mammy who I am this Evening to instruct for to-morrow, at *eleven* Mr. Linn[4] baptizes her and I must not go to Church *perhaps* you had better be here too—as you say—

—I have foolishly forgot to send for the mutton—but send Pete now—His blessing be with you, and

your *EAS*

love to Lizé[.] the eyes danced when your dear little present came—Cele is very well—

1.153 To Rebecca Seton

[January 25, 1802]

My *dearest*

Sister Willy is much better—Mammy [Huler] has been all day in bed—Eliza, Sister,[1] and all very good. [Captain George] Duplex has had a losing voyage which makes all crooked—I rejoice that your bustle is so far over. Heaven preserve you and my poor Eliza—take care of yourselves—this is indeed my wedding day,[2] it weds me nearer to my *Blessed Home*— Peace dear Rebecca—

1.154 To Anna Maria Seton

31st January 1802

Mama's dear Anna shall have a little letter for she deserves one now She is so good a girl and can write a letter herself. Papate's best love to his dear daughter and begs her to be very attentive to her Reading too

---

[4]Rev. William Linn (1752-1833) had started his career as a Presbyterian minister, but he joined the Dutch Reformed church in 1787. An able speaker and fervent believer in religious freedom, he was active in public life, holding, among other positions, that of regent of the University of the State of New York from 1787 until his death.

1.153 ASJPH 1-3-3-8:35

[1]Eliza Seton Maitland's infant daughter and Elizabeth herself

[2]Elizabeth was married January 25, 1794.

1.154 AMSV 110:10,2

good night my darling—

Your own Mother EA Seton

1.155 To Julia Scott

New York 1st February 1802

I know my friend will smile at so immediate a reply to her letter of 29th January received this morning—but an opportunity presents that cannot be refused—There are various kind of attachments in this world some of affection, without the soothing confidence of trust and esteem united—some of esteem for virtues which we can neither approach nor assimilate to our own natures, and some—the unbounded veneration, Affection, Esteem, and tribute of "the Heart Sincere"—The Bearer of this letter[1] possesses *in full* the reality of the last description in *my Heart*—and in fact I can give no stronger proof of the Affection and esteem I bear you than in expressing to you what I believe another would pervert or ridicule—

The soother and comforter of the troubled *Soul* is a kind of friend not often met with—the convincing, Pious, and singular turn of mind, and argument possessed by this most amiable being has made him without even having the least consciousness that he is so the friend most my friend in this world, and one of those who after my Adored creator I expect to recieve the largest share of happiness from in the next—

Well surely this is not for Miss Chips[2] eyes nor any thing else I write—for I am quite out of Patience with her follies and flatteries and hope with you she will at least have the merit of less[en]ing your House keeping troubles—

1.155 ASJPH 1-3-3-6:45

[1]Rev. Henry Hobart carried this letter to Philadelphia. He was visiting his mother and sister, both of whom were ill.

[2]Miss Shipton, a mutual friend

My two Boys were taken sick this morning with Symptoms of the Meazels which are very prevalent in our city—the dear Sister[3] who lessens and shares my family troubles is obliged to go to her Sister Maitland whose Husband (not a worthy) was put in the limits yesterday,[4] and whose family *six in number* my William is obliged to supply from our own store room, and every day marketing as no other part of the family will keep them from starving—or even in fire wood—

The Peace[5] has almost knocked poor Seton up—He is delighted with your *claim*, especially as he thinks I am likely to go very soon—Next September is the time I appoint for Relinquishment—but if it is true as we have heard from an intimate acquaintance and relative of yours that YOU ARE TO BE MARRIED I do not know what you will do with the Budget—but Heaven grant if it is possible they may fall in your dear hands—if that trust could *now* be confided how joyfully would I recieve my RELEASE at any moment[6]—

Poor [Colonel] Giles is pretty tired *too* I believe—his family has the Meazels—but his general Health is better—it was he told me the marrying story which he really believes to be but a story—Seton says in return for your kind compassion he means to leave (in case he goes first) his PRECIOUS STONE to you as a rich legacy. we expect him every *hour*.—If [Rev.] Mr. [Henry] Hobart is invited to your Pulpit do not neglect going to Church on that day—I believe he stays a fortnight—Many loves to your dear Children for me and remembrances to Charlott and your mother[7]—

—a thousand thanks for your remembrance of my poor Widows[8]—is it to go to the Society funds, or it is for *MY* use—I know

---

[3]Rebecca Seton, Elizabeth's sister-in-law

[4]James Maitland was to go to debtors' prison.

[5]This may refer to an impending truce between France and Britain. The Treaty of Amiens was signed March 25 with implications for American shipping.

[6]It is possible that Julia had offered to care for the Seton children in the event that anything happened to Elizabeth and William Magee. In addition Elizabeth was pregnant and expecting in September. If Julia was to be married, Elizabeth was wondering what would happen to her offer.

[7]Susanna Deshon Sitgreaves

[8]Elizabeth continued to be active in the work of aiding poor widows, serving as treasurer of the Society for the relief of poor widows with small children.

you answer as you please—indeed I have many times this winter called at a dozen houses in one morning for a less sum than that you sent for you may be sure these Meazles cause wants and sorrows which the society cannot even half supply and in many familys the small pox and meazels have immediately succeeded each other—

1.156 To Rebecca Seton

[1802]

My own Rebecca

Malta sends you last Evenings happiness—a *sweet Evening* and a Blessed day went before it—all done at Home, and safe seated long before any one came in, and then *Mr. M read. H* almost at my Elbow who with Miss *B* and Mrs. Jacobs made up all our side—to sing *his* praise and feed the Soul—hush hush—*His word is sure.*

Mammy [Huler] has been all day in bed—never mind I will settle about *10* when we meet. or *write you Saturday* our dear Willy is very anxiously uneasy about something and when I talk to him of our hope—he says he is *too much troubled*—Oh oh—*He* alone can set him right.[1]

1.156 ASJPH 1-3-3-8:24

[1]The third page of this note is torn vertically and the fragments of each line do not convey any meaning. The words that appear are:

best
you sho____
keep
shall
or shar__
Mrs. ____
wood. I'd
notice *4*
this cat_____
Pete shal__
Kit is very

1.157 To Rebecca Seton

Sunday [1802]

Dearest Rebecca—

with the *Sun* I hope we will meet again—it makes me think of when we will meet where our Sun will never be hid—but indeed I had the advantage of this world this morning as perfectly as a mortal could have—Willy carried me to the door where I sat 1/2 hour before the Bell stoped—then looking up found H[enry] H[obart] in the Pulpit—such *fervent prayers* I never heard before about *8* to join—but I am sure their *Souls* must have gone with him.

—Mine had its Peace perfect as can be recieved in this world—Our Willy is almost distracted about the times—Mammy [Huler] is very sick but Kit better and more playful the girls are *very good*—the cook wont stay[,] Pete is lazy and Mrs. Taylor *heavy. for myself*—except you have experienced—can never describe—cheerful Sorrow is not quite English, but some Souls know what it is—and he who sees in secret will remember the back must ach—but that is to sympathise with you—but no cold—do tell me the moment yours is better, for tho I do not *wish* you to live—cannot bear to think you suffer—as the Master pleases—shall I send you some *corn cobs*

—Best love to Elize and Zise[1]—Kit still sings about her—for fear she wants soup I send veal—is there any thing else.—I fear there are many things—Bless you Peace—

EAS

1.157 ASJPH 1-3-3-8:18
[1]Eliza Seton Maitland and one of her children

1.158 To Rebecca Seton

[1802]

My own Rebecca

the cook did not come this morning and all went crooked—I think little Zise¹ would eat fish try her—I long long to see you if only an hour, but not while it is so bitter cold. Sure next Sunday *we may.* Heavenly blessing what Peace it has given me— Willy is all aback about something we are all shortly to go to the *black river²* and I dare not talk of money—he owes me ten dollars and says he cant pay me [I] send you a tea pot tile the sun shines again. I could not have the Heart to touch *your* black one without asking you Mammy [Huler] keeps still better Kit is better—I am well the girls very happy—Bless you all

EAS

1.159 To Rebecca Seton

5th August 1802

Dearest Rebecca—

all is well—at church yesterday morning and afterwards to see *Sister* Mrs. *Sad* and *Dué*¹ and had to entertain the Miss Whites until past 9—wrote till twelve and slept sound till five—opened my Prayer Book with a heavy sigh and met the words *"tarry thou the*

1.158 ASJPH 1-3-3-8:19
¹One of Eliza Seton Maitland's children
²Possibly a rhetorical reference to the family's dire financial situation
1.159 ASJPH 1-3-3-8:57
¹Rebecca herself or Mary Post, Eliza Craig Sadler, and Catherine Dupleix

Lords leisure, be strong and he shall comfort thy heart"[2]—Blessed promise—O that I could be worthy to claim it.

—My soul is very very very sick—I call to my Physician every moment from the bottom of my heart—but find no Peace—

Sister told me yesterday *she* had *perfect Peace*.—Well "yet a little while and he that shall come will come and will not tarry"[3]—I speak to my soul, own Sister when I speak to you—

We have just left the Dinner *Dick at Pinery*, and Willy at Sukey,[4] all the while—but I managed very well and came off conqueror without uttering a word I was not obliged to—they are both asleep—the girls beg so hard to go out to you—do write if only a line by them—If you could have seen dear little *Mrs. Jones*[5] and I with seven children at catachism yesterday, and standing in the vestry room door a quarter of an hour afterwards—you would have said *"there was a transfer"* indeed—

What a sin it would have been if it had been *somebody* such is the force of *conscience*—Blessed be *Him* who keeps mine awake—*Bless you all love* to dear Zize[6]—

E.A.S.

1.160 To Rebecca Seton

2 Oclock Saturday 7th August

My own Rebecca—

all is well—the best thing I can tell you—sweet *Peace* to day in anticipation of to-morrow I trust—Kit looks as if my soul *must* be prepared—it is prepared if I know it, to yield even with thankfulness—I

---

[2]Ps. 27:14

[3]Heb. 10:37

[4]The children were probably restless at dinner, and she was commenting on their behavior.

[5]Possibly the wife of Rev. Cave Jones, one of the assistant ministers at Trinity Church

[6]One of Eliza Seton Maitland's children

1.160 ASJPH 1-3-3-8:28

cannot say to her "you shall weep no more, I will place you where sorrow cannot come"[1]

Ha says you liked the little girl I long to know if she does well I will send *Su* with Harriet early—5 oclock—I used not fear being asleep—Willy says he *will dine at home* tomorrow—with a significant smile—I shall be too happy if he means to keep his promise, *freely* and without any persuasion from me

best [page torn] Peace and [page torn] be with you—

1.161 To Rebecca Seton

[n.d.]

My own Rebecca—

dear Willy is to take *Ann Cele Will* and *Richard* to Breakfast tomorrow at Aunté's[1] HE CAN——then to *St. Marks,*[2] and then to Mrs. Kembles to dinner—so that *if it is possible*, you must come to *be of my party.* we have a plan almost too sweet to think of—if the children are better and you say you *can come* (of which I have doubted from your message "you did not know when you should see me")—we propose to send *Ha* out with Willy in the carriage at 8 or 1/2 past 7—and *you* return with it after it has taken them to Aunté's—if you say not *Ha* shall come out *at 6* as usual—Kit has been *out and in* all day and not so fretful as usual. Dué[3] is here reading *H's shepherd* and joying in to-morrow—all are skipping and laughing—Heaven's blessing on you[.] Sukey waits—best love to all—I wish I had something to send

---

[1] Isa. 30: 19-21

1.161 ASJPH 1-3-3-8:53

[1] Elizabeth Curson Farquhar, William's maternal aunt

[2] St. Mark's Episcopal Church in the Bowery near present-day 10th Street and Second Avenue was a daughter church of Trinity.

[3] Catherine Dupleix

1.162 To Rebecca Seton

8 Oclock Monday Morning 16 August 1802

"My cup has indeed run over"[1] my darling Soul's Sister—never would I have thought of such enjoyment in *this world* last night was surely a *foretaste* of the next—nor *pain* nor *weight* either of Soul or Body.

—This Morning I think I could walk out to *you* as easily as I did to the *chapel* yesterday. —Dué [2] is up[,] Richard says therefore I hope well—*Kit* has gone to Breakfast with her—she slept *all* night with Phoebe and did not come to me till 7—danced and sang all day yesterday—poor Mammy [Huler] is *better*—

Ha[3] looks quite serious at leaving me but *you* must not; I shall do very well—and if not *Dué* will stay with me 'till they send her back. Aunté[4] is sick and she ought to stay as long as she wishes it—*Our H[enry] H[obart]* was at St. *Marks* instead of St. Pauls—and Willy says those who heard him said he was a great contrast to the gentleman *we had*, who had given them in the Morning a *Schism* sermon. Surely *H.H.* knew nothing of *Schism* yesterday—Willy regretted very much he did not hear him—*regrets are idle things.*[5]

Oh when every regret will be forgot—*and every hope perfected.* I trust you will somehow be able to let me know how *you do* to day—

I will keep in mind *all* the christening concern—shall probably see *both* gentlemen to day. if so, will send out *Luke* or *Phoeby*—

The Blessings of Blessings be with you—

1.162 ASJPH 1-3-3-8:32

[1]Ps. 23

[2]Catherine Dupleix

[3]Harriet Seton, Elizabeth's sister-in-law

[4]Possibly Aunt Elizabeth Curson Farquhar

[5]Elizabeth is commenting on the Episcopal church in which Henry Hobart preached. Hobart's preaching style captivated many parishoners. In a day when solemn sermons were delivered from sheets of notes, Hobart's seemingly extemporaneous exhortations, springing from his own strong convictions, stirred his listeners.

yesterday shall while I have any birth days to keep always be considered the *Birth day* of the *Soul* never mind the 28th—

1.163 To Rebecca Seton

[August 17, 1802]

My darling Beka,

again I repeat *I never did feel better.* Peace of mind, and freedom from pain—Kit is as well and saucy as ever but I do not think it would be right to send so many or she should go to you with the girls—they are all singing "Going to Hobe's"—it cant be wrong to let them go and ask Him if he is to be at *St. Pauls or Trinity*[1] tomorrow—and by his answer Eliza can be governed—but tell her she would be wrong to lose a fine day for the sake of the *Minister*

you too must stay another week—and it makes *Mister* too saucy—I am to see J[ohn] W[ilkes] on business *he says* this afternoon and I will not fail to find out about the name—

dear dear Rebecca the *17th August* last year about *this time 3 Oclock in the afternoon*[2]—never mind someone will be *thinking of us* in a few years—

If Eliza could come early in the morning to town it would be better—but she will manage it best

—*Bless Bless Bless*

---

[1] Two of the Episcopal churches at which Henry Hobart might preach
[2] The anniversary of her father's death

1.164 To Julia Scott

New York 19th August 1802

I think my dear Julia must at this time be anxious to know if all is going well with us, and as I expect in a very few days to run the *gauntlet,*[1] I write you, tho' uncertain where to direct—as it is not probable you have stayed in the city during the late alarm—indeed I hope not, for I am sure if from any necessity you have done so—it has cost you a great deal of uneasiness—We have not heard one word of or about you since Miss Chippy's[2] departure, and [Colonel] Giles being out of town we have no prospect of hearing but from your own little self, therefore do say how you have managed thro' the Summer and if all is in as prosperous a train of Health and enjoyment as when Miss Chippy left you—

You know dear Julia one of the pleasures of my attachment to you has always been that I might speak my mind to you with freedom—and I freely tell you that she led me to suppose your manner of life, occupations, etc, were so different and distinct from any thing that such an old sober woman as I am could even think reasonable, that I have not thought of the pain my silence would give you, 'till now I think you are in trouble again which always restores to you your place in my *thoughts*—not affection—for that always remains the same—I am sure if you were necessitated to call for the proof you would find it so—

Seton interrupts me to say, "do not forget to tell Julia that Miss Shipton sailed the 9th June, and that I sent her out like a *Princess*—the Captain a smart little Batchelor, a handsome fortune—and a nephew to old Lady Fitch—that I will not answer for the consequences before they get there—that they have frequently been spoken with since they are out, and by this time have reached the Cape of *Good Hope.*[3] do not

---

1.164 ASJPH 1-3-3-6:46

[1]Elizabeth was ready to deliver her fifth child.

[2]Miss Shipton

[3]This is probably a rhetorical allusion expressing Elizabeth's hope that Miss Shipton would find a husband on her sea voyage.

omit to mention also that you have her Brother's letters very safe (locked in the only lock drawer) that no one but *yourself* and *myself* have seen *them*, that we were highly gratified by the perusal of them, and that I shall return them with my own hands as I recieved them from hers, as soon as the Fever season is over"—there dear you have his own words literally not one added or omitted—indeed I know I have been very unkind in keeping them so long—but the fear of their being lost by the way—partly depending on Col[onel] G[iles]—promising to find me a good opportunity, and partly neglect—all combined, have occasioned a fault which I fear has given you more uneasiness than you [have] chosen to express—

20th August 1802

Thus far, my very amiable little Friend, did our dear Eliza write last night[4] at 11 Oclock & this morning at twelve I have the satisfaction to tell you she was safely delivered of girl, *Great and Beautiful*, equalled, but not excelled by any of our others, which is all I should say of her at present and that the Mother is as well as she usually is on such occasions, *better* than would be expected for we had neither *Doctor* or *any thing of the kind*, till a quarter of an hour after the Young Lady[5] made her first appearance:—a serious day, you may depend for the twentieth day of August, but we are fortunately blessed with moderately cool weather and if it continues, the *Old Lady* hopes to write you again soon herself, in the meantime she begs me to assure you of her unalterable attachment and most sincere affection, in which I must heartily join and with best Regards to your Mother,[6] Sister C[harlotte]—and husband. begging to subscribe myself your sincere friend and Most devoted humble Servant Wm M Seton

---

[4]William Magee finished the letter which was interrupted when Elizabeth went into labor.

[5]Rebecca Seton (1802-1816), Elizabeth's youngest child, was born August 20. She moved to Emmitsburg with her mother in 1809 and became lame as a result of a fall while playing on the ice near Toms Creek. She died November 3, 1816, and is buried in the original cemetery of the Sisters of Charity, Emmitsburg.

[6]Susanna Deshon Sitgreaves

1.165 To Julia Scott

16th November 1802—

Dear Dear Julia

how many reproaches my heart makes me when I think of you—so many years I have called you dear friend, and shall your dear friend be insincere to you?—dear Julia—then I will tell you the plain truth, that my habits both of Soul and Body are changed—that I feel all the habits of society and connections of *this* life have taken a new form and are only interesting or endearing as they point the view to the next.[1]—we will never differ on this point, I know your side is the strongest and that you might use many and powerful arguments to prove the necessity of submission to the manners of the world and the recieved opinions which guide even the good and wise—Well, my dear friend—that blessed Influence which alone can renovate the heart, I pray (and pray with my whole Soul) may before it is too late convince you of *the Truth.* and if in a future day I should be so happy as to find it has done so, you will then allow and exult in acknowledging that the "way of the world" is not the way of God and as he has set us a pattern for our imitation, whenever you seek to be like that blessed pattern, you will find it is not the way *to Him.*[2]

This is not to say that my affection for you is lessened, for oh with what tender pity and love do we regard one who is dear to us when we see them walking in a path that leads to sorrow and pain, unconscious of their danger—No dear Julia—religion does not limit the powers of the affections, for our Blessed Saviour Sanctifies and approves in US all the endearing ties and connections of our existance, but Religion alone can bind that cord over which neither circumstances, time, or Death can have no power—Death on the contrary perfect that union which the cares, chances or sorrows of life may have interrupted by

---

1.165 ASJPH 1-3-3-6:47

[1] Elizabeth was apologizing for a falling off of her correspondence to Julia. She had written her few letters in the whole of 1802. She had become engaged in keeping a spiritual journal which possibly replaced some of her letter writing.

[2] "way *to Him*" is underlined twice.

opening the scene where all the promises hopes and consolations we have recieved from our Redeemer will have their triumphant accomplishment

now then dear friend I explain to you why I have not as much pleasure in Writing to you as I formerly had—why it appears to you (tho' erroniously) that I do not love you sincerely—dear Julia let it not be so always—but I know you will love me the better for saying it is so now—

I could tell you a great deal about my Darlings but my Thumb is bound up with poultice and I write with great difficulty—*Our Mammy [Huler] is gone*—O if you could have witnessed in her the comforts and consolations of a humble soul seeking the refuge of a redeemer, you would teach your children that to know and love Him is the ONLY GOOD—She was literally "born anew"—and died without a struggle or groan—as a child composed to rest in the arms of its Parent—sure of awaking secure—

My Babe is indeed a Blessing, so good and lovely that as yet she has been only a pleasure—they have all had uninterrupted Health the past summer—Seton is quite well—Anna very like *her mother in all things*—you must love her for that—yours I declare I could consider as my *own*—dear dear Maria—O how I pray that the tares may never choak her Harvest[3]—

Bless you again and again my Julia I never loved you so well as at this moment while I speak my heart freely to you—your friend *forever* EAS.

8th December—

Dearest friend, I find a hasty opportunity to send you *the dear letters* which I think so safe that it is better than waiting Seton's promise—We are all well and my Babe innoculated—Sister Post is also safe with a dear little Boy, we hear nothing of *YOU*—when we are to meet again in *this world* I see not the least prospect—we may look with joy to that meeting which will never more be interrupted—think

---

[3]Cf. Luke 8:7.

of it dear Julia and of your own friend with affection. Remember me to your Darlings

EAS

1.166 To Cecilia Seton

Cecilia B. Seton from her own Sister *EAS*—[1]

19th November 1802

Let your chief study be to acquaint yourself with God because there is nothing greater than God, and because it is the only knowledge which can fill the Heart with a Peace and joy, which nothing can disturb—

Father of all Beings how extensive are thy mercies! how great how inexpressible. It is in Thee we live and move and have our being—the lot of mortals is in thy hand—They are only happy thro' thee—Thy paternal cares are over all mankind—Thy impartial goodness causes thy sun to rise and constant blessings to descend on those even who offend and disobey Thee—by thy command the dew refreshes the earth, and the Zypher cools and revives us—thy gifts are proportioned to the wants of thy creatures but the *righteous* alone feel the sweet and salutary effects of thy Peace—

—O Thou who possessest sovereign power and givest life and enjoyment to the poorest insect which could not exist a moment but by thy Will; permit thy creature to praise and bless thy goodness, and give my Soul to thy Service

---

Blessed Saviour who gave thy life for us, and hast done every thing to engage our love and gratitude O let me never be so unhappy as to

---

1.166 ASJPH 1-3-3-8:87

[1]This note is written on the first page. The meditation that follows in Elizabeth's handwriting may not be her own composition.

offend or disobey thee willfully—Blessed Shepherd of them that seek thee O keep me in thy fold, lead me in thy paths, let me always hear and love thy voice and follow thee as a meek and quiet Lamb making it the care of my life to keep near to my blessed Master—and if ever I should lose my way or for a moment be so unhappy as to disobey thy commands O call thy wanderer *Home*—within the green pastures Beside the still waters led by our Shepherd—we ever will happy be, and find, endless rest—

As a little child relies
on a care beyond his own
Knows he's neither strong nor wise
Fears to stir a step alone
let me thus with Thee abide
as my Father guard and guide

———————

Father of Angels and of men
Saviour who hast us bought
Spirit by whom we're born again
and sanctified and taught
Thy glory holy three in one
Thy children's song shall be
Long as the wheels of time shall run
and to Eternity.

———————

Praise the Lord O my Soul, Praise the Lord—while I have my being I will Praise my God—Merciful Father, I bless and adore thy goodness for having preserved me this night past and brought me in safety to another day—grant me thy blessing that I may not offend nor disobey thee for in thee alone is my trust thro' Jesus Christ my Saviour who has taught me when I pray to thee to say—Our Father etc.—

Father of all mercies—Blessed be thy Goodness which has preserved me this day and brought me to the hour of rest—To thy merciful protection I humbly commit my Soul and Body, for thou only canst give me Peace and Safety—I supplicate thy blessing on me, my friends and Relations through Jesus Christ my Saviour—

O my Soul, there is a Heaven there is a Saviour, there is a pure and perfect felicity under the shadow of his wings—There is rest from our labours, peace from our enemies, freedom from our Sins—There we shall be always joyful—always beholding the presence of Him, who has purchased and prepared for us this unutterable glory—Let not your hearts be troubled—ye believe in God—believe also in me—

1803

1.167 To Cecilia Seton

8 April 1803 Good Friday[1]

Where He is there shall we be also = = We will be also—and the happy hours we have passed together thinking of Him and singing His praise, will then be remembered with the fondest delight = we will never more separate, never be weary, but day without night rejoice before his throne; and now we must keep our Hearts fixed on Him and try with all our souls to please our dear and blessed Lord = then when he calls us "Come up hither," we will fly with joy to our heavenly home

Your dear Sister

1.167 ASJPH 1-3-3-8:130
[1]Written on the outside: "B.C. Seton - 8 April 1803 Good Friday." This text appears to be copied from a spiritual writer or from sermon notes.

1.168 To Anna Maria Seton

3rd May 1803

My dear Anna Maria—

this is your Birth day—the day that I first held you in my arms—May God Almighty Bless you my Child and make you his Child forever—your Mother's Soul prays to Him to lead you through this world, so that we may come to his Heavenly Kingdom in Peace, through the merits of our blessed Saviour—[1]

1.169 To Anna Maria Seton

10th August 1803

My dearest Anna must remember that our Blessed Lord gave us the Parable of the Wise and the foolish virgins[1] to make us careful to choose our part with the wise ones and to keep in readiness for his coming—which will be in an hour we know not of, and should he find us dear child out of the road of our duty like sheep gone astray from their Shepherd where shall we hide from his presence who can see through the darkest shades and bring us from the farthest ends of the world—If we would please Him and be found among his Children we must *learn what our duty is, pray to Him for Grace to do it*, and then set out whole Heart and Soul to perform it—and what is your duty my dear dear Child—You know it, and I pray God to keep you in it that in that blessed day when He shall come to call us to our Heavenly Home we may see our (dear) Anna in the number of those dear children to whom he will say "Come ye blessed of my Father"[2]—Oh may He

---

1.168 ASJPH 1-3-3-18:65

[1]This note is addressed to Ann M Seton *No. 8 State Street*. It was written on the occasion of her eighth birthday. On the title page in another hand is written: "note from Mrs. William Seton to her sweet child who died the death of the Just at St. Joseph's Emmitsburg. R.P. Mrs. (afterwards) 'Mother Seton' was then a Protestant. Fr. [Charles] S[ouvay, C.M.]."

1.169 ASJPH 1-3-3-9:22

[1]Cf. Matt. 15:1-13.

[2]Matt. 25:34

grant this for the sake of our dear and merciful Redeemer—is the Prayer of your own dear Mother

EAS.[3]

1.170 To Anna Maria Seton

New York 23d August 1803

My own Anna Marie

do you not long to see me. I am sure you will not forget your promise to me, but will be good to all and do as Mary[1] tells you, and be very kind to her—Your dear Mother prays for you night and day and means to bring dear *Tat*[2] to see you next Thursday if the wind is fair. take good care of dear Papa while he is with you and do all you can to please Him—

May God Bless you now and forever.

Your own Mother

all send love to you[3]

---

[3]Written in another hand at the top: "(Yet a Protestant)".

1.170 ASJPH 1-3-3-18:66

[1]Possibly Mary Bayley Post, Elizabeth's sister, or Mary Seton, Elizabeth's sister-in-law.

[2]Rebecca Seton, Elizabeth's infant daughter

[3]This note is addressed to "Anna M. Seton Staten Island." On the title page is written in another hand: "From Mrs. Wm Seton to Anna Maria Seton, who died at Saint Joseph's Emmitsburg."

1.171 To Anna Maria Seton

[1803]

My dear Daughter

This book[1] was began when I was *fifteen* and written with great delight to please my Father—Since I have been a mother the idea of continuing it for my Childrens instruction and amusement as well as to give them an example of a good means <for their> of adding to the pleasure of Study and <strengthening> assisting the memory has been one of my favourite fancys—but fancy only it is, for in pursuing that train of reading which would afford extracts for this book I find the *soul* unsatisfied and turning with anxiety to those subjects you will find fully dwelt on in your *largest book*—works of imagination and even <those> the wonderful productions of Science carry the thoughts but to certain confines—those even that examine the beautiful order of creation are more suited to fill the mind that is making acquaintance with their great Author—but when the acquaintance is already made—the Soul filled with his immensity and only seperated by the "wall of past ties[?]" it is fully busied in holding tight the reins <of possession> and guarding against Surrounding danger or in searching all the strengthning means *his word* affords where alone it finds its refuge—in short the portion of time the Mother or mistress of a family can afford for reading is so precious that she finds the necessity of dwelling on "the needful" <and must leave that> and I must leave it to *you* my love to finish what I have begun—and recollect it as a Mothers intreaty that you <spend> give some time in every day if it is only half an hour to devotional reading—which is as necessary to the well ordering of the mind as the <careful> hand of the gardener to prevent the weeds destroying your favourite flower.

1.171 ASJPH 1-3-3-9:26

[1]Elizabeth was passing on a copybook of poetry to her daughter. It is now housed in the Archives at St. Joseph Provincial House, Emmitsburg, Maryland, as Rare Book #31, "EAS Copybook."

1.172 To Eliza Sadler

[probably September 20, 1803]

dear Eliza

I have at this time many thoughts to surpress when I write to you who have been so long accustomed to look into my heart, but would wish it laid open to you if possible as it relates to yourself, you would then find that in all the various relations it holds to different objects, and influences, that it has a real and affectionate attachment to you, and I am sure it will never cease to remember you with tenderness—I promise you it is full enough while it writes this—

The Vessel is chartered—freight procured—and the 25th appointed for departure[1]—but—every Morning sun shews so rapid a change and diminution of my Setons strength that if he is out of his bed at that time it is much more than the present prospect promises.

—do you like the plan of our dear Anna going with us—tho' I know you say she should not be parted from me, and tho she is so young the voyage will have its use to her in many ways and probably will be strongly remembered by her thro' life—You know that I go *fearless* for you know where, and how strong is my trust.

I had an unlooked for enjoyment last Thursday—Walked thro' the Quarantine garden and trod that wharf's every plank of which *His*[2] feet had been on. Sailed over the Bay in *His* Boat alone, with Darby at the Sail and William[3] who used to go with Him to get Snipes[4] at the Helm—Darby says "I never can meet such a friend again"—"the best friend I had" said William "I got out of my sick bed to row Him that last row round the Island, and then thinks I here goes the poor mans

---

1.172 ASJPH 1-3-3-7:27

[1]Elizabeth was referring to the trip the Setons were planning to Leghorn, Italy, in the hope of improving William's health. The following seven letters and notes were farewells to her children and closest friends.

[2]Elizabeth's deceased father, Dr. Richard Bayley

[3]Two of Dr. Bayley's friends from his Staten Island days

[4]A long-billed brownish wading bird

friend never mind if the row is too much for me"—the hour I was coming over was the shortest of that day—

My little William went to the church on Sunday, laid his face covered with his hands on his Grandfathers tomb[5] and nothing but shame of the people round him could get him away or stop his tears—Harriet says "indeed Sister it made my Heart ach"—dear little fellow He will often have reason to repeat his tears. Seton calls Heaven bless you

Your EAS.

Affectionate love to Mrs. *MacV[ickers],*[6] and the dear girls

11 Oclock Tuesday Morning

1.173 To Eliza Sadler

5 Oclock Wednesday 28th September [1803]

My dear dear Eliza—

Your tenderness and affection calls me back—for often often with all I have to do I forget I am here. the cloud that would overpower—can only be borne by striving to get above it— Seton has had new and severe suffering since I saw you—all say it is presumption and next to madness to undertake our Voyage—but you know we reason differently.—Saturday is Now the day every thing is ready and on board—the signature of some paper not ready detains us—

We will dear Eliza rest upon Him our only strength and my soul is thankful for surely with all the many calls we have to resign our hopes in this life we naturally without one lingering pain must seek our rest above—can it be that we will be there to seperate no more—

---

[5]Dr. Richard Bayley was buried at St. Andrew's Episcopal Church, Richmondtown, Staten Island.

[6]A friend and co-worker of Elizabeth and Eliza Craig Sadler

1.173 ASJPH 1-3-3-7:28

with the strong and ardent Faith with which I recieve and dwell on this promise—all is well and resting on the mercy of God—

May He Bless you as my Soul blesses you and raise you above the sorrow and pains with which your soul has so long struggled—dear dear Eliza my Heart trembles within me, and I can only say take my darlings often in your arms, and do not let the remembrance of any thing I have ever done that has vexed you come twice to your thoughts—I know it will not—but it seems now to me like my last hour with all that I love.

tell my dear Mrs. McV[ickers] that the thought of her affectionate good wishes [for me] add strength and comfort to my heart—I have often told Rebecca that when I think of the meeting of dear friends in Heaven Mrs. McV. always is one of the foremost in the scene—dear dear dear Eliza farewell—

1.174 To Julia Scott

1st October 1803—

My ever dear Julia

When I tell you that I have in the month of August weaned a sick Baby[1]—Broke up Housekeeping and been ever since in hourly expectation of embarking for Leghorn[2]—you will easily concieve that there has been no possibility of dwelling on the subject in a letter to you—My Setons decline is so rapid that there can be no hope of his recovery in the view of MORTAL HOPES—but knowing who holds the scale and how merciful is his guidance—My soul reposes on that Mercy and now feels the full force of those consolations I have so often wished you to know the value of—

The Signal for coming on Board is already given All my Earthly concerns are settled as if by the hour of death—and in this sacred hour

---

1.174 ASJPH 1-3-3-6:51

[1]Rebecca Seton, Elizabeth's fifth child

[2]Leghorn, Italy, the Setons' destination on their sea voyage

my Soul implores for you the friend of my first and warmest Affections—that *Peace* which God alone can give—Your *EAS.* William has put up for *you* a Box because it is marked *W.E.S.*—and a picture he thought you would like—Bless your dear children for me—and my dear Charlott and Brother [Samuel]

1.175 To William Seton

[October 1803]

My dear William

you know how dearly your own Mother loves you and how much I wish to see you good, I hope you are so particularly by so dear Godmother[1] I am glad that you go to school and learn so fast—for that will please dear Papa—who sends you much love and many kisses and so does dear Anna[2]—and

your own Mother *EAS.*

1.176 To Richard Seton

[October 1803]

My own Richard

Your dear Mother loves you more than she can tell and hopes you will be a good Boy—and mind what your dear God Mother[1] says to you and she will do every thing to make you happy—if you love me, do not plague your sweet Kate for that would make dear Maman very

---

1.175 ASJPH 1-3-3-9:8

[1] William Seton was staying with Rebecca Seton, Elizabeth's sister-in-law.

[2] Anna Maria Seton accompanied her parents on the trip to Italy.

1.176 ASJPH 1-3-3-9:47f

[1] Rebecca Seton, Elizabeth's sister-in-law

unhappy. Remember My Dick to pray for us every Night and Morning and your dear Mother and Father will pray to God to bless you and make you a good boy. Papa and Sister sends you a Kiss

Your own Mother. *EAS*

1.177 To Cecilia Seton

1 October 1803

My own dear Cecilia

Altho I leave you in the hands of your dearest friends,[1] and under the Protecting care of Our dear and Heavenly Father still my heart would dictate to you many anxious requests respecting your habitual observance of that Heavenly Christian life you have so early begun—and in order to presevere in this your first attention must be to make to yourself a few particular Rules which you must not suffer any thing on Earth to divert you from as they relate immediately to your sacred duty to God. and if you find that here are any obstacles in your way, and doubtless you will find many as every Christian does in the fulfilment of <their> his duty Still Persevere with yet more earnestness, and rejoice to bear your share in the *Cross* which is Our Passport and Seal to the Kingdom of our Redeemer—nor will your steadiness of conduct ever injure you, even in the minds of those who act differently from you, for all who love you will respect and esteem you the more for persevering in what you know to be your duty—

and may the divine Spirit strengthen your Soul in His service and make your way plain before you, that whatever are the changes in this our mortal life we may find our Rest in that Blessed Fold where dear friends will no more be seperated—but Perfect the Virtues and Affec-

1.177 ASJPH 1-3-3-8:88
[1]The James Seton family

tions which have connected them Here by the Crown of Immortal Life
and Glory—

Your own dear *EAS.*

1.178 To Rebecca Seton

Quarantine 2nd Oct[obe]r 1803[1]

My dearest Sister—

My Souls Sister—We are quietly seated at Dear Bayleys,[2] and are
not to go to sea untill 10 Oclock tomorrow—Our Willy felt the passing our Battery[3] so much that I scarcely dared wave my dear Red
Handkerchief—but since that has been very composed and better than
on shore—My Heart is lifted, feels *its treasure*[4] and the little cabin and
my cross are objects of Peace and sweet comfort—He is with me and
what can I fear—ten thousand loves to My Darlings and *most* to my
dear Girls—

I shall write you by Henry[5]—who will tell you I have had a raven-
ous Appetite and been very cheerful—Your being sick is my greatest
care—but that too must be refered to Our *All Sufficient.*

My Friend and Brothers deserted dwelling started my first
tear—the dear study windows were all I c[oul]d see—

Your own own Sis

Page is to keep Mrs. McDugals letter till Mrs. Vandeuzen[6] sends for
it—

1.178 AMSV Seton-Jevons #561-563 (photostat) No original exists.

[1]Elizabeth was at the quarantine station on Staten Island.

[2]Joseph Bayley, formerly Dr. Richard Bayley's assistant at the quarantine station

[3]William Magee Seton reacted emotionally at seeing their home on State Street as the ship left.

[4]Religious books and notes which Elizabeth brought with her

[5]Henry Seton, Elizabeth's brother-in-law, who would be returning to New York

[6]The Vanduzer family on Staten Island had a farm, sold provisions, and ran a ferry. They probably
carried mail as well.

Undated Notes and Letters

1794-1803

1.179 Draft to Lady Isabella Cayley[1]

My dear Aunt,

I am charged with a commission to You, by my Father,[2] who requests me to inform you that relying on his long established friendship for you as well as this Knowledge of your Goodness of Heart and Benevolence, he begs of you to take the trouble of drawing for Mr. Gaurineau[3] forty pounds a year (if so much is necessary to his maintanance) in quarterly payments of ten Pounds <a quarter>—<My Father is very anxious to interest you> He requests this of you as a very great favour Knowing that through you the Money will be <punctually> paid to him when you see it necessary— <[unclear] would be very happy to hear that my [unclear] health is mended,> He also wishes to know who the person is, whom Mr. John Gaurineau placed his Father with, what his Character is, and how much is due to him—I must again repeat that this is giving you too much trouble, but it is by the particular request of my Father, which I hope will plea My excuse. I hope you are well and that my Uncles[4] health is mended, I am

very affectionately yours Eliza[beth] A. Seton

If you will be so good as to let me hear from you I shall recieve any letter at William Setons No. 65 Stone Street near the Custom house[5]

1.179 AMSV 110:10,1

[1]Isabella Seton Cayley, William Magee Seton's paternal aunt, who lived in England

[2]Probably William Seton, Sr., Elizabeth's father-in-law

[3]A Mr. Guerineau was the second husband of Elizabeth Seton's paternal grandmother, but it is not known whether he had any connection with Lady Cayley.

[4]Sir Thomas Cayley

[5]There is a note on the reverse in a different hand: "This is written (I am perfectly sure) to Lady Thomas Cayley, who she always styles aunt and 'Father' is only father-in-law."

1.180 To Eliza Sadler

My dear Eliza's little Rapsody reached us last night and added a smile to the smiling scene—the company of Miss Chippy[1] this morning for 3 hours has so blunted my brighter powers that except the assurance that we are all well and remember Sad with affection I have not a word to say—Bless you—Emma[2] will tell you all about us.

Your E.A.S. Sunday Afternoon

1.181 To Eliza Sadler

My own Eliza

this little Note would have been sent you this Morning but there has been a spell on my time—Seton, my Father, Mrs. Kemble, Mrs [Mary] Wilks with whom I was obliged to spend two hours, has bewildered me—and now I can only ask you if the Cold is not too intolerable to come out, but my heart longs to be with you as it would with little Dick if I had not seen him all the day—

it is too much to ask you to come and to you I cannot go, for I am almost lame with pains, from the cold—pity the poor old woman

Your E.A.S.

1.182 To Dr. Richard Bayley

It is not the first time that Pearl has been thrown before—S ....[1]—but the cup must be full and dear Darby[2] suffered to come to us to help her finish it.

1.180 ASJPH 1-3-3-7:9
 [1]Miss Shipton
 [2]Charlotte Bayley Craig, Elizabeth's half-sister and Eliza Craig Sadler's sister-in-law
1.181 ASJPH 1-3-3-7:22
1.182 ASJPH 1-3-3-9:71
 [1]Swine, a reference to Matt. 7:6
 [2] Dr. Bayley's Staten Island friend

Still running up stairs to the spy glass—I cannot believe that so much time would be voluntarily lost by a man of business—

Shall I keep Miss D until they come She refers to me—think of Emma[3]—and if it is not indispensable to offer her the air of Staten Island

Your own own own

1.183 To Dr. Richard Bayley

Anchorite—that expresses Solitude, Leisure, and—Peace. If my Father possesses these his Betty *is*, the amount of all, Content. No gardening to day—Mr. Olive has been apparently Breathing his last these 4 days past. this Morning he is better, and my *Note of request* is to go by Mr. Cheriot this Evening if he leaves town—

The Vessel *Minerva* that took *my* and the Cramberrys kiss and Eteceteras to *my* Doux[1] arrived in 30 days. good—very good. The Birds sing so loud and so sweet one might really suppose the Season *six weeks* more advanced—

The corner of the Sofa is vacant and looks melancholy—whenever there are any Lucubrations[2] to spare think of your Betty—

Thursday Morning. *26th March*

You have 4 pine Apples and a Dolphin Cheese by Captain Niel, which will be sent tomorrow. they cannot be got at till this Evening

---

[3]Charlotte Bayley Craig, Elizabeth's half-sister
1.183 ASJPH 1-3-3-9:72
[1]Catherine Dupleix
[2]Deep meditations, ponderous thoughts

1.184 To Dr. Richard Bayley

Good Morning to my Father

Kate is better—we are all well and anxiously looking for arrivals—The Southern Papers and Your Betty's . . . .—
The *Shadan*[1] arrived, thanks

1.185 To Dr. Richard Bayley

The Papers and your Bettys enquiry if you are well with the remembrances and affection of the little circle, who are all well and delighted with the Sun shine and promise of soon going to see Grand Pappa—
Rebecca intends eating one Duck and *I* the other as knowing best the value of them, taking it for granted you shot them on purpose for us. poor Seton—

Saturday Morning 12 Oclock—

1.186 To Dr. Richard Bayley

My Father,

to say how much I am out of Patience with the Weather, or how often I have desired to share the storm with you is impossible—
Inclosed is Miss Hays[1] answer—
The question is if the Captain who is to take the Deer will be allowed to come to the Custom House dock—The bad weather delays

---

1.184 ASJPH 1-3-3-9:73
[1]Perhaps one of the ships of Seton, Maitland and Company
1.185 ASJPH 1-3-3-9:74
1.186 ASJPH 1-3-3-9:75
[1]The director of the school in Brunswick, New Jersey, which Helen, one of Dr. Bayley's daughters, attended

him til Tuesday—Will not these Easterly winds bring my
Friend—"Thought in fancy's mase runs mad"

> Bless Bless—Your Betty.
> 10 Oclock Saturday Morning

1.187 To Dr. Richard Bayley

I was in hopes this fine day would have induced my Father to have
made us a visit—The arrival from Cork[1] awakened Many Hopes, but
the *spell* yet continues and there are no letters either for me or D__.

Seton bids me say a ship arrived this Morning from England, left
Plymouth the 5th of this month. *the king* was at the point of
Death—that day reported to be dead—Mr. Pitt had refused to surren-
der his office—etc.—[2]

We are all well—Many remembrances to you—

> Your *EAS*[3]

1.188 To Dr. Richard Bayley

—Tho' I am not quite without hopes of seeing my Father this day,
the weather discourages me—on Saturday, or Sunday, Captain
Leader, in a Schooner bound to Port au Prince, owned by Mr. Hurtin,
will call for the Dear Deers—an accommodation is prepared for them,
you are to find hay and corn, and will share the net Proceeds of their
sale with the owner—

Miss Hay's[1] reply to my letter is not yet arrived—on Saturday vacation commences, and on Monday they leave school, but to-morrows

---

1.187 ASJPH 1-3-3-9:76

[1]The arrival of a ship from Ireland

[2]King George III of England (1738-1820) suffered severe attacks at this time. William Pitt
(1759-1806) became Prime Minister in 1783, left office in 1801, and returned to office in 1804.

[3]Rev. Simon Gabriel Bruté has written on the outside: "Some letters to and from Mr. Bayley her
father See his name in *Encyclopedia American.*"

1.188 ASJPH 1-3-3-9:77

[1]The director of the boarding school in Brunswick, New Jersey, which Helen, Dr. Bayley's
daughter, attended

Post will I suppose determine the day Bayley is to go for Helen[2]—Every walk Seton makes on the Battery he says "I dare say *they* will be here tomorrow"—Kate looks most Beautiful—all are on the look out for Dué[3] I have requested Miss D. to stay with us until their arrival—Bless you dear dear Sir—the little turtle was not dressed yesterday in hopes the Sun would shine to day—at 3 Oclock if I should see the door open how my heart would dance—

Your Betty.
10 Oclock Thursday Morning

1.189 To William Magee Seton

My love I send your cloaths Brush and comb which I forgot this Morning and also to remind you of the Box of Silver and the Bread Basket in my Press which will not lock—Is it possible that I am not to see you again for so long a time. Heaven Protect you, and return you again in safety. Your Darlings have enjoyed this cool day and are merry as Birds they cannot understand that Papa is not to come nor to-morrow—nor next-day nor the day after—that is for their Mother to feel—

Thomas says there is no other mat at [unclear] that he searched the garret, and every part of the House and left nothing but the drawers—I think it best to commission John to get the Pork—if you think so tell him—

I think you will have a very fair day to-morrow. I write to Beck[1] to go by to-morrows Post—

Your own E.A.S.

Old Mr. Wilks is just come to tea and I cannot finish Becks letter which I will give to Mr. W tomorrow—Dear Dear William farewell

---

[2]Dr. Richard Bayley's servant was to bring Helen home from school.
[3]Catherine Dupleix
1.189 ASJPH 1-3-3-9:69
[1]Rebecca Seton, Elizabeth's sister-in-law

1.190 To Rebecca Seton

My Rebecca can hardly imagine her own Sister *quiet* Soul and body. Anna asleep—Willy *sound,* and apparantly quite easy—he has had too much appetite and talked too much is all I have to regret for Him and I cannot help looking to the hope that he will gain strength—however you know I have no concern in my own hands they are in His who alone can guide them right—

How much I wish my own Friend could know the many comforts around me—

1.191 To Rebecca Seton

Since a *quarter* before three I have been, O how happy—come come "Souls Sister"—*let us Bless the day together one Body, one Spirit, one hope, one God.* —The Father of *All.*[1] I think our Willy will go—he has not left me five minutes since yesterday's dinner, and has had *Nelson*[2] in his hand very often—if he does, what a dinner will *to day's* be to me.

I must run for *Ha* it is near 5. all sound asleep Pinté passed a quiet night

PEACE

1.190 ASJPH 1-3-3-8:3
1.191 ASJPH 1-3-3-8:5

[1] Eph. 4:4-6

[2] Robert Nelson, *A Companion for the Festivals and Fasts of the Church of England: With Collects and Prayers for Each Solemnity* was first published in London in 1736. A revision by Rev. John Henry Hobart was published in 1804 for members of the Protestant Episcopal church in America.

1.192 To Rebecca Seton

My own Rebecca—

my Heart and Soul sympathizes with poor Eliza, and your cares and anxiety—poor girl she really has a hard trial, and I can see you with the goodness of a superior being making her troubles your own—dear dear Rebecca He who sees in secret will reward you—it is sorrowfull time indeed—and my Willy seems almost knocked up—if ever I dared indulge anticipations of Evil it would be at present for I feel worse than melancholy

whatever you get for a gown for yourself let me have the same, and if you get it made I shall prefer it—much love to Mary[1]—Richard still says God-ma come take walk—They are all very well Willy hurries me—*Heaven bless you*

Sunday evening—

1.193 To Rebecca Seton

Just got Home darling not very much heated but am troubled at not having a word from Maitland[1]—May Him above direct for the best—Blessed Blessed H[enry] H[obart]—Mr. Jones[2] had his place—and I ventured to ask if we had lost Mr. H[obart]—Poor man was the reply he has been attending *his Mother* whom Dr. Rush[3] has given over and suffers a great deal of fatigue and distress on her account was summoned to her, the Monday after *our Sunday.*—well might I see him heated, wearied and covered with dust—and your dreams will make us too supersti[ti]ous—I should like to hear some of

1.192 ASJPH 1-3-3-8:13
[1]Mary Seton, Elizabeth's sister-in-law
1.193 ASJPH 1-3-3-8:14
[1]James Maitland, Elizabeth's brother-in-law
[2]Rev. Cave Jones was one of the assistant ministers at Trinity Episcopal Church.
[3]Benjamin Rush was a prominent Philadelphia physician.

Dué's[4] visions too—Pinté is calling Rebeka all over the House—the General is just munching his Indian pudding[5] Willy has very little pain—and it is quite cheerful—Lot[6] at the Piano—Harriet trying to fill your place and Cecilia and Anna in their room—

I am going to write as usual when afraid of *self*—I wish you may be asleep at the quarter past 2. if not think of your *"Souls Sister"* and I charge you do not walk to me in the heat—Friday morning is soon enough

1.194 To Rebecca Seton

My dear Rebecca,

the cheerful fire is blazing and Dick has on his small cloaths for the *Winter*—*we* shall soon have our feet on the fender I hope and Kitten on the knee toasting—happy thoughts these are, and as Willy is cheerful I delight to indulge them. —You left Aunty[1] Monday I take it for granted, if not you must be still so near yet far off—but it dont do to reflect—My Willy talks of staying till next Tuesday therefore dont wait for his return to write—

best love to Eliza and Mary, have you heard of Vinings family—is Bun better—and how is Richard[2]—let Maitland[3] leave your little note with Willy Ogden[.][4] Abraham[5] [is] not expected till next month— a thousand blessing to you

Your own Sis *E.A.S.*
Thursday morning 8 Oclock

---

[4]Catherine Dupleix

[5]A pudding made of Indian meal, molasses, and suet; the same as hasty-pudding, frequently served in New England.

[6]Charlotte Seton, Elizabeth's sister-in-law

1.194 ASJPH 1-1-1-8:17

[1]Elizabeth Curson Farquhar, William Magee Seton's aunt

[2]Elizabeth is inquiring about Rebecca's sisters and brothers: Eliza Seton Maitland, Mary Seton, Anna Maria Seton Vining, and Richard Seton.

[3]James Maitland, Elizabeth's brother-in-law

[4]Brother of Abraham Ogden

[5]Abraham Ogden, an agent of Seton, Maitland and Company

waiting breakfast for the Health officer[6] who sings all day "Shape nor feature" I wrote Sunday by W. Ogden—and Tuesday by my Father—have you recieved?—

1.195 To Rebecca Seton

I need not tell you my dear girl that your *little* note made tears of anguish roll, indeed I never before suffered such a Struggle to show a contented face—I would travel bare foot to share your blessing—but all will not do and *all I* can do is to strive to obtain the *fruit* by applying to the means. that *you* are happy gives a comfort to *my* every hour, and I delight in tracing even while sitting in *the crowd* the Peace that now pervades the Soul of my darling Sister.—

Is it not hard to leave *J[ohn] W[ilkes]* in the hope of seeing you this Evening—to-morrow Willy will give you an account of *my day*—

Your own Sis EAS
Sunday afternoon

1.196 To Rebecca Seton

Who shall dare to distrust *His* mercy—this morning Sun found me without a *Penny*—it is now setting and *We* are worth 20 dollars in possession and the Ladies have to refund me *10.* tomorrow then we shall have 30—delightful. *the cruse does not fail*[1]

I could not find the woman in Catherine Street—and Mrs. Gibbs had moved from Ann Street[2]—but called on Mrs. Startin[3] and got the

[6]Dr. Richard Bayley, Elizabeth's father
1.195 ASJPH 1-3-3-8:23
1.196 ASJPH 1-3-3-8:31
[1]Cf. 1 Kings 17:14-16.
[2]Widows visited by the Society for the Relief of Poor Widows
[3]Sarah Startin, Elizabeth's godmother

ten—called on Parson Linn[4] who is to be here tomorrow at *12*. Willy told me a man had brought a hat here and required *2 dollars* and knowing it could not be for me and not knowing for who sent it back with the promise of sending for it if called for. *so it goes*—Contradiction. We meet at Mrs. Burrells[5] in Pine Street—best love to Lize—

your own Sis EAS

1.197 To Rebecca Seton

My own Rebecca—

an unexpected Boat offers—two Notes from Rebecca my Sis[1] two letters from Willy and 2 from J[ohn] W[ilkes] crowned the Peace of yesterday—too much for once—but your account of my poor Lidy's troubles made the ballance, and my wish to have you here, and still that you should show her the attentions and affection she must so greatly stand in need of. Father in Heaven preserve her. Bless your repentance my own Sister—Yours is Godly sorrow indeed—such is of more value than the most lively joy, and will surely be comforted with lasting Peace. the uninterrupted blessings that are to ensue will make the heavy hours and days seem only bitter momentary recollections of a past storm—I have to write to Julia Scott, who is in New York, and would "die with terror if she crossed the Bay"—Mrs. *J[ohn] W[ilkes]* too, a line—Peace be with you—His Peace—

Thursday afternoon 4 Oclock

Your own Sis *EAS*

Darlings as well as possible—they are landing one hundred sick men women and children from one vessel. 400 on board—Father of Miseries[2]

---

[4]Rev. William Linn, Presbyterian minister
[5]One of the members of the Widows Society
1.197 ASJPH 1-3-3-8:36
[1]These three words are inside a drawn box.
[2]Written on the outside: "Rebecca *'unique'* with 2 letters from WMS to keep until I see her."

1.198 To Rebecca Seton

My love

your Kate is better but still suffers more than you can imagine—She is crying for me while I write. *upon my word* I am well—but long to see you I send Miss More—Nelson and your book[1]—with ten thousand blessings to you and remembrances to dear Eliza—all are well and merry, I heard Cecilia this Morning and *she* heard the rest.

Bless Bless you

1.199 To Rebecca Seton

My own Rebecca

I inclosed a letter for Willy and a note for you to Mr. [John] Wilkes on Sunday and am perfectly melancholy at not having heard from either of you since Friday, but suppose it is owing to the uncertainty of the hour that the Boat goes, or the inattention of those who have charge of my letters for I am very sure *if all is well* there must be some—

Your Darlings are very well I am very happy in my *Dreams*, and always far happier than my *aspiring* Soul deserves to be, which ought to be content with enjoyments such as any Mortal might covet,—but—Write to me my Darling one of Eliza's weeks are almost gone—is Henry[1] come—*little* Seton returned and how is my sweet God-child and Bunzy—I wrote the girls yesterday by Miss Wall *who* came for our commands, and was to go to Brunswick[2] to

---

1.198 ASJPH 1-3-3-8:38

[1]Books Elizabeth was sending to Rebecca included Robert Nelson's *A Companion for the Festivals and Feasts of the Church of England: With Collects and Prayers for Each Solemnity.* Hannah More was a prominent English moralist and writer who published *Strictures on the Modern System of Female Education* in 1799.

1.199 ASJPH 1-3-3-8:39

[1]Henry Seton, Elizabeth's brother-in-law

[2]William's younger half-sisters were at school in Brunswick, New Jersey.

day—all goes well—there are *some* hours of Peace which are a fore-taste—come and sweeten all—

Your *EAS*
Tuesday Afternoon—

1.200 To Rebecca Seton

The afternoon yesterday (*if there had been no regrets*) was too sweet. but those regrets are part of the portion, and point the anxious thoughts to that place where they will be *no more*. Mrs. Livingstone[1] *is*—at rest with *him*. oh Rebecca— She was good and amiable, and the trial is now past—

Your Kate looks still at the door with the shake of the head. No Anta Becka[2] all is well—if you have not undone you[r] hat, it is no matter. J[ohn] W[ilkes] from some expressions will never think of it as we supposed.

The storm hangs heavy and my heart is—Ditto. Bless you *look up*—A thousand loves to Eliza and [her] darlings—Cecilia is *well*—

Your Sis

2 Oclock the linnen is all out *10 shirts*

1.201 To Rebecca Seton

My darling girl

again but a moment Thomas waits. I have had a busy day *over hauling*. but *all well*. Our disappointment will be lessened for you

1.200 ASJPH 1-3-3-8:41
[1]Mrs. Livingston, one of Elizabeth's prominent friends from the Widows Society, died in May 1801.
[2]A nickname for Rebecca Seton
1.201 ASJPH 1-3-3-8:48

cannot come to-morrow as the storm is increasing here—every blessing of the Soul be with you—

Your Sis

love to my dear Lidy—Willy is marching with *Kit* while I write—
5 Oclock 3rd vol Miss More—[1]

1.202 To Rebecca Seton

My darling—

I have been laying all the morning on the Bed with your Pinny[1]—who has a good deal of fever and sleeps all the while—Willy went for Post at *7* and it is now *12* and he had not seen her—she is still asleep and does not seem to suffer—I have heard all the girls—and given them work and was *composing* myself when Carlo told me *Mr. H[obart]* sent up to know if we were *all* well. I went down quietly as possible but *trembled* rather too much even for a Christian—told me a great deal about his mother and sister, and that he had brought home her son to educate him as his own—He says he is to read Prayers this week and probably *next* also, and *certainly* (if nothing new hinders) in St. Pauls if not at Trinity[2]—said a great deal about *my happy day*—

I told him the last 24 hours were the happiest I had ever seen or could ever expect as the most earnest wish of my heart was fulfilled—dear Rebecca if you had known how sweet last evening was—Willy's heart seemed to be nearer to me for being nearer to his God,—from absolute weariness of Body I fell asleep at *11*, and left him with *Nelson* in his hand—I read *8* chapters between 1 and 2.

—This is *dear Malta's* birth day—there are *two* big apple pies—and Richard[3] not come back—

---

[1]See 1.198 n 1.

1.202 ASJPH 1-3-3-8:54

[1]A sick baby

[2]Two of the Episcopal churches in New York

[3]Richard Seton, Elizabeth's son, or Richard Bayley, her half-brother

Post has been—and we have given the darling castor—she is in trouble enough you may be sure—take care of yourself *as much as you can*

Pinny stretches out her arm—

Heaven bless *you*

1.203 To Rebecca Seton

Mr. Woffendale[1] has just been hauling at my poor tooth and broke it short off the three prongs remaining for life I suppose—Well, that is done

—J[ohn] W[ilkes] suggested the idea this morning of your bringing the Boys to town while Eliza is away to take the range of the Battery and that you may sit quietly by poor Sis. it is a good thought—but much I fear the nay too—ask Lidy—

Sister James and James[2] were here this morning. I believe they think me an unfeeling wretch not to answer one tear—but no matter—my tears are dry—they are left with all the agonies that occasioned them on the garret floor at Staten Island—[3]

poor Hen[4] is gone—I expect you *may* come tomorrow therefore do not return the notes—certainly their writer must be very interesting—You know Rebecca how I used to wish *to go*—now I dare not—my William seems as if his life and mine were one—do come if you can in haste and pain

your Sis—
Wednesday Afternoon

1.203 ASJPH 1-3-3-8:56
[1]Her dentist
[2]Mary and James Seton, Elizabeth's sister- and brother-in-law
[3]She is probably referring to her father's death.
[4]Henry Seton, Elizabeth's brother-in-law

1.204 To Rebecca Seton

I find by Anderson that poor Maitland[1] is seriously ill—do my love send if there is any thing we have or can do—you of course cannot come, and I am satisfied—the Father of Mercies save my Rebecca. Cecilia is just asking "what was that good thing that Mary chose."[2] Sweet Celia she is my blessing
—*Will* has been already to the Bank and says Maitland must nurse himself and make himself as easy as possible.

Your EAS

James[3] is just gone with a note

1.205 To Richard Seton

dearest Richard

Mamma longs to kiss you and hold you in her arms—do not forget your duty towards God and be very good to Mary and Cele[1] and Anna take care of Kitty and do not do any thing to vex her if you love me—Pat[2] sends you plenty of kisses and so does your own Mother

---

1.204 ASJPH 1-3-3-8:58
[1] James Maitland, Elizabeth's brother-in-law
[2] Cf. Luke 10:42.
[3] James Seton, Elizabeth's brother-in-law
1.205 AMPH S-J #462
[1] Mary and Cecilia Seton, Elizabeth's sisters-in-law
[2] Probably Paté or father

Elizabeth Ann Bayley and William Magee Seton around the time of their marriage (1794)
(Courtesy, Archives of Mount Saint Vincent, New York)

Dr. Richard Bayley

The Rt. Rev. John Henry Hobart, D.D.
(Courtesy, The Parish of Trinity Church
in the City of New York)

The second Trinity Church (1788-1839), facing Broadway (Courtesy, The Parish of Trinity Church in the City of New York)

The curved and columned front of No. 8 State Street, the Seton's home from 1801 to 1803 (1859 print)

PART II

The Italian Journey 1803-1804
Letters and Journals

1803

The journal in Part II is written to Elizabeth's sister-in-law, Rebecca Seton. In this part of her writings, Elizabeth often referred to her husband, William, and her daughter, Anna Maria, both of whom accompanied her on the trip to Italy, and to her children left in New York, William, Richard, Catherine, and the infant Rebecca. She also wrote often about the Filicchi brothers, Filippo and Antonio, and their wives, Mary and Amabilia.

2.1 To Rebecca Seton

New Light House 12 Oclock 3rd October [1803]

My dearest Rebecca—

our William is quite easy without stricture of the Breast, Fever, or cough in any great degree Sweat as much as usual, but slept very well from 7 to eleven, and from 1/2 past eleven until 1/2 past three—He has more appetite than I wish as it brings on Fever invariably—but as he certainly is even now stronger than when he left Home I trust that will soon wear off—Anna has been very sick but after releiving her stomach has fallen asleep Mrs. O[1] and her child are also in their Birth and Willy is pondering over his molasses and spoon not very well able to

2.1 ASCSH Seton-Jevons #164-165

[1] Mrs. O'Brien was the wife of the captain of the *Shepherdess*, the ship on which the Setons traveled to Italy. Elizabeth refers to her and her husband as "Mrs. O" and "Captain O."

keep his legs but not at all sick—I am as usual sober and quiet[,] made my Breakfast with a great relish and it still sets very comfortable—

I feel so satisfied in my hidden Treasure[2] that you might think me an old rock—Mr. and Mrs. OBrien are really kind friends to us the steward seems as anxious to please me as even our Mary[3] could be—and a dear little child about 18 months makes me sigh for Tatle Beck[4] as I told my Bayley[5] I neither look behind nor before only up, there is my rest, and I want nothing.

—one Oclock—

Henry[6] is leaving us, all goes well—the Lord on high is mightiest—they threaten a Storm—but I fear not with Him—

Your EAS.

Bless my darling Girls for me and many loves to my little ones[7]—

2.2 To Eliza Sadler

Lighthouse one Oclock 3d October 1803

My dear Eliza will be glad to hear that after passing 24 hours on Board our ship all is well and comfortable—Seton without pain has a good appetite, and good spirits—Little Anna has been very sick the sea has a great swell and we are Rocking or Pitching without intermission—I have not the least disposition to sickness, and quietly hug my hidden Treasure[1] without looking behind or before—only upwards.—

---

[2]Probably religious books and notes which Elizabeth brought with her. In a later journal entry she spoke of enjoying "my Bible, commentaries, Kempis." She also had copies of some of Henry Hobart's sermons in a notebook.

[3]Probably a servant in the Seton household

[4]Elizabeth's daughter Rebecca was about thirteen months old at the time. "Tatle" is probably derived from the French term for a nursing child.

[5]Joseph Bayley, who worked at the Staten Island quarantine

[6]Henry Seton, a brother of William Magee Seton, was a lieutenant in the United States Navy and accompanied the Setons until their ship left New York harbor.

[7]William Magee Seton's younger half-sisters, Charlotte, Mary, Harriet, and Cecilia, as well as her own children, William, Richard, and Catherine, who were in Rebecca's care. The infant Rebecca was staying with Elizabeth's sister, Mary Bayley Post, and her family.

2.2 ASJPH 1-3-3-7:29

[1]Probably religious books and notes Elizabeth brought with her on the voyage

Peace to my dear Eliza and our dear friend MV—I was an hour at Bayleys last evening in Fathers room, in the very spot I last stood[2]—His spirit I know is with his own darling[3]—the Divine Spirit speaks Peace and what can be added—the Pangs of Parting Nature would press but He over rules all—

Your EAS.

2.3 To Julia Scott[1]

28th October 1803

We are now past the western Islands[2] which are exactly half way between N[ew] Y[ork] & Leghorn and hourly expect to meet some vessel that may take our letters Home—as I am sure my very dear Friend will be among the first enquirers of news from us, I write, tho' sure there can be little to interest you after saying that my Seton is daily getting better, and that little Ann & myself are well—If I dared indulge my Enthusiasm and describe as far as I could give them words my extravagant Enjoyments in gazing on the Ocean, and the rising & setting sun, & the moonlight Evenings, a quire of Paper would not contain what I should tell you—but one subject you will share with me which engages my whole Soul—the dear the tender the gracious love with which every moment has been marked in these my heavy hours of trial—

—you will believe because you know how blessed they are who rest on our Heavenly Father—not one struggle nor desponding thought to contend with—confiding Hope and consoling Peace has attended my way thro' storms and dangers that must have terrified a Soul whose Rock is not Christ

---

[2]Joseph Bayley, who had been Dr. Richard Bayley's assistant, was living in the house in which her father had lived before his death.

[3]Elizabeth herself

2.3 ASJPH 1-3-3-6:52

[1]Although this is part of the collection of Scott letters, it consists of only one page and does not include any outside address as found with other letters in this collection.

[2]Probably the Azores

2.4 To Richard Seton[1]

[n.d.]

My Dear Richard

your own Mother loves you dearly and is delighted to hear you are such a good Boy—and are so fond of going to school. Oh how pleased Papa will be to hear you spell. be good to little Seton and Ben and love Aunt Maitland[2]—Papa and Sister Ann send you a kiss.

your mother EAS[3]

2.5 Journal to Rebecca Seton[1]

8th November in Gibraltar Bay—

Was climbing with great difficulty a Mountain of immense height and blackness when near the top, almost exhausted a voice said—"Never mind take courage there is a beautiful green hill on the other side—and on it an angel waits for you." (at that moment Willy woke me to help him[2])

2.4 ASJPH 1-3-3-18:62

[1]Richard, William, and Catherine Seton, Elizabeth's three middle children, were left in the charge of Rebecca Seton, Elizabeth's sister-in-law, who was staying with the James Maitland family.

[2]William Seton Maitland, Benjamin Maitland, and their mother Eliza Seton Maitland

[3]Written in another hand on the letter: "Probably from Leghorn and enclosed in a letter to her sister-in-law Rebecca Seton."

2.5 ASJPH 1-3-3-3:14

[1]When the Setons traveled to Italy in 1803 for William's health, Elizabeth began keeping a journal to share her experiences with her "Soul's Sister," her sister-in-law Rebecca. In 1817 Isaac A. Kollack, of Elizabeth, New Jersey, published this as *Memoirs of Mrs. S.* without her permission. Her biographies include excerpts or passages from the journal, but most of these excerpts were edited to correct spelling, punctuation, and capitalization. In addition some passages were omitted without ellipses, and sections were combined without documentation.

The most complete versions of the *Leghorn Journal* in Elizabeth Seton's handwriting exist in the Archives at Mount St. Vincent and St. Joseph's Provincial House Archives. Mrs. Seton allowed Antonio Filicchi to keep the original of the trip to Florence; however, it is not a part of the Seton-Filicchi Collection at Mount St. Joseph. St. Joseph's Provincial House Archives has the copy made by Antonio Filicchi in exchange for the original. There are some differences among the versions, hence each has been reproduced as a separate document in Part II. The Archives at Mount St. Joseph has a copy that, while not in Elizabeth's hand, was edited by her.

[2]The page is torn at this point.

said to me Now we will part no more in time nor in Eternity—No
more repeated on who held by the hand in time nor in Eternity—

8th November Mrs. M ill in great distress—

Can I ever forget the setting sun over the little Island of Yivica [3]

11th November 1803—6 oclock Evening

My dear little Anna shed many tears on <my> her Prayer book over
the 92nd Psalm in consequence of my telling her that we offended
God every day Our conversation began by her asking me "if God put
down our bad actions in his Book as well as our good ones"—

She said she wondered how any one could be sorry to see a dear
baby die—She thought there was more cause to cry when they were
born.

Considering the Infirmity, and corrupt Nature which would overpower the Spirit of Grace, and the enormity of the offence to which the
least indulgence of them would lead me—in the anguish of my Soul
shuddering to offend my Adored Lord—I have this day solemnly engaged that through the strength of His Holy Spirit I will not again expose that corrupt and Infirm nature to the Smallest temptation I can
avoid—and therefore if my Heavenly Father will once more reunite
us all that I will make a daily sacrifice of every wish even the most innocent least they should betray me to a deviation from the Solemn and
sacred vow I have now made—

O my God imprint it on my Soul with the strength of thy Holy Spirit
that by his Grace supported and defended I may never more forget that
Thou are my all, and that I cannot be recieved in thy Heavenly King-
dom without a pure and faithful Heart supremely devoted to thy Holy
Will.—O keep me for the sake of Jesus Christ
Shepherdess—

14th November 1803

15th November—

a heavy storm of thunder and lightning at midnight—My Soul assured and strong in its almighty Protector, encouraged itself in Him,

---

[3]The island of Ibiza. Beneath Rev. Simon Gabriel Bruté wrote: "on[e] of the Balearic group." This is
a group of islands off the southeast coast of Spain.

while the knees trembled as they bent to him

—the worm of the dust <shaking> writhing at the terrors of its Almighty Judge—a helpless child clinging to the Mercy of its tender Father—A redeemed Soul Strong in the Strength of its Adored Saviour—

—after reading a great deal and <after> long and earnest Prayer went to bed—but could not rest—a little voice (my own Anna who I thought was asleep) in a soft wisper said "Come hither all ye weary Souls"—I changed my place to her arms—the rocking of the vessel and breaking of the waves were forgot the heavy Sighs and restless pains were lost in a sweet refreshing sleep—

Adored Redeemer it was thy word, by the voice of one of thy little ones, who promises indeed to be one of thy Angels—

November 18th

while the Ave Maria[4] bells were ringing arrived in the Mole[5] of Leghorn—

19th

towed by a 14 oared Barge to the Lazaretto Prison[6]—when we entered our room Anna viewed the high arches, naked walls and brick floor with streaming eyes, and as soon as her Father was composed on his mattress and they had bolted and barred us in this immense place alone for the night, clinging round my neck and bursting again in tears she said "if Papa should die here Mamma God will be with us."[7]

22nd—

Sung our Evening hymns again with little Anna—She said while we were looking at the setting sun "Mamma I dreamed last night that two men had hold of me to kill me, and as one had struck my Breast

---

[4]This probably refers to the bells which are sounded at morning, noon, and evening in Catholic churches for the Angelus, a prayer in honor of Mary.

[5]Port of Leghorn

[6]A place of quarantine

[7]Written in the right corner of the page: "dearest darling he was with us—".

with a knife, in that instant I waked, and found myself safe and was thinking so it will be with my Soul, while I am struggling with Death, in an instant I shall awake and find myself safe from all that I feared—but then FOREVER"—our Jesus!!!

2.6 Journal to Rebecca Seton

19th November [1803] 10 Oclock at night—

How eagerly would you listen to the voice that should offer to tell you where your "dear Sis" is now—your Souls Sister yet you could not rest in your bed if you saw her as she is—sitting in one corner of an immense Prison—locked in and barred with as much ceremony as any Monster of mischief might be—a single window double grated with iron thro which if I should want any thing I am to call a centinal with a fierce cocked hat, and long riffle-gun, that is that he may not recieve the dreadful infection we are supposed to have brought from N[ew] York—

to commence from where I left you last night—I went to sleep and dreamed I was in the middle Isle of Trinity Ch[urch][1] singing with all my soul the hymns at our dear Sacrament. So much comfort made me more than satisfied, and when I heard in the morning a boat was along side of our ship, I flew on deck and would have thrown myself in the arms of dear Carlton;[2] but he retired from me and a guard who I saw for the first time said "dont touch"—It now was explained that our ship was the first to bring the news of yellow fever in New York which our want of a Bill of Health[3] discovered, that the Pilot who brought us in the Mole must lose his head, our ship must go out in the Roads and my poor William being ill must go with his Baggage to the

---

2.6 ASJPH 1-3-3-8:59

[1]The church Elizabeth usually attended in New York

[2]Guy Carleton Bayley (1786-1859), the youngest son of Dr. Richard and Charlotte Barclay Bayley and half-brother of Elizabeth Seton, was employed by the Filicchis in Leghorn. He married Grace Roosevelt on November 4, 1813, and became the father of James Roosevelt Bayley (1814-1877), convert, Bishop of Newark, and Archbishop of Baltimore.

[3]Medical clearance for a vessel

Lazzaretto—at this moment the band of music that welcomes strangers came under our cabin windows and played, "hail Columbia" and all those little tunes that set the darlings singing and dancing at Home—

Mrs. O['Brien] and the rest were half wild with joy—but I was glad to hide in my birth the full Heart of sorrow which seemed as if it must break = do not judge me = you can never have an idea of the looks and tears of my poor Willy who seemed as if he would not live over the day—

—presently appeared a Boat with 14 oars—we hurried in another, with only one change of cloaths as they promised we should have the rest on Monday and the Lazaretto being some miles out of the town we were towed out to sea again and after an hours ride over the waves the chains which are across the entrance of the canal which leads to this place were let

December 4th

the word—my Bible, commentaries, Kempis,[4] visible, and in continual enjoyment—When I cannot get hours, I take minutes—Invisible, oh the company is numberless—some times I feel so assured that the guardian angel is immediately present that I look up from my Book and can hardly persuade myself I am not touched

== poor soul my J[ohn] H[enry] H[obart] would say "she will lose her reason in that Prison"—more than that I sometimes feel that his angel is near and undertake to converse with it—but these enjoyments only come when all is quiet and I have passed an hour or two with King David, the Prophet Isaiah, or become elevated by some of the commentaries—

== these hours I often think I shall hereafter wish to recall more than any of my life—

== My Father and my God—who by the consoling voice of his Word builds up the Soul in Hope so as to free it even for hours of its incumbrances—confirming and strengthening it by the hourly experience of his indulgent goodness—giving it a new life in Him even

---

[4]*The Imitation of Christ* by the fifteenth century writer Thomas á Kempis was a classic devotional work and a favorite of Elizabeth's.

while in the midst of Sorrows and care—sustaining, directing, consoling and Blessing thro every changing scene of its Pilgrimage making his Will its guide to temporal comfort and eternal glory—how shall this most unwearied diligence, the most cheerful compliance, the most humble resignation ever express enough my love, my joy, thanksgiving and Praise—

2.7 Journal to Rebecca Seton

19th November 1803—10 oclock at night—

How eagerly would you listen to the voice that should offer to tell you where your "dear Sis" is now, your Souls Sister—yet you could not rest in your bed if you saw her as she is sitting in one corner of an immense Prison bolted in and barred with as much ceremony as any monster of mischief might be—a single window double grated with iron thro' which, if I should want any thing, I am to call a centinel, with a fierce cocked hat, and long riffle gun, that is that he may not recieve the dreadful infection we are supposed to have brought with us from New York.—

To commence from where I left off last night—I went to sleep and dreamed I was in the middle Isle of Trinity Church singing with all my Soul the hymns at our dear Sacrament. So much comfort made me more than satisfied, and when I heard in the morning a boat was along side of our Ship, I flew on deck and would have thrown myself in the arms of dear Carlton[1] but he retired from me and a guard who I saw for the first time said "dont touch." It was now explained that our Ship was the first to bring the news of yellow fever in New York which our want of a Bill of health discovered, our ship must go out in the Roads and my poor William being ill must go with his baggage to the Lazaretto. At this moment the band of music that always welcomes Strangers came under our cabin window playing "Hail Columbia" and all those little tunes that set the darlings singing and dancing at

[1]Guy Carleton Bayley, Elizabeth's half-brother

home—Mrs. O['Brien] and the rest were almost wild with joy while I was glad to hide in my birth the full heart of sorrow, which seemed as if it must break—you cannot have an idea of the looks of my Seton who seemed as if he could not live over the day. presently appeared a boat with 14 oars and we entered in another fastened to it. The Lazaretto being some miles from the town we were towed out to sea again, and after an hours ride over the waves, the chains which cross the entrance of the canal which leads to this place were let down at the signal of several successive bells, and after another row between walls as high as our second story windows and the quarelling and the hollooing of the Waterman where we should be landed, the boat stopped—

Another succession of Bells brought down one guard after another, and in about half an hour Monsieur le Capitano[2]—who after much wispering and consultation with his Lieutenant said we might come out, upon which every one retreated and a guard pointed the way with his Bayonet which we were to go—An order from the Commandant was sent from our Boat to the Capitano which was recieved on the end of a stick and they were obliged to light a fire to smoke it before it would be read—My books always go with me, and they were carefully put up—but must all be looked over and the papers in the little Secretary examined—The person who did this and examined our matresses must perform as long a quarantine as ourselves—poor little Ann, how she trembled and William tottered along as if every moment he must fall which had he done no one dared for their life to touch him—We were directed to go opposite to the window of the capitano's House in which sat Mrs. P. F.,[3] in such a style—but hush compliments and kind looks without number—A fence was between us but I fear did not hide my fatigue both of Soul and Body; first we had chairs handed, rather placed for us for the chairs after we had touched them, could not go back to the house—at length we were shown the door we should enter No. 6—up 20 stone steps, a room with high arched cielings like St. Pauls[4]—brick floor, naked walls and a jug of water—The Capitano sent 3 warm eggs,

[2]A captain in the Italian military who was guarding the Lazaretto
[3]Mary Cowper Filicchi (1760-1821) of Boston was the wife of Filippo Filicchi.
[4]An Episcopal church in New York where Elizabeth often worshipped

a bottle of wine and some slips of Bread—Willy's mattrass was soon spread and he upon it. he could neither touch wine nor Eggs—our little syrrups, current jelly drinks etc. which he must have every half hour on board Ship—where were they I had heard the Lazaretto the very place for comfort for the sick—and brought Nothing—soon found there was a little closet, on which my knees found rest, and after emptying my heart and washing the bricks with my tears returned to my poor Willy, and found him and Ann both in want of a Preacher—dear puss she soon found a rope that had tied her box and began jumping away to warm herself, for the coldness of the bricks and walls made us shiver—at sun set dinner came from the Filicchi,[5] with other necessaries, we went to the grate again to see them—and now on the ship matresses spread on this cool floor my Willy and Anna are sound asleep, and I trust that God who has given him strength to go thro' a day of such exertion will carry us on—He is our all indeed—my eyes smart so much with crying, wind and fatigue that I must close them and lift up my heart—sleep wont come very easily—If you had seen little Ann's arms clasped round my neck at her prayers while the tears rolled a stream how you would love her—I read her to sleep—little pieces of trust in God—she said "Mamma if Papa should die here—but God will be with us"[6]—God is with us—and if sufferings abound in us, his Consolations also greatly abound, and far exceed all utterance[7]—

---

[5]There were two Filicchi brothers, Filippo and Antonio, and their families with whom Elizabeth was associated. Filippo Filicchi (1763-1816) spent the years 1785-1786 in the United States. It is fairly certain he was also in the United States in 1788. When he returned to Italy later that year, he was accompanied by young William Magee Seton. It was during this visit that Seton became friendly with the younger brother, Antonio Filicchi, who was studying law in Rome. In 1789 Filippo went again to the United States, and it was probably at this time that he married Mary Cowper of Boston. Late in 1789 the Filicchi house of commerce was publicly established in Leghorn. Mary Cowper Filicchi came to Italy in 1790. The couple had no children. In 1791 William Magee Seton again visited Leghorn. He had every reason to regard both Filicchi brothers as good friends. In 1794 Filippo Filicchi was honored by President George Washington with an appointment as United States Consul for the Port of Leghorn.

Antonio Filicchi (1764-1847) and his wife, Amabilia Baragazzi Filicchi (1773-1853), provided hospitality to the Setons in their home in Leghorn after the death of William Magee Seton in Pisa in 1803. Together with Filippo Filicchi, they were instrumental in Elizabeth Seton's conversion to Roman Catholicism and became lifelong friends, confidants, and benefactors to the Setons and later to the Sisters of Charity of St. Joseph's. They had ten children.

[6]Cf. 2 John 1:3.

[7]Cf. 2 Cor. 1:5.

If the wind that now almost puts out my light and blows on my W thro every crevice and over our chimney like loud Thunder could come from any but his command—or if the circumstances that has placed us in so forlorn a situation were not guided by his hand—miserable indeed would be our case—within the hour he has had a violent fit of coughing so as to bring up blood which agitates and distresses him thro' all his endeavours to hide it—

What shall we say—this is the hour of trial the Lord support and strengthen us in it. Retrospections bring anguish—press forward toward the mark and prize[8]—

20th Sunday morning

The Matin Bells[9] awakened my Soul to its most painful regrets and filled it with an agony of Sorrow which could not at first find relief even in prayer—In the little closet from whence there is a view of the Open Sea, and the beatings of the waves against the high rocks at the entrance of this Prison which throws them violently back and raises the white foam as high as its walls, I first came to my senses and reflected that I was offending my only Friend and resource in my misery and voluntarily shutting out from my Soul the only consolation it could recieve—pleading for Mercy and Strength brought Peace—and with a chearful countenance I asked Wm what we should do for Breakfast the doors were unbarred and a bottle of milk set down in the entrance of the room—little Ann and Wm ate it with bread, and I walked the floor with a crust and glass of wine—Wm could not sit up—his ague came on and my Souls agony with it,—My Husband on the old bricks without fire, shivering and groaning lifting his dim and sorrowful eyes, with a fixed gaze in my face while his tears ran on his pillow without one word—Anne rubbed one hand I the other till his Fever came on—the Capitano brought us news that our time was lessened five days told me to be satisfied with the dispensations of God etc.—and was answered by such a succession of sobs that he soon departed—Mr. F[10] now came to comfort my Willy and when he went

---

[8]Cf. 1 Cor. 9:24.

[9]Church bells announcing the pre-dawn liturgical office

[10]Either Antonio or Filippo Filicchi

away we said as much of our Blessed Service[11] as Wm could go thro'—I then was obliged to lay my head down—Dinner was sent from town and a Servant to stay with us during our quarantine—Louie—an old man, very little—grey hairs, and blue eyes which changed their expressions from joy to sorrow, as if they would console and still enliven—My face was covered with a handkerchief when he came in and tired of the sight of men with cocked hats, cockades and bayonets, I did not look up—poor Louis how long shall I remember his voice of sorrow and tenderness, when refusing the Dinner he looked up with lifted hands in some prayer that God would comfort me—and so I was comforted when I did not look at my poor Wm but to see him as he then was—was worse than to see him dead—and now the bolts of another door were hammered open and Louis who has become an object of equal terror with ourselves having entered our room and touched what we had touched had an apartment allotted him—how many times did the poor old man run up and down the nearly perpendicular 20 steps to get things necessary for our comfort next morning. When all was done I handed him a chair that he might rest—he jumped almost over it and danced round me like a mad-man, declaring he would work all night to serve us—My Wm wearied out was soon asleep Ann with a flood of tears prayed a blessing and soon forgot her sorrows—and it seemed as if opening my Prayer Book and bending my knees was the Signal for my Soul to find rest. it was 9 oclock with us—3 at Home—I imagined what I had so often enjoyed and consoled myself with the thought that tho' seperated in the Body six thousand miles—my Soul and the Souls I love were at the Throne of Grace at the same time, in the same Prayers, to one Almighty Father accepted through our adored Redeemer and enlightened by one blessed Spirit—then did it "rejoice indeed in the Lord and Triumph in the God of its Salvation"[12]—After Prayers—read my little book of Dear H's[13] Sermons—and became far more happy then I had been

---

[11]From the *Book of Common Prayer* of the Episcopal church

[12]Cf. 1 Sam. 2:1.

[13]John Henry Hobart. The Archives of Mount St. Vincent has several manuscripts in Elizabeth's handwriting: folded pages with the same watermark, sewn together. One, containing six separate sermons or commentaries, dated 1802 and 1803, is probably the "book" of Hobart's sermons.

wretched—went to bed at 12. got up twice to Prayers—and to help my poor W—

Monday—

Awoke with the same rest and comfort with which I had laid down—gave my W. his warm milk and began to consider our situation tho' so unfavorable to his complaint as one of the steps in the dispensations of that Almighty will which could alone choose aright for us and therefore set Ann to work and myself to the dear Scriptures as usual—laying close behind the dear shiverer to keep him from the ague—our Capitano came with his guards and put up a very neat bed and curtains sent by Filicchi—and fixed the benches on which Ann and I, were to lie. took down our names Signor Guillielmo, Signora Elizabeth and Signorina Anna Maria. The voice of kindness which again intreated me to look up to "le bon Dieu" made me look up to the speaker and in our Captaino I found every expression of a benevolent heart. his great cocked hat being off I found it had hid grey hairs and a kind and affectionate countenance—"I had a wife—I loved her—I loved her—Oh!—She gave me a daughter which she commended to my care—and died"—he clasped his hands and looked up—and then at my W "If God calls what can we do, et que voulez vous Signora."[14]—I began to love my Capitano—

Read and jumped the rope to warm me looked round our Prison and found that its situation was beautiful—comforted my W. all I could rubbing his hands and wiping his tears, and giving words to his Soul which was too weak to pray for itself—heard Ann read while I watched the setting sun in a cloud—after both were asleep—read prayed wept and prayed again till Eleven—at no loss to know the hours—night and day four Bells strike every hour and ring every quarter—

Tuesday—

My W was better and very much encourged by his Dr. Tutilli,[15] who was very kind to him—also our Capitano who now seemed to

---

[14]Literally, "What do you wish, Madame?"

[15]Italian physican retained by the Filicchis, who attended William in the Lazaretto

understand me a little—again repeated "I loved my wife—I loved her and she died et que voulez vous Signora."

talked with the F[ilicchi]-s at the grate and with great difficulty got my W. up the steps again—nursed him—read to him—heard Ann—and made the most of our troubles—our Louie brought us an elegant bouquet, jasmin, Jeranium, pinks etc.—makes excellent soup—cooks all with charcoal in little earthen pots—no sun set—heavy gale which, if any thing could move our wills, would certainly bring them down—the roaring of the Sea sounds like thunder—

passed my Evening as the last—quite reconciled to the Centinals watch and bolts and bars—not afraid of my candle as the window shutter is the only piece of wood about us—

Wednesday—

Not only willing to take my cross but kissed it too—and whilst glorying in our Consolations, my poor W was taken with an ague which was almost too much—he told me as he often had done before that it was too late, his strength was going from him every hour and he should go gradually—but not long—this to me—to his friends quite chearful—he was not able to go to them, they were admitted to our door—must not touch the least thing near us—and a point of our Capitanos stick warded Willy off when in eager conversation he would go too near—it reminded me of going to see the Lions—one of the guards brought a pot of incense also to purify our air.—

quiet half hour at sun set—Ann and I sung advent[16] hymns with low voice, Oh—after all was asleep said our dear Service alone. Willy had not been able in the day—found heavenly consolation, forgot prisons, bolts and sorrow, and would have rejoiced to have sung with Paul and Silas[17]

Thursday—

I find my present opportunity a Treasure—and my confinement of Body a liberty of Soul which I may never again enjoy whilst they are united—every moment not spent with my dear Books, or in my

---

[16]A period of religious preparation for Christmas
[17]In Acts 16:25 Paul and Silas rejoice even though in prison in Philippi.

nursing duty is a loss,—Ann is so happy with her rag baby and little presents it is a pleasure to see her—our Capitano brought us news, that other five days were granted, and the 19th of December we were free—poor Willy says with a groan, "I believe before then"—We pray and cry together, till fatigue overpowers him, and then he says he is willing to go—chearing up is useless, he seems easier after venting his sorrow and always gets quiet sleep after his struggles—a heavy storm of wind which drives the spray from the Sea against our window adds to his Melancholy—If I could forget my God one moment at these times I should go mad—but He hushes all—Be still and know that I am God your Father[18]—

dear Home, dearest Sisters, my little ONES—WELL—either protected by God in this World—or in Heaven—it is a sweet thought to dwell on, that all those I most tenderly love—love God—and if we do not meet again here—there we shall be separated no more—if I have lost them now, their gain is infinite and eternal. how often I tell my W "when you awake in that world you will find nothing could tempt you to return to this, you will see that your care over your wife and little ones, was like a hand only to hold the cup which God himself will give if he takes you"—

Heavenly Father pity the weak and burthened Souls of thy poor creatures, who have not Strength to look to Thee, and lift us from the Dust for His sake our resurrection and our Life Jesus Christ our Adored Redeemer—

Friday—[November 25]

A Day of Bodily pain, but Peace in God—Kneeled on our matts round the little table and said our dear Service—the storm of wind so great Carlton was admitted at the foot of the stairs and from the top I conversed with him which is always a great pleasure as he seems to me next to an angel—ventured to remind my poor W that it was our darling Williams birth day, which cost him many tears—he also cried over our dear Harriets profile—indeed he is so weak that even a thought of Home makes him shed tears—How gracious is the Lord

---

[18]Cf. Ps. 46:10

who strengthens my poor Soul—Consider—my Husband who left his all to seek a milder climate confined in this place of high and damp walls exposed to cold and wind which penetrates to the very bones, without fire except the kitchen charcoal which oppresses his Breast so much as to Nearly convulse him—no little syrrup nor softener of the cough bark and milk, bitter tea, and opium pills which he takes quietly as a duty without seeming even to hope is all I can offer him from day to day—When Nature fails, and I can no longer look up with chearfulness, I hide my head on the chair by his bedside and he thinks I am praying—and pray I do—for prayer is all my comfort, without I should be of little service to him—Night and day he calls me "his Life his Soul his dearest of Women his all"—

Our Capitano came this afternoon and seeing poor Willy in a high fever said: "in this room what suffering have I seen—there, lay an Armenian begging an knife to end the struggles of Death—there where the Signora's bed is, in the frenzy of Fever a Frenchman insisted on shooting himself, and died in agonies"—little billets of paper pasted on the doors mark how many days different persons have staid and the shutter is all over Notched—10—20—30—40 days—I do not mark ours—trusting they are marked above—He only knows best—dear, dear William I can sometimes inspire him for a few minutes to feel that it would be sweet to die—he always says "My Father and my God Thy will be done"—Our Father in Pity and compassion—Our God in power to succour and to save who promises to pardon and recieve us through our adored Redeemer, who will not let those perish for whom he has shed his precious Blood—

only to reflect—If we did not now know and love God—If we did not feel the consolations, and embrace the cheering Hope he has set before us, and find our delight in the study of his blessed word and Truth, what would become [of] us?

"Though torn from Natures most endearing ties,
"The hearts warm hope, and love's maternal glow
"[Though sunk the Source on which the Soul relies]
"[To soothe thro' lifes decline its destin'd woe]
"Though Sorrow still affecting ills prepares

"And o'er each passing day her presence lowers
"And darkened Fancy shades with many cares
"With many trials crowds the future hours
"Still in the Lord will I rejoice
"Still in my God I lift my voice
"Father of Mercies! still my grateful lays
"Shall hymn thy name, exulting in thy Praise"[19]

Capitano says "all religions are good. it is good to keep ones own, but yours is as good as mine, to 'do to others as you would wish them to do to you'[20] that is all religion and the only point"—tell me dear Capitano do you take this as a good principle only or also as a command—"I reverence the command Signora" Well Monsieur le Capitano He who commanded your excellent rule, also commanded in the first place "love the Lord your God with all your Soul"[21]—and do you not give that the first place Capitano—"Ah Signora it is excellent—mais il y a tant de choses"[22]—Poor Capitano! Sixty years of age—and yet to find that to give God the Soul interferes with "so many things"—

dear little Ann—"the child shall die a hundred years old—and the Sinner a hundred years shall be—lost."

Tuesday 29th November

was obliged to go to Bed at 10 last night to get warm in little Anns arms—awoke this morning while the moon was setting opposite our window but could not enjoy its brightness as the spray from the Sea keeps the glass always thick—laid in Bed till 9 with little Ann to explain to her our tedium—she said "one thing always troubles me mamma—Christ says they who would reign with Him must suffer with Him—and if I was now cut off where should I go for I have not yet suffered"—She coughs very much with a great deal of pain in her breast—she said "sometimes I think when this pain comes in my Breast, that God will call me soon and take me from this world where I

---

[19]The complete verses are found in ASJPH 1-3-3-3:61. The source of this verse or hymn is unidentified. Its last four lines may reflect Elizabeth's daily recitation of Psalm 118.
[20]Matt. 7:12
[21]Matt. 22:37
[22]"But there are so many things"

am always offending him, and how good that would be, if he gives me a sickness that I may bear patiently, that I may try and please Him"—My Anna you please him every day when you help me through my troubles—"O do I Mamma thank GOD thank GOD"

after Breakfast read our Psalms and the 15th Chapter of Isaiah to my W. with so much delight that it made us all merry—He read at little Anns request the last chapter of Revelations, but the tones of his voice no heart can stand—

a storm of wind still and very cold—Willy with a Blanket over his shoulders creeps to the old mans fire—Ann jumps the rope, and Maty[23] hops on one foot five or six times the length of the room without stopping—laugh at me my Sister, but it is very good exercise, and warms sooner than a fire when there is a warm heart to set it in motion—

Sung hymns—read promises to my Willy shivering under the bed clothes—and felt that the Lord is with us—and that he is our All— the fever comes hot—the bed shakes even with his breathing—My God, my Father,—

St. Andrew—30th November 1803—

William again by the kitchen fire—last night 30 or 40 poor souls of all nations Turks, Greeks, Spaniards, and Frenchmen, arrived here from a shipwreck—no matresses, cloaths, or food—great coats without shirts—shirts without coats—these sent all to one room with naked walls, and the jug of water—until the commandant should find leisure to supply them—Our Capitano says he can do nothing without orders—"Patience—que voulez vous Signora"—Anna says "for all we are so cold, and in this Prison Mamma, how happy we are compared with them and we have Peace too, they quarrell, fight, and holloo all the time—the Capitano sends us even chesnuts and fruits from his own table—these have not Bread"—dear Ann you will see many more such mysteries.

at Willys bed side we have said our daily Service—he thought it would stop his shivering—My Williams Soul is so humble it will

---

[23]A name for herself, possibly a play on "Mater"

hardly embrace that Faith which is its only resource—at any time whom have we but Our Redeemer, but when the spirit is on the brink of departure it must cling to him with increased force or where is it?

Dear W it is not from the impulse of terror you seek your God, you tried and wished to serve him long before this trial came, why then will you not consider him as the Father who knows all the different means and dispositions of his children and will graciously recieve those who come to him by that way which he has appointed—you say your only hope is in Christ what other hope do we need?—

He says that the first effect he ever felt from the calls of the Gospel he experienced from our dear H[obart]'s pressing the question in one of his sermons "What avails gaining the whole world and losing your own Soul"[24]—The reflections he made when he returned Home were "I toil and toil and what is it, what I gain, destroys me daily Soul and Body I live without God in the world, and shall die miserably"—Mr. F. D. with whom he had not been in habits of business offered to join him in an Adventure—it succeeded far b[e]yond their expectation—Mr. F. D. said when they wound it up, "one thing you know, I have been long in business, began with very little—have built a house, and have enough to build another I have generally succeeded in undertakings and attribute all to this, that whether they are great or small I always ask a blessing of God, and look to that blessing for success"—William says "I was struck with shame and Sorrow that I had been as a Heathen before God"—These he called his two warnings which awakened his Soul—and speaks of them always with tears—

O the promises he makes if it pleases God to spare Him—have had one Mate to see us from Captain OBrien—talked out of the window to him—one of the Sailors who seemed to love us like his own Soul always flying to serve, and trying to please us while on Board came with him—poor Charles he turned pale when he saw my head out of the iron bars and called out "Why dear Mrs. Seton are you in a Prison" he looked behind all the way—as he went—and shook his head at Ann as long as he could see her—Charles had lived at the quarantine at Staten Island and that without his good and affectionate heart would make

---

[24]Matt. 16:26

me love him—I shall never hear a sailors Yo Yo without thinking of his melancholy Song—He is the captains and every bodys favorite.

How gracious is my adored Master who gives even to the countenance of the Stranger the look of kindness and pity—from the time we first landed here one of the guards of our room looked always with sorrow and sympathy on us and tho' I cannot understand him, nor he me, we talk away very fast—he showed me yesterday he was very sick by pointing to his breast and throat, when the Capitano came, I told him how sorry I was for poor Phillippo—"Oh Signora he is very well off he has been two years married to a very very beautiful girl of 16—has two children, and recieves 3/6 per day[25]—to be sure he is obliged to sleep in the Lazaretto but in the morning goes home to his wife for an hour or two it is not possible to spare him longer from his duty et que voulez vous Signora"—

Good and Merciful Father—who gives content and a cheerful heart with 3/6 per day, a wife and children to maintain with such a pittance—Often let me think of Phillippo when I have not enough or think I have not—he is 22—his wife 18—thought goes to two at home most dear B and H[26]—

Went to the railings with little Ann to recieve from our Capitano's Daughter a baby she had been making for her—she was a kind good countenance and hangs on her Father's arm—has refused an offer of marriage that she may take care of him—Such a sight awakened many recollections—I hope she may meet one she loves, who will reward her.

1st December 1803—

arose between 6 and 7, before the day had dawned the light of the Moon opposite our window was still strongest—not a breath of wind—the sea which before I had always seen in violent commotion now gently seemed to creep to the Rocks it had so long been beating over—every thing around at rest except two little white gulls flying to

---

[25]The daily wage of a prison guard

[26]Elizabeth's half-brother Andrew Barclay Bayley and her sister-in-law Harriet Seton planned to marry. Barclay went to the West Indies in 1806 hoping to earn enough to send for Harriet, but when she came to Baltimore in 1809, their future was uncertain.

the westward towards my Home—towards my loves—that thought did not do—flying towards Heaven—where I tryed to send my Soul—the Angel of Peace met it and poured over the Oil of Love and Praise, driving off every vain imagination and led it to its Saviour and its God—"We Praise Thee O God"—the dear strain of praise in which I always seem to meet the Souls I love and "Our Father"—These two portions are the Union of love and Praise and in them I meet the Soul of my Soul.—at ten oclock read with W. and Anna—at twelve he was at rest—Ann playing in the next room—alone to all the World, one of those sweet pauses in spirit when the Body seems to be forgotten came over me—

in the year 1789 when my Father was in England[27] I jumped in the wagon that was driving to the woods for brush about a mile from Home[.] the Boy who drove it began to cut and I set off in the woods—soon found an outlet in a Meadow, and a chesnut tree with several young one[s] growing round it, attracted my attention as a seat, but when I came to it found rich moss under it and a warm sun—here then was a sweet bed. the air still a clear blue vault above, the numberless sounds of Spring melody and joy—the sweet clovers and wild flowers I had got by the way, and a heart as innocent as a human heart could be filled with even enthusiastic love to God and admiration of his works—still I can feel every sensation that passed thro' my Soul—and I thought at that time my Father did not care for me—well God was my Father—my All. I prayed—sung hymns—cryed—laughed in talking to myself of how far He could place me above all Sorrow—Then layed still to enjoy the Heavenly Peace that came over my Soul; and I am sure in the two hours so enjoyed grew ten years in my spiritual life—told cousin Joe[28] to go Home with his wood, not to mind me and walked a mile round to see the roof of the Parsonage, where lived—Parson of course—then I

---

[27]Dr. Richard Bayley studied medicine in London on three different occasions.

[28]Joseph Bayley (b. 1777), son of Sarah Pell and William LeConte Bayley. William LeConte Bayley (1745-1811) was the son of William and Susannah Le Conte Bayley and the brother of Dr. Richard Bayley. Elizabeth spent time as a child and a teenager in his home in New Rochelle, New York.

made another hearty Prayer—then sung all the way Home—with a good appetite for the Samp[29] and fat pork—

Well, all this came strong in my head this morning when as I tell you the Body let the Spirit alone. I had both Prayed and cryed heartily which is my daily and often hourly Comfort, and closing my eyes, with my head on the table lived all these sweet hours over again, made believe I was under the chesnut tree—felt so peaceable a heart—so full of love to God—such confidence and hope in Him and made my hearty Prayer not for the Son but The Parson himself, dwelling with delight on the hope of all meeting again in unity of Spirit, in the Bond of Peace, and that Holyness which will be perfected in the Union Eternal—The wintry storms of Time shall be over, and the unclouded Spring enjoyed forever—

So you see, as you know, with God for our Portion there is no Prison in high walls and bolts—no sorrow in the Soul that waits on him tho' beset with present cares, and gloomy Prospects—for this freedom I can never be sufficiently thankful, as in my Williams case, it keeps alive what in his weak State of Body would naturally fail—and often when he hears me repeat the Psalms of Triumph in God, and read St. Pauls faith in Christ with my Whole Soul, it so enlivens his Spirit that he also makes them his own, and all our sorrows are turned into joy—Oh well may I love God—well may my whole soul strive to please him, for what but the strain of an Angel can ever express what he has done and is constantly doing for me—While I live—while I have my being in Time and thro' Eternity let me sing praises to my God.

2nd December—

enjoyed the morn, and day break—read the commentary on 104th Psalm,[30] and sung hymns in bed till 10—a hard frost in the night—endeavoured to make a fire in my room with brush, but was smoked out—the poor strangers almost mad with hunger and cold quarelled, battled—and at last sat down in companies on the grass with cards which made them as noisy as their anger—Patience—

---

[29] A kind of porridge made from coarsely ground Indian corn
[30] Ps. 104 appears as Ps. 105 in contemporary Catholic bibles.

Ann sick, William tired out—was obliged to say my dear Service by myself—a clear sun set which cheared my heart tho' it was all the while Singing "from lowest depth of woe"—the Ave Maria bells ring while the Sun Sets, on one side of us and the Bells "for the dead" on the other—the latter sometimes continue a long while—in the morning always call again to Prayer for the "Souls in Purgatory"—Our Capitano said a good deal on the Pleasure I should enjoy on Christmas at Pisa in seeing all their ceremonies—The enjoyment of Christmas—Heavenly Father who knows my inmost soul he knows how it would enjoy—and will also pity while it is cut off from what it so much longs for—one thing is in my power, tho' communion with those my Soul loves is not within my reach in one sense, in the other what can deprive me of it, "still in spirit we may meet"—at 5 oclock here, it will be 12 there—at 5, then in some quiet corner on my Knees I may spend the time they are at the altar, and if the "cup of Salvation"[31] cannot be recieved in the strange land evidently, virtually it may, with the Blessing of Christ and the "cup of Thanksgiving" supply in a degree, That, which if I could obtain would be my strongest desire—Oh my Soul what can shut us out from the love of Him who will even dwell with us through love—

4th [December]—

Our Captain OBrien and his wife found their way to us—"must not touch Signora" says Philippo dividing us with his stick—kind affectionate Captain when I ran down to meet him the tears danced in his eyes. while poor Willy and Ann peeped thro' the grates Mrs. O began to cry—We could not see them but a few minutes for the cold.

Our Lazaretto Captain has sent hand-irons small wood etc. and I have doctored the chimney with a curtain (a sheet) so as to make the smoke bearable—have had an anxious day between Father and Ann—She was very ill for some hours—when the cause of her sufferings removed we went on our Knees together—Oh may her dear Soul long send forth such precious tears—dear dear Rebecca, how often have we nursed up the little fire at night together as I do now

---

[31]Ps. 116:13

alone—alone recall the word—my Bible, commentaries, Kempis visible and in continual enjoyment. when I cannot get hours I take minutes[.] Invisible O the company is numberless—Sometimes I feel so assured that the guardian Angel is immediately present that I look from my book and can hardly be persuaded I was not touched.

Poor soul J[ohn] H[enry] H[obart] would say She will lose her reason in that Prison Know then that I sometimes feel that his Angel is near and undertake to converse with it. but the enjoyments only come when all is quiet and I have passed an hour or two with King David, the Prophet Isaias or become elevated by some of the Commentaries—These hours I often think I shall hereafter esteem the most precious of my life.

—My Father and my God, who by the consoling voice of his word builds up the Soul in hope so as to free it even for hours of its incumbrance, confirming and strengthening it by the constant experience of his indulgent goodness; giving it a new life in him even while in the midst of pains and sorrows—sustaining, directing, consoling and blessing thro' every changing scene of its pilgrimage, making his Will its guide to temporal comfort and eternal glory—how shall the most unwearied diligence, the most cheerful compliance the most humble resignation ever enough express my love, my joy Thanksgiving and Praise—

12th December

a week has past my dear Sister without even one little memorandum—of the pen The first day of it, that dear day in which I always find my blessing was passed in interrupted Prayers, anxiety, and watching—

Monday 5th was early awakened by my poor W. in great Suffering—sent for the Doctor Tutilli, who as soon as he saw him told me—he was not wanted, but I must send for Him who would minister to his Soul—in this moment I stood alone, as to this World—My husband looked in silent agony at me and I at Him, each fearing to weaken the others Strength, at the moment he drew himself towards me and said "I breathe out my Soul to you," the exertion he made assisted Nature's remaining force and he threw a quantity from his Lungs, which had threatened to stop their motion, and so doing experienced so great a revolution that in a few hours afterwards he seemed nearly the same as when we first entered the Lazaretto—Oh that day—it was spent close by his bed side on my little matt—he Slumbered the most of every hour, and did I not pray and did I not Praise—no enquiring visitor disturbed the solemn Silence, no breakfast or dinner to interrupt the rest—Carlton came at sunset—Mrs. Filicchi they thought was dying—He thought his poor brother so—and then came our Capitano with so much offered kindness—He was shocked at the tranquility of my poor W and distressed at the thought that I was alone with Him for the Dr. had told him that notwithstanding his present relief if the expectoration from the Lungs did not return, he might be gone in a few hours—would I have some one in the room—Oh no what had I to fear—and what had I to fear?—I laid down as if to rest, that he might not be uneasy—listened all night sometimes by the fire, sometimes laying down—sometimes thought the breathing stopped—and kiss'd his poor face to feel if it was cold—and sometimes alarmed by its heaviness—well—was I alone—Dear indulgent Father—could I be alone while clinging fast to thee in continued Prayer or Thanksgiving—Prayer for Him, and Joy wonder and delight to feel assured that what I had so fondly hoped and confidently asserted really proved in the hour of trial to be more than I could hope more than I could conceive—that my God could and would bear me through even the most severe trials with that strength, confidence, and affiance which if every circumstance of the case was considered seemed more than a Human Being could expect or Hope—but His consolations—who shall speak them—how can utterance be given to that which only His Spirit can feel—

At daylight the wished for change took place—Mr. *Hall*[32] came in the morning with Mr. F[ilicchi] and the Capitano—went away with a promise to come again—and the intervening days and evenings have been spent in constant attention to the *main-concern* but from a

---

[32]Rev. Thomas Hall, the Protestant chaplain to the British consulate in Leghorn. Rev. Hall lived on the first floor of a residence located about one block from the Church of Santa Catalina. The Antonio Filicchi family occupied the second floor. Later Elizabeth Seton and her daughter Anna Maria lived on the third floor during their stay in Italy.

Singularity of disposition which rather delights in *going on*, than in retrospecting sorrow, have rather (when I could only keep awake by writing according to the old custom) busied myself in writing the *first Sermon for my dear little Dick*.

W. goes on *gently*, but keeps me busy—Ann is a Treasure—she was reading yesterday that John was imprisoned[33]—"Yes Papa Herod imprisoned Him and Miss Herodias gave him liberty,"—No my dear she had him Beheaded, "Well Papa she released him from Prison and sent him to God"—Child after my own heart

Tuesday 13th—

five days more and our quarantine is ended—lodgings are engaged at Pisa on the borders of the Arno[34]—My heart used to be very full of poetical visions about this famous river, but it has no room for visions *now*—one only vision is before it—No one ever saw my Willy without giving him the quality of an amiable man—but to see that character exalted to the Peaceful Humble Christian, waiting the will of God with a Patience that seems more than human, and a firm faith which would do honor to the most distinguished Piety, is a happiness allowed only to the poor little Mother who is seperated from all other happiness that is connected with this Scene of things—No sufferings, nor weakness nor distress (and from these he is never free in any degree) can prevent his *following* me daily in Prayer, portions of the Psalms, and generally large Portions of the Scriptures—if he is a little better he enlarges his attention if worse he is the more eager not to lose a moment, and except *the day* which we thought his last, he has never failed one day in this course, since our entrance in these *stone walls* the 19th November—he very often says *this* is the period of his life which if he lives or dies he will always consider as Blessed—the only time which he has not lost—not the smallest murmur, Oh! and lifting up of the eyes, is the strongest expression I have yet heard from him in the rapid progress of his complaint which has reduced him to almost Nothing—and from its very nature gives him no release from irritation in violent coughing, chills, oppressions, weakness and even in the

---

[33]Cf. Matthew 14:3 ff.

[34]The Filicchis arranged lodging in Pisa, a few miles from Leghorn.

weight of his own limbs seems more than a mortal could bear—"Why art thou so heavy O my Soul," is the only comfort he seems to find in words—often talks of his darlings—but most of meeting, *ONE family in Heaven*; talks of those we have left behind as if it was not yesterday and of *dear H[enry] H[obart]* whose visits and society he misses most as they would be his greatest consolation in these hours of Sorrow—

When I thank God for my "Creation and preservation" it is with a warm of feeling I never could know until now—to wait on him My W. *Soul and Body* to console and soothe those hours of affliction and pain weariness and watching which next to God I alone could do—to strike up the chearful notes of Hope and Christian triumph, which from his partial love he hears with the more enjoyment from me because to me he attributes the greatest share of them—to hear him in pronouncing the Name of his Redeemer declare that I first taught him the sweetness of the sound—Oh if I was in the dungeon of this Lazaretto I should bless and Praise my God for these days of retirement and abstraction from the world which have afforded leisure and opportunity for so blessed a work—

14th—

Said my Prayers alone while W. was asleep—did not dare remind him of them for weakness and pain quite overpower him—rain and storm as indeed we have had almost every day of the 26 we have been here. The dampness about us would be thought dangerous for a person in health, and my Ws. sufferings—Oh well I know that God is above. Capitano, you need not always point your silent look and finger there—if I thought our condition the Providence of man, instead of the "weeping Magdalane"[35] as you so graciously call me, you would find me a lioness willing to burn your Lazaretto about your ears if it were possible that I might carry off my poor prisoner to breathe the air of Heaven in some more seasonable place—to keep a poor Soul who came to your country for his Life, thirty days shut up in damp walls, smoke, and wind from all corners blowing even the curtain round his bed, which is only a mattress on boards and his bones almost

---

[35]Cf. John 20:13.

through—and now the Shadow of death, trembling if he only stands a few minutes he is to go to Pisa for his Health—this day his prospects are very far from Pisa—

But O my Heavenly Father I know that these contradictory events are permitted and guided by thy Wisdom, which only is *light*, we are in darkness, and must be thankful that our knowledge is not wanted to perfect thy work—and also keep in mind that infinite Mercy which in permitting the sufferings of the perishing Body has provided for our Souls so large an opportunity of comfort and nourishment for our eternal Life where we shall assuredly find that all things have worked together for our Good—for our sure trust in Thee—

Thursday—

finished reading the Testament[36] through, which we began the 6th October and my bible as far as *Ezekiel* which I have always read to *myself* in rotation, but the lessons appointed in the Prayer Book, to W.—to day read him several passages in Isaiah which he enjoyed so much that he was carried for awhile beyond his troubles—indeed our reading is an unfailing comfort[.] Wm says he feels like a person brought to the Light after many years of darkness when he heard the Scriptures as the law of God and therefore Sacred, but not discerning what part he had in them or feeling that they were the fountain of Eternal Life

Friday night—

a heavy day, part of our *service together*—part *alone* They have bolted us in to night, expecting to find my W. gone tomorrow—but he rests quietly—and God is with us—

Saturday and Sunday—

Melancholy days of combat with natures weakness, and the courage of Hope which pictured our removal from the Lazaretto to Pisa

Monday morning—

arose with the light and had every thing prepared for the *anxious* hour. at ten, all in readiness and at eleven held the hand of my W.

---

[36]The New Testament or Christian Scriptures

while he was seated on the arms of two men and conducted from the Lazaretto to Filichis coach, surrounded by a multitude of gazers, all sighing out *"O Pauverino"*[37] while my heart beat almost to fainting least he would die in the exertion, but the air revived him, his Spirit was chearful, and thro' fifteen miles of heavy roads, he was supported, and appeared stronger than when he set out.—My Father and my God—was all my full heart of thankfulness could utter—

Tuesday 20th December—

let me stop and ask myself if I can go thro' the remainder of my memorandum with that sincerity and exactness which has so far been adhered to—whether in the crowd of anxieties and sorrows which are pressed in so small a compass of time the overflowing of feeling can be suppressed and my Soul stand singly before my God—yes—every moment of it speaks his Praise and therefore it shall be followed

Tuesday 20th December—

My Seton was composed the greater part of the day on a sofa delighted with his change of situation, taste and elegance of every thing around him, every necessary comfort within his reach—we read, compared past and present, talked of heavenly hopes,—and with our dear Carlton (who was to stay with us four days) and then went to rest in hopes of a good night—but I had scarcely fixed the pillows of the sofa which I made my Bed before he called me to help him, and from that moment the last complaint (of the bowels) which Dr. Tutilli told me must be decisive, came on—

Wednesday—

kind of languid weakness seized the mind as well as overpowered the Body—he must and would ride. the Physician Dr. Cartelatch wispered me he might die in the attempt, but there was no possibility of refusal and it was concluded that opposition was worse than any risque, and carried down in a chair, and supported in my trembling arms with pillows—we rode—Oh my Father well did you strengthen me in that struggle—in five minutes we were forced to return, and to get him

---

[37]"O poor man!"

out of the coach, and in the chair up the stairs, and on the bed, words can never tell—

Thursday—

a cloudy day, and quiet—

Friday—

the complaint seemed lessened and ride again we must—took Madam[e] de Tot, (the lady of the House) with us, and returned in better spirits and more able to help himself than when we went out, and I really began to think that riding must be good—*but that was the last*

Saturday—

constant suffering and for the first day confined in bed—the disorder of the Bowels so violent that he said he could not last till morning—talked with chearfulness about his Darlings thanked God with great earnestness that he had given him so much time to reflect, and such consolation in his Word, and Prayer, and with the help of a small portion of Laudanum[38] rested until midnight—he then awoke, and observed I had not laid down[.] I said no love for the sweetest reflections keep me awake—Christmas day is began—the day of our dear Redeemers birth here you know is the day that opened to us the door of everlasting life—Yes he said "and how I wish we could have the Sacrament"[39]—well we must do all we can and putting a little wine in a glass I said different portions of Psalms and Prayers which I had marked hoping for a happy moment and we took the cup of Thanksgiving setting aside the sorrow of time, in the views of the joys of Eternity—oh so happy to find that those joys were more strongly painted to Him—On Sunday, OBrien came, and *my W* gave me in his charge to take me home with a composure and solemnity, that made us cold—did not pass a mouthful thro' my lips that day, which was spent on my knees by his bedside every moment I could look off of my *W*

---

[38]A sedative
[39]Holy Communion

He anxiously prayed to be released that day, and followed me in prayer whenever he had the least cessation from extreme suffering—

Monday—

was so impatient to be gone that I could scarcely persuade him to wet his lips, but continued calling his Redeemer to Pardon and release him as he always would have the door of his room shut I had no interruption, Carlton kept Anna out of the way, and every promise in the Scriptures I could remember and suitable Prayer I continually repeated to him which seemed to be his only relief. when I stopped to give any thing *"Why do you do it, what do I want, I want to be in Heaven, pray, pray, for my Soul."*—he said he felt so comfortable an assurance that his Redeemer would recieve him—that he saw his dear little Tat smiling before him, and told Anna *"Oh if Paté*[40] *could take you with him,"* and at midnight when the *cold sweat* came on would reach out both his arms to me and said repeatedly "you promised me you would go, come, come, fly,—

at four the hard struggle ceased, Nature sunk into a settled sob, *"My dear Wife and little ones"* and *"My Christ Jesus have mercy and recieve me,"* was all I could distinguish and again repeated *"my Christ Jesus"* until a quarter past seven when the dear Soul took its flight to the blessed exchange it so much longed for—

I often asked him when he could not speak, You feel my love that you are going to your Redeemer and he motioned yes with a look up of Peace at a quarter past 7 on Tuesday morning 27th December—his Soul was released—and mine from a struggle next to death—

and how will my dear Sister understand except you could concieve the scene of suffering my Wm passed thro' that I took my little Ann in my arms and made her kneel with me again by the dear Body, and thank our Heavenly Father for relieving him from his misery, for the Joyful assurance that thro' our Blessed Redeemer he had entered into Life Eternal and implored his Protecting care and pity for us who have yet to finish our course—

---

[40]Tat was a nickname for their infant daughter, Rebecca. Paté referred to William.

Now opening the door to let the people know it was finished—Servants and the Landlady all were at a loss what should be done, and finding every one afraid of catching the complaint as we should be of the yellow fever, I took two women who had washed and sometimes assisted me, and again shutting the door with their assistance did the last duties—and felt I had done all—all that tenderest love and duty could do. My head had not rested for a week—three days and nights the fatigue had been incessant and one meal in 24 hours, still I must wash, dress, pack up, and in one hour be in Mrs. F[ilicchi]s carriage and ride fifteen miles to Leghorn—Carlton and our good old Louie staid to watch and my Wm. was brought in the Afternoon and deposited in the House appointed, in the Protestant burying ground[41]—

Oh Oh Oh what a day.—close his eyes, lay him out, ride a journey, be obliged to see a dozen people in my room till night—and at night crowded with the whole sense of my situation—O MY FATHER, and MY GOD the next morning at Eleven all the English and Americans in Leghorn met at the grave house and *all was done.*—

In all this it is not necessary to dwell on the mercy and consoling presence of my dear Redeemer, for no mortal strength could support what I experienced—

My William often asked me if I felt assured that he would be accepted and pardoned, and I always tried to convince him that where the soul was so humble and sincere as his, and submission to Gods will so uniform as his had been throughout his trial, that it became sinful to doubt one moment of his reception through the merits of his Redeemer—the night before his death praying earnestly for him that his pardon might be sealed in Heaven and his transgressions blotted out, after praying I continued on my knees and leaned my head on the chair by which I knelt and insensibly lost myself—I saw in my slumber a little angel with a pen in one hand and a sheet of pure white paper in the other—he looked at me holding out the paper and wrote in large letters *JESUS* this tho' a vision of sleep was a great comfort and he was very much affected when I told him and said a few hours before he died

---

[41]The English burying ground at St. John's Anglican Church in Leghorn. The grave marker reads: "Here lies the remains of William Magee Seton, Merchant of New York, who departed this life at Pisa, the 27th day of December, 1803."

"the angel wrote JESUS—he has opened the door of eternal life for me and will cover me with his righteousness"

I had a similar dream the same night—the heavens appeared a very bright blue a little angel at some distance held open a division in the sky—a large black Bird like an eagle flew towards me and flapped its wings round and made every thing dark—the angel looked as if it held up the division waiting for something the Bird came for—and so alone from every friend on Earth, walking the valley of the Shadow of death[42] we had sweet comfort even in our dreams—while Faith convinced us they were realities—

1804

2.8 To Rebecca Seton

Leghorn January 3d 1804

My own dearest Rebecca—

I have been looking over the long history of our voyage of which I had written you a faithful account to the last day of the past year, and as it is probable that Captain OBrien will sail in a fortnight and I may be with you before this opportunity reaches Boston, and my letters yet get from Boston to you, I think, it best to take it to you myself, <and> or if it is Gods will that I do not see you, would not wish that the melancholy scenes of sorrow I have passed through should come to your knowledge as you will all feel enough at hearing that our dear William is gone—gone stretching out his arms to his Saviour, and rejoicing at the moment of his release—

---

[42]Ps. 23:4
2.8 ASJPH 1-3-3-18:43 (Seton-Jevons #37-40)

Our passage here was as comfortable as we could expect, and his prospects of recovery I think almost the same as when we left home but thirty days passed in the Lazaretto, on the sea shore, exposed to a succession of heavy storms very unusual to this climate, and a large room always cold and full of smoke, added to confinement, and the regulations of not suffering even a Physician to feel his pulse, (for whoever touched or came within some yards of us were subject to the same quarantine) all added, was more than he could bear, and eventually after having been many nights bolted in, with the assurance that he would die before morning he was carried out and put in a coach which took us *to Pisa* a ride of fifteen miles, which with pillows, cordials, etc. he bore much better than we expected, but two days before Christmas was taken to his bed with the last symptom of his disorder, a lax,[1] and from that day every thing he took passed immediately thro' him and I had to do for him as for a Baby—he suffered at times, but was generally composed and so desirous of going that every nourishment I gave him he would say "I do not want that, I want to be in heaven," and found no comfort but in having his room always shut and me on my knees by his bed side night and day to help him in his prayers.

Christmas day he continually reminded himself "this day my Redeemer took pain and sorrow that I might have Peace; this day he gained eternal life for me"—and hoped so much that he would be called that day—but Monday night about twelve the cold sweat began, he bid me carry the candle out of the room and shut the door, I did so—and remained on my knees holding his hand and praying for him till a quarter past seven when his dear soul seperated gently without any groan or struggle—I heard him repeatedly follow my prayers, and when I ceased a moment continued saying *"My Christ Jesus have mercy"*—also *"my dear wife, my little ones."* and told me tell all my dear friends not to weep for me that I die happy, and satisfied with the Almighty Will = after he was gone and dear little Ann had prayed with me by his side, I sent for the mistress of the house,[2] but found that their

---

[1]A disorder of the bowels
[2]Madame de Tot

terror of his complaint (which they look at with as much dread as we do the Yellow fever) was so great that I had no assistance to expect from them, therefore I was obliged with the assistance of a poor woman who had washed for him, to lay him out myself, which added to three nights not laying my head down and two days fasting seemed almost enough,—but not withstanding was forced to ride the fifteen miles to Leghorn with Mrs. Filicchi without even lying down, as my dear William must be carryed there to be buried, and it is a law that it must be done within the 24 hours—however by putting him in the burying house in the church yard we were allowed to wait till eleven the next day and time to send to the Americans and English in the place—they all attended, the consul,[3] and our clergyman, and every respect showed according to his own directions which he gave me in the way of conversation with the greatest composure that I might not have any trouble by being in doubt of what was right. he also sent for Obrien[4] and gave me in his charge in the most calm manner—he took a strange fancy in his mind that he had recieved a letter from the letter office in London telling him that my ticket which he had renewed there had drawn the Royal prize and that James[5] had also written to him that he had not a single bill out in the world—this was the effect of extreme weakness and I never contradicted him in it as it was a source of the greatest comfort and satisfaction to him, and he thanked God always with so much earnestness that now he was not wanted for our support he took him first that he might not see us die, and that while he was wanted he was spared—OBrien and Filicchi all agreed we must let him think so =

Here I anxiously wait my dear Sister for the day of sailing—the Filicchis do all they can to ease my situation and seem indeed that they cannot do enough—indeed from the day we left home we have met with nothing but kindness even in the servants and strangers—Mrs. F[6]__ has been in bed ever since our arrival until the day she came to fetch me from *Pisa*. and Filicchi run down with business did all he

---

[3]Thomas Appleton
[4]Captain of the *Shepherdess*, the ship on which the Setons had come to Italy
[5]James Seton, William Magee Seton's younger brother
[6]Mary Cowper Filicchi

could for us and my Carlton[7] too is all affection both to me and my Anna—

We have not heard one word from Home,—OBrien talks of going to Barcelona but as it is in the Straights and on our way home will make but a few days difference—Home—O my heavenly Father shall I once more be *there*. My Seton said "when you are all again together dont say poor William for I shall be in heaven, and trust you will come to me, and make my darlings always look for me there" + Oh how "good and gracious" has the Lord been in giving such consolation = What shall I say of love to all—an Ocean of love would not be enough—to my dear girls my darling my dear Eliza my all—

tell my dear friend J[ohn] H[enry] H[obart] that I do not write because the opportunity is unexpected and my breast is very weak after all its struggles—that I have a long letter I wrote on board of ship to him—that I am hard pushed by these charitable Romans[8] who wish that so much goodness should be improved by a conversion, which to effect they have even taken the trouble to bring me their best informed Priest *Abbey Plunket*[9] who is an Irishman, but they find me so willing to hear their inlightened conversation, that consequently as learned people like to hear themselves, best, I have but little to say, and as yet keep friends with all as the best comment on my Profession—

My William said he saw his *Tatteé*[10] while he was dying—is she too in heaven—thy will be done—how do I know how many are gone—thy will be done—*it is my Fathers*. I think I may hope to be with you on Ash Wednesday if I do not mistake the day, coming in April = not within Gods house (*but in Spirit*) since I left you, and the 27th December the first <day> night I have taken off my cloaths to sleep since the 4th of October—always watching—I shall write also to my dear Mary Post, and to every one else, my girls, Barclay, my

---

[7]Guy Carleton Bayley, Elizabeth's half-brother

[8]Roman Catholics

[9]Rev. Peter Plunkett, Irish clergyman and noted apologist, who discussed the Catholic religion with Elizabeth at the request of the Filicchis. On her return to New York, Elizabeth mentioned a daily prayer book which he had given her.

[10]Elizabeth's infant daughter, Rebecca

J Bayley,[11] etc you must explain to them that I cannot write—I write so small because it is to go by Post—which I believe will be very high.

to all the family and to Phoeby, Mary, Mammy, Dina Sur,[12] all remember me—tell James I have my Williams Journal as long as he could write, which I will bring to him—Remember me affectionately to W. D. Seton and his wife—and her family[13]—

tell Aunty F[14] *read this letter to her* that my William always talked of her and wished that she could know how happy he was—I wrote to her on Board ship also to tell her how he was—also to Eliza Sadler —all these I shall bring—If—My Soul has heavenly blessing dearest Rebecca—*"The Protecting Presence and consoling Grace of my Redeemer and God"* has never left me =

Your own own *Sister EAS.*[15]

2.9 To Rebecca Seton

Leghorn 6th January 1804

My own dearest Rebecca

Two days ago I wrote you by way of Salem (Boston) and have since heard that there is a fast sailing vessel bound to Baltimore, and think it best to write by both opportunities—though I have nothing but melancholy and sorrow to communicate = in that letter I have written you some of the particulars of my dear Williams departure, death I cannot call it, where the release is so happy as his was = it is my case that would be death to any one not Supported by the Almighty

---

[11]Mary Bayley Post, Elizabeth's sister, who was caring for baby Rebecca. "My girls" refers to William Magee's younger half-sisters, Mary, Charlotte, Harriet, and Cecilia. Barclay was Elizabeth's half-brother Andrew Barclay Bayley. J. Bayley was Joseph, who assisted her father in his medical work on Staten Island.

[12]Servants in the Seton household. Phoebe was with baby Rebecca at the Posts.

[13]This person is unidentified. William Magee Seton had a cousin, William Dalrymple Seton (1774-1804), son of Andrew and Elizabeth Seton, but according to Robert Seton he never married.

[14]Elizabeth Curson Farquhar, William Magee Seton's aunt

[15]A note follows this letter which appears to be written by Rev. Simon Gabriel Bruté: "most interesting 1. for the death of her Husband 2. account to Hobart of the efforts of Rev. Mr. Plunkett to convert her."

2.9 ASJPH 1-3-3-18:44

Comforter, but his Mercy has supported, and still upholds, and in it alone I trust. I also wrote you that Captain O'Brian[1] has appointed the 15th instance[2] for his day of sailing, but do not think it will be before the 20th and instead of Ash Wednesday which I thoughtlessly mentioned as the time I expect to be with you, I should have said the 1st April, and shall bless God indeed if it is then. once more to see my darlings seems to be more happiness *than* I dare to ask for = My William charged me always to make them look for him in heaven—and must *you* My dearest Rebecca first point it out to them—that they shall see their Father no more in this world—

I shall enclose this letter to Jack[3] and as it hurts me to write will write only to you, as I have sent by the Salem vessel letters to *My sister*, Mrs. Sad, Uncle Charlton, John Wilks,[4] and yourself I have not heard one word from America except by Captain Blagg[5] of the *Piamingo* who said that business had recommenced[6] and the inhabitants returned to New York the first November.

My dear Williams Sufferings and death has interested so many persons here, that I am as kindly treated and as much attended to both as to my health and every Consolation that they can offer to me, as if I was at Home, indeed when I look forward to my unprovided situation as it relates to the affairs of this life, I must often smile at their tenderness and precautions—Anna says "O Mamma how many friends God has provided for us in this Strange land, for they are our friends before they know us" = and who can tell how great a comfort he provided for me when he gave her to me. Richard is at Cadiz[7] and I believe does not know of our being here as he has performed a long quarantine in consequence of his having been at Malaga[8] while the Plague was there—

---

[1]Captain of the *Shepherdess*

[2]Of the present month

[3]John Curson Seton, Elizabeth's brother-in-law

[4]Mary Bayley Post, Eliza Craig Sadler, Dr. John Charlton, Elizabeth's maternal uncle and a prominent New York physician under whom Dr. Richard Bayley had studied, and John Wilkes.

[5]A sea captain

[6]Yellow fever had flared up in the summer of 1803 and many wealthy New Yorkers had fled the city.

[7]Richard Bayley, Elizabeth's half-brother. Cadiz is a seaport city in Spain.

[8]A province in southern Spain.

Carlton[9] is as affectionate as possible—he was with us at Pisa when my William died, but could not be of any use but in keeping every body away from his room as he could not have any one near him but me and even disliked to have the door opened—he was so anxious to keep his mind fixed on his approaching hour that when any one spoke <but me> it seemed as if he only felt pain and anxiety that they should be gone—again let me repeat it that in every thing that related to his dear Soul I had every comfort that I could expect and the surest grounds of Hope, through the merits of our Redeemer—

When I say I send my love to you all I send my whole heart and could almost say my Soul only that it is not mine—

I have the prospect of still <having> watching and care during my voyage, for our Captains wife is in the family way and is often very ill—she was so ill New Years night that I was obliged to go, before a carriage could be got, mud over shoes, and be hoisted up the ship to remain on board till the next day = She treated us sadly coming here, brought a baby with the Whooping cough, also a servant Boy who with the childs coughing and crying all day and most of the night and the mothers scolding was a great disturbance to my William and finally poor Ann got it too and often hindered his getting rest—for me it is all alike—but these three months has been a hard lesson—pray for me that I may make a good use of it—dear dear Rebecca heaven bless you.

Your EAS.

If there could be any faith in singularly impressive and repeated dreams our dear J[ohn] *H[enry] H[obart]* is in heaven too—how much William used to wish for him—My best love to his Wife

---

[9]Guy Carleton Bayley, Elizabeth's half-brother

2.10 Florence Journal to Rebecca Seton[1]

[January 1804]

Four days I have been at Florence lodged in the famous Palace of Medicis,[2] which fronts the Arno and prevents a view of the high mountains of Morelic[3] covered with elegant country seats, and five Bridges across the river which are always thronged with people and carriages.

On Sunday 8th January at eleven oclock went with Mrs. F[ilicchi][4] to the chapel—La SS. Annunziata[5]—passing thro' a curtain my eye was struck with hundreds of people kneeling, but the gloom of the chapel which is lighted only by the wax tapers on the Altar and a small window at the top darkened with green silk made every object at first appear indistinct, while that kind of soft and distant musick which lifts the mind to a foretaste of heavenly pleasure called up in an instant every dear and tender idea of my Soul, and forgetting Mrs. F., companions, and all the surrounding scene I sunk to my Knees in the first place I found vacant, and shed a torrent of tears at the recollection of how long I had been a stranger in the house of my God, and the accumulated sorrow that had separated me from it. I need not tell you that I said our dear service with my whole soul as far as in its agitation I could recollect.—When the Organ ceased and mass was over we walked round the Chapel, the elegance of cielings in carved gold, altar loaded with gold, silver, and other precious ornaments, pictures of every sacred subject and the dome a continued representation of different parts of Scripture—all this can never be conceived by description—nor my delight in seeing old men and women, young

---

2.10 ASJPH 1-3-3-3:15

[1]This document, the journal of Elizabeth's impressions of Florence written for Rebecca Seton, is not an original; Antonio Filicchi asked to keep the original and copied it for Elizabeth.

[2]On Via Cavour, one block from the cathedral, built in the fifteenth century, enlarged in the seventeenth century

[3]The Appenine Mountains border Florence.

[4]Amabilia Filicchi

[5]The Church of La Santissima Annunziata (The Most Holy Annunciation) in Florence contains frescoes by Andrea del Sarto and sculpture by John of Bologna.

women, and all sorts of people kneeling promiscuously about the Altar as inattentive to us or any other passengers, as if we were not there. On the other side of the Church another Chapel presented a similar scene, but as another mass had begun I passed tip toe behind Mrs. F[ilicchi]—unable to look round, though every one is so intent on their prayers and Rosary that it is very immaterial what a stranger does.

While Mrs. F[ilicchi] went to make visits I visited the Church of S. Firenze[6] and saw two more elegant Chapels but in a more simple style and had the pleasure of treading the sacred place with two of its inhabitants as a Convent is also part of the building, saw a young Priest unlock his little Chapel with that composed and equal eye as if his Soul had entered before him. My heart would willingly have followed after; here was to be the best musick—but at night, and no female could be admitted.

Rode to the Queens gardens[7] where I saw elms and firs, with edges of yew and Ivy in beautiful verdeur and cultivated fields appearing like our advanced spring: indeed it was not possible to look without thinking, or to think without my Soul crying out for those it loves in heaven or in earth; therefore I was forced to close my eyes and lean against the carriage as if sleepy—which the mild softness of the air and warmth of the sun seemed easyly to excuse.

Stopped at the Queens Country Palace and passed through such innumerable suits of appartments so elegant that each was a new object of wonder—but Solomons vanity and vexation of spirit[8] was all the while in my head.

Saw the Queen[9] twice, but as little Ann says she would not be known from any other woman but by the number of her attendants.

---

[6]St. Florence, one of Florence's few Baroque churches, constructed in 1645 by the Phillipine Fathers.

[7]Probably the Boboli Gardens behind the Pitti Palace

[8]Cf. Book of Ecclesiastes (Qoheleth) 1:2, often attributed to Solomon

[9]The "Queen" was the wife of Ferdinand III, the Grand Duke of Tuscany. Dispossessed by the French in 1799, he was reinstated in 1814 and ruled until 1824. At the time Elizabeth was visiting, the grand duchy of Tuscany was called the Kingdom of Etruria. From 1801 until 1814 it was part of Napoleon's northern Italian system.

Sunday evening Mr. Trueman,[10] Coffin, and Mrs. F. went to the Opera. I had a good fire in my room, locked the doors, and with my Ann, Books, and Pen passed a happy evening for this World—When we said our dear service together, she burst in to tears as she has always done since we say it *alone*. She says, my dear Papa is praising God in Heaven, and I ought not to cry for him, but I believe it is human nature, is it not Mamma? I think of what David said "I shall go to him, he cannot return to me"[11] Her conversation is dearer to me and preferable to any I can have this side of the grave—it is one of the greatest mercies that I was permitted to bring her for many reasons.

Monday morning visited *the Gallery*[12] but as my curiosity had been greatly excited by my Seton's descriptions, and the French have made great depredations, it did not equal my expectations. The chief d'oeuvre of D—a head scarcely to be distinguished from life, the Redeemer about 12 years of age—a Madonna holding an hour glass in one hand and a skull in the other with a smiling look expressing I fear neither time nor death—Madam[e] Le Brun a French painter—and the Baptist very young were those that attracted me most. The Statues in Bronze were beautiful, but being only an American[13] could not look very straight at them.

Innumerable curiosities and antiquities surrounded on all sides—The Sacred Representations were sufficient to engage and interest all my attention, and as the French had not been covetous of those I had the advantage of my companions—but felt the void of him who would have pointed out the beauties of every object, too much to enjoy any perfectly—*"Alone but half enjoyed"* O My God![14]

Went to the Church of S. Lorenzo[15] where a sensation of delight struck me so forceably that as I approached the great Altar formed of

---

[10]A business associate of the Filicchis. Coffin has not been identified.

[11]2 Sam. 12:23

[12]The Uffizi, which her husband had seen during an earlier visit to Italy. The French raided the gallery during the Napoleonic wars.

[13]American art did not yet depict the nude human body.

[14]"O My God!" Although the manuscript is not in Elizabeth Seton's hand, she clearly read it over because this comment is in her writing.

[15]The Church of St. Lawrence near the Medici palace after a design by Brunelleschi. It is considered an outstanding example of early Renaissance religious architecture.

all the most precious stones marbles etc. that could be produced "My Soul does magnify the Lord, my spirit rejoices in God my Saviour"[16] came in my mind with a fervor which absorbed every other feeling—it recalled the ideas of the offerings of David and Solomon to the Lord when the rich and valuable production of nature and art were devoted to his holy Temple, and sanctifyed to his service.[17] Annexed to this is the Chapel of marble, the beauty and work, and richness of which might be supposed the production of more than mortal means, if its unfinished dome did not discover its imperfection. It is the Tomb of the Medicis family, monuments of granit lapis, golden crowns set with precious stones, the polish of the whole which reflects the different monuments as a miroir and the awful *black Cosmos* who are represented on the top of the monuments as large as life with their Crowns and Scepters, made my poor weak head turn, and I believe if it had been possible that I should have been *alone* there it would never have turned back again.

Passed my Evening again in my room with dear Ann—at half past nine Mr. Coffin took the trouble to come for me from the Opera that I might hear some wonderful Trio, in which the celebrated David[18] was to show all his excellence and as it would be over at ten, and Mrs. F[ilicchi] so much desired it, I went with hat and veil, instead of the masks which they all wear—The Opera house is so dark that you scarcely can distinguish the person next to you—Ann thought the singers would go mad, and I could not find the least gratification in their quavers, felt the full conviction that those who could find pleasure in such a scene must be unacquainted with *real pleasure*—My William had so much desired that I should hear this *David* that I tried to be pleased, but not one note touched my heart. At ten I was released from the most unwilling exertion I had yet made, and returned with redoubled delight to my *pleasures*, which were as the joys of heaven in comparison.

---

[16]Luke 1:46-47
[17]Cf. 1 Chron. 29.
[18]Giacomo Davide was the most famous tenor of his time.

Tuesday saw the Church S. Maria[19] and the Queen's Palace in which she resides. Every beauty that gold, damask of every variety, and India Tapestry can devise, embellished with fine Statues, Cielings embossed with gold, elegant pictures, carpets and floors inlaid with the most costly satin woods in beautiful patterns, tables inlaid with most precious orders of stone etc. all combine to make the Palace of Pitti[20] a pattern of elegance and taste—so say the Connoisseurs—for me I am no Judge as Ombrosi says.

A Picture of the descent from the Cross[21] nearly as large as life engaged *my whole soul.* Mary at the foot of it expressed well that the iron had entered into her—and the shades of death over her agonized contenance so strongly contrasted the heavenly Peace of the dear Redeemers that it seems as if his pains had fallen on her—How hard it was to leave that picture and how often even in the few hours interval since I have seen it, I shut my eyes and recall it in imagination.

Abraham and Isaac also are represented in so expressive a manner that you feel the whole convulsion of the Patriarchs breast, and well for me that in viewing these two pictures my companions were engaged with other subjects. The dropping tears could be hid, but the shaking of the whole frame not so easily. Dear Sister—*H[enry H[obart]*—you had your sigh in reflecting how truly you would enjoy them.

Wednesday—

This morning I have indeed enjoyed in the anatomical museum and cabinet of Natural history—the "Work of the Almighty hand" in every object. The anatomical rooms displaying nature in every division of the human frame is almost too much for human nature to support—Mine shrank from it, but recalling the idea of my God in all I saw though so humiliating and painful in the view still it was congenial to every feeling of my Soul, and as my companion *Trueman* has an intelligent mind and an excellent heart which for the time entered in to my feelings, I passed through most of the rooms uninterrupted in

[19]Church of Santa Maria Novella, a Dominican church dating to 1360 with famous frescoes
[20]The residence of the Grand Duke of Tuscany from 1550 to 1859, with the Boboli Gardens behind it
[21]A painting in the Church of Santa Maria Novella

the sacred reflections they inspired—one of the rooms a female cannot enter, [several words crossed out]—and passed the door to the cabinet of natural history. The pleasures to be there enjoyed would require the attention of at least a month—In the short time I was allowed I received more than I could have obtained in years, out of my own Cabinet of precious things.

If I was allowed to choose an enjoyment from the whole Theatre of human nature it would be to go over those two hours again with my dear *Brother Post*[22] my companion [Three words crossed out.]

Visited the Gardens called *Boboli* belonging to the Queen's Residence—Was well exercised in running up flights of steps in the style of hanging Gardens and sufficently repaid by the view of the environs of Florence, and the many varieties of beautiful evergreens with which this country abounds, and prevent the possibility of recollecting it is winter except the cold and damp of their buildings remind you of it.—If the Tuscans[23] are to be judged by their taste they are a happy people for every thing without is very shabby, and within elegant. The exterior of their best buildings are to appearance in a state of ruin.—Also saw the Academy of Sculptors and the Garden of Simpla, and Botanical Garden—O O O Heaven!!!!![24]

2.11 To Rebecca Seton

28 January 1804

My Rebecca My Souls Sister—

how many new thoughts and affections pass my mind in a day, and you so far away to whom I would wish to tell all—after the last sorrowful word at Pisa[1] what shall I say—arrived at Mr. [Antonio] Filicchy's who gave the look of many Sympathys as he helped me

[22]Dr. Wright Post, Elizabeth's brother-in-law

[23]Florence and Leghorn are in the region of Tuscany.

[24]"O O O Heaven!!!!!" is in Elizabeth's hand.

2.11 ASJPH 1-3-3-8:60

[1]William Magee Seton died at Pisa.

from his carriage, and showed me to my chamber where his most amiable lady and sweet Ann looked in my face as if to comfort but my poor high heart was in the clouds roving after my William's soul and repeating my God you are my God,[2] and so I am now alone in the world with you and my little ones but you are my Father and doubly theirs—Mrs. F[ilicchi] very tired with our ride left me to rest—

Evening

—then came Parson [Thomas] Hall—a kind man indeed—"as the tree falls Mam—there it lies," was his first address to me—who was little mindful of his meaning then—our good old capitano[3] also came with a black crape on the hat and arm and such a look of Sorrow at his poor Signora—all his kindness in the Lazaretto was present, dearest Ann melted his heart again—and he ours—so many tender marks of respect and compassion and boundless generosity from the two families of Filicchys—the first night of rest with little Anns tender doating heart alone—the first night of rest since October 2—and long long before that—as you well know—

// "St. Francis de Sales Day"

(said Mr. Philippo F[ilicchi] as he entered our room) "I will give you his devout life to amuse you"[4]—amuse it truly did—how many times I was on my knees from strong impression of its powerful persuasion begging our God to make me so and so, as he said

// silence and peace enough in our chamber—Ann would say as the different enquiries would be made "could they do any thing for us, why truly Ma every body is our friend"

2nd February 1804—

This is some particular festival here[5]—Mrs. F[ilicchi] took me with her to Mass as she calls it, and we say to church—I dont know how to say the awful effect at being where they told me God was present in the blessed Sacrament, and the tall pale meek heavenly looking man who

---

[2]Cf. Ps. 63:1

[3]The man who had guarded the Setons when they were in the Lazaretto at Leghorn

[4]Saint Francis de Sales' feast day is January 29. He is the author of *Introduction to the Devout Life*, a spiritual classic.

[5]The feast of the Purification of Mary.

did I dont know what for I was the side of the altar, so that I could not look up without seeing his countenance on which Many lights from the altar reflected, and gave such strange impressions to my soul that I could but cover my face with my hands and let the tears run—oh my the very little while we were there will never be forgotten though I saw nothing and no one, but this more than human person as he seemed to me—

Now we go to Florence—Mr. and Mrs. [Antonio] F[ilicchi] are positive—ah me—that is not the way my heart goes, for it is not towards America—but Captain O[Brien] is to be ready by our return

10th February

—Well my dearest here is your Souls Sister and little Ann truly in the joyful moment—we are to sail in a few days now—I have made my little journal to Florence separate for you, as you will see—and when we meet I have so much to tell you about things you do not dream of—these dear people are so strange about Religion. I asked Mr. F[ilicchi] something I dont know what about the different religions and he began to tell me there was only one true Religion and without a right Faith we would not be acceptable to God—O my Sir then said I if there is but one Faith and nobody pleases God without it, where are all the good people who die out of it—I dont know he answered, that depends on what light of Faith they had re[ceive]d, but I know where people will go who can know the right Faith if they pray for it and enquire for it, and yet do neither, much as to say Sir you want me to pray and enquire and be of your Faith said I laughing—pray, and enquire, said he, that is all I ask you.

so dearest Bec I am laughing with God when I try to be serious and say daily as the good gentleman told me in old Mr. Popes[6] words *"if I am right O teach my heart still in the right to stay, if I am wrong thy grace impart to find the better way."* not that I can think there is a better way than I know—but every one must be respected in their own—the other day a young Englishman brought the blood from my very heart to my face in the church of Montenay[7] where the F[ilicchi]

---

[6]Alexander Pope, English essayist and poet (1688-1744)

[7]A church in Montenero built by a branch of the Benedictines, the Congregation of Vallombroso. The chapel at Montenero was thought to be the scene of many miraculous cures. No Italian ship sailed past the chapel without saluting the painting of the Virgin Mary housed there.

families took Ann and I to a lovely part of the country where Mr. F[ilicchi] had been concealed by the blessed inhabitants of the convent during some political revolution, and they invited us to hear mass in their chapel, *there* this poor young Englishman at the Very moment the Priest was doing the most sacred action they call the elevation, (after the bread you know is blessed with the prayers as they do when we go to communion)—just at that moment this wild young man said loud in my ear "this is what they call their real *PRESENCE*"—my very heart trembled with shame and sorrow for his unfeeling interruption of their sacred adoration for all around was dead Silence and many were prostrated.—involuntarily I bent from him to the pavement and thought secretly on the word of St. Paul with starting tears "they discern not the Lords body"[8] and the next thought was how should they eat and drink their very damnation for not *discerning* it, if indeed it is not *there*—yet how should it be *there*, and how did he breathe my Soul in me, and how and how a hundred other things I know nothing about.

I am a *Mother* so the Mothers thought came also how was my GOD a little babe in the first stage of his mortal existance *in Mary*, but I lost these thoughts in my babes at home, which I daily long for more and more, but they wait a fair wind—

18th Feb[ruar]y—

Oh my God—GOD TRULY MINE or what would become of me—how can I tell you Rebecca my souls Rebecca how long before we meet. We were safe on board the vessel ready to sail next morning, had parted with our most kind friends, loaded with their blessings and presents, I with gold and passports and recommendations, for fear of Algerians, or necessity to put in any of the Mediterranean ports[9]—but all that in Vain—a driving storm at night struck the Vessel against another, and in the Morn instead of hoisting sail for America, we were obliged to return on shore—most kindly indeed welcomed by the Filicchis, but heart down enough at the disappointment—and imagine

---

[8] 1 Cor. 11:17-34.
[9] Pirates were active in the Mediterranean at the time.

the rest when our sweetest Ann unable to hide her suffering was found in high Fever covered with irruptions which the Dr. pronounced *Scarlet*[10]—O My—the darling tried to conceal all she could, but little guessed the whole consequence for the doctor said the next day I must give up the Voyage or the life of the child, and could you believe I was firm in choosing the latter, that is in trusting her life and my hard case to our God since there was no other Vessel for America in Port—but Captain O[Brien] came only to say that if he took us he could not get a bill of health for Barcelona where he was forced to leave part of his cargo and a quarantine there would ruin his Voyage

—the good man may have made this more evident because from my entrance in the ship the second time a most painful circumstance had taken place *thro' my ignorance*, and I was likely to have had a truly unhappy Voyage, but what of that if I would at the end of it hold you and my darlings to my heart—

Well the hand of our God is all I must see in the whole—but it pinches to the Soul.

24th—

close work with little Ann—she is over the worst though with such care and attention of every body as would melt your heart.—my Very Soul seems in her sitting or laying all day and night by her side in this strange but beautiful land—

My Sister dear how happy would we be if we believed what these dear Souls believe, that they *possess God* in the Sacrament[11] and that he remains in their churches and is carried to them when they are sick, oh my—when they carry the B[lesse]d Sacrament under my Window while I feel the full loneliness and sadness of my case I cannot stop the tears at the thought my God how happy would I be even so far away from all so dear, if I could find you in the church as they do (for there is a chapel in the very house of Mr. F[ilicchi]) how many things I would say to you of the sorrows of my heart and the sins of my life—the other day in a moment of excessive distress I fell on my knees without

---

[10]Scarlettina, a version of scarlet fever
[11]Holy Eucharist

thinking when the Blessed Sacrament passed by and cried in an agony to God *to bless me* if he was *there*, that my whole Soul desired only him—a little prayer book of Mrs. F[ilicchi]'s was on the table and I opened a little prayer (the Memorare) of St. Bernard to the Blessed Virgin begging her to be *our Mother*, and I said it to her with such a certainty that God would surely refuse nothing *to his Mother*, and that she could not help loving and pitying the poor Souls he died for, that I felt really I had a Mother which you know my foolish heart so often lamented to have lost in early days.[12]—from the first remembrance of infancy I have looked in all the plays of childhood and wildness of youth to the clouds for my Mother, and at that moment it seemed as if I had found more than her, even in tenderness and pity of a Mother—so I cried myself to sleep in her heart

2.12 To Rebecca Seton

Leghorn 5th March 1804

My dearest Rebecca must be very anxious for letters from her own Sister after that which [Antonio] Filichi wrote J[ohn] W[ilkes] by the *Shepherdess*—It pleases God to try me very hard in many ways—but also to bestow such favors and comforts that it would be worse than disobedience not to dwell on his Mercy while I must bow to his dispensations—We were embarked on board the *Shepherdess* and to sail the next morning but a storm driving back those vessels which had sailed before us Obrien[1] could not venture out and while he waited a fair wind My dear Ann was siezed with violent fever and sore throat which proved to be the Scarlettina,[2] and OBrien was forced to leave me to my fate—She was eighteen days in bed, and the day she left it I was obliged to go to mine with the same complaint, and have this day been a fortnight, not in *great* suffering for I was too weak to receive

---

[12]Elizabeth was three when her mother died.
2.12 ASJPH 1-3-3-18:42 (Seton-Jevons #286-289)
[1]The captain of the *Shepherdess*
[2]A version of scarlet fever

any complaint violently, but suffered almost as much with that as I could have done otherways—

We came from on Board of ship to Antonio Filicchis house and have recieved more than Friendship,—the most tender affection could not bestow more, and to crown all his goodness to me he has taken my passage in the *Piamingo* Captain Blagg who sails direct for New York as soon as the Equinox is past, and accompanies us himself, as business and a wish to be acquainted with our country has long made the voyage necessary to him and now the desire of restoring his "dear Sister" to her children and those she loves best, decides him to leave his dear little wife and children = he says this is due to all my dear Setons love and Friendship for him—and is it possible I have again the hope of seeing you so soon—

My God will do all—dear dear Rebecca to tell you what he has done for me thro' my bitter afflictions will require many many happy Evenings, which if he has in store for us we will enjoy with thankful hearts, if not ____ I write only to *you*, and while I have been writing this feel so ill at my ease that I scarcely know how to go on—my whole heart, head, all are sick—but I think if I could once more be with you I should be well as ever—

Anna is very well and considered little less than an Angel here She has not improved in acquirements of general Education, but in understanding and temper the five months past are to her more than years—once more shall I hold my dear ones in my arms—Heavenly Father what an hour will that be—my dear Fatherless Children—Fatherless to the World, but rich in God their Father for he will never leave us nor forsake us—I have been to my dear Setons grave—and wept plentifully over it with the unrestrained affection which the last sufferings of his life added to remembrance of former Years, had made almost more than precious—When you read my daily memorandums since I left home you will feel what my love has been, and acknowledge that God alone could support [page torn] thro' such proofs as has been required of it—[natural] strength must have fallen the first trial—If it [pleases] God that we sail on the *Piamingo*, and nothing extraordinary happens to lengthen our passage I shall be with you nearly as soon as this, as our ship sails remarkably fast, and the season could not be more favourable—

—Dear dear Rebecca the love I should send to *all* would be endless, therefore you must do all for me—

May God bless You dear Sister as he has blessed me, by blessing you with his Heavenly consolations—pray for me as I do for you continually—*Your own own Sister.*

EAS.

8th March—

—I see you and my darlings in my dreams suffering and sorry—this is about the time you will recieve my first letters—

2.13 To Antonio Filicchi

6th April 1804

My most dear A.

We often recieve blessing from the hand of God and convert them into evils this has been my fault in respect to the very sincere and uncommon affections I have for you, and I am determined with Gods help no more to abuse the very great favour he bestows on me in giving me your friendship and in future will endeavour to shew you how much I value it by doing all I can to contribute to your happiness—on your part I intreat you will behave to me with Confidence and affection—the more you confide in me the more Careful I shall be—trust me and the Angel—

2.14 Journal to Rebecca Seton continued[1]

18th April—

Many a long day since your own Sis held the pen—the very day
Anna left her bed I had to go in her place—oh my the patience and
more than human kindness of these dear Filicchys[2] for us—you would
say it was our Saviour himself they recieved in his poor and sick
strangers—Now I am able to leave my room after my 20 days (as
Anna had hers).—

this Evening standing by the window the moon shining full on
Filicchys countenance he raised his eyes to heaven and showed me
how to make the Sign of the CROSS[3]—dearest Rebecca I was cold
with the awful impression my first making it gave me. the Sign of the
CROSS of Christ on me—deepest thoughts came with it of I know not
what earnest desires to be closely united with him who died on it—of
that last day when he is to bear it in triumph, and did you notice my
dear one the letter T with which the Angel is to mark us on the
forehead[4] *is a cross.*—All the Catholic Religion is full of those mean-
ings which interest me so—Why Rebecca they believe all we do and
suffer, if we offer it for our sins serves to expiate them—You may remember when I asked Mr. [John Henry] H[obart] what was meant by
fasting in our prayer book, as I found myself on Ash Wednesday
Morning saying so foolishly to God, "I turn to you in fasting weeping
and mourning" and I had come to church with a hearty breakfast of
Buckwheat cakes and coffee, and full of life and spirits with little
thought of my sins, you may remember what he said about it being *old
customs* etc. well the dear Mrs. F[ilicchi] who I am with never eats this
Season of Lent till after the clock strikes three (then the family assem-
bles) and she says she offers her weakness and pain of fasting for her
sins united with our Saviours sufferings—I like that very much—but

2.14 ASJPH 1-3-3-8:60

[1]This document contains material not quite identical to the second part of the Italian Journal in the
Archives at Mount St. Vincent printed above.
[2]Antonio and Amabilia Filicchi
[3]The Catholic practice of signing the cross on one's person
[4]Cf. Rev. 7:3

what I like better my dearest Rebecca (only think what a comfort) they go to mass here every morning—ah how often you and I used to give the sigh and you would press your arm in mine of a Sunday evening and say *no more till next Sunday* as we turned from the church door which closed on us (unless a prayer day was given out in the week)—well here they go to church at 4 every morning if they please—and you know how we were laughed at for running from one church to the other *Sacrament Sundays*,[5] that we might recieve as often as we could, well here people that love God and live a good regular life can go (tho' many do not do it) yet they can go *every day*.

—O my—I dont know how any body can have any trouble in this world who believe all these dear Souls believe—if I dont believe it, it shall not be for want of praying—why they must be as happy as the angels almost—little Ann is quite well now and so am I—but little prospect of home—

Oh joy joy joy a Captain B[lagge][6] will take us to America—and only think of Mr. Fi[licchi]'s goodness as this Captain is a very young man and a stranger, and many things of war or danger might happen on the Voyage Mr. F[ilicchi] will make it with us—Ann is wild with joy—yet often she whispers me "Ma is there no Catholicks in America, Ma wont we go to the Catholic church when we go home"—Sweet darling she is now out Visiting some of the blessed places with Mrs. F[ilicchi] children and their governess—would you believe whenever we go to walk we go first in some church or convent chapel as we pass which we always forsee by a large CROSS before it and say some little prayers before we go further—Men do it as well as women you know with us a man would be ashamed to be seen kneeling especially of a week day—O my but I shall be with you again—

Two days more and we set out for HOME—this mild heavenly evening puts me in mind when often you and I have stood or rather leaned on each other looking at the setting sun, sometimes with silent tears and sighs for that HOME where sorrow cannot come—Alas how may I perhaps find mine—sorrow plenty—I was speaking of it the

---

[5]Sacrament Sundays were held about six times a year in the Episcopal church at the time. The service included eucharistic prayer and communion as part of Sunday worship.
[6]The captain of the *Pyomingo*

other evening to Filicchi and he said in his dry English "my little sister, God, the *Almighty*, is laughing at you he takes care of little birds and makes the lilys grow, and you fear he will not take care of you[7]—I tell you he will take care of you."—

So I hope—dearest Rebecca you know we used to envy them that were poor because they had nothing to do with the world—

last hour in Leghorn—

Oh think how this heart trembles—Mrs. F[ilicchi] came while the stars were yet bright to say we would go to Mass and she would there part with her Antonio—oh the admirable woman—as we entered the church the Cannon of the *Piamingo* which would carry us to America gave the signal to be on board in 2 *hours*, MY SAVIOUR—MY GOD—Antonio and his wife their separation in God and Communion—poor I *not* but did I not beg him to give me their Faith and promise him *all* in return for such a gift—little Ann and I had only strange tears of Joy and grief—we leave but dear ashes—

—the last adieu of Mrs. F[ilicchi] as the sun rose full on the balcony where we stood, and the last signal of our ship for our parting—will I ever forget—now poor Antonio is tearing away—and I Hastening to you and my angels.[8]

"The 8th of April, at half-past four in the morning, my dear brother[9] came to my room to awaken my soul to all its dearest hopes and anticipations. The heaven was bright with stars, the wind fair, and the *Piamingo's* signal expected to call us on board—meanwhile the tolling of the bell called us to mass, and in a few minutes we were prostrate in the presence of God. Oh, my soul, how solemn was that offering—for a blessing on our voyage—for my dear ones, my sisters, and all so dear to me—and more than all, for the souls of my dear husband and father—earnestly our desires ascended with the blessed sacrifice, that they might find acceptance through Him who gave himself

---

[7]Cf. Matt. 6:25-34.

[8]The first edition of Rev. Charles I. White, *Life of Mrs. Eliza A. Seton: Foundress and First Superior of the Sisters or Daughters of Charity in the United States of America* (New York: Edward Dunigan and Brother, 1853) 106-112, contains the following passages about the return voyage. It varies somewhat from the account of the last hour in Leghorn printed above.

[9]Elizabeth frequently refers to Antonio Filicchi as brother from this point on in their relationship.

for us—earnestly we desired to be united with Him, and would gladly encounter all the sorrows before us to be partakers of that blessed body and blood. O my God, spare and pity me.

"We returned home with hearts full of many sensations—on my part, sorrow at parting with the friends who had been so kind to me, and the dear little angels I tenderly love, struggled with the joy of once more embarking for home—while I gave dear Amabilia a farewell embrace in the balcony, the sun rose bright and glorious, and called out thoughts to that hour when the Sun of Righteousness would rise and reunite us forever.

"The signal had been given, the waterman waited for us, and my dear brother passed the struggle like a man and a Christian—dear manly soul, it indeed appeared to me in the 'image of God.'

"Philip Filicchi and Carlton[10] waited for us at the Health Office, and letters for America.

[Filippo] Filicchi's last blessing to me was as his whole conduct had been—that of the truest friend. Oh, Filicchi, you shall not *witness against me.* May God bless you forever, and may you shine as the 'stars in glory,'[11] for what you have done for me.

"At eight o'clock, was quietly seated with little Ann and dear Antonio, on the quarter deck. The anchor weighed, sails hoisted, and dear yo, yo! resounding on all sides, brought to remembrance the 2d October, 1803,[12] with a force as strong as could be borne—most dear Seton, where are you now? I lose sight of the shore that contains your dear ashes, and your soul is in that region of immensity where I cannot find you. My Father and my God—and yet I must always love to retrospect thy wonderful dispensations—to be sent so many thousand miles on so hopeless an errand—to be constantly supported and accompanied by thy consoling mercy, through scenes of trial which nature alone must have sunk under—to be brought to the light of thy truth, notwithstanding every affection of my heart and power of my will was opposed to it—to be succored and cherished by the tenderest friendship,

---

[10]Guy Carleton Bayley, Elizabeth's half-brother
[11]Cf. Sirach 43:9.
[12]The date when the Setons set sail from New York to Italy.

while separated and far from those that I loved—my Father and my God, while I live, let me praise—while I have my being let me serve and adore thee.[13]

19th April, 1804.

"The Lord is my refuge—my God is the strength of my confidence. If the Lord had not helped me, it had not failed but my soul had been put to silence; but when I said my foot had slipped, thy mercy, O Lord, held me up.[14] For four days past, the trial has been hard—oh, Lord, deal not with me in displeasure—let not my enemy triumph—have mercy on us, for Jesus Christ's sake.

"So many days on board, and could not find courage to begin my journal.

"O my God! graciously hear my prayers; accept my tears. Shouldst thou deal with us as we deserve, where should we hide from thy presence? Lift us from the dust, thou Lord of Righteousness, and though we are tied and bound by the chains of our sins, let the faithfulness of thy mercy loose us for the sake of Jesus Christ our Saviour.

"20th April—This day thirty-seven years ago, my Seton was born—does he pass this birth-day in heaven? Oh, my husband, how my soul would rejoice to be united with yours—if rejoicing before his throne, how joyful—if in the bonds of justice, how willingly it would share your pain to lessen it. My Saviour and my God, be not angry with me; consider my desire and have mercy.

"My dear, dear little children, no feast of mirth to-day; my own Rebecca, sister of my soul, something strongly tells me that you too are in heaven.

"21st—'Ye shall not be tempted above what ye are able, but with the temptation there shall be a way to escape.' This way, Lord, I must seek or I am lost; there is no possibility of outward means, and in thy holy name alone must be my refuge. Once more then, we set out again—(+ to God is the mark)—trusting in thee alone, under thy

---

[13]Subsequent editions of White's biography ended at this point. What follows was omitted in all editions after the first, published in 1853. The excerpt reprinted here contains numerous scriptural allusions.

[14]Cf. Ps. 46 and Ps. 38:16.

banner and bearing thy cross. Since we cannot fly the monster, we must face him, calling on thy name, Jesus! Jesus! Jesus!

"The madness that leads us from thee is without excuse, the blindness that keeps us from following thee, leaves us a prey to the destroyer; but, O Lord, let it be so no longer; have mercy upon us and strengthen our souls, or all our resolutions will prove but delusive words. Lord Jesus Christ, have mercy. When a soul whose only hope is in God, whose concern and desires are so limited that it would forsake all human beings, and account the dearest ties of life as foolishness compared with his love—when this soul sincerely desirous of serving and obeying him, is beset by the lowest passions of human nature, and from tears and prayers of earnest penitence can, by the apparently, most trivial incitements, pass to the most humiliating compliances to sin—apparently, for until the effects are experienced, it would be too incredible that the commonest affections and unintentional actions should produce a confusion and disturbance in the mind that is exalted to the love of God, and destroy every impression but momentary gratification—this can only be the work of the enemy of our souls—our souls that have so often declared inviolable fidelity to God—so often prayed to him for grace and mercy, and while lamenting our errors, and trying to gain mutual strength, have solemnly declared that we would embrace our cross, follow our leader, and valiantly oppose the enemy of our salvation. Most dear Antonio, a thousand times endeared to me by the struggles of your soul, our Lord is with us—once more the mark is—+ to God.

"23d—We have passed this day opposite the Pyrenees. Their base, black as jet, and the dazzling whiteness of the snow on their tops, which were high above the clouds that settled round them, formed a subject for the most delightful contemplations, and spoke so loudly of God, that my soul answered them involuntarily in the sweet language of praise and glory. The gentlest motion of the waves, which were as a sheet of glass reflecting the last rays of the sun over the mountains, and the rising moon on the opposite shore—and more than all, that cheerful content in my soul that always accompanies it when it is faithful to its dear Master, has recalled the remembrance of precious hours, and makes me incessantly cry out, my God! my God! do not forsake me, for certain it is, that whatever enjoyments are separate from that heavenly peace his favor gives, are only bitterness to me, even whilst their delusions would make me forget the only source of all blessing. The Pyrenees divide Spain and Portugal from France—and Oh! how many miles divide me from the dear Highlands of *Home*. If the Pyrenees would form a bridge for me, what hardships would I think too great in crossing them. God—Patience—Hope.

"24th April—We have passed the Straits, and again I have seen Gibraltar, with the thousand bitter recollections that must always recur to my thoughts when I think of the sufferings of my William when we passed it together.

"I have not mentioned two days which I wish to remember—one in view of the towering Alps, which separate Italy from France; also the day we were becalmed opposite the town of Valencia,[15] and surrounded by Lord Nelson's fleet. We were boarded by the *Belle-Isle*, and the evening before by the seventy-four *Excellent*.[16]

"Oh, my God, if I should die in the midst of so much sin and so little penitence! how terrible it will be to fall into thy hands! I have sinned against heaven and before thee, O my Father. Oh that I could wash out my sins with my tears, and expiate them with my blood. I know I deserve death as the punishment of my sins, and therefore accept with submission the decree of thy justice; let this body formed of the earth return to the earth, but oh, let the soul created in thy image, return again to thy bosom. My hope, O Father of mercies, is in thee, for I know thou desirest not the death of a sinner, but would rather he should be converted and live, and while I receive from thy hand the stroke of death, I will bless thee and hope in thee. Oh, that I may bless and love thee eternally, and be accepted through the merits of Jesus Christ. Let me never forget this mercy above all mercies, and though shame and sorrow must attend the recollection, let it be always present to me that I have been so blinded by sin as to forget its deformity—that upright soul so in love with its God and devoted to his service could forget his presence and laugh while he was angry—and if he then had

---

[15]A city in Spain

[16]France and England were hostile to each other, and a British fleet sailed the Mediterranean.

left me, how dreadful would have been my fall; but oh, my merciful Saviour, in that hour of darkness thy beloved voice still called and invited me back, and when prostrate on my face in sorrow, and shame, lifted me from the dust, and led me back to thy fold, so gently, so mercifully, as if my wickedness was to be rewarded instead of punished—and shall I ever be so wretched as to leave thee again? O my God! my God! save me from this worst of misery.

"25th—Lord of all mercy, I have sinned, I have offended thee, and the remembrance of my sins and offences overpowers my soul with sorrow; often I have confessed them, and detested them, as I have thought, with real sincerity of heart—still they are ever before me, and what shall I say to thee, Lord of all mercy? What can I do but throw myself again at thy feet, and implore thy pity on a soul whose only hope is in thy mercy, and the merits and sufferings of its Redeemer! Vouchsafe to apply them to that poor, afflicted soul, to cleanse it from its iniquities. It is by thy blood alone, adored Redeemer, they can be pardoned. Give it a sincere sorrow, and a constant, effectual resolution to avoid all occasions of offending thee, and seal its pardon through thy infinite merits and righteousness.

"I am ashamed, O Lord, to come to thee, even to thank thee for thy mercy—thy mercy in so long having patience with my repeated sins and disobedience to thy holy word—but whatever I am, though so miserable and hateful even to my guilty self, thy attributes can never change, thy goodness and mercy know no bounds, and feeling as I do, that I am entirely unworthy even to speak of thee, yet if even now my poor soul is condemned, if this day is the last of my wretched life on earth, my soul must still praise thee for so long sparing the punishment so justly due it, must still adore that infinite mercy that has given me so many means of grace, though my corrupt nature has made so bad a use of them. Oh, Lord Jesus Christ, still be merciful to a miserable sinner.

"12th of May, 1804."[17]

«Le corail dans l'Océan est une branche d'un pâle vert. Retirez-la de son lit natal, elle devient ferme, ne fléchit plus, c'est presque une pierre. Sa tendre couleur est changée en un brillant vermillon: ainsi de nous, submergés dans l'océan de ce monde, soumis à la vicissitude de ses flots, prêts à céder sous l'effort de chaque vague et de chaque tentation.»

«Mais aussitôt que notre âme s'élève, et qu'elle respire vers le ciel, le pàle vert de nos maldives espérances se change en ce pur vermillon du divin et constant amour. Alors nous regardons le bouleversement de la nature et la chute des mondes avec un constance et une confiance inébranlables.»

["The coral in the ocean is a branch of pale green. Take it from its native bed, it becomes firm, bends no more, it is almost a rock. Its tender color is changed to a brilliant red: so too we, submerged in the ocean of this world, subjected to the succession of the waves, ready to give up under the stress of each wave and temptation.

"But as soon as our soul rises, and it breathes toward heaven, the pale green of our sickly hopes is changed into that pure bright red of divine and constant love. Then we regard the disruptions of nature and the fall of worlds with an unshakable constancy and confidence."

---

[17]The original notebook containing journal entries of Mrs. Seton's return journey was sent to Madame Hélène de Barberey and never returned. Madame de Barberey's biography, *Elizabeth Seton et les commencements de l'église catholique aux États-Unis* (Paris, 1868), includes much of the Italian material. Cf. Joseph B. Code's English edition of de Barberey's text, *Elizabeth Seton* (New York, 1927). According to Annabelle Melville, *Elizabeth Bayley Seton* (New York: Charles Scribner's Sons, 1951), 322 n 59: "The journal Mrs. Seton kept of the voyage home is not available. In the 1902 *Diary of Robert Seton*, now in the possession of the New-York Historical Society, Seton states, 'I gave Madame de Barbery (Rome '66) a little book all written Mother Seton's hand . . . My aunt Catherine gave me the book. Mme de Barbery is dead and the book is, now, God knows where. I remember only that it had some notes of her return voyage from Leghorn to New York after her husband's death.'"

This passage from de Barberey, pp. 156-57, found in the May 25 entry, is also found in Code's work, p. 97, but not in any of White's editions.

2.15 Draft to Rev. John Henry Hobart

[written at sea, n.d.]

as I approach to you I tremble and while the dashing of the waves and their incessant motion picture to me the allotment which God has given me the tears fall fast thro' my fingers at the insupportable thought of being Seperated from you—and yet my dear H__[obart] you will not be severe—you will respect my sincerity and tho' you will think me in an error and even reprehensible in changing my religion I know that heavenly Christian Charity will plead for me in your Affections—you have certainly without my knowing it been dearer to me than God for when my reason, my Judgment and every conviction used their combined force against the value of your esteem the combat was in vain until I considered that yourself would no longer oppose or desire so severe a struggle which was destroying my mortal life and more than that my peace with God—Still if you will not be my Brother—if you[r] dear friendship and esteem must be the price of my fidility to what I believe to be the truth—I cannot doubt the Mercy of God who by depriving me of my dearest tie on earth will certainly draw me nearer to him—and this I feel confidently from the experience of the past and the truth of his promise which never can fail—

Amabilia and Antonio Filicchi

Elizabeth Seton, from a copy of a 1796 engraving by Charles Fevret de Saint-Mémin
(Courtesy, St. Joseph's Provincial House Archives)

View of the port of Leghorn (Courtesy, Archives of Mount Saint Vincent, New York)

House appointed in the Protestant burying ground —
Oh oh Oh what a day — close his eyes lay him out ride a journey be obliged to see a dozen people in my room till night — and at night crowded with the whole sense of my situation — Oh my Father and my G[

Elizabeth Seton's journal entry for December 27, 1803, the day of her husband's death (excerpt) (Courtesy, Archives of Mount Saint Vincent, New York)

PART III

Spiritual Conflict and Conversion 1804-1805

1804

In Part III Elizabeth makes frequent reference to her deceased husband, William, and to her children, Anna Maria (Anna), William, Richard (Dick), Catherine (Kit), and Rebecca. She refers to her sister and brother-in-law, Mary (Sister) and Wright Post (Brother Post), and to her sisters-in-law Harriet and Cecilia Seton. Among her friends she often refers to Antonio Filicchi (Brother, Mr. F., Tonio, Tonierlinno) and his wife, Amabilia; to relatives of Julia Scott: her children, Maria and John, her siblings, Charlotte Sitgreaves Cox (Sister) and Samuel Sitgreaves (Brother), and her niece Hitty; and to clergymen: Bishop John Carroll (the Bishop), Rev. John Henry Hobart (Mr. H.), and Rev. Matthew O'Brien (O.B.). In addition she speaks of John Murray and Sons (Murrey), the Filicchis' business agent in New York.

3.1 Journal to Rebecca Seton continued

4th June 1804

Do I hold my dear ones again in my bosom[1] —has God restored all my Treasure—even the little soul[2] I have so long contemplated an

---

[1] Returning from Europe, Elizabeth had just been reunited with her children after being separated from them for seven months.

[2] Baby Rebecca about whom Elizabeth had been dreaming and feared dead

angel in heaven—Nature crys out they are Fatherless—while God himself replies I am the Father of the Fatherless and the helper of the helpless—My God well may I cling to thee for "whom have I in Heaven but thee and who upon Earth beside thee, My heart and my flesh fail but thou art the Strength of my heart and my portion for ever"[3]—

My soul's Sister[4] came not out to meet me, she too had been journ[e]ying fast to her heavenly home and her spirit now seemed only to wait the consoling love and tenderness of her beloved Sister[5] to accompany it in its passage to eternity—to meet her who had been the dear Companion of all the pains—and all the comforts—of Songs of Praise and notes of sorrow, the dear faithful tender friend of my Soul through every varied scene of many years of trial—gone—only the Shadow remaining—and that in a few days must pass away—

The Home of plenty and of comfort—the Society of Sisters united by prayer and divine affections—the Evening hymns, the daily lectures, the sunset contemplations, the Service of holy days, the Kiss of Peace, the widows visits—all—all—gone—forever—and is Poverty and Sorrow the only exchange My Husband—my Sisters—my Home—my comforts—Poverty and sorrow—well with Gods blessing you too shall be changed into dearest friends—to the world you show your outward garments but thro them you discover to my Soul the palm of victory the triumph of Faith and the sweet footsteps of my Redeemer leading direct to his Kingdom—then let me gently meet you, be recieved in your bosom and be daily conducted by your councils thro' the remainder of the destined Journey. I know that many Divine graces accompany your path and change the stings of penance for the ease of conscience and the solitude of the desert for the Society of Angels—the angels of God accompanied the faithful when the light of his truth only dawned in the World—and now, that the day spring from on high has visited and exalted our nature to a union with the Divine will these beneficent beings be less associated or delighted to

---

[3] Ps. 73:25-26
[4] Rebecca Seton, Elizabeth's sister-in-law
[5] Elizabeth herself

dwell with the Soul that is panting for heavenly joys, and longing to join in their eternal Alelujahs—Oh no I will imagine them always surrounding me and in every moment I am free will sing with them Holy Holy Holy Lord God of Hosts, heaven and earth is full of thy glory.—

Sunday morning [July 8]

This is my Rebecca's Birth day in heaven[6]—No more watching now my darling Sister—No more agonizing sufferings—the hourly prayers interrupted by pains and tears are now exchanged for the eternal Hallelujah. the blessed angels who have so often witnessed our feeble efforts, now teach your Soul the Songs of Sion.—dear dear Soul we shall no more watch the setting sun on our knees, and sigh our soul to the Sun of Righteousness, for he has recieved you to his everlasting light—no more sing praises gazing on the moon—for you have awakened to eternal day—that dear voice that soothed the widows heart, admonished the forgetful Soul, inspired the love of God, and only uttered sounds of love and Peace to all shall now be heard no more among us, but the reward of those who lead others to Righteousness now crowns his promise who has said "they shall shine as the stars forever"[7]—

The dawning day was unusually clear, and as the clouds recieved the brightness of the rising sun Rebeccas Soul seemed to be aroused from the slumbers of approaching death which had gradually composed her during the night, and pointing to a glowing cloud opposite her window, she said with a cheerful smile dear Sister if this glimpse of glory is so delightful, what must be in the presence of our God—

While the sun arose we said our usual prayers, the Tedium, the fifty first psalm,[8] and part of the Communion Service "with Angels with Archangels and all the Company of Heaven we praise thee"—She said "this is the dear day of rest, suppose Sister it should be my blessed Sabbath, Oh how you disappointed me last Evening when you told me my pulse was stronger—but he is faithful that promises that I may

---

[6]Rebecca died July 8, 1804.

[7]Dan. 12:3

[8]The *Te Deum* is a traditional prayer of praise attributed to St. Ambrose. Psalm 51, known as the *Miserere*, is a traditional prayer of repentance.

well say." we then talked a little of our tender and faithful love for each other and earnestly prayed that this dear affection begun in Christ Jesus on earth might be perfected through him in Heaven—"and now dear Sister all is ready shut the window and lay my head easy that I may Sleep." (these were her express words) I said my love I dare not move you without some assistance, "why not" she repeated "all is ready" (she knew that I feared the consequence of moving her) at this moment Aunt F[9] entered the room and she was so desirous of being moved that I raised her head and drew her towards me—Nature gave its last sigh—she was gone in five minutes without a groan—

He who searches the heart and knows the spring of each secret affection—He only knows what I lost at that moment.—but her unspeakable gain silences Natures voice and the Soul presses forward towards the mark and prize of her high calling in Christ Jesus.

3.2 To Antonio Filicchi

[n.d.]

My dearest Antonio

I cannot resist the desire of hearing from you since I cannot see you—and was so unhappy as to lose you in the crowd this Morning dear dear Brother why did you not look for me as I did for you if it had been only in exercise of your usual Charity knowing how much I should be disappointed at returning home without your Fraternal Benediction—

If you are too lazy to write me a line send me a word of kindness by Mary[1] and she shall make you her best curtsey—tell her also when you

---

[9]Elizabeth Curson Farquhar, William Magee Seton's aunt

3.2 AMSJ A111 019

[1]Possibly Mary Gillon Hoffman Seton, Elizabeth's sister-in-law

go, and do do love your poor Sister if not for her sake and for the love she bears you, yet for His Sake whose law is love.

Yours forever E A S
Morn[ing]

3.3 To Antonio Filicchi

Saturday afternoon 1804

How happy I shall be dear Antonio if you are not gone—my woman has been sick I could not send before—a few lines from Carlton[1] inclosing a short letter from Mrs. Filicchi mentions a little box of Elixer for children, which I wrote for soon after my return, therefore the hats cannot be for me and you had better leave them with Murrey till called for—

May His Blessing which is above every blessing be with you and protect you thro' every danger—Mrs. F[ilicchi]s letter may amuse you and I send it hoping you are not gone—

Your Sister

3.4 Draft to John Wilkes

[July 1804]

My dear friend

Your brother Charles gave me yesterday the unwelcome intelligence that you have been detained at Albany and suffered very much—perhaps of knowing that you were [unclear]—he was so kind

---

3.3 AMSJ A 111 020
[1]Guy Carleton Bayley, Elizabeth's half-brother, was working at the Filicchi firm in Leghorn.
3.4 ASJPH 1-3-3-3:39

as to pass an hour with me for which jaunt [unclear] he thinks <line crossed out>—He was quite pleased with my little House[1] and my darlings whom he found eating their bread and milk with a very good appetite but I observed that he was really so affected at the tolling of the Bells for the death of poor Hamilton[2] that he could scarcely command himself [written over] <feelings>—how much you will be distressed at this melancholy event—the circumstances of which are really too bad to think of—Patience in this world is the constant lesson—

You will have heard before this of the departure of our dear Angel[3]—She suffered extremely for about an hour, on Friday night so much, that we thought all was over, but recovered her senses again became perfectly composed seemed free from pain—on Sunday she was delighted with the beauty of the morning and pointed to the clouds that were brightening with the rising Sun and said Ah my Sister that this might be my day of rest—shut the windows and I will sleep—I raised her head to make it easier, and immediately without the least strain she gave her last sigh—[my] dearest companion is gone, but I must be satisfied that she does not share my fate which she would certainly have done had she lived—with a grateful soul I thank God and you that my life is as comfortable as it is, but cannot be so selfish as to wish her to partake with me the many cares that must necessarily attend it[4]—

---

[1]John Wilkes, Dr. Wright Post, and Mrs. Sarah Startin, Elizabeth's godmother, had rented a house for the Setons on a temporary basis. This may have been the house on North Moore Street listed in the 1805 City Directory as Widow Seton's residence. North Moore Street was north of Duane and Jay Streets, running eastward from Greenwich Street.

[2]Alexander Hamilton (1757-1804), secretary of the treasury during George Washington's presidental administration, was a neighbor of the Setons. He died July 12, 1804, after being fatally injured in a duel with Aaron Burr on July 11 and is buried in Trinity churchyard.

[3]Rebecca Seton, Elizabeth's sister-in-law

[4]Written at the bottom of the page horizontally: "1st To rise as early as the season"; in another hand: "some time in July 1804."

3.5 To Julia Scott

15th July 1804

My dearest Julia

The tenderness and affection of your expressions brought many quick and bitter tears from my very heart—I find so many changes and reverses in my singular fate that I did not look for your kindness or value your friendship as I ought accustomed to find every one occupied in their own concerns I thought Julia is enjoying and pursuing, and I will not remind her there is a being so burthened with sorrow as I am—My Seton has left his five darlings and myself wholly dependent on the Bounty of those individuals who have loved and respected him = happily for us both entirely unconscious of the desparate state of his affairs he died quite happy in the idea that we would have a sufficiency when his books were brought up[1]—but on the contrary there is even a great deficiency, and if John Wilkes did not continue a faithful friend to us I should see my dear ones in a state of absolute poverty—but my Brother Post and Mrs. [Sarah] Startin unite with him in our maintenance for this year as my Rebecca is so young, after which if I live I am to pursue some personal exertion towards it myself—

I am so happy amongst all my difficulties to meet with a small neat house about a half mile from town where we occupy the upper room and will let the lower floor as soon as I can find a tenant—we eat milk morning and evening and chocolate for dinner, always with a thankful heart and a good appetite—my dearest companion and friend,—my Souls Sister[2] departed for the happier world this day week, and with her is gone all my interest in the connections of this life—it appears to me Julia that a cave or a desert would best satisfy my Natural desire. but God has given me a great deal to do, and I have always, and hope always, to prefer his Will to every wish of my own. he has been most gracious to me in returning me all my dear ones in health, and

---

3.5 ASJPH 1-3-3-6:53

[1] Accounts and financial status of Seton, Maitland and Company which was in bankruptcy

[2] Rebecca Seton, Elizabeth's sister-in-law

providing a roof to cover us—most gracious in giving both to my husband and sister[3] that Peace in their last hours which assures me they are free from all sufferings and inheriting his promises—most gracious in raising my Soul above all the changing events of my mortal existance—Why then you will say my friend do you declare you are burthened with sorrow—next week I will write you Why—

I anticipate your first question to me my dear Julia, can you not share with me your portion?[4] can you not add to the contributions of those friends who support me?—in answer to these questions which I am sure of from you, I assure you that for the present there is no necessity, I spend much less than even those friends imagine, and delight in the opportunity of bringing up my children without those pretentions and indulgences that ruin so many.

Your idea of my making you a visit you will readily see is impracticable—h[ow mu]ch I wish to see your dear children and yourself I cannot express, but I put that among the many other wishes that I set aside as not to be gratified, for your coming to me at this Season cannot be right—The Father of Blessings bless you my love remember me to Charlotte—Hitty and Maria and be assured of my sincere and grateful affection

---

[3]Rebecca Seton, Elizabeth's sister-in-law
[4]Julia invited Elizabeth to come to Philadelphia to live, and in July when she visited New York, she tried to persuade Elizabeth to let Anna Maria return with her to Philadelphia.

3.6 To Bishop John Carroll[1]

[26 July 1804]

Reverend Sir

The inclosed letter from Mr. [Antonio] Filicchi will acquaint you with the motive which leads me to take the liberty of addressing you—He has indeed most kindly befriended me in endeavoring to enlighten and instruct my mind—the first impression I recieved from him that I was in error and in a church founded on error Startled my Soul and decided me to make every enquiry on the subject—the Books he put into my hands gave me an intire conviction that the Protestant Episcopal Church was founded only on the principles and passions of Luther, and consequently that it was seperated from the Church founded by Our Lord and his Apostles, and its ministers without a regular succession from them—Shocked at the idea of being so far from the truth a determination of quitting their communion and uniting myself with yours became the earnest desire of my Soul which accustomed to rely Supremely on Divine Grace was easily satisfied on those points of difference and peculiarity in your Church when it was persuaded that it was the true one—under these impressions it remained until my arrival in New York—It was my friend Filicchi's wish, and a respect due to those Pastors and friends from whom I had

---

3.6 AAB 7N2

[1] John Carroll (1735-1815) was a native of Maryland, educated in Europe, and joined the Society of Jesus (Jesuits). He returned to Maryland in 1773 when the Jesuits were suppressed. He was later named the first Catholic bishop in the United States (1789) and the first archbishop of Baltimore (1811-1815). Bishop Carroll first met Elizabeth Seton when he administered the sacrament of Confirmation to her May 25, 1806, at St. Peter's Church on Barclay Street in New York. Elizabeth looked to Carroll as her spiritual father and he became her confidant. She turned to him for advice, support, and direction during the beginning years of the Sisters of Charity. Carroll surrendered his immediate superintendence of the new community to the Sulpician Fathers in 1809. In 1812 Carroll, as ecclesiastical superior, approved a modified version of the *Common Rules of the Daughters of Charity* for use by the community, then called the Sisters of Charity of Saint Joseph's.

The Society of Jesus (Jesuits) is a religious order founded by St. Ignatius Loyola in Spain in 1540. French, Spanish, and English Jesuits came to the New World with the explorers in the sixteenth and seventeenth centuries. The first Jesuits came to Maryland in 1634, and during the colonial period English Jesuits bore the major pastoral responsibility for Catholics in British territory on the east coast of North America.

recieved my first principles and affections to state my objections to their Communion—but I assure you that in the believe of those first objects I mentioned (that they proceeded from Luther and were without a regular succession from Christ and his Apostles) I felt my Soul so determined, that it appeared a wicked insincerity to give them any hope of changing me—when to my great astonishment they give me the most positive testimony that I have been decieved in those points—

—You will naturally observe to me that I must have expected an opposition where parties are opposed—certainly, and had the opposition rested on Transubstantiation or any point of faith be assured that my Faith would not have stopped at any point that your church has yet proposed to me—but in the decided testimonies that are given me by the clergy of the Protestant Episcopal Church that they are a True Church I acknowledge that the foundation of my Catholick principles is destroyed and I cannot see the necessity for my making a change—It is necessary to inform you that I have felt my situation the most awful manner and as the Mother and Sole parent of five children have certainly pleaded with God earnestly and I may strictly say incessantly as it has been the only and supreme desire of my Soul to know the Truth—I know that I have besides the natural errors of a Corrupt nature added many Sins to the account he has with me—indeed often in the struggles of my Soul I should have thought myself deservedly forsaken by him had I dared to impeach his mercy to one who desires above all things to please him and has the greatest sorrow for having offended him—indeed all other sorrow is Joy to me, and in the many severe trials he has been pleased to send me I have feared nothing but the fear of losing his favor.

—With the Sincerity with which I lay my heart before him I must declare to you that <the motive of my> I feel my mind decided in its original Sentiments respecting my Religion

—Mr. A Filicchi who has accompanied me to America has requested me to make this Statement to you—and I have promised him to defer every further step until you will favour me with an answer—and must intreat you to consider that my present divided situation from every Communion is almost more than I can bear, and that it will be an act of the greatest charity to forward your sentiments as soon as your liesure will permit—I am with very great respect

Your [unclear][2]

3.7 To Antonio Filicchi

30th August 1804

This day compleats one week since my most dear Brother left me—which week I have passed without seeing any one but little Cecilia and Harriet for a few minutes—I have thought of you incessantly, indeed I cannot think of my Soul without remembering you—and as certainly the greatest part of my days and nights are occupied in solicitude and watching over that poor soul consequently you are the constant companion of my thoughts and prayers—when I began the Litany of Jesus[1] this afternoon the plural number put it in my mind to say it for you also, and praying heartily for you made me resolve to write to my dear Brother altho' it appeared to me that you did not encourage the idea of writing to you often—

The Bishops letter has been held to my heart, on my knees beseeching God to enlighten me to see the truth, unmixed with doubts and hesitations—I read the promises given to St Peter and the 6th chapter John[2] every day and then ask God can I offend him by believing those

[2]Antonio Filicchi, writing to Bishop Carroll, July 26, 1804, explained this enclosure in the following P.S.: "Mrs. Seton had written to you, but her Bishop [Benjamin Moore] has prevailed on her not to enter into any more discussion I enclose to you the original *minuta* of the letter that she had prepared for you as a history of the circumstances. As notwithstanding whatever I could be able to say to her she appears decided in maintaining her former communion, and was but with great difficulty prevailed upon to wait the result of my present application to you, I must beg you with all my Soul to hasten to come to my relief with the proper direction and answer.

"I had just written so far, when the two add[r]essed notes are brought to me, one from Mrs. Seton, the other from Mr. Hobart. I am bound in honor to comply with the request of Mrs. Seton: and at a loss what better to do, I have left with Rev. M[atthew] O'Bryan the manuscripts in question, who has promised me that he will be able for this same evening to have them perused and answered. Pray, console me with your direction." (AAB 3S2)

3.7 AMSJ A 111 021

[1]*The Litany of the Holy Name of Jesus* was found in Catholic prayer books from the sixteenth century on.

[2]Cf. Matt. 16:18-21; John 6.

express words—I read my dear St Francis,[3] and ask if it is possible that I shall dare to think differently from him or seek heaven any other way. I have read your Englands Reformation[4] and find its evidence too conclusive to admit of any reply—God will not forsake me Antonio, I know that he will unite me to his flock, and altho' now my Faith is unsettled I am assured that he will not disappoint my hope which is fixed on his own word that he will not despise the humble contrite heart which would esteem all losses in this world as greatest gain if it can only be so happy as to please him—

2nd September—

I begin now wishfully to watch for J[ames] Setons chair,[5] every evening hoping that he will bring me a letter from you—this you may think childish dear Antonio but remember you have not a female heart, and mine is most truely and fondly attached to you, as you have proved when I have been most contradictory and troublesome to you—fearing too much not to possess your invaluable affection—

I was willing to embrace an excuse for not going to town last Sunday in compliance with your advice—and my Brother Post came to visit me—Our conversation turned accidently on the subject that engrosses my Soul, and led me to an explanation with him very interesting and I believe surprising to him as I fixed my argument on litteral words rather than human fancy—his cool and quiet Judgment could not follow the flight of my Faith, but was so candid as to admit that if before God I believed the Doctrine of the Church to be true, the errors or imperfection of its members could not Justify a seperation from its communion—

But still these hidious objects will present themselves Which disturb my Soul and unsettle my faith, and tho' God is so gracious as to give me the fullest assurance that thro' the Name of Jesus my prayer

---

[3]St. Francis de Sales' *Introduction to the Devout Life* (1609)

[4]Robert Manning's *England's Conversion and Reformation Compared*, a Catholic work of apologetics, first appeared in Antwerp in 1725.

[5]James Seton was Elizabeth's brother-in-law and a partner in Seton, Maitland and Company. Sedan chairs were a common method of conveyance in New York City. Elizabeth received mail sent through the public channels in care of James Seton. Most people preferred to send letters by travelers because of the element of safety and to avoid the excessive postage charges the recipient paid.

shall finally be answered yet there seems now a cloud before my way that keeps me always asking him which is the right path—indeed my Brother when the rem[em]berance of my impurities and unholiness before God strikes my memory with their fullest conviction I only wonder how we can expect from him so great a favor as the light of his truth until the sorrow and penance of my remaining <years> life shall invite his pitying mercy to grant it—remember to pray for me—

8th September—

day after day passes without one line from you but I trust in God that you are safe and only defer writing from multiplied engagements and the pleasure of new acquaintances—This is the Nativity of the Blessed Virgin and I have tryed to sanctify it begging God to look in my Soul and see how gladly I would kiss her feet because she was his Mother and joyfully show every expression of reverence that even my Antonio would desire if I could do it with that freedom of Soul which flowed from the knowledge of his Will—

Mr. H[obart] was here yesterday for the first time since your absence and was so intirely out of all patience that it was in vain to show the letter. He says "the Church was corrupt, we have returned to the Primative doctrine and what more would you have when you act according to your best judgment"—I tell him that would be enough for this world but I fear in the next to meet another question. his visit was short and painful on both sides—God direct me for I see it is in vain to look for help from any but him—

12th September—

Your much wished for letter of 7th Instance is arrived and I have thanked God with my whole soul that you are safe—I can find but one fault in your letter which is that a whole side of it is blank—you meet with that hospitality in Boston[6] which my jealous heart would have desired you should have recieved from all to whom I belong—If you should meet with General Knox,[7] his wife or daughter they were kind friends to me before my connection with Seton—take care of the

---

[6]Antonio Filicchi was travelling in the United States on business.

[7]Probably General Henry Knox, a Revolutionary War general and secretary of war in George Washington's first cabinet.

Thermometer I charge you—my prayers for you are most ardent on that point—

Three of my children have the whooping cough and as I watch them the greater part of the night my prayers are often repeated—but Oh Antonio when will my poor Soul be worthy to be heard, and make its direct applications with that liberty of spirit which the light of truth alone can give to it. I repeat to you pray for me it will benefit us both—and when you wish to add a cordial drop of sweetness to my cup write some of the thoughts of your Soul to your dear Sister who loves you with most true and unceasing affection—

EAS

3.8 To Antonio Filicchi

September 19 [1804]

My most dear Brother

The 13th Inst[ance] I sent a letter for you to the Post office and hope you have not only recieved it but that there is now another from your dear hand on the way in reply to it—you say you must know all my concerns interior and exterior—as for the latter they are easily related—I have seen no one since I wrote you but my Philadelphia friend Mrs. [Julia] Scott whose tenderness to me is unremitted—Mrs. [Eliza] Sadler who cannot enter into the spirit of our cause,[1] and Captain Blagg[2] who came to offer his services if I had any commands in Leghorn or Paris. Mr. H[obart] and all the other Misters have left me to my contemplations or rather to my "best judgment" I suppose—but, I rather hope to God—so much for exterior to which I only add I am very well tho' quite oppressed with fatigue occasioned by my poor little childrens Whooping cough.

3.8 AAB 7N3

[1] Elizabeth's growing interest in Catholicism
[2] Captain of the ship on which Elizabeth returned to New York

In order to disclose to you the interior I must speak to you as to God—to him I say—when shall my darkness be made light—for really it would seem that the Evil Spirit has taken his place so near my Soul that nothing good can enter in it without being mixed with his Suggestions—In the life of St. Augustin[3] I read that "where he is most active and obstacles seem greatest in the Divine Service there we have reason to conclude that Success will be most glorious."—the hope of this glorious Success is all my comfort for indeed my spirit is sometimes so severly tried it is ready to sink—This morning I fell on my face before God (remember I tell you all) and appealed to him as my righteous Judge if hardness of heart, or unwillingness to be taught, or any human reasons stood between me and the truth—if I would not rejoice to cast my Sorrows on the Bosom of the Blessed Mary—to intreat the Influence of all his Blessed Saints and angels, to pray for precious Souls even more than for myself, and account myself happy in dying for his Sacred Truth if once my soul could know it was pleasing him—I remembered how much these exercises had comforted and delighted me at Leghorn and recalled all the reasons which had there convinced me of their truth, and immediately a cloud of doubts and replies raised a contest in this poor Soul and I could only again cry out for mercy to a sinner and implore his Pity who is the source of life light and truth to enlighten my eyes that I sleep not in death—that death of sin and error which with every power of my Soul I endeavor to escape—

after reading the life of St. Mary Magdalen[4] I thought "Come my Soul let us turn from all these Suggestions of one side or the other and quietly resolve to go to that church which has at least the multitude of the wise and good on its side, and began to consider the first steps I must take—the first step is it not to declare I believe all that is taught by the council of Trent,[5] and if I said that, would not the Searcher of hearts know my falsehood and insincerity—could you say that you would be satisfied with his Bread and believe the cup, which he

---

[3]St. Augustine of Hippo, a fourth century Christian apologist and writer (354-430)

[4]Possibly St. Mary Magdalen de Pazzi (1566-1607), a Florentine Carmelite and mystic

[5]The Council of Trent (1545-63) was a major church council which clarified Catholic doctrine and teaching.

equally commanded unnecessary—could you believe that the Prayers and Litanies addressed to our Blessed Lady were acceptable to God tho' not commanded in Scripture, etc. etc. by all which I find and you my Antonio will be out of Patience to find that the tradition of the Church has not the true weight of authority in my mind[6]—do not be angry—pity me—remember the mixtures of truth and error which have been pressed upon my Soul—and rather pray for me than reproach me—for indeed I make every endeavor to think as you wish me to, and it is only the most obstinate resistance of my mind that prevents my immediately doing also as you wish me to, and all I can do is to renew my promise that I will pray incessantly and strive to wash out with tears and penance the Sins which I fear oppose my way to God—again I repeat pray for me—

22nd September—

Your most flattering and kind letter of the 15th September is safe in my possession, I read it over and over and smile to think that the heart of Man knows itself so little—but God knows it, and it is enough—you will recieve mine of the 12th September I hope before your jaunt to Portland[7]—and it will reassure you of the constancy of that affection on which you so justly rely—that affection my dearest Tonierlinno which notwithstanding all my doubts and fears, I must yet hope will be perfected in Paradise—I tremble at the thought of your Brothers[8] next letter and yet very much wish to have one both from him and your lovely Amabilia—as to your letters they are so free from mistakes and so perfectly well expressed that I shall imagine you have found some kind Directress to supply the deficiency of her you left behind you—She may be more happy in many respects and worthier of so distinguished a favor, but certainly can never excell in truth or affection—and when you return must yield her claim to a more ancient pretention—

---

[6]The Council of Trent affirmed the authority of tradition along with scripture.
[7]Portland, Maine
[8]Filippo Filicchi

I reiterate your Solemn Benediction from the bottom of my Soul and pray earnestly that "Almighty God" may bless and preserve my dear Brother—and restore [him] safe to his own true friend and Sister

EAS.

3.9 To Antonio Filicchi

September 27 [1804]

Most dear friend and Brother

It is necessary to lay the restraint of Discretion on my pen while I thank you for your letter of the 20th which though but two hours ago recieved has been already read over many times—the pen is restrained, but the heart which is before God blesses and adores him in unbounded thanksgiving for such a friend—Your goodness to me he only can reward—

to answer you fully now would not be proper in any way, especially as you see my poor Soul is still more unsettled and perplexed from day to day, not from any failure in its prayers or intreaties to God which are rather redoubled than neglected, but like a Bird struggling in a net it cannot escape its fears and tremblings—

This afternoon after dismissing the children to play, I went to my knees in my little closet to consider what I should do, and how my sacred duty would direct—Should I again read those Books I first received from Mr. H[obart] my heart revolted, for I know there are all the black accusations and the Sum of them too sensibly torment my Soul—should I again go over those of the Catholick Doct[rine] though every page I read is familiar to me and my memory represents in rotation the different instructions and replies?—Since your absence I have read the book your Brother first gave me and the one you also gave, with the most careful attention—not only with attention but always with Prayer—and now must look up to that as my only refuge,

---

Prayer at all times, in all places—really Antonio my most dear Brother to whom I can speak every secret of my Soul, I have and do pray so much that it seems every thought is Prayer, and when I awake from my short sleeps my mind seems to have been praying—and the poor eyes are really almost blind with incessant tears—for can I pray for such a favor without a beating heart and torrents of tears—My children say "poor Mamma," continually and really are better than they were that they may not add to my Sorrow—Yet sweet are these tears, and sweet are the Sorrows, great is my comfort, that though the Almighty source of Light does not visit me with his blessed light, yet he does not leave me Contented and insensible to my darkness—

29th

This day has been a feast day to the children and a holiday from school that I might give the greatest portion of the hours to God—you would have been pleased to hear their questions about St. Michael[1] and how eagerly they listened to the history of the good offices done to us by the Blessed angels, and of St. Michael driving Lucifer out of heaven etc. They always wait on their knees after prayers till I bless them each with the Sign of the Cross and I look up to God with a humble hope that he will not forsake us—

I could tell you many things my Brother but must wait for the much wished for hour when we shall be seated with our big book at the table[2]—I could cry out now as my poor Seton used to Antonio Antonio Antonio, but call back the thought and my Soul cries out Jesus Jesus Jesus—there it finds rest, and heavenly Peace, and is hushed by that dear Sound as my little Babe is quieted by my Cradle song—The Jesus Psalter in the little Book you gave me is my favorite office because it so often repeats that name—and when thought goes to you Antonio and imagines you in the promiscuous company you must meet, without any solid gratification—fatigued by your excursions, wandering in your fancy etc. etc. etc. etc. Oh how I pray that the Holy Spirit may not leave you, and that your dear Angel may even pinch you at the hour of Prayers rather than suffer you to neglect them.

---

[1] An angel mentioned in the Christian scriptures whose feast is celebrated September 29
[2] The Bible

You charge me not to neglect the lives of the Saints—which I could not if I would, for they interest me so much, that the little time I can catch for reading is all given to them, indeed they are a relaxation to my mind, for they lessen all my troubles and make them as nothing by comparison—when I read that St. Au[gus]tin[e] was long in a fluctuating state of mind between error and truth, I say to myself, be Patient, God will bring you Home at last—and as for the lessons of self denial and Poverty If St. Francis De Sales[3] and the Life of our dear Master had not before pointed out to me the many virtues and graces that accompany them I should even wish for them to be like those dear dear Saints in any respect—Antonio Antonio why cannot my poor Soul be satisfied that your religion is now the same that theirs then was—how can it hesitate—why must it struggle—the Almighty only can decide

—do my Brother tell me something about yourself you certainly must know how grateful even the smallest particular is to an absent friend always anxious for your happiness and wellfare—I am ashamed of my own letters they are all Egotism but my Soul is so intirely engrossed by one subject that it cannot speak with freedom on any other—day after day passes and I see no one, indeed I can say with perfect truth at all times I prefer my Solitude to the company of any human being except that of my most dear A. you know my heart you know my thoughts, my pains and Sorrows hopes and fears—Jonathan loved David[4] as his own Soul and if I was your Brother, Antonio I would never leave you for one hour—but as it is I try rather to turn every affection to God, well knowing that there alone their utmost exercise cannot be misapplied and most ardent hopes can never be disappointed—

The idea you suggested to me of writing to B[is]h[o]p C[arroll] was suggested by a good or an evil angel immediately after your departure—the Protestants say I am in a state of temptation, you must naturally think the same—the Almighty is my defence in either case, not from any claim of mine, but thro' the name of Jesus Christ—Is it

[3]Elizabeth was reading *Introduction to the Devout Life.*
[5]Cf. 1 Sam. 18:1.

possible I can do wrong in writing to him sanctioned by your direction—at least I will have a letter prepared by the time you come—

your EAS.
30th September

3.10 To Antonio Filicchi

9th October 1804

Five days are passed my dearest Brother since the usual period of recieving your letters, which have not exceeded the interval of nine days—but I am quite sure there is one on the way for me or perhaps in the Pocket of some forgetful gentleman, sometimes I think Antonio himself is on the way and begin to watch the door expecting the welcome visit, dear dear friend how my heart will rejoice in that hour—if God pleases, if you are preserved from sickness and other accidents which my anxious and busy imagination so often presents—

11th October

I have your letter of the 8th Instance before me—you must not know that I placed it in my Bosom until I had given thanks and said my Prayers before it was opened—and judge of my disappointment when only a few lines rewarded my anxious anticipations—however at the foot of my cross I found consolation and kissing it over and over I repeated and repeat, There only I am never disappointed—but if my letters interest you as much as your flattering encomiumns express I will delight in continuing them as a means of giving pleasure to my dear Brother and endeavouring to prove as much as is possible that affection which is inexpressible—

This is the first time since our correspondance by letter commenced that the pen goes heavily. I have nothing new—the poor Soul goes through nearly the same exercises day by day always drifting on the Ocean without any perceptable approach to its haven of rest but supported by its hope in God that he will not leave it to perish—a letter but not a very satisfactory one is prepared for our Bishop C[arroll] your application will I hope prevent the necessity of addressing it—of this however my dear A. shall judge—

The secret bias of my heart was clearly discovered to me last Saturday whilst I passed half an hour with the sick man who is a Catholick for whom you gave me the ten dollars—the pleasure of consoling him and conversing with the poor honest family he lives with recompensed the trouble of my walk ten fold, and when he prayed for me and for my dear Brother it seemed to me sure that his prayers would be heard—also passing the Roman Church I stoped and read the tombstones lifting up my heart to God for pity, appealing to him as my judge how joyfully I would enter there and kiss the steps of his Altar—every day to visit my Saviour there and pour out my Soul before him is the supreme desire—but Oh Antonio my most dear Brother should I ever dare to bring there a doubtful distracted mind, a confusion of fears and hesitations, trembling before God, in anguish and terror least it should offend him who only it desires to please—in the sure confidence of your mind you must smile at your poor Sisters expressions as the effusions of a heated imagination—but Oh my Soul is at stake—and the dear ones of my Soul must partake my error in going or staying—far different is my situation from those who are uninstructed—but my hard case is to have a head turned with instruction without the light in my Soul to direct it where to rest—Still there is only one remedy the constant prayer "Show me the way I shall walk in, I give up my Soul to Thee"[1] and with the poor Sinner in the Gospel "Lord what would thou have me to do"[2]—

The friends once so much interested on this subject seem to have given me up to God also for I see them no more—Mr. H[obart] sent some messages about a lame foot and I am very happy to be excused from unavailing conversations—

17th October When you write to Leghorn remember me most affectionately to your best Beloved[3]—I believe I must not write until I

---

[1]Ps. 32:8
[2]Matt. 19:16
[3]Amabilia Filicchi

hear from them—how often, indeed almost continually my thoughts wander there realizing my room under your roof, the appearance of every object from the window and the smile of the little darling Pat[4] on his tip toe asking questions of his Signora Seton—sometimes too I am obliged to make the sign of the cross and look to God for Pity. The happiest hour I can now anticipate in this world is that in which I shall hear that you are again in that dear place in the arms of the still dearer objects it contains—

I trust you will not suffer from the severity of our winter—the storms have already begun and the wind blows my candle while I write—however they have no other effect than reminding me more forcable of my journey's end and pointing every wish and sigh to that Eternal Spring where storms cannot reach—can it be Antonio that God will let me perish, will he ever say that dreadful word—GO—to me? certainly in the operation of his Justice that must be my wretched doom, but that Justice is always tempered with Mercy or where should I be now—often I think the barren fig tree is spared yet one year more[5]—this may be the last part of that Year, and yet how barren of all fruit it is—often the thought presses so strong upon me—to be banished from him—to hear no sounds but blasphemy—that would be infinite torment without the devouring flame—what would become of me if he did not see my heart and know all its struggles and desires—He sees it, and sees there also the constant prayer for your Soul as earnestly offered as for my own—

Your own friend and Sister EAS

3.11 To Antonio Filicchi

Thursday Evening 16th November 1804

Your letter of 7th Instance is this moment recieved, and has been read twice, I never drempt of repr[o]aching you Antonio though a

---

[4]Patrizio Filicchi, Antonio and Amabilia's son
[5]Cf. Matt. 21:18-19.
3.11 AMSJ A 111 023

month and two weeks are past since I had your few lines of 7th October. My heart has jumped almost out of me every time our street door opened, and trembled so much at the sight of Mr. [John] Wilkes, J[ames] Seton[1] or any one who might inform me of you that I have scarcely been able to speak—however all this is an excess of folly that deserves the just punishment it recieves and I ought only to thank God that by depriving me of confidence in any human affection he draws my Soul more near to its only center of rest—

3rd December —These were my Sentiments my Brother when I received your letter of last month, nor are they changed by the few lines delivered to me this Evening since the above period my woman has had a severe illness and I have had all the work to do—of making fires, preparing food, and nursing her, added to my usual occupations which fatigue has been attended with violent cold on my breast with pains etc.—yet I have written to you and had sealed the letter ready for the Post—but considering with my own heart, its errors, its wanderings and still added sorrows which all call to it with an irresistable force to give itself to God alone, I ask why then deliver it, or even lend it to the uncertain influences of human affections, why allow it to look for Antonio to be made happy by his attentions or disturbed by his neglects—when those moments spent in writing to or thinking of my Brother are given to my J[esus] He never disappoints me but repays every instant with hours of sweet Peace and unfailing contentment—and the tenderest interest you ever can bestow on me is only a stream of which he is the fountain—

This on my part—on yours, the multiplicity of business, laziness of temper diffidence of disposition, inconvenience in writing English with other Etcetera's, are an all sufficient acknowledgement however delicately expressed, that writing to your Sister must be a sacrifice which her affection for you would rather dispense with than constrain[2] you to perform. I hope your new Engagements in Boston will supply to you fully the loss of my letters in instructing you in our language as

---

[1] Elizabeth's brother-in-law
[2] Constrain is underlined twice

doubtless the 2 or 3 weeks you purpose still to remain there will lengthen to months as easily as those that are past—

Immediately on Mr. Wilkes return to New York he proposed a plan to me for my future maintainance which by every possible evasion I have withheld my consent to having for two months past expected your return here, and been anxiously desirous of not accepting any terms without the consent of him who next to God my heart owns to be its sole controler; but pushed by necessity, and compelled by my unprovided condition and another offering to take the situation unconditionally which I have so long hesitated to accept, I have yielded to circumstances I could not avoid and engaged to take the charge of 20 Boys as Boarders[3] in a house a little further out of town near their school—the Establishment is to commence the beginning of the year—I believe it is certain and will yield to me some independence—My heart feels so really bowed down that I cannot either fear or hope on the subject, but pray and fast, and try to keep both Eye and Soul fixed on God ready to meet his Will. Oh how eagerly they both stretch out to gain his blessed favour always in life and in Death

your own most Affectionate Sister

3.12 Draft in French to an Unidentified Woman[1]

20th November 1804

Ma chere ami Mamma

Mon coeur vous a ecrit bien des Lettres depuis notre separation—ce separation qui a ete suivi de tout des malheurs, exquis, nous avons partagé vos peines. Mon Wm. a donné bien dis Soupiers pour la

---

[3]This plan involved Elizabeth taking as boarders the children of John Wilkes and his brother, Charles, as well as a dozen more from the school conducted by Rev. William Harris, the curate of St. Mark's Episcopal Church in the Bowery. Although Elizabeth seemed pressed to make a decision, this plan did not materialize for another year.

3.12 ASJPH 1-3-3-4:57

[1]Written at the top in another hand: "Sur Sa Conversion" [Upon Her Conversion]

sort de votre chere mari et les suite funist qui vous avez prouvé soutout au moment qu'elle a senti ses soufrances dans les siens, et bien j'ai sente les votres chere mamma et aussi, bien des circonstance amers que j'espere en Dieu ne peut jamais vous toucherez

—Je ne sais pas se l'adversite a la meme effet pour vous—pour moi, il me semble que en perdant mon Pere, mon Mari et Rebecca tout et fini—je regard mes petites Enfans comme des tresors cest vrai, mais avec peur de fixer meme lesperance de bonheur sur des objects qui change si vite et a qui l'existance est si incertain—certainment cest pour qui un Mere pouvez bien si soutenir sous des pains and d'leau ils sont toute dans une santé parfait bien bonne et carressant et parlant a chaque jour de leur cher Papa et l'heureuse moment que dont nous receivoir

vous avez bien Jugé qui notre bien faisent ami ma donez tout les secours possible, et il a fait un arrangement pour moi que peut me donnez quelque independance si le bon dieu me conserve ma Santé pour un vie si fatigant cest de receivor ces garcon[s] celle de son frere et encore un douzain, pour la compensation necessaire pour la maintenance de ma famille. —l'establishment sera pres de leurs Ecolle, et je crois que ce sera un vie aussi doux qui je peut esperé dans mes circonstances—

Si Mr. Wilkes n'avez pas puis tant d'interest dans ma situation j'avais quitté mon payie presque au meme moment de mon retour en consequences de froideur que j'ai eprouvé de mes amis en general au cause de mes sentiments Catholic. Je ne sais pas Mamma si vous avez remarqué la force de la religion dans ma disposition quand nous etions ensemble, certainment les evenments dupuis ce temps la a bien augmenté cette affection—et ce n'est pas necessaire de vous donez un excuse pour etant Catholick surtout chez des catholick—il me ga[g]net l'ame et la coeur si bien que si ce n'etait pas pour mes devoirs a mes Enfants j'avais retiré dans une couvent au moment qui a fini la vie de mon mari—mais en arrivent ici la clergé ma fait un attack sur la question en parlant de l'antichrist, l'idolatries et un torrant d'objections qui en meme temp quils[?] ne pouvet pas me changez les opinions que j'avais adopté; ma assay[?] effrayé pour me tenir dans un hesitation, et me voila dans les mains de Dieu prient nuit et jour pour sa l'ami - qui seul fuit m'amenez droit J'instruire mes Enfants dans cette Religion tout, qui je peut sans prenant la parti dicisive—et tous les desires de mon ame est la, et je trouve mon plus grand soulagement en ma placant en imagination dans leur Eglises

—Prie pour moi chere ami—c'est possible dont que je vous ai fait un si longue detail - dans une mannier aussi qui a peine vous pouvez comprender—cest la primiere letter que j'ai jamais ecrit en Francais—la seul excuse que je peut offris pour tout les defauts et cette difficulté de me fais comprandre est l'unique raison que vous navez pas recu de moi un lettre par chaque Batiment depuis votre depart—Oh qui je serais content de savoir tout vous ce que vous est relative - de vous, vous cheres enfants Notre William Seton le petite ange Harriett Henrique Aglai Adele—objets que me serais toujours chers[?]—Souvent je chant tres bas quand les enfant[s] dont les petite air, «vien tendre amour» et «Sainté Marie» les pleurs coule bien vite sous l'anguille en face des recollection presque insoutenable—Mes freres et sœurs sont tout bien, par ici et par la comme des agneaus sans maitre

—Madame Sadler parle de vous avec un interest bien sincere—J'ai vu notre ami Chenot aujourdhui pour le primiere fois depuis mon retour, mais il ma donnez la main de l'ancient amitié—chere ami de tout mon cour

EAS.

November 20, 1804

[My dear friend Mamma,[2]

My heart has written you many letters since our separation—that separation followed by so many painful misfortunes; we have shared your sorrows. My William sighed a great deal over the fate of your dear husband and its dreadful aftermath for you, which you experience especially at the time he experienced his sufferings in his own.

---

[2]Annabelle Melville names the addressee in this letter as "Olive."

Ah well, I have experienced yours, dear Mamma, and also many bitter circumstances which I hope in God will never touch you.

I do not know if adversity has the same effect on you. As for me, I think that, losing my Father, my husband and Rebecca all is finished. True, I look upon my little children as treasures, but with the fear of even placing the hope of happiness on objects that change so quickly and whose existence is so uncertain. Certainly, that is enough to make a mother go on bread and water. They are all in perfect health, good, and affectionate and speaking every day of their Papa and the happy moment when we will be reunited.

You have judged correctly that our benevolent friend[3] has given me all possible help and has made arrangements for me which allow me some independence. If God preserves my health for such a fatiguing life, it is to receive these boys of his brother's and another twelve or so, as the settlement necessary for the maintenance of my family. The establishment will be near their school, and I think it will be a life as easy as I can hope for in my circumstances. If Mr. Wilkes had not taken such an interest in my situation, I would have left my country at almost the very moment of my return, because of the coldness I experienced from my friends in general because of my Catholic sentiments. I don't know, Mamma, if you noticed the strength of religion in my disposition when we were together, certainly subsequent events have greatly increased this ardor—and it is not necessary to give you an excuse for being Catholic, especially with Catholics.

It has won me over, heart and soul, so much so that, were it not for my duties to my children, I would have gone into a convent[4] as soon as my husband died. But, when I arrived here, the clergy attacked me on the question, speaking of the antichrist, idolatry, and a torrent of objections, which, even though they could not make me change the opinions I had adopted, frightened me enough at the same time to cause me some hesitation. So, here I am in the hands of God, praying night and day for the friend who alone can guide me straight. I am instructing my children in this religion as best I can, without taking the decisive

[3] John Wilkes
[4] It was common practice for widows to board in convents as a sheltered setting.

step. My entire soul desires this and I find my greatest consolation in placing myself in imagination in their churches.

Pray for me, dear friend. Is it possible that I have written you in so much detail—in a manner you can scarcely understand—This is the first letter I have ever written in French, the only excuse I can offer for all the mistakes, and this difficulty in making myself understood is the only reason you have not received any letters from me on every boat since your departure.

Oh! how happy I would be to know everything about you—you yourself, your dear children, our William Seton, the little angel Harriet, Henrique, Aglai, Adele—subjects that will always be dear to me . . . Often I hum the little air "come tender love" and "Holy Mary." Then the tears begin to fall very quickly on my needle at the almost unbearable remembrance.

My brothers and sisters are all well, here and there like lambs without a master. Mrs. [Eliza] Sadler speaks of you with very sincere interest. I saw our friend Chenot today for the first time since my return, but he gave me the handshake of our former friendship.

Dear friend, I love you with all my heart.

EAS.]

3.13 To Julia Scott

28th November 1804

My dear Julia

You have had time to arrive at Home, to be married,[1] according to the report of the World, and to have fulfilled all the etceteras etceteras, and yet I do not hear from you—is it true that you are so seriously engaged, or have you been reading my memorandums and concluded that any intercourse with the mad Enthusiast is loss of time—I have

---

3.13 ASJPH 1-3-3-6:54
[1]Julia Scott visited Elizabeth in September, but she never remarried.

been constantly busy with my Darlings mending up and turning winter clothes—they have in turn all been sick <too> from the change of weather added to their whooping cough—the old Mammy too has been sick—in short dear I have been one of Job's Sisters[2]—and from all appearances must long look to his example = Well, I am satisfied = to sow in tears if I may reap in joy,[3] and when all the wintry storms of time are past we shall enjoy the delights of an Eternal Spring—In the mean time I should wish to know if you are alive, how your Domestic affairs (in which you interested me very much) go on. Something about you all, but more than all a little of your dear interior self would be most acceptable as your Soul is most dear to me dear Julia—in that only can I hope to perpetuate my affection for you as in all exteriors we are and must continue to be wholly Separated—There is nothing new in my prospects since your departure except a suggestion of Mr. Wilkes that in order to avoid the boarding School plan I might recieve Boarders from one curate of St. Marks[4] who has ten or twelve scholars, and lives in the vicinity of the city—which would produce at least a part of the necessary means to make the ends of this year meet with my manner of living—Filicchi has not returned from Boston—his letters are full of extravagancies—very much the reverse of the above ideas—such as my heart would grasp at, but Reason must not listen to = God Almighty will I trust direct it—my mind is but little occupied with the Subject, so much I confide in his pitying Mercy—

Your and Maria's visits to me last summer appears like a vision.—little Kit often speaks of Aunt Scott and Anna sighs so pitifully at the mention of your name that my heart involuntarily answers hers, and though fully convinced in every point of view of the value of your affectionate kindness to her, Nature will sometimes prove her power and I shrink from the promise which reason and gratitude has sealed = she is a singular child and requires so many amendments in her disposition and habits that I fear she will call the whole force of your affection for me in exercise—but do not think of it, God will bless your

[2]Cf. Job 1:4 and Job 42:11.
[3]Cf. Ps. 126:5.
[4]St. Mark's Episcopal Church in the Bowery

kind intentions to a Fatherless child—and however rough or unhinged my mind may be, my Soul must be attached to you tenfold forever—

Remember me to your children and Mother[5]—and affectionately to Charlotte and Brother Sam

Your EAS

3.14 To Julia Scott

13th December 1804

Your letter my dearest Julia should have been answered immediately, and would have been, if I could have commanded the time for writing as readily as my heart dictated, but in this as in many other instances it must trust to your goodness whilst it is fully sensible how little it deserves the tenderness of your Friendship.—your gift of love[1] to my dear ones will I fear be expended in wood and Bread for us all, for with even pinching Economy those two articles must be very heavy—but all goes infinitely better than I could have expected and while my health is so much mended, that blessing supplies the place of many—Yet dear if you could see your friend turn out at day light in the coldest mornings, make fire, dress and comb, wash and scold the little ones, fill the kettle, prepare breakfast, sweep, make beds, and the etcetera work, nurse the old woman, keep the school, make ready dinner, supper and put to bed again, you will say could she go through it, all the while looking up too—and this I am always liable to as my poor old woman is subject to complaints which has confined her in bed for a week together during the severest weather—You will say where are all the friends, but must consider every one has their own occupations and pursuits and often for ten and twelve day[s] I see no one—My Italian friend[2] has been detained in Boston but doubtless will soon be on his way to your city and of course introduced to you—

---

[5]Susanna Deshon Sitgreaves
3.14 ASJPH 1-3-3-6:55
[1]Julia regularly sent Elizabeth financial contributions for the family.
[2]Antonio Filicchi

Your visionary scheme of love and kindness like many other sweet imaginations will do to dream of—while I am in this part of the world, where my Sister is, there I must be—Julia Julia dear Julia do not forget my question, and when you imagine the voice let it be animated by love, intreaty, supplication for Oh when I think of you in that point of view, I could fasten you in my Bosom and drag you, compel you, and when sure of your consent fly with you to the feet of our Saviour and Judge—yes Judge he must and will be, and then though I should be eager to share my Oil with you I shall find there is only enough for my own little lamp[3]—dear dear dear friend consider, and when you consider resolve, and then [qui]ckly go to him, tell Him you are in want of ever[y thi]ng—beg for the new heart, the right spirit, and that He will teach you to do the thing that pleases Him—

Well, there are fine Preachers in this life—but my dearest if you possessed a little glass thro which you could discern the finest country and one you tenderly loved neglected to look thro' it and would perhaps forget the way, you would be ready even to pain them rather than let them wait till the clouds and storms gathered round and the road should be either hidden or lost—and if you take your darlings astray too take care Miss Julia—you say write—I will indeed when I can, even though it should be a scrawl like this as fast as the pen can drive = there is nothing more done in the new arrangement but I believe it will certainly take place—how I wish John Wilkes and yourself had been cut out for each other—but perhaps you have already chained the Batchelor—you said you were not affraid in the main point. write to me, tell me—send my papers, and be assured of the tenderest affection of

your EAS.

---

[3]Cf. Matthew 25: 1-9.

3.15 To Antonio Filicchi

13th December 1804

I had Just taken my little secretary on my lap and was reading one of your most kind letters when the most kind one of the 6th December was brought to me—and certainly I was obliged to make the dear sign[1] to help me in my good resolution of trying to be indifferent—I should wish earnestly my most dear Brother never to think of you with tenderness but when calling on Almighty God to bless you, then often indeed my heart overflows and exhausts the sighs and tears of affection which at all other times are most carefully repressed—and so far from feeling less interest for you or less value for your Affection it has never so earnestly so anxiously prayed for you as during the few weeks past in which it has been pained by your neglect—

Antonio, you ought indeed to pity me for at times the sense of my real situation presses so strong upon my mind that it almost overpowers me—not the care or interest of my temporal concerns, for those thro' Gods pitying mercy do not in the least affect or trouble me; but the horror of neglecting to hear His voice, if he has indeed spoken to me through you, or of resisting him if all these warnings and declarations on the other side are truth—the Scriptures once my delight and comfort are now the continual sources of my pain, every page I open confounds my poor Soul, I fall on my knees and blinded with tears cry out to God to teach me—

Twelve months ago when six days were past,[2] I joyful looked to the dear Sabbath as a full reward for whatever sorrow or care I had passed through in the week—Now I look fearfully at the setting sun dreading least a fine morning should leave me without excuse for going to church—and when I pass over the street that leads to your church my heart struggles and prays O teach me teach me where to go—indeed before I leave home I pray always for forgiveness, if indeed I pass by

---

3.15 AMSJ A 111 024

[1]The sign of the cross

[2]This time the previous year the Setons had been quarantined in the Lazaretto at Leghorn scarcely one week.

where He dwells, and light and grace to know his Will—When in church how often my Soul is called back from the little chappel in Santa Catharina's[3] where beside your Amabilia I see the Priest you used to say said the long Mass every feature and action is before me I hear the Bell and see the cup elevated and my Spirit lays in the Dust before God—

If your Church is Antichrist your Worship Idolitrous my soul shares the crime, though my will would resist it, for O my Brother, if you could know the shocking and awful objects presented to my mind in opposition to your church, you would say it is impossible except a voice from Heaven directed, that I ever could become a member of it.

truely I say with David Save me Lord for the waters go over my Soul I am in the deep mire where no ground is[4]—and you can easily concieve that as the view of my sins always rise against me as the vail between my soul and the Truth that I most earnestly desire that God will keep me from all created beings that by a broken and contrite heart I may find mercy through my Redeemer—also when some hours of consolation come I think hard as the trial is yet it is sweet—I never knew till now what prayer is—never thought of fasting—though now it is more a habit than eating, never knew how to give up all, and send my spirit to mount calvary nor how to console and delight it in the Society of Angels—Patience says my soul He will not let you and your little ones perish and if yet your life is given in the conflict at the last he will nail all to his cross and recieve you to his mercy—

this letter you will easily see is only to unburthen my heart to its dearest Friend—how much that heart desires that you may be Blessed can only be known to Him who sees it—you say nothing of yourself, I say all—and say sincerely that until you mentioned the Law suit[5] detaining you in Boston, I thought that something else did—May God preserve your Soul and Body—

Your own friend and Sister EAS.

---

[3] A local church in Leghorn frequented by the Filicchis

[4] Cf. Ps. 69, a cry of anguish and great distress.

[5] Antonio instituted a lawsuit on behalf of his brother Filippo.

1805

3.16 To Antonio Filicchi

2nd January 1805

I wrote you my dear Brother 13th December a full sheet of paper, but as it was one of those pictures of my troubled heart you have so often recieved the letter remains in my Secretary. and now wish only to remind you of your Sister and to reassure you of often repeated sentiments of truest affection. Will you not return? October, November, December and January began, I have been watching and still watch for the footsteps of the only one I can welcome with my heart within my doors—this must sound shocking to you, but think only of a part of the contradictions to that heart, and you who know its most secret thoughts will not wonder if it desires to dwell in a cave or desert. but no more of this, it must go back to its lesson of "Thy will be done."—

Mr. [John] Wilkes made me the New Year visit this Morning and says the plan I mentioned to you in my last letter will not be put in operation until May; Who knows by that time God may take me Home and I shall escape from all these struggles—I do not offer New Year wishes to my Brother, for every day every hour my Soul sends up its purest most fervent wishes for the Blessing of your Soul and Body, but for your Soul as for my Own.

do not think because I say nothing of my soul that it is less active or desirous to know the truth, its desires though less impatient as submitted to the source of truth, were never more ardent constant and incessently in action then they are now. I think if I had the treasures of the World at my command I would give them as dust for one hours conversation with Bishop C[arroll] or one of his character—

Bayley[1] has returned, and is going in a few weeks again—he intends writing to you that you may prepare your commands—

Your own Sister most truely most affectionately EAS.

3.16 AMSJ A 111 025

[1]Richard Bayley, Elizabeth's half-brother, was working for the Filicchi firm in Leghorn. He was in New York for a few weeks and called on Elizabeth to pick up messages for Italy.

3.17 Draft to Filippo Filicchi

[after 1/6/1805]

My dear Filicchi,

I find from Antonios letters you expect to hear from me, tho' from your not answering my first letter I concluded you were too much dissatisfied with me and that I had intirely forfieted your Friendship. This could not be the case if you knew the pitiable situation to which my poor Soul has been reduced, finding no satisfaction in any thing, or any consolation but in tears and prayers. but after being left intirely to myself and little children, my friends dispersed in the country for the Summer season, the clergy tired of my stupid comprehension, and Antonio wearied with my Scruples and doubts took his departure to Boston; I gave myself up to God and Prayer encouraging myself with the Hope that my unrighteousness would be no more remembered at the foot of the Cross, and that sincere and unremitted asking would be answered in Gods own time. This author and that author on the Prophecies[1] was read again and again; the texts they refered to read on my knees with constant tears, but not with much conviction. They had told me from the beginning, that my strong belief in your Doctrine must be a temptation, and as I know the old gentleman[2] would naturally trouble a heart so eagerly seeking the Will of God I resolved to double the only weapons against him, humility, Prayer, and fasting, and found my mind gradually settle in Confidence in Christ and the infinite treasures of his Mercy. for some months I have stood between the two ways looking steadily upwards but fearing to proceed, never crossing the street that led to your Church without lifting up my heart for mercy and often in the Protestant Church finding my Soul at Mass in Leghorn.[3] this was my exact situation when the New year commenced, and without any other intention than to enjoy a good sermon

---

3.17 ASJPH 1-3-3-10:6

[1]This probably refers to Thomas Newton's *Dissertations on the Prophecies* which Rev. Henry Hobart had recommended to Elizabeth.

[2]The devil

[3]The city in Italy where Elizabeth visited the Filicchis

on the season, I took down a volume of Bourdaloue[4] who speaking of the wise Mens enquiry "where is he who is born King of the Jews,"[5] draws the inference that when we no longer discern the Star of Faith we must seek it where only it is to be found with the Depositors of his Word. Therefore once more I resolved after heartily committing my Cause to God again to read those books on the catholick faith which had at first won me to it and in consequence of so doing would certainly with a helping hand give my Seal to it. I have endeavoured to see Mr. OBrian[6] but been disappointed, have written to Bishop Caroll, but his Silence to Antonios letters makes me hesitate in sending mine.—yet even under these strong impressions I could not make any dicision in my own Soul without asking some questions for its relief and comfort; when Antonio returns (if he ever returns here) we will try to do so; if not, I am sure that God will help me by some other means—you know it would be wicked to doubt, (tho' I am so utterly unworthy) that thro' Jesus I shall recieve this dearest favour having already recieved so many.

3.18 To Antonio Filicchi

24th January 1805

The first emotion I felt on reading your letter my dearest Brother was joy and thankfulness that you were not travelling in this severe weather. the children crowded round me as they always do when a letter comes from you with the repeated question "when will he come Mamma," and I was obliged to pretend that you had sent a message of love to each of them; indeed every one wonders at your stay, and think

---

[4]Rev. Louis Bourdaloue (1632-1704) was a French Catholic spiritual writer whose collected sermons delivered in Paris fill dozens of volumes.

[5]Matt. 2:2

[6]Rev. Matthew O'Brien came to New York from Albany sometime before 1802. Elizabeth mistakenly believed he was the only Catholic priest in New York. He eventually was the priest who received her profession of faith as a Roman Catholic at St. Peter's Church, Barclay Street, in lower Manhattan March 14, 1805.

3.18 AMSJ A 111 026

that now I am safe, tho' I always speak explicitly whenever questioned as to the state of my Soul and certainly must have some eloquence on the subject from the effect produced—

but oh my Brother religion here has a sandy foundation indeed, and the best instructed minds on other Subjects know little of that which should be their all. God be merciful—I may as well tell you as I have so long thought it, I could not help imagining that some extravagance such as that which "once bound you to your sister," influenced your stay in Boston—do not say it was ungenerous as the source of these imaginations you must most easily discern; but your word is sufficient—

you speak most highly of the catholic Priests of Boston[1] perhaps it would be best you should give a short history of your dear Sister to the one you esteem most. as I may one day find the benefit of your doing so, for it is plain that if the gracious God should bless me so as really to unite me to your communion tho' I might persevere thro' every obstacle myself, I could never seperate my children from the influence of my connections, and must try every way for the best. This like everything else is in the hands of God.

The Bishop of Meaux[2] has written some address to Protestants and observations on the Apoc[a]lyps[e][3] which I desire much to see. I tell you as you may perhaps bring it with you.—Is it possible that you can excuse yourself to me on the score of diffidence and ignorance of our language—this is indeed so like the language of a stranger to a stranger, and throws me at so great a distance from your affection that I should wish to burn every letter of yours containing those expressions—you surely could neither feel nor express them to one you really love—but no more on that

[1]Rev. Francis A. Matignon (1753-1818) was an emigré from France and doctor of the Sorbonne (1785) who arrived in Baltimore in 1792. While serving in Boston, he was a trusted advisor and friend of Elizabeth Seton.

Rev. John Cheverus (1768-1836), another emigré from France, became the first bishop of Boston in 1808. He befriended and advised Elizabeth Seton after her conversion. After resigning as bishop of Boston, Cheverus became the archbishop of Bordeaux (1826-1836) and was named cardinal shortly before his death.

[2]James Bossuet (1627-1704). Filippo Filicchi recommended his *History of the Variation of Protestant Churches* to Elizabeth.

[3]The Book of Revelation

subject—your Boston weeks I find very long, but certainly they must one day have an end—Wherever you are you have the sincere affection and most ardent prayers of your

EAS.

3.19 To Julia Scott

March 5th 1805

My dearest Julia

It is almost incredible that your most affectionate letter has been six weeks in my possession unanswered—the love and tenderness it expresses brought me to my knees I ask God with tears of joy and thankfulness have I indeed such a friend, indeed Julia it has made me saucy for my mind often involuntarily turns to some pleasures which before I should not have had a thought of accomplishing—not exactly those you wished for me, for it seems I must fulfil the engagement with Mr. [John] Wilkes, but I think in consequence of your generosity and love I may procure a person who will rid me of the dreaded burthen of patching and darning and that I may be able to give a large portion of my time to my Anna in communicating to her what I know of Music and French which is as much and perhaps more than she would attain in another situation, for I am persuaded and have experienced that in those acquirements which require so much patience and application, a Mother is by far the most desirable preceptress at least I have an earnest wish to make the experiment with her and think I can trust to my sense of duty to her and to you who will afford me the means for a regular attention on my part—therefore dearest friend let your three hundred be 150 dollars which will amply pay the woman and supply Anna with cloathing.

I have run the gauntlet, and persuaded Filicchi that this is not the time for my entering into his fascinating schemes—tho' I do not see my duty to my dear ones in a clear view either way. I could go almost mad at the view of the conduct of every friend I have here except yourself. It would really seem that in their estimation I am a child not to be trusted with its daily bread least it should waste it—but never mind all will come right one of these days, and you know penance is the purifyer of the Soul, therefore I drive every thought away and meet it all with the smile of content, which however often conceals the sharp thorn in the heart—a thorn I can give you no name for; I should be sorry to think it pride or disappointment for I can have no claim on any one except what God opens their hearts to do for me—Peace peace rebellious Nature—how much worse do you deserve =

—Your assurance of dear Brothers [Samuel] interest in me and my affairs brought Home many a remembrance of time past, I can see him, speak to him, read his heart, and would throw myself upon his pity and affection securely and with out reserve as if I was still his little B[etty] Bayley. but that too must be hushed, and I must jog on the allotted path thro' all its windings and weariness till it brings me Home where all tears shall be wiped away and sorrow and sighing be heard no more[1]—in the mean while dearest, courage, LOOK UP.—

—Is your dear little hea[r]t still filled with contradictions - or has the Birth of the new darling been propitious[2]—how I should like to witness your every day scene without your knowing it, dearest Julia I fear it would present a picture less free from care than even my own, yet your Maria must be a precious blessing to you, and I hope will be the friend of your heart and your comfort—My Anna is almost an a[n]gel to me.

Antonio Filicchi will present this to you—You will find him very much the gentleman—but too diffident a character to engage acceptance on first acquaintance tho I am sure you will give him credit for the excellent qualities I have found in him and for my sake show him your affable side as his curiosity is really excited with respect to you.

—dear dear dear Julia what will you think of my not writing you—tho indeed if you knew the daily domestic scene you would

---

[1]Cf. Rev. 21:4

[2]Possibly the child of Julia's niece, Hitty Cox Markow, who was married the previous year

soon forgive—the old Mammy half her time sick her Daughter lain-in³ in my house with many other Etceteras—yet do not think this a picture of my Soul—it is as quiet as your tenderest Affection could wish it—and with its tenderest affections prays for the Peace of yours and that the same sheltering Wing may at length recieve us both—united forever.

Your EAS.
March 25th

3.20 Draft to Rev. John Cheverus¹

[After March 25, 1805]

Dear and Reverend Sir,

My joyful heart offers you the tribute of its lively gratitude for your kind and charitable interest in its sorrows when it was oppressed with doubts and fears; and hastens after completion of its happiness to inform you that thro' the boundless Mercy of God and aided by your very satisfactory council,² my Soul has offered all its hesitations and reluctancies a Sacrifice with the blessed Sacrifice of the Altar on the 14th March³ and the next day was admitted to the true Church of Jesus Christ with a mind grateful and satisfied as that of a poor shipwrecked mariner on being restored to his Home.

I should immediately have made a communication so pleasing to you, but have been necessarily very much engaged in collecting all the powers of my soul for recieving the pledge of eternal happiness with which it has been blessed on the happy day of the Annunciation,⁴

---

³A term for childbirth

3.20 ASJPH 1-3-3-1:1

¹This is the only extant example of many letters Elizabeth Seton wrote to Rev. John Cheverus. The actual letter she sent in 1805 was apparently destroyed along with all the correspondence Cheverus had received during his years in America as a priest and later the bishop of Boston when he was shipwrecked off the French coast in 1823.

²Elizabeth and Rev. John Cheverus had been corresponding.

³Elizabeth made her profession of faith in the Catholic church March 14, 1805.

⁴Elizabeth made her First Communion in the Catholic church March 25, 1805, the feast of the Annunciation.

when it seemed indeed to be admitted to a new life and that Peace which passes all understanding—with David I now say "Thou hast saved my Soul from death, my eyes from tears, and my feet from falling," and certainly desire most earnestly to "walk before him in the land of the living"[5] esteeming my priviledge so great and what he has done for me so beyond my most lively hopes that I can scarcely realize my own blessedness—you dear Sir could never experience but may picture to yourself a poor burthened creature weighed down with sins and sorrows recieving an immediate transsition to life liberty and rest. Oh pray for me that I may be faithful and persevere to the end. and I would beg of you advice and council how to preserve my inestimable blessings—

true there are many good books, but directions personally addressed from a revered source most forcably impress—for instance many years I have preferred those Chapters you appoint in St. John—but from your direction make it a rule to read them constantly. the Book you mentioned "the following of Christ"[6] has been my consolation thro' the severest struggles of my life and indeed one of my first convictions of the truth arose from reflecting on the account a Protestant writer gives of Kempis as having been remarkable for his study and knowledge of the Holy Scriptures and fervent zeal in the service of God—I remember falling on my knees and with many tears enquired of God, if He who knows his Scriptures so well and so ardently loved him could have been mistaken in the true faith, also in reading the life of St. Francis de Sales[7] I felt a perfect willingness to follow him and could not but pray that my soul might have its portion with his on the great day—the Sermons of Bourdaloue[8] have also greatly helped to convince and enlighten me, for many months past

---

[5]Ps. 116

[6]*The Following of Christ* by Thomas à Kempis is a classic on Christian spirituality.

[7]A seventeenth century bishop and writer

[8]Elizabeth was using the published sermons of Rev. Louis Bourdaloue as a text. It is also known that Rev. John Cheverus provided her with the *Roman Catholic Manual, or Collection of Prayers, Anthems, Hymns, etc.* (Boston, 1803) which he had had printed. This book is now in the University of Notre Dame Archives but the title page is missing. In addition he sent her a book of sermons by Jean Baptiste Massillon. Massillon was rated with Bossuet and Bourdaloue as one of the great French writers of sermons. The first printed edition appeared posthumously in 1745. It is not possible to determine which edition Cheverus sent Elizabeth.

one of them are always included in my daily devotions—these books and some others Filicchi who has been, and is, the true friend of my Soul has provided me with—if he did not encourage me I do not know how I should dare to press so long a letter on your time so fully and sacredly occupied—pardon me in consideration of the relief it gives my heart to express itself to one who understands it whilst it earnestly prays that you may long be the instrument of Gods Glory and the happiness of his creatures—Most respectfully and affectionately,

EAS.

3.21 To Antonio Filicchi

[March 31, 1805][1]

My dearest Brother.

I cannot recollect Mrs. [Julia] Scotts direction[2] but Mr. Cox[3] her Brother-in-law is very much known, and she lives nearly opposite to him.* With my whole soul I pray to God to direct you in all your ways. and shall not go to the Altar in spirit or in reality with out remembering my most dear Brother.

ever Yours most Sincerely EAS.
*I think in Second street.

3.21 AMSJ A 111 027
[1]Written on the outside in another hand: "31 March 1805"
[2]Address
[3]James Cox was married to Charlotte Sitgreaves Cox, Julia's sister.

3.22 To Antonio Filicchi

6th April 1805

By this time I trust my dear Brother the fatigues of your Journey are over, and hope that the dearest and most active principle of your Soul will soon be directed where it will meet a grateful welcome—Not knowing your direction,[1] I wait to receive it from you, and in the mean time would say to you that every day I am more assured of the truth of your assertion that the exclusive right of real friend and Brother is solely yours. that you have led me to a happiness which admits of no description, and daily even hourly increases my souls Peace, and really supplies strength and resolution superior to any thing I could have concieved possible in so frail a Being—

The so long agitated plan is given up,[2] and in consequence I am plagued for a House, wearied with consultations about what would be best for me etc, and certainly the painful ideas suggested by my present circumstances would weigh down my spirits if they were not supported and so fully occupied by interior consolations—in the midst of all the different conversations of the good ladies and my Brother P[ost] my heart is free of all concern, redoubles its prayers, prepares for its dear Master,[3] and this morning after a half hours consolatory communication with O.B[rien], recieved Him happy, grateful, joyful, and most truely Blessed. do not think you was forgotten in that hour dearest Antonio, no aspirations of my Soul are more ardent than those it forms for your true happiness, indeed how can it be otherways when every enjoyment of my own reminds me of what I owe to you.

9th April—

Perhaps you expect to hear from your sister, and naturally must go to the Post office for Murrey's letters, therefore this may take its

---

3.22 AMSJ A 111 028
[1] Address
[2] John Wilkes' plan for her to take in boarders
[3] Reception of Holy Communion

chance and will at least prove to you that I would not omit doing any thing that might give you even the least pleasure—

I have made acquaintance with your Mr. Morris,[4] who enquired very kindly of you—he invited me with my children to his seat in church[5]—My Boys are mad with Joy at going where they can see the cross at St Peter,[6] William is always begging to be a little Priest (meaning the little Boys who serve at the Altar) he says "I would rather be one Mamma than the richest greatest man in the whole world," indeed I had so much pleasure in seeing them sign themselves and kneel so devoutly that it compensated the pain of seeing your seat vacant. I hope my dear Antonio your heart will fully share the blessings of this week, so as even to exclude from your thoughts the greater enjoyment you might recieve by being in Boston though I assure you mine often involuntarily turns to your interesting description of [Rev. John] Chevrous and his manner of Instruction, for it requires indeed a mind superior to all externals to find its real enjoyment here. a Stranger has assisted the last week, but certainly is not any acquisition in that respect, I am forced to keep my eyes always on my Book, even when not using it—never mind these things are but secondary as your dear eloquence has taught me, but it is my weakness to be too much influenced by them, yet my grateful Soul acknowledges that its dear Master has given me as I think the most perfect happiness it can enjoy on Earth and more and more it feels its joy and glory in the exchange it has made—dear dear Antonio May God bless you bless you, bless you for the part you have done in it.—

---

[4]Andrew Morris, a wealthy chandler, was among the founders of St. Peter's, the first Catholic parish in New York City. The first Catholic office-holder in New York City, he was assistant alderman of the First Ward from 1802 to 1806.

[5]It was customary to pay rent for the use of pews in church.

[6]St. Peter's Church on Barclay Street, established in 1785, is the oldest Catholic church in New York. It was built on land purchased from Trinity Episcopal Church at the corner of Church and Barclay Streets. This first Catholic parish was organized soon after New York's Anti-Priest Law of 1700 was repealed in 1784. According to this law, any Catholic priest entering New York had been subject to arrest and life in prison. Catholics had been prohibited from voting, holding public office, or serving on juries.

Elizabeth Seton was received into the Roman Catholic church at St. Peter's March 14, 1805, by Rev. Matthew O'Brien.

Have you seen my friend[7]—does your patience bear the trial it must receive from those merchants—how often it pains me that you must think of my Seton with so much vexation—if I had a world to pay you with you know it would be all yours—

Do at least send me your blessing if you cannot afford another word, you know that may be given without the trouble of painting. Most truely, really, sincerely, simply without exaggeration, I am yours, all that is mine to give Your Sister Friend Servant

EAS

3.23 To Antonio Filicchi

15th April [1805]

My dearest Tonino.

In the morning I wish for sunset hoping for what it may bring, but all in vain, a fortnight is past and I have not even the happiness of knowing if you are safe arrived in Philadelphia—Patience—thought flies on to the approaching time when I shall see you no more, and hear once or twice only in twelve months—Nature cannot stop at the Recollection, and the desiring soul flies even beyond to the sweet garden of Paradise where you first promised to call for your dear Sister, and where she shall enjoy your beloved society forever.

I hear you say how much you have been engaged and vexed with your troublesome business, you have had many letters to prepare for Leghorn—strangers are pressing and inviting you—Confession, Communion all have engaged your time and attention—

You would be pleased to know how happy I have been last week, and how even more and more I am satisfied with my Director.[1] Saturday last I had a very painful conversation (certainly for the last time)

[7]Julia Scott
3.23 AMSJ A 111 029
[1]Rev. Matthew O'Brien

with Mr. H[obart], but was repaid fully and a thousand times on Sunday morning by my dear Master at Communion, and my Faith if possible more strengthened and decided than if it had not been attacked. My Mrs. [Catherine] Duplex goes on very fast—every day some one of the kind ladies sheds tears to her for the poor deluded Mrs. Seton, and she always tells them how happy she is that anything in this world can comfort and console me—

Whoever speaks to me I tell them instantly with a cold decided countenance that the time of reasoning and opinions is past, nor can I be so ungrateful to God after the powerful conviction he has so graciously given me, as to speak one moment on the subject as it would certainly offend Him—

I have taken part of a very neat House, about half way to town near Greenwich Street[2]—for £ 50. the one I am in is 80—thirty pounds will buy winter cloths, and what is best of all, I shall be able to go every morning before breakfast to visit my Master[3]—

19 April—

Really now I am seriously uneasy about you and if tomorrow brings no news from you will write Mrs. [Julia] Scott to enquire about you—for tho' you said you would not write yet if it had been in your power you would have sent at least your direction. Often my heart cries out to God for you and if I did not commit you wholy to him I should be very unhappy. O.B[rien] has twice asked me about you—John Wilkes has made me some sharp yet gentle reproaches for my "imprudence in offending my uncle[4] and other friends"—he said nothing of my religion but that he knew the "Evidences of the Christian religion were all on that side" and my sentiments made no difference to him—Sister says "tell me candidly if you go to our church or not" I answered, since the first day of Lent I have been to St. Peters—

But why do I say these things to you when it is uncertain that you will even recieve this letter—very well Antonio I fear your charity has passed New York and gone on to Boston—but I shall be satisfied with

---

[2]The city directory gives her address as North Moore Street.
[3]She moved within walking distance of St. Peter's Church.
[4]Dr. John Charlton, the brother of Elizabeth's mother

every thing if you are only well—I am your true your own your most
affectionate Sister

EAS.

3.24 To Amabilia Filicchi

April 15 1805

My very dear Friend

You must have long ago expected a reply to your last letter of
_____ but this is the first opportunity your Antonio has pointed out,
and he says the only direct one there has been for some months, indeed
dear Amabilia your upright and happy Soul can never imagine the
struggles and distresses of mine since I left you, or you would not
wonder if I avoided writing or speaking on the source of its unhappi-
ness, and certainly it was not easy to write to one as dear to me as you
are without expressing it.

—but all now is past, the heavy cloud has given place to the sun
shine of Peace, and my soul is as free and contented as it has been
burthened and afflicted, for God has been so gracious to me as to remove every obstacle in my mind to the true Faith and given me
strength to meet the difficulties and temptations I am externally tried
with—You may suppose my happiness in being once more permitted
to kneel at his Altar, and to enjoy those foretastes of Heaven he has
provided for us on Earth. now every thing is easy, Poverty, suffering,
displeasure of my friends all lead me to Him, and only fit my heart
more eagerly to approach its only good. How your dear charitable
heart so often lifted to God in Prayer for me will rejoice, I know that it
will with those also of Gubbio[1] who have so tenderly kept a poor
stranger in remembrance If I could make them understand me I would
thank them most affectionately and beg them still to brighten their

3.24 AMSJ A 111 030

[1]City in Italy where the Filicchi family had relatives, two of whom were nuns.

crown and pray that the one their prayers have helped to gain for me may not be lost—

Your Antonio is now in Philadelphia. Oh how you would be pleased to see him so well, so handsome, so delighted with your sweet picture as scarcely to permit any one to hold it in their hands—and certainly the expression of it is just such as you would have wished tender and sorrowful as if lamenting your separation—he feels it so, and speaks as tenderly to it as if you were present—he also talks of his Patrick as if he had seen him but yesterday of his dancing and shaking himself so drolely and all his little lovely ways—for me I always see my Georgino[2] with his dear arms stretched out to me, and sweet inviting smiles—Oh if ever I should hold him to my heart again how happy I should be, but that happiness with every other wish and desire must all be referred to Paradise for here in all human probability they will not be accomplished.

Yet I must often think of you all, of the dear girls and of you dear Amabilia and all the unmeritted kindness I have recieved from you—God only can reward you.

Well we may bless Him for keeping your Antonio free from the danger of the Fever in both countries and his health here is so perfect that not withstanding the severity of the winter he has not had even a headach, as no doubt he has told you for he speaks of it as a most gracious Providence. Oh with what a thankful soul I shall adore that Providence if he is only restored safe and well to you. He will tell you that he took the figs and one basket of the raisins you so kindly sent to me, as he wished them for a friend and one basket was abundance for my Darlings, I boil them in rice for them and it makes an excellent dinner—You speak with so much ceremony about sending them my dear friend that surely I ought to have made many Apologies for so great a liberty as I took with you when I sent you some things so triffling—but let not such language be known between us—God sees my heart to you and knows it loves you most sincerely, and respects

---

[2]Patrizio and Georgino were the Filicchis' sons whom Elizabeth had known while she was in Italy.

your virtues more then ever I can express—If ever it is in my power most gladly will I prove it to you.

How much I thank your Brother Gaspero[3] for his kind recollections, and beg you will return them for me as also to the dear Rosina and all your family—Antonio knows how often I have wished to transport some fine Apples to Dr. Tutilli[4] his kindness I must always remember with the most lively gratitude and beg you to offer him my affectionate compliments—

Is Sibald and Belfour still of your party, will you remember me to them, and kiss your Darlings for me a thousand times little Ann is much improved—she always speaks with delight of Leghorn, and of your dear girls as if she was with them only yesterday. When Antonio showed her your picture she was in a rapture and said afterwards, Oh Mamma how I wish to hold it in my hands and kiss it.

dear dear Amabilia may Almighty God bless you do remember me particularly to Mr. Hall[5]

your E A Seton

3.25 To Antonio Filicchi

22nd April 1805

My dear dear Brother

Your most welcome letter arrived this Evening I set the Piano wide open and let the children dance till they were tired— You are to be sure a counsellor of the first order and open your cause as a Plaintiff, when I thought opening your letter let me see Antonio's Defence—but you men when once convinced of you[r] consequence are saucy mortals

---

[3]Gaspero Baragazzi, Amabilia's brother

[4]The Italian physician who attended William Magee Seton in the Lazaretto

[5]Rev. Thomas Hall was the British chaplain who attended William Seton on his deathbed in Italy and conducted his funeral services. Hall lived on the first floor of the building where the Filicchis had the second and where Elizabeth occupied the third floor during her stay in Leghorn.

3.25 AMSJ A 111 031

that is well known—three weeks to day since you left your Sister without any direction to you, in a state of utter uncertainty if your neck was broke or not, or if perhaps you had not stole a march on me and gone to the Northward instead of to the Southward, and then you very modestly commence an accusation, in answer to a letter containing a most humble and earnest address to your charity and compassion—but never mind I shall learn by experience what to expect from so Philosophic a Spirit, and leave you to your Apathy while I shall uniformly follow the suggestions of my duty and affection—Yet if I thought it is his general character—but so well knowing your ardor where you are really interested, absolutely my Patience is tried—

Tonino, Tonino—how I long to meet you in your state of perfection, where I shall receive the transfusion of your affections without your exertions—but to be done triffling—let me tell you that one reason why you have not heard from me oftener is that from circumstances of particular impressions on my mind I have been obliged to watch it so carefully and keep so near the fountain head[1] that I have been three times to communion since you left me—not to influence my Faith, but to keep Peace in my Soul, which without this heavenly resource would be agitated and discomposed by the frequent assaults which in my immediate situation are naturally made on my feelings—

the counsel and excellent directions of O.B[rien][2] also, if even I was sensible of them before, strengthen me, and being sometimes enforced by command give a determination to my actions which is now indispensable—early the same morning you say you were happy, I was also—making only the Acts of Faith, etc—sometimes I am really affraid to go to Him having so little or nothing to say—for tho' there is a cloud of imperfection surrounding every moment of my life yet for those things that have a name my soul would be too happy in being so free from them if it did not dread the hour of temptation, knowing too well its frailty to even hope such a state should last—Yet even in that case, thro' Christ Who strengthens we can do all things.[3]

---

[1] The Eucharist and the Roman Catholic church
[2] Rev. Matthew O'Brien
[3] Cf. Phil. 4:13.

pray for me, my Brother, pray for me—you little know how much I pray for you, so much that if the command was not added to the inclination I should ask my soul how it dared—I now look every day for an answer from your [Rev. John] Chevrous—as my letter went in the post office the day you left N[ew] York—My letters for Leghorn are gone to Murrey not waiting your information when the ship would sail—

23rd.

In reading again your letter I smile to myself and say do not be flattered by Antonio's commendation—remember he paints and colours as a thing of course—but O.B[rien]. did not exaggerate in his opinion of you this morning—he said you were an "upright excellent character," and other things that made your little Sisters heart dance with pleasure, for so I would have every one think of you he also spoke of Philippo [Filicchi] as a miracle, but I would only allow he was your superior as a Merchant and that only in his department—This was in the Vestry room where he invited me to give me a Book of his Sermons—I cannot express to you how kind Mr. [Andrew] Morris is to me—he also always inquires of you very particularly—

I have passed thro' a fire today in the number of people I accidentally encountered—every one smiled some with affection, some with civility—and when I get alone again I recollect with delight how "gently He clears my way" and say with Blessed David "Tho' I walk thro' the Valley and Shadow of Death I will fear no evil, for thou art with me."[4] I am pleased that my dear little friend Mrs. [Julia] Scott is attentive to you and thank God with every power of my soul for the favourable prospect in your business— dear dear Brother may he Bless you in all things, and reward your generous soul for the kindness with which you have, and do comfort mine—His three fold Peace be yours, as I am yours

EAS.

---

[4]Ps. 23:4

3.26 To Antonio Filicchi

30th April 1805

Your dear Sister has been doing Penance this week past, cheerfully tho', and with a sweet hope that it will be accepted—my woman has been again sick these five days and I have been deprived of the dear morning visit to my Master[1]—on Sunday I was so weak as not to be able to walk to town with my other fatigues, but sent the children, and they were all called in the Vestry room, and many kind Enquiries made about Mamma—tomorrow at 7 oclock I hope to go and really long for it as a child to see its Mother.

And how are you my Brother? do you meet any Elegant Friends in Philadelphia, any Pupils for the Italian language, any Sirens—God preserve you—I pray that your good angel may have no cause to turn from you, and that you may be faithful to all his admonitions—perhaps your [Rev. John] Chevrous is preparing some kind instructions for me, and I impatiently wait to hear from him—Shall I enclose his letter if he writes or only tell you the particulars?—

My old friend Mr. H[obart] thinks it is his duty to warn all my friends here of the falsity and danger of my principles, and of the necessity of avoiding every communication with me on the subject—I told him if he thought it his duty he must act in conformity to it, as I on my part should do mine to the extent of my power—knowing that "God can bring to nothing the wisdom of the World."[2] however we must keep the Divine Precept of doing as we would be done by, and consider how much reason Mr. H. has for being embittered on this occasion—

Wednesday 1st May

The desired happiness was granted and my soul really comforted—but could not have all as O.B[rien] is absent, and the French Priest[3] too much engaged—afterwards took coffee with Mrs.

3.26 AMSJ A 111 032

[1] Attendance at morning Mass
[2] 1 Cor. 3:19
[3] Rev. Mr. Vrennay, a French Catholic priest, was in New York in early 1805.

[Catherine] Duplex who has suggested an idea of which I wish your opinion—A Mr. [Patrick] White an English gentleman of very respectable character and a compleat scholar but in reduced circumstances is endeavouring to establish a school for young Ladies, and perhaps Boys also, in which his wife will assist—He has seen my children and is interested for us—he has offered to teach them, and receive me as an assistant in his school in case it succeeds, of which there is every prospect as he is well recommended and a school such as he proposes is very much wanted—I should have a good prospect for the education of my boys—quiet my conscience by doing something if every so triffling towards our maintenance—and my Anna would recieve more instruction than I can give her,—but as in taking Medicine for a Disease I should willingly take it looking up to God for its success, so my mind recieves this proposal very quietly tho' certainly desirous that it might be accomplished, particularly if it has your approbation—if you can prevail with yourself do exercise your charity in communicating your sentiments.

dear dear Antonio why must I speak to you in a manner so little conformed to the feelings of my heart—but you know yourself drew the line, and the kindness and sweetness of affection must be veiled—from the searcher of hearts it cannot, and it delights me to consider that he also sees its sincerity, simplicity and holiness—Is it possible to retrospect the past, realize the present and meditate the heavenly Hope set before us, without freely and firmly yielding every power of my Soul to perform his Blessed Will and devoting every Affection in gratitude and love for such unmerited Mercy—Pray Pray that your dear Sister may attain the heavenly Grace of Perseverance—as my Whole Soul begs it for you—

EAS

tell me if you hear from your sweet Amabilia?—

3.27 To Julia Scott

6th May 1805

dear dearest Julia—

My Heart has turned to you many many times though my pen so seldom, for it seems sometimes as if there is a spell upon my writing—When I recieved Filicchi's first letter expressing your kind attention to him, while I blessed you for it in my Soul I thought another week shall not pass without repeating to my friend at least that I am her own Betty B[ayley] in affection, for fondly as I loved you then it could not be a comparison with the love of my Soul for you now which would give a part of itself, to make you a part of itself—there you dear mad creature is Logic for you the explanation of which is that I would ever wish you at any Expence I could make the purchase to be a partaker in my Fanatasism, Enthusasism, any thing You may please to call it, to call you back from your delusions and point your views to your next existance before you are called to it. so it is. you think I am in delusion, I know you are in delusion. I ask you "Julia where are you going." you are uncertain, you must either laugh or weep you cannot reflect on the subject or pause on it without a sigh—dear dear little Soul—Oh that it could see the things that belong to its Peace—

—Write to you once in two months and then only to scold Patience, dearest, I must let thought take its way at least to you—O how many thoughts crowded on me when I met poor [Colonel Aquila] Giles the other day, forlorn, dejected, shabby, and so changed from what he was— not changed in his kind heart however, for it seemed to feel a convulsion on seeing me and many a reproach for not having done so before. —they tell me his fortune is embarrassed and he has a miserable life—Father of Mercies, so goes this World—Let me tell you that in the hope of bettering my Property (that is my children) I have entered into an engagement with an English gentleman[1] and his wife (who have failed in their schemes in the interior of our country) to

---

3.27 ASJPH 1-3-3-6:57
[1]Patrick White

assist them in an English Seminary they are now establishing and which has a prospect of Eminent success—my profits are to be a third of whatever this plan produces and includes the Education of my Children—as I shall have no responsibility or trouble in organizing the plan, I could certainly find no situation more easy—especially as you are to pay the woman I shall employ to mend and to darn[2] and when I have a leisure hour it will be for my self—

My friends relatives etc who have been uniformly cool and composed in relation to all my concerns, are not less so in this instance, but as I shall take care to be distinct in all circumstances of contracts and agreements I cannot if the worst should happen be more their dependant than I am now—especially as I have so great a desire if only to taste a bit of bread of my own earning if it might be so—but in this I repeat the daily Prayer "thy will be done"—

How is Charlotte and Brother S[amuel] does your dear Maria continue so good and amiable, is your domestic Economy the same—is your Health better—how is the Bachelor[3]—what are you going to do this Summer—my heart would rejoice if your jaunt should be this way. in every way and All ways God Bless you, His Peace be with you, as is the sincere affection of Your EA.S.

My Darlings are quite well—Anna always speaks of you sweetly, affectionately, "My Aunt Scott." Cate says "she is mine too." Rebecca is a cherub. but my saucy Boys almost Master me—

3.28 To Antonio Filicchi

6 May 1805

Dear dear Brother,

How kind you were in complying so immediately with my request, my heart thanks you for this as well as the many many proofs you give

---

[2]This is a reference to a previous letter (3.19) in which Elizabeth talks about wanting to "procure a person who will rid me of the dreaded burthen of patching and darning" in order to devote more time to teaching music and French to her daughter Anna Maria Seton.

[3]Possibly the man who was courting Julia

and have given of your interest and pity for your poor little Sister—certainly you would be amused if you could know the events of the last two or three days in my history—

As soon as the report was circulated that there was a school intended of the description I mentioned to you, it was immediately added according to the usual custom of our generous world, that this Mr. and Mrs. [Patrick] White were Roman Catholicks and that Mrs. Seton joined herself in their plan to advance the principles of her new Religion. Poor Mr. H[obart] in the warmth of his Zeal flew to the Clergyman who had given the certificate of Mr. Whites abilities to reproach him for his imprudence and told every one who mentioned the subject of the dangerous consequences of the intended establishment—My Mrs. [Eliza] Sadler and [Catherine] Duplex finding that the scheme was likely to fall through, waited on the clergymen and explained that Mr. and Mrs. W. were Protestants and Mrs. Setons only intention was to obtain Bread for her children and to be at Peace with all the world instead of making discord between Parents and children—Mr. H[obart] was so very kind as to say after this explanation that he would use his influence for the school—

Mr. Post and Mr. [John] Wilkes give their cool assent—and I am satisfied that my situation cannot be worse than to be a dependent on such Philosophic Spirits. When I consulted O.B[rien] he promised his interest, and authorized me to say conscientiously that my principles and duties in this instance were seperate, except the former were called for—so it is my Brother—Patience—if it succeeds I bless God, if he does not succeed I bless God, because then it will be right that it should not succeed.—

Mrs. John Livingston[1] enquired very much about you, lamented that she had not known that you had returned to New York—hoped that she would not be gone again to the country before your return to Philadelphia etc. etc., and behaves to me really with the tenderness of a Sister—

Nothing yet from [Rev. John] Chevrous—perhaps he is collecting some good advices for me—I wish we could know if the new Pupil[2]

---

[1] A former neighbor and associate of Elizabeth

[2] Elizabeth herself

makes any progress towards the calendar—but that he would only tell to you.

I fear dear Brother if you must have recourse to the law that you have flattered me in your hopes of the issue of your business—Well my Soul prays with all its power that God may bless you in it—and most happy I shall be if you do indeed succeed—

—9th May

I have written my little Mrs. [Julia] Scott and thanked her for her attention to you—dear dear Antonio that has been the hardest pinch on my feelings of all I have yet encountered, the little, indeed the total want of attention to you on the part of those I call my friends, but if they had been such according to my ideas, they would have thought no care no kindness sufficient towards one who had been so much to me—but there is another scene of things—Where the Friend, the Protector, the Consoler of the Widow and the Fatherless, will recieve according to what they have done and these luke warm Souls find that they have been asleep—Where my most dear Brother will be rewarded as my heart desires and beyond even what its most fervent imagination can concieve—

Tomorrow will be my happy day so much distraction in mind and occupation in temporals must be counterbalanced or the poor little Soul is disturbed by every Shadow, but when its powers are stretched to that exalted object all others are but passing clouds in the Horizon which may for a moment obscure the glorious lustre of the Sun, while it goes on its course above them undiviating, in the will of its Master—May He bless you—and bless us with the final Blessing of his Children—is the first wish of the Soul of Your own Sister

EAS

3.29 To Antonio Filicchi

New York Sunday Evening 17 May 1805

My dearest Antonio

Judging your Heart by my own you will be pleased that I enclose you [Rev. John] Cheverous letter which I beg you will keep as Gold untill we meet again—I cannot part with it without reading it many times—and while my soul is lifted in thankfulness and joy for its privilege of asking and recieving advice and being numbered among the friends of so exalted a Being as your Cheverous its sensibilities are increased and every power brought in action in the remembrance that it is to my Brother, Protector, Friend, Benefactor that I owe this, among the numberless favours it has pleased God to bestow on me thro' you—Well may I pray for you—but He alone can recompense you.

Are you nearly disengaged from your Business—and thinking of your return to New York—You will find your little Sister in possession of part of a neat and comfortable House in which also the intended school will be kept and the fatigue of walking will be spared—also it is within one street of my dear church[1] which is the greatest luxury this World can afford me as I shall be enabled every morning to sanctify the rest of the day—O. B[rien] and Mr. [Andrew] Morris spoil me, their kindness and attention is more than I can express—If you see my dear little friend[2] tell her I have recieved her letter with a grateful Heart, and will write her very soon—have you no news from Home I long again for letters—could you spare time to tell your Sister you are well—it would be considered as a very great favour—and also consider that having no letters from you, you must excuse the Egotism of mine—and the shortness of this apply to the true

---

3.29 AMSJ A 111 034
[1] St. Peter's Catholic Church on Barclay Street
[2] Julia Scott

cause, moving, hurry etc. and the wish that you should be possessed of the enclosed as soon as possible—Your own most affectionate Sister

EAS.

3.30 To Antonio Filicchi

Saturday 1st June 1805

My most dear Brother has I hope exercised his much charity to his Sister and not condemned her for the omission of her weekly communication—I have recieved your kind letter and am very greatful for its contents tho' my Heart must ask for your dear Amabilia. Your account of the children delights me particularly the idea of Georgino's[1] loveliness pleases me as if I was indeed his Parent—if ever I should have the happiness of holding him to my heart again it would experience one of the sweetest pleasures I can hope for in this life—

May God bless all you do, and the angel of his presence accompany you in all your purposed Journeys, and restore you at last to the happy heart which claims you for its own—Yet my prayers go far beyond even that desired felicity and anticipate the period when time and place shall be no barrier to dear affections and your little Sister too may claim her share in the participation of your happiness, and enjoy the blessing of being one of your inseparable companions forever—

did not the dear letter delight you—besides the kindness that related it to me—the communication to you was no doubt food enough for the day on which you recieved it—O. B[rien] continues my kind friend and purposes to introduce me tomorrow to the Society of the Holy Sacrament which he recommends I should be associated with as it embraces many rules that may aid in the attainment of the much desired perfection at least as near an approach to it as my frail nature will admit of—He admits me every Sunday Morning to communion and there tomorrow my Soul will particularly plead for yours that it may

---

3.30 AMSJ A 111 035
[1]Georgino Filicchi

recieve the Spirit of Grace and Holiness—dear dear Antonio open your heart to Him, seek his blessed presence now that He may dwell in you eternally—

I long very much for your return here—you will scarcely find my Establishment begun—altho' I have recieved some young Ladies last week in my immediate care untill the return of Mr. White who has gone to Albany for his family—

Mrs. Livingston and Miss Ludlow[2] made me a very kind visit yesterday. I found one object of it was to ascertain if I had really resolved on not interfering in the religious principles of those committed to my charge—I told them plainly that if I had not taken the advice of my Director on the subject, and felt that I was not to be considered a "teacher of Souls" I would not for any consideration have subjected myself to the necessity of returning ingratitude for the confidence reposed in me—she said that generally a connection with even a Deist was not feared while with a Roman Catholick it was thought of with horror—I told her it was a curious contradiction in principles which allowed every Sect that could obtain a name to be right and in the way of Salvation—she believed the heart only was required by God—I believed the heart must be given, but if other conditions were required too, the Master certainly has a right to exact them—they mentioned some nonsense from Miss Lynch that sixty or eighty Prayers repeated obtained her the full forgiveness of all her sins—I appealed to their reason, and they begged that the subject might not be mentioned between us—as transient conversations seldom seldom have good effect—

My Brother my dear Brother pray for me that God will carry me through these briars and thorns to His kingdom of rest and Peace—May He bless you forever—Your Own Sister—

EAS.

---

[2]Mrs. John Livingston and Miss Ludlow, who formerly had been neighbors of the Setons

3.31 Journal to Amabilia Filicchi

19th July 1804

Here I am dearest Amabilia—released from the anxious watchful care of my beloved Rebecca[1]—her most lovely Soul departed yesterday morning—and with it—but not to stop on all that, which at last is all in order since it is the will of our God, I will tell you what I know you have at heart to know, that the impressions of your example and the different scenes I passed through in Leghorn are far from being effaced from my mind, which indeed could not even in the most Painful moments of attendance on my beloved Rebecca help the strong comparison of a sick and dying bed in your happy Country where the poor sufferer is soothed and strengthened at once by every help of religion, where the one you call Father of your Soul attends and watches it in the weakness and trials of parting nature, with the same care you and I watch our little infants body in its first struggles and wants on its entrance into life—

dearest Rebecca how many looks of silent distress have we exchanged about the last passage, this exchange of time for Eternity—to be sure her uncommon piety and innocence and sweet confidence in God are my full consolation but I mean to say that a departing soul has so many trials and temptations that for my part I go through a sort of agony never to be described, even while to keep up their hope and courage, I appear to them most cheerful—oh my—forgive these melancholy words they were here before I knew it—your day and mine will come too—if we are but ready!—

The children all asleep—this my time of many thoughts—I had a most affectionate note from Mr. H[obart] today asking me how I could ever think of leaving the church in which I was baptized—but though whatever he says to me has the weight of my partiality for him, as well as the respect it seems to me I could scarcely have for any one else, yet that question made me smile for it is like saying that wherever

---

3.31 ASJPH 1-3-3-10:3a
[1]Rebecca Seton, Elizabeth's sister-in-law

a child is born, and wherever its parents placed it there it will find the truth, and he does not hear the drole invitations made me every day since I am in my little new home and old friends come to see me—for it has already happened that one of the most excellent women I ever knew who is of the Church of Scotland[2] finding me unsettled about the great object of a true Faith said to me "Oh do dear Soul come and hear our J. Mason[3] and I am sure you will Join us"—a little after came one I loved for the purest and most innocent manners of the Society of Quakers, (to which I have been always attached) she coaxed me too with artless persuasion, Betsy I tell thee thee had best come with us.—and my Faithful old friend Mrs. T of the Annabaptist meeting says with tears in her eyes Oh could you be regenerated, could you know our experiences and enjoy with us our heavenly banquet, and my good mammy Mary the Methodist groans and contemplates, as she calls it, over my soul, so mislead, because I have yet no convictions.—

But oh my Father and my God all that will not do for me—Your word is truth, and without contradiction wherever it is, one Faith, one hope, one baptism I look for, wherever it is and I often think my sins, my miseries hide the light, yet I will cling and hold to my God to the last gasp begging for that light and never change until I find it.

August 28th

long Since I wrote you the little word, for there is a sad weariness now over life I never before was tired with—my lovely Children round their writing table or round our evening fire make me forget a little this unworthy dejection which rises I believe from continual application of mind to these multiplied books brought for my instruction, above all Newton's Prophecies[4]—Your poor friend though is not so easily troubled as to the facts it dwells on, because it may or may

---

[2]The Presbyterian church

[3]Rev. John Mason was pastor of the Scotch Presbyterian Church in New York. He was unsurpassed in his power as a preacher and held important civic posts including provost of Columbia College.

[4]Thomas Newton first published his *Dissertations on the Prophecies* in 1754-1758. Rev. John Henry Hobart recommended that Elizabeth read the work.

not be, but living all my days in the thought that all and every body would be Saved who meant well, it grieves my very Soul to see that Protestants as well as your (as I thought hard and severe principles) see the thing so differently, since this book so Valued by them, send[s] all followers of the Pope to the bottomless pit etc. and it appears by the account made of them from the Apostles time that a greater part of the world must be already there at that rate—

Oh my the Worshipper of images and the Man of Sin are different enough from the beloved souls I knew in Leghorn to ease my mind in that point, since I so well knew what you worshipped my Amabilia, but yet so painful and sorrowful an impression is left on my heart, it is all clouded and troubled, so I say the Penitential Psalms if not with the Spirit of the royal prophet at least with his tears, which truly mix with the food and water the couch of your poor friend, yet with such Confidence in God that it seems to me he never was so truly my Father and my all at any moment of my life—

Anna coaxes me when we are at our evening prayers to say Hail Mary and all say oh do Ma teach it to us, even little Bec tries to lisp it though she can scarcely speak; and I ask my Saviour why should we not say it, if any one is in heaven his Mother must be there, are the Angels then, who are so often represented as being so interested for us on earth, more compassionate or more exalted than she is—oh no no, Mary our Mother that cannot be, so I beg her with the confidence and tenderness of her child to pity us, and guide us to the true faith if we are not in it, and if we are, to obtain peace for my poor Soul, that I may be a good Mother to my poor darlings—for I know if God should leave me to myself after all my sins he would be justified, and since I read these books my head is quite bewildered about the few that are saved, so I kiss her picture you gave me, and beg her to be a Mother to us.

September—

I have Just now the kindest letter from your Antonio—he is still in Boston and would not have been well pleased to see me in St. Pauls Church[5] to day, but peace and persuasion about proprieties etc. over

---

[5]St. Paul's Episcopal Chapel

prevailed—Yet I got in a side pew which turned my face towards the Catholic Church[6] in the next street, and found myself twenty times speaking to the Blessed Sacrament there instead of looking at the naked altar where I was or minding the routine of prayers. tears plenty, and sighs as silent and deep as when I first entered your blessed Church of Annunciation[7] in Florence all turning to the one only desire to see the way most pleasing to my God, whichever that way is—Mr. H[obart] says how can you believe that there are as many gods as there are millions of altars and tens of millions of blessed hosts all over the world—again I can but smile at his earnest words, for the whole of my Cogitations about it are reduced to one thought is it GOD who does it, the same God who fed so many thousands with the little barley loaves and little fishes,[8] multiplying them of course in the hands which distributed them? the thought stops not a moment to me, I look straight at my GOD and see that nothing is so very hard to believe in it, since it is He who does it—

Years ago I read in some old book when you say a thing is a miracle and you do not understand it, you say nothing against the Mystery itself, but only acknowledge your limited knowledge and comprehension which does not understand a thousand things you must yet own to be true—and so often it comes in my head if the religion which gives to the world, (at least to so great a part of it) the heavenly consolations attached to the belief of the Presence of God in the blessed Sacrament, to be the food of the poor wanderers in the desert of this world as well as the manna was the support of the Israelites through the Wilderness to their Canaan,[9] if this religion says your poor friend is the work and contrivance of men and priests as they say, then God seems not as earnest for our happiness as these contrivers, nor to love us, though the children of Redemption and bought with the precious blood of his dear son, as much as he did the children of the old law since he leaves our churches with nothing but naked walls and our altars unadorned

---

[6]St. Peter's Catholic Church
[7]The church of SS. Annunziata in Florence, Italy
[8]Cf. John 6: 1-15.
[9]Cf. Exod. 16.

with either the Ark[10] which his presence filled, or any of the precious pledges of his care of us which he gave to those of old—

they tell me I must worship him now in spirit and truth, but my poor spirit very often goes to sleep, or roves about like an idler for want of something to fix its attention, and for the truth dearest Amabilia I think I feel more true Union of heart and soul with him over a picture of the Crucifixion I found years ago in my Fathers port folio than in the—but what I was going to say would be folly, for truth does not depend on the people around us or the place we are in, I can only say I do long and desire to worship our God in Truth, and if I had never met you Catholics, and yet should have read the books Mr. H[obart] has brought me, they would have in themselves brought a thousand uncertainties and doubts in my mind—and these soften my heart so much before God in the certainty how much he must pity me, knowing as he does the sole and whole bent of my Soul is to please him only, and get close to him in this life and the next, that in the midnight hour believe me I often look up at the walls through the tears and distress that overpowers me, expecting rather to see his finger writing on the wall[11] for my relieve than that he will forsake or abandon so poor a creature—

November 1st—All Saints

I do not get on Amabilia—cannot cast the balance for the peace of this Poor Soul but it suffers plenty and the body too. I say daily with great confidence of being one day heard the 119th Psalm,[12] never weary of repeating it and reading Kempis[13] who by the by was a Catholic writer, and in our Protestant preface says "wonderfully versed in the knowledge of the holy scriptures" and I read much too of St. F[rancis] de Sales[14] so earnest for bringing all to the bosom of the Catholic Church and I say to myself will I ever know better how to please God than they did, and down I kneel to pour my tears to them and beg them to obtain faith for me—then I see FAITH is a gift of God

[10]Cf. Exodus 25: 8; 40:34.
[11]Cf. Dan. 5:5
[12]In contemporary Catholic bibles Ps. 120
[13]Author of the *Imitation of Christ*
[14]Author of many works including *Introduction to the Devout Life* (1609) and *Treatise on the Love of God* (1616).

to be diligently sought and earnestly desired and groan to him for it in silence since our Saviour says I cannot come to him unless the Father draw me—so it is—by and by I trust this storm will cease how painful and often Agonizing he only knows who can and will still it in his own good time—

Mrs. [Eliza] S[adler] my long tried friend observed to me this morn[ing] I had penance enough without seeking it among Catholics—true but we bear all the pain without the merit, Yet I do try sincerely to turn all mine for account of my Soul—I was telling her I hoped the more I suffered in this life the more I hoped to be spared in the next as I believed God would accept my pains in attonement for my sins—she said indeed that was very comfortable Doctrine she wished she could believe it. indeed it is all my comfort dearest Amabilia—worn out now to a skeleton almost Death may over take me in my struggle—but God himself must finish it.

January 1805

Many a long day since I wrote you dear friend for this perpetual routine of life with my sweet darlings says the same thing every day for the exterior, except that our old servant has had a long sickness and I have had the comfort to nurse her night and day as well as do her work of all kinds for the snow has been almost impassably high and even my precious Sister P[ost] could not get to see us,[15] You would not say we were not happy for the love with which it is all Seasoned can only be enjoyed by those who could experience our reverse, but we never give it a sigh, I play the piano all the Evening for them and they dance or we get close round the fire and I live over with them all the scenes of David, Daniel or Judith etc.[16] till we forget the present intirely—the neighbours children too beset us to hear our stories and sing our hymns and say prayers with us—dear dearest Amabilia God will at last deliver—

now I read with an agonizing heart the Epiphany Sermon of Bourdalou—alas where is my star[17]—I have tried so many ways to see the Dr. O[Brien] who they say is the only Catholic priest in New York

---

[15]The next six lines are blacked out and unreadable.
[16]From the Scriptures

where they say Catholicks are the offscourings of the people, somebody said their congregation [is] "a public Nuisance" but that troubles
not me, the congregation of a city, may be very shabby yet very pleasing to God, or very bad people among them yet cannot hurt the Faith as
I take it, and should the priest himself deserve no more respect than is
here allowed him, his ministry of the sacraments would be the same to
me if dearest friend I ever shall recieve them, I seek but God and his
church and expect to find my peace in them not in the people.

—Would you believe Amabilia in a desperation of Heart I went
last Sunday to St. Georges Church,[18] the wants and necessities of my
Soul were so pressing that I looked straight up to God, and I told him
since I cannot see the way to please you, whom alone I wish to please,
every thing is indifferent to me, and until you do show me the way you
mean me to walk in I will trudge on in the path you suffered me to be
born in, and go even to the Very sacrament where I once used to find
you—So away I went my old mammy happy to take care of the children for me once more till I came back—but if I left the house a
Protestant I returned to it a Catholick I think since I determined to go
no more to the Protestants, being much more troubled than ever I
thought I could be while I remembered GOD IS MY GOD—but so it
was that the bowing of my heart before the Bishop[19] to recieve his Absolution which is given publickly and universally to all in the church I
had not the least faith in his Prayer, and looked for an Apostolic
loosing from my sins, which by the books Mr. H[obart] had given me
to read I find they do not claim or admit—

then trembling to communion half dead with the inward struggle,
when they said the Body and blood of Christ—Oh Amabilia—no
words for my trial—and I remember in my old Prayer book of former
edition when I was a child it was not as now, said to be Spiritually
taken and recieved,—however to get thoughts away I took the daily
exercise of good Abbe Plunket[20] to read the prayers after COMMU-

---

[17]The scriptural allusion to the Epiphany star refers to Matthew 2:2. Elizabeth was reading one of
the sermons of Bourdaloue.

[18]St. George Church is a daughter church of Trinity, located at Second Avenue and 14th Street,
near Stuyvesant Square.

[19]Episcopal bishop, Rev. Benjamin Moore

NION, but finding every word addressed to our dear Saviour as really present and conversing with it, I became half crazy, and for the first time could not bear the sweet caresses of the darlings or bless their little dinner—O my God that day—but it finished calmly at last abandoning all to God, and a renewed confidence in the blessed Virgin whose mild and peaceful love reproached my bold excesses, and reminded me to fix my heart above with better hopes—

Now they tell me take care I am a Mother, and my children I must answer for in Judgment, whatever Faith I lead them to—that being so, and I so unconscious, for I little thought 'till told by Mr. H[obart] that their Faith could be so full of consequence to them or me, I WILL GO PEACEABLY and FIRMLY TO THE CATHOLICK CHURCH—for if Faith is so important to our Salvation I will seek it where true Faith first begun, seek it among those who recieved it from GOD HIMSELF, the controversies on it I am quite incapable of deciding, and as the strictest Protestant allows Salvation to a good Catholick, to the Catholicks I will go, and try to be a good one, may God accept my intention and pity me—as to supposing the word of our Lord has failed, and that he suffered his first foundation to be built on by Antichrist, I cannot stop on that without stopping on every other Word of our Lord and being tempted to be no Christian at all, for if the first church became Antichrist, and the second holds her rights from it, then I should be affraid both might be Antichrist, and I make my way to the bottomless pit by following either—

Come then my little ones we will go to Judgment together, and present our Lord his own words, and if he says You fools I did not mean that, we will say since you said you would be always even to the end of ages[21] with this church you built with your blood, if you ever left it, it is your Word which mis led us, therefore please to pardon Your poor fools for your own Words sake—

I am between laughing and crying all the while Amabilia—Yet not frightened for on God himself I pin my Faith—and wait only the coming of your Antonio whom I look for next week from Boston to go

---

[20]Abbé Peter Plunkett, an Irish priest and apologist whom Elizabeth met in Leghorn
[21]Cf. Matt. 16:18.

Valliantly and boldly to the Standard of the Catholics and trust all to
God—it is his Affair NOW

[February 27th 1805 Ash Wednesday][22]

A day of days for me Amabilia I have been—where—to the
Church of St. Peter with a CROSS on the top instead of a weather-
cock—that is mischevious, but I mean I have been to what is called
here among so many churches the Catholic church—when I turned
the corner of the street it is in, here my God I go said I, heart all to
you—entering it, how that heart died away as it were in silence before
the little tabernacle and the great Crucifixion over it[23]—Ah My God
here let me rest said I—and down the head on the bosom and the knees
on the bench—if I could have thought of any thing but God there was
enough I suppose to have astonished a stranger by the hurrying over
one another of this offscoured congregation, but as I came only to visit
his Majesty I knew not what it meant till afterwards—that it was a day
they recieve Ashes the beginning of Lent and drole but most Venerable Irish priest[24] who seems just come there talked of Death so famil-
iarly that he delighted and revived me—

[March 14th 1805]

After all were gone I was called to the little room next the Altar and
there PROFESSED to believe what the Council of Trent[25] believes
and teaches, laughing with my heart to my Saviour, who saw that I
knew not what the Council of Trent believed, only that it believed
what the church of God declared to be its belief, and consequently is
now my belief for as to going a walking any more about what all the
different people believe, I cannot, being quite tired out. and I came up
light at heart and cool of head the first time these many long months,

[22]Elizabeth telescoped her account. The following events took place February 27, March 14, and March 20, but she listed all under March 25.

[23]The large painting of the Crucifixion is by the Mexican artist José María Vallejo. Rev. William O'Brien, the pastor of St. Peter's, had studied in Bologna, and one of his fellow students eventually rose to an archbishopric in Mexico. In 1789 Rev. O'Brien traveled to Mexico, seeking assistance for his church. He brought back nearly $6000 and several paintings for the completion and adornment of St. Peter's. It is likely that the Vallejo Crucifixion was one of these paintings.

[24]Rev. John Byrne

[25]The Council of Trent was a sixteenth century council of the Catholic church.

but not without begging our Lord to wrap my heart deep in that opened side so well described in the beautiful Crucifixion, or lock it up in his little tabernacle where I shall now rest forever—Oh Amabilia the endearments of this day with the Children and the play of the heart with God while keeping up their little farces with them—Anna suspects—I anticipate her delight when I take her next Sunday—

So delighted now to prepare for this GOOD CONFESSION[26] which bad as I am I would be ready to make on the house top to insure the GOOD ABSOLUTION I hope for after it—and then to set out a new life—a new existance itself. no great difficulty for me to be ready for it for truly my life has been well called over in bitterness of Soul these months of Sorrow past.

[March 20th 1805]

IT IS DONE—easy enough— the kindest most respectable confessor is this Mr. O['Brien] with the compassion and yet firmness in this work of Mercy which I would have expected from our Lord himself—our Lord himself I saw alone in him, both in his and my part of this Venerable Sacrament—for Oh Amabilia—how awful those words of unloosing after a 30 years bondage—I felt as if my chains fell, as those of St. Peter at the touch of the divine messenger[27]—

My God what new scenes for my Soul—ANNUNCIATION DAY[28] I shall be made one with him who said unless you eat my flesh and drink my blood you can have no part with ME—

I count the days and hours—yet a few more of hope and expectation and then—how bright the Sun these morning walks of preparation—deep snow, or smooth ice, all to me the same I see nothing but the little bright cross on St. Peters steeple—the children are wild with their pleasure of going with me in their turn.

25 March

At last Amabilia—at last—GOD IS MINE and I AM HIS—Now let all go its round—I HAVE RECIEVED HIM [29]—the awful

---

[26]The sacrament of Reconciliation

[27]Cf. Acts 7.

[28]On March 25 the Roman Catholic church celebrates the feast recounted in Luke 1:35.

[29]Roman Catholics believe that the body and blood of Jesus Christ is present in the Holy Eucharist and received by the faithful in Holy Communion under the form of bread and wine.

impressions of the evening before, fears of not having done all to prepare, and yet even then transports of confidence and hope in his GOODNESS—

MY GOD—to the last breath of life will I not remember this night of watching for morning dawn—the fearful beating heart so pressing to be gone—the long walk to town, but every step counted nearer that street—then nearer that tabernacle, then nearer the moment he would enter the poor poor little dwelling so all his own—

and when he did—the first thought, I remember, was let God arise let his enemies be scattered,[30] for it seemed to me my King had come to take his throne, and instead of the humble tender welcome I had expected to give him, it was but a triumph of joy and gladness that the deliverer was come, and my defence and shield and strength and Salvation made mine for this World and the next—

now then all the excesses of my heart found their play and it danced with more fervour—no must not say that, but perhaps almost with as much as the royal Prophets before his Ark, for I was far richer than he and more honoured than he ever could be—now the point is for the fruits—so far, truly I feel all the powers of my soul held fast by him who came with so much Majesty to take possession of this little poor Kingdom—

[April 14]

—an Easter COMMUNION now—in my green pastures amidst the refreshing waters[31] for which I thirsted truly—but you would not believe how the Holy Week puzzled me unless at the time of the Divine Sacrifice so commanding, and yet already so familiar for all my wants and necessities—that speaks for itself, and I am All at home in it, but the other hours of the office having no book to explain or lead I was quite at a loss, but made it up with that only thought, My God is here, he sees me, every sigh and desire is before him, and so I would close my eyes and say the dear litany of JESUS or some of the psalms, and most that lovely hymn[32] to the Blessed Sacrament "FAITH for all defects sup-

[30]Possibly a reference to Ps. 82
[31] Cf. Ps. 23:2.
[32]A traditional Catholic hymn for benediction of the Blessed Sacrament, *Tantum Ergo*.

plies, and SENSE is lost in MYSTERY—here the Faithful rest secure, while God can Vouch and Faith insure"—but you would sometimes enjoy through mischief, if you could just know the foolish things that pass my brain after so much Wonderful Knowledge—as I have been taking in it about idol worshipping etc. etc. even in the sacred Moments of the elevation my heart will say half serious dare I worship you—Adored Saviour—but he has proved well enough to me there, what he is—and I can say with even more transports than St. Thomas MY LORD and MY GOD[33]—truly it is a greater Mystery how Souls for whom he had done such incomprehensible things should shut themselves out by incredulity from his best of all Gifts, this Divine Sacrifice and Holy Eucharist, refusing to believe in [the] spiritual and heavenly order of things, that WORD which spake and created the Whole Natural Order, recreating through succession of ages for the body, and yet he cannot be believed to recreate for the soul—I see more mystery in this blindness of redeemed souls than in any of the mysteries proposed in his Church—with what grateful and unspeakable joy and reverence I adore the daily renewed virtue of THAT WORD by which we possess him in our blessed MASS, and Communion—but all that is but Words since Faith is from God and I must but humble myself and adore—

Your A[ntonio]—goes now for England and will soon be with you I trust—Much he says of my bringing all the children to you[r] Gubbio[34] to find peace and abundance, but I have a long life of Sins to expiate and since I hope always to find the morning MASS in America, it matters little what can happen through the few successive days I may have to live for my health is pitiful—yet we will see—perhaps our Lord will pity my little ones—and at all events, happen now what will I rest with GOD—the tabernacle and Communion—so now I can pass the Valley of Death[35] itself.

Antonio will tell you all our little affairs—Pray for your own

EAS.

---

[33]Cf. John 20:28.
[34]Filicchi relatives lived in the Italian city of Gubbio.
[35] Cf. Ps. 23:4.

St. Paul's Episcopal Chapel

St. Peter's Catholic Church, circa 1831

Crucifixion scene by Vallejo, St. Peter's Church

Archbishop John Carroll, by Gilbert Stuart
(Courtesy, Georgetown University)

Bishop John Cheverus
(Courtesy, St. Joseph's Provincial House Archives)

PART IV

New York Catholic Widow and Mother
July 1805 - June 1808

1805

In Part IV Elizabeth makes frequent references to her children, Anna Maria (Anna), William, Richard (Dick), Catherine (Kate, Kit), and Rebecca (Bec, Beck). Her sister, Mary Bayley Post (Sister, Mary, Sister Post), and brother-in-law, Dr. Wright Post (Brother, Brother Post, Post), also appear frequently, as do her sisters-in-law, Cecilia Seton (Celia, Saint Cecilia, Cilia, Ceci, Cicy) and Harriet Seton (Hatch, H, Ha), and her young cousin, Eliza Farquhar (Zide).

In her letters to Julia Scott, Elizabeth refers to members of Julia's family: her siblings, Charlotte Sitgreaves Cox (Lott) and Samuel Sitgreaves (Brother, Brother Samuel), and her children, Maria and John (Jack) Scott. In her letters to Antonio Filicchi, Elizabeth frequently mentions Antonio's wife, Amabilia; his sons, Georgino and Patricio; and his brother, Filippo. She also frequently refers to New York Catholic friends, the Barrys: James, Joanna, and their daughter Ann (Nancy). Murray and Sons is the New York financial agent for the Filicchi firm.

Elizabeth refers to a number of clergy in this section, often using the appellation Mr. They are Rev. John Tisserant, Rev. John Cheverus, Rev. Matthew O'Brien (O.B.), Rev. Francis Matignon (Dr.), Bishop John Carroll (Bishop C., the Bishop), Rev. Michael Hurley, O.S.A. (St. M., M., why so), Rev. Louis Dubourg, S.S., and Rev. Louis Sibourd.

4.1 To Julia Scott

10th July 1805—

dearest Julia

My heart is by your bedside recalling all the tenderness and affection with which it used to watch and console you—if I had my choice of being by a wish any where in the World, that spot I would eagerly fly to. Your friend Mrs. Seaman says you have been very ill, and while I have imagined you enjoying some sweet summer retreat or jaunt of fashion—the poor little head and heart have both been aching and oppressed with suffering—dear dear Julia how much I wish to be with you—tell Maria I beg it as a mark of affection that she will write me a line. I hope you will leave the city as soon as possible, happy I should be if your excursions may lead to me—for altho' my time is occupied, it would be much more convenient for you to see me now, [than] when you were here last summer—My situation is very comfortable, the family I am with are very friendly,[1] but the school makes no appearance—three scholars added to our 9 children is all.[2] Many are promised in the fall—well, succeed or not succeed it must be right—my case cannot be worse. nor can it be better for my real enjoyment than it now is while I have you, Mrs. [Sarah] Startin, and [Antonio] Filicchi that is saying a great deal but it is truely so. nothing can be worse than a state of dependence, but if it is my allotment it cannot be better than when supplied by the hand of real friendship—

You would have received a letter from me acknowledging your mark of love received the 18th May but I have had a succession of trouble first in the prospect of losing my sweet Kate with an inflamatory Fever and afterwards with my poor bones wearied out almost refusing to go any more, or if obliged to make the effort overpowered with faintness and a giddy head.—Mrs. Startin has helped very much to restore me with the simple remedy of a glass a wine

---

4.1 ASJPH 1-3-3-6:58

[1]Mr. and Mrs. Patrick White

[2]The nine children were her own and the Whites who were students in the school.

every day—and now the suffering is nearly past, I wish I could know you were as well—Do beg Maria to write me—Kate is recovering fast. the other darlings are quite well and my heart loves you most sincerely

EAS.

remember me to dear Charlotte and Brother[.] Filicchi offers you his "grateful and respectful compliments"

4.2 To Antonio Filicchi

28th August 1805

My most dear dear Brother

Certainly it was a most unexpected and grateful surprise when your letter of 12th Instance was handed to me this morning, you had even said "My Sister do not write to me," but I gladly and with redoubled affection comply with your last request of writing to you immediately. Your safety so far on your perilous voyage[1] lifts my heart with thankfulness and joy and you may be assured the warmest prayers it can concieve are already formed in it, and will be constantly employed in union with the many more efficacious ones which I know are put up for your Welfare in the old World as well as the New, which added to those we hope are exercised in the World of Spirits and presented to so indulgent so gracious a Master may be presumed (if you are tollerably faithful on your part) to form a strong barrier against the dangers that await my dear Antonio, yet I shall be truely rejoiced to welcome you again in New York and should be less unwilling to trust you to the Ocean than to your present dangerous expedition. do do dear Antonio keep your promise of letting me hear from you at Montreal.

4.2 AMSJ A 111 036

[1] Antonio Filicchi traveled from Philadelphia to Canada during the summer of 1805. He stopped in New York en route.

Many Many troubles have pressed upon me, and my poor head has gone thro' almost as many difficulties as you have experienced in your Journey—almost immediately after you left me Mr.[Patrick] White informed me that he could not pay his share of the house rent for the next quarter, and consequently I was obliged to remove on a few days notice to hinder the landlord taking my things for payment. Mr. Post hurried me out of town to his country seat[2] and I found myself separated in a few hours from my Liberty in every respect. the dear early Mass etc. etc. no Saturday confession, Sunday Communion, or word of consolation from any one—but God is so rich in Mercy and so pitiful to a poor desolated Soul that these deprivations are made up in many respects, and at all events, I must and do adore his Almighty Will in every case, begging only for a happy exit and to recieve my portion where no disappointments or sorrows can intervene—

I have written twice to Mr.Tisserant[3] with all the energy of my heart, but have not yet had the happiness of an answer—O.B[rien] has been very dangerously ill but is again recovered. he speaks of you with perfect veneration and most Affectionate enquiries—dear dear Antonio take care of yourself think often of the many many who love and value you besides the strong endearing ties of Nature which call so loudly to you—

---

[2]Dr. Wright Post, Elizabeth's brother-in-law, had a residence at Greenwich on Blessing Street (now Bleeker Street), Greenwich Village. This village was about two miles outside the town of New York and was considered to be a healthful region to which many residents fled during outbreaks of disease in the city. In fact the Setons left the city just as the yellow fever epidemic of 1805 was taking on alarming proportions.

[3]Rev. John S. Tisserant, a French emigré and a friend of Rev. John Cheverus of Boston, became Elizabeth Seton's spiritual advisor during the first year after her conversion and was her sponsor at Confirmation when he served in Elizabethtown, New Jersey. From June 1805 to June 1806 when he returned to Europe, they wrote frequently. Elizabeth hoped for his return, and on January 9, 1810, she mentions the possibility of him as chaplain for the Sisters of Charity. Tisserant's letters to Elizabeth are preserved in Emmitsburg; hers to him have not been found.

4.3 To Julia Scott

28th August 1805

When I look at the date of your most Affectionate letter I can scarcely believe that it is not yet answered. I did not recieve it tho' for many days after it was written owing to my removal at my Brother Posts at Greenwhich—Unexpectedly indeed it came to me, for the straight story I had had from my blundering [Antonio] Filicchi of your illness, added to the long silence which succeeded the pressing intreaties I had addressed to both yourself and Maria for only one line led me to immagine the worst, and I even dreaded to hear from Philadelphia. judge then my delight on recieving a letter from your own dear hand.

two days preceeding Quarter day[1] Mr. [Patrick] White informed me that he had been disappointed in the receipt of money he had expected and could not pay his rent after the present quarter, consequently the house must be given up to the landlord and I must be off to prevent his securing my little possessions—Post hurried me to his country seat and in a few hours I found myself in a new state of existance most desirable in many respects but in some most inconvenient, yet the ballance is far on the best side as it respects my health and that of the darlings. I had become so feeble as to be subject to excessive faintness on the least exertion—good Mrs. [Sarah] Startin nursed me with candle and old wine daily, but I believe the change of air was so indispensable that if necessity of one kind had not forced me to it another would. and tho my health is certainly mended here I am but a shadow, and all my anticipations are pointing to my only Home—

dear Emmas[2] death gave me a heavy blow, sitting up with her and seeing her struggles was almost too much—you may well my love make the retrospect of what once was, and how is it possible my dear dear Julia you can divest your mind of what must be—Patience—but

---

4.3 ASJPH 1-3-3-6:59

[1] Probably refers to the end of the financial quarter, June 30
[2] Charlotte Amelia Bayley Craig, Elizabeth's half-sister, died July 22, 1805.

you must forgive me if I feel unceasing solicitude on this subject—Eternity my precious friend is a long long day—and I have seen
so many hurried off with scarce a pause to contemplate the dreadful
object, that it is impossible to think of you with the tenderness which
will accompany your image in my Soul without its enquiring with agony is my Julia to be one of those. or when the spirit is left to linger in a
wasting frame its powers inact[ive and s]adened with the accumulated
infirmities and pains of our Human Nature, how shall it form or progress in the union with the Divine Nature which we are well assured
must form the happiness of our future existance—or if permitted—but stop dear friend you say, I know all these things—you do
know them my darling, and therefore you resist that Divine Spirit
which would then speak Peace to your Soul, and with heavenly consolations sooth every pang of parting Nature while it guided you to the
eternal blessings you will so earnestly covet—

I have had the indiscribable satisfaction of attending Mrs. Bayley[3]
in her last hours—I believe I have expressed to you my pleasure in
recieving from her since my return Home every mark of Peace and
reconciliation, which also gives me the double enjoyment of the confidence and affection of the dear girls Helen and Mary[4]—their situation is truely melancholy—indeed I feel more than I can tell for
them—Sister Craig's little darling[5] is all she would have wished and
the only comfort of its almost inconsolable father—there is so great an
alarm about Fever that I feel this may be the last letter you may recieve
from me for a long while.

—Your Anna and sweet Kit are quite well—Anna is with Mary[6]
trying to console and amuse her—they are extremely attached—I
hope you will never reproach me for the little use I have as yet made of

---

[3]Charlotte Amelia Barclay Bayley, Elizabeth's stepmother, from whom she had been estranged
since her youth, died September 1, 1805. Elizabeth often took several days to complete her letters,
which accounts for the incongruence of dates.

[4]Helen and Mary Fitch Bayley, Elizabeth's half-sisters. Mary Fitch Bayley was the daughter of
Dr. Richard and Charlotte Barclay Bayley. About 1817 she married Sir Robert Henry Bunch and
lived in Nassau in the Bahamas.

[5]Henry Craig was Charlotte Amelia Bayley Craig's newborn son who survived his mother by
only a few months.

[6]Mary Fitch Bayley, whose mother had just died

your goodness to her—I will write you more fully my dearest friend when I am able—May God protect and bless you, forever—

your EAS.

4.4 To Antonio Filicchi

9 September [1805]

My own dear Brother—

my letter has been interrupted by a summons to attend the last hours of my poor Mother-in-law, Mrs. Bayley[1]—which has detained me many days in town.—Well may I love you and lift up my hands to God for you every hour of the day when he has chosen you to be the dear friend of my Soul who has conducted me to the light of his blessed Truth—When I see these poor souls die without Sacraments, without prayers, and left in their last moments to the conflicts of parting Nature without the divine consolations which our Almighty God has so mercifully provided for us, I feel then while my heart is filled with sorrow for them as if my joy is too great to be expressed at the idea of the different prospect I have before me in that hour thro' the divine goodness and mercy—but with this subject I could fill many sheets and yet never express what is in my heart—

The Yellow Fever has made its appearance in so malignant a form that the City is nearly Evacuated—My God be merciful.—Oh how thankful I am that your absence is at this time, for Philadelphia being in the same situation, you could not have chosen a better period for your visit to Montreal—no doubt the same good angel who directed you then will continue to protect you, which my soul prays with all its power—

I am and always must be your most affectionate grateful friend and sister EASeton

---

4.4 AMSJ A111 037
[1]Charlotte Amelia Barclay Bayley, Elizabeth's stepmother, to whom she refers as her mother-in-law according to nineteenth century usage

the children very often speak of dear Filicchi—they are very well—Bayley[2] is not come, his ship has returned with Brandus, direct to me still thro' Mr. Morris—again I repeat take care of yourself—

4.5 To Antonio Filicchi

Greenwich 2nd October 1805

My Conscience really reproaches me, dear Tonino that I have not written you at Boston as you directed me, but to tell you the identical truth I have been so busied in preparing Winter cloathing for my Children that altho' I am at work till midnight and sometimes till one oclock yet the hour I would have given to writing my best Brother has been always called for some other way. If you could imagine the occupation of mending and turning old things to best account added to teaching the little they learn and having them always at my elbows, you would believe me that it is easier to pray than to write; also I clean my own room, wash all the small clothes and have much more employment in my present situation than ever. This you must know to excuse myself from the scolding I know I deserve, but have pity on me dear Antonio—remember your little Sister is in a constant Warfare and your displeasure would grieve her very very much.

Rather tell me you are happy that the dear friends whose society and affection is so pleasing to you are well, and that you feel with thankfulness how good God is to you in sparing your city while Ours is the seat of desolation and sorrow. very often I thank Him you are not here and that you left us before the moment of surprise, for it seemed to be very little expected and my dear Tonino might have staid a day too long—The dear Angels whose day I have been commemorating[1] as well as I could in my poor Heart, hastened you away, have kept you safe I trust thro' your adventrous Journey, and are still with you in the dangers that every where await a Christian especially one who fights

---

[2]Andrew Barclay Bayley, Elizabeth's half-brother, was in Italy working at the Filicchi firm .
4.5 AMSJ A 111038
[1]October 2 is the Catholic feast of the Guardian Angels.

to be as good as you do. Morning and Evening my darlings all lift their hands for Blessed Mr. [John] Tisserant and dear Filicchi. "That God would give them grace to do His Holy Will and bring them to His Heavenly kingdom," indeed I often ask it with tears. We delight even to speak the name of Mr. Tisserant and a letter I received from him since I wrote you I keep as a part of myself.

It is very very painful to be so separated from all. I cannot write to him because I can no more see Mr. [Andrew] Morris who is the only person to whom Mr. Tisserant has given his direction. You cannot imagine a creature more forlorn in externals no dear church, nor any comfort connected with it. but with all the accumulated difficulties that surround me for the present and in prospect, He who lives in my Heart never suffers me to forget that the seed I am now sowing in tears shall certainly be reaped in joy,[2] and this certainty is so ever present with me and bears me up so lightly over the briers and thorns that I often stop in the midst of hurry and beg my dear Saviour to assure me that it is not temptation, and that he will not let my enemy persuade me there is Peace where there is no Peace—He always answers do not fear, while your Peace is in Me alone it cannot be false. When I was dear [William Magee] Setons wife and he lamented that I did too much, I delighted in telling him "love makes labour easy" and how much more may I delight in repeating it to Him who is Father Husband Brother Friend.

As you know I can have nothing to tell you dear Brother but of my worthless little self you must forgive all this Egotism and after the same example tell me all you can of your Soul and your Body; and now dearest Tonino prove your true love to me by exerting your utmost power in getting my poor Boys to Baltimore[3] if it is possible. If you could know the situation they are in here only your love for Souls independent of any personal interest for me would induce you to pity

---

[2]Cf. Ps. 126:5.

[3]Elizabeth was trying to arrange for her sons, William and Richard, to be educated at St. Mary's College in Baltimore. Antonio Filicchi had promised to help pay for the boys' education.

In 1791 the Seminary of St. Sulpice in Baltimore (later known as St. Mary's Seminary) was founded by Rev. Charles F. Nagot, S.S. St. Mary's College, adjoining it, was opened by Rev. Louis William Dubourg, S.S., in 1799.

them in the redicule they are forced to hear of our Holy religion and the mockery at the church and ministers, besides their minds are being poisoned with bad principles of every kind which I cannot always check or controul. Mr. Tisserant has promised me to write, but it may be a long time before I hear from Him again. do direct me can I do any thing in it?

I was grieved to hear of the Indisposition of Dr. [Francis] Maitinon to whom I beg you to present me with most affectionate respect, and also to our dear Mr. [John] Chevrous. I purpose writing to him next week enclosed to you—dear dear Antonio take care of yourself and pray very often be assured I do not bend my knee without offering for you also.

your E A Seton

direct to me at Dr. Post's Greenwich[4] and I shall recieve it as the office is close by us. I wrote you a letter to Montreal and was obliged to put the one you enclosed me for O.B[rien] in the post office as I may not see him in many weeks. I hope I have not done wrong. I directed his number and street.—do write soon for charities sake, or do it for penance only do but write—

My dear Antonio I have forgotten your direction excuse me to Mr. Cheverus for the liberty of directing to Him—

4.6 To Cecilia Seton[1]

October 7th 1805

The sweetest and even the most innocent pleasures quickly pass in this life—and the dear moments of Peace and love enjoyed with my

---

[4]Elizabeth and her children were residing with her sister and brother-in-law, Mary and Wright Post, in Greenwich.

4.6 ASJPH 1-3-3-18:3

[1]This document exists with minor differences in spelling and punctuation in a slightly different form also in Elizabeth Seton's handwriting as ASJPH 1-3-3-8:89, the first three pages of which are in another hand, perhaps Anna Maria Seton's.

Cecilia this morning appear only as a dream but as a dream pleasing and soothing to the mind often gives it a foretaste of something it earnestly covets, so my heart turns to the dear Hope that it may one day enjoy your Society even in this World.[2] or if otherways ordered by Our dear and Heavenly Father the more certain Hope of an eternal union before his Throne cannot fail us but by our own Negligence and perversion, against which we must pray literally without ceasing—without ceasing, in every occurence and employment of our lives—you know I mean that prayer of the heart which is independent of place or situation or which is rather a habit of lifting up the heart to God as in a constant communication with Him—as for instance when you go to your Studies you look up to him with sweet complacency and think O Lord how worthless is this knowledge if it were not for the enlightening my mind and improving it to thy Service, or for being more useful to my fellow creatures, and enabled to fill the part thy providence may appoint me—When going into society or mixing with Company appeal to Him who sees your heart and knows how much rather you would devote every hour to him, but say dear Lord you have placed me here and I must yield to them whom you have placed me in subjection to, O keep my heart from all that would seperate me from thee. When you are excited to impatience, think for a moment how much more reason God has to be angry with you than you can have for anger against any human being, and yet how constant is his patience and forbearance

—and in every disappointment great or small let your dear heart fly direct to Him your dear Saviour throwing yourself in his arms for refuge against every pain and sorrow "He will never leave you nor forsake you."

—and in that little secret[3] we mentioned, let your dear Lord be your first confident and never dare to cherish a sentiment which you can not dwell on while laying your heart before him. Next to Him you have promised your dear Sis.

---

[2] Cecilia came to live with Elizabeth when she was seven years old and was greatly influenced by her. Under the present circumstances they were separated.

[3] Cecilia's discernment about becoming a Roman Catholic

—O my Celia love me, think of me as most truly your Sister, your faithful friend, who loves you in my very soul, loves you for the past and for the present, for Earth and for Heaven. You are to me as my dearest child, I never attempt it or can express the sentiment of tenderest love that lives in my heart for you dear dear Girls[4] and which is always connected with every hope even of my future and eternal existance. May God make you his Own is the pray[er of] my Soul

your EAS.[5]

4.7 To Antonio Filicchi

[New York 11 October 1805 in a different hand]

My most dear Brother

your letter has so cheered and comforted my heart that you must excuse my immediate reply to it, I say excuse as your little sister has but the old story to repeat to you how much she loves you and that she is fighting among the Philistines[1] as usual—They have hard run me to go and hear some of their fine preachers today, but a decided denial, and a real necessity not to leave my Children brings me through the Sunday quietly, generally with particular blessings of spiritual consolation and pleasure in instructing the little ones, but the joy my Soul anticipates if ever again it is allowed to wait at the Altar will surely be a fortaste of the joy of the Blessed—if ever your lazy spirit should tempt you to be careless of your sweet privilege of going there every day, think of your Banished Sister and praise God for your happiness.

---

[4]The younger half-sisters of William Magee Seton for whom he and Elizabeth had provided after the death of their father

[5]Written on the outside: "Thursday Morning The dear girls passed yesterday afternoon with me Oh how we longed for you—Bless Bless Bless my darling Girl your own Sis"

4.7 AMSJ A111 039

[1]Reference to a story in the Hebrew Scriptures of hostilities between the Hebrew people and outsiders in Judges 14 and 15. Elizabeth was referring to the hostility of her relatives to her conversion to Catholicism.

O.B[rien] wrote me a very kind letter this morning in consequence of one I was obliged to address to him to help me for the present out of my difficulty in our Friday and Saturday abstinence.[2] My Sister procures fish with so great expense and difficulty (really as if for the greatest stranger) that my Bread and Water Spirit is ashamed to partake of it and as Mr. Tisserant had told me in my particular circumstances I must conform to necessity with a humble heart The case was easily explained to Mr. O.B. and he has written me a very affectionate letter and dispensation which however with Gods Grace shall never be used but to keep Peace.—I am a poor creature, before I was in the blessed Ark[3] could fast all day on Friday, now can hardly wait from one meal to the other without faintness.

dear Tonio do not forget the promissed letter, you may scold, or what you will, only do not forget me. Your idea of the Canada Seminary[4] frightens me, I have a little secret to communicate to you when we meet (a sweet dream of imagination) which if you meet my opinion and views would render the Baltimore plan[5] every way most preferable—but all is in the hands of God—I know it will go right—

With this you will find a letter for our dear and respected Mr. [John] Chevrous. I always tremble when I cannot show my letters to you, lest there is not sufficient respect in the expressions, you know my heart sometimes leaps beyond discretion and if it has in this instance beg indulgence for me.

do tell me when you have news from Leghorn what our dear Amabilia says of your long absence and all the etceteras you know I would be so glad to hear. also say something to me of your dear friends in Boston whether your Calender of Saints[6] is increased, if you have any new Scholars, and if the old ones improve and above all things dear Tonino if you try earnestly to "be good" which is my greatest interest. You remember the first letter you ever wrote me you said your

---

[2]Both Friday and Saturday were days of abstinence from meat in the Catholic church at the beginning of the nineteenth century.

[3]The Roman Catholic church

[4]A school in Montreal which Antonio Filicchi had recommended for her sons

[5]The plan was to send her sons to school at St. Mary's College in Baltimore.

[6]The official listing used as a reference in liturgical celebrations in order to honor the memory of holy men and women whom the Catholic church recognizes for their sanctity

soul would call for me in Paradise, and now I declare I believe St Peter would let me pass as soon as you tho' I am at the eleventh hour, and perhaps listen to my entreaty not to shut the gate till Antonio enters. This sauciness is not a specimen of my Humility, but to make you put on your consideration cap, and not be too sure because you have been always an Israelite,[7] and of all things do not trust to the prayers of others so much. You know you are without excuse if you do not practice the good you have so successfully taught—yet the prayers of your Sisters Soul is always yours, often so earnestly that conscience checks and enquires if so great a Sinner has any plea for another certainly none but its own only Hope and refuge and thro that dear precious plea I beg for you as myself—

as far as you can with propriety present me to Dr. [Francis] Matignon—do dear Antonio beg for me his blessing and prayers.—

Your EAS.

4.8 To Anna Maria Seton

[n.d. October]

My own Ann

all goes well—Eliza[s] Mother[1] is quite a Lady—am going down to-morrow tho' no dear daughter to take my place—Kiss the dear Girls[2] for me a thousand times and pinch Uncle Sams[3] ear for me. You must play your best to amuse Uncle James[4] and learn something sweet for me—

---

[7]Cf. John 1:47, an "Israelite without guile." On her entreaty to keep the gate open until Antonio enters, cf. Matt. 25:1-13. Note her free and familiar use of biblical references to make a serious point.

4.8 ASJPH 1-3-3-9:23

[1]Eliza Farquhar, a cousin of the Setons, became closely associated with Elizabeth's family during this period. Her mother was Elizabeth Curson Farquhar.

[2]Elizabeth's younger sisters-in-law, Harriet, Cecilia, Mary, and Charlotte Seton

[3]Samuel Waddington Seton, Elizabeth's young brother-in-law

[4]James Seton, Elizabeth's brother-in-law, with whom her daughter, Anna Maria, was staying

Your Mothers heart felt Blessing is always with you forever

Tuesday Evening

it is useless to say how much I share your happiness—

4.9 To Anna Maria Seton

16 October 1805

My own Darling

your little letter gave Joy to my heart which loves you more than I can express and earnestly prays to our dear Lord Jesus to bless you and make you his own—

if you have an opportunity come home to-morrow it is time to begin your lessons again. Kit and Bec each send a kiss, and your dear Mother her blessing from her Soul.

EAS

4.10 To Antonio Filicchi

25th October 1805

My dear Antonio—

You must pay the penalty of being my "best Brother" and be troubled with the communication of all my concerns—how far the present object is worthy [of] your regard time only can prove—but I wish you to be made acquainted with it tho' it is now only an idea—

Mr. J[ohn] Wilkes called on me this morning to propose the old scheme of superintending his, and his Brothers Boys with some others added—nothing definite is planed but it was necessary to ascertain if I would enter in it before other measures are taken—with my usual diffidence in opposing, and eager desire of doing something towards the maintenance of my children I did not give it the negative, and next week I am to hear more on the subject They are not sure that Mr. Harris[1] (the School Master) will be associated with a Catholick, nor that Parents will commit their children to my care to live with me—

I heard these suggestions with Humility and secret gladness that I might bear the reproach in His Name and said that I would do anything honest for a living. and to relieve my Sister of the burden of my family—indeed dear Antonio anything is preferable to entering in the scenes of company etc., besides the natural dissimilarity of my Sisters disposition with those duties and engagements which compose my part in life. All these I would have encountered without any other calculation than a simple desire of doing the Will of God, if I could in no way escape it, but I cannot think it his Will if any other way presents, especially one which would place me in my proper station instead of an indulgence of a life of inactivity and being made a Lady of for a Winter.

Some proposals have been made me of keeping a Tea store—or China Shop—or Small school for little children (too young I suppose to be taught the "Hail Mary"—). in short Tonino, they do not know what to do with me, but God does—and when His blessed time is come we shall know, and in the mean time he makes his poorest feeblest creature Strong.—Joy will come in the morning[2]— and now they look with surprise at one whose impatience could not be controuled but a few years ago—always smiling at the difficulties they so sensibly sympathise in—here I go, prattling to you as if you were by my side, not considering that by this time you are well tired—but you must know all, that you may think for me.

How do you do my best of Brothers, does your heart never reproach you for taking such a burden on it as the six such helpless desolated mortals—look beyond the present scene, to that hour when the cup of cold water given for His sake will be rewarded[3]—much less the

---

[1]Rev. William Harris, an Episcopalian clergyman in New York, operated a school. Elizabeth hoped to take in boarders from among his students.

[2]Cf. Ps. 30:5.

[3]Cf. Mark 9:41.

stores of kindness already heaped on your poor little Sister from your hand—

Your dear promised letter is I hope on the way one for our dear Mr. Chevrous inclosed to yourself was forwarded last week—My heart beats at the very thought of recieving the answers—

Will you come early in November—but you know your Bostonian promises are not to be trusted, or at least must be allowed a latitude of some weeks, if not months—poor me—must not think of the pleasure of your Society for where dear friend shall I again enjoy it—Where you first called for it, in Paradise, I believe—my portion is not here but am very thankful you have so much success in the kind endeavours you have made to put my poor Wandering Soul in the sweet way to it—your cares will be your gain, even if I should be so wretched as to lose—

Pray for me my Brother and beg those prayers for me which we so much confide in—

Your EASeton.

4.11 To Julia Scott

20th November 1805

My dear dear Julia

What passes in your dear heart respecting your poor Friend—you do not call her ungrateful—forgetful—but rather consider the most probable cause of her long silence and attribute it to its true reason a heavy head and heavy heart whenever it would address one who has all its Affection and confidence—having had nothing but cares and anxieties to communicate to you either as it related to myself or others, whenever affection suggested write to Julia the same affection pleaded—what, to grieve and pain her? but now that a Home and Home comforts again are mine,[1] and life and cheerfulness are

---

4.11 ASJPH 1-3-3-6:60

[1] In November 1805 Elizabeth and her family moved to Stuyvesant Lane in the Bowery near St. Mark's Episcopal Church.

reanimated, it is sweet to relieve you from the solicitude which I know my peculiarly hard case must have Occasioned in the heart that so truely loves me—It seemed as if there was no escape from the Inconveniences and trouble I was necessitated to give the family of my Brother [Wright] P[ost] the more kind they were to me, the more painful was my sense of it, but according to the old principle by constant looking up, and reinforcement of patience the poor Spirit was broken down to bear every thing as it happened and prepared with silent resignation for the future, when most unexpectedly Mr. J[ohn] W[ilkes] made the proposal of the old scheme of recieving the Pupils of St Marks School[2] as Boarders—This plan so much dreaded before I had drank deep of my cup was now embraced with eagerness, and I am removed with my Treasures to a very pleasant dwelling two miles from the city and on Monday next expect twelve or fourteen Children committed to my care to Board, Wash and mend for—Your provision for my Anna ennables me to pay a good old Woman whom I have know[n] for many years, to take a great part of the burden off me and to keep my darling companion and comfort at Home, a Mothers pen must not be trusted to describe what my Anna is to me, her mind and Intelligence has progressed these last twelve months as much as her loveliness and grace of features—

6th December

My Julia must consider for me how difficult it is to catch even half an hour from my bee hive—we begin at the dawn of day, and by the time all is done I actually fall asleep even at my prayers. but my heart has been lifted with thanks to God and melts with tenderness inexpressible at the thought of all your love and tenderness to me—tears will start when you say that I have still a place in the heart of Brother Sam—is it possible that he has so large a share of sorrow too—earnestly I pray that it may draw his Soul to the source of Consolation—Oh how pleased I should be to be always near him in our future existance—since in this I have been allowed so small a taste of his dear society—and you my darling friend—Shall we be forever united

---

[2]The school conducted by Rev. William Harris was located at St. Mark's Church.

there—but stop my eyes are blinded by these questions—and I must now tell you that our sweet dear little blossom is withered and gone, Our precious little Henry Craig is gone to his Mother[3]—such is the inscrutable dispensation—and his Father is now only a shadow—an image of wretchedness—Mrs. [Eliza] Sadler suffers almost as much—dear Helen [Bayley Craig] is very much recovered, but scarcely can bear this privation of her little darling—

When you tell me of your exertions and cares you never say how the little tender frame supports the burthen—dear dear Julia much I fear you will not consider how much you try it until it is too late—and will our dear John Scott soon become your Protector your friend and comfort too I trust—which added to Marias excellent Mind and affectionate attentions will I hope repay you a part of the indiscribable cares and Solicitudes you have borne for them—I rejoice that you are so near Charlott this Winter, but do not let the World run too much away with you sometimes say "Julia where are we going"—I hope this happy season will find you both as happy as it does me, scarcely can that happiness be realized which has given me again a Home—three dollars a week for each Boy[4] with washing and mending paid for will help at least to make Us less a burthen—and the pleasure of doing something for my darlings makes every labour easy—they already have their comfortable cloathing in anticipation of your love and care—Kit is the gayest little being you can imagine with a very quick capacity—Rebecca is doated on by us all—the 100 dollars laid by safely—it is a store for necessity—Anna will attend an excellent dancing Master at Mrs. Farquhar's[5] (who is our near neighbour) on the strength of it—not for the steps but to obtain a little polish and to please Aunt Scott—

This blotted scratching is unpardonable but indeed dear I have not time to copy it—

---

[3]Charlotte Amelia Bayley Craig died in childbirth in July 1805. Although her son Henry survived, he died four months later.

[4]Elizabeth's boarders from Mr. Harris' school

[5]Elizabeth Curson Farquhar, Elizabeth's aunt by marriage

4.12 To Cecilia Seton

Christmas Eve 1805

Oh that I could take the Wings of the Angel of Peace and visit the heart of my darling darling Child—pain and sorrow should take their flight, or if ordained to stay as messengers from Our Father of Mercies to seperate you from our life of temptation and misery and prepare you for the reception of endless blessedness, I would repeat to you the story of his sufferings and anguish, who chose them for his companions from the cradle to the grave—I would help you to seperate all worldly thoughts from your breast, to yield the sinful Body to the punishment it deserves, and to beg that sanctifying grace which will change temporal pain to eternal glory—and then I would again remind you of those sweet instructions and Heavenly precepts which we read together the happy night we last enjoyed—

My Cecilia—my Sister—my friend—my dear dear child I beg, beseech, implore you, to offer up all your pains, your Sorrows, and vexations to God that he will unite them with the Sorrows, the pangs and anguish which Our adored Redeemer bore for us on the Cross[1]—place yourself in spirit at the foot of that cross, and intreat that a drop of that precious blood there shed may fall on you to enlighten strengthen and support your Soul in this life and ensure its eternal Salvation in the next—He knows all our weakness and the failings of our hearts—as the Father pities his own children he pities US and has himself declared that he never will forsake the soul that confides in his Name—think of our Sweet Rebecca[2] how meekly she bore her burden and earnestly looked up to the cross—she was given to us to teach us how to live and taken from us to learn us how to die. Blessed Angel she doubtless intercedes for us even while we sleep, and in the light of His countenance is pleading that an emanation of that light may cheer us in our banishment and guide us to our Home == dear dearest Soul

---

4.12 ASJPH 1-3-3-8:137

[1]As Cecilia's desire to become a Catholic deepened, she became troubled by the probable consequences and her health deteriorated. She was living at James Seton's house at the time.

[2]Rebecca Seton, Elizabeth's sister-in-law, who died in July 1804

let us work while it is day, and trim our lamps and prepare the oil for that hour when none can work[3]—at this blessed season he especially manifests Himself to those who love him with fervent love—the blessings he has afforded my poor Soul are boundless and unutterable—May he hear its most earnest prayer and grant you his peace forever—forever

your EAS.

1806

4.13 To Julia Scott

20th January 1806—

Every day since the beginning of the year I have thought this Evening I will write to my Julia, but weariness or some interruption has always disappointed me—This season finds me so much more comfortable and happier in every respect than the last, that your dear heart would rejoice if it could witness the change—My food is sweetned with the thought that I do my part to obtain it, and love and gratitude to Him who has ordered it so, that it nourishes and strengthens the poor old body while often the heart so overflows as to communicate its delight to all around it and the plainest materials form a Luxurious feast—Think of me sometimes when your cook does not do her duty—think of me some times when little wasps of vexation beset you—think of me sometimes when your heart feels the futility of earthly enjoyments and sighs for a possession it can never find here—then remember that your friend never calls at the throne of Mercy without pleading for yours as for her own Soul—

Ah Julia Julia, when that inevitable hour comes the moments you now give to Him will be the only time remembered with pleasure, and when you see the tears of your dear children you will then feel that you

---

[3]Cf. Matt. 25: 7 and John 9:4.
4.13 ASJPH 1-3-3-6:61

have been only as the Mother of their Bodies while the divine image in their souls has been disfigured if not sullied by a mistaken Education which while it fits them for an uncertain and transient existence leaves them uninstructed or indifferent for the one which must be eternal—Since you know it dearest, and why repeat it—how can I write without showing my heart, and how conceal one of its most earnest desires which is that you will reflect and resolve in time. lean your head on that dear little white hand, close your eyes and imagine the present routine of your life past and your guardian spirit introducing you in your future state of existance—dear dear Soul it will be no dream—an Account must be given and He who is now our compassionate Redeemer will then be the inexorable Judge—but the handsome Establishment Equipages,[1] fashionable friends, decided habits, bent of the mind etc etc etc etc etc are all in the way. Your dear little Soul is imprisoned in its body and both in the World out of which it cannot be released without many a painful struggle. —never let it enter your mind that you cannot be good in the station you are placed in—on the contrary that is the very place God has appointed, and a performance of the duties of it would insure your Salvation, the only danger my darling is, your abuse of it, for to be rich, honorable, and distinguished are all of his appointment, but the giving them the service of the Soul as well as the Body is contrary to the convictions of your own upright mind as well as to every principle of a Christian Spirit

—is the plan the same as formerly—Mother with you—Hitty still happy—does not Charlotte grow old—tell me of Maria, of Harriet—dear Brother,[2] and most of all of your dear precious Self—send me a close written letter for a New Years gift and do tell me all, as if seated by my side—I love to draw a picture when I think of you. your dear John Scott is then in the character a Mothers heart so fondly anticipates—with every promise of a Friend and Protector pictured in his countenance if it is as when he used to ask petchy Pailey[3] for a

---

[1] Fancy carriages
[2] Julia's relatives: Susanna Deshon Sitgreaves, her mother; Mehitabel Cox Markow; Charlotte Sitgreaves Cox; Maria Litchfield Scott; Harriet Sitgreaves, Julia's niece; and Samuel Sitgreaves.
[3] Childish name for Betsy Bayley

Kiss—sweet fellow how I should like to give him a dozen now—make them think of me dear, as their true friend—

You asked me long ago about my Religious Principles—I am gently quietly and silently a good Catholic—the rubs etc are all past, no one appears to know it except by showing redoubled kindness only a few knotty hearts that must talk of something, and the worst they say is—"so much trouble has turned her brain"—well and I kiss my Crucifix which I have loved for so many years, and say they are only mistaken—

So we go dear Julia—travelling on—take care Miss where you stop—think, you may meet a tender Father who will say "my Child was lost and is found. come Home—here is rest."—but if He should say "I have called, and you would not answer—Go"[4]—think! think about it. May He Bless you, love you and make you his Own forever and ever—is the Prayer from the Soul of Your EASeton.

[Antonio] Filicchi will hand you [this—He has] taken upon Himself the expense of my Boys Edu[cation and pro]mises them the same situation my Brothers Richard [Bayley] and [Guy] Carl[eton Bayley have had] with the Friendship he had for their Father—this [is a bur]then off my mind—they will go to the Colledge[5] immediately if he can obtain them a situation—

4.14 To Antonio Filicchi

Tuesday Evening 25th March 1806

My most dear friend and Brother—

After passing the 14th[1] (the day in which your idea must necessarily be connected with my very prayers and thankfulness to God) without disobeying your injunction of not writing, it would seem easy also to pass the present happy hour of retirement and rest without

---

[4]Cf. Luke 15: 32 and Matt. 22: 1-14.

[5]St. Mary's College in Baltimore, administered by the Sulpician Fathers

4.14 AMSJ A111 041

[1]March 14 was the anniversary of Elizabeth's profession of faith and reception into the Roman Catholic church.

expressing my heart to you—but after Celebrating (in my Soul) the Anniversary of our most dear Mother,[2] and the delight and joy of my first Communion—you must not be angry if your Sister addresses a few words of enquiry and affection to you as the Instrument of Mercy and deliverance appointed by Divine Providence to bring the poor little stray sheep to his fold—for can I drink of the fountain of Life[3] and not think of the hand that led me to it—yes Antonio my last recollections and most fervent supplications will be given for you, not only as my true and affectionate friend, but as the Guide, Protector, and preserver of my Soul thro' Him. but it is vain to attempt in Words to convey an idea of the extent of your Benefactions—first I must have the power of disclosing to you the happiness experienced at His altar and indeed in every circumstance the sum of the favours received—

By a letter from our dear and reverend Bishop to Mrs. Barry[4] I heard with delight that you had jumped over your usual delays and already arrived in Baltimore and that you were the next day to dine with him and consequently I may hope you are well, as well as safe,—My good Angel I know will keep me near your heart which is the more earnestly desired as since you left me My Health is very much altered, and the debility and weakness of my frame is so great that really it is necessary to force my thoughts from the consequences which so naturally present themself to my mind—the kind Protesters[5] say it is only the consequence of keeping Lent, but that is not the truth as really every precaution has been taken—but God knows—and will direct it—

When you are shut up some stormy day, and Charity Wispers write a line to your little sister, hear her with Patience, and without the

---

[2]March 25 is the feast of the Annunciation; cf. Luke 1: 26-38. On this date Elizabeth made her First Communion as a Roman Catholic.

[3]Cf. John 10:1-18 and Ps. 36:10.

[4]Joanna Barry was married to James Barry of New York. They had two daughters. James Barry was a merchant of Washington and Baltimore whose business had carried him to New York and Canada. In the fall of 1805, the family had been at the Narrows, Long Island, when their daughter Mary became seriously ill. They took her to New York where she died November 17, 1805. The Barrys remained in New York until James Barry's death in January 1808. They were relative strangers in New York society when Elizabeth met them. Their second daughter, Ann (called Nancy), died in 1808 shortly after her father. They were friends of Bishop John Carroll and became friends of Elizabeth Seton after her conversion to Catholicism.

[5]Probably some Protestant relatives

trouble of minding your pen kindly lay the paper before you and I will trust your good heart for the rest—I have prayed for you lately more than ever, so you must not bring the old accusation—Oh if they were Accompanied with as much Grace as Sincerity how good you would be—

Shall I dare present myself thro' you to Our Reverend Pastor[6]—Mrs. Barry has communicated his kind expression of me and made my heart cry out to God. Oh if he knew what is known to you how different would be his impressions—looking so much at a fine picture Mrs. B. has of him has familiarised me as to Mr. Tisserant, and I have really a delight in praying for him—poor Sister pray, pray, pray, it is all she can do—and much easier than to express how much she is and ever must be

Your gratefully affectionate EAS.

28th

a heavy snow in March is quite a novelty but it has compleatly shut us up for three days and I hardly know if my letter will now reach you—but hazard.[7]

4.15 To Antonio Filicchi

28th April 1806

My most dear Friend and Brother

Your kind letter was a most grateful and unexpected favour as I had heard from Mr. Kelly of Georgetown[1] the uncertain state of your mind

---

[6]Probably a reference to Bishop John Carroll.

[7]This play on words relates to the Seton coat of arms which traces its origins to that of Sir Robert Avenel of the twelfth century. In the usage of the time it reads, *Hazard Zit Forward* which contemporary English would render, "At whatever risk, yet go forward."

4.15 AMSJ A 111 042

[1]Thomas Kelly was a lay instructor at Georgetown College near Washington which Bishop John Carroll had established in 1791 as a school for boys. Carroll also had a goal of providing a seminary to train native clergy.

on the subject so interesting to me—also a letter from Our dear Bishop to Mr. [James] Barry gave the same Intelligence—adding that the Boys could be received at G[eorge] Town for two or three years. Mr.Tisserant has passed some hours with me, and suggests the plan to you of placing them there for that time if it accords with your views for them.

The Mr. Kelly you saw there has offered every assistance and attention in his power, and Mr. Barrys[2] residence being so near, is another object. but my dear Antonio I very unwillingly, and only in obedience to Mr. Tisserant make these observations to you, well knowing that you only can be the proper Judge of what is right and it would make me very unhappy to add voluntarily in any way to the trouble you already have for your poor Sister—but be Patient, My Poverty in this World will gain you a store of Riches in Heaven—

The Bishop Speaks of you in a manner which Christian Friendship must not repeat as your heart could not resist such flattering encomiums He earnestly desires you should be know[n] to my Mr. [James] Barry who on his part very much regrets his ill health and the sorrowful situation of his family prevented his waiting on you before you left us.

Your Friend Miss Nancy [Barry] sits again opposite to me in Church, how often I look for you near her, and wish to enquire of her some particulars of our St. D. Mr. Chevrous has again written and enquired of you—Mr. Tisserant has gone to take leave of Him as his departure for Europe is decided for the end of May.[3]

and you dear Antonio will depart too—and to God alone I must look, beyond all the deprivations of this scene of regrets, and as it must be, for our Amabilia I shall rejoice and imagine Her joy with your Darlings, when I read the discision we meet no more.—words which I cannot write without tears or think of without earnest prayer. always and forever

Your EAS.

---

[2]Robert Barry, nephew of James Barry, was the Portuguese consul in Baltimore.
[3]Rev. John Tisserant left for London June 9, 1806.

4.16 To Cecilia Seton

Exaltation [May 3, 1806]

My sweet Darling

If you could but see Ann—her little Tea Urn (once the Coffee urn)
Kits Equipage, the poisoned cake etc.—all the merry giggers round
ten in number[1]
—were you at the side of Poor Sis, who has been wishing for you
all day it would be a galla day indeed.
—how long will Our poor Ann rejoice on her Birth day with her
present Peace and Innocence?—Alas!—but we must do all we can.
He will hold her in his dear hand. once I rejoiced like her, but when the
birth day now returns it is but to press the load of Sin and Sorrow still
heavier. But it will not always be so—will it darling—the day of deliverance will come!—so then you are daring to Calculate, Naughty
Child—you who know so well that he has it all ordered even now for
us, so sweetly, so many dear consolations whether we stay or go—and
as to the idea of staying as it is, that is the last thing to be expected. but
patience—it is best to know nothing—
have you been aspiring to day?—I hope so—Oh that I could have
one dear kiss of the lilly neck and hear the dear sound "Sister"—Eliza
[Farquhar] passed more than an hour here yesterday; more extravagant
than ever, said she loved me better than you do—I said your love was of
a different kind—true dearest how can she or any one else know of [the]
bands of our love who have never known their sweetness
He alone who has tied them can know. May he bless us forever forever forever Amen Amen Amen

Your MEAS[2]

4.16 ASJPH 1-3-3-8:134

[1]May 3 was Anna Maria's eleventh birthday.

[2]At her Confirmation, May 25, 1805, Elizabeth took the name Mary and began adding it or the
initial M to her signature. This symbolized her desire to take the three most significant mothers in the
Christian scriptures—Elizabeth, the mother of John the Baptist; Ann, the mother of Mary; and
Mary, the mother of Jesus—as her models. In 4.19 Elizabeth says they "contain the moments of the
Mysteries of Salvation."

4.17 To Antonio Filicchi

Sunday Evening 12th May 1806

My dear Antonio,

Your Sister has a foretaste of Paradise in the relief from care and anxiety which she has so long experienced for her little Boys[1]—Mr. [James] Barry takes them under his care—it would seem that it is so ordered to complete my satisfaction—and will himself conduct them to Georgetown.—If all was not refered to God I should now indeed be in danger of becoming an Idolater and be tempted to give you more honor than I ought, and must, and always shall consider you as my good angel, the Instrument of my Salvation, and guide to every good I can hope for in this Life or the next—

I have written to Mr. [Thomas] Kelly to procure whatever may be indispensably necessary for the children which I may have omitted—also have written Bishops Neal[2] and Carroll—a task you may be sure performed with a trembling hand—

You know you are to be amongst the "highest stars in glory" therefore my wishes can add nothing but your little Sisters heart crys out to God for you almost without the operation of the Will forever and ever may He Bless you—as I shall be forever and ever

Your EASeton

If you think it best to send the Boys to see My Mrs. S[cott] give them the Inclosed[3]—if not it is of no consequence—

4.17 AMSJ A 111 043

[1]Antonio had written May 2 that he approved the Georgetown plan for the education of Elizabeth's sons, William and Richard. William was then about nine and a half years old and Richard was almost eight. They were enrolled at Georgetown from May 20, 1806, to June 22, 1808.

[2]Rev. Leonard Neale (1746-1817), president of Georgetown College from 1791 to 1806, was named coadjutor for Bishop John Carroll in 1800 and became the second archbishop of Baltimore, serving from 1815 to 1817.

[3]This letter, along with another of the same date to Julia Scott, appears to have been hand-carried by Elizabeth's sons to Antonio, then in Philadelphia.

4.18 To Julia Scott

Sunday Night 12th May 1806

My darling dear Julia

My heart is almost too happy to write you—My Darling Boys are on their way to Georgetown College with Mr. James Barry of Washington City and may stay a few days in Philadelphia—

The Bearer of your last letter must be an odd genius, after delivering it in a moment of great hurry when I was giving my great family their dinner he promised to call again which he did three weeks after on Thur[sday] morning the only day of the week I go to town, staid an hour with my old sewing lady, played the Piano, and went away before my return leaving word he would call again and not having done so, I suppose the affair is finished—as must this handsome scrawl, being greatly greatly hurried—

your Own dear EAS—

Kiss my Boys 100 times for me.

4.19 To Antonio Filicchi

28th May 1806

My dear dear Brother will think me very negligent in not sooner replying to his kind letter, but not having any intelligence to transmit you from Mr. Tisserant have been every day waiting the answer of my letters to him, and this day am favored with a long message from him to you, the substance of which is that—"there is every expectation of his departure with Mr. and Mrs. B[1] in ten days on Board the *Science* [under] Captain *Havard*—but that it was not absolutely decided and that he still hopes in the possibility that you may accompany them,[2] and concludes with saying it is the wish of Mr. and Madame Belasis that you should know they desire your company extremely and very particularly wish to be known to you, adding they are acquainted with your character from some intimate friend—you know how partial friends are Tonino.

Imagine how happy I have been this week under the direction of our very dear Bishop [Carroll] and in the long wished for gift at W[h]itsunday[3]—believe me your presence only was necessary to complete so many favours—Mr. Tisserant could not be here and Mr. Hurley[4] was proxy for him and added the Name of Mary to the Ann Elizabeth which present the three most endearing ideas in the World—and contain the moments of the Mysteries of Salvation

are you coming—oh do make haste before the Bishop goes—dear Antonio, and shall I see you again only to part until admitted by St

---

[1] Rev. John Tisserant seems to have been a tutor in the family of a Mr. and Mrs. Belasis with whom he visited in the United States and then returned with them to England. Tisserant wrote Elizabeth Seton from London August 28, 1806.

[2] Antonio did not accompany Tisserant but sailed for Europe soon after.

[3] Pentecost Sunday, May 25 that year, on which Elizabeth received the sacrament of Confirmation from Bishop John Carroll

[4] Rev. Michael Hurley, O.S.A.(1780?-1837), was raised in Philadelphia although he was probably born in Ireland. He entered the Augustinian order in 1797, becoming its first candidate from the United States. Educated for the priesthood in Italy, he was ordained in 1803 and then returned to serve at St. Augustine's Church in Philadelphia, the first Augustinian foundation in the United States. He came to New York to assist at the time of the 1805 yellow fever epidemic. He served at St. Peter's in New York until 1807 when he was recalled to Philadelphia. Elizabeth grew to admire and respect the young priest who became her spiritual advisor. She and Cecilia Seton often called him "St. Michael," "St. M," or "why so." He later became pastor of St. Augustine's in Philadelphia (1820) and superior of the Augustinians in the United States (1826).

The Order of Saint Augustine (O.S.A.) was a mendicant order commonly known as Augustinians. They began in the thirteenth century when a number of semi-eremitical groups in presentday Italy, Spain, Germany, France, and England were consolidated under the rule of St. Augustine (354-430), bishop of Hippo and doctor of the Church. The first Augustinian friars came to the United States from Ireland in 1794 and settled in Philadelphia.

Peter—This letter must go, it must make haste or you will be still re-proaching me another Post—

Bishop C[arroll]—says you must make as much haste as possible that he may see you—

Yours forever MEAS

4.20 To Cecilia Seton

[June 20, 1806]

Your mother could not have rejoiced more in the hour of your Birth than I rejoice this day,[1] not indeed as she did in the uncertain conse-quences of your existence—but in the first assurance that you are among the chosen of the most high, and that the special Graces he has already evidenced in you are but the preludes of the eternal crown

May you always be clothed in Righteousness—and largely partake the blessings you procure for others—

4.21 To Cecilia Seton

St. Peter and St. Paul [June 29,1806] 2 Oclock

Dear Darling Child—

Your Peace is from God, it is the Sweet Reward he has promised to his Children—Docile to his commands and fervent in their Love their Very Sacrifices become their pleasures, being Accompanied by the conscious Joy of pleasing Him they Love above all—My soul has felt this Joy in Unison with Yours, but it has been the Joy of tears—such as

---

4.20 ASJPH 1-3-3-3:80,5

[1]Cecilia Seton was received into the Catholic church June 20, 1806, by Rev. Michael Hurley, O.S.A. She was fourteen years old.

4.21 AMSV 110:10,3

We experienced together When Adoring in his presence "Our hearts burned within Us"[1]—

—If for a moment We compare this treasure with the passing Joys of a fleeting existance, and realize the moment when the Miserere[2] must be sung—and then the precious Salutaris Hostia[3]—Oh Heavenly Mercy—the very thought Makes Nature strong and triumphs over the pangs of death—they are but Shadows to a soul that truly Loves—

Shall we be together in that hour—Shall we be seperated—or so, or not—He will cover us with his Shield and trust to blissful Peace—will wipe the streaming eyes, soften the agonies of Nature and reposing in the faithful breast give it the foretaste of Eternal rest—Eternal rest—rest with Jesus—hush ——Sister Spirit come away[4]—

Do not say St. Peter would keep you—no no my darling—Your reception is most sure—I have begged hard to day for a portion of his Spirit of Faith and Repentance—to-morrow I hope—tho' I do not like to go out of rule—more probably Wednesday! except there is threatening of rain—

Be Faithful in the dear heart and fear Nothing. You will conquer all the weakness of feeble nature either by being delivered, or by bearing them so as to add to the Treasure—I hope you will hear Mr. Lacey[5] Sunday—if not—His voice will supply all instruction—Bless Bless Bless—

forever Yours MEAS

[1] Luke 24: 32
[2] Ps. 51
[3] "O Saving Victim," a hymn traditionally sung at Benediction of the Blessed Sacrament
[4] Possibly a book given to her by Rev. Michael Hurley, O.S.A. Cf. 4.22.
[5] Rev. Michael Lacey was serving at St. Peter's Church, Barclay Street, in New York.

4.22 To Cecilia Seton

Friday [1806]

Precious precious dear Child of my Heart—

oh that Sister had had a pang in her finger or a thorn in her heart—any thing rather than have written a pain upon Yours—how silly to set your little brain to work and threaten it with a storm that may never come,[1] or if it reaches you may drive you still further in your interior castle[2] and point out to you the path of future Peace—And do you think I would leave you without seeing the coast clear that is your situation established in some way or other—as you are never—death alone can take your Sister from you while there is the least probability you may want her sheltering heart. Peace—Peace how unfortunate I should not meet my much loved[,][3] an unhappy woman of our household detained me—and having overslept five Oclock as usual owing to a restless night did not get in till St. M's Pater Noster—received Our All from Blessed Why so[4]—dear dear Cis you must not let timidity stop your blessing, tho' necessity must have all the claim—Well the ways of Providence are mysterious indeed as to the human Nature but most clearly we may distinguish in them the progress of the Divine, persuading all, lifting the child of mortality above its sphere and making darkness Light

—If only we may experience that constant separation from the Spirit of the world which now bestows such sweetness and rest to conscience, we ought most freely and thankfully yield ourselves as Osiers[5] in that dear Hand which only intends to sever the Grain from

---

4.22 ASJPH 1-3-3-8:92

[1] Cecilia feared the negative reaction of her relatives to her conversion, a premonition that proved correct.

[2] Elizabeth may have been aware of the spiritual classic of the same name written in 1577 by St. Teresa of Avila (1515-1582).

[3] Cecilia herself

[4] Both names refer to Rev. Michael Hurley, O.S.A. Elizabeth was very late for Mass but did receive Communion.

[5] Willows

the Chaff[6] and will one day put us in his treasure house—Sweet Cecil—

Sister is waiting with "Sister Spirit come away" open before her (the gift of St. M)[,][7] two little penseés pinned upon her heart which is full of your dear image, supposing that you are on your piazza or surrounded by your little charges[8] in some pleasant corner could I be near you at least the look of love might be exchanged, the sigh re-echoed—but fancy wanders—rather let us say how blessed is the offering of a Peaceful Spirit to . . . resigning the most innocent and dearest joys of its existance without a sigh but that which ascends for his Love to supply the place of All—He is all—Heavenly Treasure unfailing and unfading Joy—Bliss of Eternity—

Saturday afternoon

Where are you how are you my dearest—the clouds gather, the thunder rolls but the sun of the soul is bright, spirits gay— I would have a good frolick if you were here—what a sweet day to me—all all Peace. and when the thought of my Cecil would disturb it one look up to Him who rules the waves of sin and sorrow makes me hope you are offering up the willing sacrifice—brightening your crown and making the angels smile at your triumph over the tormentor—

the Hope of tomorrow is very sweet even if it is even Eleven—how I long to see you—forever[9]

---

[6]Matt. 3:12

[7]Possibly a book given to her by Rev. Michael Hurley

[8]The eight children of the family of James Seton

[9]Written on the outside, probably by Rev. Simon Gabriel Bruté, S.S.: "after her conversion some most beautiful thoughts."

4.23 To Anna Maria Seton

23rd July 1806

My Darling Daughter

you must not be uneasy at not seeing me either yesterday or to day[1]—to-morrow I hope to hold you to my heart which prays for you incessantly that God may give you Grace to use well the precious hours of this week, and I repeat, you have it in your power to make me the happiest of Mothers and to be my sweet comfort through every Sorrow, or to occasion the heaviest Affliction to my poor Soul that it can meet with in this world, and as your example will have the greatest influence on your dear little Sisters also and you do not know how soon you may be in the place of their Mother to them your doing your duty faithfully is of the greatest consequence besides what you owe to God and your own Soul—

Pray Him, Supplicate Him, to make you His own and to keep you His forever—which is the earnest prayer of your dear Mother

There are so many enquiries for Anna we are quite lost without you, but when you return it will be no longer my little Anna but my Friend and Companion—Oh how it delights me to think of it—Rebecca and Kit send their loves and you have a thousand from my Heart.

I hope Mrs. B. and poor Nancy is better, show them by every attention in your power how sensible you are of their kindness, and remember me to them affectionately—Remember that Mr. Hurley[2] is now in the place of God to you, recieve his instructions as from Heaven as no

---

4.23 ASJPH 1-3-3-9:28

[1] Anna Maria had gone to stay with James and Joanna Barry and their daughter Ann (Nancy) in order to be closer to St. Peter's Church where she had been receiving instructions to prepare her for her First Communion.

[2] Rev. Michael Hurley, O.S.A., had been instructing Anna Maria for her First Communion which she made July 16, 1806, at St. Peter's.

doubt your dear Saviour has appointed them as the means of bringing you there.

once more your own Mother.

4.24 To Antonio Filicchi

August 10th 1806

When I recollect the last kind look of my dear Tonino and his unwearied constant affectionate regard to his poor Sister I hope he will not be displeased at being so soon troubled with a letter from here tho' it does not contain any communication of absolute necessity—My heart has followed yours in the passage of the Atlantic[1] and many many prayers of sincere Affection it has poured forth for your Safety.

I have been in a sea of troubles since you left me but the guiding star is always bright, and the master of the storm always in view—the anger and violence of the Setons, Farquhars, Wilkes etc.[2] when they found Cecilia was not only a Catholic but as firm as the Rock she builds on, cannot be described. They threatened that she should be sent from the country, I should be turned out a beggar with my children, and many other nonsenses (as you call them) not worth naming, assembled a family meeting and resolved if she persevered that they would consider themselves individually bound never to speak to either of us again or suffer her to enter the House of either of them. She quietly tied up her clothes in a bundle and came to me very early in the morning of the day she was to be turned out if she did not consent to their wishes, and has been followed by the most abusive letters and charges against our "Faith, Bigotry, Superstition, wicked Priests," etc. etc. etc.—Mr. Hurley has behaved like an Angel and our true friend, or how could your poor little sister have known how to

---

4.24 AMSJ A 111 045
[1]Antonio was in London.
[2]Relatives of Elizabeth by marriage

act—but Almighty God always provides, and to Him I commit my cause—

After your departure I recieved a letter from Mr. Tisserant written at the Hook[3] in which he laments not having seen you the day of his departure, and expresses an earnest desire that when in London you would inquire for him at Dr. Silburns and leave your address, if he should not meet you there—he adds something about meeting you at Signor L'Eveque de St. Pol's—but it is written in such haste I cannot decipher it. Immediately after your departure Mr. [James] Barry wrote to the Bishop [John] Carroll requesting he would rectify the mistake[4] in regard to my Boys and make arrangements necessary for the regularity of future payments—We have not heard any more on the subject except that the Bishop would do so.

If you were now here my dear Brother I think you would exert your Friendship for us and obtain the so long desired refuge of a place in the Order of St. Francis for your converts.[5] They have made so many objections to Cecilia remaining with me, (and what else she can do I cannot imagine) little Ann is in so interesting a situation with respect to her Protestant relatives and in truth all my poor little girls if the Almighty God should remove me, that often as a Mother I feel my responsibility for trusting to so dangerous a situation if it is practicable to change it even at the expence of any human inconvenience which might happen in consequence—certainly when my Boys remove to Montreal it will be very difficult for me to remain behind.[6]—to God and to you I trust all—

I have waited many days unwilling to close my letter hoping to communicate something new from Mr. J[ohn] Wilkes who sent me a

---

[3]Rev. John S. Tisserant wrote Elizabeth from Sandy Hook, a spit of land in New York harbor and the last mail drop-off before ships set out across the Atlantic.

[4]James Barry had been handling negotiations for the Seton boys' entrance into Georgetown. The "mistake" had to do with financial arrangements and with items the boys were expected to bring with them. The Georgetown ledger, 1803-1813, gives a full account of the Seton accounts from their entrance, May 20, 1806, to withdrawal, June 22, 1808.

[5]The Franciscan Order was prominent in Gubbio, Italy, where the Filicchis had relatives who were nuns.

[6]The option of sending the Seton boys to school in Montreal when they were better prepared educationally remained a possibility. If realized, Elizabeth hoped to go there also and obtain a teaching position.

message that he wished a particular conversation—but day after day he does not call, and you will already think your dear Sister negligent— My Brother Richard [Bayley] arrived here two weeks ago and imagine the surprise and astonishment occasioned by the unexpected appearance of Carlton [Bayley]. I have seen him but once and cannot understand any reason for his return except a wish to assist his Brother and endeavour to do something for himself I believe also some discontent with Trueman.[7] Oh Antonio I hope they have not behaved ungratefully. —I have no letters—but he says they expected you to leave America in April, and daily looking for your European letters dear Amabilia preparing the House, and Georgino and Patrichio[8] as well and lovely as possible. Amabilia would have met you in England, but was uncertain of the time of your arrival—

Will you remember your dear Sister when your happy days return—poor Sister—she will try all she can to do penance for those that are past, and as it must be done you know, Tonino, happy if she may do it—Here—Our little Cecilia is trying to be a Saint—St Cecilia St Delia—handsome American names should it be so—I have not heard from Mr. Chevrous, nor recieved any answer from Dr. Matignon whom I addressed soon after your departure and you may be sure did not fail to assure him you had left your most Affectionate regrets at Boston—

Will you please write to me dear Filicchi when you can, your Sister would be honored, gratified, blessed by a letter from you. and in the mean while is praying for that day which will unite us (the Gate of St Peter past) in that sweet country when we will part no more Always and forever

Your MEA Seton

---

[7]A business associate of the Filicchi brothers in Italy, where both Richard and Guy Carleton Bayley were employed

[8]Antonio Filicchi's wife and and two sons

4.25 To Cecilia Seton

[Fall 1806]

My darling Ceci

perhaps Much Loved[1] may come and therefore the little word shall be ready—You are to dine at Simonds, he says but I hope it is going to rain hard—at six or half past shall be filling cups and quite pleased at having the lowest place at the feast[2] as it excuses going in. Why so shall put a piece thro' the ring for you—perhaps you may have another delightful dream—

Sunday Mr. Lacey[3] from Norfolk preached for us a sermon made for you; his subject "the advantages of crosses and contradictions"—"the foundation of all spiritual blessings dear Christians is Humility and this precious Virtue is the Daughter of Adversity, nor can she be perfected but by the influence of her harsh and severe Parent."—also he insisted that where Souls were so privileged as to be uncorrupted by the love of the World which affliction was generally sent to counteract they were equally necessary to preserve them from the danger and made the personal appeal full of conviction.

—precious Child—your Soul is indeed privileged—and I trust in God you will recieve the bitter preservation to the glory of His blessed Name—how I long to have you in my arms—is your breast better—Oh take care of that which is so every way precious—Bless Bless Again and again[4]

4.25 ASJPH 1-3-3-8:121
[1]Samuel Waddington Seton, Elizabeth's brother-in-law
[2]Cf. Luke 14:7-11.
[3]Rev. Michael Lacey
[4]Written on the outside: "16 day of same Memorable"

4.26 To Julia Scott

November 10th 1806

My dearest dearest Julianna

When I would write to you my heart presents a thousand tender expressions which it dares not utter and you would scarcely recieve with pleasure as you are quite unconscious of the many combinations which give rise to them, but this my dear friend you surely know that your steady unremitting affection in my worldly shipwreck is a sweet consolation, and one of the very few remaining endearments of this life, which added to past remembrances—the idea of Husband, and Father—I could lay myself at your dear little feet, and hold them in my bosom—

—Are you once more arranged at Home—and has not the fatigue exhausted you—no heavy cold—aching head or heavy heart—My Julia, what a toil—and how mixed with care and vexation, if the object is attained; but that neither you nor I can alter while your immediate situation must necessarily create them, your daily occupations and the objects around you unavoidably produce a succession of them, but Julia dear, you bear the chain and love it too.

Friday 20th November

—My darling Friend you must write to me—do not say "She is an Outré[1] creature and cannot enter into my views" She does enter into them my love, grieves that you are under certain influences which are with so much difficulty controuled, and commits you to God with a tenderness of affection which can be expressed to Him alone—

How is Maria, Our saucy J[ohn] and your dear little self. is Mrs. C[ox], or rather let me say dear Charlotte better from her summer exertions are there any consequences do you hear from Brother S[amuel] is H's love returned.[2]

4.26 ASJPH 1-3-3-6:63

[1]Exaggerated or strange (French)

[2]Elizabeth was inquiring after either Mehitabel "Hitty" Cox or another niece, Harriet Sitgreaves.

How is your personable Friend, as [Andrew Barclay] Bayley calls him—is Home in the same position as it relates to _____ many many questions I would ask you—and you who feel so much for my position would ask as many in return—which are answered by simply saying, as you left me—except that J[ohn] W[ilkes][3] is married as you probably know and of course I am the more interested not to trespass more on his Benevolence—

—A gentleman of very great respectability from Baltimore[4] the Superior of the college there has endeavoured to interest me in the establishment I have heard you mention with approbation in Philadelphia, Madam I do not know who, who keeps the celibrated boarding school[5]—but the aim of my desires if I were to change the present situation is very different, tho certainly the idea of going to Philadelphia or rather to you would be delightful to me—but no more of that—

Your Anna and Kit are quite well—I have the most consoling accounts from my sweet Boys my strength has I believe increased since my favourite season has commenced—again I repeat tell me all you can of little precious self and love your poor friend as your own your true friend—

forever EAS

---

[3]John Wilkes' first wife, Mary, had died in 1801.

[4]Rev. Louis William Dubourg, S.S., (1766-1833), was born in San Domingo, educated and ordained in France, and came to America as a result of the French Revolution. He joined the Sulpician community and became President of St. Mary's College in Baltimore. His invitation to Elizabeth Seton to come and teach in Baltimore led to the establishment of the first native sisterhood in the United States, the Sisters of Charity of St. Joseph's in Emmitsburg, Maryland (1809). He briefly served as the community's first Superior (1809). As first bishop of Louisiana (1812), Dubourg invited the first priests of the Congregation of the Mission (Vincentians) to begin a mission in North America in 1816. He resigned his Episcopal See in 1826 to return to France where he became bishop of Mantauban (1826-1833) and archbishop of Besançon (1833).

The Congregation of the Mission (Vincentians) was founded in France in 1625 by St. Vincent de Paul (1581-1660) to evangelize the poor in country districts through parish missions. Their ministry soon expanded to include priestly formation through seminaries, ministry among the sick and poor, and foreign missions.

[5]This may refer to a well known French school for girls on Mulberry Street in Philadelphia run by a Madame Grelaud, which many students from Maryland attended.

4.27 To Bishop John Carroll

26th November 1806

Dear and Reverend Sir,

Trusting to the Indulgence you have already shown me and the Interest you have so kindly expressed for my dear little children I must trespass a few moments on your precious time and beg your direction in a case of the greatest moment to my happiness here, and my eternal happiness—Accidently meeting Mr. Duburgh as he passed thro' New York he entered into conversation with me respecting my little Boys and my intentions for them—I told him Mr. [Antonio] Felicchi's earnest wish was to place them at Montreal and mentioned also that he had given me a distant hope that I might myself, with my little girls be recieved in a convent there, and perhaps be so happy as to make myself useful as an assistant in Teaching, as that employment was, (from the particular Providence in which I have been placed) familiar to me, and most suitable to my disposition This Hope which had hitherto been but as a delightful dream to me and appeared too much happiness for my earthly pilgrimage, Mr. Dubourgh brought in the nearest point of view and has flattered me with the believe that it is not only possible but may be accomplished without difficulty.[1] I could not venture to take a further step in so interesting a situation without your concurrence and direction which also I am assured will the more readily obtain for me the blessing of Him whose will alone it is my earnest desire to accomplish—

—My situation since I had the happiness of seeing you is very, very painful as it respects all my connections. One part of them never suffer even their Children to speak to me or mine—the other, tolarate my coming in their doors as a favour—Mrs. [Catherine] Duplex is totally seperated from me—and I should return home without a Breakfast

[1] Although Dubourg seemed to encourage Elizabeth in her desire to go to Montreal, he was also discussing with Revs. Matignon and Cheverus a plan to allow her to remain in the United States and fulfill her hope.

from my dear Church if Mrs. [Joanna] Barry or Mr. Hurley did not open their doors and hearts to me—and this for refusing the unreasonable request to persuade my Sister Cecilia to relinquish the Catholic Faith after she was united to the church—and then recieving her under my roof after their Solemn Avowel that She should never re-enter theirs, or be suffered to see any one of her family again—I know that you will be very much pained by these circumstances—but I assured you I would do every thing for Peace, and have yielded every point that was possible consistent with my Peace for the hour of Death—and for that hour my dear Sir I now beg you to consider while you direct me how to Act for my dear little Children who in that hour, if they remain in their present Situation, would be snatched from Our dear Faith as from an Accummulation of Error, as well as misfortune to them.

For myself—certainly the only fear I can have is that there is too much of self seeking in pleading for the Accomplishment of this object which however I joyfully yield to the Will of the Almighty, confident that as He has disposed my Heart to wish above all things to please Him, it will not be disappointed in the desire whatever may be his appointed means—the embracing a Religious Life has been from the time I was in Leghorn[2] so much my Hope and consolation that I would at any moment have embraced all the difficulties of again crossing the Ocean to attain it, little imagining it could be accomplished here—but now my children are so circumstanced that I could not die in Peace (and you know dear Sir we must make every preparation) except I felt the full conviction I had done all in my power to shield them from it—in that case it would be easy to commit them to God—

If you had recieved the packet of thanks and ack[nowledge]ments my heart has written to you my dear Sir in overflowing gratitude for your goodness to my Darling Boys you would acquit it of any omission in the most affectionate respect to you—and very very often in the intention of transcribing it the idea of intrusion on your sacred time

[2]Elizabeth had been in Leghorn, Italy, in 1803 and 1804.

which I knew from Mrs. Barry was burthened with Correspondants, deterred me—

Mr. [James] Barry will no doubt tell you every particular of his family—I passed a very cheerful hour with them this morning. their spirits are at least more composed, tho' really it appears from Mr. Barrys Situation new trials are preparing for them, dear Ann [Barry] I fear has already the most painful presentiment—Your friendship and affection seems to be their only earthly consolation.

I am most gratefully dear Sir Your Obedient Servant

MEASeton

You will be pleased to hear Mr. Filicchi is safe in London and mentions Mr. Tisserant is well I have letters from them both—Mr. Tisserants some weeks ago, Filicchi's of much later date—

4.28 To Antonio Filicchi

4th December 1806

My most dear Brother—

Your letter of the 5th September from London was a cordial to my heart made me feel bold, and while I read the last Paragraph to the Barrys, and some other of my friends certainly could not help exulting in the certainty of such a friend—not so much dear Antonio for human Considerations, because you know Providence always protects the poor and defenceless, but that you the best, the truest tenderest friend are the instrument of his Mercy to us, whilst thrice blessed it reflects again to your own breast, and also declares still more his honor and glory.—

I write you now for Leghorn in the hope that you are safely lodged in the arms of your Amabilia sweet Patrichio, and the rest of your dear ones—and have given before this a hundred kisses to my precious

Georgino for his poor Signora Se[ton]—whose only hope of seeing him again is thro' the medium of St. Peter[1]—is it possible Antonio that I shall not see you again in this World—Merciful Heaven I must not dwell on that thought but as an incitement to strive the more for Paradise which was if you remember the first invitation you ever gave me—There my Brother my every hope is centered as you know, and to meet you and yours there one of my most earnest desires—

I have written you a part of the curious events that have occured since your departure. if you have received the letter it is well, if not, certainly it is not worth while to call it over especially as I have told the tale to your Philippo—I was never so contented and satisfied with the daily dispensations at any time of my life—I hope it is my time of Harvest, as every hour admits of some Sacrifice—my unruly Boys[2] are still more ungovernal since they have lost a portion of respect for me which it was impossible to avoid whilst we were the laughing stocks of their dinner tables at Home and the talk of the neighbourhood here—Mrs. Farquhars[3] children being forbid entering the house occasioned a great deal of amusement to them—Your Friend Chevrous and Dr. Matignon opposed every wish of quiting so unfavourable a situation (tho certainly I never explained it in its extent to them) and I rest satisfied that in obeying them I shall do the will of God which is the only object.

You cannot imagine how much pleasure I have in the acquisition of Mr. Duburg's acquaintance (the superior of Baltimore College)—He would have sent me to Montreal in a moment, and shows us an interest and kindness more than I can express—Mr. Tisserant has written me from London several times, says a great deal of you, and gives every hope of his return in the spring—one expression of the Charity of any one of those gentlemen to me is of more worth than all the narrow hearts I have lost.

My Boys write me that they are very happy, as I also hear from every one who sees them. Bishop Neal has resigned his place and Mr.

---

[1]Elizabeth often spoke of Saint Peter when she referred to eternity or heaven.

[2]Boys from Mr. Harris' school who boarded with Elizabeth

[3]The Farquhars were paternal cousins to Elizabeth's children. They were forbidden to enter Elizabeth's house because of the furor over Cecilia Seton's conversion to Catholicism.

Molleneux is President.[4] Mr. [James] Barry and Mr. Hurley says the College will be much better conducted. Bishop [John] Carroll speaks very favourable of my Boys and has paid the whole sum he promised in advance, also forwarded the account in which it appears the sum additional which you disapproved is made up in extra charges. Mr. Barry begs that nothing more may be said on the subject as Bishop C[arroll] is much interested in forwarding the establishment and it would hurt his feelings after he has paid his 200 Dollars—

Mr. Wilkes, Post and Mrs. Startin are all silent as to their subscriptions[5]—in my present situation until the storm is blown over I am advised to be silent too. Mrs. Startin has lost her Patience intirely, tho' she rejoices that Cecilia's conversion will prove to the World how little our principles and our Priests are to be trusted—I thought that had been proved long ago—I had 200 Dollars (partly of Mrs. [Julia] Scotts) not in use, and have given them in charge to Mr. Morris—I shall not draw on Murrey again until I know the general conclusion of these good people except I should really want—and if in any thing I am wrong dear Antonio do not be angry with your poor Sister, that is the last evil I should be willing to encounter.

I have heard a great deal at Mrs. Barrys of the intended marriage of your young Murrey to Miss Rogers of Baltimore—I am sorry your perhaps better intention for him will be disappointed. but perhaps also— Our St.[6] may meet a good Catholick—tell your Most Amiable I shall love her forever, though so unworthy of her love she must pray for me and teach sweetest dearest Georgino to lift up his innocent hands to Jésu for his absent friend who loves him next to his dear Mother and if he ever comes to America will be his Mother here. Also let your darling and the dear girls pray for me. Antonio pray for your Sister.

---

[4]Rev. Robert Molyneux succeeded Bishop Leonard Neal as president of Georgetown College.

[5]John Wilkes, Dr. Wright Post, Elizabeth's brother-in-law, and Sarah Startin, Elizabeth's godmother, had agreed to support Elizabeth and her fatherless household for at least a year because the age of her youngest child prevented Elizabeth from becoming self-supporting. This subscription consisted of annual pledges of the following amounts: Julia Scott, $200; the Wilkes brothers, $200-$300; Wright Post $200; Sarah Startin, $200; the Filicchi brothers, $400.

[6]Cecilia Seton, Elizabeth's sister-in-law, who was a recent convert to Catholicism

A mob on Christmas Eve assembled to pull down our Church[7] or set fire to it—but were dispersed with only the death of a Constable and the wounds of several others—they say it is high time the cross was pulled down, but the Mayor has issued a proclamation to check the evil. Our Gentlemen near the church has had a sad time of it.

In Peace, or War, in life, or death, my Brother I shall never cease to pray for you, and love you with my Whole Heart.

MEASeton[8]

1807

4.29 To Julia Scott

12th January 1807

My darling Julia

I wrote you five or six weeks ago perhaps more, and do not now remind you with reproach, but with a real apprehension that you may be ill, or that there is some serious reason for so long a silence, which if occasioned by your usual unwillingness to write and the coldness of your dear little fingers, might have been supplied by the warm heart of you[r] gallant Jack[1] who I know would willingly relieve anxiety in any one, and readily in his old friend, tell him I challenge him in Prose or verse, short or long, any measure that will assure me you are well.

---

[7]An anti-Catholic protest at St. Peter's Church, known as the Highbinders' Riot of December 24-25, 1806. Some fifty men gathered in front of St. Peter's Church intending to disrupt Christmas Eve services. Andrew Morris, a trustee of St. Peter's as well as a member of the city council, persuaded the mob to disperse, but they returned and continued a menacing presence. Irish parishioners arrived the next day to defend their church, and a riot broke out which resulted in the death of a constable. Only the arrival of the mayor, De Witt Clinton, brought an end to the event.

[8]The following note appears on the outside of this letter: "New York 1806 Mrs. Seton 4 December/29 May R is going Brig *Naturo* Pisa 20 Ag 1888. Mrs. Seton letter of the 4th December 1806 to Ant. Filicchi received by the Brig *Neptuneon* the 15th of June in Leghorn. Patrizio Filicchi, Son of Ant. Filicchi"

4.29 ASJPH 1-3-3-6:64

[1]John Scott, Julia's son

I am unusually well this Winter, quite contented with the necessity of the case, sometimes doubtful though as it respects my darlings whether it is not a duty to take them from the influence of my rude and unmannered inmates—but God will direct. Anna is almost as much a woman as her Mother and much more discreet, and considerate—Your Cate is a Treasure of amiable disposition and promising talents. My sweet Sister[2] rewards my former attention to her by every assistance in her power for their instruction. We are all prospering dear, except poor Bayley who is hugging the hope of his little arm-full with a heart discontent and quite uncertain of his future prospects.[3] how much happier is his "poor Sis" whom he so much pities. looking up steadily spares the pains both of retrospection and anticipation, but on my part I greatly pity him, as I having been behind the curtain of all this sweet happiness he looks for so naturally, certainly have a very different opinion of it from that his imagination so warmly pictures. and you my darling if you had the Job to do again would also I believe take it rather gently.

—How is my Brother Sam, I suppose he has come to his senses or rather his right senses before this time. my dearest best and oldest strongest love to him when you have the opportunity. I have many fears for the health of dear Charlotte this winter and if not sure that any sorrow pressing on your heart would have induced you the more readily to write me, should have been apprehensive her complaints had increased

—Will you plese to tell me if your personable friend is still your Humble Servant, or if you are any nearer in the sense of St. Paul to becoming his.[4] O do dear Julia write me if but in short hand—my best and tenderest love are always yours

EAS.

remember me to dear Maria—and to Harriet.[5]

---

[2]Cecilia Seton, Elizabeth's sister-in-law, was helping with school lessons for the Seton children while she was living with them.

[3]Andrew Barclay Bayley, Elizabeth's half-brother. She was possibly referring to his management of his inheritance or to his courtship of Harriet Seton, Elizabeth's sister-in-law.

[4]Elizabeth was asking Julia if she planned to get married. Cf. Eph. 5:22.

[5]Julia's niece.

4.30 To Bishop John Carroll

23 January 1807

Dear and Most Honoured Sir,

From the last letter you have written our excellent and dear Mrs. [Joanna] Barry I think it may be a relief to your mind to hear from a third person and one whom you must be convinced shares her sorrows and watches their effects with solicitous Affection, that neither her health or spirits are in so bad a state as might be supposed—from the first hour of recieving her last severe trial she has had the fullest conviction that the whole strength of dear Ann [Barry] depended on her exertions, and she has shown a uniform firmness which the Almighty alone could have supported. her internal struggles may have been the greater, but certainly I can assure you that I have seen her every other day, dined with her, breakfasted, in short been with them at all times except after sun set. She has read to me his letters (at least whatever regarded the interesting subject) with composure, and calculated the hopes and fears that might be admitted in every point of view. both Mrs. B and beloved Ann have given vent to their feelings to me seperately and I assure you that so far from dwelling on their affliction they have not only been willing I should play the fool but been willing also to join in every nonsense to drive away thought. What a sight for the admiration of Angels, to behold these two virtuous hearts a constant sacrifice to mutual tenderness—the Mother drys her tears not to pain the child, the child to spare the Mother smiles through hers, and like a heroine indeed (not such as you in so flattering a manner mentioned in your letter to Mrs. Barry) scarcely suffers herself to weep before God, lest her fears might be attributed to their natural cause—

Oh dear Sir what are my trials borne ALONE—what anguish has affliction when it is not reflected to a heart dearer than our own—to suffer with Jesus alone how sweet, how consoling, to Him no constraint, no reserves, the more we weep the more He rejoices foreseeing the salutary effects of our grief—but the sufferings of our friend has every aggravation—He alone can carry her through them—Your letters are greater consolation to her than any human resource, and I beg you, while your writing is so essential to her not to think of me but in the moments when in charity you plead for your flock—though dear Sir a letter from you would give the greatest pleasure I could recieve I am very sensible your claims must be so numerous as to make writing a very great fatigue—the same Charity which interested Mr. Debourg for the poor converts while passing through New York has no doubt engaged him to communicate to you the result of his consultation with his friends in Boston relative to us[1]—to wait the Manifestation of the Divine Will—the will of a Father most tender who will not let go the Child afraid to step alone.

—perhaps dear Sir this letter may be an unnecessary intrusion, as you are so intirely acquainted with the dispositions of our dear sufferers, but you will recieve the intention I am sure in its true meaning—as to Anns health she has declared to me most solemnly she has no complaint whatever, You know the footing on which their tenderness has placed me authorizes any appeal to Ann on the subject of her duty in nursing herself, which she recieves most affectionately—her colour is good, and appearance certainly no worse than when You were here, I often think it is much better. If I dared envy any one it would be that Lady who is so happy as to nurse their Idol and gain so much of their love. If you should find a favourable Occasion my dear sir will you be so obliging as to remind him of th[at] warm Affection of his Madame Perpignan, French Nun, or Odd Fish, Jigger, or any other name he pleases[2]—

This is taking a very great liberty but I dare not write himself, tho' indeed it might be my duty to contradict the scandal which Ann threatens to have written against me—I believe also a part was to have been addressed to You—but am quite sure you will not judge a cause With only one evidence or at least so doubtful a one—

---

[1] Rev. Louis William Dubourg, S.S., had invited Elizabeth to come to Baltimore to teach. He had discussed this plan with Rev. John Cheverus and Rev. Francis A. Matignon in Boston.

[2] Elizabeth, using humorous names for herself, is asking Bishop Carroll to remind Rev. Dubourg of her regard for the latter.

I am dear and honoured Sir with the most affectionate respect Your Grateful and humble Servant

MEASeton

My noisy Boys[3] turn my head, pray excuse my incorrectness, I have not time to copy

4.31 To Antonio Filicchi[1]

14th March 1807 New York

My most dear Antonio

This day cannot be passed over without offering some part of it to my most dear Brother, who has so largely shared the happiness it commemorates[2]—do you remember when you carried the poor little wandering sheep to the fold? and led it to the feet of its tender Shepherd?—Whose warning voice first said "my Sister you are in the Broadway, and not in the right one?" Antonio's. Who begged me to seek the right one? Antonio! Who led me kindly, gently in it? Antonio. and when deceived and turning back whose tender persevering charity with held my erring steps and strengthened my fainting heart? Antonio's and who is my unfailing Friend, Protector, Benefactor? Antonio, Antonio. Commissioned from on high. The Messenger of Peace, and instrument of Mercy. My God, My God, My God, reward Him—The Widows pleading voice, the Orphans innocent hands are lifted to you, to bless him. They rejoice in his love, O grant him, the eternal joy of yours.

---

[3]Elizabeth's boarders

4.31 AMSJ A 111 046

[1]The following note appears with this letter which Antonio Filicchi copied: "Copy of the Original forwarded to Rev. White 20 October 1846 at Baltimore." The papers of Rev. Charles I. White, author of the first biography of Elizabeth Seton, appear not to be extant.

[2]This letter was written on the second anniversary of Elizabeth's reception into the Catholic church.

You may be sure Tonino I have been to Communion this morning, imagine what my heart said for you, and Filippo.[3]—it is not easily expressed, and our little Saint Cecilia is as fervent in her prayer for you as in her Religion, to which she is really a most beautiful ornament of innocence and Piety and the admiration of even those who think her Wisdom Folly.

We have lately been obliged sometimes to meet our old relatives and friends at the death bed of our poor Mrs. Maitland.[4] the fatigue of nursing her was very great and her parting affection being chiefly centered in Cecilia and myself, our services were willingly accepted to share the burthen. No doubt they would have been more acceptable if they could have made us mute for the time, but it passed off very well by my going always at night /like the bird of wisdom you know/ and Cecilia in the day. They have been delighted with her sweet submissive manner and prudent behaviour, and she has received invitations from all her Sisters and from Mrs. James Seton[5] to come and visit them, which she will do quietly and at leisure,—whenever it happened I met with any of them I appeared as if I had seen them but yesterday, and now the poor sufferer gone [,] shall probably see them no more.—I was the only one with her, and closed her dying eyes Antonio—Oh my Brother—how awful, without prayer, without Sacrament, without Faith. Terrified, Impatient, wretched.—How shall we ever praise enough that mercy which has placed us in the Bosom of our Mother.[6]

Easter Monday [March 30]

Happy Resurrection to you my most dear Brother.—May you spiritually now anticipate that which will bring us once more united—no longer to be divided by Gulfs, Seas, Straights, and Da[r]kness—Will you not rejoice in that bright morning to be sure, and the smiles of our

---

[3]His brother

[4]In her last illness Eliza Seton Maitland, Elizabeth's sister-in-law, asked for Elizabeth and Cecilia to nurse her. This opened the way to reconcilation with the Seton relatives. Eliza Maitland died in March 1807, leaving five children.

[5]Mary Gillon Hoffman Seton, Elizabeth's sister-in-law. Cecilia had been living with the James Seton family prior to her conversion. She was put out when she became a Catholic, but now was invited to visit them.

[6]The Roman Catholic church

friend St. Peter will encrease our joy. Tell dear Amabilia the little lamb—the dinner at her dear Mothers, with herself and dear ones—Rosina, the Brides, her Brothers,[7] the little Chapel by the large Cross, were all present to my mind yesterday, and painted by remembrance with many regrets—but most I regretted how unworthy I then was of her kindness and affection.

I passed my day at Church, and with the dear Barrys, whose tenderness, and attention to the poor fanatic is my sweetest earthly pleasure—My Breakfasts and Dinners are always with them or our Mr. Hurley who is always the same, as to myself, but very much improved in his official Character, and quite freed from those singularities we used to lament in him—He is my rigid, and severe friend in a calm, but whenever I have any trouble the most indulgent and compassionate—We have also a Mr. Kelly[8] who is a very very great acquisition to our Church—Mr. Chevrous and Dr. Matignon have written in their consolatory, and heavenly style with the same patience, and charity I used to find from Mr. Tisserant, who they suppose must be on his way to us, how happy happy I shall be to see him again.—upon my word it is very pleasant to have the name of being persecuted, and yet enjoy the sweetest of favours, to be poor and wretched, and yet be rich and happy, neglected and forsaken, yet cherished, and most tenderly indulged, by God's most favoured Servants, and Friends. If now your Sister did not wear her most cheerful and contented countenance she would be indeed a Hypocrite. "Rejoice in the Lord always"[9]

10th April

Your dear precious letter announcing your safe arrival Home is in my Bosom dear Brother, and what could I do but say Te Deum,[10] first carry it to Mrs. Barry, then to Mr. Hurley, or rather, to our family of Pastors, who shared my joy, gave thanks for your escape,[11] and admired the Providence who provided such a Brother for the poor little

---

[7]People whom she visited while in Italy

[8]Rev. Matthias Kelly of Dublin had arrived at St. Peter's Church by 1806.

[9]Phil. 4:4

[10]An ancient prayer of thanks to God attributed to St. Ambrose

[11]In his first edition of Mrs. Seton's life, Rev. Charles I. White quotes Antonio Filicchi's description of escaping a fall from a precipice on the summit of Mount Cenis during a snowstorm.

forsaken Woman and permitted her to go the next morning to Communion, to offer the thanksgiving of inestimable Value—with my whole Soul I did so—You are then in the arms of Amabilia, and your darlings—blessed be God. You will no doubt be much pleased to hear of the union of your friend Murrey with so amiable a partner, and so worthy a family. The Barrys, who know them very well, esteem them as the best connection in Baltimore—

It is many weeks since I have had letters from my Boys—Mr. Kelly[12] was at the College at the time of the last examination and says that they excelled other Boys who had studied much longer, and in the Latin were above some who were older both in study, and years. Mr. Barry certainly is much pleased with their situation, as there are professors of the most distinguished talents lately united to the College from Europe, and a new President.[13] he was there a short time ago, and gives me every hope that they are doing very well in all subjects—

The orders from Rome have not arrived it seems, which are to establish Dr. Matignon[14] with us—He means I believe to make your Sister his private Secretary, from the letters, and advice he has sent me through Mr. Dubourg, and again latterly by Mr. Chevrous letters, who does not leave me any hope to their consent to my Canada Scheme[15]—but God will direct it—and that is enough—Destined to forward the progress of his holy Faith /such is their opinion/ the very idea is enough to turn a stronger brain, but I know very well He sees differently from Man, and as obedience is His favourite Service, and cannot lead me wrong, according to the old rule I look neither behind nor before but straight upwards without thinking of human calculations—this to you Antonio, who understands the sincerity of your poor little Sister's heart and that it all all belongs to God—

Will you remember, and write to your own Sister as often as you can—Oh Antonio Antonio, does the wide Ocean divide me from

---

[12]Thomas Kelly, a professor at Georgetown College, reported on her sons' progress.

[13]Rev. Robert Molyneux

[14]There was a question of Rev. Francis Matignon being appointed to serve in New York, but that did not happen. Elizabeth understood that she was to be his secretary.

[15]Neither Rev. Louis William Dubourg, S.S., nor Rev. John Cheverus was in favor of Elizabeth's plan to send her sons to school in Montreal.

you—but nature trembles, and my eyes are clouded at the thought, dwelling on it a moment makes them overflow, but the struggle concludes by a fervent prayer for our eternal Reunion—Always remember me to Dr. Tutilli[16]—I never can forget him—Tell your Brother [Filippo] to send his benediction since the fruits of it are so precious, it cannot be denied, embrace all you[r] dear ones for your true Sister and friend

MEAS
20th April

I will send this to your Messrs. Murrey my Antonio, and beg them to forward it as soon as possible—

4.32 To Cecilia Seton

Lady Day [April 6, 1807][1]

My best beloved Cicil

Your own sister has past the day between the Altar and the bedside of dear Ann [Barry]—sweet sweet most sweet and to crown all had hardly done kissing the dear ones before precious Hatch was in my arms—So you dear gypsey you stole my treasure—and can it be possible I had not even missed it—bad Sister! My Darling not to trifle with yourself I charge you go to dear Jo if the thumb is not better—do you not know when your finger pains my heart Achs? be good and obey your Mammy

I was told to day to remember the pattern of purity and to dare even to imitate perfection—poor me that is a high hill indeed—but my sweet little dear I Echo to you the good instruction and beg you to

[16]An Italian physician who attended William Magee Seton before his death
4.32 ASJPH 1-3-3-8:136

[1]Originally, Our Lady Day was a day kept in celebration of some event in the life of the Virgin Mary. At this time it referred to March 25, the Annunciation, but formerly it also applied to December 8, the Immaculate Conception; September 8, the Nativity of the Virgin Mary; and August 15, the Assumption.

drive the old lady[2] out of your head and keep her only in your Heart with Xst [Christ] "be strong." there seems to be trouble in the wind from sweet Hatch's account but you have the secret that is with them that fear Him Blessed be his Name

I am engaged—good night even in the very center of the heart of your own own own own own

give All the dear ones a hug for Aunt Wm and dear Em a kiss too[3]

4.33 To Julia Scott

10th April 1807

My much loved Julia

If you are not out of Patience with your friend it is much more than I deserve as it is not probable that you are acquainted with the Melancholy Reason of my long silence which really has been unavoidable, and you will say so, when you know that for several weeks now, and sometimes three nights of the week, I have been obliged to sit up and watch the dying hours of our poor Eliza Maitland.[1] You know love that persons in sickness and pain wish for the presence of those who are experienced in them, and this poor Sister found or thought she found more comfort in my nursing than in the attention of any one else, and you may be sure in such a moment I could not add a pain to the dear parting Soul, and—

One more added to my list of Agonies—She has left five as helpless little beings as ever wanted a Mothers care. their Father is an unfortunate man,[2] and the Family will take charge of them—poor little Lambs—

---

[2]Elizabeth herself

[3]Written on the outside: "Sweet Lucy Do you not know"

4.33 ASJPH 1-3-3-6:65

[1]Eliza Seton Maitland, Elizabeth's sister-in-law

[2]James Maitland, Elizabeth's brother-in-law, had been involved in Seton, Maitland and Co. which suffered bankruptcy.

Julia my precious Friend—this dear Eliza did not love the world, she had a bitter portion in it, and you would say a life passed in the slavery of poverty and secluded from those allurements which commonly endear us to the present scene would have ensured her at least a peaceful Death—some Nights before her last in an interval of ease she conversed with me and observed herself that such had been her situation—but added, how is it that until we are just going we never think of the necessary dispositions to meet Death—I made some consolatory reflections to her, but altho' she said but little on the subject during her Illness which was long and painful, and her mind naturally quite uninterested in it, her Fears and dread continued to the last. Oh Julia Julia Julia "the last last last sad Silence" The soul departing without Hope, its views, its interests centered in a World it is hurried from, No Fathers sheltering arms,—No Heavenly Home of Joy—My Julia Julia Julia—Eternity—a word of transport, or of Agony—Your Friend, your own, your true, your dear Friend begs you, supplicates you in the Name of God—think of IT. O if she should see your precious Soul torn, dragged, an unwilling Victim—what a thought of horror.

—15th April

Do not be angry with me dearest Friend—say not the intreaty is from a heart torn with misfortune or depressed by melancholy—not so—never was a more chearful or contented heart than your friends—absolutely reposed in the Bosom of the tenderest of Fathers.

How I wish I was near you I would sing and laugh for you my darling Julia, and show you how sweet how very sweet it is to look over the hills that surround Our Valley—and then you know as we are both past thirty we might form some plans between this and sixty—but the truth is that I have never felt myself bound to my dear little Sister P[ost], at any time half as much [as at present] and tho' often two weeks together elapse without our having the least communication, yet except some plan occured of certain advantage, I must jog on, and rest quiet in the certainty of encountering difficulties in every allotment, and let the current take its cours[e]—He who sits above smiles at the anxious calculating heart, and makes every thing easy to the simple and confiding. I may well act upon this plan having found it the only source of real Peace.

—No doubt poor Harriet[3] is signed and sealed before this—and perhaps gone—dear child, the beauteous Vision will vanish, but it is all in the course of things—May God protect and bless her—Is your dear Maria improved by her visit—What strange recollections the name of Caton[4] give rise to in my silly fancy I could laugh like a fool even with myself at the remembrance of an Evening Mrs. C passed with us in Wall Street[5]—She was one of my Williams[6] favourites and my friends the Barrys are attached to her. therefore I say to Folly, Hush.

I cannot tell you, dear Julia how your generous attention presses on my heart and when your letter containing the remittance comes the comparative view will present itself—as certainly it is not the plan of Brother Post that we should recieve the sum subscribed except there was more necessity than the present—you wait neither calculations nor receipts but the expanded Heart flies before all—the dear Children you love most, promise most—Anna is a piece of Harmony in mind and Person both—Kit has a most amiable disposition with very superior abilities.

Will you tell dear Lott[7] I love her dearly and wait in anxious expectation of the NEWS. surely she will not be contented with one pair.

I suppose Brother has an Army by this time—prosperity attend Him, how dearly dearly I should love to have a peeping corner among you all—I guess I should see queer things—remember me to your dear ones—think of me—love me—take care of yourself go on your dear little knees before you put away this letter and lift up your heart—Adieu love ever

yours EAS

---

[3]Julia's niece, Harriet Sitgreaves

[4]Possibly Mary (Polly) Carroll Caton (1770-1846) who was a daughter of Charles Carroll of Carrollton and a niece of Bishop John Carroll. She married Richard Caton in 1786, and they were the parents of Emily, Louisa, and Mary Caton who later attended St. Joseph's Academy at Emmitsburg.

[5]The Setons formerly lived at 27 Wall Street in lower Manhattan in New York.

[6]William Magee Seton, Elizabeth's husband

[7]Charlotte Sitgreaves Cox had given birth to twins.

4.34 To Julia Scott

22nd April 1807

If I did not feel my Heart full and overflowing with tenderest, truest love to my Julia I should be sure it was no longer in my Bosom—dear dear Friend, can it be that—I have so faithful so dear a heart still left from the wreck of past blessings—while mine retains one throb of life it cannot forg[e]t to love you.

Your Dr.[1] I believe borrowed a look and smile from you—or at least the sight of him recalled your smile of mischief so strongly to my fancy that I could not retain the character or personify the stranger to Him—you know that in facto your friend is never that to any one—the heart flies out so quickly—but it is time to be circumspect, and sometime at least to behave, but never mind, it must go in the course of things—

On Saturday last the 18th my long looked for reply to you was put in the post—I have observed that Mrs. [Sarah] Startin (who is not more regular in her affairs etc than your dear little self) always requires of me a Receipt for whatever money I recieve from her, in order to keep her books correct, and told me that I should enclose yours without any question—but as I do not know how to date the beginning of your remittances you must direct it yourself dear friend.

My precious merry little Cis is gone,[2] and I may truely say I am lost—Anna's disposition is so different—she knows how to put her cheek to mine and mix a silent tear, but to turn that tear to a smile is only the province of sweet Celia. Mrs. Setons[3] confinement which has lately taken place separates us now—for how long I know not—she has the power and disposition to make herself so useful to them that most probably we shall be separated

---

4.34 ASJPH 1-3-3-6:66

[1]Dr. Bollman, the bearer of this letter

[2]Cecilia Seton, Elizabeth's sister-in-law, had returned to James Seton's household.

[3]Mary Gillon Hoffman Seton, wife of James Seton

—Eliza Farquhar[4] is going fast to heaven—with the most angelic dispositions that ever met in a being so circumstanced I believe—Consumption—

—Patience—turn and turn about as the children say.—

Good Night dear Julia dear—My love to your darlings—the Book will be a great Acquisition to my Sweet girl who really improves in every thing and has no fault so dangerous as her loveliness—tell your Saucy J[ohn] how much I thank him. farewell farewell ever ever

yours E A.S.

Thursday night—

4.35 Draft to Rev. Michael Hurley[1]

[5/n.d.]

The Rising of the full Moon and the "certain invisible bonds" strongly draw my thoughts to the traveller this evening—the Moon excited the Prayer to the Sweet Virgin Queen of Heaven, the Reflected Rays of the Eternal Son to Bless you with her Influence—and for my own poor Soul for the hour of Death—Oh St. Michael—for the hour of Death, you feel too the horror, and the bliss connected with that thought which are naturally most powerfully awakened in my Soul by immediate circumstances, as well as the liveliest sentiments of adoration and joy in the view of that Infinite mercy which has so long waited for the ungrateful wanderer, and now affords so consoling a prospect for that hour in the place of the awful and gloomy blank—the lost of so many less favoured by his Providence.

Your voice of admonition here adds the necessary precaution—Beware—and Conscience "tremblingly alive" can only answer Blessed Friend Pray for Me—

---

[4]Eliza "Zide" Farquhar, a cousin of the Setons.

4.35 ASJPH 1-3-3-1:31

[1]According to Rev. Charles I. White, Elizabeth Seton's correspondence with Rev. Michael Hurley, O.S.A., was lost when the Augustinian church was destroyed during the anti-Catholic riot in Philadelphia in May 1844.

but to change this subject will you indeed return to us—As Mrs. W. says I do not like your Philadelphia visits[2]—Pitying Mercy if you should not when would we find the Expletive to the Chasm, "Surely then the scourge would fall heavy. Almighty God arrest it, and rather send you to the lost sheep of Israel not only to protect and guard them but with a brain full charged and lips touched with the burning coal[3] to drive Old Tom and his apostates to their den and give them a foretaste of the Infinite Woe and infinite despair" but the Litany of the Saints is unsaid and it is past ten Good Night to the poor traveller in the stage Peace and with you

4.36 To Cecilia Seton

Thursday Night—Corpus Christi 28th May 1807

My dear dear Darling—

Ann and your MEAS were an hour and quarter getting to Town this morning, the showers so often stoped us—She prepared for Sunday—I at the very moment the clock struck ten recieved ALL your Soul and mine holds dearest. the anticipated Joy of Eternity

—my poor prison walls seem to have been falling ever since you left me—not one moment I believe free from pain—we must sing with the leper, but the Soul is in a dead calm, quite awake, but only alive at the though[t] of the Miserere[1] behind the pillow.

Blessed St. M.[2]—I fear his Mother is gone—May she find Mercy in life or death—the new man is expected to-morrow and I hope for a letter. and am quite certain some one has taken one out of the post office

—Patience—Patience—Patience

---

[2]Rev. Hurley had gone to Philadelphia to visit his sick mother.
[3]Cf. Matt. 10:6 and Is. 6:6.
4.36 ASJPH 1-3-3-8:139
[1]Ps. 51
[2]Rev. Michael Hurley, O.S.A., had recently left New York for Philadelphia where his mother was seriously ill.

—Is it possible sweetest Hatch is with you—how that pleases me—with her and my much loved[3] you need only think of me to wish I shared your dear society. I envy you the pleasure of mending his stockings and the many opportunities of pleasing Him, send him whenever you can if only to give me a look tho' that look is never separated from the sigh to departed love—Nature is full to the brim good night my beloved Child—look up I am going to the foot of the +[4]

tell precious Hatch if ten thousand Worlds were mine I would give them all to share my Blessings with her—

4.37 To Cecilia Seton

Last day May—Sunday Night. Paddy [1807]

My precious Darling

tho' I parted with you in anguish of Heart, it has been a sweet sweet day—Kate has been an example of that love I owed, as well as the pride of my heart—the letter you gave was from Bishop [John] Caroll and such a one as may well encourage a fainting soul and make it glory in being of His fold—and to my great delight who should appear to say the Eleven Oclock prayers but Our dear Father Burns[1]—the Sermon from Why so was most grateful as well as elegant on the Parable of the Supper[2]—after church made a short cut to the Old lady's; was glad to find who was out, and entered the Convent with sweet Kate and the fondest Anticipations of a Mothers heart knowing that Mr. B. had just left my Boys[3]—dined on Beefstake and claret alone with Him and was truly feasted with a full and most flattering account of my dear ones and plenty of sweet letters from them and Mr. K.[4] You know

---

[3]Samuel Waddington Seton, Elizabeth's brother-in-law

[4]In the text Elizabeth has drawn a cross.

4.37 ASJPH 1-3-3-8:148

[1]Rev. John Byrne of Ireland was an assistant at St. Peter's Church on Barclay Street in New York.

[2]Cf. Luke 14: 15-24.

[3]Rev. John Byrne had just returned from Georgetown where he had visited Elizabeth's sons, William and Richard.

[4]Thomas Kelly, a professor at Georgetown College

His conversation so instructive and such multiplied enquiries of my Celia[.] Dick sends his usual quantity of loves but love to you twice on the same page—Vespers sung by why so—the organ Hymns and Benediction with the heavy rain out doors and the still quiet state of interior Peace in His Divine presence placed the Soul in Excelsia

—happy happy Soul—Merciful God is it so—and how many would enjoy it still more than US perhaps could they taste the Bliss of Faith—the rain detained the M an hour after service and was it not delightful—What would I not give for the sign of my Own Own Celia close—My My Celia—look up—

—found the Darlings all well—Ann as usual—she returned at one—Peace Peace Peace Peace Peace "May He whose service is your delight and whose love is your reward Protect and guard You!"

Sincerely Your Friend M[5]

Ann says no letter has been recieved there and there must be one somewhere for me—Patience

4.38 To Cecilia Seton

Saturday 7th June 1807

My Darling Child

Our secret bands are particularly soothing to my Soul this day—You suffer, I also, Your longing heart pants for Home, and Oh does not mine—but the Sum of all is, the dear Heavenly Friend is treating us as he does always those he loves best—and would our coward feeble hearts choose another portion—No—no—no—no—no. by those five blessed pleas, let but our dwelling be in them and Heaven is Ours—Eternity JESUS—

---

[5]Elizabeth sometimes referred to herself by her Confirmation name, Mary.
4.38 ASJPH 1-3-3-8:100

How my heart bounded at the sight of my much loved and the black hat—but when H's[1] face appeared under it—the sigh flew straight upwards—tho, next to you I would have hailed her welcome—but that chasm—it is a dreary Gulf, we must commit it to God.—

Your Angel Watched me last Night I believe—I slept so well—am really better to day—the sigh still pains, but the fever much lessened—shall not go to-morrow except it is fair—you and I both must be thankful for the past and yield all with peaceful resignation.—I hope to get a letter tomorrow from some quarter or other—

—am delighted with your musical fancy—"soft remembrances" was quite a favorite with my W M.[2] mind the E flat—before you begin to play any thing examine every note and make yourself sure of the flats and sharps—

I have always found when under any particular trial of Patience a great consolation in the Litany of our Blessed Mother, after renewing promises to our dear Lord which we know we have often broken, and fear to break again it is sweet to intreat her who bore Him in her Bosom of Peace to take our case in hand—if she is not heard who shall be—

Precious dear Cecilia/My hearts Darling cherish that emanation of Love and Kindness to every one which He gives you from Himself that it may adorn the Cross you bear in his Name. the preaching of example is most efficacious, and those who make the Noble Aim must always keep the eye upwards—the Name of Christian without His spirit will only make the Account greater—and Sweet Humility must be the friend and companion of your Soul—the day will come when she will give you an everlasting Crown—

Write me to morrow, to be in readiness—my heart hangs upon every little word—how precious is our love—so seldom found in the mire of this World—and best of all, it pleases Him Who is Our All—

read this little Book with attention it delights me let it accompany you on the Piazza as it has me on the pillow

Yours forever MEAS

---

[1] Possibly Harriet Seton, Elizabeth's sister-in-law
[2] William Magee Seton, Elizabeth's deceased husband

4.39 To Antonio Filicchi

June 22nd 1807

My dear Brother

There has been a spell on my communications with you through the disappointment occasioned by Captain Blaggs repeated promises to call for my letters—whether he is gone to your Port or is going, it will be my surer plan to send them to Murrey as I first intended as before this time you must have accused your poor sister with inattention and neglect—A letter from Mr. Cheverus mentions your having written him as late as ____ and a little paragraph from it proves your continued affection and interest for your American family—The Lord reward you—He only can.

My last letter of April mentions the death of Mrs. Maitland and this the still more melancholy one of Mrs. James Seton[1]—which event has removed me from the sweet society and consoling affection of my Cecilia—who was immediately taken Home to take charge of the children—her trial on the occasion is so severe it will probably soon put a period to her pains, but she lives in the midst of every contradiction like an Angel of Peace—the Governess of the Family has endeavored already to persuade Mr. Seton[2] that Cecilia is instilling our principles in his eldest daughter, which has occasioned a great deal of trouble and torn open all the painful wounds made at her conversion, and makes us once more the subject of conversation etc. for I have no words to express the situation we are in as objects of remark and ridicule which affects her as little as it does me except the real distress of hearing Our Faith misrepresented, and grief for the darkness of those who despise it—but it is in the hands of Him who makes darkness light, and makes us rejoice in the testimony of conscience, for we would neither of US change the least portion of Our Treasure for a

---

4.39 AMSJ A 111 047

[1]Two of Elizabeth's sisters-in-law had died, Eliza Seton Maitland in March 1807 and Mary Gillon Hoffman Seton in June 1807.

[2]James Seton, Elizabeth's brother-in-law

thousand Worlds, much less for one which sets us at Liberty by the severity of its treatment—

I repeat to you Antonio (as you may be anxious on the subject) these are my happiest days—sometimes the harassed mind wearied with continual contradiction to all it would most covet Solitude, Silence, Peace—sighs for a change, but five minutes recollection procures an immediate Act of Resignation, convinced that this is the day of Salvation for me and if like a coward I should run away from the field of battle I am sure the very Peace I seek would fly from me, and the state of Penance sanctified by the Will of God would be again wished for as the safest and surest road—My Health is very much as when you left me—when I eat and drink, and laugh I am as well and gay as at fifteen—This is all to satisfy your anxiety which I know you once experienced and hope still possess for your dear sister.

Our Mr. Hurley has just returned from Georgetown and confirms the good account already given you of the Boys—Mr. Cheverus says you promise yours may come to America—Oh Antonio if that should be in my day I would travel over every state of it to meet them—they would find a Mother this side of the World too—

Do you not mean to write me any more, your last letter is that which mentions your happy return—and possession of that felicity you so much deserve—dear happy Amabilia must be in extacies indeed after so many bitter hours of separation—I heard from Mrs. [Joanna] Barry a very interesting history of a young man so amiable that he might have served for a model of Romance—he was engaged to a very lovely and amiable daughter of Mr. Mason of Boston—who is now heart broken and shut up in her room, because her beloved was obliged to fly to another climate when they were on the point of marriage to recover his health, and who should this wonder of perfection prove to be but your old friend Patrick Grant who buried the wife you saw with him, or rather saw him with, mourned for her with all his heart, and a few months after addressed this Miss Mason who is certainly from Miss Barrys account of her a second Delia. laugh at me if you will for telling you such a history, it is very correct as I have seen Mr. Masons letters to the Barrys—it has interested me very much—So goes the world dear Brother—the curtain has droped to me but you see sometimes I take a peep behind it, which never fails to make me more and more delighted with my interior retreat—

I hope you continue to be good after all your fiery trials—3 times a week I beg for you with my whole Soul in the hour of favour when nothing is denied to Faith—imagine your poor little wandering erring Sister standing on the Rock, and admitted so often to the spring of Eternal Life—the healing balm of every wound, indeed if I wore a galling chain and lived on bread and water I ought to feel the transport of gr[ace], but Peace of Mind and a sufficient share of exterior comfort with the inexhaustible Treasure[3] keeps My Soul in a state of constant comparison between the Giver, and reciever, the former days and the present, and Hope always awake wispers ["]Mercy for the future, as sure as the past["]—Antonio who planned this picture for me first loosened the bandage from my eyes—I need not answer

I wish you would tell me something about your Filippo—the same sentiment fills my heart to you both, but you only know all the curious combinations of my fate—and—Oh how much Patience you have had with me—

May the Almighty God bless you and yours forever—Your sister prays for you continually always always it is all I can do and it is one as naturally as for myself.

Yours forever MEAS

1st July 1807

I have Just now a letter from Bishop [John] Carroll such as a tender Parent would address to his child—every body is so good to me—every body whose love is in the right channel—

Love me too Antonio—Pray for me—tell Signor Phillipo to send me his Blessing.

So much Noise of War and crooked politicks[4]—I shall fly to Canada if it continues—

---

[3]The Eucharist

[4]Elizabeth was referring to the political and economic conditions created by the Napoleonic Wars.

4.40 To Cecilia Seton

1st July 1807

my Lovely

did your heart beat true to love at 1/2 past 7 yesterday Morning. When the clock struck 7 was on the knees to St. M. recieving the dearest consolation this world can afford—at half past in the exact spot we were on Sunday when H[arriet] and Zide were in our hearts—Blessed why so said in "vitam eternam"[1] with such a voice as no one has but Himself—you was in the beating heart and helped to swell it larger—but oh how could it contain half the Joy and Blessing and not burst—hush hush

—Mrs. [Sarah] Startin compleatly took me in, and docility for once was my punishment—what with storms and excuses, and visiting Widows she detained me till late in the afternoon and then John Wilkes came and stayed an hour, Sister came to take me to Mrs. Tenbrocks and it was 9 Oclock before the Litany was said—this I tell you that you may know I was in bondage as well as yourself—but Who can bind the Soul which God sets free—it sp[r]ang to him fifty times—have scarcely a moment without being turned to him while the Voice and eyes were answering down below—sweet sweet . . .

My darling Soul—think of him love him, and look to him, and never mind the rest—all will be well—

—St. M. has changed his mind about the Canada Scheme[2] and said a great deal about it—talked it over with Sister P[ost] her heart melted, but she said whoever loved me must wish it therefore YOU[3] are now my only draw back—the Lord will direct

---

4.40 ASJPH 1-3-3-8:138

[1]Eternal life

[2]The possibility of sending the Seton boys to school in Canada

[3]"You" is also written above and below this capitalized YOU.

When will you come—dear dear dear Child—if I could hold you to my heart this Morning how merry it would be—to-morrow is the Visitation,[4] I hope to go [on the] wings of Aurora[5]—be with me

Yours forever[6]

4.41 To Cecilia Seton[1]

8 July 1807

How often have I felt my Soul awakened by thy Light, and warmed by the fire of thy Love—then I approach Thee—I find Thee—but alas instantly after I lose Thee—often I think myself recieved—then fear I am rejected—and in this constant change of interior dispositions I walk in darkness and often go astray—I desire and know not how to desire, I love, and know not how to love,—nor how to find what I love.

Thus my Soul loses itself without ceasing to hope in Thee—It knows by its own experience that it desires much, and is unable to do any thing—Thou seest its trouble O Lord—and in that happy moment when fatigued with so many Vicissitudes it falls at last into entire diffidence of itself then Thou openest its eyes and it sees the true ways to Peace and Life—it knows Thou wast nearer than it imagined—Thou instructest it all at once without Voice or Words, it thinks only of what possesses it, abandoning all things else, it then possesses Thee—It sees without knowing what it sees, it hears and is ignorant of what it

---

[4] The feast of the Visitation, formerly on July 2, commemorates Mary's visit to her cousin Elizabeth. Cf. Luke: 1: 39-45.

[5] Roman goddess of the dawn

[6] Written on the outside: "much loved [Samuel Waddington Seton] will have your Basket 1st July 1807"

4.41 ASJPH 1-3-3-8:142

[1] This reads like a spiritual journal and may not be Elizabeth's original thoughts but sentiments copied from a spiritual book. One possible source is the writings of Thomas de Andrade, also called Thomas of Jesus, an Augustinian hermit who died in prison at Sagena, Morocco, where he had authored the work *Os Trabalhos de Jesus*. He is not to be confused with St. Thomas of Villanova (1488-1555), who sent the first Augustinian missionaries to the Americas (Mexico). Elizabeth Seton's friend, Rev. Michael Hurley, O.S.A., provided Augustinian works for her reading and reflection.

hears, it knows only Who he is to whom it is attentive, it contents itself with loving Him, it loves Him continually more and more—Words cannot express, nor the mind comprehend what it recieves from THEE O MY GOD even in this place of BANISHMENT—

How happy is that moment O divine JESUS! how pure is that Light—how ineffible is that Communion of thy Blessings! Thou knowest O Lord how precious that gift is, and thy Creature that recieves it knows also—Ah! if It were faithful, if It never departed from Thee—if It knew how to preserve the Grace it had recieved, how happy would it be! and yet this is but a drop of the infinite Ocean of Blessings which thou art one day to Communicate to It . . . O Soul of my Soul—what is my Soul and what Good can it have without possessing Thee . . . Life of my Life! what is my Life when I live not in Thee . . . Is it possible that my Heart is capable of possessing Thee—of enjoying Thee all alone—of extending and dilating itself in Thee— . . . can thy Creature thus be elevated above itself to repose in thy Breast, and after that depart from Thee? bury itself in the Earth? . . . Ah Lord I know not what I ought to say to Thee: but hear the Voice of my Love and of my Misery; live always in me, and let me live perpetually in Thee and for Thee as I live only by Thee.

I offer Thee O Divine Jesus! all that Thou art pleased to be for the Love of me: I offer Thee Thy most Sacred Body, thy most pure Soul, and thy Divinity which is the source of all happiness and Wisdom I offer myself to thy Father by Thee—to Thyself by thy Father, and by thy Father and Thee to the Holy Ghost who is the Mutual Love of Both.

Enlighten me O Divine Light!
Conduct me O Supreme Truth!
Raise me again O increated Life!
Seperate me from every thing that displeases Thee
Suffer me to remain at thy Feet
There it is that I find any happiness O Divine JESUS!—my Joy, my
Delight, that Peace of God which surpasses all Understanding—[2]

---

[2]Cf. Phil. 4:7. Written vertically just below this line: "+ . . . Copy of the Soul written at Midnight 8 July 1807. . .+"

O my Blessed Mother Obtain from Him what is necessary for my/our coming to Him—that I/we may one day possess Him with You—for Eternity

C.B.S. MEAS[3] (St. Thomas of Jesus)[4]

4.42 To Cecilia Seton

[July 18]

My dear dear most dear Child—

Your little precious word of love fills my heart to over flowing—the tears have not dried since they flowed to meet J . .[1] at 7 this morning. St. M. Our St. M. never known till lost, nor did we know our love and value for him until the blow is struck—He leaves US on Monday to return NO MORE[2]—the rector of his St. Augustine Church has left it to Him and is going away in ill health

—hush hush hush Nature—He wishes extremely to see you Sunday Morning—to share your cares and wipe your tears my Angel would be my Supreme earthly desire—but—Almighty God protect us—the tears fall too fast Sam[3] will see them—my beloved my darling Celia look to God with a steady Soul he will as surely uphold and deliver you as he is God—FOREVER forever

Your Own

the Children will be-all with Dué[4] to-morrow—I sleep at the Barrys—pass Sunday in Church—Sister's Soul longs for you 2 Oclock Saturday

---

[3]These initials are enclosed.

[4]Written on the outside: "to be read every day *for a week* Sweet Peace"

4.42 ASJPH 1-3-3-8:123

[1]Jesus in Holy Communion

[2]Rev. Michael Hurley, O.S.A., had been recalled to Philadelphia by his superior, Rev. Matthew Carr, O.S.A.

[3]The devil

[4]Catherine Dupleix

4.43 To Julia Scott

20th July 1807

My darling Julia—

How is it that strong minds, weak minds and all sorts of minds I believe are subject to melancholy and unaccountable forbodings often without being able either to trace their source or resist their impressions—scarcely more than one days Journey seperates us—yet like a fool fancy often pictures you suffering in mind or Body, and certainly in all events sighing and wearied with real or ideal evils which are, and ever must be the certain attendants of a life which seeks its pleasures every where but from Within—

Affection, fervent, anxious affection would make enquiries, but the pen drops on the reflection, "dear little Soul it is a pain to her to write—she has a thousand Occupations"—and indeed sometimes I am so sure you will again take the fashionable rout[e] that I expect to hear you are in town from day to day, and Anna often has said I do believe there is Aunt Scott's carriage—

The most painful, cruelly painful circumstance and circumstances of poor Mary Setons death (Mrs. James Seton)[1] has been more sensibly felt by myself (tho' apparently the person least interested) than can be imagined, and once more compleatly covered every power and faculty of my mind with the veil of Sorrow—so many painful combinations never before united in the death of any one of the many I have been so nearly connected with—nor deprived my Soul of those cheering consoling reflections which have always accompanied its deepest Afflictions—but as in every other instance now too, I look up in silent acquiesence adoring that dear hand which will one day shew every apparently dark and mysterious event in the most beautiful and perfect perspective of Wisdom and Harmony—The much loved darling Cecilia by this sudden change is removed from me—her poor Brother

---

4.43 ASJPH 1-3-3-6:67

[1]Mary Gillon Hoffman Seton, Elizabeth's sister-in-law, had died in June probably as a result of childbirth.

[James Seton] finds his greatest consolation in her faithful and unwearied attentions to himself and his children (he has 8 - five girls)—therefore my deprivation is easily reconciled having many comforts he has not.

Mrs. [Eliza] Sadler and Mrs. [Catherine] Duplex are on the point of embarking for Ireland—Sister Post is at her summer residence on Long Island—My dear Barrys at the Springs—Mrs. [Sarah] Startin at Brunswick—I can lay my hand sweetly on my Heart, look up to God and say I am ALONE with you dear Lord and my little children—

4th August

My dearest Friend—Your letter of 28th July was sent to me this afternoon by one of my Neighbors, how long Brother Post has had it I know not—it is a great relief to me altho you have evidently very little of the sweet Peace your friend wishes for you as the Choicest gift of Heaven—poor darling Julia—in how many ways you must be tormented, the Widows friend would indeed have gloried in chastising the Rascal who usurps your right—Surely the fear of being hooted at might have hindered so dishonorable an action—it rouses my Bayley blood. how glad I am Brother will make your cause his own—

—You say nothing of your health in the Battle—when will the letter come which you promise shall tell me of your dear children—a Gentleman mentioned that dear Maria had been in N[ew] Y[ork] on her way to the Springs with Mrs. Somebody is it so—is our Trojan John the same? No views of Europe in his head?—our dear Charlotte must have felt the Parental pang most keenly—but He knows best—

Every body is talking of War[2] here and it has seemed impossible for me to feel an interest in the subject supposing it one of the Whirlgigs of our changeable existance which would not be permitted to produce Good or Evil but in subservience to the great plan—Your letter has awakened now the most Solicitous desire as if Julia who is so small a speck was indeed the whole world to me—or as if the same All directing Providence would not shelter her in that hour as in the present—it will—the promise is sure—

---

[2]This was the era of the Napoleonic Wars.

You[r] continued remittance which I am no more in want of than the great Mogul, is now a real pain to me—did I want it I would fly to you sooner than any Earthly resource I have—but not in the least want, obliged indeed to put it at interest while I am persuaded the multiplicity of demands on you must make the command of ready Money often difficult = I would beg you dearest friend at least to suspend it—I have All and more than I want[.] [Antonio] Filicchi pays the whole of my Boys expenses and 200 dollars besides the [John] Wilke's Signiture goes to my house rent and 300 dollars a year from my Inmates[3]—Judge than if I have not more than I want—Mrs. Startin has given once a hundred dollars—Post is silent—

The greatest difficulty I have to encounter is the loveliness of my Anna—she is indeed a Being formed to please—Patience—must take it cooley—little Kit is every day more knit in her Mothers Affections—She learns without any of the labouring up Hill so common to children—every thing she does is with ease and sweetness, and a little smile of love the only reply to the most difficult task that can be given her, her assiduity is often a strong contrast to poor Anns Indifference—Natures Plants are indeed various—Rebecca reads and sews without any other Instruction than being present at the lessons of her Sisters—the Boys are said to be the most docile and Obedient of all their companions—Bishop [John] Carrol writes me they are extremely beloved and progressing very fast. See how many good things I have to tell you

poor Bayley[4] has gone to sea again half distracted—without prospect or view but to try for his daily Bread—his Beloved is an amiable little creature, and her situation truly interesting—

You do not say any thing of Brothers Progeny—do they multiply—is his health [good] I suppose he has long since Numbered me among the Lunatics—therefore [give] him my hair-brained Affection in its Primative Warmth—I met a very Personable man in the street the other day who I could have Vowed was himself, and like to have fallen on his neck—it would have been a fine business to be sure—

---

[3]The boys whom Elizabeth was boarding
[4]Andrew Barclay Bayley, Elizabeth's half-brother, who was engaged to Harriet Seton

poor Harriet[5] the sigh involuntarily rises at the thought of her—her fate however may (if she has chosen a generous heart for a partner) be eventually more happy than Mrs. Markoes[6] surrounded by her Relatives—

When will Maria compleat the picture, how different her character must be from either of her cousins, and I am well persuaded will require many more ingredients to form her happiness.

are you in retirement, or only at the distance convenient for Visitors dear dear Julia how I should love to be near You in some hidden situation humble and neat where I could catch your hour of leisure—not scold you but console and chear your dear heart—sometimes when you are in haste softly wisper Julia where are you going—hush, hush, Peace to you love forever Yours—

You see this letter was to have gone to you 2 weeks ago, the person who was to take it disappointed or rather I missed the opportunity—and procrastination our sympathetic complaint finished only the first page—the recipe was simply 10 drops of Laudanum one or 2 of Oil peppermint according to its strength to an Ounce vial of water sweetened—

4.44 Draft to Rev. Michael Hurley, O.S.A.

28th July 1807

You are then safe—well—and running your course with Hope—no doubt to terminate in Joy.—Blessed be God. While applying the two first verses of the 120th Psalm to my own poor Soul, most fervently it addresses for you the remaining five[1]—may the Lord indeed keep your going out and coming in from hence forth now and forever.

---

[5]Julia's niece
[6]Mehitabel Cox Markow, Julia's niece
4.44 ASJPH 1-3-3-1:130
[1]In contemporary Catholic editions of scripture this refers to Ps. 121.

a letter from Dr. Matignon by Mrs. Montgomery[2] in the post office on Saturday gave me the cheering hope of finding her on Sunday and conversing of our absent friend—could I be so happy as to meet her my heart would go before all words, but enquiring at the Broadway lodging house had the disappointment to find her gone on Friday—how proud I should have been to have taken her in dear Anns corner—and doing something you would have wished done—patience—passed a very heavy day—could not help thinking of "the bottle in the frost," or more expressively in the smoke. dined with our excellent Mrs. Wall—the old gentleman kept us in order. "Remembrance waked with all her busy trials"—

So many many enquiries after you—Mrs. Morris asked if I carried a bowl to catch the tears for your departure—the laugh went against me, but without losing composure simply answered they stream from my heart tho' it rejoices in the happiness he has gained—all was Silence—the old gentleman leaned his face on the back of a chair, the young people seemed not to hear—but yesterday they remarked "we are very lonely without Mr. Hurley"[3]—and there it finished, most probably not to be renewed, certainly not by me, as it is your wish, and I cannot but revolt at hearing a name my Soul reverences always pronounced in a manner which indicates Insincerity—

Mr. Lacey[4] gave the neither hot nor cold from Revelations[5] a complete raking and many instructions for the scrupulous—the hard threat of being "Spewed out," often repeated as I was really sick, increased the nausia—Oh dear St. Michael pray for me that it may not be realized.

---

[2]Rachel Montgomery, a Catholic convert of Rev. Michael Hurley, O.S.A., in Philadelphia
[3]Rev. Michael Hurley had been recently recalled to Philadelphia.
[4]Rev. Michael Lacey, preaching at St. Peter's
[5]Cf. Rev. 3:16.

4.45 To Cecilia Seton

[July n.d.]

My Souls Darling—

Your dear Sister would not take off your burthen if it could be done even by a simple wish but she prays fervently that you may be faithful to that grace which is ever ready to support it—as sure as we have an adored Master so sure he has appointed this the day of your Salvation[1]—Your precious humble Soul will be exalted to his very bosom while even the most perfect life exercised in that heavenly Virtue will be found to wait at his feet—

—remember St. M. the last morning you saw him (or did you notice) how earnestly he said to us Sursum Corda[2]—the words had so strong an impression at that time that they often sound to me when sinking Nature seems deaf to every other remembrance—

besides like natural storm[s] those of the spirit prepare the Blessed Harvest—He said, "Peace be still"[3]—He will say it again—he says it this Moment to your precious heart, and while He seems absent, still is there Glory to his Name—

the little rose I saved for you since Friday is fallen preserve the beautious leaves I have part of them—Kate is more precious since she came from Cecil what a treasure—

Yours forever, ever

4.45 ASJPH 1-3-3-8:119
[1]Cf. 2 Cor. 6:2.
[2]Latin for "Lift up your hearts" said during Mass
[3]Mark 4:39

4.46 To Antonio Filicchi

New York 10th August 1807

My dearest Brother

How is it I hear no more from you—the tears of Affection often suggest many things—but one thought never can be admitted of your having less interest or affection for your poor little sister—Two letters I sent Messrs Murrey to forward for me about eight weeks ago I hope have reached you—many have been addressed to you since the date of your last which announced your happy arrival in Leghorn.[1] Dr. Matignon has enclosed one from Mr. Chevrous who gave it to some Captain going to your port before he went on his Mission to the Northward who afterwards changed his voyage and returned the letter in the state it is now sent to you. Those blessed gentlemen continue their kindness to me—from the high principle on which they act no doubt they ever will.

I have lost my friend and Director Mr. Hurley who has removed, ordered by the Bishop [John Carroll] to the church of St. Augustine in Philadelphia much regretted by his friends here—and we have in his place a regular Superior Mr. Sibourg[2] a particular friend of Dr. Matignon and highly approved by the Bishop—The Barrys whose house is now the only place I go, are extremely desirous for the execution of my Canada scheme,[3] Mr. Barry has already taken some steps toward it—but still as you have left me so much in the charge of our Bostonian friends I will do nothing without their full consent.

There is continued account of the good conduct and improvement of my Boys—the little girls give me great happiness in their progress in their Religious instructions and impressions—Alone in the world

---

4.46 AMSJ A 111 048

[1]Antonio Filicchi had just returned to his home. He had been in the United States since June 1804 when he had accompanied Elizabeth on her return to New York.

[2]Rev. Louis Sibourd, a French priest who came to the United States about 1798 and became pastor of Saint Peter's Catholic Church in New York in the summer of 1807. He later ministered in New Orleans.

[3]The possibility of sending the Seton boys to school in Montreal

(litterally, as to any claim or interference any one has in my actions) I commit All to the Almighty alone. accustomed now to think the poor creatures head is turned with religious folly, no one asks a question, or pretends to trouble me any more.

Mr. [John] Wilkes pays my house rent with the subscription of himself and Brother [Charles]—Mr. Post says nothing—Mrs. [Sarah] Startin is I fear tired of her promise she is very distant and re-served—visits me no more, tho' you may be sure I behave as usual to her—she has once since you are gone given me one hundred dollars—Mrs. [Julia] Scott is more warm than ever in her friend-ship—regularly transmits her sum which I give to our old friend Mr. Morris (with proper receipts) on interest—Before you went away you made me draw on Murreys for two hundred dollars. Two weeks ago have drawn on him for the same sum to pay the Georgetown ac-count—Mr. Barry has some vexation with Bishop Neal and refuses to correspond with him and Mr. Hurley was so good as to forward the money for me.[4]

These details must be tedious to you dearest Antonio—and in part will be vexatious I fear, as I positively promised you to send in regular receipts for the subscriptions your friendship gained me but I am sure if you knew all that has happ[en]ed since and my exact situation you would not require it.

My beloved Cecilia (our shining convert) is settled at her brothers James Seton—He is sensible of her merit tho' naturally very fearful of the influence of her example on his children—how long she will be there He who rules all, only knows.

So much for the external affairs—for the internal, the Peace and consolation I daily, hourly and constantly experience in the Divine principles my Brother has taught me, their influence over my Life and sweet promise in Death, make all secondary considerations appear tri-fling, or at least put them in their true point of view, as passing clouds which can only obs[c]ure the sun a few moments while he calmly and with steadiness pursues his course—If you could exactly imagine my

---

[4]William and Richard Seton were students at Georgetown College. Bishop Leonard Neal had been president of the college until December 1806.

position my dear Brother you would know that there is no real sorrow but sin, no pain but that of not advancing in the Service I am engaged—I never was so happy—in the brightest years of my life, never experienced an enjoyment to be compared with a moments Blessedness at communion—this you cannot judge of dearest Tonino as you have always dwelt in the Bosom of that dear Mother[5] whose tenderness is yet new to me—

How is your dear Amabilia—have you no more Treasures to share the smiles of Georgino and Patrichio. What pleasure it would give me once more to share their sweet smiles—and witness the improvements your dear girls have made. Pray dear Antonio write me. so often the question is asked have you heard from Mr. Filicchi I am mortified to say not these seven, eight months—besides that really my affection de[sires] it as necessary support and consolation which you must give and when you are most unwilling to take the trouble offer it as a Penance—

You know me too well my Brother not to excuse the foolery of having mentioned the wish to have some of the black stuff such as your dear Amabilia bought for me—a recollection how much trouble it might give soon made me regret the request and I beg you will forget it has been made—

Dear dear Brother farewell—I beg your Filippo's blessing, as I know we have his charitable affection and good wishes—if our prayers are heard, they will be a thousand fold rewarded

I cannot tell you a word of news as I never enter any house but the Barrys. Church and the Barrys, is my world. Mrs. [Eliza] Sadler and Mrs. [Catherine] Duplex have gone to Ireland—the latter is more and more desirous of embracing our Faith—but one alone can give the grace to sacrifice all and be turned out of doors as she absolutely must be. Pray for us dear brother. I pray for you with all the fervour of my soul—forever

Yours M E A Seton

---

[5]The Catholic church

4.47 To Cecilia Seton

14th August 1807

Dearest Darling

our little Hospital is cheerful this Morning after a sad night—gladly ac[c]ompanied our adored in spirit through the streets of Jerusalem[1] all night—when the heart is all his how easy is pain and sorrow or rather pain and sorrow becomes purest Joy—

the hand trembles as you may see, but the Soul is all Peace—I wish I could know exactly how you and your dear charge are—commit you with full confidence to Him, for I know he is always with you—dreamed the sweetest dream that I held the blessed Host[2] close to my heart making earnest acts of adoration and love—mixed with great fear of it being lost in a quantity of almond and raisins which were thrown in my lap—you know how fond I am of them—earthly affections

precious dear child may he Bless you forever and bring us soon to our sweet happiness—

forever yours MEAS

4.48 To Cecilia Seton

15th August 1807

Is not "the Spirit willing"[1] this day—gladly most gladly would it fly—but the Adored hand holds it and silently sweetly it waits his will—pain and uneasiness only makes it more sensible of the balm of

---

4.47 ASJPH 1-3-3-8:144

[1]Refers to Jesus' way of the cross. Cf. Mark 15.
[2]The Eucharistic bread of Holy Communion

4.48 ASJPH 1-3-3-8:146

[1]Matt. 26:41

his dear Love—Love—the Love of Jesus—Merciful Saviour what a gift?

My darling Child that dear Peace which is so precious to weak nature you know is uncertain, it is not always to be desired if we wish to do our work in a short time—but your trial of patience and confidence is the sure, the certain means of being perfected—ask yourself if you would not pity the little ant, much less He who is love and pity itself—

speak all your dear heart to your own—I am well persuaded it is going thro' that crucible which all His most favoured servants have passed, nor can there be a more perfectly acceptable offering to Him than a heart feeble but willing, as his own in our human Nature once has been—

Yet I am very very earnest in the intreaty that you will do your part to get rid of all depression. as to softness and sensibility of feeling at the thought of our Pilgrimage and absence from Him it is the souls repast, try at least to turn the stream of sorrow there—

10 Oclock

Our much loved makes us all alive again—He say[s] you gave them Breakfast but very unwell—dearest dear Cicil could I be with you—my aching bones would yet support You—the hope for to-morrow is faint indeed—Patience—think how well for us the vacation comes—

darling of my heart pray for Your own—her whole soul begs for you—

forever yours MEAS[2]

4.49 To Cecilia Seton

[before August 28, 1807]

If to snatch a little look only on the road is so sweet—how sensible shall we be to the Joy of never never losing sight of each other my own

---

[2]Written on the outside: "Kate sends a cross"
4.49 ASJPH 1-3-3-8:125

own dear Dearest darling—My day was a struggle of poor nature's weakness and delight of the spirit once more to enjoy its only rest on Earth—for you precious child, your sacrifice whether more or less still must have been another thorn for the wreathe Glory to his Name—Oh if I could give your dear Soul the fruits of my experience how thankful you would be for the privilege of Offering all to his Will—but when I was as you now are—Sister[1] could not bear it half so well—Patience—

4 Oclock

the smile of much loved once more—[I] am writing to St. M. for his Birthday—mine Thursday, no Friday oh that I could have you early early early—

—love me—it is not possible as I love you—but love poor Sis and pray for her with your whole Soul.

Kiss the dear ones for me—Your Kits had no fever last night and bled but little—do you find the charm I do in Thomas[2]—I hope so—.

cannot hear from the Girls[3]—and feel more sensibly than usual a separation so often affirmed Bless Bless Bless Ned[4] is come—

Yours forever

4.50 To Eliza Sadler

28th August 1807

My dear Eliza,

I have deferred to the last preparing the little letter which is not the first addressed to you in the mind since your departure.[1] the Spirit of regrets takes its privilege and excites imaginations and reflections

[1]Herself
[2]Thomas de Andrade, also called Thomas of Jesus, an Augustinian author
[3]Probably refers to Harriet Seton and Eliza Farquhar
[4]Edward Augustus Seton, Elizabeth's brother-in-law
4.50 ASJPH 1-3-3-7:31
[1]Eliza Craig Sadler had left for Ireland in July. Catherine Dupleix was also in Ireland at the time.

which only prove the contradiction of the human heart in always multiplying evils and refusing to dwell on the fair and harmonious picture presented by reason—or rather the divine influence which points out the tranquil path of Resignation—

My Friends—Heavenly Mercy—If I would count them where are they—and where am I wandering by the question the soul that is pressing on must not stop a moment but you must let it [be] known particularly and minutely how you and dear Du have passed thro' the storms—yet I am sure your Sun will keep its course with steadiness whatever are the clouds that surround it.

—how much I would give to attain your height—and gladly give up the few years of difference in age to reach the shelter you have found—Oh teach me the use of your weights and measures, and clear off the mist which weakens my sight—a little note of yours written when I lived at Greenwich[2] and the great question was agitated if I was to remain with Brother P[ost] struck my eye the other day among the papers of value—and contains such advice, so worded, and peculiarly expressed that reading it over and over and in silence it seemed to me I was kneeling to our Reverend Friend,[3] and actually listening to his voice of Peace and reconciliation—it will please you to know that my new Reverend friend[4] is of the same kind—what a resource to me, it acts like a charm to put all things in their proper order—

You are now more than half your way over the dear Ocean—What a World of Wonder and delight it was to me—my horizon now is equally limited and my dear ones are within it—therefore away that regret—and for you Eliza dear my whole soul prays that Peace may accompany you—pray for one another is the sacred word, if then for All, how fervently does affection plead—

It is so that both the end and view of your Voyage are unknown to me, but one sacred end is certainly computed—the seeing the objects

---

[2] A section of New York where Elizabeth had lived temporarily with her sister, Mary Bayley Post. Eliza Sadler had written: "Does your Sister and her husband really desire your remaining with them? Of this I think there can be little doubt, however some inequalities of temper may seem to contradict it. Were this not the case, I am inclined to rely upon the good judgment of Post that he would put an end to such domestic inquietudes."

[3] Probably Rev. John Tisserant who was a friend of Eliza Sadler's

[4] Rev. Louis Sibourd, the new pastor of St. Peter's Church

of your first affection, and holding in your arms the remnants of those that are gone—the tribute will be paid but your mind will be soothed—do do make believe I am at the back of your chair and give me a picture of the reality—and I then will close the eyes and imagine I see my sober Sad once more in the land of Social cheerfulness, sharing the smile and look of love from Beings perhaps inexpressibly dear to her—if our dear dear Dué could always be one of them how sweet it would be—My sweet smilers are well Kit more Weak and thin from her Influenza—but I hope the cold weather will brace us again—farewell dear Sad

I shall write you very soon again—

Yours always EASeton

4.51 To Cecilia Seton

Thursday [September 3, 1807]

It is one of the Miracles of Divine Grace and Wisdom that every state of life which is not reproved by the Law of God may be referred to our Salvation—experience daily shows that the actions which we perform for discharging the duties of our state, though they seem sometimes very distracting of themselves bring US NEARER TO GOD than they remove us from him—that they augment the desire of his presence, and that He communicates himself to the soul in such a manner by secret and unknown Ways in the midst of NECESSARY distractions that it is never delayed thereby—

By carefully elevating the mind to God often in the day—resigning ourselves to Him—blessing his holy name—thanking him for his favours imploring his help—speaking to him affectionately—and sighing after the possession of Him we perpetually entertain the fire of Divine Love—and it frequently happens at these moments that God will grant what we do not obtain by hours of prayer to teach us that it is

to his Good we owe Our happiness, more than to our own case—"and
that all he asks of us is the Heart"

These sweet instructions, dearest, I transcribe for you from (St.
Thomas of Jesus one of the Hermits of St. Augustine[1]) that they may
comfort you as they have me—he says also (most for my consolation)
that our dear Lord often seperates us from Whatever we love most,
that Himself may take their place in our hearts—divesting us of every
thing else that we may be alone with Him, and thereby enjoy unutterable Peace; while we dwell on Earth, converse with Heaven—and
lead an angelic Life in our Prisons of Clay—also the happiness of the
soul consists in the Unity of its love—and its misery in the multiplicity
of its desires—

—Is not this delightful—Blessed Father Thomas has taken the
place of all other reading and almost all other prayers for his works are
a continual prayer I hope you will soon be of our party

—precious dear Cecilia—sigh to the Blessed Baptist[2] to obtain for
you a portion of his spirit that we may take our Penance
chearfully—Since the evening of his anniversary My soul has felt in a
new existance, and I mean to beg particularly during his Octave—Will
we go Sunday morning—is it possible—I dare not think of it—

to-morrow I hope to be padding with early steps—the Soul has already gone before—

Look up sweet Love—"God is wonderfully adorable in his ways
and as I am persuaded they are all founded in equity and that Salvation
is alone his work, I submit to whatever trials he may please to expose
me"—(St. M. one of the Monks of St. Augustine[3])

—These Augustines have certainly a very sweet spirit, I rejoice he
is my Patron Saint in the chronological order[4]

---

[1]Thomas de Andrade, also called Thomas of Jesus
[2]August 29 is the feast of the beheading of John the Baptist.
[3]Rev. Michael Hurley, O.S.A.
[4]Elizabeth was born August 28, feast of St. Augustine (354-450), convert, bishop, and doctor of
the church.

—Cicy what should we fear Heaven is for us—what should be against us,[5] Old Lucifer cannot gain a step but what we give Him—we will Watch, with . . .

Yours Forever

4.52 Draft to Rev. Michael Hurley, O.S.A.

9th September 1807

My dear Friend—

I have been ill or should have immediately expressed the most grateful Acknowledgments for your letter—After suffering suceeds a quiescent state both to the mind and Body which is perhaps the most favorable moment to address one whose society I only anticipate in Heaven—in this world I believe no more—

Your goodness in writing Cecilia could only be repaid by a Knowledge of the effect it has had on her—it has changed the tone of her mind and harmonized it like a message from the skies—with all her excellent acquirements of Patience etc. she has like someone older than herself a pliancy of temper apt to yield to present impressions and without a palliative to mitigate the constant irritabilities of Nature we should both be interiorly wretched, whatever the external presented. You are too well acquainted with human weakness to ask why a letter of yours often reverted to should console when the highest resource is ineffectual. it is simply explained by the figure of the Ladder—Blessed be his mercy which has brought us to the steps—I have not seen the inclosed letter, she says in a little note "I have written [,] Sister, as a Child to its Father."

Our friend [James] Barry has had the alarming Cholera Morbus[1] which has frequently succeeded Influenze, and was almost too much

---

[5]Cf. Rom. 8:31.
4.52 ASJPH 1-3-3-1:32
[1]A gastrointestinal disturbance usually resulting from overeating or consuming contaminated foods

for him—but was much better when I was last in town and must still be so or should have known it. perhaps he has written you himself—he makes speeches to the Trustees,[2] which his odd genius alone can reconcile—and laughs them over at Home with a mischievous pleasure—Mrs. B—still throws up the appealing look and says "Who can miss Him as we do Yet I must rejoice that he is gone"[3]—

Will you not (You see your indulgence increases confidence) some day when the moment is your own, explain for me the verse You have applied. the only commentary I have on the Psalms is Bishop Horn[4] who of course is not very well able to lighten my darkness, being blind himself—I should not in this instance or in any other have indulged the freedom of my heart to you but in the fullest confidence that you read my letters like any others of the hundreds you must transiently recieve, and with perhaps the distinction of one sigh more to human weakness and error—therefore dear St. M have pity—I will not go in forbidden fields any more indeed since my Birth day I have taken my station where[5] . . .

. . . and from thence look out at the World thro the medium indeed of that love which procures us the refuge, but I hope in a seperation from its spirit forever.

pray for me my true friend that I may keep the station—Mr. Dubourg told me to take St Augustin for the daily companion of my pilgrimage—little thinking how familiarized my soul is to the instruction—which however was most grateful—

4.53 To Cecilia Seton

Monday morning [September 28, 1807]

Your own dear Sister took you with her—presented all your wants and dear wishes. Precious darling Child will go to the little Island one

---

[2]There was a long history of discord between the clergy and lay trustees at St. Peter's.

[3]Joanna Barry was still lamenting the departure of Rev. Michael Hurley.

[4]In 1802 Rev. John Henry Hobart had given Elizabeth his personal copy of *A Commentary on the Book of Psalms* by the Anglican bishop George Horne (Philadelphia: William Young, 1792). Elizabeth later gave it to Rev. Simon Gabriel Bruté, S.S., with her extensive marginal notes. It is in the collection of the Old Cathedral Library, Vincennes, Indiana.

[5]The next one and a half lines are blank.

of thes[e] days—lost Vespers and Benediction—at Sister Post—all sick—My whole Soul prays for you and loves you too much MEAS. J.O.

to morrow Ann and I (Oh that I could say you too) go to Him at 7—to commemorate and honor St. M.[1] and all Angels—

4.54 To Eliza Sadler

October 6th 1807

My dearest Eliza—

a procession of interruptions in the usual routine occasioned by the illness of my Anna, Sister P[ost] and finally a tedious ague in my face has hindered the little word of Remembrance and affection from being prepared. Sister has lost again;[1] moving is fatal to her She hastened from the country to change the air for poor Helen[2] who has been reduced to a shadow by fever ague—but is recovering fast since she has been in Town—Sister was so ill I stayed several nights and days by her bed side.

—Well dearest—so we go—the wheel goes round—precious inestimable privilege,—may [we look] up all the while—

I have Breakfasted sometimes in Courtland Street[3] since you are gone—it is said you have been twice spoken at sea, but Craigé[4] does not seem to give much credit to it. He is so much as usual that my heart achs only to look at his dejected sorrowful countenance never changing from its fixed expression—perhaps it is more so to me who must unavoidably occasion him painful remembrances—He says he is

---

[1] The feast of St. Michael the Archangel, patron of Rev. Michael Hurley, O.S.A., was September 29.

4.54 ASJPH 1-3-3-7:32

[1] Possibly Mary Bayley Post had a miscarriage.

[2] Helen Bayley Craig, Elizabeth's half-sister

[3] The Sadlers lived on Cortland Street. One of Eliza Craig Sadler's brothers, William or Samuel, may have lived there also.

[4] William Craig, Elizabeth's brother-in-law, had been married to Charlotte Amelia Bayley (Emma), who died in July 1805.

quite well—Sam Rod and J.[5] look cheerful and give me a very kind welcome to the hot rolls—Sam [unclear] out gravity for the little plate of tongue and—all agree that I make better tea than the dear being whose place I fill—

Where are you Eliza? When you were surrounded by your Books flowers and retirement at Home tho' many cares were mixed with them, the necessity that separated me from you and seemed almost habitual was considered among the privations of my fate—since I no longer know you are well and that I may see you at any time I would follow you w[h]ere ever you go, and wish to know all those pains or consolations which neither my solicitude could lessen or affection increase—

Such is the provision dear bountiful nature has [page torn] for the changes of our state, bringing the [page torn] perfect accord out of the contradictions of so inconsistent a temperament as mine—not yours my friend, it has as I believe been long beyond the influence of this ill shaped spirit if it was ever in any degree subject to it in earlier years—from my youth upwards what have I been to God and man this question tho' so familiarized—always starts a tear—Yet perhaps without the pleading of self-love it may be admitted that circumstances have been always against me in the effort to acquire that Charity, order and harmony of conduct which is assuredly the garb of Virtue and perfection of the Christian character—My Director[6] always tells me "begin again to day, what is lost must not cause dejection, what you have gained will be lost if you do not begin again as if nothing had been done"—twice a week I get this lesson in some shape or other, and with so many helps I may hope to get at least up part of the mountain—but oh dear Eliza how weak the poor Soul and Body are when strength is called for—how courageous and assured when suffered to rest—Patience Patience Patience—this is a stolen subject not intended.

Not one word of our Revered Friend[7]—Am going to write and will give you half a side—

---

[5]Possibly Samuel Craig and children or servants

[6]Rev. Louis Sibourd

[7]Rev. John Tisserant

All is well I do not know anything changed since you are gone—the dear ones are well—Kit is rosy but excessively thin if my spirit could advance as fast as dear Anna's you would be astonished on your return—the oak and vine how different—The dear Barrys[8] are still deeper in Affliction—his strength lessens daily—

—McV.s still out of Town—Mrs. Hart also[9]—little Cilia as you left her—they are looking for a house in town. James[10] walked in my room the other morning, took me in his arms like one of the children, asked some questions about a bundle at the custom House, and seemed to have met me every day of the twelve months I have not seen him—I like that—so all the world should do—dear dear Eliza farewell always

your EASeton

4.55 Spiritual Journal to Cecilia Seton

August 10 to October 16, 1807

This[1] first time to [page torn] every affection of the [page torn] for Him who justly claims [page torn] Unusual sweetness and consolation at Communion the more sensibly felt, because ungrateful self indulgence kept me absent the two former appointed days—renewed the entire sacrifice fervently yielded All and offered every nerve fiber and power of Soul and Body to sickness, Death, or any and every appointment of his blessed Will.

—Passed a day of heavy Penance the last at poor Dués[2]—How is it then O my adored that I am called and so many left—it is not that Thy voice is silent to them, but their hearts sleep—Keep mine Sweet

---

[8] James Barry was seriously ill.

[9] New York acquaintances of both women

[10] James Seton, Elizabeth's brother-in-law, had formerly been estranged because of the conversion of Elizabeth and Cecilia Seton.

4.55 ASJPH 1-3-3-8:145

[1] At this time Elizabeth resumed her practice of keeping a journal. Parts of the corners of pages 1 and 2 have been torn away.

[2] Catherine Dupleix

Mercy ever on the watch let it never know a moments repose but in Thee—turn its dearest joys to sorrows, its fondest hopes to anguish, only fasten it forever unchangably to Thyself—

11th

What are the workings of fancy in sleep,[3] whose secret finger weaves the web—it was but a web—yet I sensibly pressed the Adored Host close to my heart after saving it from the hand of one who rediculed my faith in its Divine essence and whilst I was lost in adoration and love, but much agitated [page torn] smile who first [page torn] (almonds and raisins [of which I am] very fond) in my life [page torn] broke off part of my Treasure which was so mingled with them, I awoke in my anxious endeavours to separate them—human affections how difficult to separate—

12th

A night of Watching and fever, with many "Glorias"[4]—how joyfully Faith triumphs—it is in the hour of pain and affliction it feels its Joy—while working the passage how sweet to see him always before beckoning the harrassed Soul to bear up its wing and press forward.

13th

pain and Resignation instead of the Treasure this day—but He is then most near—while Weeping under his Cross we are there content to stay

14th

The Soul with the Body is overpowered, the one wants rest the other sleeps when it should wake—Can it be indifferent that it will not be to-morrow under the Banner of its Blessed Mother while so many Faithful ones are offering up their vows—Divine Communion which neither absence nor Death (except the eternal) can destroy, the bond of Faith and Charity uniting All—

---

[3]Cf. 4.47 for another reference to this dream.

[4]A traditional Christian prayer of praise to the Trinity

15th

Assumption—Blessed Lord grant me that Humility and Love which has crowned her for Eternity—happy happy Blessed Mother, You are reunited to Him whose absence was your desolation—pity me—pray for me it is my sweet consolation to think you are pleading for the wretched poor banished Wanderer—

16th

The first Sunday of exile from his Tabernacle since He placed me two miles from it[5]—all the dear ones sick—lead in all my limbs—sweetness and inexpressible tenderness in the heart (Thomas of Jesus, Sufferings of Christ) and litanies, Rosaries and prayers for the Blessed Sacrifice in which all are offered absent and present "that it may obtain for them Eternal Life" fill up the hours of absence if it can be absence while He is ever present.

every Body out—doors and windows all shut—all day with the dear ones and Peace . . .

17th

Offered up my own Kate[6] with my whole soul—could I be unwilling to see her an Angel—and know that she would never be so wretched as to offend Him—precious child your Mother's doating heart begs him to cast you down as the early Blossom rather than live to once offend Him—what is Sorrow what is death they are but Sounds when at Peace with Jesus—Sorrow and death?—their real sense is the loss of his dear Love.

18th

pain and debility—irritability—poor poor Mortality—Sin and death spread the snare—who shall deliver the things of Heaven, Earth and Hell shall bow to His adored Name—He will deliver again the willing offering is renewed. All the combination of this poor Body so fitted for pain this feeble heart awakes to sense of keenest sufferings the Soul which turns to thee in anguish—Blessed Lord what is pain what is

---

[5]Elizabeth had moved farther away from St. Peter's Church where the Blessed Sacrament was reserved in the tabernacle.

[6]Catherine Seton, Elizabeth's daughter, who was sick

anguish while it lies at your feet dear feet can there then be actual sorrow in that soul which can confidently say "my Lord and my God"[7]—

19th

At Peace—Beloved Cicil how the very soul longs for you—But how earnestly I have often begged Him to turn my most innocent sweets to Bitters if it would bring me nearer to Him—this day I can lay my hand on my heart and say I am alone with God

the innocent ones are playing in a corner Rebecca appealed to me with most powerful eloquence hands and eyes all in motion, "did I not tell Amelia right, if we have the Crown of thorns in this world will we not have the roses in the next"—dear love if at 5 years you know this truth that is, the lesson of the Cross, what may not an experience of their precious thorns produce in you.

20th

Once more disappointed in the hope of going to Him. a strong apprehension of some serious complaint in my dear Kate—yet what can separate US—her soul is spotless—there is the point—could mine, sin sick and defiled, hope to follow hers—Jesus, Jesus adored Physician—renew that poor poor Soul—It must become a little child or it cannot enter Thy kingdom[8]—beloved Kate I will take you then for my pattern and try to please Him as you to please me—to grieve with the like tenderness when I displease Him, to obey, and mind his voice as you do mine—to do my work as neatly and exactly as you do yours, grieve to lose sight of him a moment, fly with joy to meet him, fear he should go and leave me even when I sleep—this is the lesson of love you set me, and when I have seemed to be angry, without petulance or obstinacy you silently and steadily try to accomplish my wish, I will say dearest Lord give me grace to copy well this lovely image of my duty to Thee—

23rd

"In the multitude of Thy Mercies I have again entered Thy house—and worshipped in Thy Holy Temple" [9]—

---

[7] John 20:28
[8] Cf. Mark 10:15.
[9] Ps. 5:8

Recieved the Longing Desire of my soul—Merciful Lord what a
Privilege—and my dearest Anna too—the bonds of Nature and Grace
all twined together The Parent offers the Child, the Child the Parent
and both are United in the source of their Being—and rest together on
Redeeming Love.—May we never never leave the sheltering wing but
dwelling now under the Shadow of His Cross we will chearfully
gather the thorns which will be turned hereafter into a joyful crown—

28th August [Feast of] Saint Augustine—

and my happy Birth day the first in course of thirty three years in
which the Soul has sincerely rejoiced that it exists for Immortality.—When Hope has ventured to step forward she has never been
separate from fears, apprehension, sighs, and the tremblings of Nature—to day She exalting exclaims "Thou has drawn me from the
mire and clay and set me upon a Rock. Thou hast put a new song in my
mouth, the song of salvation to my God."[10] O order my goings in Thy
way that my footsteps slip not.

If the empty vessel is best fitted for thy Grace, O my divine Redeemer, what did you find to obstruct your entrance in my free heart
set free in the Liberty of your Children.[11]—this day you have entered
in, and having sent before thy own Benediction, it was waiting for its
dear Master with many sighs of longing desire—did any thing else
possess it—not even a remnant of Human Affection, not a thought or a
wish which did not speak Jesus—

and now—the sacrifice of all again renewed—it awaits thy will in
certain Hope—pressing forward to eternity—reaching for the things
before looking steadfastly upwards—how sure how real its happiness—quiet and resigned in affliction—it finds no bitterness in Sorrow unmixed with Sin—Keep me only from its Sorrows dearest Lord,
and for every other Glory to Thee forever—

Having walked with my Blessed Patron[12] in the paths of Sin and
darkness and been brought like Him to Light and Liberty—guide me
also with thy Almighty hand thro' the dangers of my pilgrimage and

---

[10]Ps. 40:2-3
[11]Rom. 8:21
[12]St. Augustine

tho' I have not strength to reach the heights of his Glory, or even to climb the lowest steps Grant that thro' His merits whose Glory is the Blessedness of the least and the greatest that I may be associated with them who have left us here the Te Deum of Joy,[13] and be permitted to join that which they will resound to thee through Eternity—

September 8th . . . Nativity of B[lessed] V[irgin] M[ary]

passed in the bed not without many sighs and aspirations to Her whose pattern has been so often set before me—her Humble, Meek and Faithful heart—will it ever be, can I now so contrary even approach to the smallest resemblance—My God, my God, my God have Mercy—

10th

celebrated the dear Festival with my whole Soul—and that of St. Nicholas[14]—(Augustine order) Merciful Lord give me the spirit of Penance, Humility, and Meekness which crowned him even while on earth, and gave him the appearance of a Seraph, make my poor soul a sharer in his Merits and number me among the family of my Blessed Patron—thro' Him, who redeemed me and lifts the lowest from the dust.

Exaltation of + 14th The heart down—discouraged at the constant failure in good resolutions—so soon disturbed by trifles—so little Interior Recollection—and forgetfulness of his constant presence the reproaches of disobedience to the little ones much more applicable to myself—

So many Communions and confessions with so little fruit often suggest the idea of lessening them—to fly from the fountain while in danger of dying with thirst. but in a moment he lifts up the Soul from the dust

16th

at the Tribunal of Reconciliation received strength Father S[ibourd] assured the feeble Soul and warned warned it of the Lecherous Fiend who would tempt the little Child from the arms of its

---

[14]St. Nicholas of Tolantino (1245-1305), an eloquent Augustinian

Mother—Dear Dear adored Redeemer as the suffering disobedient and ungrateful child, but wretched and lost without your reviving and pitying tenderness and Pardon—I have lain and still remain at your Sacred feet—the abundance of tears there shed will, mixed with your precious blood, feed and nourish the Soul that faints and pants for deliverance from its chains—and hopes in your Mercy alone—

My neighbor Mrs. P has given me a journal of the illness and death of her Niece the unfortunate Mrs. W—it concludes with their parting scene in which the dying woman expresses the utmost despair, and declares her mind in doubts of her Salvation had sought for consolation in the writings of Voltaire and Rousseau[15] which had been her ruin, and warned all her friends to beware of them—

My Merciful Saviour I too have felt their fatal Influence and once they composed my Sunday devotion—dazzled by the glare of seductive eloquence how many nights of repose and days of deceitful pleasure have I passed in the charm of their deceptions—

Mrs. W_ is gone—hopeless and convinced there is no mercy for her—I remain the daily subject of that boundless Mercy—the mists of Night and darkness dispersed, and if even at the Eleventh hour, Yet permitted to share in the Vineyard and gather the fruits of Eternal Life[16]—glory glory glory forever forever and forever—

Clouds and darkness surround him[17]—but—"Watch, Watch my Soul"—in the great harvest Mrs. W. may be gathered—thyself bound among the tares those who have known his will and done it not, shall have many stripes.[18]

18th St. Thomas Villanova +—Augustinian order

Remember my Soul this Blessed day—the head cleaving to the pillow—the slothful heart asleep, how unwillingly you were roused to go to your Lord—who has so often overflowed the cup of Blessing at the very moment of Insensibility and ingratitude—so this day—when he was approached more as a Slave goes to regular duty than the

---

[15]Voltaire (1694-1778) and Rousseau were leading French writers of the Enlightenment. Cf. references to Rousseau in several 1799 letters of Elizabeth to Eliza Sadler.

[16]Matt. 20:1-16

[17]Cf. Ps. 97:2 and Mark 14:34.

[18]Cf. Matt. 13:30.

perishing wretch to its deliverer—how sweet how mercyful was the reception he gave—how bountiful and abundant thy portion—what a reproof to the Soul that loves Thee Adored Master—and how mercifully too it was awakened to recieve it—what was its reply—it can only be understood by the unutterable Love and intelligence of a spirit to its Creator—Redeemer—God, but it must remember the Ardour with which the offering was renewed of all all for the attainment of Thy dear Love—imagining the corrupted heart in Thy hand, it begged Thee with all its strength to cut, pare, and remove from it, (whatever anguish it must undergo) whatever prevented the entrance of Thy Love—again it repeats the supplication, and begs it as Thy greatest mercy—cut to the center, tear up every root, let it bleed, let it suffer any thing, every thing, only fit it for Thyself, place only Thy Love there, and let Humility keep centinal and what shall I fear—what is Peace, Sorrow, Poverty, Reproach—Blessed Lord they all were once thy inmates, thy chosen companions, and can I reject them as enemies and fly from the friends you send to bring me to your Kingdom—Lord I am dust—in sweetest pitying Mercy scourge me, compel my coward feeble Spirit, fill it with that fire which consumed the Blessed Saint (this day Commemorated) when he cryed out for thy Love declaring that all torments and fatigues should joyfully be borne to obtain it—unite my unworthy soul to his earnest intreaty. "O omnipotent Jesus give me what thyself commandest—for tho' to Love Thee be of all things most sweet Yet it is above the reach and Strength of Nature but I am inexcusable if I do not love Thee for Thou grantest thy Love to all who desire or ask it.—I cannot see without Light, yet if I shut my eyes to the noon day light—the fault is not in the sun but in me"

29th [Feast of] St. Michael—

The sigh of the wretched hails you Glorious Friend—My Soul claims Your patronage by its fervent affection, and confidence in your protection against its Enemy

—how he triumphs in that poor soul—poor poor soul in the hour of peace and serenity, how confidently you asserted your fidelity, how sincerely embraced pain and suffering in anticipation and now that only one finger of His hand, whose whole weight you deserved, is laid on you, recollection is lost—nature struggles—you sink—sorrow overpowers and pain takes you captive—Oh my Soul!

Who shall deliver—My Jesus Arise! and let thy enemies be scattered[19]—shelter my sinking spirit under his banner who continually exclaims "Who is like God"[20]

[Feast of] St Therese [of Avila] 15th October

Holy Mother you called yourself a Sinner—the worst of Sinners—What then am I—the sins of your whole Life would be balanced by the sum of any one of my days—

My Almighty God! what then am I—and if in the short and feeble sight of mortality so deeply dyed—what then in the searching light of Thy truth and Justice—My Saviour My Jesus hide me—Shelter me, shelter the shuddering trembling Soul that lays itself in thy hand—Yes again I begin—nothing is done—Oh give me that clean heart—give me thy Spirit—Oh my God how short may be my time help me, draw me on—how much of my day is past I know not—save me let not the night overtake—

Blessed saints of God pray for the wandering weary soul who has staid so far behind—You have reached the Summit—pray for me.

16th

There is a Mystery the greatest of all mysteries—not that my adored Lord is in the Blessed Sacrament of the Altar—His word has said it—and what so simple as to take that Word which is the Truth itself—But that Souls of his own creation whom he gave his Life to save—who are endowed with his choicest gifts in all things else—should remain Blind, insensible, and deprived of that light without which every other blessing is unavailing!—and that the ungrateful, stupid, faithless being to whom He has given the Free, the Bounteous heavenly gift shall approach his true and Holy Sanctuary, taste the sweetness of his presence, feed on the Bread of Angels—the Lord of Glory united to the very essence of its Being and become a part of itself, yet still remain a groveler in the Earth!—is my poor poor

---

[19] Ps. 68
[20] Ps. 113:5. The meaning of "Michael" is "who is like God."

Soul is what we too will experience while lost in wonder of his for-
bearing Mercy and still more wondring at our own misery in the very
center of Blessedness—Jesus then is there we can go, recieve Him, he
is our own—were we to pause and think of this thro' Eternity, yet we
can only realize it by his conviction— that he is there (Oh heavenly
theme!) is as certainly true as that Bread naturally taken removes my
hunger—so this Bread of Angels removes my pain, my cares, warms,
cheers, sooths, contents and renews my whole being—Merciful God
and I do possess you, Kindest tenderest dearest Friend, every Affection of my Nature absorbed in you still is active, nay perfected in their
operations thro' your refining love.—hush my Soul—we cannot
speak it—tongues of Angels could not express our Treasure of Peace
and contentment in Him—let us always wisper his Name of Love as
the antidote to all all the discord that surrounds us—we cannot say the
rest the Harmony of Heaven begins to us while silent from all the
World we again and again repeat it—Jesus Jesus Jesus Jesus Jesus

and how many say the Adored Name looking beyond him while
looking for him—deny him on his Altar—who then is the Author of
the Religion I adore?—is man then wiser in his inventions than Eternal Wisdom—did he contrive a method to relieve the wretched, to
support the feeble, to recall the sinner and secure the inconstant
Which of us having once tasted how sweet the Lord is on his holy Altar and in his true Sanctuary, who finding at that Altar our nourishment of soul and strength to labour our propitiation, thanksgiving,
Hope and refuge can think with sorrow and anguish of heart of the naked, unsubstantial, comfortless worship they partake of who know not
the treasure of Our Faith—theirs founded on Words of which they
take the Shadow While we enjoy the adored Substance in the center of
our Souls, theirs void, cheerless, in comparison of the Bliss of Our
daily offering where Jesus pleads for us.

Oh my Soul when our corrupted Nature overpowers, when we are
sick of ourselves, weakened on All sides, discouraged with repeated re-
lapses, wearied with Sin and Sorrow, we gently, sweetly, lay the whole
account at his feet, reconciled and encouraged by his appointed representative,[21] yet trembling and conscious of our imperfect dispositions,

---

[21]The priest, acting in his role as confessor

we draw near the sacred fountain—securely the expanded heart recieves its longing desire, then wrapt in his Love, covered with his Righteousness we are no longer the Same, Adoration Thanksgiving love Joy Peace contentment—unutterable Mercy— take this from me—tho' now the happiest of poor and banished sinners—then most most wretched desolate—what would be my refuge—Jesus is every Where, in the very air I breathe—Yes every where—but in his Sacrament of the Altar as present actually and really as my Soul within my Body in his sacrifice daily offered, as really as once offered on the Cross—Merciful Saviour can there be any comparison to this Blessedness—could any other plan satisfy offended Justice, form an Acceptable oblation to thy Eternal Father, or reconcile us to Thyself?

adored Lord, increase my Faith—perfect it—crown it, Thy Own, thy choicest, dearest Gift, having drawn me from the pit and borne me to Thy fold, Keep me in thy sweet pastures—and lead me to Eternal Life Amen Amen Amen

4.56 To Filippo Filicchi

2nd November 1807

My dear Filicchi—

Your letter is indeed a cordial, I often read it to encourage and strengthen me in the disappointment of not being permitted to fulfil the so long anticipated removal of my family to Canada—which plan originating in the Benevolence and precautions of your Antonio[1] for our wellfare had been long contemplated in my female fancy (which you know must be active) as one of the sweet dispositions of Providence among the many it has effected for us thro' him—but your opinion added to the united sentiments of those persons whose will is my law[2] has banished even the thoughts of it (voluntarily indulged) tho

---

4.56 ASJPH 1-3-3-10:36

[1] Antonio Filicchi, Filippo's brother, supported Elizabeth's dream of moving to Canada.

[2] Her priest advisors were encouraging her to move to Baltimore instead.

naturally they present themselves in every occasion of difficulty so frequent in the particular situation in which we are placed—quite sure I am many would await us there, but they could scarcely be combined of materials so repulsive to my Nature—You will congratulate me for being quite in earnest in seeking "the Pearl"[3] it is best to be obliged to conquer the principle most apt to blind me in my pursuit, and my daily object is to keep close to your first advise (with St. Francis) [de Sales] to take every event gently and quietly, and oppose good nature and cheerfulness to every contradiction, which succeeds so well that now it is an acknowledged opinion that Mrs. William Seton is in a very happy situation and Mr. [John] Wilkes says speaking of his profession "yet Providence does not do so much for Me as for you as it makes you happy and contented in every Situation." Yet—indeed for how can he build who has not the Rock for his foundation[4]—but Mrs. William Seton is obliged to watch every moment to keep up the reality of this appearance, You know Filicchi what it costs to be always humble and satisfied, tho really when this disposition is familiarized it is the true treasure—do do pray continually for that Soul whose salvation has already cost you so much care. While enjoying the greatest happiness on Earth[5] which I obtain sometimes three times a week, (the weather and children sometimes deprive), imagine the effusions of warm and ardent affections at that moment of Grateful Joy and triumph, conscious that nothing on Earth can add or take from this infinite good which supplies the place of all others to the confiding Soul, whose very desolation in human possessions is the best foundation for this unfailing happiness—and then how came this knowledge to my Soul, whose blessed hands guided it to its only Treasure, who encouraged it when sinking and drew it on when affraid of its own Salvation—and my darling children—I teach them to consider you two the Source of all our consolation—They remember Antonio perfectly, but number you among the Beings of another region except Annina who has many

---

[3]Cf. Matt. 13:46.

[4]Cf. Matt. 7:25.

[5]Elizabeth's director allowed her to receive the Eucharist frequently.

remembrances of a gay and merry kind always wishing for a romp with you once more. She is as lively as a Bird and a very good child— Our Honored Bishop Carroll is quite well—and writes the most favourable Account of my Boys—The Mr. Hurley who acknowledges so many obligations to you is making brilliant conversions in Philadelphia[;] a Mr. Cooper[6] of great intellectual attainments waited a few weeks ago on Bishop White[7] and other clergy of note enquiring their reasons of Separation and finding them as they are, was received on the Visitation at St. Augustines Church—he is of family and fortune and therefore makes a great noise as also the conversion of one of their most fashionable women, a Mrs. [Rachel] Montgomery—but many are added from time to time peaceably and without noise—Mr. Hurley says ["] I could not have been a Priest but for Mr. Filicchi, ["] and his talents being a singular acquisition, the Church owes you an extensive blessing—is the Reverend Mr. Plunket[8] still with you I will never forget his Charitable interest for us nor the great kindness of Dr. Tutilli—pray present me to them. You do not say a word of your dear Marias[9] Health—I would write her but have so little to interest her more than that we are well, if she suffered me to recall what I owe to her goodness the theme would be futile indeed, but that a heart like hers never suffers—do remember me to her affectionately—

My gowns are safe received and will serve me several winters—I should never dared have purchased as handsome here but when I simply say Filicchi sent them it is all right—yet it was very wrong to ask for any thing difficult to procure I imagined the materials very common in Leghorn and low priced—you shall not be plagued again so foolishly. pray remember me to your Camilla and the [one entire line

---

[6]Samuel Sutherland Cooper (1769-1843) was a former sea captain and Catholic convert of Rev. Michael Hurley, O.S.A., in Philadelphia. Cooper was ordained a priest in Maryland in 1818. As a seminarian he became a significant benefactor of Elizabeth Seton and the Sisters of Charity through his donation of $6,961 for the purchase of 269 acres of land in Emmitsburg, Maryland, in 1809.

[7]Rev. James White (1748-1836), an Episcopal bishop and spiritual mentor of Rev. John Henry Hobart

[8]Abbé Plunkett was an Irish priest who helped Elizabeth in Leghorn. Dr. Tutilli was the physician who attended William Seton in Leghorn.

[9]Mary Cowper Filicchi, Filippo's wife

is inked out] if it was His Will,—have written Antonio by a former opportunity as it was best not to send both letters in the same Ship.

Always Yours MEASeton

4.57 To Bishop John Carroll

November 13, 1807

Dear and Honored Sir

How much I was delighted once more to see your writing in the hands of dear Mrs. B[arry] is impossible to tell you—from the very bottom of my heart I have prayed constantly for your recovery and in every communion that for his honor and glory you might be restored to us. the dear Beings for whom you beg the choicest favours of Heaven are preparing for them through a thorny path of sorrow indeed, Our poor [James] Barry appears to be going rapidly—the pale and dejected looks of his Angelic Wife and daughter, thin forced smiles and hidden tears is truely a heart rending sight—but that these sorrows are purifying them for the Kingdom of Peace silences all repining.

I must now trouble you on an unworthy subject dear Sir but it is the wish of Mrs. Barry (supposing the case her own) and the express direction of Mr. Sibourg that you should be made acquainted with the immediate situation of myself and children[1]—Your kindest expressions in your most valued favour of May last[2] that you considered yourself in the place of a Parent to us are inexpressibly consoling, and gives me the fullest confidence that you will forgive this additional trouble to your many engagements—Imagining you then in your elbow chair and my poor self at your honored feet repeat to you what I

4.57 ASJPH 1-3-3-1:46

[1]Though aware of Dubourg's proposal to relocate her to Baltimore, Elizabeth was still drawn to her "Canada scheme." Perhaps it seemed a more immediate way to resolve her current difficulties.

[2]Bishop Carroll had written to Elizabeth on May 23, 1807, that, although unfamiliar with the specifics of Dubourg's plan, he fully approved of it because Matignon and Cheverus agreed.

believe you already know that when Mr. [Antonio] Filicchi mentioned his resolution that my Boys should go to Montreal it was considered by us both as also a shelter for my little girls—you know their
situation and danger with respect to their connections—it is useless to
mention it, or my own desire of advancing my own Salvation—The
means of executing this plan amounts to six hundred dollars yearly
which is sure, and I am authorised by subscription obtained by
Filicchi to demand twice that sum. I have also now some hundred dollars in the hands of Mr. Morris—is there not a hope that my talents
such as they are might be useful in the instruction of children and assist our maintenance. I am now very much in advance for our annual
maintenance, my Boarders do not clear the expences by some hundred
dollars and are besides very unfit associates for my Girls—their Parents have found my inability to controul ten Boys from ten to sixteen
years of Age and lament that the advantages of their institution is lost
from the irregularity of their conduct with me therefore my present situation is a matter of favour—the time appointed for the termination of
their school is three years from this month.

The sacrifices I should make in leaving this place are centered in
the dear converted sister who now lives with her Brother[3] and the
other dear girls (though not permitted to see me)—the dear Barrys
who are individually dearer to me than any connection I have. my
friends have so much distrust of my character considering, and justly
that every Action is involved in my religious principles that they
would certainly rather consider it as a relief if they knew I was in a situation conformable to my own Peace—

Filicchis last letter expresses his willingness that my dear Boys
may remain at Georgetown "as long as may be thought advisable" and
your assurances of their wellfare in all respects thro' Mr. Sibourg has
changed all uneasiness with respect to them in thankfulness and
joy,—and if you think best to wave all delicacy with respect to the
Gentlemen who employ me, and not leave my place without their
dismission and make the best of circumstances until some Providential change takes place I shall feel every thing reconciled by your

---

[3]Cecilia Seton, Elizabeth's sister-in-law, was living with her brother James Seton.

decission and in every event be convinced it is the Will of God—if you think the Boys may properly be removed to Montreal and that I may remove with them it will be my greatest security to be authorized by your Judgment and permission which however I shall not mention to any one but Our dear Barrys and those reverend gentlemen who interest themselves in our eternal Welfare—[4]

I am most respectfully dear and honored Sir your Affectionate Child in God

MEASeton[5]

4.58 To Eliza Sadler

November 13th 1807

My dearest Eliza

I remember you said "if only one line" it would be grateful to you—Why cannot I tell you that I have lately seen Craigé[1]—but my sweet Cate has obliged me always to hasten home and to go away late—so that I could not stay till his dinner hour or be early enough for Breakfast—Monday last I called but he was gone—the Woman (housekeeper I believe) said he was quite well.

I have had a sad trial lately from the Parents of my Boys[2] who are quite dissatisfied with my not managing them better, and still leave me in doubt if I am to remain in my present situation or not—at first I was quite apprehensive least I had failed in some duty to them but Mr. Harris[3] assures me I have no blame in the business that can be imputed without great injustice—How earnestly I now look for that guide who would direct so painful a situation—whether to stay (as Mr. [John]

---

[4]Revs. Louis William Dubourg, S.S., Francis Matignon, and John Cheverus
[5]Documents ASJPH 1-3-3-1:47 and 1-3-3-1:48 are drafts of this letter.
4.58 ASJPH 1-3-3-7:33
[1]William Craig, Eliza Craig Sadler's brother
[2]Her boarders
[3]Rev. William Harris, the schoolmaster

Wilkes explicitly said the advantages of their being with Mr. Harris is lost by their disadvantages with me and indeed the whole attention of my mind is always directed to giving them a cheerful and comfortable Home)—or depart—where—how—when—if He was here how soon it might be decided—Patience.

How goes your Journey dearest—it is smiling—gloomy?—tolerable?—how anxiously I await the arrival of Duplex.[4] Not a word from you yet [nor] probably will be until his return—[the] suggestion that Dué will return with him only impresses not that I even expect her until reflection on the improbability of her quiting her friends chases the delusion—but she is guided by a Vane consequently any thing [may happen]—precious Being who can tell what to wish for her.

Mary is enjoying her vacation—Anna has not seen her—Cate is so constantly suffering that I cannot spare her in Town the dear little being is I believe gradually going as her fever and debility shows something is materially wrong. there is only Peace in the thought to me—if He wills it, she is certainly the dearest of my Treasures, and this is the best proof I can give of my love—is it not so—

Always yours MEAS

I have heard Mrs. [Sarah] Startin lament the want of a board at the meeting of your Orphan Society,[5] she began her complaint "Mrs. Sadler is gone"—she has herself purposed a Voyage to escape the winter and recover from complaint in her breast she is no longer a manager for the poor Widows—but there is no perceptable change in her health—Little Beck is resting and lovely as perfect health and sweetness can be and calls her clasping her little Arms round her neck with kisses—O wonderful Providence—it walks a[lways] after her by her finger repeating Mamma—I always wish to contemplate them for an hour if possible—

---

[4]Captain George Dupleix and his wife, Catherine
[5]Both Sarah Startin and Eliza Craig Sadler were members of the Society for the Relief of Poor Widows with Small Children, as Elizabeth had been prior to her voyage to Italy.

There is now a prospect that my Angelic friend Ann Barry will go very soon after her Father—Merciful God. wonderful indeed it is a scene of Mute Affliction—Eliza Eliza dear Farewell

4.59 To Bishop John Carroll

Sunday Evening 22d November 1807

Dear and honoured Sir

Mrs. [Joanna] Barry this morning expressed a wish that I would write to you on a Subject which it is scarcely possible she can herself dwell on at this moment—the most painful and disturbing that can be concieved. The best most amiable and excellent of Daughters [Ann] has been within a few weeks a subject of even more solicitude than her Father. a lingering cough the remains of Influenza occasioned the first alarm, a sore throat added confined her to the house, Dr. McNeville did not think it dangerous, but Dr. Servantes who attended her Father intreated her dear Mother to attend immediately to the state of her health. many of her acquaintance called to recommend Dr. Bergerre who is very much celebrated and has been very successful in similar cases—He has declared her situation critical, and Mrs. Barry is convinced from their combined opionions that they think Ann is in a rapid decay and in more immediate danger than her Father—the effect of this You, dear Sir, can too well judge of—a voyage is desired—but [James] Barry cannot bear even to go in a carriage with the windows closed—this morning after Sermon dear Ann and her Parents brought me home in a carriage quite shut, he had two great coats (altho the day was quite mild) yet was chilly and evidently uncomfortable—Ann seemed easy during her ride, is unusually cheerful, and as you know assiduously hides her pains but her altered countenance and very Smiles and unusual exertions for conversation betrays her. She is on milk diet (which she has a great aversion to) but has totally lost all Appetite—

The Pattern of Women looks at one and the other covering the anguish of her Souls by every cheerful exertion that is possible to human nature. She commands the Reverence of a Superior Being, and did she not evidence the strength from on High in all and every Action I should doubt my own senses when I look at her. how pure how Acceptable must be the offering of both Mother and child. She earnestly desires you should immediately know these particulars that Ann may have an added portion of your Prayers.

how sad is this task—a person is waiting while I write to take my letter to Town—some excuse I hope for its hurried expression—besides that of an aching head and heart for the Sorrows of these dear beings, particularly as both Mother and Daughter suffer me to share what each would hide from the other, are a renewal of many that are past to Me. but sweetly gently every sigh is hushed in the certainty that All is leading upwards—

with every affectionate sentiment of Reverence and Respect I am dear Sir

Your MEASeton.

4.60 To Julia Scott

29 November 1807

My dearest Julia—

From some mistake of Brother P[ost] I did not recieve your letter until this Morning—The tenderness and affection it repeats is most consoling and grateful, and effectually reproves my Silence tho really it would have been most difficult to express my heart within the last three months, and more difficult to supress to you its inquietude and embarrassment. but some how or some how (as Betty B[1] used to say) inquietude knocks long at my door without admittance, or if she

---

4.60 ASJPH 1-3-3-6:68
[1]Herself

surprises me she finds no room for her restless disposition—in other words Dear your friend is so tired she can rest even upon thorns—tired of contradictions most compleatly—this is the Prologue my love, and the comedy is that the Parents of my young Boarders who were ten in number have expressed much dissatisfaction at the Liberty their children enjoy in my Family and have roasted me handsomely for not keeping them in better order—to which civility I could only reply that the business had been misunderstood as I supposed my only responsibility was the care of their cloathing, food, and a comfortable Home—however tho' I tried to laugh it off and pretended not to believe they were in earnest I have lost three, which is a large drawback in my income which at best was three hundred dollars short of my expenditure—but let it go round—I can but decamp you know my incumbrances are not weighty. sometimes the thought of Philadelphia cheers the scene—but at others the whole heart flies upwards and I would not give a sigh for any thing in the interval, and Peace my dear sober friend says we will jog up the hill as quietly as possible and when the flies and musquetoes bite wrap the cloke round and never mind them they can only penetrate the surface—Darling Julia how I wish you would buy such a cloke,[2] it costs a good deal at first but it wears so well and is so comfortable that it is really worth twice the sum, and—but you can imagine its convenience—the only difficulty is that it is not in Fashion, and I know I sometimes look shabby enough in Mine—the little sheet grows short (good Irish) I must leave a large space to thank you for the Interesting particulars of your letter which gives me some actual idea of your dear ones as they are.

8th December—

My friend thinks as usual, and justly too that she has bestowed her affectionate kindness on an unworthy and careless creature—every Morning and every Evening it has been part of the plan to dismiss this shabby little scrawl, and here it still is—stormy weather, wet walking, a stiff neck, work upon work—how sweet it is to hear from yourself that you have an unusual share of health, that vexations at least are not

---

[2]For a time Elizabeth attempted to interest Julia in becoming a Catholic.

increased—you never speak of one person who has the power of diminishing or adding essentially to your comfort if she still resides with you. —how I should delight in passing twenty four hours with you—but—a Prisoner, I sigh—yet in dearest company—my dear ones are at the different ages productive of Hope rather than the anxiety yours must excite[.] Anna is making rapid progress in her music she often plays off simply what I am obliged to study—you talk of taking her from me—dearest friend if it was difficult two years ago—imagine now—softly, softly my heart—hereafter we may wish what now we pronounce impossible My fate Julia is as uncertain as the World we are thrown upon—Patience—look to the clouds—

Your Bills my kindest friend are safe, I am always unwilling to change them, when I do it is for comfort—Three hundred and fifty dollars for this house per annum, three dollars for every load [of] wood put up, four dollars per week for Bread—what an extravagance to meet 13 hundred dollars income—and maintain nine young giants besides our little selves—Patience—if they will but allow Peace, at best it must be such as I used to find in my cabin during a Storm. Adieu adieu adieu May the best of blessings be yours forever MEAS

Stuyvesants lane, Bowery, near St. Marks Church two white houses joined, left hand[3]—children the sign of the dwelling—no number—well dearest are you wiser, how I shall rejoice in that day you give this direction to your coachman—

12th December

Anna an ulcerated sore throat—Kit sick—sweet little self wearied, faint and good for nothing—the little letter remained in the Secretary for want of a carrier to town where I have been only once since I received yours—do not be angry with me indeed you must forgive.

[3]Elizabeth's current address

4.61 To Bishop John Carroll

16th December 1807

Honored and Reverend Sir—

I have received your letter, and offer you many thanks—for two weeks past wet weather and Indisposition has confined me Home intirely or your wish to hear of the Dear Barrys should have been complied with.

—Yesterday I had the consolation of seeing them, not indeed essentially better, but suffering less than usual, [James] Barry has a general swelling of the legs which makes it very difficult for him to move, the skin of them has burst in flakes—but his Physicians still declare it does not threaten immediate dissolution but is the effect of intire debility, and recommends his making an immediate Voyage with Ann who is so unconscious of the intention that she has intreated to be permitted to accompany him, yet offering to remain with Mrs. Howard or who they please rather than cross him in his wish—she has not the least idea that the Voyage would be for her and her dear Mother endeavors to blind her to the situation as much as possible—Mrs. Barry says she has not spirits to write you dear Sir—her mind is harassed every way, her family has been driven from Lisbon, at least had chartered a Vessel to leave it—

Mr. Barry enquired particularly if you had said any thing of your own health in your last letter, but you did not my dear Sir,—may we hope that you are free from the effects of your last illness—

You will have the goodness to excuse this short and incorrect tribute—if any thing new should occur to our most valued friends it shall be immediately communicated

I am your humble servant and affectionately

your MEASeton

Partition Street Tuesday morning Ann has been once more at church

---

1808

4.62 To Bishop John Carroll

3d January 1808

Dear and Honored Sir

My whole family have been sick and myself in bed so that it has not been possible to make you any communication relative to the much loved Barrys—but Mr. Sibourg was so kind as to come with a carriage and take me to them to day. Mr. Barry recieved the last Sacraments on New Years Eve so composed and intirely resigned that he expressed his wish that the next hour might terminate—since then he peaceably awaits his summons and Ann and Mrs. B are shut up in his room kneeling or Reading—they positively refuse every assistance and tho Anns cough and pain in the side continues they are unheeded—

Mrs. Barrys mind is on the very stretch of exertion, the dignity of her Sorrow is supernatural—she dismissed me with carresses which cut me to the soul absolutely forbidding all intrusion—Blessed Woman how glorious may be the reward of so much Virtue—

Dear and Revered Sir I am always

Your humble servant and Affectionate child MEAS.

Monday Evening a messenger from town has just brought word that no particular change has taken place—

4.63 To Julia Scott

January 16th 1808

My dear darling Julia

my heart has flown to your little Bosom a hundred times since this year began, it would wish there to read what perchance may not be written—to see if the sweet Character of Peace and content are plainly inscribed, if the little corner so long occupied by your poor hair brained friend is undisturbed by the bustle and intrusions of the day, for it is at the hours of midnight when see sawing the chair and humming to my poor darlings I have thought of you most. for several weeks an ulcerated sore throat has had possession of us alternately as soon as one recovered another was seized untill it had made the round—but we are all recovered and merry again—as it was an Epidemic we had it all to ourselves, so much the better—

I have met with a very serious loss in the Death of Mr. James Barry Who I believe I told you sought me out with his dear wife and presented themselves intire strangers solely for the love he had had for my Seton[1] a plea which at once opened my whole heart to them and from that hour they have shown me and my darlings the most uniform Unwearied Affection I have ever known except that so precious from my Julia. Miss [Ann] Barry is in a decline and her Mother will take her [on] a Voyage as soon as this cruel embargo is raised. —then—Adieu to every inducement to go to town independant of St. Peters [Church]—

Sister and Helen[2] (who is thought among the sweetest and handsomest girls in N[ew] York) have become voteries of fashion—they are very much in publick and Sister P[ost] makes every sacrifice to make her happy. I know it will please you to know this.

—and your dear I in the corner is not more molested by the Bountiful Gentlemen who have left me and my Young Gentlemen to manage

4.63 ASJPH 1-3-3-6:69

[1]William Magee Seton, Elizabeth's husband
[2]Helen Bayley, Elizabeth's half-sister

each other—how long I know not. Their school Master is much terrified at the idea of War[3] that they have no idea of his remaining if it takes place—are you agitated with the rest of the World on the subject, your last letter expressed some uneasiness—My poor Brother James[4] has once more to begin the world again with his eight children—how the poor Setons are melted down—but he bears it as a man and is universally respected and pitied. Cecilia he says is his greatest comfort, her health is greatly mended—

Will you please my dear Mrs. Glorianna[5] to send me a few lines to let me know that you are well and hope that I'm the same. do do do for pitys sake.

Give John Scott a New Year smack for me and tell him I hope he may live until he is wedded to Wisdom which I believe will require an extension of time quite equal to his wishes—saucy Mrs. Seton remember me to dearest Maria tenderly affectionately and offer Mrs. C[harlotte] the "glowing fervor" of my Bayley-Heart. Bless you forever Your EAS.

My sweet Kit and Rebecca send you messages of love when they find I am writing Aunt Scott. Anna is at James Setons for some days—

4.64 To Cecilia Seton

19th January 1808

My much loved Cecil

I did not think I could have thought of you at the Wilderness[1] more than usual but these two days the picture of your dear circle and my

---

[3]Rev. William Harris was troubled by the continuing European conflicts.

[4]James Seton, Elizabeth's brother-in-law

[5]Affectionate name for Julia Scott. Glorianna is also the name of the Faerie Queen in *The Faerie Queen* by Edmund Spencer. Elizabeth was probably familiar with this famous allegorical epic containing themes related to virtue.

4.64 ASJPH 1-3-3-8:147

[1]James Seton's country place was called "The Wilderness." It was located on a neck of land on the banks of the Hudson River near presentday 43rd Street and 11th Avenue in New York.

three solitary dear ones have made a continual contrast in imagination—could they have been united how sweet it would be—but—

is the Mountain still groaning or the secret in the wind—had some hope of you coming to-day—tomorrow I shall be off, but home at eleven I hope. dear dear dear Cecil *five* times dear.

is Anna[2] a good child—she must be good—I have thought of her without a moments pain tho generally her absence is worse than a blister

4.65 To Cecilia Seton

[February 28, 1808]

At 8 this morning at the Altar with dear A[nn Barry] and her Mother. at ten on Board their vessel received the last Adieus. You dearest was affectionately remembered in them. My eyes smart and heart Achs—yet there is a heavenly Comfort in turning to him at such an hour above all others

—a Treasure from St. M.[1] and the promise of the precious likeness soon.—how are you my own how I would love to lean my wearied head on your dear shoulder. how much more to kneel with you on Sunday.—will it be—dear dear Lord comfort US. is there now any thing so dear to us as hope. heavenly hope, cherish it my darling and it will carry us through triumphant

—do you remember the last chapters of the Spiritual Combat[2] if not let me send it to you.—not a word of Sweet Hatch—perhaps she is at Mary H's[3] do do write much very much

Friday—

---

[2]Anna Maria Seton was visiting Cecilia at James Seton's home.

4.65 ASJPH 1-3-3-8:110

[1]Rev. Michael Hurley, O.S.A., was forwarding a picture of himself at Elizabeth's request.

[2]*Spiritual Combat* by Dom Lawrence Scupoli was a spiritual treatise first published in 1610 and a favorite book of St. Francis de Sales.

[3]Harriet Seton, Elizabeth's sister-in-law, was possibly visiting her sister Mary Seton Hoffman.

You will send little Pages clothes as soon as you can—I often imagine you nursing the poor sick girl—it is trouble sent by Sister but it will be rewarded by Our Jesus—our all—Oh my darling is it possible he loves us and accepts even Our most imperfect actions—do you wish to have the devotions again Mrs. [Joanna] B[arry] has given me hers and you shall have it as long as you wish—

My very heart and Soul longs to see dearest—

forever Yours

4.66 To Bishop John Carroll

Sunday 28th February 1808

Dear Revered Honored Sir,

It will be some consolation to you to know that tho' the dearest and Best of woman is gone,[1] she departed with the exterior of cheerfulness and Hope which even called the Smile and jest from Her Ann, and kept all our tears locked up until we could no longer be seen by them. Since she had written you so lately, no doubt you know more than I can communicate, for I know her strongest tie and only living regret in this country was Yourself—her former friends she rather dreaded than wished to see, but in every anguish of her heart clasping her hands and directing her eyes to Heaven she would say "and O if we were near the Bishop, how different it would be."—tho' Mr. Sibourg was as a Father to them, this was her constant regret. The Pilot brought a most cheerful line from Ann saying she was now in her turn nursing her Mother who was excessively sick, but herself enjoying the brown biscuit and pears—Dr. Bergerre her Physician is pleased that she was not sick at first and is sure she will be when they are further out. but indeed dear Sir her disease appears to be more from the mind than constitution—the morning before she sailed an Apostrophy escaped her

---

4.66 ASJPH 1-3-3-1:51b

[1]Joanna Barry and her daughter Ann had sailed to Madeira.

(tho alone with me) which expressed too much "Well at least there is Peace in the Grave"

Accustomed to continual suppression of feelings so acute as hers must have the worst effect, but as so great a favour as her recovery must come from the Almighty alone—to him alone we look—To speak of my privation is useless [or] of the pang of Nature in looking around this desolated mansion—only the weeping Belone and good good Mrs. Lefever, she is to answer all for the resigning the house and then proceed to Washington—

My dear Sir my weak Mother[s] heart is now longing to see my Boys[2]—and it is some measure necessary as it respects [Antonio] Filicchi and some friends who yet interest themselves in repeated enquiries after them—could I but ascertain if it would be proper they should come to me, a Mr. Barry[3] is to come for some Valuables here and might be prevailed with to take them in charge as he will come about the time of Easter holidays, and Mrs. Lefever would take them back—if they may not come to me, in August Vacation I may go to them. Why trouble you about this—only that you know if it would be proper and would direct their coming if it is so. one word in reply in any communication you make Mr. Sibourg as I know you have so little time for writing would satisfy me what is best—

How much I wish for your blessing and the happiness of seeing you once more I cannot express. I am always With Affectionate Respect and veneration Your child and servant

MEASeton

Mrs Lefever begs to be remembered

---

[2]William and Richard, Elizabeth's sons, were at Georgetown College in Baltimore.
[3]Possibly Robert Barry from Baltimore, a nephew of James and Joanna Barry

4.67 To Julia Scott

March 8 1808

My Friend—my dear dear Julia—

can it be your letter is so long unanswered tho my heart made so warm a reply on its first reception,—and never thinks of you without a thousand emotions of affection, gratitude and tenderest remembrances, and how often these thoughts arise you would scarcely believe from the nature of my Occupations except you could know the force of those affections which so many years have rivetted to you, independent of your unremitted and precious Friendship—let my Julia feel one consolation in the changing scene that surrounds her—You have a friend who would fly to you from any part of the World, leave children every thing, on the smallest intimation she could be useful to You. I would think the distance between us but a speck if I might hold your dear head when it ached or banish one hour of sorrow—that dear all ruling hand which has granted me so many favours will I trust hear my earnest prayer that I may one day be able to prove to you how true, how heart felt my Attachment is—of all the many attachments I have had you are the only one on Earth who my heart turns to in the simple unrepressed warmth of confiding love—every other is shackelled with hesitations, doubts, calculations etc so contradictory to my nature—but what is all the world to one who bears no part in it but the charge of five innocent docile children.

Your Annas progress in Music is uncommon for her age and every new lesson she excells in pictures to me the delight they who are gone would have had in hearing her, and the only check to these regrets is the anticipation of the pleasure She may in a future period afford to my Julia—she is very neat at her needle and pen, and translates French with facility and pleasure, her lessons of geography are limitted to Turner and Morse which is as much as is necessary for a general idea of it—she is fond of Occupation, but like her poor Mother only attached to reading and writing—her strength and health would delight you and that reserved quiet manner the result of natural temper saves her from a thousand difficulties I encountered at her age—yet there never was a wilder romp when she meets her favorite companions her Aunt Celia and Emma Seton (James eldest daughter)

—Sweet Kate who forms every Action and thought from the eyes and words of her Mother is a different disposition, always in earnest, diligent in every thing she thinks may please, every heart leans towards her—mine, too much, because her health is very delicate—how can I write you dearest always of these darlings—who or what else can I speak of—for weeks together I see no one else—the dear interesting family of the Barrys to whom I was indebted for so much comfort and unceasing attention are gone—the Father to Heaven (for he was very very good) the only dear daughter quickly following is now with her excellent Mother on their way to Medeira in hopes of benefit from a Sea Voyage—

Your account of Charlott grieves me—dear amiable Being—may she be happy in life or Death—Harriets[1] fate awakens many melancholy ideas Parental care and love cherishes uncertain Hope indeed—sweet Sister Helen[2] is engaged to marry a Mr. Kerney of independent fortune, which is the only particular I have yet heard of him, nor have I seen him but hope he will supply to her the many ties she has lost, her sweet and interesting manner promises every thing, but Oh dear Julia what a faithless prospect is that she now contemplates—

poor [Colonel] Giles stopped me in the street about five minutes but in that time said a volume about your not being yet married, his surprise that you were not, his doubts if you ever would consent to it etc etc etc etc—which I answered with a positive assurance you never would be - and who gave me this assurance? Well at least it seemed to brighten the poor soul who looks as if he lived in a ditch—his Madame is sick—Unfortunate beings—most truly unfortunate—

how are Marias ideas directed, to the glittering, or solid views of life I think she must have too much discernment to be led by a Meteor

---

[1] Either Elizabeth's sister-in-law or Julia's niece

[2] Helen Bayley, Elizabeth's half-sister. It is not known whether she married Mr. Kerney. She later married Samuel Craig June 1, 1814.

yet at her age we could not even wish her to be correct in her estimate—

dear dear dear Julia let us love while we live at least. a thousand blessings be with you, Remember me to Brother S and dear J[ohn] when you write them and tell dear Charlott I wish my spirit could be infused in some of her remedies and they would soon very soon relieve her—never will I forget the charm of a day I once passed with her in her chamber her tears of pain and smile of affection—gone gone forever—

You find the paper is larger—the note is not changed but carefully put by, destined to fulfil on some future day a fervent wish of my heart—dearest friend how many of its desires you have enabled it to indulge.

always yours most affectionately EASeton
March 20

I have been sick dear friend or this would have been forwarded many days ago.

4.68 To Eliza Sadler

March 20th 1808

Did you dear friend give a moments thought to the effect of your leaving poor little I out of the number of those you remembered in America—that you did not—nor did you know good Mrs. [Sarah] Startin and Mrs. Sarah Hoffman[1] would take me in the number of their Visitations and with solemn interjection condole with me that I had no letter, but this was momentary and the little Lady expatiated so much on your attention in sending the gown and writing to her that I forgave her the first pain—She is now in much better health than when I last wrote you but has always some irritation of the breast. Rebecca[2] is

4.68 ASJPH 1-3-3-7:34

[1]Mary Gillon Hoffman Seton's mother
[2]Rebecca Seton Maitland, who was adopted by Sarah Startin after her mother's death

such a creature as one might expect in a Vision of Fancy but is too sweet to be an object of human Affection, and I believe dear Mrs. S[tartin] would suffer every thing next to a Mother in losing her—but the Darling is the picture of health.

My Cate is "doucement"[3] neither ill nor well, languid, and restless in sleep—I offer her up with an effort of daily resignation which I trust will be accepted, but she is also daily more precious.

8th April 1808

My dear Eliza I have heard that the Packet closes this day and the pen flies to thank you for your two letters which our dear Craige[4] brought me a few days ago—but O how they grieved me in the account of dear dear Dué.[5] Wonderful indeed are her trials precious being—Duplex left us in the full expectation of her meeting him in England—but how will it be possible. All calculations but those of anxiety are silenced for her, and Affection such as we have for her can only show its willingness to share her sufferings if it were permitted. Mr. McVickers told me yesterday he thought that at all events she could not return with Duplex—how anxious I shall be to hear from them.

And you are then really dear Eliza taking a rest from your many cares for how can you be otherways than happy from the sweet picture you drew—Yet the Home you have left must intrude to deprive you of a part. Craige expressed himself to me as if he was only enduring existance and nothing in this world had the power to give more or less.—but you certainly have an influence over his happiness perhaps more than he is sensible of except he was deprived of your society intirely—but you will return—the motive that determines you is certain. He will have told you many things no doubt of dear Helen,[6] most interesting indeed, she has evidenced the most amiable discretion and delicacy of conduct I ever heard of in so young a person—how proud I

---

[3]Gently
[4]William Craig, whose wife, Charlotte Amelia Bayley, had died
[5]Catherine Dupleix
[6]Helen Bayley, Elizabeth's half-sister

should be if my Anna ever imitates it. little Sister admires her as some-one wonderful.

No precious letter from London. it is thought by Mr. Cheverus that the return[7] is more uncertain than ever—I have written a long para-graph for you in my last letter. —All goes the same with me—quiet and regular—the dear ones improve, and are daily more consoling and endearing to poor Mother. I sometimes fear I do not understand Anna sufficiently, but beg Him to direct me who alone can remedy the evil. perhaps we may improve each other in the end—

perhaps my sweet Boys may be in my arms in a few hours Mr. Dubourg[8] from the Baltimore Seminary is to bring them if he could get permission of the President. how my heart beats at the thought. fare-well dear dear Eliza Peace be with you forever always

yours MEASeton

4.69 To Cecilia Seton

[Saturday, March 26, 1808]

My dear Darling—

Your not coming to day was a great disappointment but the reason is so good—Yesterday (the blessed Annunciation) was to me all that Heaven on Earth could give. and to-morrow was arranged to go down at ten with Cate and Rebecca—if I judge you would be willing to be without Sister is it wrong? if you wish her to be with you on account of the tremblings stop an instant as you go down and I will follow you immediately—but be sure not to go without Breakfast—dear Mrs. W. will rejoice to see you—if you can wait you do not know how sweet it is to go after 8 Oclock and then, recieve when all are gone, then also

---

[7]Rev. John Cheverus thought that the return of Rev. John Tisserant to New York was unlikely.
[8]William and Richard did not accompany Rev. Dubourg.
4.69 ASJPH 1-3-3-8:132

Mr. S[ibourd] will surely be alone—this is all supposing I am not with you—dearest—

You are a good child but if we could pass a day or night together I would show you how to be better—tell your own heart continually "pray for poor Sister." how much I wish to write the dear girls a letter—but that must not be—how I love them is known to Him alone—[If you can] stay till 11 tomorrow, or can remain the day how precious it will be—you might beg it as a favour—

forever ever Your MEAS
Friday 4 Oclock—[1]

do not give the inclosed, only show them and kiss the dear ones for me—how I rejoice darling Nick is better.

4.70 To Cecilia Seton

Impromtu [after April 17, 1808][1]

On hearing the Rev. Dubourgh's sermon on the Resurrection, on Easter Sunday at St. Peter's Church[2]—

*"He is risen from the dead."[3]
The great Dubourgh exclaims
in sounds seraphic and in holy strains!—
"The Saviour is risen—"
Dare infidels deny,
The power omnipotent of him on high,
Go man of God—
To all the world proclaim—*

---

[1]It appears she wrote this note Saturday, March 26, not Friday, because March 25 was a Friday in 1808.

4.70 ASJPH 1-3-3-8:156

[1]Easter Sunday was April 17 in 1808.

[2]Rev. Louis William Dubourg, S.S., had come to New York to help with Holy Week and Easter services.

[3]Matt. 28:7

The splendid glory of his act and name,
Apostle like thou'rt gifted from above
and Christians hail thee as the coming dove

4.71 Draft to Mrs. Hill of Philadelphia

19th April 1808—

It is not possible My dear Mrs. Hill[1] to convey to you the least idea of the sensations which crowded round my heart when Mrs. [Sarah] Startin silently put your letter in my hand this morning—not to be remembered in it, or to be kindly remembered, how could I bear either—strange inconsistency of human nature, that I should quietly resign your esteem, suffer you to think me deluded, perverted—and offering the sacrifice in confidence that the Divine Mercy would support me through that and the many others which are daily required without even an attempt to vindicate either my motives or principles—yet to be no longer remembered by you with kindness would have caused a pain of real anguish—for the time when once you promised that whatever was the distance of the head, still the heart should be ever near is often recurred to with delight, and your last endearing expressions when we parted in Mr. H's[2] hall gave me the fullest confidence that you were (not as the world) my friend. Sweetly the sentence appropriated for me in Mrs. S[tartin's] letter enlivened that confidence—how little do I deserve such kindness—dear and amiable friend—O that it was in my power to convince you of my sense of it. the letter you speak of as unanswered would have recieved an immediate reply but for the peculiarity of my situation which affords very little time indeed for writing or at least for epistolary writing and some correspondants of absolute necessity fill the few hours of the week or month often with a pain and weakness which converts the employment into an absolute punishment and

---

4.71 ASJPH 1-3-3-7:75

[1]Mrs. Hill, apparently a friend of Rev. John Henry Hobart, must have known Elizabeth before her conversion to Catholicism. The tone of the letter suggests that Mrs. Hill disapproved of Elizabeth's conversion.

[2]Rev. John Henry Hobart

is always stolen from the hour of rest—yet should your letter have been answered, but from day to day deferring sickness of myself or family often intervening—it was left intirely.

Your Health then still remains imperfect and you speak of a Suffering which I have always heard is the most painful in Nature. O that I could hold your head, and exchange the look of love and sorrow with you dear friend but all must be submitted—our dear Mrs. Startin will recieve a consolation denied to me—She hopes to see you soon and tho' she is now very much weakened and quite a sufferer, I cannot help hoping that a jaunt to you would soon restore her—her sweet little angel you will doat on—My darlings are a treasure indeed—their dispositions are most promising, and their improvements more than even a Mothers Hope—Anna is my companion, friend and diligent assistant—little Kitty claims more affection than should be given to Earthly mold, and is always very delicate in her health—Rebecca is Health and Life itself—My William and Richard have many encomiums for their amiable and docile attention to their studies in which they have progressed beyond any boys of their age in the College.

—Your tender affectionate nature is interested for us all, and therefore this detail, which would be triffling to another—recieve in its intention this tribute of affection and overlook its inaccurate and hasty performance—and believe me with earnest prayers for your happiness to Him we best love

Yours truly EASeton

4.72 To Bishop John Carroll

19th April 1808

Dear dear and Honored Sir,

Your letter by Mr. Dubourg[1] contained every consolation in itself—that you should with even Parental indulgence interest yourself

---

4.72 ASJPH 1-3-3-1:52

[1]Rev. Louis William Dubourg, S.S., had come to New York from Baltimore.

(and at a moment when you were pressed by so many demands) even in our very wishes is an additional proof of that affectionate regard for us which is indeed the Pride of my heart—yet little did I expect, or intend to give you so much trouble, Nature certainly had blinded reason or the request would not have been so earnestly made, as it is denied so justly I hope it is to prove the means of my making a visit to our much loved Mrs.[Joanna] Barry in case she should return to Washington where in every case it is most probable she will go if she survives this last dreadful trial—How well you know the heart of beloved Ann [Barry], which she has often declared was as free as an Infants—but the sorrow to which I alluded in the sentence that excited attention was that continual and most painful supression of her feelings which forced them back upon her heart with redoubled weight. She particularly mentioned some instances at the time of her Fathers Death which had nearly deprived her of her senses, in one she did actually faint for a long while, and that Virtuous Sacrifice to each others feelings has been I believe more injurious to both the Mother and Daughter than any excess of bodily pain could be. but—what can be said of two such perfect Beings—no doubt their reward will be infinite—their loss to us is inexpressible the lustre of their example will not easily be supplied, indeed it must be so in whatever place they may go—for my dear ones and self their absence is a desolation—Oh the sweet the precious hours that dear family bestowed on us.—the subject is too much Yet I must tell you good Mrs. Lefever is well and at the house of the worthy Mr. Idley whose attachment to the dear Barrys likewise is extreme—

When shall I again recieve your Blessing and present once more my darlings to you dear Sir, If so great a favour is ever granted it will be most precious—

With all the affection of my heart I am Honored and dear Sir, your child and humble servant

MEASeton

4.73 To Julia Scott

April 25th 1808

How well you know the heart of your own friend my Julia when you bade me pause and ponder on the flattering question it proposed—you find how patiently I have waited the discreet moment but I assure you not from any hesitation in replying to it—one of Brothers Children, a piece of himself, his darling, given to my arms and heart[1]—Oh the crazy brain turns at the thought—but my dearest, my dwelling of 350 dollars rent is exchanged for one of 150,[2] which tho' very convenient and in the street on a line with the one we are in yet obliges me to contract my personal accommodation and we are five in a room and closet, which might be disagreeable to you in placing the darling

—the Boys who remain with me are only five—they leave me as they prepare for College, and my means is much deminished yet as they never afforded me any other advantage than daily Bread neither paying house rent nor fuel I have not much to regret—and so sweet is the Providence that overrules us, at this very moment of solicitude for our destination when the present means fails Mr. Dubourg[3] the President of St. Marys College in Baltimore to whom I communicated my delemma has offered to give me a formal grant of a lot of ground situated close to the College which is out of the town and in a very healthy situation and procure me immediately the charge of a half dozen girls and as many more as I can manage, added to this he will take my boys in the College, and the intire charge of them for a very small consideration in order that [Antonio] Filicchi's money may assist me in another way—much as this offer delighted me I urged my want of talents etc, he assures me that Madame La Comb[4] whom he established in a

---

4.73 ASJPH 1-3-3-6:71

[1]Apparently Julia proposed to send one of Samuel Sitgreaves' children to board with Elizabeth.

[2]Elizabeth had moved or was about to move to a smaller and less expensive house on the same street.

[3]Rev. Louis William Dubourg, S.S., had first broached this subject to Elizabeth in a general way in November 1806. It was not until April 1808 that Dubourg presented this concrete plan involving Baltimore.

[4]A woman who ran a school for girls in Baltimore

much more unfavourable footing has now more than one hundred young persons in charge of the first families

—do you shake your dear head, or is the smile of pleasure predominant—how much I wish to know. do write me as soon as you can, as yet I have not consulted my Brother P[ost] or Mr.[John] Wilkes, but I am sure they foresee the burthen We shall be to them when this present living is over, and will readily approve—yet much must depend on procuring if possible the money my Uncle [Dr. John] Charlton[5] left me that a house may be provided on my lot dearest, and the affair so managed that it may be secured to the children—unfortunately I did no[t] go at the proper moment and can neither see my Brother nor Mr. Wilk[e]s but next week we must conclude on something—

Filicchi left me an unlimited credit on John Murrey and Son but it will not do to abuse their kindness, the four hundred dollars per annum is already a great deal. We will see—it will all be right, perhaps God may deny my wish of being so near my darling Boys for some good purpose—but indeed the thought of joining them gives a strength and courage to my soul which bears it over every impediment.

And now to speak of your dearest self there is a passage of your letter which would excite the attention of a heart much less attached to you than mine "Poor girl she knows not how soon etc"—You have told me a War would derange your plans it is true, but surely your melancholy expression indicates more than a mere lessening of property which as it would affect the general state of affairs as much as your own would never deprive my dear Julias family of the distinction they have ever held—What is it dear dear friend, how I long to see you and know your whole heart—that dear and Virtuous child will never give you pain therefore your words are mysterious. how soon will you write? do do, dear Julia. and of all things tell me of yourself, of your health, spirits, every thing—

—Is there any news of Harriet—and dear Charlotte[6] is she better? her ill health must be a great deprivation to you both are there any more Pairs on the way—dear dear Charlotte—offer my tenderest

---

[5]Elizabeth's uncle and benefactor. According to the terms of his will, both Mary Post and Elizabeth were to receive $2,500, but this did not happen.

[6]Julia's niece and Charlotte Sitgreaves Cox, Julia's sister who had given birth to twins

remembrances to your interesting amiable Maria—her friend you speak of is said to be very beautiful etc and saucy-box came home to see her—no doubt he has a good taste, Marias friendship is a solid recommendation, and I wish his studies may proceed with the same facility as before. tell the dear fellow he has the best wishes of his ancient sweetheart.

Sunday Evening

My dearest I must either close this now or it may be long delayed a thousand Blessings, be with you—

Your EAS.

4.74 To Julia Scott

1st June 1808

My darling Julia

Your letter should have been answered by return of Post had I not been daily expecting to communicate the final decision of Mr. [John] Wilkes and my Brother P[ost] respecting my removal to Baltimore, that decision is now obtained and with it the most cordial desire of forwarding my plan there, and a pressing advice for my immediate departure, as at this season the house I occupy may be easily let, and a convenient one can now be procured for me in the vicinity of the College at Baltimore[1] which is out of the city—in short the time, day, and manner of our departure would have been concluded on this very morning had I not expressed an earnest wish to hear first from you therefore do if only in ten lines by return of Post tell me how you are circumstanced—are you yet in Affliction, is your poor Mother worse or better? could the presence of your own friend relieve you from a moments sorrow—on your answer depends either my going round by Sea, or coming to you in two or three weeks by land.[2] but be sincere in

---

4.74 ASJPH 1-3-3-6:72

[1] St. Mary's College, directed by Rev. Louis William Dubourg, S.S.

[2] In fact Elizabeth did go by sea and did not see Julia on her trip to Baltimore.

your statement as they tell me it will be much less expence to go by Water, and I know so many of us must be an embarrassment to you—certainly I shall not indulge my wish of seeing you unless the foregoing questions recieve an Affirmative—

—in pain weariness and haste I am

Your Own Friend EAS

Undated Notes and Letters

Elizabeth Seton did not date many of her notes to Cecilia Seton. In them she often calls herself "Sister" or "Aunt William." Some notes name Rev.Michael Hurley, O.S.A., as "St. M" or "Why so"; "Much loved" was Elizabeth's name for Cecilia's brother Samuel, and "Ned" was her brother Edward Augustus. Both boys often carried messages between Elizabeth and Cecilia. "Hatch" or "H" was Harriet Seton, Elizabeth's sister-in-law, and "Zide" was Eliza Farquhar, her cousin.

4.75 To Cecilia Seton

1

all approved, and much the hour and quarter of writing and reading on such a day, for remembrances oftener drives the heart still closer than any present object or instruction could do

—All right my Cecilia—while you keep Martha close by Mary[1] to be ready at a moment call

—Peace my dear one

2

—I see you all around—at the foot of this tabernacle where the love of our Jesus has so long waited for many of you—but also I see the awful and dreadful account in his judgment of the use of this grace my dearest girls[2] if you should even one of you be so unhappy as to abuse it—but I rather hope every heart is in earnest—you know

4.75 ASJPH 1-3-3-3:25,1,2
[1]Cf. Luke 10:38-42.
[2]The younger Seton girls, Harriet, Charlotte, and Cecilia, Elizabeth's sisters-in-law

already when it was prepared for you—when it was merited for each
Soul in particular

4.76 To Cecilia Seton

My dear dear Child

my Heart is by your bed-side watching, soothing and waiting on
you with the tenderest love—Oh my Saviour it is to you I commit her,
and submit my poor soul that is not permitted to do as it would. I fear
my darling you have been very ill tho' I knew nothing of it till Will
brought your note. I would leave all the world to be near you—but
must still in this case as in so many others must look beyond the present pain to that dear hour when we shall not be separated either by distance or Sorrow, We may rejoice in that hope my darling thro' every
distress, and now I know you Glorify your dear Masters name by
showing how sweetly his Spirit of Peace and patience consoles and
strengthens his dear Children in every situation—
—Barclay[1] really alarms me for you this evening. Oh my darling
perhaps He will wing your way over the toilsome Journey and Slip
you gently in his Blessed fold before we thought your sorrows more
than begun—dear dear Cecilia my soul is bowed to his Will while it
hovers near you as a Mothers by her darling child.
How much it pleases me that our Souls Sister[2] is with you, if only
for a few hours, they will be sweet ones I know[.] you have both been
with poor Solitary Sis at his footstool, my Heart melts and covers my
face with tears while I stretch out my hands to beg and implore with
unutterable love that He will bless you bless us all and gather us in his
dear pastures of eternal life and bless [page torn]—think of our darling

---

4.76 ASJPH 1-3-3-8:90

[1]Possibly Andrew Barclay Bayley, Elizabeth's half-brother; however, since he was in the West
Indies for several years, it could refer to a servant.

[2]Since Elizabeth used this term for her sister-in-law, Rebecca Seton, who died in July 1804, this
reference is unclear. It could be construed as a reference to Eliza Farquhar, Elizabeth's cousin by
marriage, or to Harriet Seton, Elizabeth's sister-in-law, who was lamenting the long absence of her
fiancé, Andrew Barclay Bayley.

Rebecca how she must wait and wish for that happy hour when "the final consummation" shall unite us forever, thro' His Merits—His righteousness—His adored Name by which alone we can persevere until the Contest shall be done, and the storm overpast—Now let us take shelter under his blessed wing and while we are sowing in tears bless and adore him for the Hope of reaping in Joy[3]—

I am interrupted May he bless you, E[liza] H[arriet] all forever your EA Seton

Monday morning—Emma[4] says you are not better—ever dear dear Sister how I wish I were with you—[paper torn] love with When you see our darling Hatch Kiss her for me—

4.77 To Cecilia Seton

Tuesday morning 12 Oclock

Your sweet little note this morning and a sight of my much loved, was like sunshine after rain—the long sigh yet comes with soreness and irritation—but the fine weather and to-morrow morning 7 Oclock will make all well—contrary to rule—am to dine at Sister P[ost]s

tell Hatch to come and see Helen[1]—so sweetly Alfred said dear Aunt this morning with so affectionate a manner he started the tears I wished to hide—dear Child, God bless Him keep my Widows tears, the little purple flower, by itself—every morning a new one will blow these leaves and the colour of humility, the long green leaf, the band of Hope—

all are well—Kit loves you too much, Rebecca insisted when she waked this morning that she had seen Aunt Celia in her black gown kneeling by me at the bed side—

---

[3]Cf. Ps. 126:5.

[4]James Seton's daughter

4.77 ASJPH 1-3-3-8:91

[1]Helen Bayley, Elizabeth's half-sister

I wish I could be a chair or any thing for a little while to be near you my Darling—but hush Nature eternal love and Joy succeed present separation and sorrow—

Yours [unclear] M

4.78 To Cecilia Seton

Two days are gone without a line from my dear one—but look out with delight for the smile of my well beloved and the little note—

Caroline brought little Elizabeth here yesterday and said Hatch was to come to-day of course you are a Prisoner—but it is a "Prisoner of the Lord," [1] Blessed be his Name—it could not be so without his immediate permission—nor without that permission could your darling Sister be consuming with the daily and mighty fever and burning breast—How sweet and Peaceful is His Spirit which pours the Oil of Patience and joyful Resignation—could not go for my treasure this Morning but Hope is always on the Wing—

I beg you do not tell any one I am not well—

2 Oclock

better—dearest—Mrs. Pollock has given me some of the Balsom of Life. a good thing if it is of the General kind—God Bless you I want to look at Sam—Be good—hush—

Yours forever

4.78 ASJPH 1-3-3-8:93
[1] Eph. 4:1

4.79 To Cecilia Seton

3 Oclock Monday—

one little word from my own darling would be very precious—the impression You left on me yesterday was sorrowful, or the day would have been too sweet—that Peace the World knows not possessed my Whole Soul—and may it rest with my own, He knows best—you will have it dearest when it is for the satisfaction of that dear Soul so precious to Him—when your warfare is further fulfilled—

Tuesday Evening

What can it mean neither much loved nor N[ed] for two days—my silly heart would imagine some evil, but calls itself back and offers all to Him
—Hope to go Early to the Fountain—precious precious Cecil I carry you in my heart.
farewell dearest—Peace I must write a line to Zide—Ann is going again to-morrow to see the Babe—she was there this afternoon and Zide better—dear Hatch well—

Your forever MEAS

If the girls have any story books to lend your Cate they shall be taken care of and returned She is always wishing for some

4.80 To Cecilia Seton

My darling Cecil

Your own Sister has now the compleat trial of the Sincerity of her confidence in Him whose sheltering wing is our refuge—Or how could I know you were sick and in sorrows and go two miles further from you—and begin this day again without any hope of even hearing from you—

Your pains must have been very very great indeed if they Were greater punishment to you than the sad hours I passed yesterday with poor Dué[1]— Oh my darling how greatly exceeding Blessed is that heart fortified by His Sweet love and presence enabled to view pain and Sorrow only as an effect of that love, rather than a scourge and torment—

how I rejoice Brother[2] is better—but my hearts darling could I know that you were so—or even trying to be so—Patience—and hope—

4 Oclock

how my heart rejoices your better and I cannot wait a moment

4.81 To Cecilia Seton

My darling Sis is better—do all you can for Peace—your own discretion must direct

forever yours
Ned has not a moment

4.82 To Cecilia Seton

My most dear Cis

the heart that longs for you still rejoices that you are absent—highly honored indeed is that Soul and much to be envied whose every action and thought is a sacrifice to . . .

---

[1]Catherine Dupleix
[2]Probably James Seton, Elizabeth's brother-in-law
4.81 ASJPH 1-3-3-8:96
4.82 ASJPH 1-3-3-8:97

happy happy Celia—weigh you[r] blessing let no portion of it be lost for want of a right estimate—ever[y] page that is unfolded in your destiny proves more and more that he has chosen and marked you for his Own my soul rejoices that it is your Sister in spirit and in Nature—

—I trust you will come before Sunday—if it is his Will—but courage dear Soldier—what will we not do or yield to please Him—think of me, pray for me, Love me—my heart and soul is bound to yours—it never says ME any more but all ways US you are itself

forever yours MEAS

4.83 To Cecilia Seton

Wednesday morning

My darling

I could tell you a Volume of Yesterday—but that must be for the happy hour we meet—you were regretted by the dear little Mage to the last minute—She behaved sweetly, and all all was done with so peaceful and solemn a manner by Whyso that the very tones of his voice gave her confidence—

I was within the door at the moment only of the Ceremony—had a nice little room to myself sent in the tea—assisted at the Benediction of the Bridle bed—ring etc and tied on the Surplus with trembling fingers—poor little I how many remembrances crowded—came Home at ten after receiving the tears of the Bride, and the perfectly Enthusiastic acknowledgments from Will Cocks—he is to be sure, "a charming fellow"

—said my litanies with a peaceful content the fruits of Comparative happiness for my Joys can never fade—but fairies I believe kept the mind afloat and concluded it was best to banish present Ideas by the society of the Irish girl, offering the intention to my dear Lord—and oh Cisy do I acknowledge it to you it was past three before it was closed—shame, shame, shame—but such is the Mystery of poor Human Nature—how many times did rapturous Joy and adoration fill the whole Soul of thanksgiving that I am permitted to dwell in this divine region of "Superstition" as the English-man calls it—to be a Catholic—Heavenly Mercy I would be trampled on by the Whole World—

to-morrow will offer All again and pass part of the day in town from Necessity—Why so is delighted with the promise that WE will dine with Him on Sunday—Father Burns[1] is gone to Norfolk you must must must come on Saturday.

—a thousand Blessings on you My darling I shall send Ann to see Eliza—She and your angel send love and love and love—

yours forever MEAS

Mage is gone to the falls—again this Morning she said "best love to Celia, dont forget"—send you a little bottle of _____ used at the Nuptial Benediction—Whyso charged me to take care of it—[2]

4.84 To Cecilia Seton

dear darling Child—

it is useless to repeat to you that every day and hour increases the love of that heart for you which feels you are a part of itself—perhaps the warmth of its expression Oversteped Prudence this afternoon—but forgive the pain which love alone occasioned and particularly as the remembrance may be a Preventative.

had written so far when Hatche and Ann entered they tell me you were cheerful—triumphant Grace—that alone could make you so—and hear the voice of Sister begging you to take some precautions about your throat—Your Life is most precious whatever you may

---

[1] Rev. John Byrne, a priest at St. Peter's Church

[2] A note, probably written by Bruté on the cover page: "See the last lines of the 2nd page—M. 'Why so' (M Hurley I think)"

4.84 ASJPH 1-3-3-8:99

think of it because sealed by that Very Grace which even in the World may yet procure US sweet and smiling hours of Peace—and will repay present sorrow ten-fold

Our Ganganelli says (writing to his Sister) "the troubles you speak of ought to be more precious than pleasures if you have Faith, Calvary is in the World the proper place for a Christian, if he mounts on Tabor[1] it is only for an instant"—You feel the force of these Words I know darling—but like poor sister the Heart Will sometimes faint while even most desirous to acknowledge their Truth—but we must Remember we have made many Offerings and many Vows and now must accept the trial of our fidelity as the certain forerunner of our reward if it is proved by Humility and Patience—

—"thro patience we shall Inherit the promises"—little sleep says "Come" but love such as mine for you NEVER SLEEPS—PEACE—

Saturday morning

Your note of this morning comforts me dearest altho' it is so sad—are you then to be sick and absent from your Own—but He is, and always will be with you—Lift the silent the silent soul of Faith to Him.

If you can without Imprudence come to-morrow, Mrs. M being alone you can ride both down and up with her that is certain. and besides if your little heart is prepared you can pass from the Ark to the tribunal[2] I will manage it all for you—but if you are not better do not think of it—Bless Bless Bless you a thousand times

Your Own EAS[3]

---

[1] Cf. Matt. 27:33 regarding Calvary. Tabor is traditionally the mountain of the Transfiguration; cf. Matt. 17:1-8.

[2] The place of confession

[3] Written on the outside: "Ann Reed, Mage, and E Winthrop have just called and all send you best love—take care of my little sweet *William*"

4.85 To Cecilia Seton

Dearest Sister

my heart is too heavy about Ann—but He knows a Mothers Heart—I am anxiously waiting in hopes Post will call for me as I wrote him to do—perhaps he cannot—and You must only be careful to keep her quite warm and plenty of drink—it must have its course—will see you depend as soon as possible send you Old Buchan in case I do not come this afternoon—

> forever Your MEAS
> 2 Oclock Wednesday[1]

4.86 To Cecilia Seton

> Wednesday

My Darling Child—

it is a little mystery to me how your precious heart can be so long in the ditch—pray look up as quick as possible and give me a better account of yourself—you would be quite amused with a letter from St. M. he says "I am on a secret expedition seeking an expletive to a chasm when that is found you will see me, and after emancipating from the gloom the darkness the Enemy has conjured up round me I shall be better able to lay any that may sympathetically assail you"—these are His own words, what an odd genius—he also charges "Be not anxious Leave all to God"

Helen[1] and Sister have been here—Eliza is gone to stay a week in town—and you my precious little Sister is your Cell yet built—I am writing you by twilight your heart I hope is a step higher—Kiss the Kit

---

4.85 ASJPH 1-3-3-8:101
[1]Written on the outside: "Cecilia Write me by the Boys"
4.86 ASJPH 1-3-3-8:102
[1]Helen Bayley, Elizabeth's half-sister

for me You can say an Avé with your face hid in her soft back—do but reflect a moment how precious the constant aspirations of that little Virgin heart of yours must be to its Master and you will not be sad a moment at any privation

Thursday Night

all [unclear] sweet sleep do not go down to-morrow morning but at 9 Saturday with poor Mage to recieve her nuptial Communion—and I Oh Cecy dear if it was mine what a sweet passport it would be to present to St. Peter—but we must wait in patient Faith—

—how is your dear little heart—mine is calling out for you and has dwelt on you too much this afternoon being more alone than usual the children gone to Cratons—

never mind—the day will come look up—drop by drop the angel pours, Our Cup may be nearer full than we imagine—Good night sweet love Peace

MEAS[2]

4.87 To Cecilia Seton

Thursday—

My Cecil

is it a dream that I have seen you—dear dear Sister of my Soul I brought You only added pain instead of cheerfulness and consolation. but Mothers heart had been fighting against its feelings so long—All uneasiness about my own Ann ceases in the remembrance of every thing about her and her precious nurses—she is much more comfortable than I could make her, and I am sure your care must equal mine—Yet the unbidden tears stand ready at every thought of her—how inconsistent and weak is frail nature—

---

[2]Written on the outside; "*all is well* Friday morning"
4.87 ASJPH 1-3-3-104

poor Ann Barry was here a few minutes after my return—looked wretched—we treasure in this life a fleeting Shadow—how soon to vanish—Oh my Darling let us fix the eye upwards.—I shall see you again very soon—poor Styve says he will take me at any time, Mrs. Pollock also—how kind—Where do his Mercies fail.

What would I give to pass some hours with you—but hush covetous Nature

4.88 To Cecilia Seton

My darling

the only proper reply I think you can insist on it—the very great inconsistency in not having been to Mr. [John] Wilkes and the rude appearance to him—how could you meet them?—Sister is not well—no matter—hope every thing for Sunday—love love a thousand times

forever yours

4.89 To Cecilia Seton

My Darling Cis—

for once in my Life I was willing to let you go yesterday fearing that any delay might hinder our future happiness—happiness—true happiness—unchangeable and a certain anticipation of eternal Blessedness

—Breakfast with Mr. Lacey[1]—the communication was a Sermon—what an odd genius—saw Sad—Dué[2] and E and home at 12—what an escape—

4.88 ASJPH 1-3-3-8:105
4.89 ASJPH 1-3-3-8:106
[1]Rev. Michael Lacey
[2]Eliza Craig Sadler and Catherine Dupleix

—dearest dearest creature write to me—make a visit to Aunty that I may see you even [an] hour— Will you come can you come Sunday—cheer up that precious heart—keep it with Him—O how glorious the reward He prepares for its fedelity besides present Peace—but He tells you a great deal more than Sister can

Thursday 3 Oclock

Your sweet little note and a look from Much loved makes me too happy—May you be blessed—blessed in Him forever—my Soul is in the prayer dearest Child—I told St. M yesterday with Truth that you were/are more to me than All my Children love me Write your own forever forever[3]

4.90 To Cecilia Seton

dear darling—

This is Saturdays note ready for dear much loved who did not come—Yesterday was a Prisoner—wrote till half past 12 too happy had you been in the corner—had enclosed your note for H but taken it out to give it myself—dear dear dear Cecil write me kiss all for me and Bless dear Ann for her Mother—the three lonely ones are waiting Heavens dear and endless blessing be yours forever

your MEAS

4.91 To Cecilia Seton

Sister is better my Darling—I hasten to tell you so the moment poor Tat[1] is out of my arms—she too is better but still has fever—how

---

[3]Written on the outside; "write me about little W—"

4.90 ASJPH 1-3-3-8:107

4.91 ASJPH 1-3-3-8:108

[1]Rebecca Seton, Elizabeth's youngest child

sweet the moment will be when I shall hold you to my heart is known to me alone—but oh do do be prudent and careful—

> forever yours—
> Monday Evening

4.92 To Cecilia Seton

My own own dear Child—

at 5 I awoke as you say rejoicing—it began to rain in earnest as I turned the corner of Barclay Street—heard three[1] as happy as any remembered—was consoled and encouraged in the tenderest manner and obtained the Souls desire[2] at Eight—

the Neighbors carriage was coming up empty—and I was most happy found all well—and had I you have every wish for this world that I dare ask—

The happiness of a Soul reaching forward to eternity—how sure, how real quiet and resigned thro' its Journey nothing but sin can Afflict it—and is this my portion darling darling Sister—may it be yours is my Birth day prayer,[3] and to the hour of my death will still be offered—

there was something in Yesterday which will not soon return to us my sweetest—it is like a dream—we may pass many hours together but they can hardly be more precious—much loved crowned it so nicely the big bowl will always be my favorite—

you should rather warn Sister not to love you too much, considering we daily offer each other to Him

a thousand thousand thousand Blessings on you my Own

> Yours FOREVER MEAS

4.92 ASJPH 1-3-3-8:109
[1] Elizabeth attended three Masses at St. Peter's Church
[2] Holy Communion
[3] Elizabeth's birthday was August 28, Cecilia Seton's was August 9.

do not neglect the Journal—mine is going on[4]—it is good for the Soul if it is offered to Him, and in simplicity of Heart—Peace—Peace—Love—forever

4.93 To Cecilia Seton

Precious being—

Sister has not a moment but to say what you so well know, how dearly she loves you and longs for the sweet hour of Peace—but first the battle must be won, the thorny road passed—dear dear darling look up—He is every moment looking at you—write something prepared—so [shall] I—Commit all to Him.

forever

4.94 To Cecilia Seton

My good Angel must surely have left me yesterday morning Love or I should not have been sleeping while your precious soul was waiting for me—Well, Patience—got in the Ark[1] before the Offering—recieved Our All at nine—passed a very heavy day after eleven—one hour of it in St. M's room among his books alone with sweet Kit—was not well—am not well—but what of that—We ought to be well pleased with every inconvenience which lessens our period of absence from OUR HOME

When I think of my children the Mother's tears are dried by the certainty that God will have his own—

If your throat is not better to day, I shall think you are quite ill—and that is worse than all to me—

---

[4]Elizabeth kept a journal for Cecilia from August 10 to October 16, 1807.

4.93 ASJPH 1-3-3-8:113

4.94 ASJPH 1-3-3-8:8:115

[1]St. Peter's Church, where Elizabeth arrived in time for the second half of Mass and received Holy Communion

"The Lord will deliver." Write my darling in trust

your own Sister
Monday morning. the longest day of the year

4.95 To Cecilia Seton

My dear darling

The days are long and tedious without seeing you—what would I give for one little still Evening—I hear of you—that you are well—little cheat—May his dear sheltering wing be over you thro' all the storms—it is—and when your dear wearied heart sinks and does not feel the immediate influence then tho' hidden He is nearest, may your dear angel in the heavy hour inspire your thoughts to rise to their dear Standard—think when it comes in Glory how we shall triumph in having spent our few and fleeting years in its Service—Eternity—dear Love—think of Eternity—with . . .

Saturday night—

Your own

4.96 To Cecilia Seton

Saturday Morning 10 Oclock

Dear loved-much loved-best beloved Child—

Sis has her ups and downs as well as you—Sometimes and oftenest in the spirit—never mind—ten years hence.—did not go yesterday Kate was sick—and a heavy fog—the Soul clouded too—poor Brother[1] how my heart pities Him—You will be his ministering

---

4.95 ASJPH 1-3-3-8:116
4.96 ASJPH 1-3-3-8:117
[1] James Seton, Elizabeth's brother-in-law

Angel, as welcome a sacrifice to Our dear Lord as if adoring at his Altar. pray pray my darling do not hear to any prospect of coming while he is in the least indisposed. if you can persuade him to soak his feet and put some bran in the water—take care of yourself

to-morrow my soul will be wrapped in yours they are one at the moment of Divine Union. His own. perhaps I too may be detained—but what can impede the Spirit, glory to his Name and infinite mercies—He is every Where—

Be confident in Jesus—do not suffer yourself to dwell on the changes and variations of your own dear heart while you simply feel it is his, do not mind any other disposition, his most favoured Servants are most subject to these imperfections which are an accompaniment of the struggles of Nature and Grace—He who conquered for us has his sheltering wing now over my darling, and in the proper house will crown her triumph—in the mean while keep close to your Kempis[2]—So says St. M in his last letter "let it be a part of your daily Bread"[3]—he will direct your heart to that prayer of the Spirit which neither occupations nor pain can drive from it—tho' it may not be active still it is there—Bless Bless

Your MEAS

go on gently with Why so for the present Anna also will do so—

4.97 To Cecilia Seton

My Blessed—

the flowers the note—the smile of my Beloved are all so many precious delights to poor Sis—Rich Sis have been [to] Breakfast with Dué,[1] and got a little rose from Margaret—

[2]*The Imitation of Christ* by Thomas à Kempis
[3]Cf. Luke 11:3.
4.97 ASJPH 1-3-3-8:118
[1]Catherine Dupleix

dear darling will have a note ready for next time—was unusually weak Yesterday—better to day—

God Almighty bless you was obliged to let Why so take your book he says he will return it immediately

You are and have been with me all the morning

once more Adieu

4.98 To Cecilia Seton

The Girls will have Ann[.] I fear Brother[1] will think it too much—but know not how to deny them—

Shall go to-morrow if a fair day and if you can come down with the dear finger bring it at J.OBs. at ten and you will meet your own, if you cannot must be satisfied with hope dearest tho' it sometimes makes me sigh—if the weather is not quite as clear will wait till next day—as I must call on Madge—

—Ann Hoffman[2] has just been here, wonders cease not—My little dwelling is taken—it is going to rain I fear—cheer up my Sole—Peace—remembrance what would I give to tuck you up to night in the little bed—to wrap up the dear finger and sign the dear forehead but—this is not the Season—do you not know that—never mind—strange Sister—

Your Own—

poor Ann how she would interest you with her blisters and fever so sweet and peaceful talked over all her distress thro the last weeks of misery—they are going to Charleston or Somewhere immediately She spoke of you as an Angel, my angel darling dear dear Child May He Bless you forever

---

4.98 ASJPH 1-3-3-8:120

[1]Anna Maria Seton was probably staying with James Seton's family.
[2]Possibly a relative of Mary Hoffman Seton, Elizabeth's sister-in-law

4.99 To Cecilia Seton

My darling love

the Witches have hindered me from writing you and dear Ann T. to day tho' I have intended it a dozen times—but here is my blessing and ten thousand loves—for yourself and the Darlings—

forever Your MEAS

4.100 To Cecilia Seton

My Own Darling—

perhaps much loved may call—and the little word must be ready though I hope to be on the wings of the morning[1] could you bear my Company it would make up for the sad necessity of going down wards instead of returning straight Home. Patience—

your last dear Note pierced my very Soul—Cisy Cisy dear You un-happy—Oh contradiction—you His dear Lamb, whom He holds in his arms with tenderest Watchful care—yet so it is, to be mortal and the companion of sorrow and care is one and the same meaning—but I must always repeat to you to weigh your case in comparison—Eliza for instance—she has been here a few minutes—full of hope that she recovers fast—ah dear Lord—and sweet H what a prospect compared with Your possession

I cannot help hoping my dear one that another page will soon be turned over—and at all events how Safe we are under the Shadow of the Cross.

Blessed Blessed Lord keep US always in your company, and force our coward hearts when they are unwilling to go on

---

4.99 ASJPH 1-3-3-8:122
4.100 ASJPH 1-3-3-8:124
[1] Ps. 139:9

My darling say Amen good night—good morning—good day
Eternal forever

your MEAS[2]

4.101 To Cecilia Seton

Monday 10 Oclock [September 7]

I cannot tell you how I was troubled at the idea yesterday morning
that you would remain from early to one Oclock without leaving our
Ark—Sister little thought you was at the Wilderness[1] and you that I
was in anguish over poor Ann who was very very ill but Nature made a
powerful effort and she is now playing in the Baby house with Kit—so
it is Dearest—Hope ever on the Wing—but Death and eternity the
only certainty—Hoping still for tomorrow the Nat[ivity] of our
Blessed Mother

but the wrath threatens—Patience—Love and Jesus—as you
say.— am not the more content since your confab as it will only make
more discord in the family—but let US gently put all in his hands the
little notes now and then, not too often cannot be amiss—and do not
my dearest harken to any proposals of my dear ones coming to you or
going to us except it comes from Brother Himself—Your sweet discretion will always know—

Hatch guarded by Sam F[arquhar] passed an half hour with us last
Evening—to see poor Ann—it was sweet tho' constrained—dear dear
Hatch how my Soul loves, and pities her situation[2] yours even as it is,
is perfect freedom in comparison—

---

[2]Written on the outside: "Thursday night *ten*. Father of Soul"
4.101 ASJPH 1-3-3-8:126

[1]James Seton's country place

[2]Elizabeth was referring to the the uncertainty of Harriet's future since her fiancé, Andrew
Barclay Bayley, had been gone for some time.

We shall all be free by and by Blessed be his name for ever ever ever

Your Own Sister MEAS

how very very few can we say so to dearest

4.102 To Cecilia Seton

My Own Darling Child

The Soul that loves you as itself feels deeply your hard trial—but who can tell how much future Peace and reward is to be the consequence of your sweet sacrifice—most acceptable indeed it must be to Him who himself was weighed with the very sorrow which now bears you down—but make every exertion in your own power do not attempt to restrain its expression to Him your dear dearest Friend who sees it long before you give it vent—"He will deliver" —thought of you too much yesterday—soon soon may the leaf turn if it is his dear Blessed will—Dearest write I charge you—Bless you a thousand thousand times—pity me Wednesday as I shall you—let us put on our Shield the sigh is heard as effectually as the prayer—

Your own forever

4.103 To Cecilia Seton

My Darling

I cannot contrive what you mean by Thursday except much loved has been so mischievous as to tell you that I have thought all the week that Thursday was 28th—be it as it may when you come my heart and

---

4.102 ASJPH 1-3-3-8:127
4.103 ASJPH 1-3-3-8:128

soul will rejoice—Hope to go to-morrow, as I have missed so many times—and this Friday will come in order—especially if you do not go to [unclear] on Thursday—yet if you intended Sister to go then will gladly be there Thursday also—

How much it delights me to see these dear Girls I cannot tell you—Oh that it could often be so—had a long confab with Mr. Harris[1] last Evening and disclosed to them my Canada Scheme[2]—but he is determined on keeping the school for three years more so probably I shall have to stick to it.

—He above will order all many an event may take place in that time—dear dear dear Cecilia one thing is sure death and life Eternal the next sure and certain thing I can know is that I love You even more than Myself—Peace—Jesus - Love—eternal

Love MEAS
1 Oclock—

My darling—be it understood I meet you in Town Thursday Morning—and we will walk home together to Breakfast—Sweet most sweet it will be Yours forever

4.104 To Cecilia Seton

—In the hope of seeing dear much loved once more the little notes are brought out—how long it seems since that little momentary look at my Cecil and Ann—Tomorrow what is our prospect, for me my only chance is to be off at day light—sure you might leave Ann to Em if the roads are passable—had they been so to day I should have coaxed Mrs. P. —some day next week I hope she will take me to you.

dear dear dear Cecil you have borne the pain and watching that belonged to Sister, but it is all written above—My heart is like lead these

---

[1] Rev. William Harris, who superintended the school for which she provided boarding facilities
[2] Elizabeth's plan to send her boys to school in Montreal and teach there herself
4.104 ASJPH 1-3-3-8:129

many days but after eight to-morrow will it not fly—Oh that we could fly together.

Kiss my dear dear Ann after prayers for Mother, how I long to see her open the Piano once more—

Saturday afternoon

Yours and hers forever[1]

4.105 To Cecilia Seton

Sunday Morning

My precious Darling

Nine Oclock bells have rung and here am I yet—the wet and a sore throat wont agree—but Ann and I will try it presently—

—thought so much of you yesterday—perhaps too much—but it was to Jesus "He will deliver." this is the day of Salvation—for you in your desert as well as for the most favoured in externals—you are always with Me but—this day in a special manner—let your Heart shine on your Countenance in Silence and Resignation—take it with Humility and make Necessity your Sanctification which it assuredly will be if you recieve it as a Penance—When once in your situation (and much worse) I offered all willingly acknowledging how many hours I had spent in his Temple and presence without using the blessing as I ought, and am sure the sighs of my Soul was then accepted as surely yours must be my Darling—

Rejoice in Hope—it will all—pass—how many pain[s] are gone—and the Joy to come is Eternal there we will adore and bless Him for having here numbered Us with his own Children—

How did you get over yesterday—never mind—that too is gone

Dominus Vobiscum[1] and your own MEAS

---

[1]Written on the outside: "Cecil Wafers are Scarce"

4.105 ASJPH 1-3-3-8:131

[1]Latin for "The Lord be with you"

4.106 To Cecilia Seton

Precious dear Child—

do do contrive to come to morrow or the first of the week. beg Brother[1] to spare you for Pitys sake. love love ten thousand times All was decided yesterday for as soon as possible dear dear dear Darling LOOK UP—

forever Yours
Kiss My dear Girls[2] for their own Aunt W—

4.107 To Cecilia Seton

Wednesday Evening

My darling

poor Sister is indeed comforted and tho' sorely disappointed at not seeing my own Ann yet am very thankful, and will say my Te Deum[1] with a joyful heart, as I may hope she only now requires Prudence and great attention to avoid cold—the painful idea of giving it to the dear ones of the Wilderness I must take as St. Francis[2] says in humility tho' certainly with much regret—

You did not tell me what Post said about your finger—Oh that I could nurse it—but hush—Shall we ever go together again? extravagant question, we will, When He only knows—

Send me your Novice if you can and return me my friend Buchan[3] who I dare say is worth a dozen of it—tell sweet Emma[4] I know she is

---

4.106 ASJPH 1-3-3-8:133

[1]James Seton, Elizabeth's brother-in-law

[2]The children of James Seton

4.107 ASJPH 1-3-3-8:135

[1]A hymn of praise

[2]St. Francis de Sales

[3]Books that Elizabeth and Cecilia were reading

[4]Emma Seton, Elizabeth's niece

the dearest Nurse and tenderest friend to my Anna as I always see her watching and comforting her in imagination happy happy Could it be in reality—

Bless and kiss her for her own Aunt Wm I would cherish and love her next to the one she loves if ever we are so blessed as to be together—dear dear most dear Cicil good night—

Your MEAS

4.108 To Cecilia Seton

Friday Night

My Darling—

so it is—Kate suffers more and more must go to Post at his Breakfast hour and try to get something for her—Sweet Angel—will soon be home = Oh if I should find you here—too good—

—Received My all, OUR ALL,[1] from St M this morning—did I not think of you dear dearest of all precious ones which step of the ladder is the poor heart on—take care hold on, I am waiting for you—too too too happy Sister who possesses the dearest earthly blessing almost with Indifference—but I may fall—poor human Nature always changing we must bear with—but we WILL WATCH dearest farewell

forever yours

4.108 ASJPH 1-3-3-8:140
[1] Holy Communion

4.109 To Cecilia Seton

My darling

Do you not know that you are climbing up the Mountain of Ararat on which the Ark[1] rested—it would be very sweet indeed to have one hand always in the dear Muff to support each other on the path of Ice we certainly must pass over [unclear]

Saturday Evening

well dearest but almost sick to see you and Ann—thought of walking this Morning but the snow storm—Hatche was here last night quite well—Oh do do write poor Sis

4.110 To Cecilia Seton

Saturday Evening

My darling precious—

Your dear note yesterday was a sad reproof—to slothful Sister who did not go because she had a stiff neck, stiff heart to let that hinder and the clouds etc. etc.—to morrow too has a dark prospect bad bad Sister!

My sweet love were you me—how many walks you would take to him which I do not—this thought sometimes rouses me—Well perhaps we may take some short walks some of these days.

Greenwich[1] would yet be nearer than [the] Wilderness,[2] it certainly must be there or in Town—Well—Peace to the changeable Heart let ours rest on one object and all will be well—poor sweet Hatch how different is her divided fate—Ours my dear one cannot be moved by

---

4.109 ASJPH 1-3-3-8:141

[1]Cf. Gen. 8:4. Noah's ark was said to have rested on Mount Ararat.

4.110 ASJPH 1-3-3-8:143

[1]Country home of Elizabeth's sister and brother-in-law, Mary and Dr. Wright Post, located in Manhattan

[2]Country home of James Seton where Cecilia, then fourteen, was caring for his eight motherless children

human caprice, happen what will our Tabernacle is always firm—Sunday last sweet precious memorable hours what has human Joy to show in comparison even if it was not frail and treacherous—

My dear dear dear dear dear Cecil? my heart melts at the thought of how dear we are to each other and the tie which binds us—and will it be so FOREVER? shall we get out of this stormy Ocean and rest at His feet? heavenly thought it sends me to them now to anticipate it—farewell sweet love.

Your MEAS[3]

4.111 To Eliza Farquhar

My most dear Eliza—

It is not possible to tell you half the pain it give[s] me to hear from our C[1] that you are so unhappy—So long you have reposed yourself in the arms of your heavenly Father and drawn the sweetest consolations from the love of your Saviour, and now that you are called upon to exert that love and confidence will you be alarmed, and seek for Human Support from so frail a creature as your poor Sister—has not our love been sanctified by the strongest views of the Divine Mercy, how eagerly you have recieved the lessons of Peace and confidence in Him, assured that He would give us strength for every trial, and deliver Us from all our Sorrows in the good time, and will you now suffer the weakness of nature to triumph, and forget that precious moment when on your knees you promised your "soul's sister"[2] to look to the Almighty alone—since then my Eliza you have suffered other ideas to possess your mind, and forget how weak you now are both in mind and Body, and also that the wisest and best of Gods Servants have contradicted those assertions which so much interest you, with their Blood.—how can you then Judge from one view if you had the

---

[3]Written on lines on the outside: "Hatch/Cicil/dear/dear/dear/dear/Sis S. Dear A.M.J."

4.111 ASJPH 1-3-3-7:96

[1]Cecilia Seton, Elizabeth's sister-in-law
[2]Elizabeth herself

opportunity of both views, you would be sinful in not using it, but circumstanced as you are you only irritate and disturb your mind, and eventually will find the worst consequences.

By that dear Affection which we hope to enjoy beyond the grave, do my beloved Eliza endeavour to keep your heart with God and in your weak state instead of your long attention to Prayer, try rather to think of our dear Saviour as in your heart and speak its pains to Him with that reliance on his love and mercy you have so long experienced not one sigh or pang is unnoticed by him—but you must not anticipate his Providence which hereafter you will find was in this your most sorrowful hour directing all for the Salvation of your soul, most precious to Him if you are sincere in the protestations you have so often made—the blessing you seek is His gift alone, beg for it, plead for it, but do so with intire reliance on Him and the offering of your Whole Soul in life and death.

When all Hearts are made known, you will know how dearly my Eliza I love you, and how much I would do to prove that love—trust to my sincerity and truth and spare the repetition that you are less dear to me—surely it is useless to repeat Why I do not write—spare spare me dear Eliza

—I am and must be yours in dearest and kindest Affection "happen what may" I pray for you with more earnestness than for myself—You are remembered you know where it is the greatest blessing to be remembered—every promise of Hope and love you may claim from your dear Lord, and the greatest Sin you can commit is to fear he will forsake Your dear Soul when it is struggling to be His— "look up" my love there we will reap in Joy, and thank Him for our present pain

Your own Sister (E.A.Seton)

4.112 To Eliza Farquhar

My Darling Eliza

Your own Sisters tenderest love and Blessing accompanied with a thousand thousand prayers for Your Peace in God and advancement in His dear love is yours—I think of you constantly—to-morrow will present you to Him when He will be in the midst of my Heart and with Him you will there remain in every prayer and desire it offers
Be but faithful to Him with your whole heart, and never fear. He will support, direct, console, and finally crown your dearest Hope. precious precious child how does he distinguish you by that love and confidence He has put in your Heart for Him—only let me repeat to you leave all to Him, all you have to do is Pray pray. and we pray with and for you with all our Souls and most in that sweet hour when our adored Intercessor is offering himself with and for us sanctifies all our requests—Always and forever

Your own MEAS

4.113 To Eliza Farquhar

My own Eliza

I wish I could change my whole self into the little lock. it is a little one for it is almost all gone.
—my Darling do not carry your resignation too far. Tho' a Heavenly Virtue in itself, in your situation it must be limitted—I may submit to Slavery as a dispensation of Divine Providence but yet must not cease to sigh for Liberty if it would enable me to serve Him better—stretch out your arms towards His Holy Altar beg Him, supplicate Him on Sunday that He will permit you to recieve with true

Faith the sweet Substance instead of the Shadow[1]—Merciful Jesus must my Eliza be there. I presented you again my own darling to Him while in the midst of my Heart this morning—oh Heavenly Bliss delight past all expression how consoling how sweet the presence of Jesus to the longing Harrassed Soul, it is instant Peace and balm to every wound. Three times this week and next Sunday too. Oh that you two Darlings could be with us. dearest truest love to sweet Hatch.

forever and forever your MEAS[2]

4.114 To Eliza Farquhar

Sweet Sweet Sweet Eliza

I can only say to you as to our Blessed Jesus "my soul longs for you"[1] at Communion to day when I presented you to Him again in the midst of my tenderest love and most earnest desires, He seemed to say Peace poor heart your prayer is heard she is mine and in my own good time I will Seal her so—my Eliza how we would mix our Prayers and tears together there, at least my darling meet Him there in spirit make it your unceasing request to be admitted to the dear reality. at half past six every morning meet the Soul of your own Sis at His altar, it is the exact time of the Communion of Blessed H[2]—dear dear dear Eliza no expression can ever reach my love for you. how sweet it is to say and feel it will be eternal

yours MEAS[3]

---

[1]Elizabeth was comparing her experience of receiving Holy Communion as a Catholic and as an Episcopalian.

[2]Written below: "St Peters Zide"

4.114 ASJPH 1-3-3-9:99

[1]Ps. 42:1

[2]Rev. Michael Hurley, O.S.A.

[3]Written on the next page: "Zide St. Peters"

4.115 To Eliza Farquhar

sent with a little present by a dear Protestant child—oh do pray for her (my Eliza)—she lives in New York watched carefully by poor Mr. Hobart[1]—

4.116 Draft To Mrs. Eliza Curson Farquhar

My dear Aunt

When I consider all your Kindness to me it grieves my heart that you should be pained by such fears as Mary James[1] has expressed to the dear girls[2] in her late conversations with them—and tho' He who knows all hearts knows that either of the three are dearer to me than myself I am willing rather than give you uneasiness to Sacrifice the happiness I enjoy in my intercourse with them and beg you not to consider my feelings but to prohibit it if it is necessary to yours—
    <Sorrow must accompany me to the grave, but I would wish to be spared that of afflicting you>

EAS

4.117 To Harriet Seton

My own dear Harriet's little little letter was like Blessed oil to the many pains and wounds your own sister has recieved in this storm of sorrow—the worst is past when you tell me that you love what I so

---

4.115 ASJPH 1-3-3-7:101
    [1]This note in Elizabeth's hand was written on the second page of a letter to Elizabeth Seton from Eliza Farquhar.

4.116 ASJPH 1-3-3-7:77
    [1]Mary Gillon Hoffman Seton, wife of James Seton and sister-in-law of Elizabeth
    [2]Mary Seton feared that Elizabeth was exerting a Catholic influence on the young Seton girls, Harriet, Charlotte, and Cecilia, and on Eliza Farquhar, their cousin.

4.117 ASJPH 1-3-3-8:66

much love and still also love me as much as ever altho' certainly in His providence I have occasioned you much pain dear dear child—I would at any moment suffer a thousand rather than give you one, but His will, which if we make a right use of it, is always for our true happiness must take place of all—and we by patiently submitting will obtain his dear love which is worth every other possible blessing—

My darling girl Keep always in view the end of every Hope and remember our heaviest affliction or greatest happiness is but very short compared with that eternal state which depends wholly on our present fidelity to Him—As I know you must be sincere in what you wrote me—take care how you deny it by word or letter we are not always obliged to declare, but always on every penalty forbid to deny; which to our dear Barclay[1] I know you will find difficult but evade all you can and rather let him suffer the pain of suspecting than offend your all. for what can supply to you his denying you —which you know must be if you deny his words. Your own with truest love and eternal affection

MEAS

4.118 Draft To Bishop John Carroll

—a few moments yesterday morning provided a store for memory which life only can terminate—some expressions of weariness and disgust occasioned by the unavoidable confusion of such a period was succeeded by a congratulatory apostrophe "Well at least there is rest in the grave, Soul and Body both will then be quiet." we were alone and the silence was long indeed— "Have you no letter from Mr. Hurley"[1] summed our conversation. the Mother in haste and Hope which however is not always predominant I will try to refer its Value

---

[1]Andrew Barclay Bayley, Elizabeth's half-brother, was engaged to Harriet Seton, her sister-in-law.
4.118 ASJPH 1-3-3-3:32
[1]From the context Elizabeth was speaking with Ann Barry. Cf. 4.66 (ASJPH 1-3-3-1:51b).

to the first original I do not say the one from which the painter takes it—it will never answer me.

Tomorrow this will be closed in the desolated roof—Belona, Mrs. L[e]F[ever], can it be—but perhaps they are not gone—

4.119 Draft to Mrs. Sarah Startin

My dear Mrs Startin

Your kind consoling letter makes me again ask the question to my heart can you call yourself poor or desolate while solaced and comforted with such uninvited Affection—My Heavenly Father succours me in so many ways both interior and externally that I feel like a hypocrite to the world which regards her as an unfortunate and pitiable object and when your practi[c]al goodness magnifies the mist of my Resignation it is but to adore His mercy which while it is the source of that <resignation> makes it the riches and Joy of its happy possession

we never can calculate it then until that useful hour when it will be known how much is regarded and how much been [received] when those who know their Lords will and did it not shall visit them many stripes—

the desire of Peace and Rest is a vain on my part asking of the vain desires of the world—it is the will of God that my circumstances does not permit me to enjoy them for certainly this is not the place of rest much less of Peace in an enemies country[1]—it may be found in the decisive day that this time of patience and forbearance has been the best employed of my whole life.—[2]

4.119 ASJPH 1-3-3-3:33

[1]Reference to the anti-Catholic bigotry Elizabeth was experiencing as a result of her conversion
[2]Written at the bottom in a different hand: "1806"

4.120 Draft to Unidentified Person

did your Angel wisper you this morning at half past eight—the idea that your spirit hovered round the Awful scene added to it impressive tenderness—the Parents pleading love —the meek and innocent Victim, every feature speaking Peace and Resignation—the Altar pitying of Mercy—when He descended there—imagine—

- -

Where the sofa was opposite the Bishops Picture stands the Altar Mr. Sibourg Mr. Idley simple neatness—the Father in a corner by the fire side—the Mother opposite by the middle door olde Mrs Lynn who received in the center

—Innocence and Peace personified under the Bishops Picture (Servants at his left hand) at her right by her side the Sinner. Not a sigh nor the smallest sound of interruption Sacred Sorrow—fervent Hope "waked all the tuneful Soul of love"—the harmonies of the angel's choir were round it and the thought that we should adore forever dissipated every present grievance Oh that your dear Soul may be now infused with the sweet Affiance, and peaceful Hope which then took possession of mine and still holds it—for tho' many hours are since past that hour retains its lively impression—say not this is inconsistent <with> the flight <beyond> of ardent feelings—no the views and hopes of that dear Being are centered in Eternity—every passing moment is preparing the cherished objects of his love for that period—This is an offering fit for Heaven—unfitted to stem the torrent of human Contradictions which excellence such as hers must meet with the calculations of the good she may obtain uncertain the Sorrows and tribulations Sure—this view of the truth will not dry the gush of anguish nor check the agonizing sigh which Nature forces from the heart that loves her

The Sacrafice is offered—the necessity and reasonableness of the offering evident yet its price and value is not the less estimated nor the charms and power of sympathy less acute—

4.121 To Eliza Sadler

My own dear Eliza

I fear you did not understand sufficiently my meaning in the use of those little prayers I gave you—which was to impress on your mind the necessity of preparing for a Blessed Death. this does not require a sadness or painful exercise of mind, on the contrary considering through faith and hope in the Merits of our Divine Redeemer we are his children and the purchase of his blood, we more naturally anticipate with Joy that [page torn] which will deliver us from the [page torn] constantly experience [page torn] will then and [page torn] happiness [page torn] are each

should we make a practice of considering with calm and dispassionate meditation that that hour must come to all whether they reflect or not—its uncertainty with respect to time—the pains, weakness, and often extreme anguish our parting Nature must experience, and what is still worse the possibility that we may be summoned without any warning at all, it would be taking no more precaution than we would allow to the commonest events of life if we were to allow Our Souls a few minutes of every day to beg for Mercy and Grace in that momentous [page torn] the soul enjoys [page torn] in a prayer [page torn] powers and [page torn]

I have observed dear that any good resolutions or exercises begun on the period of our Birth are more seriously impressed, and chose this for you at this time, as reflecting on a Birth day on Earth more easily transfers our thoughts to the Birth day of our future existance. and it is very useful to make use of that day from year to year to examine our souls account in full on the progress we have made in approaching that Heavenly example of [page torn]

4.122 Draft to an Unknown Person

My dear Sir

The old story of reading novels again supersedes All other amusement, at least with William Wilkes, King, and McVicker[1]—It is my duty to let you know it, but as I have both scolded and intreated on the subject, must beg you to spare me as you have always done and not let them know that I have done so and as they pass a great deal of time at *Bedoes* library they will not be surprised that you observe it.

4.122 ASJPH 1-3-3-3:21,6

[1] This note may have been written to Rev. William Harris with regard to several of Elizabeth's young boarders who were students in his school.

APPENDIX

A-1.6a Description of Dr. Richard Bayley

"The following portraiture is to be found among Mrs. Seton's papers, in her own handwriting, and most probably refers to her father.

"His voice is peculiarly adapted to cheer the desponding and encourage the trembling sufferer, who shrinks with fastidious delicacy from any of the remedies of the healing art. Nor is its influence less salutary to the being who, shaken by the tempests of the world, yet struggles to brave them, and support a claim to reason and fortitude. Nature has endowed him with that quick sensibility by which, without any previous study, he enters into every character, and the tender interest he takes in the mind's pains as well as the body's, soon unlocks its inmost recesses to his view, and fits it to receive the species of consolation best adapted to its wants. It may be said of him, as of the celebrated and unfortunate Zimmerman, that he never visited a patient without making a friend."

A-1.71 To Lady Isabella Cayley

New York, December 1799

My first letter was written from Wall Street, from which we were driven by the yellow fever. My William was the only one of the family who suffered in the least; which as it is so numerous, was almost a miracle. We did not venture to town as inhabitants, until the first of November, when we removed immediately to the family house in Stone

---

A-1.6a Cited in Charles I. White, *Life of Mrs. Eliza A. Seton* (New York, 1853), 469 n. 6. [The original cannot be located.]
A-1.71 Excerpt from Robert Seton, *An Old Family* (New York, 1899), 286-288.

Street. My husband, with the general consent of the family, sold the greater part of the furniture, as most of it had been in use ever since my father's first marriage, and we have abundance of our own since we were married. The things that were not sold were valued by competent judges, and the plate was divided.

Mary and Charlotte, the two girls next [to] Rebecca, are placed at an English boarding-school established in Brunswick, State of New Jersey, about thirty miles from New York; and the two younger girls passed the winter at home, where Rebecca and I taught them spelling, reading, and writing, until her health made it impossible to give them the necessary attention. When Mary and Charlotte returned after their spring vacation, they took Harriet with them to school, and Cecilia, the youngest accompanied Rebecca. She is a very delicate child, and one of the most amiable little creatures in the world. Samuel and Edward, whom my father used to call his little pillars, and always had one on each side of him at table, are the most promising lovely boys that ever were, and have a marked elegance and grace in their appearance and manners that distinguishes them from any boys of their age I ever saw, and a sweetness of disposition unequaled.[1] They are under the care of the Rev. Mr. Bowden, in Cheshire, State of Connecticut; although we hear from them once a week we are very sorry to have them so far from home; but it is inconceivable how difficult it is to educate children in our city, although it is the reservoir of people of all nations, and you would suppose from its being one of the capital cities of America it could command any thing. The general want is good schools, and many families that can not part with their children are really suffering from it.

Brother James and his family are at present in the country, that is, five miles from town. He has lost a lovely boy, five years of age, this spring, at the moment of the birth of a daughter. John and his two little daughters reside in Virginia. Henry is in the American navy, a lieutenant on board the *Baltimore* sloop-of-war[2]

---

[1] The letter here continues where the previous draft ends.

[2] William Magee Seton's brothers James, John, and Henry Seton

Mrs.Vining[3] remains in Delaware. She has a fine family of boys, and enjoys better health than formerly. Aunt [Margaret] Seton, is very happy in Albany in the society of her three daughters; two of whom presented her, each, a second grandchild but a few days ago, and she hourly expects to hear that Mrs. Chancellor has also increased the number. I think, my dear aunt, I have given you a pretty good account of us all, except my own three sweet children, who I can *reasonably* assure you are not surpassed by any. My Anna-Maria is the very model of all we could even wish for; and perhaps my change of life may be one of her greatest advantages, as it has altered her young mother into an old one,[4] better calculated to watch the progress of her active little mind. William grows so wonderfully like his grandfather, that you would scarcely believe it possible a child could be so much like a parent; and appears to have as many traces of his disposition and manners as he has of his features. Richard, our youngest, is, if possible, lovelier than either. I am his nurse, as I have been to all the others, and although he is able to stand up and lay his head in my bosom, I cannot find courage to wean him yet.

Your kind confidence, my dear aunt, in my good qualities is very flattering and grateful to me—particularly if I may hope that it has been communicated from the pen of him whose good opinion I so much valued. I can never lament the season of youth; for that of middle age is much more desirable and lasts much longer, particularly if it properly prepares the way to honorable old age, and accumulates such materials as will make that happy. All my leisure hours have that aim; and if the point anticipated is never reached, it certainly occupies the present moments to the best advantage, and if 'their memory remains' it will be a source of the greatest pleasure. I am not yet five and twenty, but the last year has made both William and me at least ten years older. In order to give you a more perfect idea of what we are like we forwarded to Mr. Maitland,[5] a few months ago an engraving of us both to be sent to you. They are good likenesses, but disfigured by the dress of

---

[3] Anna Maria Seton Vining, Elizabeth's sister-in-law

[4] Elizabeth was probably referring to the added responsibility for William's younger half-sisters and brothers she assumed when William Seton, Sr., died.

[5] The head of the London branch of Seton, Maitland and Co.

the hair. If ever you go to London you will see at Mr. Maitland's a portrait of our father,[6] the greatest likeness imaginable, copy of one done by an eminent artist, of the name of [Gilbert] Stuart, who made his appearance in his city a few months previous to his death. It was precisely what he was, as well in feature as in figure. The original is in our possession, and is all to us but himself, for whom its uncommon resemblance. This is altogether a family letter, and of such length that I will defer to my next many little communications you might wish for. It is necessary you should know something of every individual of the family in America, that you may be better able to trace us in idea, until some fortunate chance will bring us nearer to you, or you to us; but I fear the immense ocean between us will be an everlasting barrier to a meeting I so much desire. My William says he will add a few lines, if it is only to acknowledge the receipt of an affectionate letter he received from you on the 4th of August, many months after it was written.

A-1.86 To William Magee Seton

[n.d., summer 1800]

Father says you are a Jonas,[1] but I rejoice you had even so short a passage. Morris came to breakfast with us soon after you were gone. He told me a great deal about Henry,[2] and although he is to set out immediately for the city of Washington, as he is to command the frigate New York, I wish you would make it a point to call on him, because he has been very much Henry's friend. He reinstated Marcelline this morning, but poor Duer[3] must be tried for his life, and he says every circumstance condemns him.

---

[6]William Seton, Sr.

A-1.86 Excerpt from Robert Seton, *Memoir* I (New York, 1869), 62-63.

[1]Cf. Jon. 1.

[2]Henry Seton, William Magee's brother, was an officer in the United States Navy and first lieutenant on the *New York.*

[3]William Duer, born in England, came to New York in 1768. He was a friend of Alexander Hamilton and served as assistant secretary of the Treasury. By the 1790s he was a speculator and was imprisoned, owing creditors more than $750,000.

INDEX

The following references are indexed to page numbers.

A

Albany, New York: 61, 91, 116, 118, 311, 342, 366
Alexandria, Virginia: 83, 111
Alps Mountains: 302
America, Americans: 275, 290, 291, 297, 298, 316, 416, 444, 548
Ann Street (NYC): 235
Antichrist: 333, 339, 374
Antwerp, Belgium: 318
Apostolic Succession: 315, 369
Appelton, Thomas: 278
Appenine Mountains: 283
Azores Islands: 245

B

Baltimore, Maryland: 55, 74, 76, 84, 85, 154, 249, 263, 280, 315, 343, 387, 391, 401, 402, 404, 406, 419, 423, 428, 429, 432, 479, 496, 504, 506, 508
Baltimore Gazette: 153, 154
Bank of New York: 2, 5
Baragazzi, Gaspero: 355
Barcelona, Spain: 279, 292
Barclay Street (NYC): 315, 342, 350, 364, 410, 440, 524
Barry, Ann (Nancy): 379, 402, 404, 413, 422, 427, 433, 486, 491, 492, 494, 495, 505, 522, 542
Barry, James: 379, 402, 404, 406, 407, 413, 415, 422, 424, 431, 432, 436, 444, 449, 451, 456, 457, 458, 465, 469, 482, 483, 484, 486, 490, 491, 492, 495, 498
Barry, Joanna: 379, 402, 403, 413, 421, 422, 427, 431, 436, 444, 449, 451, 458, 466, 469, 482, 486, 490, 491, 492, 494, 495, 498, 542

Barry, Mary: 402
Barry, Robert: 404, 496
Battery (NYC): 8, 15, 29, 151, 159, 163, 188, 225, 231, 240
Bayley, Andrew Barclay (brother-in-law): 51, 65, 197, 263, 280, 386, 419, 426, 452, 512, 530, 542
Bayley, Catherine Charlton (Mrs. Richard) (mother): 4, 12, 134
Bayley, Catherine (sister): 4
Bayley, Charlotte Amelia. *See* Craig, Charlotte Amelia Bayley
Bayley, Charlotte Amelia Barclay (Mrs. Richard) (stepmother): 32, 50, 58, 59, 65, 75, 77, 249, 384, 385
Bayley, Grace Roosevelt: 249
Bayley, Guy Carlton (half-brother): 197, 249, 251, 258, 268, 272, 274, 279, 282, 299, 311, 401, 416
Bayley, James Roosevelt: 249
Bayley, Dr. Joseph: 49, 149, 162, 166, 167, 175, 185, 190, 225, 231, 244, 245, 264, 280
Bayley, Helen. *See* Craig, Helen Bayley
Bayley, Mary Fitch (Bunch) (half-sister): 384
Bayley, Richard (half-brother): 32, 48, 50, 65, 164, 197, 239, 281, 340, 401, 416
Bayley, Dr. Richard (father): 3, 4, 7, 9, 11, 12, 13, 14, 18, 22, 24, 25, 29, 32, 37, 41, 42, 44, 45, 46, 50, 52, 53, 59, 60, 61, 63, 65, 75, 77, 90, 94, 96, 97, 99, 105, 110, 112, 113, 114-19, 118, 121, 123, 125, 126, 130, 133, 134, 135, 137, 139, 141, 146, 148, 149, 150, 152, 153-54, 157, 159, 160, 161, 162, 163, 164, 166, 167, 170, 171, 173, 175, 176, 180, 181, 182,

— 558 —

Pitt, William: 230
Plunkett, Abbé Peter: 279, 280, 374, 481
Pollock, Mr. and Mrs.: 78, 475, 514, 522, 532
Pope, Alexander: 290
Port au Prince, Haiti: 230
Portland, Maine: 322
Portugal: 302
Post, Catherine Charlton (niece): 12, 50, 115,
    188, 189
Post, Edward (nephew): 12
Post, Lionel (Leo) (nephew): 12
Post, Mary Magdalen Bayley (Mrs. Wright)
    (sister): 1, 12, 15, 17, 18, 23, 45, 47, 48,
    50, 58, 105, 115, 116, 117, 124, 125, 127,
    139, 182, 183, 188, 199, 213, 218, 223,
    244, 280, 281, 307, 337, 372, 388, 394,
    434, 435, 446, 451, 462, 466, 467, 492,
    507, 513, 536
Post, Dr. Wright (brother-in-law): 3, 6, 8, 15,
    18, 42, 45, 50, 52, 80, 86, 117, 118, 152,
    158, 182, 188, 199, 239, 240, 280, 288,
    307, 313, 317, 349, 362, 379, 382, 383,
    388, 396, 424, 436, 451, 462, 487, 507,
    508, 520, 534, 535, 536
Prayers
    Gloria Patri: 470
    Hail Mary: 248, 266, 369, 394
    Jesus Psalter: 324
    Litany of Our Blessed Mother: 442
    Litany of the Holy Name of Jesus: 317,
    377
    Litany of Saints: 439
    Matins: 254
    Memorare: 293
    Miserere: 410, 439
    Our Father: 411
    Rosary: 284
    Service, Daily: 257, 258, 261, 266, 271,
    283, 285, 286, 308
    Sign of the Cross: 296, 297, 328, 338,
    528
    Te Deum: 431, 474, 534
    Vespers: 441, 467
Presbyterian Church: 200, 368
Protestant: 232, 402, 415
Provoost, Rev. Samuel: 2, 184
Pyrenees: 301, 302

Q

Quakers, Society of: 153, 368

R

Ramage, John: 92
Religious Life: 421
Richmondtown, Staten Island, (NYC): 184
Riots (anti-Catholic): 425, 438
Roach, Regina Marie Dalton: 99
Rousseau, Jean Jacques: 76, 81, 90, 95, 96,
    99, 176, 475
Rules, Common Rules of the Daughters of
    Charity: 315
Rush, Benjamin: 233

S

Sacrament Sunday: 251, 266, 297, 309
Sacraments
    Confirmation: 315, 382, 405, 408, 441
    Eucharist: 273, 289, 291, 292, 293, 297,
    298, 341, 349, 356, 365, 370, 373, 377,
    378, 382, 385, 402, 410, 413, 441, 445,
    446, 448, 449, 458, 459, 467, 469, 471,
    477, 478, 480, 514, 515, 524, 525, 527,
    535, 539, 540
    Reconciliation (Penance): 376, 382, 474,
    519
    Viaticum (Last Sacraments): 491
Sadler, Eliza Craig (Mrs. Henry): 3, 4, 6,
    7-13, 14-19, 20-21, 27, 33, 50, 58, 59, 73,
    75, 76-77, 80-82, 84, 85, 86-88, 90-91,
    94-96, 97-99, 105, 125, 127, 135, 137,
    142, 157, 159, 161, 167-68, 171-172,
    175-76, 189, 190, 192, 193, 195, 197,
    205, 220-21, 227-28, 244-45, 280, 281,
    320, 332, 334, 362, 397, 451, 458,
    461-63, 467-69, 484-86, 499-501, 522,
    545
Sadler, Henry: 3, 9, 12, 16, 17, 50, 80, 85, 87,
    89, 91, 94, 95, 98, 99, 125, 127, 168, 193,
    467
Saint Joseph's, Emmitsburg: 217, 218, 219,
    436
Saint Mary's College and Seminary: 1, 14,
    387, 391, 401, 419, 423, 501, 506, 508
Saints
    Ambrose: 474
    Augustine: 321, 325, 408, 438, 447, 461,
    464, 466, 473, 474
    Bernard of Clairvaux: 293
    Francis de Sales: 289, 318, 325, 347, 371,
    480, 494, 534
    Ignatius Loyola: 315